# THE NEW AGE MOVEMENT
# AND THE BIBLICAL WORLDVIEW

# The New Age Movement and the Biblical Worldview

*Conflict and Dialogue*

John P. Newport

WILLIAM B. EERDMANS PUBLISHING COMPANY
GRAND RAPIDS, MICHIGAN / CAMBRIDGE, U.K.

© 1998 Wm. B. Eerdmans Publishing Co.
255 Jefferson Ave. S.E., Grand Rapids, Michigan 49503 /
P.O. Box 163, Cambridge CB3 9PU U.K.

Printed in the United States of America

03 02 01 00 99 98     7 6 5 4 3 2

**Library of Congress Cataloging-in-Publication Data**

Newport, John P.
The New Age movement and the biblical worldview: conflict and dialogue /
John P. Newport.
p.     cm.
Includes bibliographical references and index.
ISBN 0-8028-4430-8 (alk. paper)
1. Christianity and other religions — New Age movement.
2. New Age movement — Relations — Christianity.
3. New Age movement — Controversial literature.
I. Title.
BR128.N48N48 1998
239'.93 — dc21                            97-45909
CIP

# Contents

*Acknowledgments*     vii

*Preface*     ix

1. The New Age Movement     1

2. Tracing the Origins of New Age     19

3. A Worldview Crisis     40

4. Consciousness and Radical Transformation     53

5. Spiritism and Channeling vs. Biblical Revelation
   and Prophecy     145

6. Magic, Witchcraft, Neopaganism,
   and the Goddess Movement     212

7. Ecology and the New Age     274

8. Health and the New Age Worldview     324

9. The World of Business     382

10. Education     418

11. Science                                               446

12. The Arts                                              470

13. The Meaning of History                               499

14. Modern Satanism and Black Magic                      533

15. New Age: Critique and Transformation                 596

    *Index*                                               608

# Acknowledgments

The intellectual and practical context at Southwestern Seminary, Baylor University, New Orleans Seminary, and Rice University, where I have spent several years immersed in the study of the philosophy of religion, has been especially helpful in the writing of this book.

I am grateful to Kenneth Hemphill, president of the seminary and professor of New Testament, and Paula A. Hemphill for their encouragement and support of this project.

While he was president of Southwestern Seminary, Russell Dilday supported my research and writing in many theoretical and practical ways.

Southwestern Seminary professors Steve Lemke, Keith Putt, and Ted Cabal, and Yandall Woodfin, professor emeritus, all members of the Department of Philosophy of Religion, made important contributions toward the framing and development of my approach and thought.

Professor Niels Nielsen, Jr., chairman of the Department of Religious Studies, emeritus, at Rice University, played a significant role in this study's early stages of development.

In recent years, George H. Gallup, Jr., chairman of the George H. Gallup International Institute, has broadened the scope of my work by inviting me to speak at and attend annual institute meetings dealing with topics considered in this book.

Special appreciation is in order for three secretaries and a doctoral student who helped with this project: Amy Boll, Brenda Cargile, Emily Wilcher, and Fred Smith.

I especially wish to thank Sam Eerdmans, Vice President of Sales and Marketing at William B. Eerdmans Publishing Company, for his vision in taking on this book, and Managing Editor Charles Van Hof and Assistant Managing Editor Jennifer Hoffman for their guidance in seeing it through. The expertise of editor Jane Haradine has also been invaluable.

I have also been encouraged and helped by my three children, Martha, Frank, and John, Jr.

But above all, I express appreciation to my wife, Eddie Belle, who has supported this project in so many ways and who, more than anyone else, has made this study possible.

JOHN P. NEWPORT

# *Preface*

During the 1980s and continuing into the 1990s, there has been much talk about the New Age. The New Age movement, which found acceptance in the counterculture of the later 1960s and early 1970s — when the New Age was known as "the Age of Aquarius" — has become reasonably well established. The term "New Age" has even entered popular vocabulary.

A person's initial impression is of an eclectic hodgepodge of beliefs, practices, and ways of life. The mysticism of Buddhism, Hinduism, Islam, and Taoism enters the picture. So do elements from "pagan" teachings, including Celtic, Druidic, Mayan, and Native American. And an exceedingly wide range of practices — Zen meditations, Wiccan rituals, enlightenment seminars, management training, wilderness events, spiritual therapies, and forms of positive thinking — also fall under the New Age rubric.

In spite of the popularity of the term, however, the actual content of the New Age movement remains vague. Why? Because New Age is not a centrally controlled organization. There are no official doctrines, standard religious practices, or even dominant leaders in official capacities.

Despite this vagueness, however, we find that underneath all of this variety is a remarkable constancy. Again and again, turning from practice to practice, from publication to publication — indeed, from country to country — one encounters the same (or very similar) ideas about the world and the people of the world, the problems and the solutions.

New Agers say the world is facing a crisis brought on by our reliance on science, our confidence in our own reasoning, and certain practices of Christianity. They offer New Age as a necessary "third option" which doesn't reject religion or spirituality or science or rationality. Instead, it combines them in a "higher" form.

ix

The New Age promotes what has been called "Self-spirituality." The Self, defined as "the divine Ego," is considered sacred. As spirit guides speaking through well-known New Ager Shirley MacLaine have put it, "If everyone was taught one basic spiritual law, your world would be a happier, healthier place. And that law is this: Everyone is God. Everyone."[1]

An awareness that the New Age movement has become a major phenomenon is reflected by the sheer number of books and articles written about the movement in recent years. New Age frequently attracts the attention of the media, giving rise to a proliferation of articles in newspapers and magazines, and reports on television and radio. Because these articles and reports focus on the sensational and the controversial, they seldom go beyond a superficial look at the topic. Unfortunately, these are the only sources most outsiders have for their information on the New Age.

Another group of New Age publications is written from the perspective of religiously committed outsiders, almost always of a Christian persuasion. We find here the whole gamut, from attempts at serious theological dialogue between Christian churches and the New Age to extremely hostile attempts to unmask the movement as satanic.

Another type of article or book is written from the "skeptical" point of view. These writers, who have been focusing on New Age since the second half of the 1980s, tend to criticize its practices on the basis of a secular-humanistic ideology.

Finally, in contrast to all these works written by outsiders is the literature written from New Age perspectives.

In this book I seek to put the New Age movement into its proper historical context in order to build a foundation for properly interpreting its worldview and theology. To do that, I detail religious traditions in both Western and Eastern cultures that form a background for the New Age.

The main emphasis will be on the New Age movement as it emerged in the second half of the 1970s, came to full development in the 1980s, and is still growing in the 1990s as we approach the new millennium.

New Age was originally a movement of modern Western industrialized society. Its foundations lie in the United States and Western Europe, although there are signs that New Age ideas have begun to spread beyond these areas. However, in the New Age subculture there is much influence from various aspects of Buddhism, Hinduism, Sufism, Jewish mysticism, gnosticism, and Native American religions, as well as comparative mythology and traditional folklore.

New Age must not be confused with a much broader group of new religions. The main way to tell the difference is that these new religious groups

1. Paul Heelas, *The New Age Movement* (Cambridge, Mass.: Blackwell, 1996), 2.

have generally recognized leaders, normative doctrines, and specific practices, and New Age does not. However, some of these religious groups do describe themselves as New Age.

There also are those movements often associated with New Age by others that refer to themselves by more specific designations: Transcendental Meditation, Hare Krishna, and Rajneeshism.

The New Age movement occupies a cultic milieu, or pattern, united by the shared ideology of "seekership." This concept applies to persons who have adopted a problem-solving perspective and have defined conventional religious institutions and beliefs as inadequate. The basic New Age claim is that what is wrong with the person and the world can only be dealt with properly by encountering and thereby unleashing that which lies "within." The New Age claims that "Self-spirituality" can make a difference to what it means to be human and fulfilled. This belief translates into practices of healing, work, relationships, community life, politics, sex — indeed, all areas of human experience.

New Age clearly transcends the boundaries of a specific religious organization while leaving room within its domain for such organizations to develop and to disappear. New Age has now become conscious of itself as constituting a more or less unified movement.[2]

The increasing commercialization of the New Age movement in the 1980s had, by the beginning of the 1990s, brought negative connotations to the name "New Age." As a result, many erstwhile New Agers now deny any link. For example, James Redfield, author of *The Celestine Prophecy*, which the *New York Times* reported was the best-selling fiction book in the world in 1996 and some critics called "New Age pop psychology," tries to distance himself from that identification. "*The Celestine Prophecy* isn't New Age nonsense," he has said. "Wherever there's a counterfeit, there's also the real thing. This book puts into words how to experience spirituality."

But no matter how much Redfield denies association with the New Age, he is espousing the same concepts that New Age leader Shirley MacLaine did ten years earlier. Such protest against any association with New Age does not necessarily imply that these protestors no longer see themselves as part of the "movement." It simply means that they don't like the term "New Age."[3]

---

2. Wouter J. Hanegraaff, *New Age Religion and Western Culture* (Leiden: E. J. Brill, 1996), 517, 1-3, 13-17. Cf. Heelas, *The New Age Movement*, 4.

3. David Jeremiah, *Invasion of Other Gods* (Dallas: Word Publishing, 1995), 14-15, 17.

# A PERSONAL PILGRIMAGE

The roots of my realization of the importance of New Age are complex. My more intense interest began when I was invited in the early 1970s to be a professor at Rice University, a secular, scientifically oriented school. Theoretically, I was brought to the university as an evangelical voice in a Ph.D.–granting Religious Studies Department that had a wide variety of professors with diverse backgrounds. Ironically, one of the first courses I was asked to teach was one devoted to a comparison of the New Age and biblical worldviews. Student interest was so great that enrollment had to be limited. A student committee helped to screen the many applicants. The chairperson of that committee was a campus leader with a New Age perspective. The course enrollment was largely confined to students already involved in various facets of the New Age movement.

Out of this experience and later opportunities to teach the same course, I wrote a book called *Christ and the New Consciousness.* "New Consciousness" was one of the terms used at that time for the New Age worldview.

My background for interest in dialogue between the biblical and New Age worldviews began much earlier in my life. Coming from the so-called Bible Belt, I entered Southern Baptist Theological Seminary and, after some 5½ years, finished a doctorate in New Testament studies with an emphasis on the apocalyptic literature of the Bible and the Intertestamental Period. This study aroused my interest in the biblical view of the future. Later I wrote a book entitled *The Lion and the Lamb* on the book of Revelation.

After finishing theological studies, I accepted the pastorate of a college church directly across the street from a Christian liberal arts college. There I found that many of the professors who were doing graduate work in secular universities dominated by the Enlightenment and the secular worldview were having great difficulty relating their Christian faith to their studies.

Realizing a developing need in the evangelical world, I determined to pursue further graduate work in the fields of philosophical theology and Christian apologetics. I left the United States for Europe, where I studied at the University of Edinburgh in Scotland and at the Universities of Basel and Zurich in Switzerland. Scotland had earlier faced the Enlightenment, and study there was especially helpful. In my period of study at the University of Basel, I encountered Karl Barth, who had had a rather radical reaction to the Enlightenment. I also studied with Emil Brunner at the University of Zurich. Brunner had a deep interest in Christian apologetics.

It was at Basel that I encountered the darker side of the occult world. Martin Nieden, my roommate in an international theological hostel, had been in the Hitler Youth Corps before his dramatic conversion and entrance into the Lutheran ministry. In his earlier years, Martin had been active in every form of the occult and satanism in the Hitler youth movement. Dialogue with Martin aroused my interest in the area of black magic and satanism and the darker side of the occult.

While in Basel and Zurich, I became interested in Carl Jung, the eminent psychiatrist. Jung was born in Basel and studied in Zurich. His pastor father had great difficulties with his Christian faith, and his mother was involved in many forms of the occult. Jung himself is one of the key persons related to the psychological aspects of the contemporary New Age movement.

In later years, my interest in the occult world was heightened by a lecture tour in South America where I encountered various forms of the occult. I was especially impressed with the power of the Macumba and Quimbanda religions in Brazil. Macumba is a strange admixture of primal religion and Roman Catholicism.

In a study trip in the Caribbean I encountered the Mayan culture. Other study programs in Mexico led me deeper into the background of the darker side of satanism and witchcraft. These movements have grown in recent years in Mexico and in the United States, especially in Texas, Florida, and California. As a result of these experiences, I wrote a book entitled *Demons, Demons, Demons.*

A Rockefeller program and post-doctoral fellowship at Harvard University pushed me more deeply into the area of world religions. The Center for the Study of World Religions at Harvard was just being started. At nearby Massachusetts Institute of Technology, Huston Smith was lecturing on the increasing impact of world religions on America and the influence of these religions on our culture through the New Age worldview.

As a result of this increasing interest in world religions, I had an opportunity during a sabbatical to study in the Middle and Far East. I encountered Hinduism at Hindu Benares University. I also studied Buddhism and other Far Eastern religions in Thailand, Hong Kong, Taiwan, Korea, and Japan. Some years later I conducted two study tours in China, where the Confucianist and Taoist religions and their derivatives were seen in context.

While at Harvard, I also had an opportunity to study with Paul Tillich, who emphasized the "kairos" concept, which has a renewed significance as we face the millennial year 2000. New Age leaders have drawn ideas from Tillich, who attempted to combine the Christian faith and the philosophy of Hegel, Schelling, and other German idealistic and existential philosophers. As a result of my study with Tillich, I was asked to write a book on Tillich in The Makers of the Modern Theological Mind series. Tillich also stimulated my interest in mysticism and the arts. I was later to edit a book on mysticism and to write a book entitled *Theology and Contemporary Art Forms.* The New Age has shown interest in these areas.

In the 1960s and 1970s, I encountered leaders of various facets of the

New Age movement in the San Francisco area. While teaching and lecturing there, I witnessed the influence of Charles Manson and his followers and visited the Church of Satan.

Studying at Union Seminary in New York City on a sabbatical, I visited the Greenwich Village area to hear Swami Prabhupada, the founder of the International Society for Krishna Consciousness (ISKCON), on his first visit to the United States. Sometime later I taught in the summer school of Princeton Theological Seminary and took my class to New York City to interview the leaders of the Hare Krishna and the Unification movements.

To acquire background for dialogue with New Age adherents, I became a member of the Noetic Institute, a prominent New Age organization, and gained new insights attending some of their conferences, including one on the goddess movement.

More recently, I attended an international conference on the New Age movement and alternative religions under the direction of J. Gordon Melton, sponsored by the University of Santa Barbara in California. There I met leaders and critics of the New Age movement from around the world.

Much of the growing interest in the New Age movement is rooted in its call for a transformation of people's views of society. As we will see, the New Age movement is a sophisticated monistic system which is a close cousin to (if not an identical twin of) primal religion. The ancient shaman is returning in scientific disguise.

As the year 2000 approaches, there is also a revival of interest in the Christian faith. On the left are liberation theology, feminism, and African-American theology. To the right there is a renewal of fundamentalism and the Religious Right. For mainline denominations, there is an interest in feminism and the Jesus seminar. Evangelicalism is also experiencing revival and renewal.

These developments in both New Age studies and the biblical area are related to a new understanding and a new interest in the importance of worldviews. In this study, I will concentrate on two basic worldviews as we move toward the millennial year 2000. One is called the New Age worldview. It combines new physics, transpersonal psychology, and the human potential movement. It is holistic. It is related to Far Eastern religions. The other is the biblical worldview.

It is interesting to note that New Age leaders claim the biblical worldview is closely related to what they designate as a Christian male god dominance and an ecological emphasis that has ripped humans from nature. The biblical view also has been associated with negative aspects of technology. New Age leaders then say that these attitudes and practices constitute a large part of society's problem.

Biblical scholars respond that New Age advocates have distorted the biblical view, picking some of the worst exponents of the biblical view to critique. However, many biblical advocates admit that followers of the biblical worldview have distorted and failed to live up to an enlightened understanding of the implications of the biblical view. These discerning biblical advocates want to return to the basic teachings of the biblical worldview as properly understood. They are willing to set up criteria for evaluation, dialogue, and transformation. These biblical leaders also deplore scientism and materialism.

Biblical advocates affirm that it is important for New Age advocates and biblical adherents to have an understanding of the worldview of each perspective. They grant that there are lessons to be learned and evaluations to be made and hope that transformations will occur as dialogue and evaluation occur.

In this study, I will use incidents from my own religious and cultural pilgrimage to help an evangelical readership discover its own history, learn from the errors of the past, and face up to the challenges of the future.

My personal struggle has been to help evangelicals to allow their faith to shape their understanding of the world. I have sought to show evangelicals the coherence and viability of their beliefs. To construct an edifice, one must first be assured of the reliability of its foundations. My teaching and writing, especially my book *Life's Ultimate Questions: A Contemporary Philosophy of Religion*, have aimed to secure the public acceptance of the intellectual adequacy and sufficiency of evangelicalism in terms both of its own internal criteria and in terms of the alternatives in the modern Western world. We must continue to help shape and renew the Christian mind and heart.

This study, approached from an evangelical perspective, is designed to provide a basis of study for churches, colleges, seminaries, and laypeople. In 1996, under the leadership of Tom and Karen Cowley, some thirty-five evangelical churches in the San Francisco Bay area conducted a lay-led seminar based on the contents of this book. I was a leader and respondent. The success of that seminar revealed how dialogue can open an avenue to a fresh understanding and appreciation of the biblical worldview.

Unfortunately, many professed Christians are caught up in certain phases of the New Age movement without realizing that the New Age worldview is contrary in most of its teachings to a basic biblical perspective.

This study, which describes and evaluates the New Age and biblical worldviews in eleven key areas, should give Christians and New Age advocates alike a better understanding of both sides. Of central concern throughout are the nature, structure, and increasing impact of the New Age worldview.

# CHAPTER ONE

# *The New Age Movement*

"New Age" is a spiritual movement seeking to transform individuals and society through mystical union with a dynamic cosmos. Its advocates hope to bring about a utopian era, a "New Age" of harmony and progress that some say has already begun.

The New Age movement offers the world a new frame of orientation. It seeks to replace both traditional biblical religion and secular humanism. It promises hope for a new future through personal and social transformation. It involves new types of psychological techniques that often are nothing more than updates of older approaches. It capitalizes on our concerns for our health, the environment, nuclear power, and women's issues.

Today's Christians need to understand the meaning of the New Age. They need to understand what makes it so attractive to so many people, especially young people. They need to understand how it differs from traditional biblical Christianity. And finally, Christians need to understand why New Age advocates insist the world is "in crisis," a crisis they say can only be solved by the New Age movement.

## A NETWORK OF ORGANIZATIONS

New Age is merely an umbrella term. There is no central headquarters that you can contact. There are no national officers. Instead New Age should be understood as a network, or a network of networks — an extremely large and

1

loosely structured group of organizations bound together by common assumptions and a common vision.

The New Age movement emerged in Western society in the late 1960s and, during the 1980s and 1990s, has shown itself to be an important new force in the ever-changing Western culture. While freely accepting new perspectives from the East, the movement has deep roots in Middle Eastern and Western philosophy and life.

All New Age religion has been defined as a criticism of dogmatic Christianity as well as a criticism of rational and scientific ideologies. New Agers contend that the clash between Christianity and scientific and rational beliefs has put the world in "crisis." The solution, they say, is a "third option" which does not reject religion and spirituality or science and rationality, but combines them. New Age advocates, in fact, insist that the world crisis will be resolved only if this third New Age option becomes dominant in society.[1]

Before we can understand both this "world crisis" and the solution promised by New Age, we must understand the New Age movement. There are two New Age camps, or groups. The "mainstream" aspect enters our culture through the areas of health, psychology, art, education, and business. It packages itself in culturally attractive and appealing wrappings. This group includes thinkers with environmental, transformational, and holistic-health agendas.

The "occult" side becomes part of our culture by more openly appropriating exotic spiritual beliefs. Members of this group immerse themselves in channeling, or receiving messages from spiritual masters risen to beyond-the-earth realms. Actress Shirley MacLaine, who has written a book on her New Age beliefs, and people who are involved in magic and witchcraft are examples of the occult side.

While separating themselves from what is termed "fortune-telling," many so-called sophisticated New Age people accept and rely on some traditional occult practices as they try for greater awareness of themselves and of the world. In this context, most New Agers have no hesitancy to consult astrologers, tarot card readers, and professional psychics. New Age astrologers focus on how astrological charts can guide in self-understanding and transformation.

New Agers tend to avoid spiritualist mediums who consult the dead, but have little difficulty with individuals who are in contact with higher spirit teachers, conceived as ascended masters, the "great White brotherhood," or the "higher self" of a medium.

The name "New Age" was coined in recent years and came from astrology's prediction that we are moving into an Aquarian, or millennial,

---

1. Wouter J. Hanegraaff, *New Age Religion and Western Culture* (Leiden: Brill, 1996), 517.

2

age which will come at the close of this century. Believers in this theory contend that for the past two thousand years the earth has been influenced by the sign of Pisces, the fish. During this period, they say, legalistic and restrictive Christianity has been dominant. Occult knowledge has been undervalued. They see the new Aquarian Age as one of brotherhood and occult happenings. Shirley MacLaine and others believe that the Aquarian Age has already begun.

## STRONG UNITY OF IDEAS

It is easy to get caught up in examining the growth of New Age at the "micro" level of dozens of individual groups. Instead, we need to stand back and realize that, seen as a whole, the New Age collection of ideas displays an amazing unity.

Like the term "evangelicalism," New Age is not tied to any particular organizations but is linked by a set of common worldview assumptions, a way of understanding reality. Its worldview is one of occult mysticism spelled out in secular terms — an ancient wisdom updated and expressed with a modern vocabulary. For many Christian authors, the New Age movement is seen most significantly as a sophisticated, contemporary representation of the same old spiritual kingdom that has always stood in stark opposition to the kingdom of Jesus Christ (see Acts 13:8-12).

Carl Raschke, of the University of Denver, states that "The [New Age movement] is a codification, an updating of the idealistic fervor, religious experimentation, anti-intellectualism, millennialism and self-immersion of the earlier counter-culture. It is a mystical utopianism. It has an implicit political vision with totalitarian overtones."[2]

In reality, New Age is an alternative belief system. It creates and uses its own language. And its belief system is affecting the way an increasing number of individuals and groups see reality and life.

The traditional biblical belief system has been undercut over the years by science and legalism. New Age took advantage of that vacuum, capitalizing on what is called "scientific" holism in order to create a new "religious" holism.

Although the various New Age groups may put their main focus on different things, certain assumptions cannot be separated from the basic New Age belief system. The movement places more importance on experience than it does on beliefs. Beliefs last only as long as they are functional and

2. Carl Raschke, "The New Age: The Movement toward Self-Discovery," in *New Age Spirituality* (Louisville, Ky.: Westminster/John Knox, 1993), 106-9.

helpful. While there will be frequent clashes of ideas, a belief is seen as a matter of preference rather than of "truth."

In contrast to a religion like Christianity, where the truth comes from God and is spelled out in the Bible, the New Age movement has numerous ways of arriving at truth. These are distinguished by their efficiency more than their rightness. For the New Ager it is a matter of choosing a preferred method from among many equally suitable options rather than discovering the single best and correct means.

# BASIC NEW AGE IDEAS

Even though beliefs are secondary, there are some basic ideas that are readily identifiable and held by most people in the movement.

## "All Is One" (Monism)

The New Age bottom line can be stated in three words: "all is one." The cosmos is seen as a pure, undifferentiated, universal, energy-interconnected process. This premise is known as "monism," where distinctions of apparent opposites disappear. There is no line between the creation of material and the force or energy that creates it. This reduction of all reality to energy is derived from theories of matter and light related to quantum physics. The New Age movement denies any separation between humanity and nature — or even between humans and God.

The New Age teaching about the nature of the world and human life can be seen as a modern-day version of the theory of "correspondence." The universe, from this perspective, is the source of life's many manifestations and, as such, possesses an intelligence that guides and guards humans on life's pathways.

The relation of the universe to individual human beings is not the same for New Age religion as the traditional relationship between God and his creatures is for the biblical view. Rather, the New Age universe contains all of life. New Agers emphasize their conviction that the notion of separateness, of discrete existence, is illusory. In New Age belief, human beings are all expressions of one another and of the universe. New Age theology puts forth the idea that matter and energy are different manifestations of one encompassing reality.[3]

3. Douglas Groothuis, "New Age or Ancient Error?" *Moody Monthly*, February 1985, 20.

4

This energy goes by many names: prana, mana, odic force, orgone energy, holy spirit, the ch'i, mind, and the healing force. Regardless of the name, this energy is the force believed to cause psychic healing. It is the force released in various forms of meditation and body therapies that energizes individuals mentally and physically. It is the force passed between individuals in the expression of love. It is the underlying reality of the universe encountered in mystical states of consciousness.[4]

## Everything Is God (Pantheism)

Most New Agers identify God with the "Ultimate Unifying Principle" that binds the whole together and is the power that gives it a dynamic. This is called "pantheism" because it states that all things, all plants, and all humans partake of the one divine essence. The One, or God, is beyond personality. In New Age, God is more an "it" than a "he" or "she." God is seen as an impersonal energy force or consciousness. God is in all and through all.

This vibrating energy which is God is viewed as a "higher" manifestation of the universe than is matter. New Agers combine the language of quantum physics with age-old mystical imagery and symbolism and see this vibrating energy as "light."

In New Age, God, or ultimate reality, manifests itself in creation as a dynamic interaction of polarities: light/dark, male/female, good/evil. These polarities, however, are not absolute but only different facets of that single reality from which all creation emanates and in which all creation is united. In spite of appearances, all is one.

## God Is within You

Based upon their idealistic or spiritual understanding of the nature of the universe, New Age devotees frequently or usually affirm their own godhood and/or the self as god. Persons are viewed as individualized manifestations of god — gods and goddesses in exile.[5] As one New Age writer says, "It is time that God be put in his place, that is in man." We are God in disguise. Only ignorance keeps us from realizing our divine reality. Another New Age writer says, "Honor and worship your own being. God dwells in you as You."

---

4. J. Gordon Melton, *New Age Encyclopedia* (Detroit: Gale Research, 1990), xvi.

5. Melton, *New Age Encyclopedia*, xvii; see also Paul Heelas, *The New Age Movement* (Cambridge, Mass.: Blackwell, 1996), 19ff.

This is one theme in actress Shirley MacLaine's book *Out on a Limb*, which explores and defends the New Age. She writes of a friend telling her, "Each person is a universe. If you know yourself, you know everything."

All knowledge, power, and truth are within us and waiting to be unlocked. Another leader states, "We are as gods and might as well get good at it." "I am God," shouts Shirley MacLaine on the Malibu beach.

Few aspects of the New Age have shocked traditional religious sensitivities more (or invited more ridicule, even from non-religious quarters) than Shirley MacLaine's notorious "I am God" exclamations. Clearly intended to be provocative, her statement contains an argumentative edge that is absent in most other authors. More importantly, within the wider context of MacLaine's beliefs, the phrase "I am God" can be seen as containing a whole metaphysics in a nutshell. If the whole is contained in each of its parts, then each part *is* the whole.

MacLaine's radical "I am God" belief is directly derived from one of her main influences, J. Z. Knight/Ramtha. Ramtha sees it as his most important task to convince the members of his audience that each of them is God. On the back cover of *Ramtha: An Introduction* is a photograph of J. Z. Knight staring the reader straight in the face, accompanied by this text: "You never knew how beautiful you were, for you never really looked at who and what you are. You want to see what God looks like? Go look in a reflector — you are looking God straight in the face."[6]

As a primary effect of such an affirmation, New Agers frequently report a sense of self-affirmation, a release from guilt, and an acceptance of life (very similar to the experience of a Christian who discovers a new identity as a child of God the Father). In the realm of ethics, New Agers often affirm that all is god, hence all is good. Evil is usually tied to ignorance and seen as a lack of enlightenment.[7]

## Reincarnation and Karma

Within New Age, personal transformation is a way of life. Hence, each person will choose a *sadhana*, a path of growth and spiritual development. But since almost no sadhana can be completed in one lifetime, a common belief in reincarnation and karma provides a long-term framework in which to view individual spiritual progression.

The prospects for spiritual evolution beyond physical death are not at all limited to physical rebirth on our (or even on another) planet. The universal

6. Hanegraaff, *New Age Religion*, 207-9.
7. Melton, *New Age Encyclopedia*, xvii.

element in New Age ideas about survival is "progressive spiritual evolution," considered a process which starts before birth and continues beyond death. Reincarnation is a crucial part of this larger process.

You must progress through many lifetimes to reach oneness with the One — to be reunited with Ultimate Reality. If you accumulate good karma (the fruit of your actions), positive benefits will accrue in later lives. Bad karma produces future punishments. The final goal is to merge with the cosmos, or God, and end the repetitious and painful birth-death-rebirth process.

Of the most commonly accepted opinions within the New Age movement, few are held with such passion and even dogmatic certainty as the belief in reincarnation and karma. For many, the passion derives from their experience of transformation which included a renunciation of the Christian doctrine of hell and damnation.

But in the New Age worldview, a view in which the believer is no longer dealing with an ongoing relationship with God, karma and reincarnation serve numerous intellectual functions. They explain the inequalities and negativities of life, allow obviously needed additional time for spiritual growth, and provide a never-ending source for speculation on past lives, soul mates, and life after death.[8]

## Changing Your Consciousness

From a New Age perspective, your problem, to begin with, is that you have an illusion that you are limited and finite. A New Ager will tell you that you are separated from God only in your own consciousness. You need to be enlightened. You have forgotten your true identity. You are the victim of a false sense of a separate identity which blinds you to your essential unity with God. This is the cause of all your problems. In the words of Eliade, a historian and philosopher who has written numerous books on world religions, "The wretchedness of human life is not owing to divine punishment or to an original sin, but to . . . metaphysical ignorance."[9]

The transformation from an ignorant state to an enlightened one releases the individual from the consequences (karma) of ignorance and brings forgiveness and/or understanding of the former experience of unpleasantness, what the mundane world calls evil. The enlightened being then lives beyond what this world calls good and evil.

8. Ibid., xvi.
9. Karen Hoyt, *The New Age Rage* (Old Tappan, N.J: Revell, 1987), 20.

# PSYCHO-SPIRITUAL TECHNIQUES

In New Age, you are responsible to change your own consciousness. Humans are not depraved or dependent on any outside source for deliverance or strength. A person's blindness, which is the root of all of his or her problems, can be eliminated by a change, or transformation, of consciousness. A person needs to have the experience of knowing the One and his or her own essential deity. This experience is brought about by psycho-spiritual techniques. These techniques involve balancing polarities, manipulating energy, and ridding consciousness of the fragmenting effects of rational thinking and the predefining limitations of old religious beliefs.

New Agers see human action in the world as a series of lessons to be learned. In this concept, the pilgrim is understood more as a student, and the world has become a New Age schoolhouse. The answer is to realize that we ourselves are god. Your slumbering "higher self," or "divinity," can be aroused.

There are a number of psycho-spiritual techniques to help you realize your own divinity. These include meditation, Yoga, chanting, mood-altering music, mind-expanding drugs, and religious mysticism. The list also involves guided imagery, balancing and aligning "energies," hypnosis, body disciplines, fasting, and martial arts. Other techniques include consciousness-raising seminars such as Erhard Seminar Training (est), "rebirthing," Silva Mind Control, and body therapies such as rolfing and bio-energetics.

New tools are being developed and announced regularly. Of special importance among these tools are crystals. Occult attention to gemstones and crystal substances goes back many centuries, when they were valued as healing agents. Now, through the medium of channeling, crystals have been assigned an unprecedented central role in the transformation process. That central role began with Edgar Cayce, who is the most widely known American channeler. In the 1980s, Frank Alper, a longtime Spiritualist medium who had become attuned to the New Age, gave detailed instructions on the personal use of crystals to tap into the cosmic powers that facilitate transformation.[10]

New Agers, with their strong preference for synthesis, often follow multiple disciplines at the same time. For example, a person who seeks to practice the code of forgiveness specified in the *Course in Miracles* may also regularly receive Trager bodywork, a form of massage that aims to facilitate meditative and even mystical states. That person may also be following the recommendations of an astrologer and practicing vegetarianism as a part of a spiritual discipline. The same person may also be incorporating into daily life other suggestions of a particular New Age teacher. One can practice Zen meditation without being a Buddhist or joining a zendo.

10. James R. Lewis and J. Gordon Melton, *Perspectives on the New Age* (Albany, N.Y.: State University of New York, 1992), 23.

8

# THE ROLE OF THE GURU

The question of techniques raises the issue of the role of the teacher or, to use the Indian term, the "guru." A guru is a person believed to be experienced in spiritual matters — one who is mature and capable of introducing a pupil to spiritual reality. In order to adopt and use a spiritual practice, one must learn it. For many practices, the learning process is simple and straightforward and may be self-taught from a book. However, some are believed to require the personal tutoring of a guru. A number of techniques are taught in the context of what is seen as the transfer of energy from guru to pupil. Thus, for the average New Ager, gurus may assume a variety of functions. For some, the guru may even become a lifelong master teacher. But some New Agers avoid all gurus and advocate the adequacy and sufficiency of those practices not related to a guru. Most revere gurus as mature teachers from whom they can learn, but to whom they do not offer any personal allegiance. Thus at a typical New Age event, gurus will be present, and New Agers will partake as they please from their offerings.[11]

# TRANSFORMATION AND REALIZING YOUR GODHOOD

When New Age transformation occurs, you realize your godhood. This is the path to self-realization, cosmic consciousness, and enlightenment. Your self is a cosmic treasure of wisdom, power, and delight. Realization of oneness and divinity leads to spiritual power and well-being. Transcendental Meditation even promises that advanced students can achieve the ability to levitate, fly, and become invisible.

Through transformation, the limitations of the supposedly finite and imperfect human being turn into limitless potential for the truly enlightened being. Expanses in parapsychology become open. There are many names for this transformation, such as God-realization, self-realization, enlightenment, illumination, nirvana, satori, and "at-one-ment."

Getting in touch with one's own unconscious is the first step toward godhood. The personal unconscious, however, is only a localized region of the "collective unconscious" which connects all individual human consciousnesses. This collective unconscious is a realm of the mind where we can get in touch with the universal archetypes. In Jungian fashion, the traditional group of "gods" are often interpreted as archetypes, and conversely the archetypes of the collective

11. Melton, *New Age Encyclopedia*, xv.

unconscious are seen as powerful, spiritual realities. In other words, traditional religious concepts are reinterpreted in psychological terms. However, because psychology itself is embedded in an encompassing religious framework, New Age authors can avoid the conclusion that the gods are unreal because they exist "only in the mind." They *do* exist only in the mind, of course, but if God as well as all reality is ultimately the mind, then where else could the gods be if not in the mind?

The New Age movement follows Carl Jung, rather than Freud, in regarding the unconscious as much more than just a storehouse of repressed emotions. The unconscious has some remarkable "talents" of its own. However, because unconscious impressions exist in a prereflective and nonverbal state, we have to translate them into words and images.

This translation requires the use of our intuitive faculties. Both intuition and the unconscious are associated with the right brain, which functions on holistic principles. The left hemisphere, in contrast, is analytic, intellectual, and verbal. New Age sources never tire of repeating that most of us rely heavily on only the rational, and neglect the intuitive. They say it is important to develop our "right-brain" faculties to an equal level as those of our "left brain." In this way we not only gain access to knowledge stored in the unconscious, but also to the superconscious, or transpersonal, realms.

The emphasis on the unconscious world of symbols and archetypes as the *only* way to reach the divine (and the corresponding concentration on art, myth, and ritual) is particularly characteristic for neopaganism. Nevertheless, the view of the unconscious as the connection between human and divine consciousness (via the higher self) is a general New Age tenet.[12]

Theoretical ideas about universal and earthly correspondence, buttressed by the concept of the transformational nature of matter-energy, lead to the idea that everything is everything else. This means that everything can impinge on everything else. Hence, the New Age universe and planet are conceived as places of magic and miracle. Transformation in the New Age is often assumed to be sudden, dramatic, and strongly perceptible.

This New Age idea of transformation relates conceptually to the biblical view of conversion. New Agers see the human situation as, in some ways, deficient, and the perfection that is possible is not yet present. There is, indeed, a millennial ring to New Age theology, as its name itself suggests. Followers think of present-day humans as existing in states that are metaphysical equivalents of sickness or sin. Sometimes, in New Age understanding, that sickness or sin finds material, or physical, expression. At other times, its expression is largely mental, or "spiritual." In both cases, the description of the human situation — in need of healing — echoes, in nontheological ways, biblical notions of original sin and the need of conversion.

12. Hanegraaff, *New Age Religion*, 216-18.

# HELP FROM SPIRITUAL BEINGS
# THROUGH CHANNELING

Channeling, or spirit contact, is seen by some as possibly the single most important and definitive aspect of the New Age. It is certainly the activity which has had the greatest success in mobilizing support for the movement as a whole. It also provides an excellent illustration of the manner in which the movement has interacted with the older esoteric groups already established in the culture.

New Age spirit contact is no different in form than that practiced in Spiritualism for the last 150 years. However, channeling distinguishes itself from Spiritualist mediumship in its purpose and content. In Spiritualism, the mediums have specialized in contact with the "spirits of the dead" for the purpose of demonstrating the continuance of individual life after death. Within the New Age movement, channeling has been accepted and redirected to the goal of facilitating the personal transformation of the channelers' clients.[13] For example, Shirley MacLaine stated that her life, in earlier years, was guided by Ramtha. He is described as a 35,000-year-old ascended master. He was once a barbarian warrior king, later a Hindu god, and is now beyond even deity itself.

Spiritual beings are usually regarded as human beings who differ from us only in having progressed beyond the earthly plane. They have completed the cycle of incarnations on earth and are now further developing in higher realities. From their comparatively exalted perspective they can help and advise brothers and sisters who are still struggling for spiritual understanding within the perimeters of matter. But it is equally possible that they have another background. For example, they may have come from other planets or from other dimensions. In all cases, they are essentially like us: evolving spiritual beings who are engaged in a cosmic process of learning by experience.

Ramtha and other ascended masters such as Mafu now have no physical existence; that is, they are spirits or spirit-beings. They are mainly interested in dispensing their philosophy of life to human beings. They operate through selected humans by temporarily assuming control of a human body during a trance. People who subject themselves to such entrancement and control are called "channelers," or simply "channels." The controlling spirit or entity will lecture, counsel, teach, or otherwise advise its human audience through these channelers.[14]

13. Lewis and Melton, *Perspectives on the New Age*, 21-23.
14. Hanegraaff, *New Age Religion*, 200.

11

## ALL RELIGIONS AS ONE

In the New Age, it is believed, people will recognize only one universal religion. The enlightened ones of all the great religions — Jesus, Buddha, Krishna, and others — have taught an experience of that same oneness. There are many paths to the one truth, many methods to become one with the One, but all differences are superficial and external. This is called "syncretism," or the perennial philosophy. It is also called "revelational indeterminacy." This is the belief that the truth may be revealed in diverse ways and through diverse agents. No individual or collectivity possesses a monopoly of the truth.[15]

I attended a "goddess" conference sponsored by the Isthmus Institute of Dallas, Texas. One woman testified that she had once been taught that she could be "saved" only by trust or faith in Jesus Christ. However, since embracing New Age teaching, she had found enlightenment and God-realization through the Hindu god Kali, the Red Lady of the Choctaw Indians, and the Egyptian Selamet. Jesus of Nazareth, she said, should not be considered the only begotten Son of God, the God-man, the Lord and Savior of the world. She explained that he is only one of many appearances or manifestations of God throughout the ages.

According to the New Age movement, Jesus and the other significant religious teachers, like Buddha and Krishna, were particularly transparent as bearers of the Divine, or Christ, Principle. Such teachers, according to New Agers, appear regularly throughout history to illustrate the aware, or fully realized, life, to teach individuals the goal of awareness, and to train them in particular techniques that facilitate self-awareness of one's inherent divinity.[16]

Christ, they say, is separate from Jesus. The "Christ" is the perfect god idea — the awareness of the divinity within. Jesus had "Christ-consciousness" or the "Christ Spirit" as much or more than anyone, but everyone can have the Christ Spirit. To use popular New Age phrases: we, too, may share the "Christ consciousness" or "the cosmic Christ Spirit."

Although New Age believers may talk about the "second coming of the Christ," they do not necessarily believe that this event will involve the appearance of a visible person. Some of them do (for instance, the Scottish New Age theosophist Benjamin Creme, who has been announcing "Maitreya the Christ" for two decades), but most expect the second coming to be a purely spiritual event which will be felt and experienced within rather than seen with physical eyes.[17]

---

15. Lewis and Melton, *Perspectives on the New Age*, 7.
16. Melton, *New Age Encyclopedia*, xvii.
17. Hanegraaff, *New Age Religion*, 101.

This Christ principle concept means that Christianity is not distinctive. In fact, some New Age leaders talk about a lost Christianity which turns out to be little different from Eastern mysticism and occultism. This idea is partially based on the Gospel of Thomas, a noncanonical book discovered at Nag Hammadi in Egypt.

## A GLORIOUS NEW AGE FUTURE

The majority of New Age advocates are filled with optimism and hope. As the New Age teachings gain ground and infiltrate with the gospel of cosmic unity, it is predicted that humanity will be ready to take over the reins of evolution. Teilhard de Chardin, a Jesuit paleontologist, prophesied a progressive evolutionary harmonization and unification of world consciousness that will eventually reach "the Omega Point."

The modern education system in the West has helped to promote the idea that the mythology of "evolutionism" can provide answers to ultimate human questions about meaning and purpose. This "evolutionism" was picked up by a wide cross-section of New Age leaders who say that we are poised on the brink of a massive transformation. The current period is unique in history and represents the beginning of a change of the quality of human existence. Christ-consciousness, or cosmic-consciousness, is awakening in millions of Christians and non-Christians. The Messiah within each of us, they say, will lead all of us forward into a glorious future.

## ASTROLOGY AND PREDICTIONS OF CHANGE

In 1987 an art historian named Jose Arguelles announced that his studies of ancient Mayan calendars showed that the "materialistic" world could end on August 16, 1987. This was the time when three planets would line up with the new moon. The requirement was that the proper number of true believers (144,000) would gather in various sacred sites around the world and "resonate" sufficiently to bring in a New Age of peace and harmony. In August 1987, far more than that number gathered in so-called sacred sites around the world. For Arguelles and his followers, the idea of an Aquarian Age assumes that through overwhelming natural cosmic forces, symbolized by the stars and planets, the New World is coming.

This prophecy approach is but one example of the widespread conviction in the New Age movement that humanity is poised at the crossroads. It is ready to leap forward and emerge as an entirely new creature, no longer constrained by the limitations and evils of the old order.

The New Age movement pursues the theme of "cosmic evolutionary optimism." New Agers believe that this change is potentially as sweeping as the Renaissance or the Protestant Reformation. They believe the world is on the verge of a profound breakthrough. The limited, finite Old Order will give way to a glorious, unlimited New Order of peace, prosperity, and perfection. Scientist Fritjof Capra has written a book entitled *The Turning Point*. This widely read book is representative of numerous books that affirm that this dynamic New Age is being born.

Many people within the New Age movement, primarily those with a theosophical background, see the need for a world teacher — a new avatar, an embodiment of God, a being of the status of Jesus or Gautama Buddha. This new world teacher will be a master of the highest order who comes to earth to facilitate the transformation into a new eon.

The idea had its most recent expression in the predictions of Benjamin Creme concerning the return of Maitreya, the Buddhist bodhisattva (master). Independent theosophist Alice Bailey, founder of the Arcane School, has been an energetic advocate of this position, and her students have circulated thousands of copies of a prayer, "The Great Invocation," which calls for this avatar's appearance.[18]

# YES AND NO TO HINDUISM

In most respects New Age can rightly be classified as a Western expression of classic Hinduism. The most basic beliefs are the same, as are the mystical experiences that are at the heart of both. Many of the New Age spiritual techniques that produce these experiences have come directly from India, brought here and taught since the 1960s by Hindu swamis and gurus. In spite of these commonalities, however, New Age differs from Hinduism in that it is life- and world-affirming.

One reason the New Age movement rejected the traditional Hindu view of the world is that it desires to change the world, not drop out of it. It also desires personal (earthly) as well as spiritual fulfillment. Neopaganism, which is part of the New Age movement, tends toward a stronger this-world-liness than does the rest of New Age.[19]

18. Melton, *New Age Encyclopedia*, xvii.
19. Elliot Miller, "The New Age Movement: What Is It?" *Forward*, Summer 1985, 20; see also Hanegraaff, *New Age Religion*, 365.

# NEW AGE OUTREACH

New Age is religious, but not solely a religion. Indeed, many New Age groups are clearly not religious groups. Some are political. Others are educational. Some are engaged in social issues such as ecology or peace. And many New Age organizations are simply businesses, intending to make a financial profit, perhaps while promoting New Age concepts.

## New Age "Churches"

An important concern for people in the biblical tradition is proper identification of New Age groups that are religious in scope. One stream of New Age activity does find expression in "churches" that resemble conventional churches, at least in form and building styles. Congregations in the New Thought lineage (Christian Science, Unity, Science of Mind) have existed for more than a hundred years. They are not necessarily typical of most New Age activities, and they often try to dissociate themselves from certain aspects of New Age. However, numerous New Age seminars are held in Unity churches.

The last decade has seen the rise of what we call independent New Age churches. They have names like the Church of Spiritual Healing, the Church of Ageless Wisdom, Radiant Light Interfaith Church, the Church of the Earth Nation, and the Church of Truth.

## New Age Institutes

However, churches are developing less frequently now than are groups of people who gather around institutes, study centers, seminars, trance channelers, psychics, teachers, healers, and expositions. All of these interrelate, or "network," with one another.

The New Age institutes seem to fulfill at least three functions. First, the institutes, usually privately or corporately owned, perform a service to clients. That service may be instruction in a New Age technique, counseling, or health care. Second, the institutes provide a place for people to gather and study New Age concepts. Third, the institutes encourage people to gather for fellowship, food, recreation, testimonies, and sharing in meditation, yoga, and astral dreaming.

Many of these New Age small groups, seminars, and retreats become functional substitutes for a church. In a great many ways, these strategies may be more efficient than some institutionalized churches and denominations. These New Age strategies have certain appeals for people, particularly for those who have been disappointed by, overlooked by, or for any reason turned off by traditional Christian churches.

Few leaders in New Age have formal theological or ministerial training. The movement does have gurus and professional ministers, but often these portray themselves as pilgrims on a spiritual path. By this experience and identification with ordinary people they gain a following. Women are visible and influential in New Age activities, both as participants and as leaders. Most of the trance channelers are women; most of the psychics are women; and most of the healers are women.

A number of academic institutions now offer degrees and programs on New Age topics at the bachelor, master, and doctorate levels.

## A Business

Despite the fact that some of its philosophical and theological background is Hinduism and Eastern thought, contemporary New Age is heavily European-ized and Americanized. New Age people have replaced the simplicity and slow pace of Hinduism with the efficiency and pragmatism that characterizes Americans and western Europeans.

New Age is a business, and nowhere is that more evident than in the array of consumer goods New Age groups produce and sell. They sell a myriad of products to enhance worship, meditation, or whatever one follows to transform consciousness: prayer mats, yapa beads, incense, clothing from natural fibers, crystals (and special lights to intensify them), health foods, vitamin pills, portable massage tables, meditation goggles, subliminal tapes, herbal teas, and herbal sleeping pillows. One salesman reported, "We're selling Buddha in a can."

There are also expositions and psychic fairs, which bring together companies, organizations, and practitioners who show their wares and their views to the general public.

# THE CONFLICT

Thus we see that the New Age world and the biblical world are in philo-sophical and religious collision. The New Age movement is not a deviation of the biblical view. Its use of biblical symbols and language is just a superficial use of culturally popular words and phrases for the purpose of introducing and interpreting the dynamics of the New Age movement to people who have some Christian background. The New Age movement is not a cult, by any of the popular definitions. To label and respond to the New Age movement as a cult is merely to trivialize the serious challenge which it presents to the biblical world and to substitute name-calling for honest analysis.

The New Age vision offers people a distinctly different approach for coming into a right relationship with Ultimate Reality. There are, of course, some similarities: the need for change, the promise of a new eon dominated by values such as love and peace, the assertion that spiritual values are more important than political, economic, and technological ones.

But there the similarity ends. The differences, which are more substantial, center on the contrasting views concerning the Ultimate Reality in the Universe, the human condition, and the solution to the basic human problem.

The New Age offers a vision of a universe united — a diverse chaotic visible world underlain by a mystical Oneness and universal power. This Oneness can be known by individuals as they awaken their inner senses. It is best described by impersonal terms such as Principle, Mind, Power, Light, Love, and Truth.

The biblical view, in contrast, offers the God of the Scriptures, a very personal deity whose basic characteristic is a loving relatedness, within himself as Trinity and toward humanity through creative action. The biblical view invites people to a personal relationship with a loving, caring God. Within the Christian tradition, mystical experience has an important place, but it is always judged by its relation to the God of the Scriptures.

Fundamental to the collision between the New Age and biblical worlds is the view of the human condition. New Agers see humans as basically the pinnacle of the creative process. However, they believe that humans have been slowed and blocked by various cultural conditions which, if removed, can be quickly surpassed. These hampering factors on an individual level include parent-inflicted psychological trauma, bad living habits, and the effects of a poisoned environment. On the social level they include corporate dominance of people, war, processed food, addictive chemicals, and dogmatic religion. Evil can be reduced to a list of human-produced factors.

The biblical view has a more profound understanding of the human condition. Humans have an essential warping within their nature, and human evils are seen as the product of that warping. That warping separates humans from God, binds the will, and perpetually leads to the reemergence of idolatry and self-centeredness, thus defeating or distorting all attempts at reform. Human history demonstrates that as one manifestation of evil is overcome, a new one arises to take its place.[20]

20. J. Gordon Melton, "The New Age Movement: A Survey and Christian Response" (Atlanta: Interfaith Witness Department, Home Mission Board, SBC, March 1985), 12-13.

# THE SOLUTION

For a solution, the New Age movement looks for the transformation of humans and human society by overcoming the personal and social evils which humanity has created. The force of the universe will propel the human race into a New Age, though the details of the process are a matter of debate among members of the movement. Some, who have an evolutionary scheme, see the gradual development of society, propelled forward at significant moments by a Christ figure, an avatar, or a God-man. This will appear to release a new burst of spiritual energy. This will facilitate large numbers of personal transformations which in turn will transform elements of society. As the transformations reach a crucial mass, the whole is thrust forward to the New Age.

Christians, with their understanding of the human condition, affirm that the problem of humans requires outside intervention to correct the warping and to reestablish contact with the Ultimate Reality in the universe, the Living God. That outside intervention occurred in Jesus Christ, who alone, as the instrument of the grace of God, can correct the human situation. Thus, while Christians honor the contributions made by other groups to culture and society, they assert that in the long run these groups fall short of the Divine. While these other groups may be able to make some changes in society, they will fail in their goal of transforming society at any profound level.

In like measure, all "religions" are not the same, either in some set of lowest common denominator teachings or as differing paths to the same goal. There is certainly room for interreligious cooperation on issues of mutual concern, from hunger to the prevention of war. But that does not negate — and it frequently highlights — the very real incompatibilities.[21]

Christians also assert the uniqueness of Jesus. He is not one avatar among many. He is God. He did not manifest a Christ Principle, a modern abstraction of New Age values; rather, he fully incarnated God. He is not primarily a moral example (though he is certainly that as well), but *the* connecting link by which humanity, warped and unable to fulfill the divine intention, is brought back into touch and fellowship with God and finds salvation.

21. Ibid., 13-14.

# CHAPTER TWO

# Tracing the Origins of New Age

New Age thinking goes back a long way — to before the time of Christ — and can be traced through a wide range of alternative religions and cultic movements.

Broadly speaking, the New Age movement encompasses many religious movements that would not generally be categorized as such. Among these is Mormonism. Joseph Smith was deeply involved in spiritualism and had frequent communication with spirit guides. There is also considerable New Age philosophy in Christian Science, New Thought, Unity, the Children of God, the Unification Church, the Hare Krishnas, Scientology, and many lesser-known cultic movements such as Rosicrucianism, Swedenborgianism, est, Eckankar, the Church Universal and Triumphant, Silva Mind Control, Yoga, the Rajneesh Ashram, and the Divine Light Mission.

Thus, despite its relatively recent appearance, the New Age movement should not be viewed as a startlingly new phenomenon in Western culture. Rather, it is more adequately seen as the latest phase in occult/metaphysical religion, a persistent tradition that has been in constant contrast to the Judeo-Christian tradition through the centuries.[1]

1. Ruth Tucker, *Another Gospel* (Grand Rapids: Academie, 1989), 320.

# THE OCCULT IN THE BIBLICAL
# AND HELLENISTIC ERAS

Even prior to the rise of biblical religion and continuing during its development, there was an alternative occult tradition. For example, in the Old Testament period, the occult view dominated Egypt, Assyria, Babylon, and Persia, as well as the beliefs of the Canaanites.

For students of religious history, it is well known that Christ lived and taught in a time of religious change and crisis similar to that of today. The background of Christ's ministry was complex. Some people in his time were attracted to the one God concept and to the demands of the Hebrew religion. Others found the secret initiations of the mystery religions, with their dying-rising gods, meaningful. The universalism of Stoicism was widely acclaimed. The nature and fertility gods were continuing their influence. Paul faced the religion of Diana and Aphrodite in Ephesus and Corinth.

Roots of the occult world can also be found in the Hellenistic world during the first three centuries of the Christian era. This was a world in which a mixture of Greek, Roman, Christian, Jewish, and other elements fused in various ways to produce a cosmopolitan religious and cultural synthesis.

By the end of the Hellenistic period, in the fourth century, Christianity won out and became the official religion of the Roman Empire. However, elements of the older Hellenistic beliefs provided the ingredients for an alternative occult view that persisted.

## Gnosticism

First, as a system, there was Gnosticism, a religious teaching and practice that had grown on the fringes of both the Jewish and Christian traditions. A Gnostic was, literally, one who knew. The Gnostic was thought to be someone within whom the saving spark of knowledge was planted. By means of the spark of knowledge, the Gnostic could start the long journey leading to reunion with his or her divine counterpart within the Godhead. The goal was mystical merging.

## Neoplatonism

Plato had taught that the real world was the world of Ideas, or Forms, on which the physical, material universe was modeled. For Plato, there was a hierarchy among the Ideas, and the ultimate among them were the Good, the True, and the Beautiful.

Neoplatonism retained Plato's theory of Ideas and the vision of a hierarchy among them. However, it saw the ultimate Idea as the One, followed by Nous, or Mind, which was in turn followed by the World Soul. From the World Soul came individual souls and, even lower in the hierarchy, the many-ness of the material world. The religious task, as Neoplatonists understood it, was to reclaim oneself for the One, retracing the path of downward emanation from the One by an upward ascent of the soul. Like the Gnostic, it was clear that the Neoplatonist desired and sought mystical experience — union with the One.[2]

## Hermeticism

The religious philosophy called Hermeticism brought together Gnosticism, Platonism, Neoplatonism, astrology, and various other religious philosophies from ancient Greece. It offered mystical teachings from pagan sources and established a cult that exalted the mind as intuition and had magical lessons.

Although most Christian church fathers such as Augustine (A.D. 354-430) preached against the Hermetic texts, other Christians passed on their teachings.

## Alchemy

Some church fathers engaged in Alchemy, an occult system with religious overtones. For religious alchemists, the process of creating gold was an external symbol for an internal change the person sought. Here the understood task of the alchemist was to discover the divine spark identified as the Self. The alchemist then sought a reunification with that spark and a merging with the All that was considered divine. In the twentieth century, Swiss psychiatrist Carl Jung drew heavily from Alchemy.

## Celts

In the Middle Ages, the Christians in Europe confronted the so-called pagan movement rooted in the Celtic tradition of England. (See Chapter 6 for more on magic, witchcraft, and the neopagan movement.)

2. Catherine L. Albanese, *America: Religions and Religion* (Belmont, Calif.: Wadsworth, 1992), 253-54.

# THE RENAISSANCE

Through these five systems and other practices, the various occult disciplines found their way into the lives of those who carried on the alternative tradition and transmitted it to the Renaissance. This cultural rebirth called the Renaissance began in northern Italy in the fourteenth century and helped spread occultism throughout Europe over the next two centuries.[3]

By the middle of the eighteenth century powerful dissenting forces were massed against the traditional order in the West. From the salons and cafés of pre-revolutionary France, especially, a working alliance of secularists, political revolutionaries, and occultists emerged. This alliance was later vividly portrayed in pictures of the first president of the United States in his Masonic garb and in the placing of occult symbols on the new country's national seal.

A powerful Christian community remained in the United States and in many western European countries, but through a bewildering variety of religious dissent, the occult view came out into the open as well.

# FREEMASONRY

Possibly the largest of these earlier dissenting movements was Freemasonry, which spread a new gnostic spirituality. Since it was not a "church" and did not openly compete with Christianity, it could spread unopposed to every city and town. Although opposed by the Catholic Church and some conservative Protestants, it was generally not seen as a competitor to orthodox Christianity, and many church members and leaders joined. In America, where only 20 to 30 percent of the population were church members in the nineteenth century, Freemasonry functioned as a spiritual home to the religiously unaffiliated.[4]

# SWEDENBORGIANISM

As a Rockefeller Visiting Scholar at Harvard in the 1950s, I would walk past a small group of frame buildings on the Harvard campus that obviously were out of place among the large classroom and museum edifices. Learning that

3. Albanese, *America: Religions and Religion*, 255; cf. also Paul J. Stern, *The Haunted Prophet* (New York: Dell, 1976), 190-95.
4. Timothy L. Miller, ed., *America's Alternative Religions* (New York: State University of New York, 1995), 347-48.

the small buildings constituted the Swedenborgian Seminary, I immediately sought more information about the philosophical and theological roots of this school.

Emanuel Swedenborg (1688-1772) was one of the leading scientists of Sweden. He would likely be lauded today for his scientific accomplishments had his name not been deleted from the history of science after he left that career to become a "seer." In the face of growing materialism, he championed the primacy of the invisible spiritual world. He suggested that the world he explored in his dreamlike states had greater metaphysical reality than the visible world more properly explored by science, which he considered an inferior, shadowlike realm. But Swedenborg stated his conclusions in such a way that the science of his day was neither contradicted nor discounted, merely put in its proper "secondary" place. This world was the product of the divine influx, the ultimate origin of power and life.

Swedenborg analyzed the relation between the two worlds in his treatment of the "scientific" law of "correspondences." Everything in the visible material world corresponded to something in the spiritual world, though in a lesser sense. Disposing of the outmoded three-story universe (that of heaven, earth, and hell), his correspondence theory gave the metaphysical community a modern scientific restatement of the old Hermetic principle, "As above, so below." In other words, the Divine and the natural exist both in God and in Man. Everything that exists visibly, in day-to-day experience, reflects patterns laid out in the spiritual world and is the end product of spiritual force.[5]

# MESMERISM

The idea of "influx" was given a more precise and "scientific" formulation by Franz Anton Mesmer (1733-1815), a Viennese physician. If Swedenborgianism offered a unitive view of existence, Mesmer provided the very principle interconnecting the human and spiritual realms. He proposed the existence of what he termed "universal magnetic fluid." Though he was rebuffed by the French Academy of Science, his disciples experienced the mysterious flow of energy of which he spoke, and some, such as Karl von Reichenbach, devised numerous experiments to prove its existence. The fact that the experiments proved unconvincing to the larger scientific community became less important than Mesmer's articulation of a scientific-like model in which to restate old

5. Miller, *America's Alternative Religions*, 63; cf. also W. J. Hanegraaff, *New Age Religion and Western Culture* (Leiden: Brill, 1996), 424-29.

claims about a magical power or a healing power or a sacred spiritual energy. In the nineteenth century it became known as animal magnetism, astral light, odic force, and psychic energy.[6]

## SPIRITUALISM

The significance of Spiritualism was that it proposed that it could scientifically demonstrate the survival of individual humans after death. Not content to talk to angels, Spiritualists talked to the spirits of the so-called dead, among the first being no less than Swedenborg himself, who had died in the 1770s. The means of communication between the living and the dead was by means of a self-induced trance. The entranced said they could hear, and many did. And the popularity of Spiritualism grew.

Orthodox Christians were horrified by the fact that Spiritualists ignored biblical injunctions against conversing with spirits. Some scientists, unable to reconcile the faith of their childhood with the new discoveries they were making, devoted their lives to researching the claims of the Spiritualists with more or less positive results for the psychical researchers.[7]

## HINDUISM

Another significant component of the unique synthesis of religious traditions and social movements that became the New Age is the South Asian religious tradition, particularly certain strands of Hinduism. The Hindu influence is clearly evident in the Indian yoga and meditation techniques as well as in certain key notions, such as chakras and karma, that are important within the New Age subculture.

The first impact was almost purely literary. In the latter half of the eighteenth century, a group of scholar-officials working for the British East India Company translated some of the more important Hindu religious scriptures into English. The ideas contained in the texts directly influenced the Transcendentalist movement and, both directly and indirectly, influenced New Thought, the movement devoted to spiritual healing and the creative power

6. Miller, *America's Alternative Religions,* 63; cf. also Hanegraaff, *New Age Religion,* 430-35.

7. J. Gordon Melton, *New Age Encyclopedia* (Detroit: Gale Research, 1990), xxiv; cf. also Hanegraaff, *New Age Religion,* 435-37.

of constructive thinking, and Theosophy, in which a person is believed to be able to master nature and guide his own destiny.[8]

# TRANSCENDENTALISM

The occult tradition of the Far East, especially Hinduism, entered the United States in the nineteenth century. In New England, the religious dissent was spearheaded by Ralph Waldo Emerson. The influence of Hinduism on the Transcendentalist movement is evident in Emerson's "Over-Soul" essay.

The pilgrimage of Emerson, who became Transcendentalism's major spokesperson, took him from Christian orthodoxy to Unitarianism to a new religious vision that brought angry responses from even his most liberal colleagues. Enthusiastic over the new translations of the holy books of Hinduism, especially the *Bhagavad Gita,* Emerson created a uniquely American form of what might best be seen as a pagan nature mysticism. Emerson left behind a workable mysticism to compete with that which he called dualistic Christianity and materialistic nineteenth-century science.

Emerson also utilized the Swedenborgian idea of correspondences, which states that every aspect of the material universe is reflected in — or corresponds with — the inner spiritual life of the soul.[9]

The resultant movement was called Transcendentalism. This was the first substantial religious movement in North America with a prominent Asian component. Its emergence signaled the arrival of an alternative religious tradition in America which has grown up and existed alongside the more prominent Christian bodies. This alternative tradition values mysticism and Eastern religious wisdom. It also integrates Western values, particularly individualism and success orientations.

The side of Transcendentalism which influenced the New Age world was that side which pointed to a divine presence in the world and an exalted human nature. For Emerson and other Transcendentalists, humans were using only part of the full range of powers they possessed, and there was great optimism regarding their innate goodness and their capacity for reforming society.[10]

Individual effort in self-actualization, intuition, and imagination all

8. James R. Lewis and J. Gordon Melton, *Perspectives on the New Age* (Albany, N.Y.: State University of New York, 1992), 48-49.

9. Miller, *America's Alternative Religions,* 82; cf. also Hanegraaff, *New Age Religion,* 458ff.

10. Albanese, *America: Religion and Religions,* 129.

became qualities of life designed to pierce the restricting shell of the human body and usher the initiate into direct contact with the Oversoul. Above all, the Transcendentalists were role models for an eclectic future that would combine different beliefs. Dissatisfied with Christianity, even in its liberal Unitarian form, they picked and chose from what was available to them to build their own religious response to life.

Transcendentalism passed on its emphasis on mystical experience and Eastern religion to several popular movements: Spiritualism, Theosophy, New Thought, and Christian Science. Christian Science and New Thought appeared in the 1870s and 1880s, respectively, developing their programs around a "practical" application of Emerson's ideas. Both groups enjoyed immediate, enthusiastic popular responses and quickly built national organizations despite the fact that they were not recognized as Christian by the established churches. Metaphysical books by such authors as Ralph Waldo Trine and Henry Wood became nationwide best-sellers. In the early twentieth century, Spiritualism and New Thought divided and produced new organizations, some of which became national in scope. The membership of these groups supplied the initial support for the New Age vision.[11]

# A PROTESTANT HINDUISM

In the Far East, especially in India, there were developments in the Hindu religion that would eventually affect the United States. As a result of the Christian missionary movement, the Hindus began to respond to Westerners' critiques of Hindu worship of more than one god and village religion with its local deities. The result was a Protestant Hinduism stripped of the deities and the extraneous additions of traditional Indian religion. This change transformed the ashram, originally a small isolated residence of the guru, into a communal structure similar to that of a Christian congregation. The reformers sought to appropriate knowledge of the West and drew upon Western religious leaders.

Swamis Vivekananda and Yogananda, two outstanding products of these new developments in Hinduism, planted Hinduism in America. In fact, Swami Vivekananda, who visited the United States in 1893, was the most popular speaker at the World Parliament of Religions in Chicago. He eventually gathered enough support to establish the Vedanta Society in New York, an organization which, because of its publishing activities, has had an influence

11. J. Gordon Melton, "The New Age Movement: A Survey and Christian Response," Interfaith Witness Department, Southern Baptist Convention, March 1985, 2.

out of proportion to its membership. Swami Yogananda organized the Self-Realization Fellowship. In addition, his *Autobiography of a Yogi* inspired thousands of Westerners to undertake Eastern spiritual disciplines.[12]

# THEOSOPHY

Although its Western intellectual roots were in nineteenth-century German idealism, the New Age movement drew its inspiration more immediately from the end-of-the-world hopes that were taking different forms in occult circles. Emerging as the most important nineteenth-century forerunner of New Age was Theosophy. New Thought and Christian Science were peculiarly American and not spectacularly successful elsewhere, but the Theosophical Society, founded in 1875, spread worldwide in its first generation and spawned many similar groups, some of which would eclipse it in membership.[13]

Emerging as a prime example of a Western alternative religion, Theosophy stepped into the midst of the Hindu renaissance when its founders, Madame H. P. Blavatsky and Col. Henry S. Olcott, moved to India in 1878. Once settled, the Theosophical Society began to inform its members and the general public about Eastern wisdom and to integrate Eastern thought into Western life.

# THE MASTERS

In an early book, *Isis Unveiled* (1877), Blavatsky sought to show that the Brahmanism of early India and, later, Buddhism were the sources for the other religions. In writing her vast work, Blavatsky claimed that she was aided by the Mahatmas, members of a select brotherhood of individuals who, while still human beings, had evolved to degrees of perfection beyond those normally reached by others. They possessed magical abilities to materialize at will or to communicate by letters that arrived at their destination as soon as they were sent. Blavatsky claimed that they helped her to write *The Secret Doctrine* (1888).

In that book, Blavatsky gave an occult account of the origins of the world and of human life. She told, too, of a "law of becoming" in which each

---

12. J. Gordon Melton, *New Age Encyclopedia*, 49; cf. also Hanegraaff, *New Age Religion*, 455-62.

13. Miller, *America's Alternative Religions*, 347-48.

individual reaped what he or she had sowed and was periodically reincarnated to grow in spiritual maturity. Finally, she subscribed to the unity of all souls in the Oversoul, a belief that Ralph Waldo Emerson had already described.[14]

It is hard to overestimate the importance of the masters, the "ruling spiritual elite," in the development of Theosophy. The masters were the ones who really controlled the cosmos. From their lofty realms they constantly seeded society with new scientific ideas, and they periodically called humanity to higher levels of moral and spiritual attainment by sending one of their number to walk among the merely mortal.

Under the leadership of Annie Besant, belief in the masters led the society to mobilize hope in the appearance of a savior figure in the near future. According to many of the members of the early Theosophical movement, its real occult purpose was to prepare the way for a coming world teacher. The initial appearance of this world teacher was made through a young Indian boy, Jiddu Krishnamurti, whom Besant sent to England for his education and, in 1925, proclaimed to be the Messiah. He later renounced his role in the endeavor, much to the chagrin of his worshipers.[15]

Theosophy became the seedbed that nurtured the important new movements that emerged so forcefully in the twentieth century. Several hundred new occult organizations can be traced directly to the Theosophical Society. For example, drawing upon the work initiated by Theosophy, ritual magicians have attempted to attain the mastery of the world through occult means in a measure only hinted at in theosophical circles. Through the success of theosophical disciples such as Edgar Cayce, reincarnation reached a broad audience and earned the acceptance of the vast majority in the metaphysical community.[16]

In the late nineteenth century, Theosophists introduced a language of expectation for a "new age." And that theosophical concept has had a good deal to do with the shape and style of the New Age movement.[17]

After the death of Blavatsky, Theosophy splintered into a number of factions. Early in the twentieth century, Alice Bailey left the Theosophical Society to found the Arcane School. During the 1930s Guy Ballard founded the I AM activity. Each of these groups has further subdivided, producing scores of new organizations, preparing the way for the New Age movement.

While teaching the vision of the essential unity of religion, Theosophists also proposed the vision of a coming new world religious teacher who

---

14. Albanese, *America: Religions and Religion,* 267; cf. also Paul Heelas, *The New Age Movement* (Cambridge, Mass.: Blackwell, 1996), 44ff.; Hanegraaff, *New Age Religion,* 443-44, 448-55, 470-73.

15. Melton, *New Age Encyclopedia,* xxv.

16. Ibid., xxv-xxvi.

17. Albanese, *America: Religions and Religion,* 268.

would teach the nations the new religious truths. These new truths were being revealed to theosophical leaders by the spiritual masters. Alice Bailey gave impetus to the vision in her book *Reappearance of the Christ*, published in 1948. She equated the coming of the world teacher with several prophesied religious events, the second coming of Christ and the return of the Buddhist Bodhisattva Maitreya.

Alice Bailey and the Arcane School popularized the practice of what today is called "channeling," in which information is conveyed to those on earth. Bailey broke with the Theosophical Society in America because she was channeling material from the masters. Her books found a devoted audience, and, in the years since her death, others have discovered their ability to channel from either the masters of Blavatsky's hierarchy or other exalted beings — God, disembodied spirits, the collective subconscious, or flying-saucer entities.

Another theosophical offshoot, the I AM religious movement, emphasized the importance of light (a common element in many reports of mystical experience) and added an emphasis upon the spiritual, or occult, significance of color. The attention paid to color, especially as experienced in the light of gems, underlies the love of crystals in recent decades.[18] I AM has now been translated into Christ the Savior Brotherhood.

# NEW THOUGHT AND SPIRITUAL HEALING

New Thought, the movement devoted to spiritual healing and the creative power of constructive thinking, stressed metaphysical concerns without occult elaboration. The seed for New Thought was contained in the teaching and healing practices of Phineas P. Quimby (1802-1866). Quimby was the mental healer who played a significant role in the life of Mary Baker Eddy, the founder of Christian Science.

Quimby launched a completely new healing ministry based on an integration of scientifically demonstrable mind healing and Christian teachings. It was Quimby who first came up with the term "Divine Mind" for God. He went on to teach that the Christ was the spirit of God in all human beings and, when properly attuned, a channel for ailing humans to connect to emanations of health, happiness, prosperity, and abundance. Limited material thinking produced limited experience; spiritual thought generated abundance. A controversy rages to this day concerning the question of whether Quimby should rightfully be considered the "founder" of the "Chris-

18. Melton, *New Age Encyclopedia*, xxvi.

tian Science" concept and the intellectual and spiritual source of the metaphysical movement.[19]

# CHRISTIAN SCIENCE,
# A FORERUNNER OF NEW AGE

Mary Baker Eddy's Christian Science emerged as a unique religious phenomenon in American culture during the tumultuous latter decades of the nineteenth century. Her delineation of a "sustaining" metaphysical reality found a ready audience in believers who had lost faith in traditional Christian beliefs that had been challenged by scientific and social revolutions.

Members, past and present, of the Christian Science movement claim Mary Baker Eddy's truths to be part of a unique and final religious revelation. However, most outside observers place Christian Science in the metaphysical family of religious organizations with roots "both in the idealistic philosophy of the nineteenth century and in the search for alternative means of healing at a time when the healing arts were still in a primitive state."[20]

In Christian Science, the broad descriptive term "metaphysical" takes on a different meaning, denoting the superiority of Mind as *the* controlling factor in human experience. At the heart of that perspective is the affirmation that God is perfect Mind, and human beings, in reality, exist in a state of eternal manifestation of that Divine Mind.

Here's the reasoning: If God is Mind and the substance of being is Spirit, then humans, as the perfect reflection or expression of Mind, can be and must be as perfect as God. Contrary to Protestant beliefs, Christian Science teaches that it is not original sin that causes human beings to experience suffering, insecurity, lack, illness, and death but a profound error in thinking. Health, security, and prosperity, they contend, are qualities of God's unchanging expression that human beings will enjoy once they depart from faulty mortal thinking. Healing, both of sin and sickness, became a focus of the Christian Science religion.

The Christian element in Christian Science emerges in the teaching that Jesus was the ultimate "Christian Scientist" who overcame sin, sickness, and death through his superior perception of the allness of Spirit and the nothingness of matter. Jesus was seen not as a unique savior who atoned for human sin, as traditional Christianity teaches, but as the first human being

---

19. Miller, *America's Alternative Religions*, 64; cf. also Hanegraaff, *New Age Religion*, 485-87.
20. Ibid., 61.

to understand and fully express Divine Mind. The real lesson of the Gospel, according to Christian Science, finds Jesus as nothing more than an example — a human being who attained Christ consciousness and was then, scientifically, able to demonstrate mastery over sin, disease, and death.[21]

According to William Swaim of the Religious News Service, the First Church of Christ, Scientist, has gone New Age. Church officials and their rank-and-file supporters deny that's their precise intention. But they admit they're hoping church founder Mary Baker Eddy's 119-year-old classic, *Science and Health with Key to the Scriptures,* will benefit from the success of New Age best-sellers such as *The Celestine Prophecy.* To accomplish this, the Boston-based church is sending speakers to such unlikely theological outposts as The Phoenix Bookstore, purveyor of New Age literature to denizens of Santa Monica, California.[22]

## UNITY SCHOOL OF CHRISTIANITY

Unlike Christian Science, which claimed a basis in divine revelation, proponents of New Thought sought a foundation in philosophy for their ideas. New Thought not only sought to help people to get well but also, by thinking correctly, to become prosperous and successful. The Unity School of Christianity, with its vast publishing enterprise and ministerial training program, became probably the best known of the New Thought institutions. Unity circulated publications far beyond its own adherents. Issued by commercial publishers, writings of leading metaphysical authors Emmet Fox, William Walker Atkinson, Walter Lanyon, Stella Terrill Mann, and others have reached millions of readers unaware of the authors' spiritual affiliations.[23] Other New Thought denominations, such as Divine Science and Religious Science, also helped to spread the belief.

## POSITIVE THINKING

Christian Science and New Thought so influenced liberal Protestantism that many who were part of the mainstream absorbed their ideas and values and

21. Ibid., 62.

22. William Swaim, "Christian Scientists March Reluctantly into New Age," *Baptists Today,* March 23, 1995, 10.

23. Melton, *New Age Encyclopedia,* 348.

began to spread them. Norman Vincent Peale, with his *Power of Positive Thinking*, published in 1952, brought mental healing and the success ethic to millions of people outside the movement, while his other books and magazines continued the trend.[24] John Simmons maintains that Robert Schuller has taken the mind-over-matter, "positive thinking" message of Christian Science and New Thought and adapted it to a quasi-orthodox Protestant Christian theological stance. Protestant, Catholic, and Jewish religious writers have produced books that top the charts while offering thinly disguised Christian Science ideas. These include Bishop Fulton Sheen's *Peace of Soul* and Rabbi Joshua Liebman's *Peace of Mind*.[25]

These groups and other occult-metaphysical groups which followed them became even more entrenched in Western culture in the twentieth century. By the time the vision of the New Age began to unfold in the early 1970s, the occult-metaphysical community, consisting of the members and constituencies of several hundred alternative metaphysical religions, formed a large potential audience. The membership of these metaphysical groups became the first to be told of the New Age and the first to become enthusiastic about the movement's vision.

The initial support given the movement by the many older Spiritualist, Theosophical, and New Thought groups explains the seeming quickness of the movement's emergence and expansion. The older occult-metaphysical community also provided a host of additional ideas and practices that gave the new movement increasing substance.[26]

# STUDY OF ALL WORLD RELIGIONS

Another factor promoting the interest in Eastern religions was the growth in Western scholarly circles of the study of world religions. The dramatic beginning of this was the Parliament of Religions in Chicago in 1893, sponsored by the League of Liberal Churchmen as part of the celebration of the 400th anniversary of Christopher Columbus's arrival in the New World. The Columbian Exposition, named for Columbus, drew more than 27 million people from at least seventy-two countries to its specially erected buildings in Chicago. Speakers at the Parliament of Religions included Theosophists, Hindus, Buddhists, and followers of Bahai.

24. Albanese, *America: Religions and Religion*, 269-72.
25. Miller, *America's Alternative Religions*, 67.
26. Melton, *New Age Encyclopedia*, xxvi; cf. also Hanegraaff, *New Age Religion*, 441-42.

The Parliament of Religions not only introduced most Eastern religions to the United States but led to the establishment of the first Hindu, Buddhist, and Islamic organizations in this country. A similar celebration commemorating the centennial of the 1893 Parliament of Religions was held in Chicago in August 1993.

## EFFECT OF IMMIGRATION POLICY

Another factor in the spread of Eastern religions was the removal in 1965 of the Asian Immigration Exclusion Act, which had been in effect since the early twentieth century. The Asian and Middle Eastern countries were put on the same immigration quotas which had always been given to Europe. Each year since then, tens of thousands of Asians have moved to the United States. Since 1965, numerous teachers have either moved to America or taken advantage of generous visa regulations to build followings in the United States. Many of these teachers came not to work within the new Asian-American communities, but to spread their teaching among Westerners. The last days of the 1960s saw the launching of a major missionary thrust of the Eastern religions toward the West. It was not centrally coordinated. However, it grew out of a popular idea within all the religious communities in Asia, from Japan to India, that the West was ready for and in need of the wisdom which the East possesses. I heard Swami Prabhupada (Hare Krishna) and Maharishi Mahesh Yoga (T.M.) bring this emphasis to American audiences.

While this spiritual subculture of the seventies was comprised of Buddhists, Sufis, and other non-Hindu groups, Indian spiritual teachers were the most numerous as well as, in the long run, the most influential. This spiritual subculture, which in many ways succeeded the counterculture of the sixties, has been integrated into the New Age movement of the 1980s and '90s.[27]

## THE FAR EAST AND SECULAR GROUPS

In this same period of the 1960s and 1970s, Western secular groups developed which utilized ideas from the Far East. These include Scientology, Silva Mind Control, and the Erhard Seminar Training groups called "est."

During this general period, Christian-related groups, such as the Unification Church and various Jesus-people groups, became active. There were

27. Lewis and Melton, *Perspectives on the New Age,* 49.

also movements which are related to Mexican Shamanic groups. This includes the work of anthropologist Carlos Castaneda and his explanation of the work of a Mexican shaman called Don Juan.

New Agers have felt attracted to shamanism for a variety of reasons. A major factor in this attraction is that, while the shaman is a kind of mystic, the focus is on the forces of nature rather than an otherworldly mysticism. Also, traditional shamanism's stress on healing is very much in line with the New Age tendency to combine the quest for health, both physical and psychological, with the quest for spirituality. Other attractions are the use of mind-altering drugs, including peyote, and the romanticized images of nature.[28]

About the same time, American Indian teachers began to communicate parts of their spiritual traditions. Native teachers like Sun Bear (Chippewa) and Rolling Thunder (Cherokee and adopted Shoshone) taught beliefs and practices from their traditions to non-Indian Americans. The Bear Tribe Medicine Society, which Sun Bear founded in 1966, flourished with mostly nonnative membership.

New Agers appropriated Native American rituals like the sweat-lodge ceremony in various versions. They borrowed American Indian rattles and drums; wore and used feathers, beads, and gemstones; engaged in variants of native pipe ceremonies; made pilgrimages to Indian sacred sites; and worked to practice shamanism. Sweat-lodge ceremonies, in fact, became prototypical New Age rituals, and shamanism became a pervasive technique and model for efforts in imaging, mental "journeying," and healing.[29]

# THE CONTEMPORARY "NEW AGE" MOVEMENT

As all these new movements progressed through the 1970s, we witnessed one other tremendously influential development, designated as the New Age movement. Baba Ram Dass was the first recognized national exponent of New Age consciousness. A former professor of psychology at Harvard, the Jewish-born Richard Alpert (later called Ram Dass) accompanied his colleague Timothy Leary through a period of experimentation with psychedelic drugs before going to India and finding his guru. Alpert reappeared as Baba Ram Dass, a guru in his own right, just as the New Age was being announced. His extensive Western academic background, transformed by his newfound

28. Miller, *America's Alternative Religions*, 384.
29. Albanese, *America: Religions and Religion*, 359-60; cf. also Heelas, *The New Age Movement*, 49-54.

Eastern faith, made him the perfect symbol of the New Age. The movement consumed his popular books: *The Only Dance There Is* (1973), *Grist for the Mill* (1977), *Journey of the Awakening* (1978), and *Miracle of Love* (1979).

Two other prominent leaders were Marilyn Ferguson with her visionary survey of the movement entitled *The Aquarian Conspiracy* (1980), and David Spangler, who originally directed the Scottish New Age community at Findhorn.[30]

After three years as co-director of the Scottish community at Findhorn, Spangler returned to the United States and founded the Lorian Association, a New Age community near Madison, Wisconsin. His early volume, *Revelation, the Birth of a New Age* (1976), has provided one popular statement of New Age perspectives.

In 1975, *A Course in Miracles,* transcribed between 1965 and 1973 by Helen Schucman, was published. This course was promoted by the newly formed Foundation for Inner Peace under the leadership of Judith Skutch, an early New Age advocate in New York City. The multivolume *Course,* a simple restatement of New Thought metaphysics using the metaphor of "miracles," became a very popular study book throughout New Age circles, and several hundred groups were founded across North America during its first decade in print. Other popular New Age teachers include George Leonard, Jean Houston, Barbara Marx Hubbard, Norman Shealy, and Sam Keen.[31]

# NETWORKS, COMMUNES, AND SOCIAL STRUCTURES

Thus we see that many ingredients came together to form the emerging New Age synthesis. A new self-consciousness among participants developed and was reflected in the designation "New Age," which came to stand for the general collection of beliefs and behaviors within the movement.

However, not every person who identified with the name "New Age" shared every belief or engaged in every behavior that characterized the movement as a whole. Rather, individuals appropriated different elements from the available pool, so that New Age expressed diversity and fluidity in membership.

30. John Newport, "Why Our Culture Is Ripe for Alternative Religions," *Search,* Spring 1993, 56; cf. also Hanegraaff, *New Age Religion,* 104-7.
31. Melton, "New Age Movement," 5-6; cf. also Hanegraaff, *New Age Religion,* 37-38.

The New Age movement has a cohesiveness that is often overlooked. What is often seen by the casual observer is "a disjointed collection of stories and idea-stories of UFOs, hauntings, predictions, premonitions, ghosts, mysterious happenings, psychic powers and ESP." What is not recognized is that, when "seen as a whole, the New Age rag bag of ideas displays an amazing unity. It is not a deliberately created system, but rather a pattern that is reinforced by sheer repetition."[32] Virtually every aspect of the New Age movement, such as channeling and the use of crystals, has its historical antecedent in some practice that dates back centuries.

Once the basic idea of the New Age was expressed, early exponents began to build the networks of those groups and organizations that seemed to be aligned either ideologically or practically. The early directories included not only the centers for the various occult, Eastern, and mystical religions, but also health food stores, metaphysical bookstores, antivivisection societies, yoga teachers, parapsychology research organizations, psychic-development interest groups, communes, and alternative health care facilities.[33]

Many New Agers have come to believe in what is popularly termed the "hundredth monkey concept." The concept was derived from a tale of anthropologists observing a community of monkeys learning a new task. The concept poses the idea that through short-term diligent effort, enough people will commit to New Age concepts so that what amounts to a critical mass will be reached and the obviously correct ideal will spread quickly, as if by magic, through the human race.[34]

Admiring cooperation over competition, New Age exponents have tried several social structures to embody their ideals. Communes were a natural option. Some older communes, such as the Lama Foundation in New Mexico, were among the first groups to identify with the New Age perspective. Particularly in the field of health, national professional and referral associations have been founded to bring some order to the competition among numerous forms of therapy (some of dubious value) being offered by individuals with highly varying qualifications. Among the most prominent are the American Holistic Medical Association in Washington, D.C., and the Association for Holistic Health in San Diego, California.[35]

32. Tucker, *Another Gospel*, 321.
33. Melton, *New Age Encyclopedia*, xxviii.
34. Ibid., xxi.
35. Ibid., xxix.

# AN EMPHASIS ON TRANSFORMATION

Personal transformation has become one of the distinguishing characteristics of New Age. That emphasis was promoted by Gordon Melton, who recognized that New Agers have either experienced or are diligently seeking a profound personal transformation from an old, unacceptable life to a new, exciting future. One prominent model for that transformation is healing, which has given rise to what is possibly the largest identifiable segment of the movement, the holistic health movement.

Having experienced a personal transformation, New Agers project the possibility of the transformation not of just a number of additional individuals, but of the culture and of humanity itself. They claim that transformation is not just a possibility but a present reality. The New Age, they like to point out, is emerging in this generation. This healing, projected into the larger social context, has become a movement to heal the earth, the ideological foundation for the movement's support of peace and ecological activism.[36]

This personal transformation experience has a few common characteristics:

- New Agers leave a life dominated by a set of negative aspects — oppressive "orthodox" modes of thought, dysfunctional exploitative relationships, poverty, illness, boredom, purposelessness, and/or hopelessness.
- The experience almost instantly transforms their lives. Even everyday life for New Agers becomes one of new openness and new equalitarian relationships with a sense of abundance, regained vitality and health, excitement, intensity, new meaning, and a new future.
- For many, transformations occur in the form of a profound mystical experience, often emerging amid a personal crisis or as the culmination of a lengthy spiritual quest.
- It is also characteristic for New Age leaders, as they reflect upon their experience, to seek a means to share the transformative event with others. In their analysis of the experience, leaders can isolate the specific agents that led to their change and can recast the experience into a repeatable system to facilitate change in others.[37]

The most important elements of the New Age movement are the many individuals, organizations, and businesses which have arisen to facilitate the process of transformation. Every metropolitan area has scores of individuals

36. Ibid., xiii.
37. Ibid., xiii-xiv.

who teach transformational techniques, from meditation to martial arts, and who practice the various forms of alternative medicines, body therapies, and psychological processes. *American Demographics* magazine in June 1997 reported that the number of New Age bookstores in the United States now exceeds five thousand.

## UNIVERSAL RELIGION HAS STRONG APPEAL

One of the appeals of New Age is the fact that it says there is one universal religion which will assume many different forms and draw from all present religious traditions. This faith finds inspiration in nature and in the changing seasons and in the growth and development of individuals through the common cycles of life. It also places an emphasis on self-knowledge, inner exploration, and participation in a continual transformative process.

Since few individuals complete their transformation in one lifetime, the commonly accepted belief in reincarnation and karma provides a long-term framework in which to view the individual's spiritual progression. The significance of Jesus and the other prominent religious teachers such as Buddha and Krishna is that they were particularly transparent as bearers of the Divine, or the Christ Consciousness.

Not only will one universal religion be recognized in the New Age, there will be an allegiance to the planet and the human race which will supersede loyalty to the more limited groupings of clan, nation, race, or religion.

The more sophisticated exponents of New Age want to separate themselves from certain far-out occult techniques. However, they do accept some traditional occult practices such as channeling and astrology as tools in the acquisition of a greater awareness of themselves and of the world.

Because the New Age movement primarily is an updating of longstanding occult and metaphysical traditions in American life, it can be expected to have a bright future. This metaphysical community has been present in North America for at least 150 years, and the number of people attracted to it has grown measurably, decade by decade, and at a heightened pace since the early 1970s. The continued influx of Asians into the United States also gives strong support.

Unlike older forms of the occult in previous decades, the New Age movement has been able to penetrate and even develop its largest constituency among single, young, upwardly mobile urban adults. They accept the process of transformation, which they believe naturally accompanies career success. At their youthful age, they still tend to believe that utopian social visions can be realized. In this connection, a 1993 article in the *New York Times Sunday Magazine* about the social vision of Hillary Clinton emphasized just such a utopian social view.

The density of population in the urban centers where New Age followers dwell allows them the freedom to develop their own particular variation of New Age in the company of others of similar vision. New Agers are, as an affluent social group, among the most capable of providing firm support for a growing movement, then passing it along to the next generation, as yet unborn, and spreading the movement among those who are influential in the culture.[38]

Ruth Tucker, a well-known New Age critic, asks the question: "Is New Age merely an age-old form of the occult that will taper off in popularity as the fad loses its luster, or is it truly a movement that has only barely begun to make its all-encompassing mark on the world?"[39]

The answer to this question is one of the very few things the most ardent religious critics and the devoted disciples of the movement agree on. Both sides envision a future one-world religion united under the banner of New Age, and both speak of the enormous impact the movement is making on every aspect of modern life.

38. Ibid., xxx.
39. Tucker, *Another Gospel*, 323.

# CHAPTER THREE

# A Worldview Crisis

When I moved to Houston, Texas, and assumed a professorship at Rice University, I found that the concept of "futurology" was everywhere. The original futurology group, the Club of Rome, even met in Houston. Various Rice University departments sponsored futurology lectures. I was asked to teach a course on futurology and religion.

To learn more about this popular concept, I began to attend conferences. At one international conference, Fred Polak, author of *The Image of the Future*, was the center of discussion. Polak contends that the most urgent problem facing humankind as we approach the year 2000 is to find or develop a worthy model or worldview to guide and empower us and to give positive shape to our future.

## THE POWER OF WORLDVIEWS

Each of us has a worldview, or vision, of life. It may or may not be organized, but it makes up the framework of fundamental considerations which give context, direction, and meaning to our lives. What is new and remarkable today is our increasing awareness of how worldviews affect both our perceptions of the world and our actions. Conflicts in life and even in science, we are discovering, come down to differences in underlying worldviews.

There are many attempts in our time to refurbish old worldviews, while other impassioned voices insist that our world can be saved from total collapse only if we adopt a new worldview. In *The Turning Point: Science, Society, and the Rising Culture,* Fritjof Capra pleads for a New Age synthesis of modern physics and Eastern mysticism as the only viable escape from the collapse of the dominant Western and biblical worldviews.[1] On the other side of the issue is Wheaton College professor Arthur Holmes, who calls for a renewal of the biblical worldview as the answer to our needs.[2]

## THE WORLDVIEW CONCEPT

Worldview is a vision of life and of the world that helps us make sense of life. James Olthuis describes it as "a framework or set of fundamental beliefs through which we view the world and our calling and future in it." A worldview helps us understand our role in the historical perspective of good and evil. It tells us who we are and why we are here.

It is also important to note that worldviews have a religious dimension. A worldview is rooted in beliefs that are ultimate in character because these beliefs are answers to what Stephen Toulmin has called "limit" questions. Such questions are at the limits of our rationality or, to change the metaphor, they are the ground of our rationality. Their answers provide us with what Nicholas Wolterstorff has described as "control beliefs."[3]

## RISE OF THE MODERNIST VIEW

The modern era in Western civilization began with the scientific revolution in the seventeenth century. The discoveries in astronomy and physics by Copernicus, Kepler, Galileo, and Newton not only changed our picture of the cosmos, but also radically altered the way we think. A new concept of how we come to know the truth about reality found expression in the philosophical systems of Bacon and Locke. No truths were taken for granted without careful examination. Any proposition that we couldn't prove through the five senses, such as religious beliefs, was banished to a status of inferior knowledge. Some philosophers even considered religious statements "meaningless" or, at best, unverifiable.

1. Paul A. Marshall, Sander Griffioen, and Richard J. Mouw, eds., *Stained Glass: Worldviews and Social Science* (Lanham, Md.: University Press of America, 1989), 39.

2. Arthur E. Holmes, *Contours of a Worldview* (Grand Rapids: Eerdmans, 1983).

3. Brian J. Walsh, "Worldviews, Modernity and the Task of Christian College Education," *Faculty Dialogue,* Institute for Christian Studies, Toronto, vol. 18 (1992): 19.

Modern science offered the language of facts, which it proclaimed to be "really true." Before long most people gave "unthinking priority to the world of scientific fact as the world of the really real."

The main thesis of this modern era was progress. People believed that the world would get better solely through human effort. This myth promised us an earthly paradise. Instead, some of our "progress" has left us with a despoiled wilderness, an environmental crisis. We also are hearing the voices of women, of aboriginal peoples, of colonized peoples who say that this progress was good news for only certain segments of the world's population and came at the expense of others.[4]

# BREAKDOWN OF THE MODERNIST VIEW

Following the Enlightenment of the eighteenth century, in which traditional religious, social, and political ideas were rejected, Western culture became dominated by a materialist, rationalist worldview coupled with a competitive, male-dominated power structure.

Scientific reductionism, the theory of explaining the workings of human beings in the same way as a chemical reaction, led to the view that a human being has no significance beyond being a functioning collection of chemicals. Industry harnesses these "organic machines" to work in a way similar to that of mechanical machinery to make products that supposedly enhance the quality of life. In this system, the consumer is manipulated and dehumanized as much as the producing worker.

As we face the new millennium, there is extensive evidence that this dominant worldview which the West has embraced for several centuries is in crisis. A gap has developed between the Western worldview and our actual experience. In such a situation the very ground on which we stand is uncertain. We are no longer sure of who we are, what the meaning of life is, what we are to do, or where we are going. Questions that once had some form of ultimate, faith-committed answers are reopened, and what we find is usually disturbing.

Jeremy Rifkin describes this crisis as a widespread cultural angst:

> When a particular worldview begins to break down, when it can no longer adequately answer the basic questions to the satisfaction of its adherents, faith is broken, uncertainty and confusion set in, and the individual and the masses are cast adrift — exposed, unprotected and above all frightened.[5]

4. "How Porno Can You Go," *Academic Alert* 4.2 (Spring 1995): 1.
5. *Christians Scholars Review* 14.2 (1985), 153-64.

Such a situation is now at hand. The culture of modernity, the culture of the progress myth, is entering such a crisis period. Robert Heilbroner, in his disturbing book *An Inquiry into the Human Prospect*, says we have come to the end of the Enlightenment. The Enlightenment dream of progress attainable through the autonomous exercise of human reason translated into technological power and economic abundance has been proven not only to be an illusion, but is dangerous. It has not only lied to us about the world and ourselves, it has cursed us and cursed future generations.[6]

## FLAWS OF MODERNISM

The belief of modern thinkers that we can think things straight by using our own independent powers has drawn criticism from those who say that people aren't completely objective in their approach to knowledge. They say we can never get outside of our own knowledge in order to check its accuracy against "objective" reality. We have a certain viewpoint. And our interpretation of facts is based on that viewpoint, colored by our own interests.

Some postmodern thinkers typically deny that there are any features of this "world" to which we could appeal that could function as independently existing "norms" or "criteria" for truth and goodness. Any criterion we might come up with is itself a human construction.[7]

Modernism with its faith in totally objective reason tends to have a totalizing view which is actually oppressive. Western conquest and political superiority are given legitimacy. It is a metaphysics of violence. And that violence, deconstructionists explain, is the direct result of seeking to grasp the infinite, irreducible complexities of the world as a unified and homogeneous totality. All such "totalizing" seeks to reduce the diversity of reality to a system which we can grasp by "repressing what doesn't fit and erasing the memory of those who have questioned it." We must inquire about what and who have been left out, silenced, or suppressed in all constructions that aspire toward a "total" accounting of reality.[8]

There is the assumption that by means of objective reason Western culture has the truth, and that marginalizes all others who somehow don't have it. What deconstructionists are saying is that the sort of homogenizing and naturalizing approach to otherness and difference that is illustrated by U.S. immigration policy

6. Walsh, "Worldviews," 22.
7. Timothy R. Phillips and Dennis L. Okholm, *Christian Apologetics in the Postmodern World* (Downers Grove, Ill.: InterVarsity, 1995), 134-35.
8. "How Porno Can You Go," 1.

has characterized Western thought and culture as a whole and modernity in particular. The differences of women, the otherness of non-Western cultures, and the very complex heterogeneity of the world have been dissolved or repressed into a totalizing vision. Such a vision is inherently violent because it necessarily excludes not just elements of reality that do not fit, but any person or group who sees things from a different perspective. "When convinced of the truth or right of a given worldview," notes Kenneth Gergen, "a culture has only two significant options: totalitarian control of the opposition or annihilation of it."[9]

Deconstructionists say this has in fact been the legacy of the last five hundred years of Western history in relation to women; to non-Western, particularly nonwhite, peoples; and to nonhuman creation itself. It is no wonder, therefore, that postmodern author Jean-François Lyotard tells us that modernity has given us "as much terror as we can take." Renouncing the nostalgia for a total scheme of things because it is both unattainable and inherently violent is a characteristic postmodern theme.[10]

## REACTIONS AND RESPONSES

This crisis related to the modern era has dismantled the faith underlying the modernist worldview. Many people experience a sense of lostness and betrayal in our post-Enlightenment culture. Such people are looking for a new faith and a new worldview.

Some become more entrenched in their old views in a time of crisis. According to Brian J. Walsh, rather than creatively dealing with the crisis, cultures and individuals tend to dig in their heels and hang on to what they have. A survivalist mentality emerges, and we witness a recommitment to the Enlightenment worldview and the very faith that seems to be discredited by historical development. At times, such a recommitment takes on the character of a revival service — give me that old-time religion of faith in human progress and the American dream of life, liberty, and the pursuit of happiness.

This is the view of liberal optimism of futurist Herman Kahn: "On the whole . . . this problem-prone, super-industrial period will be marked by rising living standards and less rather than more sacrifice. Eventually, almost all of the problems will be dealt with reasonably satisfactorily, so that at the end of the transition period, the true post-industrial society can emerge."[11]

9. Phillips and Okholm, *Christian Apologetics*, 138.
10. Ibid.
11. Herman Kahn, "The Economic Future," in Frank Feather, ed., *Through the '80s: Thinking Globally, Acting Locally* (Washington, D.C.: World Futures Society, 1980), 208.

# NEW AGE OFFERS ANSWER

In any case, this time of crisis is calling for a different worldview than that of modernism and secular humanism. Russell Chandler, religion editor of the *Los Angeles Times,* states that the leaders of the New Age movement have stepped forward to contend that their movement offers the best hope for a cultural consensus for the 1990s and beyond into the new millennium. They claim to offer the best alternative to secular humanism and materialism, on the one hand, and what they call the now outmoded, fragmented, and repressive orthodox biblical tradition on the other.[12]

According to Brooks Alexander, an editor of the *SCP Journal,* a broad survey of the many different concerns that make up human culture reveals a common and emerging vision in secular society in general, an important cultural transformation of substantial magnitude called the New Age.[13]

We can get a sense of the interdisciplinary nature of this New Age conviction very quickly. Lansela White, a physicist and biologist, has written in his book *The Universe of Experience,* "This book suggests that the human psyche is about to turn a corner and enjoy vistas never seen before. It attempts to share a radical metamorphosis of the psyche already underway, particularly in the West."

George Leonard, senior editor of *Look* magazine for seventeen years, writes in his book *The Transformation,* "The current period is indeed unique in history and represents the beginning of the most thoroughgoing change in the quality of human existence in some five thousand years."

Teilhard de Chardin, the French Jesuit who is a world-renowned paleontologist, wrote in *Building the Earth,* "Humanity has just entered what is probably the greatest transformation it has ever known."

John Platt, a professor of physics and research biophysics, writes, "A recent era of change may be converging within this generation to a unique historical transformation to a totally new concept of life."

Willis Harmon, a former professor of engineering at Stanford University, director of the Center for the Study of Social Policy at the Stanford Research Institute, and president of the Institute of Noetic Sciences, stated, "This change is not just an evolutionary development from one phase of history to another. Rather, the evidence suggests that the technologically advanced nations of the world may be approaching one of the greatest transformations in history."

Lewis Mumford, analyzing the transformations that have occurred throughout human history, says, "All such changes have rested on a metaphysi-

---

12. Russell Chandler, *Understanding the New Age* (Dallas: Word, 1991), 18-19.
13. Brooks Alexander, Spiritual Counterfeits Project, tape.

cal and ideological base or rather on deeper stirrings and intuitions whose rationalized expressions take the form of a new picture of the cosmos and of the nature of man."

It is this New Age picture of the cosmos and new picture of the nature of humanity that is emerging in our time. Some call this movement the third Great Awakening. The editors of *The New Age Journal* call it the "new consciousness movement."[14]

The New Age movement is widespread and will undoubtedly survive current waves of faddishness. J. Gordon Melton indicates that the New Age movement is a symbol of the growth and maturing of the esoteric and metaphysical religious traditions of the modern West. These traditions have spread to all parts of North America and Europe and have begun a marked diffusion around the world. The New Age movement is still having to contend with important pockets of intense opposition but has found space to operate openly.

James R. Lewis contends that New Age is merely the most visible part of a significant cultural shift. While the popularity of phenomena like channeling and crystals may well be on the decline, the larger spiritual subculture which gave birth to these particular phenomena is growing steadily. These impressions are reinforced by Gallup Poll statistics which indicate that one out of five Americans believes in reincarnation, which is an essential concept of the New Age worldview. Similar surveys taken in the United Kingdom turn up the interesting statistic that 30 to 35 percent of the British population believe in reincarnation.

To judge by the size of the New Age and Christian sections of most bookstores, the New Age movement today has far more popular appeal than Christianity. Its influence is pervasive.

We are no longer talking about a marginal phenomenon. Rather, we appear to be witnessing the birth of a new, truly pluralistic mainstream. This especially seems to be the case in northern California, where a recent newspaper survey found that roughly 25 percent of San Francisco Bay area residents agree with certain key New Age ideas, such as the notion that "nature, or Mother Earth, has its own kind of wisdom, a planetary consciousness of its own."

Lewis concludes by stating that if we think in terms of the larger spiritual subculture in which the New Age is rooted, the cultural shift anticipated by New Agers (usually under the rubric of a "paradigm shift") has already occurred — though most people have not yet recognized it as a *fait accompli*.[15]

---

14. Gordon R. Lewis, "The Church and the New Spirituality," *The Journal of the Evangelical Theological Society*, December 1993, 433.

15. James R. Lewis and J. Gordon Melton, *Perspectives on the New Age* (Albany, N.Y.: State University of New York, 1992), 4-5.

# IMPACT ON MAINSTREAM DENOMINATIONS

The New Age spiritual subculture is difficult for scholars to study because it is so amorphous and ever-changing. It also has crossed certain taken-for-granted boundaries and infiltrated groups that one might anticipate would be hostile to nontraditional spirituality. There are, for example, many members of mainstream religious denominations who practice yoga and meditation, explore alternative healing practices, follow astrological advice, and even believe in reincarnation. Such people often continue to consider themselves good Methodists, Presbyterians, Catholics, or whatever and thus are easy to miss in surveys that classify populations into mutually exclusive categories.

A significant number of professional people are said to keep their unorthodox spiritual orientations "in the closet" to avoid possible negative ramifications for their professional practices. The presence of large numbers of New Age movement participants at elite levels of society is thus not immediately evident to the casual observer.[16]

There is also a growing camp of "New Age Christians." More and more Christians see God as working only within the mind, or the consciousness. They give religion a therapeutic role that has as much to do with self-improvement in the here and now as it does for eternal salvation. They think of themselves as Christians but are moving beyond classic Christian beliefs. Authority in mainline churches is even shifting from God to that which lies within the self. Some claim that even Evangelicalism has been affected. Themes having to do with self-empowerment, including "self-actualization," have become important.

Another indication is that relatively few Christians are content simply to heed religious teachings or remain faithful to particular organizations. Christians exercise their own authority to decide what to believe in the Bible, not infrequently deciding to combine Christian teachings with those drawn from other sources. The religion practiced by an increasing number of Americans may be entirely of their own manufacture.[17]

All this change in beliefs is causing some to dig in their heels. We hear calls from many fundamentalist pulpits to "go back" to the Judeo-Christian heritage of our culture, the very biblical view and way of life that is crumbling.

But many see the church as having lost real spirituality, distracted by attention to its internal machinery and its attempts to maintain its own power rather than saving souls. Many people do not expect to find spiritual meaning in the church.

16. Ibid., 5.
17. Paul Heelas, *The New Age Movement* (Cambridge, Mass.: Blackwell, 1996), 164-65.

Perhaps the biggest problem with developing a Christian response to the New Age movement is that Christians are often at the forefront of defending the status quo. One researcher points to the perverse, if not heretical, gospel-of-wealth doctrine that characterizes much of televangelism and even many fundamentalist churches. Certainly such Christians oppose certain elements in our culture (like abortion, pornography, and liberalized education) because of their Christian faith, but hang on to our commodity-oriented lifestyle, our technological superiority, and our military power, and look at others with an unjust, often racist, attitude. Such a stance, this researcher contends, is spiritual bankruptcy — a belief that one can indeed serve two masters.

## EVANGELICAL CALL FOR RENEWAL

In response to this fundamentalist and orthodox entrenchment, a number of evangelical leaders are calling for professing Christians to take a new look at the Bible as the divinely authored and inspired story of God's amazing work. The Bible, they emphasize, was divinely authored as a total work, not as bits and pieces of infallible material communicated to individual authors.

The Scriptures also relate a worldview, not just stories of events in one locality.[18] It is difficult to see how one could take the biblical presentation of creation, fall, and redemption as merely a local tale. Indeed, it is difficult to find a grander, more comprehensive story anywhere. Christianity is undeniably rooted in a grand tale that claims to tell the true story of the world from creation to the end — a tale of cosmic proportions.[19]

To be an authentic adherent of the biblical worldview, there must be a constantly renewing submission to the authority of Scripture. That means that a person actually has to read the Bible.

The transformation called for by the biblical worldview is never guaranteed. It is not a mechanical function of the Scriptures, but depends on the response of the individual. It means we must take the text of Scripture seriously, more seriously even than our specific religious beliefs, which are often not entirely biblical. It means that we must be willing to let the biblical text judge our point of view, to call us into question, to convert us.[20]

18. Roger E. Olson, "Postconservative Evangelicals Greet the Postmodern Age," *The Christian Century*, May 3, 1995, 481.

19. Phillips and Okholm, *Christian Apologetics*, 141-42.

20. Ibid., 154.

It is true that among some traditional Christians, much is made of submission to the authority of the Bible, yet in many cases the Bible plays a limited role. They tend to ignore the Christ-centered structure and character of the Scriptures. Instead of the biblical story becoming a force within them, they tend to pull out of the Bible various kinds of "timeless truths." In that way, people don't have to read the Bible because they already know what it says.[21]

The biblical worldview presents truth for everyone. Yet some say that the biblical worldview is as totalizing and oppressing as was modernism. Those who believe that are ignoring two fundamental biblical themes that check the oppressive effects of Scripture.

1. One dimension is sensitivity to suffering. God hears the cries of the oppressed Israelites and intervenes to set them free. Jesus on the cross, God incarnate, faces suffering. It is central to the biblical story that God attends to human suffering. This sensitivity to suffering pervades the stories of the Bible from the Exodus to the Cross.

2. The other key theme is that Israel's God is the creator of all people from all nations. So the biblical worldview has to take into account that all people in some sense started at the same place. We cannot exempt anyone from the possibility of redemption. Rooting the story in creation indicates that it is not simply a local story of the Christian church, true only in some corner of the universe, but the story of the world, which includes all peoples without suppressing their genuine differences.[22]

Others have pointed out the biblical balance of nature and grace. Nature, though fallen, is never abandoned by grace; grace, though supernatural, pervades nature. They say this world of nature is our home for now, and we should see ourselves as created cocreators with God, caring for creation on the way to its final redemption. Some press for an evangelical theology of nature that encourages biblical activism as a spiritual discipline.[23]

The broad biblical worldview also rejects triumphalism, and in that context there is a need for greater modesty, tentativeness, and flexibility.

Christians talk about truth in terms of a gift and a call. On the most fundamental level, truth is merely received as a gift. Jesus is the truth, so truth comes to us as a person as well as in the inspired biblical text. Yet we are also called to study our world in a constant process and to earnestly share the biblical worldview with all peoples.[24]

---

21. "How Porno Can You Go, 4.
22. Ibid., 2.
23. "Postconservative Evangelicals," 482.
24. "How Porno Can You Go," 2.

# THE PLUSES OF EVANGELICALS

According to British theologian Alister McGrath, the biblical worldview presented by the Evangelicals is now being supplemented by increasingly rigorous theological foundations, and its intellectual credibility has been enhanced by the growing number of academic theologians within its ranks. According to McGrath, one of the most significant contributions to contemporary philosophy of religion comes from a group of American writers, including Alvin Plantinga and Nicholas Wolterstorff. Their discussion on the theme of "faith and rationality" has become a landmark in recent debates centering on this theme.[25]

Head and heart are being brought together in a movement that is looking forward to the future with a sense of expectancy and anticipation. The future seems to beckon to Evangelicalism, inviting it to advance and mature still further.[26]

One reason why Evangelicalism has continuing attractiveness is that it has refused to modernize Christianity. The progressive Evangelicals felt that the best way to ensure that Christianity remains relevant to the modern world is to be faithful to the biblical worldview and articulate the faith in terms the world can understand.

In contrast, mainline denominations appear to have proceeded on the assumption that there was an urgent need to jettison any aspect of the Christian faith that causes people problems, such as the idea of a transcendent God. In many mainline churches, Christianity has become little more than a pale and vaguely religious reflection of secular cultural trends.

McGrath contends that the future of Christianity may come to depend on Evangelicalism and other versions of Christianity that provide an attractive alternative to New Age and secular worldviews. The very public failure of liberalism and the questioning of the New Age worldview have led many to look for a version of Christianity that makes sense and stays faithful to the biblical vision.[27]

They are finding their answer in Evangelicalism. One attraction is the commitment to evangelism — that is, the proclamation of the gospel in the full confidence that it contains something God-given that will enable it to find a response in the hearts and minds of men and women. Evangelism is natural to evangelicals. "The church," wrote Emil Brunner, "lives by mission

---

25. Alister McGrath, "Why Evangelicalism Is the Future of Protestantism," *Christianity Today,* June 19, 1995, 121; cf. also Alister McGrath, *Evangelicalism and the Future of Christianity* (Downers Grove, Ill: InterVarsity, 1995), 97.

26. McGrath, "Why Evangelicalism Is the Future of Protestantism," 18.

27. Ibid., 20.

as a fire lives by burning." Evangelism is something intrinsic in the biblical worldview — something that is part and parcel of its very being, not an optional extra. The attraction is Jesus Christ.[28]

A central task of evangelism is to make Christianity credible in the modern world. The area of Christian thought that has dealt with this matter is apologetics — the "defense of the faith," to give a rough translation of the Greek word "apologia," used in 1 Peter 3:15. A good working definition of apologetics would be "the attempt to create an intellectual climate favorable to Christian faith." Evangelicalism is becoming increasingly confident in its presentation. The biblical worldview is not only attractive but it rests securely in the knowledge of its truth.[29]

However, Evangelicalism needs to purge some of its less desirable and theologically dubious aspects and pay attention to its weaknesses. Only then will evangelicals have an even larger appeal in an era when people are searching for a new worldview.

This will go a long way toward ensuring the future well-being of the evangelical movement in particular and of the Christian faith in general.[30]

## VALUE OF DIALOGUE

There is a collision in worldviews, but there is value in dialogue. Many Christians are fearful of the New Age movement because it merges into the occult, and so reject any dialogue. This effectively allows the New Age movement to hijack various images, practices, and insights that are ethically neutral or even originated in the Judeo-Christian tradition.

Along with the challenge to the biblical view, the New Age movement comes with a word of judgment. At least three accusations are made against the Christian view. The first and foremost accusation is that many Christian churches are not places of transformation. The Christian church is seen as an anti-intellectual cultural accretion and a spiritual dry hole. While many within the evangelical community may respond that such is the description of liberal Protestantism, it is also true of many evangelical congregations. While we question the beliefs and practices of New Age groups, we must with equal vigor seek to live up to the Christian profession and speak with humility.

The New Age also accuses Western forms of Christianity of selling out to nineteenth-century rationalistic, technological values. In addition, New

---

28. Ibid.
29. Ibid., 22; see also McGrath, *Evangelicalism and the Future of Christianity*, 102.
30. McGrath, "Why Evangelicalism Is the Future of Protestantism," 23.

Age advocates point out that in spite of Christians' allegiance to a supposedly loving and liberating God, Christians have often been warlike and destructive of human life. They also say that Christians are sexist and racist, prone to religious wars, and intolerant of those who disagree with them.

## TOWARD A BETTER UNDERSTANDING

Despite what Christians see as a heretical ideological perspective in the New Age movement, they must recognize the New Age emphases that are latent in the biblical view. For example, the New Age movement has adopted and advocates a number of nonconventional alternative medical and psychological practices. With few exceptions, these practices can stand or fall quite apart from the New Age ideological system in which they may be encased. In like measure, humanistic and human potential psychologies are a vital corrective to more traditional psychotherapies. They should be evaluated quite apart from the religious superlatives placed upon them within some popularly marketed systems. For example, hypnosis, stripped of the metaphysics of animal magnetism, has proven to be a quite natural and valuable medical tool. This is also true of some of the nonconventional therapies and the various processes for assisting individuals to discover their latent and suppressed talents, interests, and abilities.

In our new pluralistic culture, the Christian efforts to confess, share, and communicate the biblical worldview, centered on Jesus Christ, must be accompanied by a studied and sophisticated understanding of the New Age world.

Subsequent chapters of this study will point out the weaknesses of the New Age worldview in eleven areas — transformation, channeling, witchcraft and neopaganism and the goddess movement, ecology, health, business, education, science, art, history, and modern Satanism and black magic.

We will also show the way in which a renewed biblical worldview understanding and commitment provide a divinely revealed and fulfilling answer to the current worldview crisis.

# CHAPTER FOUR

# Consciousness and
# Radical Transformation

New Agers believe in the all-pervasive nature of consciousness as a primary force in the universe. They also believe in the ability of human beings to tap directly into this consciousness.

And now a Stanford University professor says consciousness gives rise to matter. Put simply, if you can think it, you can create it.

Sound incredible? Willis Harman, who was emeritus professor of engineering-economic systems at Stanford and president of the Institute of Noetic Sciences, confessed that this statement did sound incredible. But he contended that this view of reality was nothing new. For thousands of years the priority of consciousness has been the basis of reality in most of the world's spiritual traditions. He explained that the mystical writings of most spiritual traditions — Christian, Jewish, Sufi, Hindu, and Buddhist — all speak of an understanding of reality similar to this view.

All he did, he explained, is simply substantiate this view with his research in metaphysics, that field of study defined as "mind beyond physical reality."[1]

Harman didn't say that this is the only way of looking at reality. What he did say was that this view is "more congenial" to the total human experience than is the scientific approach, that a major transformation is taking place at the most fundamental level of the belief structure of Western industrial society.

1. George A. Maloney, *Mysticism and the New Age: Christic Consciousness in the New Creation* (New York: Alba House, Society of St. Paul, 1991), 13.

53

He maintained that this concept of reality is as profound as the scientific revolution was four centuries ago when it forever altered the way we view the world.[2]

This inner enlightenment of "gnosis" — that is, an awakening from out of sleepy darkness to live in the light of new awareness in unity with God and the entire universe — has been called the "perennial wisdom."

The work of translating the highly technical, difficult to understand ideology of this new physics into more popular New Age terms has been undertaken by a host of writers. None has been more successful, however, than Fritjof Capra. In *The Turning Point — Science, Society and the Rising Culture,* he maintains that science is now offering us a new standard that has the potential to heal us.

Capra explains that the worldview emerging from modern physics "can be characterized by words like organic, holistic, and ecological. The universe is no longer seen as a machine, made up of a multitude of objects, but has to be pictured as one indivisible, dynamic whole whose parts are essentially interrelated and can be understood only as patterns of a cosmic process."[3]

Capra says this new vision of reality is known as the "systems view" and that it looks at the world in terms of relationships and integration. Thus, Capra seeks to "transcend" the age-old dispute between mechanism and vitalism (that is, the belief that organisms are animated by a nonscientific force) and come out on the side of *both* materialistic biology *and* Eastern/occult mysticism.[4]

In *The Aquarian Conspiracy,* Marilyn Ferguson has probably done more to promote New Age ideology on a popular level than any other author with any single book. She gives an overview of a vast array of contemporary ideas and activities, and suggests that they may all be converging to produce a far-reaching personal and social transformation — the "New Age."

Ferguson contends that the New Age transcendental monism view has triggered a new way of thinking. It is a "new mind" that gathers into its framework human potential psychologies, nuclear physics, and Far Eastern religions.[5]

---

2. Willis Harmon, *Global Mind Change* (Indianapolis: Knowledge Systems, 1988), 34-35, 38-39.

3. Fritjof Capra, *The Turning Point* (Toronto: Bantam, 1982), 2.

4. Elliot Miller, *A Crash Course on the New Age Movement* (Grand Rapids: Baker, 1989), 63.

5. Miller, *Crash Course,* 56. Cf. W. J. Hanegraaff, *New Age Religion and Western Culture* (Leiden: Brill, 1996), 106-7.

# HINDUISM AND NEW AGE TRANSFORMATION

In some respects, New Age religion can rightly be classified as a Western expression of classic monistic Hinduism, called Vedanta. Their most basic beliefs about God, the world, human beings, and salvation are the same, as are the mystical experiences that are at the heart of both. Much of the New Age spiritual technology that produces these experiences has come straight from India, brought here and taught since the 1960s by Hindu swamis and gurus. Their followers make up a sizable — though by no means dominant — contingent of the New Age movement itself.

In spite of these common features, the New Age movement, including its Oriental components, is very different from traditional Eastern mysticism. The key to this difference lies in the fact that New Agers are life- and world-affirming.

In traditional Hinduism the earthly is set in direct conflict with the spiritual. Those who are serious about seeking God and salvation are expected to renounce the world of temporal pleasures and responsibilities. This world is illusion, called *maya*, and is considered a formidable obstacle to eternal bliss. In the enlightened state, all is seen as God, or Brahman. Events in the world, because they are illusory, have no ultimate importance. Historic Hinduism is therefore world-denying.

In keeping with their Western heritage, New Agers have rejected this aspect of Eastern mysticism. They affirm the value of the realities of this world: people, nature, culture, education, politics, even science and technology. In fact, contemporary New Age thought represents an effort to graft the fruits of higher learning onto the various branches of mystical beliefs.

In order to go beyond any world-denial emphasis, some New Agers have proposed a "transmaterial" worldview, which they claim is neither non-materialist (as with Hinduism) nor materialist (as with secular humanism). This view agrees with the Hindus that on a certain level of consciousness, the "spiritual state," all is seen as one, and there are no distinctions between, for example, subject and object, or good and evil. It would also agree that on another level the materialist's perspective is valid.

New Agers argue for a third level, which incorporates both. Mark Satin writes, "In this state, objects, events, and self are neither separate, as in the material state, nor identical, as in the spiritual. Objects, events, and self are seen as separate *and* as flowing into a larger unity. In this perspective, the diversified created order can be viewed positively.... The world, therefore, has value and purpose."[6]

6. Miller, *Crash Course,* 21-23.

According to J. Gordon Melton, the New Age is among the most difficult of the recently prominent spiritual movements to grasp, primarily because it is a movement built much more around a vision and an experience rather than around doctrines or a belief system. As a decentralized movement, it will entertain contradictory ideas. Among its more important spokespersons are people who voice opinions completely unacceptable to the movement as a whole.

## TRANSFORMATION IS CENTRAL
## TO NEW AGE BELIEF

The central vision and experience of the New Age is one of radical transformation. On an individual level that experience is very personal and mystical. It involves an awakening to a new reality of self such as a discovery of psychic abilities, the experience of a physical or psychological healing, the emergence of new potentials within oneself, an intimate experience within a community, or the acceptance of a new picture of the universe.

However, the essence of New Age is the imposition of that vision of personal transformation onto society and the world. Thus the New Age is ultimately a social vision of a world transformed, a heaven on earth, a society in which the problems of today are overcome and a new existence emerges. There is a wide range of opinion about the nature of that New Age and the means of bringing it about, but the symbol of the New Age is grounded in the individual's personal experience of transformation, which gives the movement its vitality and appeal.

The power to bring about the necessary transformation of both individuals and society comes from "universal energy." Members of the New Age movement assume the existence of a basic energy which is different from the more recognized forms of energy (heat, light, etc.) and which supports and permeates all of existence. This energy goes by many names — prana, mana, odic force, orgone energy, holy spirit, the ch'i, the healing force. It is the force believed to cause psychic healing to occur. It is the force said to be released in various forms of meditation and body therapies which energizes the individual mentally and physically. It is the force New Agers believe is passed between individuals in expressions of love.[7]

7. J. Gordon Melton, "The New Age Movement: A Survey and Christian Response," March 1985, 6-7.

# TECHNIQUES FOR THE SPIRITUAL PATH

The emphasis upon continual transformation will lead New Agers on a *sadhana,* a spiritual path. For some that will mean commitment for a period or a lifetime to the practices taught by a single spiritual teacher. Others will continually sample transformative practices, picking and choosing from them, and thus develop a very individualized and constantly changing sadhana.

Meditation, or "creative visualization," and several other techniques for altering the consciousness play a pivotal role in the New Age movement. Such "psychotechnologies" are capable of interrupting or even bringing to a halt one's normal patterns of conceptual thought without extinguishing or diminishing consciousness itself. For the responsive subject, these altered states of consciousness can produce a profound mystical sense of "transcendence" of individuality and identification with everything. Such experiences of undifferentiated consciousness suggest to the seeker that ultimate reality itself is undifferentiated; everything is One, and the nature of the One must be consciousness, since at the peak of the mystical state consciousness is virtually all that is experienced.

R. M. Bucke, a turn-of-the-century psychiatrist who popularized the term "cosmic consciousness" to describe these states, emphasized that this consciousness shows the cosmos to consist not of dead matter governed by unconscious, rigid, and unintending law; it shows it on the contrary as entirely immaterial, entirely spiritual, and entirely alive.

Those who actively pursue or passively submit to an altered state of consciousness are setting themselves up for nothing short of a religious conversion: They will likely come out of their experiences persuaded that metaphysical reality is something similar to what Bucke described.

It can therefore be observed that altered states of consciousness are either a passageway to reality or a passageway to delusion, but they are hardly a neutral phenomenon to which one can repeatedly subject oneself while retaining a detached, "scientific" frame of mind. Their impact on the psyche is too powerful, producing a subjective entanglement in the dynamics inherent to the experience.

Although New Agers do not generally repudiate normal reasoning processes, they do believe that they have experienced something that transcends them. Thus it is very difficult for rational arguments (such as arguments concerning the dangers of subjectivism) to penetrate their mind-set: they simply assume that those challenging the experience have not had it — or they would "know."

Altered states of consciousness can have an especially profound impact on secular humanists who either never were exposed to, or have long since given up on, traditional Christian spirituality. After languishing in the arid

57

wastelands of godless naturalism, and then encountering the spiritual realm directly through an altered state of consciousness, the former skeptic's entire world is shaken. Ecstatic feelings, psychic power, even contacts from spirit entities all create hope for a more purposeful, satisfying life.[8]

The sadhana, or spiritual path, thus has as its goal the production of a mystical consciousness or awareness. This is frequently called by such names as higher consciousness, self-realization, or Christ consciousness. It is an awareness of the universal energy which undergirds existence and of the metaphysical unity which underlies the appearance of diversity. Most (but not all) New Agers identify God with that Ultimate Unifying Principle which binds the whole together and the Power which gives it a dynamic. Thus most New Agers identify God and the world as one reality. Using metaphysical speculations derived from Einstein's identification of matter with energy, they tend to reduce all reality to energy.

New Agers from a wide variety of disciplines and backgrounds seek to "matchmake" a union of science and Eastern/occultic religion. Not only would such a marriage vindicate the mystical worldview in their minds, it would offer powerful propaganda in a culture where whatever science says is given much weight.

Abraham Maslow, who is considered the "father of the human potential movement," has observed that "science is the only way we have of shoving truth down the reluctant throat."[9]

Others, especially those influenced by Far Eastern groups, will tend toward a form of dualism which sees spiritual reality as ultimately good and real, and matter as the evil which must be left behind in the spiritual-mystical life.

People thus see themselves as participating in God as individualized manifestations of that Ultimate Unifying Principle and as channels of the universal energy to the world. Jesus and the other significant religious teachers, such as Buddha or Krishna, were particularly transparent as bearers of the Divine, or Christ, Principle. Such teachers appear regularly throughout history to illustrate the aware, or fully realized, life, to teach individuals the goal of awareness, and to train them in particular techniques to reach the awareness of their own divinity. Some New Age people see the need to find a living guru who is a fully realized teacher. Such a teacher is judged mainly upon perceived awareness, or enlightenment, rather than on more mundane questions of a particular religious tradition, personal behavior (unless it becomes scandalous or outrageous), or teaching idiosyncrasies.

---

8. Miller, *Crash Course*, 36-37.
9. Marilyn Ferguson, *The Brain Revolution* (New York: Bantam, 1973), xiii.

# THE BIBLICAL VIEW OF TRANSFORMATION

Like New Age, the biblical emphasis is also on transformation. When carried out along biblical lines, the emphasis on transformation should be applauded. For the Christian the problem with the New Age approach to personal transformation is the metaphysical and spiritual context in which the transformation concept is understood and pursued.

In the Bible, spiritual growth is equated with increasing dependence on Christ and conformity to his will. (See 2 Cor. 3:4-5; Jas. 4:13-16; Eph. 4:15.)

In contrast, New Agers offer definitions such as: "The personal and spiritual growth of a person can be described as the transformation from a dependent human being to one who knows and feels that he/she is in charge of his/her life and acts upon it."[10]

# CREATUREHOOD AND SINFUL NATURE

Since the distinction between Creator and creation is absolute and permanent for the biblical view, the limited creature must always depend on and obey the all-sufficient, sovereign Creator. Though personal growth may involve increasing independence on a human level, our relationship with God operates differently.

For the New Ager, the distinction between "creator" and creation is illusory, so that which is all-sufficient and sovereign must be the self. In such a case, growth or transformation would logically involve recognizing this fact and acting on it, in ever-increasing self-sufficiency and control over one's own life.

# RESPONSIBILITY TO GOD

From the biblical perspective, the New Age appeals to human beings' primordial, sinful desire to be gods, independent of the creator God (Gen. 3:4-6). When New Agers talk about "taking responsibility" and "being accountable," Christians can be disarmed, since these terms are part of their own vocabulary. Actually, the word *responsibility* can be used in very different contexts.

10. Miller, *Crash Course*, 25.

To the Christian a human made in God's image is responsible and accountable to external authorities, beginning with God, and including those human authorities that God has instituted (for example, Rom. 13:1-2).

The New Ager, on the other hand, defines "taking responsibility" and "being accountable" ultimately in terms of the self. We have the power to create our own reality, but it will be created by external forces if we do not take responsibility for whatever happens to us. This is why human-potential seminar graduates have been known to blame such adversities as cancer and rape on the people who suffer from them. New Age belief in unlimited human potential — our power to "take responsibility" and shape our own future — is increasingly being applied not just to the individual but to society as a whole.

The New Age emphasis does not have the biblical view of humanity's basic sinfulness and need of a personal Divine-Human Savior. The worldview of New Agers compels them to say that Jesus is no more God than anyone else. The difference between Jesus and the rest of humanity must therefore be that he more fully realized and demonstrated the divine potential we all have. His value to us becomes primarily one of example. New Agers say that Jesus wanted us to become his equals, not to worship him.

Christianity is a faith focused in the person of Jesus Christ as the unique God-man (2 Cor. 4:5; 11:2-3), and the highest spiritual attainment has never been mystical identification with God, but fellowship with the Son of God and, through him, with the Father (1 John 1:1-3; John 17:3; Phil. 3:8).

# NEW AGE TRANSFORMATION

New Age beliefs draw upon Eastern religious and philosophical traditions, mystical aspects of the Judeo-Christian tradition, and elements of the magic worldview. These practices include, among others, yoga, various forms of meditation, crystal healing, macrobiotics, reincarnation, the Western esoteric tradition, tantra, and trance channeling.[11]

In fact, we can say that the term "New Age" is strongly influenced by a gradual adaptation and utilization of an "Eastern worldview" in the West. It is not limited to people who have actually joined Eastern-related movements, but it is visible in a vast variety of cultural institutions. In hospitals, for example, doctors are discovering the importance of the breathing and concentration practices associated with yoga to reduce high blood pressure. Nurses are taught Therapeutic Touch in their nursing schools. Holistic therapies abound. In

11. James R. Lewis and J. Gordon Melton, eds., *Perspectives on the New Age* (Albany, N.Y.: State University of New York, 1992), 87, 192.

schools, children may learn relaxation exercises or guided visualizations. In health clubs, women and men practice not only aerobics, but yoga, for physical fitness. People may undertake psychotherapy to discover their own inner resources, or "human potential." Even in some more liberal churches, ministers might speak of "realizing the Christ within their own consciousness."

The New Age movement is not constituted by a few young people who are "turning east" by joining marginal religious movements, but by a whole culture influenced by the East.

Beyond particular movements, with their particular insights or their particular failings, is the wider issue of the encounter of worldviews in a world where East is no longer East, West is no longer West, where the twain have met, and where the outcome of that meeting is of the utmost consequence for the future of humankind.[12]

## Alternative Typologies

New Age groups can be divided into those that bear the imprint of Western psychology and therapeutic subculture and those related to Asiatic religions.

Among these movements drawing on values and techniques of Western psychology and therapy are some, such as Scientology, that are geared to the pursuit of traditional Western values like individual success, superiority, domination of circumstances, and "how to win friends and influence people." Their ideal is self-improvement rather than self-realization.

Others are committed to the "expressive" values of humanist psychology and the "Human Potential movement," focusing on human growth and the exploration and realization of the self. Erhard Seminars Training (est) seems to cover both aspects. Both Scientology and est have incorporated elements of Eastern religions (reincarnation, Zen, etc.), whereas some Indian guru movements like Transcendental Meditation and the Bhagwan movement have gone through the reverse process and now represent a blend of Eastern religion and Western psychology, either of the self-improvement (TM) or the self-realization (Bhagwan) type. Even groups like those coming from Tibetan Buddhism have succeeded in interpreting themselves and in being understood in psychological terms in the West. Obviously it is difficult to draw a clear dividing line between religious movements related to Asia and "psycho-movements."[13]

The new Spiritualism, on the other hand, is a phenomenon occurring in the relatively affluent postmodern society and reflects the need for the

---

12. Allan R. Brockway and J. Paul Rajashekar, eds., *New Religious Movements and the Churches* (Geneva: WCC, 1987), 154.
    13. Ibid., 19-20.

freedom of the human spirit from a technologically and rationally controlled society. It is a quest for human possibilities. It must be pointed out that there may be a tendency to manipulate or utilize spirits for this worldly happiness and success at the mass level, and this has led some observers to point to a kind of "magicalization" of religion.

# COMMON IDEAS

But in all types of New Age radical transformation there are common ideas:

- Knowledge *is* salvation, though this knowledge is intuitive, not rational. To be enlightened through mystical intuition, or higher consciousness, about the true reality of our oneness with God is in itself to be saved.
- Ignorance is the source of evil. If knowledge is salvation, the cause of the problems from which we are saved is our own ignorance. This emphasis is a primary theme of the many seminars that promote the new awareness necessary for enlightenment. Famous examples include the est training sessions of Werner Erhard (some of the programs are now designated as the Forum) and the Esalen Institute in California.
- Salvation through human effort. The New Age affirms various techniques for arriving at true knowledge, the mystical experience of enlightenment that is salvation. This new consciousness must come through our own initiative but it can be achieved in a number of ways. This fits the pluralistic, do-your-own-thing tendencies of the New Age movement. New Agers believe that any religion can help you find truth. Follow the Buddha, Krishna, Jesus, or one of many others. They all teach the same basic message.

In this view, the teachings and example of Jesus — not his unique deity or sacrificial death or physical resurrection — are what New Age proponents consider important. The New Age radio program "Dimensions" states these ideals in its Introduction: "It is only through a change of consciousness that the world will be changed. This is our responsibility."

## The Primal Approach to Transformation

The New Age movement looks back to primal societies for techniques of transformation. The term "primal" refers to those religions which began before the great historic religions and continue to reveal many of the basic and primary features of religion. This definition allows one to apply the concepts not only to isolated tribal societies but also to pagan beliefs which are currently emerging within Western society. If we speak of the "primal worldview," this term encompasses a set of similar but distinct worldviews belonging to particular groups. Anglican specialist in world religions Stephen Neill estimates that the worldview of at least 40 percent of the world's population holds this primal view. To be transformed, you must know how to avoid disturbing the spirits and how to manipulate spiritual powers. This is the work of the shaman.

Although revival of interest in Native American spirituality began with the 1960s counterculture, it did not become a major phenomenon until the arrival of the New Age movement of the late 1980s. It should be noted that common fundamentals underlie the various approaches of Native Americans to mysticism and transformation.

Foremost is the Native American view that the Earth is sacred, and that it is a living, intelligent being with holy powers. "Earth Mother," as the land is often called, is treated with great respect.

Native Americans feel a particular kinship with animals and in many respects regard them as superior peoples because they were placed on Earth before humans.[14]

There is a growing attraction in New Age circles to an "Earth Mother" deity, as opposed to a heavenly Father.

Spiritually adventuresome New Agers say they want something a little closer to home than, say, Tibetan gong meditation. Throughout North America, Native Americans are building sacred structures, such as dance arenas and underground sweat lodges, and creating sacred fires, rock walls, and medicine wheels related to the acquisition of power by shamans. Seekers of "mystical visions" open themselves to "cosmological forces" in high country training, often fasting and dancing for hours at a time while shouting to the "spirits."

New Agers see these rites as an integral part of a Western society that has teetered on the edge of extinction and which, like the condor, must be saved. New Age leaders contend that a rediscovery of certain motifs of shamanism is an effective counter to the technological, rationalistic culture.[15]

A leader in this endeavor is Sun Bear, a Chippewa Indian teacher and medicine chief, who has a vision that medicine wheels should return as places for teaching, sharing, and "channeling love and healing energy to the Earth Mother." He states: "The invisible powers that are the spirit-keepers come to

14. Rosemary Ellen Guiley, *Harper's Encyclopedia of Mystical and Paranormal Experience* (Edison, N.J.: Castle Books, 1991), 388-89.
15. Russell Chandler, *Understanding the New Age* (Dallas: Word, 1991), 98-99, 95.

us, and when we lock ourselves into their energy we conduct it; we are working together, like electricity when it flows through certain kinds of crystals."[16]

Leslie Gray, a Cherokee who holds a Ph.D. in psychology from Harvard, contends that "the United States, not the Himalayas or Tibet, is the Holy Land." Shamanism in the 1980s and 1990s, she says, "is what Zen and yoga were in the 1960s and 70s."

Characteristically, the shaman is a healer, a psychopomp (someone who guides the souls of the dead to their home in the afterlife), and more generally a mediator between the community and the world of spirits, most often animal spirits and the spirits of the forces of nature.

Lynn Andrews, known as the "Beverly Hills medicine woman" and the "female Carlos Castaneda," has put many upscale suburban women on the path to Native American spirituality. Though not an Indian herself, Andrews spent the better part of fifteen years as an apprentice to indigenous women shamans, all the while gathering material for her five best-selling books on adventures of enlightenment. Her counseling techniques include the use of rattles and bells "to balance the electromagnetic energy field surrounding the body."[17]

Many contemporary New Agers have thus come to adopt some of the trappings of American Indian shamanism. The popularity of Native American spirituality has, however, evoked hostility from certain Indian groups. These Indian groups assert that whereas the European and American invaders stole the land, the new invaders are trying to steal the religions of native peoples. Their concern is understandable. Just look at the advertisements in New Age magazines through which one can purchase by mail everything from medicine rattles and sacred pipes to a complete "Course in Shamanism" on cassette tapes. Ads also offer "Pilgrimages to Places of Power," as well as innumerable workshops on vision quests, sweat lodges, and the like.[18]

# CASTANEDA AND DON JUAN

Who is Don Juan? Carlos Castaneda tells us about the Yaqui Indian sorcerer-warrior Don Juan. Castaneda is an anthropologist and author of a number of books purported to be his true experiences learning lessons from Don Juan about the mystical worlds. Castaneda was born in Peru in 1925. He enrolled at the University of California at Los Angeles and majored in anthropology.

16. Lewis and Melton, *Perspectives on the New Age*, 196.
17. Chandler, *Understanding the New Age*, 100-101.
18. Timothy Miller, ed., *America's Alternative Religions* (Albany, N.Y.: State University of New York, 1995), 384.

In 1960, on a research trip to Mexico, he was directed to Don Juan, who was said to possess the knowledge Castaneda sought. The next year, Don Juan took Castaneda on as an apprentice and introduced him to another sorcerer, don Genaro Flores, a Mazatec Indian, who would serve as his tutor.

Castaneda wrote three books about his experiences, covering the teachings of Don Juan. The third, *Journey to Ixtlan,* was accepted as his doctoral dissertation.

Many reviews of his books have been favorable, yet there has been much debate as to whether the books are documented fact, embellished fact, or entirely fiction.[19]

Castaneda has drawn on the European philosophical movement of phenomenology, initiated by Edmund Husserl, to explain Don Juan's teachings. According to the phenomenologists, what we perceive as reality depends on the interpretation we have been led to place on an ultimately mysterious universe. If we can bracket out our normal ways of perceiving the world, we can see how arbitrary previous interpretations are. The thrust of Don Juan's teaching is to break down Castaneda's conviction that the ordinary world with its limits is the only field of human experience. The eventual goal, at least for the strong and brave, is to obtain a new view of reality and a new set of interpretations.

Castaneda criticized Timothy Leary for having a naive view when Leary said psychedelic drugs alone have the power to alter the world. Castaneda said that to alter the world something else, such as sorcery, is required. Drugs comprised only the initial phase of his apprenticeship; Don Juan later taught him to achieve the same results without drugs.[20]

For help in obtaining a new consciousness, Swiss psychiatrist Carl Jung points to societies such as the Pueblo of North America and the African people he visited on one of his trips.

# THE HINDU APPROACH

Many Westerners are looking to the East and India for a New Age "turn on." The sacred scriptures upon which modern Hinduism is based, the Vedas, are written in Sanskrit and are thought to be at least three thousand years old. These ancient writings speak of many deities, all of whom are manifestations of Brahman, or god. Other sacred writings celebrate devotion to an incarnation of Brahman, Lord Krishna, and praise the discipline of Yoga.

19. Guiley, *Harper's Encyclopedia,* 82.
20. Ibid., 83.

The religious philosophy of India reached high points in the ninth and twelfth centuries after Christ. Perhaps the most basic intellectual philosophy of India, known as Vedanta, was developed by Shankara in the ninth century A.D. A more personal approach was developed by the bhakti movement in the twelfth century.

# AMERICA AND HINDUISM

Scholars have traced an American interest in the religions and philosophies of the Orient back to the nineteenth century in letters regarding Hinduism exchanged between John Adams and Thomas Jefferson. Spirituality with an Eastern flavor was also particularly influential on the New England Transcendentalist movement, especially influencing Ralph Waldo Emerson and Thoreau. The World Parliament of Religions held in Chicago in 1893 introduced Indian Swami Vivekananda of the Ramakrishna Mission and Soyen Shaku, representing Japanese Zen, to the United States.

Swami Vivekananda was the first Hindu teacher to attract widespread attention in the United States. On September 11, 1893, he gave his first address to the Chicago Parliament. The conference continued for seventeen days. Dressed in vivid orange and red robes and turbans, and speaking in an aggressive style, Vivekananda made a strong impression. He was thirty years old. The response was good. Later, a disciple reported that people began to ask, "Why send missionaries to a country which produces men like this?"

After the parliament, Vivekananda continued to receive extensive newspaper coverage of his lectures in the United States and in England. He conducted classes and lectured in New York City and Boston. He emerged as a vigorous defender of the value of Hindu thought who was ready to cross verbal swords with Christian missionaries. The first Vedanta Society was organized in New York City in 1896.

His message, which he termed Vedanta, was that each individual is able to achieve the direct experience of God-realization. He explained that the diversity of various religions and sects merely meant that there were different paths to the same goal.

When Vivekananda returned to India in 1896, he was welcomed as a hero who had reversed the tide of Christian proselytization by winning American converts to Hinduism. Vivekananda returned to the United States and in 1899 to 1900 spent six months lecturing to Unitarian and New Thought groups in the Los Angeles and San Francisco areas.[21]

21. Timothy Miller, *America's Alternative Religions*, 176-77.

Many of the early Europeans were shocked and disgusted by much of Hindu culture. The blatant idolatry, animal sacrifice, child marriage, and untouchability appeared primitive in Western eyes.

Countering that, Vivekananda idealized the Hindu world, including its religion and philosophy. This picture of India gradually filtered out into American culture and was thus readily available to the fifties Beats, the sixties counterculture, and the New Age movement of the seventies and eighties.[22]

### Yogananda and Devotional Hinduism

The same year that Vivekananda addressed the Parliament of Religions, an infant who would become Paramahansa Yogananda was born. Although a fellow Bengali, Yogananda was a very different personality. Vivekananda, "the cyclonic Hindu," presented Hinduism as a "manly" religion. He stressed the need for self-reliance in the struggle toward enlightenment. In contrast, Yogananda, with his round face and shoulder-length wavy hair, evoked a softer presence in his appearance as well as in his teachings. He emphasized the devotional aspects of the Hindu tradition. Yogananda has presented his life's story in his *Autobiography of a Yogi,* which was first published in 1946 and has since been translated into eighteen languages.

He attended the Scottish Church College in India for two years, completing his A.B. degree at Serampore College, which was affiliated with Calcutta University. After his graduation, he took *sannyasa,* becoming Swami Yogananda — one who has bliss through divine union.

In 1920, Yogananda received an invitation to address the International Congress of Religious Liberals convening in Boston under the auspices of the American Unitarian Association. Funded by his father, Yogananda traveled to the United States. He delivered his address, "The Science of Religion," on October 6, 1920.

Yogananda found Boston to be receptive to his message and he settled there for three years. In 1924, he began a transcontinental speaking tour, attracting large crowds in major cities. In January 1925, the three-thousand-seat Philharmonic Auditorium in Los Angeles was filled to capacity for Yogananda's lectures, with thousands turned away. During this time, the California horticulturalist Luther Burbank became Yogananda's disciple. Two years later, Yogananda attracted record crowds to his lectures in Washington, D.C., and was received by President Calvin Coolidge at the White House. Yogananda's organization was incorporated in 1935 as the Self-Realization Fellowship.

The work of Ramakrishna swamis and Yogananda helped to establish

22. Lewis and Melton, *Perspectives on the New Age,* 56.

Hinduism in America as a viable religious alternative. Their work set the stage for the growth of American interest in Hindu philosophy, meditation, and yoga that blossomed in the 1960s and '70s and has continued into the 1990s.[23]

This explosion of Hindu gurus, or religious teachers, appearing on the American scene has emphasized a direct turning on to spiritual reality. Light, color, incense, music, and touch have been widely used to induce religious experience.

## BASIC HINDU CONCEPTS

Although the worldview and religious methods of the Vedanta movement and the Self-Realization Fellowship are not identical, their common roots in the Bengali Neo-Vedantic renaissance make them similar enough to warrant outlining some of the basic concepts which they offered to Americans.

First and foremost, they offered to the West a positive understanding of human nature. The view that each human partakes in divinity was forcefully expressed by Vivekananda at the Parliament of Religions as an alternative to the Christian doctrine of original sin:

> The Hindu refuses to call you sinners. We are the Children of God, the sharers of immortal bliss, holy and perfect beings. It is a sin to call a man [a sinner].

Vivekananda was expressing the Hindu concept that the true human self, the "atman," is eternally free, perfect, and divine. It is identical with the unmanifest Absolute, "nirguna (without qualities) Brahman." The material world, including the body, is a secondary, impermanent, and deluding existence (maya). Yogananda was fond of explaining that Jesus Christ was not the only Son of God. Jesus' command, "Be perfect, therefore, as your heavenly Father is perfect" (Matt. 5:48), should be taken seriously by every person, since each has the capacity to realize the Christ Consciousness within and to know oneself to be the perfect child of God.

These Hindu groups took to an extreme the basic New Age idea that the only god one can find is within. Words are seen as secondary to an atmosphere which ignites the interior experience. When words are used, it is usually in a chanting or repetitive way. Turning from social concerns, the new Hindu groups emphasized an individual's inner spiritual development by means of meditation, yoga, chanting, and demonstrations of love for one

23. Timothy Miller, *America's Alternative Religions*, 177-79, 187.

another. Charismatic gurus offered specific techniques and methods of spiritual awareness. The mass media as well as books and magazines were used to share their optimistic messages.

There are significant differences in organization and practices among Hindu New Age groups. The root worldview, which underlies most Hindu groups, is known as Vedanta or pantheistic monism. This view undergirds the thought of Transcendental Meditation as well as of some Buddhist groups. Hare Krishna modifies the more abstract Vedanta view by declaring that reality is more personal.[24]

## HARE KRISHNA

In the 1970s, the International Society for Krishna Consciousness (ISKCON) became for many people the symbol of the invasion of Asian religion into Western society. In 1965, at the age of seventy, a former pharmacist from Bengal sailed to New York. His name was A. C. Bhaktivedanta Swami Prabhupada.

As a visiting scholar in New York City in 1965, I went down to lower Manhattan to hear the 69-year-old Swami Prabhupada. Hare Krishna represented the devotional form of Hinduism (bhakti yoga), emphasizing that love and devotional service to God, or Krishna, were the means by which one could gain spiritual realization. Instead of seeing him as one of several gods, this view made Krishna the supreme manifestation of God. In a major split from other forms of Hinduism, Hare Krishna preached that all people, regardless of their caste or station in life, could be self-realized through activities performed in the service of Krishna.

This approach developed another practice unique to Hinduism, which has proved a trademark of the Krishna movement in America. Growing out of intense religious passion, this approach initiated "sankirtana," a practice requiring followers to venture out into the streets to dance and sing their praises of Lord Krishna. In this way, preaching, book distribution, and chanting in public became the principal means of spreading Krishna Consciousness.

The spiritual goal of Hare Krishna devotees is to escape birth in the material world and go back to Godhead. Because of material contamination, the soul is forced to assume a continuous succession of rebirths. To escape the laws of karma and break the cycle of reincarnation, devotees seek to perfect their spiritual lives by controlling their senses. This is done under the direction of a guru. The bhakti yoga process involves a number of religious practices directed toward purifying the soul. Central to this process of self-realization

24. Ibid., 180.

is chanting the Hare Krishna mantra: "Hare Krishna, Hare Krishna, Krishna Krishna, Hare Hare, Hare Rama, Hare Rama, Rama Rama, Hare Hare." George Harrison wrote "My Sweet Lord" in praise of Krishna.

Since its introduction to America in 1965, the fortunes of the Krishna movement have changed rather dramatically. From very humble beginnings in New York City, Prabhupada and his followers recruited thousands of members. Along with success, however, came public scrutiny and controversy that caused a downturn in both recruitment and economic fortunes. Hare Krishna began to decline as a religious organization. Prabhupada's death, in 1977, added to the crisis.

And out of crisis, came change. The ISKCON undertook a number of strategies that altered its relationship with the surrounding culture. ISKCON relaxed its formerly rigid boundaries to allow its members to seek outside employment. It also began building a congregation of East Indian members. These changes made ISKCON inclusive and pluralistic, its members as much involved in the conventional society as within ISKCON. Further changes and a growing secularization seem likely to threaten ISKCON's uniqueness and overall mission.[25]

## TRANSCENDENTAL MEDITATION (TM)

Transcendental Meditation has become the most successful of all the meditation groups. The movement was founded by Maharishi Mahesh Yogi in 1957. The bearded, white-robed yogi popularized his simplified Hindu meditation techniques under the initials TM. TM was presented as a technique, like speed reading, that could help the practitioner perform more effectively in the world. The costly fallout from the 1960s drug-induced consciousness revolution motivated Americans to find a safe way to "expand the mind" that would be a lawful alternative to dangerous drugs. Scientific studies conducted by R. Keith Wallace, Herbert Benson, and others suggested that TM does produce an altered state of consciousness — one marked by deep rest which restores energy and may be of general benefit to physical and mental health. By the early 1970s the means, the motivation, and the moment had converged to make TM seem to be a panacea that could deliver America from all sorts of individual and social problems.

The number of new initiates to TM per year in the United States reached its peak in 1975, after Merv Griffin heavily endorsed it on his television program, bringing the cumulative total of Americans who had begun the practice to about a million. By then TM had an American center for higher education, Maharishi International University, founded in California

25. Ibid., 216.

in 1971 and moved to Iowa in 1974. The world headquarters and two institutions for advanced study, Maharishi European Research University and
Maharishi Vedic University, were established in western Europe. The
Maharishi settled there, seldom visiting the United States, and from 1972
onward formulated visionary plans for a world government based on higher
consciousness.

In 1982, Maharishi announced his world strategy to set up 3,600
centers, one for each million people of earth. Each of these centers would
have one TM teacher per 1,000 people in the general population. It is claimed
that as soon as 1 percent of the world's population practice TM, the world
will be saved from war and destruction.

The progressive optimism of the TM movement has been evident
recently in medicine. The TM version of the traditional healing system of
India, called Maharishi Ayur-Ved, has been made available to the public
through consultation and treatment at holistic health clinics in major cities
and in products sold in health food stores and by mail order. As we will see
in the chapter on health, the best-known medical advocate of the system and
its benefits is Deepak Chopra, M.D. His workshops and popular books offer
the possibility of "quantum healing" and "perfect health."[26]

For TM, as in much of New Age thinking, the Logos, or the Word,
that creates the cosmos is not God's wisdom or reason, but vibrations. These
vibrations can be tapped into by the practice of mantra — the use of a word,
or rather a sound, separated from meaning or reason. Maharishi Mahesh Yogi
explains mantra as "chanting to produce an effect in some other world, [to]
draw the attention of those higher beings or gods living there."

Mantra is not prayer, at least as the Christian understands it. Prayer is
a meaningful personal conversation with our Creator. Mantra is a deliberate
annihilation of meaningful language by mechanical, nonpersonal repetition of
a word or sound. As Eliade says, "All indefinite repetition leads to destruction
of language; in some mystical traditions, this destruction appears to be the
condition for further experiences."[27]

The significance of mantra is justified by a belief in occult correspondence. The cosmos is nothing but vibration. And what is sound? Pure vibration, once it is severed from reasoned communication or language. Language
keeps us entangled at the level of maya, or illusion. Sound can take us to the
source of cosmic vibrations.

26. Ibid., 194-95.
27. Vishal Mangalwadi, *When the New Age Gets Old: Looking for a Greater Spirituality* (Downers Grove, Ill.: InterVarsity, 1992), 113-14.

# A CHRISTIAN CRITIQUE

The new world promised by many devotees of the Maharishi's technique sounds extremely promising and appealing. In practice it does not match the promises. From a Christian perspective, the method has serious philosophical and theological flaws. There is an open and explicit element of worship in the required initiation ceremony.

Another weakness of TM is that it seeks the answer to humanity's problems from within humanity himself. The basic precept of the Maharishi is that we can find god *within* us as a spark of the divine. TM fails to recognize humanity's biggest problem: sin. According to biblical teaching, sinful hearts and the roots of their minds do not yield thought bubbles of divine wonder and intention but wicked devices and selfish ends, all in revolt against the sovereignty of God.

The Maharishi does not give any guidance for morality nor does he give any standard of ethics. The primary requirement is to sink a shaft of light (your mantra) into your mind; then your mind will gravitate to the light to find "absolute bliss." When you gain pure consciousness, you automatically perform right actions.

## The Major Hindu Yoga Systems

For the purpose of transformation, yoga is the basic emphasis coming from India. Yoga is a Sanskrit word literally meaning "to unite." It has the connotation both of submission to discipline and of union. Probably spiritual discipline is the best translation of the term. There are six major yoga systems.

### HATHA — YOGA OF BODILY CONTROL

The word "Hatha" is made up of the syllable "ha," meaning sun, and "tha," which means moon. The reason for this is that yogis believe that two warring impulses are set in motion every time we breathe. The moon impulse begins in the heart and ascends up to the brain. The sun impulse starts at the solar plexus and heads downward to the anus. The discord between these contrary pulls causes the restlessness we experience in mind and body.

Hatha yoga tries to harness these two sets of currents and, by making them unite, to still both body and mind. The person would then be free to concentrate upon one's true "self." The breathing exercises are all designed to create the uniting of these two currents. What should then happen is that the concentration of energy is pushed down to the base of the spine. Here there is one of the seven "chakras," or spiritual energy centers, of the body, and also the entrance to the "sushumna," the central spinal canal.

For most people the "sushumna" is never opened as long as they live. Yet when the yogi manages to push energy through the "sushumna," he suddenly finds that spiritual life has become all at once much easier. This, then, is what the physical exercises of yoga are really for. Any physical fitness benefits are secondary. Many yogi regard Hatha as merely the preliminary exercises to be gone through before real yoga begins.[28]

Classic commentaries on yoga issue dire warnings for those who practice Hatha yoga for purely physical ends, rather than for spiritual discipline. Yoga is definitely not just another form for gymnastics or just a means of relaxation. In fact such statements are bluntly offensive in relation to yoga. Hatha yoga puts into practice the idea that "this body" is the means of liberation.

Hatha yoga tells of the five main techniques by which one can get full control and mastery over the elements by manipulating the chakras. These yogic techniques are used in order to take control over the Force, the Kundalini-power, so that it can "regain its lost empire" and gradually rid itself of "the human condition" and achieve divinity.[29]

## JNANA — YOGA FOR THE INTELLECTUAL

Jnana yoga is for the intellectual type. It is a way of knowledge and wisdom. It emphasizes self-analysis and awareness. It involves discrimination, indifference to sensual objects, and calmness of mind as ways of completely identifying with the divinity within.

## KARMA — YOGA OF ACTION

Karma yoga is the yoga of work and everyday life. The logic is that all people must act, but the wise man acts in a detached manner without "self" involvement. The actions are therefore no longer his actions since they are not performed for self-gratification. The process of karma is thus terminated, and the person is free. The principle is inaction in action. The best-known karma yogi was Mahatma Gandhi.

---

28. David Burnett, *Clash of Worlds* (Eastbourne: MARC, 1990), 80-81.
29. Brockway and Rajashekar, *New Religious Movements*, 52-53.

## BHAKTI — YOGA OF DEVOTION

The best-known Hindu cult is that of the Bhakti form. The Hare Krishna people are well-known representatives. Bhakti means "devotion." In this form of yoga, the adherent is supposed to achieve union with the ultimate reality by giving his love and worship unremittingly to one of the personal forms of God. Hindus believe that although Brahman is impersonal, he/it may be worshiped as a person. One way of devoting oneself is to repeatedly chant the sacred form of words, called mantra. By incessant chanting, it is believed, one loses attachment to material things and is drawn away from the fascinations of "maya" to fall in love with reality itself.[30]

## KUNDALINI

Kundalini teaches that a potent nucleus of vital energy, a repository of physical and sexual power, dwells at the base of the spine. Kundalini is visualized as a small serpent lying in a spiral of three and a half coils at the base of the spine. Through certain yogic techniques this power can be awakened and aroused and drawn up the spinal column. As we will describe later in detail, Tantra yoga Kundalini is an aspect of Shakti, divine female energy and the consort of Shiva.[31]

These Kundalini techniques to draw the power up the spinal column include many of the major techniques of yoga. Awakening the Kundalini calls for bodily posture, hand gestures (mudra), mystic syllables (mantra), breath control, eye focusing, symbolic diagrams (yantra), and super concentration. Breath control is especially important.

In the process of moving the Kundalini up the spine, certain chakras are opened. The chakras are seen as a lotus center of dormant psychic energy. They are further described as psychic dynamos or centers of superphysical energy. They have no physiological existence and cannot be laid out on a dissecting table. They can only be known through meditation experience. The chakras are similar to the Chinese pressure points which are pricked in acupuncture. The chakras are part of the Hindu concept of humans' "subtle body," which surrounds the physical body but cannot be seen by the human eye.

The chakras are located along the spinal column at such places as the base of the spine, the region of the sex organs, the heart, the neck, above the eyebrows, and just above the crown of the head. They are arranged along a shaft of the "subtle" body called the Rod of Brahma.

30. Burnett, *Clash of Worlds*, 81-83.
31. Guiley, *Harper's Encyclopedia*, 319.

According to Hindu advocates, the Kundalini lies asleep in the average person. This is good. If disturbed or ignorantly raised, the Kundalini will cause an abnormal arousal of the baser instincts and passions. To seek to raise the Kundalini or open the chakras apart from a spiritual purpose is both pointless and hazardous.[32]

A proper raising of the Kundalini is said to produce remarkable states of awareness. The first awareness of Kundalini's awakening is a sensation of warmth which grows from warmth to a burning heat. Each chakra pierced and opened brings a new experience, new power, and a new vision. Oftentimes strange sounds are heard.

Individuals who have experienced Kundalini say it is beyond description. The phenomena associated with it vary and include bizarre physical sensations and movements, pain, clairaudience, visions, brilliant lights, super-lucidity, physical powers, ecstasy, bliss, and transcendence of self. Kundalini has been described as liquid fire and liquid light.

The final objective of Kundalini raising may take many years. It is achieved when the Kundalini, or serpent power, reaches the final chakra point inside the skull. With a psychic explosion it is said to awaken a ten-thousand-petal lotus. This is a graphic way of describing complete cosmic consciousness and god-realization. Descriptions are vivid. Brilliant stars and flaming tongues are seen. A realized person sees an entire world inside of his head complete with its own miniature mountain, lake, sun, and moon. In the midst of this world, the god Siva is seen enthroned. This is union, absorption, identity. The transcendent state of being-consciousness-bliss has been reached.

Gopi Krishna (1903-1984) devoted much of his life to learning everything he could about Kundalini. He considered it "the most jealously guarded secret in history" and "the guardian of human evolution." He believed it to be the driving force behind genius and inspiration. Gopi Krishna was eager to see kundalini awakening cultivated, especially in the West.

Since the 1970s Kundalini awakenings have been reported with increasing frequency in the West. There are perhaps two major reasons: more people have been undertaking spiritual disciplines likely to liberate the energy, and more people are aware of what Kundalini is, and therefore more likely to recognize the signs of it.

Scientific research of Kundalini remains embryonic, hampered by the nonphysical nature of the energy and its unpredictability.[33]

32. Benjamin Walker, "Kundalini," in *Man, Myth, Magic,* ed. Richard Cavendish (New York: Marshall Cavendish, 1970), 12.1586.

33. Guiley, *Harper's Encyclopedia,* 319-21.

## THE SCANDAL OF TANTRISM

Most forms of yoga involve discipline, but the Tantric texts suggested the possibility of using some of the natural impulses of the body in yoga rather than suppressing them. Sex, especially, was seen as a possible route to reality. Prolonging the sexual act, it was claimed, generates a flow of sexual energy between the two partners so that both begin to experience the ultimate Oneness of reality.

Most orthodox Vedanta Hindus were scandalized by these ideas. They had in general ignored bodily processes, especially sexual intercourse. Frequent sexual intercourse was regarded as resulting in a loss of spiritual power. The Hatha form of yoga was probably stimulated as a counteraction to Tantrism which made prolonged sexual intercourse a route to enlightenment.[34]

The term "Tantra" has many meanings. It is used as the collective name of certain Indo-Tibetan scriptures, and of the religious practices and yogic techniques taught by those scriptures. Tantra may also refer to the religio-philosophical tradition that results from those scriptures, teachings, and practices.

In Indian history Tantra seems to have emerged around A.D. 600. By A.D. 900 at least sixty-four scriptures were already in circulation. And by the year 1000 Tantric art had begun to dominate the cultural scene in India. But historians believe that Tantra's roots reach back into Indian pre-history — in pre-Aryan, magical, mystical fertility cults that seem to have worshiped the goddess and the female power of generation.

Tantra accepts the classical Hindu view that reality is one. Before the beginning, beyond time, was pure consciousness, existing in perfect unity or equilibrium, having no polarity, no form, no thought, no distinction. Something disturbed this primeval, pure, and still ocean of consciousness. The divine stability then turned into an oscillating instability, imbalance, or insanity. God was divided. The first duality to appear as a result of this "insanity" was male and female. The consciousness of this original duality produced a series of waves, further disturbing the tranquil surface of the sea of bliss. A crisscrossing of these waves created elaborate patterns. The farther these waves were removed from their original state (as divine consciousness), the "grosser" they became, appearing finally as condensed matter, the world of sense experience. The cosmos, then, is divine devolution — densified frequencies, or compacted waves of consciousness, that can conceal their divinity because they are convoluted divine emanations. Thus the original polarity of male and female manifests itself finally as the polarity of mind and matter.

Physicists such as Fritjof Capra find this Tantric view of the ultimate oneness of mind and matter to be a mind-blowing insight for scientists.

---

34. Burnett, *Clash of Worlds*, 84.

Capra thinks that it is utterly remarkable that after centuries of painstaking research, scientists should arrive at the same conclusion, that matter and energy are one!

Because the finer "consciousness" and the grosser "body" coexist in a human being, we are, according to Tantric thought, microscopic versions of the cosmos. Polarity is therefore the key to existence. The gender division of male and female, being the basic polarity in the human race, is therefore the key to our human existence: its reunification in sexual intercourse is our point of contact with the cosmic powers.

The idea that we can have spiritual experience through sex was introduced to millions of people through the 1984 movie *Indiana Jones and the Temple of Doom*. The hero rescues the "Shankara stone" from a Tantric sect to deliver it to its rightful possessors. The Shankara stone is "Shiva-lingam" (i.e., the god Shiva's phallus), more worshiped than understood by the Hindus. In the movie the villains had found three primeval Shiva-lingams and were searching for the other two so as to unite them with Kali (Shakti), the female consort of Shiva.

Mircea Eliade, author of *Yoga: Immortality and Freedom*, suggests that Tantra might represent the spiritual counterattack of an indigenous mother-cult, suppressed earlier by the invading Aryans.

Amaury de Riencourt sees in Tantra a human, if not a historical or racial, counterattack. It is a manifestation of the human instinct for self-preservation, an attempt to save India from the destructive consequences of Hindu and Buddhist outlooks, which view life as suffering, if not illusion.

This fundamental opposition to mainstream Hindu thought was responsible for Tantra's persecution by the Aryan establishment. Its morally suspect practices, sometimes indistinguishable from black magic, also invited fierce Muslim opposition. The persecution drove Tantra underground.


# BODY, SEX, AND TRANSFORMATION

It is important but ironic that Tantra has become a main Hindu influence on the New Age movement in the West in spite of its marginalization in India. The late Bhagwan Shree Rajneesh, in the summer of 1981, packed up his large commune at Poona in India and reassembled it on an immense, isolated cattle ranch in central Oregon known as "the Big Muddy." It was his teaching, contained in his books such as *From Sex to Superconsciousness*, which made headlines because of what went on at his ashrams at Poona in the 1970s and then in Antelope, Oregon, in the United States.[35]

35. Mangalwadi, *When the New Age Gets Old*, 109-13.

Those who have watched, whether in person or on film, the meditations practiced by the followers of Rajneesh must have wondered how such insanity can lead to God. The answer is that if you were to understand that creation itself is the insanity of God, then you would cease to depend on the sanity of reason. For reason can only keep you in the bondage of maya and karma. As Capra puts it:

> To free the human mind from words and explanations is one of the main aims. As long as we try to explain things, we are bound by karma; trapped in our conceptual network. To transcend words and explanations meant to break the bonds of karma and attain liberation.[36]

Rajneesh taught that the human mind is our "chief villain," for it acts like a prism, dividing one ray into many. The mind is the source of bondage because it can only see an object by separating it from others, by labeling or categorizing it. Therefore, according to Rajneesh, the aim of our religious quest should be to "kill the mind," in other words to choose insanity.

A number of scholars have pointed out that the shocking uniqueness of Tantra is that while it admits, with the rest of Hinduism, that this world is maya (illusion), it does not scorn this world as a source of temptation, but embraces it as the raw material of enlightenment. For Tantra, the realm of maya is the only available context of liberation.

The belief that the material body is consciousness is given concrete description in Tantra, which asserts that the body is a network of channels for cosmic (divine) consciousness. Where these channels interact they create pulse points or psychic centers called "chakras." Though there are about 88,000 such chakras, seven of them are most important for Tantric practice. These seven are situated not in our physical body, but in the "subtle" body, along the central axis that runs from the tailbone to the skull.

The divine polarities of male and female lie at the opposite ends of these seven chakras. Traditionally it has been taught that the female, called Kundalini, or the serpent power, lies dormant at the base of the spine, separated from her divine lover Shiva, the masculine counterpart who dwells in the crown chakra in the head. Some New Age mystics consider this to be a patriarchal perversion of mysticism.[37]

According to actress Shirley MacLaine, the top three chakras are yin — feminine or spiritual energy. The lower three chakras are yang — masculine or physical energy. The central heart chakra is the most important one, because it is androgynous. The heart chakra, MacLaine claims,

36. Fritjof Capra, *The Tao of Physics* (London: Flamingo, 1990), 322.
37. Mangalwadi, *When the New Age Gets Old*, 113, 115.

is the seat or the home of the soul or Higher Self, and it is perfectly balanced in its yin and yang expressions. The Higher Self is connected and interfaced with God energy, which also is perfect in its balance of creating and manifesting the yin and the yang.

Therefore, the more we each resonate to the perfection of the Higher Self, the more we are reflecting perfect balance in ourselves, the more androgynous we are.[38]

Thus we see that the Tantric understanding of the anatomy of the "subtle" human body has undergone a fundamental change to facilitate the New Age understanding of femininity.

## MYSTIC ONENESS BEYOND SEXUAL UNION

Contrary to the New Age approach of MacLaine, traditional Hindu Tantra does not focus on the heart chakra or the Higher Self. The goal of the Tantric mystic (usually a celibate) was to awaken the dormant (female) Kundalini through secret practices borrowed generally from various yogic traditions such as Hatha yoga. As Kundalini rose to meet her lover in the crown chakra, it gave the Tantric intense psychic experiences as it passed through the different chakras. The enlightenment occurred not when an androgynous Higher Self was discovered in the heart chakra, but only when the god and the goddess were united in a psychic-sexual embrace. The veil of illusion then vanished and the unity of all polarities was perceived.

Sexual ritual in Tantra is called "maithuna." During maithuna a male disciple usually favors having a female Tantric who takes over the role of the guru. But it is not essential for a man to have a woman companion for Tantra, for the objective of maithuna is not to achieve physical release through ejaculation and orgasm. Rather, it is to seek psychic experiences by the "threefold immobility" of semen, breath, and consciousness. Tantric transcendence takes place when the mind is completely still but focused, breathing has ceased, and sexual arousal is arrested at the point of maximum tension. Thus maithuna first stimulates and then traps the energies of sexual arousal to be able to release them through the channel of a still mind. This "spiritual orgasm" does not seek to make a man and a woman "one flesh." On the contrary, its aim is to help fuse a Tantric's own inner polarities into one; that is, to give him the mystic experience of oneness.

38. Shirley MacLaine, *Going Within* (New York: Bantam, 1990), 187.

## CELIBACY

Most Hindu/Buddhist Tantrics practice celibacy. They do not seek an abiding, growing, fulfilling love-relationship with a member of the opposite sex because, as Rajneesh says, Tantra treats sex as "Simply a door. While making love to a woman, you are really making love to Existence itself. The woman is just a door; the man is just a door."

Once you have learned to reach samadhi, or superconsciousness, through sex, Rajneesh says, you do not need a woman (if you are a man), for you can have sex with the whole universe — with a tree, with the moon, with anything. Or you can simply shut yourself in a room and reach superconsciousness using the female Kundalini within you.[39]

Vishal Mangalwadi, well-known Hindu scholar of New Age teachings, gives reasons why elements of the philosophy and practice of Tantrism are attractive in the West. In particular, many sensitive young people coming out of a Christian and especially a Roman Catholic tradition experience an instant conversion to "Eastern" mysticism when they are confronted with the beauty and magic of Tantric art. As we have seen, a great part of Tantra, though by no means all of it, seeks the experience of self-realization through actual or symbolic sexual rites. These are often depicted not in underground pornographic literature, but in explicit erotic sculpture in the temples of religious worship and religious literature. This type of erotic sculpture was quite a shock to me when I was a student in India.

To portray a goddess naked and in the sexual act is the extreme opposite of Catholic art, where the highest portrayal of a woman is as the "Holy Virgin." By implication, holiness is equated with virginity, and the ascetic denial of sensual pleasure is exalted as a religious virtue.

The Protestant Reformation, however, revolted against this distortion of biblical teaching. It reaffirmed that the Bible taught that Adam and Eve were created as male and female to "cleave to each other" and be united as "one flesh" even before they fell into sin. Thus sex was part of their original blessing in paradise, given not simply for procreation, but also for their enjoyment, for bonding them into oneness, and for personal fulfillment.

The Bible did not exalt Mary because she was a virgin. Her greatness was seen in that she was willing to trust and obey God at great personal cost. She was engaged to be married to Joseph. For her to be willing to become pregnant meant that in order to give birth to the Savior of the world she was willing to forgo the pleasure and security of marriage. She was not living in a society where being an unmarried mother was acceptable. No one would believe that she had not been sexually immoral and that her conception was

39. Mangalwadi, *When the New Age Gets Old*, 116-17.

the result of the creative work of the Holy Spirit. Mary knew that she would be ridiculed, scorned, and punished. The punishment of immorality could extend to being stoned to death.

Mary's greatness lies in the fact that displaying astonishing faith and humility, she said, "I am the Lord's servant. May it be to me as you have said" (Luke 1:38).

This aspect of the Protestant revolt did not just result in a Catholic monk like Martin Luther choosing marriage rather than celibacy, it also made it possible for Rembrandt to paint his nude wife waiting for him in bed.

According to Mangalwadi, Tantra undoubtedly helps liberate those men and women in the West who, as a result of unbiblical Christian traditions, are unnecessarily bound by guilt and shame about their own sexuality.

As a native of India, Mangalwadi points out that the positive contribution of Tantra in a culture such as India's is even greater than what it can ever give to the West. Hindu-Buddhist thought has rarely affirmed the metaphysical goodness of the physical creation, including our bodies as male and female. On the contrary, it has generally seen physical life as intrinsically evil, bondage, and suffering. That is why Amaury de Riencourt is one of many who point out that Tantra saved Indian society from itself.

The life-denying vision of the Vedantists would have destroyed Indian society if the great bulk of the people had not instinctively counteracted it with the help of life-affirming creeds emphasizing the positive side of things. In Tantra we see finally the bankruptcy of the life-denying philosophers. The Indian people would have disappeared from the face of the earth if they had all adopted the Vedantic outlook. From the "Apollonian" attitude of the Vedanta, the Tantric devotee travels all the way to the "Dionysian" acceptance of life with all its joys and sufferings, with its refusal to make a cowardly escape from the coils of a now venerated matter. The sensuous and spiritual aspects of the world are now viewed as indivisible, and through full enjoyment of the world (through food, drink, and sex), the Tantric disciple (sadhana) can hope to overcome the world of dualism just as well as those [Vedantins] who frown upon them.

However, the Tantric view in the deepest sense does not celebrate life. "Even in its affirmations," writes Brooks Alexander, "Tantra is haunted by paradoxes. The naturalness of human life is affirmed, but only as a means for its ultimate dissolution. Human existence is validated, but only as a platform for leaving humanity behind."[40]

As Rajneesh says, in sex a Tantric does not make love to a woman. He uses her merely as a door, as a means for his own enlightenment. Shirley MacLaine admits that sex in Tantra is not meant to fulfill two people by

40. Ibid., 117, 123-26.

uniting them into one bond, but rather is used by each partner to discover his or her own completeness as an androgynous being so that each may become complete without his or her partner. When a Tantric uses a woman to reach maximum arousal for himself, and then withdraws without ejaculation, he may be seeking higher bliss for himself but he is certainly condemning his partner to frustration.

Tantra does unabashedly embrace human sexuality in its spirituality. But because it uses it for individual gain rather than for binding two people in love, it turns sex into frustration. It does not fulfill men and women as sexual beings, nor does it celebrate life. It seeks to deny or transcend the essence of what we are as male and female.

## The Biblical Approach to Sexuality

Biblical groups have traditionally had difficulty in dealing with the dynamics of sexuality and femininity. To use Chinese terms, the West, under the influence of the biblical tradition, has expressed yang, or the male force, most strongly. Our God is Jehovah, our Father in heaven. There has been a patriarchal emphasis.

The Far East, in contrast, has expressed yin, or the female emphasis. It has emphasized the mother principle. Many see the current interest in the Far East as an interest provoked by an attempt to restore a missing female emphasis to the West.

Christians respond to such discussions by emphasizing the basic Hebrew emphasis on the goodness of the body. Jesus, as God's Son, was incarnated in a body. Jesus displayed both masculine and feminine qualities. He taught that God was both holy and love. Holiness has traditionally been associated with the male and love with the female. Women were some of Jesus' earliest and most loyal followers. In a first-century world that seemed to either worship or despise the body, Jesus neutralized the body and sex. They are inherently neither good nor evil. The important thing is how they are used.

The church is described in the New Testament as the bride of Christ. The Holy Spirit is known as being tender and intimate in his appeal. In the midst of a patriarchal society, the apostle Paul, at a time when some of his earliest and most loyal folowers were women, wrote to the Galatians that in Christ "there is neither male nor female" (Gal. 3:28).

Despite its inherent affirmative attitude toward the body and sexuality, the evangelical Christian tradition can learn from Tantric Hinduism. For careful study of that tradition reveals resources for a balanced view of the human body and sexuality.

82

## Christianity and Hindu Groups

Certain of the Hindu-related New Age groups claim a complementary function in relation to Christianity. TM, for instance, presents its meditation technique as a means to deepen the realization of God within the churches, although its attitude toward Christianity is in fact quite negative. On the whole, these groups demonstrate a high awareness of religious pluralism and at the same time present themselves as a unique way of overcoming it by harmonizing and unifying denominational and religious divisions and diversities. Certain groups will concede that Jesus was also a master, but only during his lifetime, so that Christians would need to be initiated by a present master if they wanted to attain the highest level of god-realization. They deny the finality of Christ and make him appear a religious figure of the past, superseded by the new Guru-Avatar, or Living Master.[41]

The movements and figures we have discussed are only a few of the many Hindu New Age groups active in the United States and Western Europe and other places. Each group or person emphasizes a certain spiritual path. Despite its practical physical squalor, India continues to attract those seeking a New Age turn-on. It is a land of religious extremes. It combines color, festivity, and devotional fervor with asceticism and isolated meditation.

As we have seen, Hindu philosophy and religious presuppositions are quite different from that of the biblical tradition. For most of the Hindu groups, god in his essence is impersonal. Human beings, essentially divine, emanate from god; they are not created and essentially personal. Salvation is related to enlightenment and union with god. Sin is ignorance and lack of enlightenment — not rebellion. Immortality is natural or innate. History is cyclical. Matter is essentially illusory.

## Buddhists and Radical Transformation

Buddhism was founded during the life of Siddartha Gautama, the Buddha (563-483 B.C.E.). But Buddhism is taught differently, depending on the cultural context. This has meant a great deal of regional variation among Buddhists around the world, under three major movements.

Theravada, or Southern Buddhism, the Path of the Elders, has preserved the teachings of the Buddha in the original Pali texts. It is all but gone from India, where it began, but is now to be found in Sri Lanka and Southeast Asia. Mahayana, or Northern Buddhism, the Greater Vehicle, spread to East Asia, especially to China, Korea, and Japan. Its scriptures, such as the Lotus

41. Brockway and Rajashekar, *New Religious Movements*, 26.

Sutra, the Perfection of Wisdom Sutra, and the Pure Land Sutras, were recorded in Sanskrit. It includes the Zen and Nichiren schools. The third major movement is Vajrayana, the Diamond Vehicle, also known as Tantric Buddhism. Tibetan and Mongolian Buddhism are Vajrayana Buddhism.[42]

## THE FOUR NOBLE TRUTHS

In spite of the differences, there is a central core of teaching on which all are agreed. Based on central teachings, Buddhism continues to provide techniques for radical transformation for the New Age movement. In Hindu thought, we saw that the world or self is identical with god, or Brahman. Buddha went one step further. If the self is simply the same as the one universal, impersonal Brahman, it is also "no self" (anatman) in any individualistic sense. Man is not a personal being but a bundle of sensations, thoughts, and feelings in a state of flux.

The idea of "no self" is a fundamental clue to the meaning of the four noble truths which Buddha taught:

First, according to Buddha, all life is to be seen as suffering. This truth tells us that life is frustrating and unsatisfactory and getting worse and worse.

Second, we are to understand that life is suffering because we try to cling to things such as objects, ideas, and persons which are partial and not permanent. We are constantly anxious over the prospect of losing these objects. We have selfish cravings or desires.

The false idea behind our suffering and grasping is that we are separate, individual selves. Instead of selves or souls stuck in bodies, we are simply five entities (skandhas) temporarily brought together. We are just mental compilations of five transient conditions: the physical body, ideas or understanding, will, feelings, and pure consciousness.

We will come apart because the law of karma, a universal force or law of action and reaction, keeps everything moving and changing. When you die, there is nothing like a soul taken from your body and put in another body. The karmic waves, however, which you have made in this life by your actions and thoughts, continue to operate until they put together another set of five elements. If you have left good waves, the new set of elements will be a positive reincarnation. For bad waves, there will be something deplorable reassembled.

Buddha's third truth is that the cessation of suffering and negative reincarnations can be reached by forsaking desire.

The fourth truth of Buddha is constituted by his eightfold path. The path involves eight basic steps to stifle desire. This path will help you to end all desire and achieve Nirvana, which means freedom or emancipation. Nir-

---

42. Timothy Miller, *America's Alternative Religions*, 161-62.

vana is achieved by meditating and acting in harmony with the onrushing waves of the spirit of Buddha. Proper acts which lead to Nirvana include unlimited friendliness, compassion, joy, and even-mindedness. Nirvana means the blowing out of all the fires of desire and the illusions of self which constrict us. One can thus break out into a Nirvanic ocean and ride the tides of the infinite. One can see all and know all. One Buddhist leader states that people are relieved when they learn that they are nothing, that they do not exist.

## Northern Buddhism and the Buddha Spirits

Northern, or Mahayana, Buddhism developed in Tibet, China, Korea, and Japan. It is more flexible. The historical Gautama Buddha, although respected, is relatively deemphasized in this type of Buddhism, which teaches that all reality is full of Buddhas. There are many ways of turning on or finding enlightenment.

For Northern Buddhism, there are thousands of Buddhas called bodhisattvas, or "enlightenment beings." These beings are on their way to final enlightenment. But they delay to help others until all are enlightened. They are skilled and compassionate. A bodhisattva can come down as an apparition in the form of a monk, abbot, orphan, beggar, prostitute, or rich man to help the unenlightened. He cannot change karma or the law of judgment at a single stroke. But the enlightened being can help you, by his wise teaching and helpful experiences, to make new resolutions and eliminate desire.

### MIND-ONLY BUDDHISM

An even more subtle development in Buddhism was the rise of mind-only, or consciousness-only, Buddhism. According to this view, there is fundamentally only one field of consciousness, which is the Buddha-nature, or Nirvana. The mind-only approach developed various positive means of realizing Nirvana and transforming consciousness. One method, developed by Zen, utilizes still meditation. Another method was developed in Tibet as Tantric Buddhism. It uses sacred and powerful words, gestures, and hard meditation. One of its guidebooks is the *Tibetan Book of the Dead.*

All of these forms of transformation are utilized or adopted in one form or another by the New Age movement. Zen fosters the satori experience. Satori is the mystic state in which you appreciate your own original inseparability with the universe. In American Zen sessions, after periods of meditation, group chanting is emphasized. The Heart Sutra is often used: "Form is emptiness, and emptiness is form. . . . The wisdom that has gone beyond, and beyond the beyond; O what an awakening, all hail!"

Religion scholar Huston Smith, recently retired from the University of California at Berkeley, credited Buddhism's growing popularity to its "practical emphasis on liberation in a rational, psychological sense over transcendence requiring belief in a mystical, redeeming God, which is foreign to Buddhist thought."

Buddhist-style meditation has also been taken up by Christian contemplatives — the late Roman Catholic Trappist monk Thomas Merton being the most famous — who often combine it with their own tradition's meditative practices. The inroads made by Buddhist meditation among Catholics has been visible enough for the Vatican to warn against it on more than one occasion.

I shall never forget a series on Zen led by Alan Watts in which I participated. The sessions took place in the dramatic setting of a houseboat moored in the shadow of the Golden Gate Bridge in the San Francisco area.

Zen is also used by those who practice the "inner game," treating sports such as golf as a spiritual discipline while becoming more effective in the sport. Phil Jackson, coach of the NBA's Bulls, has taken Zen meditation into the locker room, where his athletes employ it to filter out distractions and focus their minds on the game.

It is obvious that most Zen teachings are quite different from the emphasis of evangelical Christianity. Zen is a self-help religion. For Zen there is no god in the Christian sense. There is no sin, because human beings are part of the ultimate. There is no need for a divine savior. People need only a way-shower. Salvation comes from self-understanding. Buddhist compassion is that of an enlightened person feeling sorry for the ignorant. For Christianity, the human's problem is related to rebellion against God and egocentricity and pride. Salvation for the Christian must come from someone not caught up in humanity's vicious circle.

According to Harvey Cox, the features of Asian spirituality that most attract young people today, not only in the West but in Asia itself, are not their theologies but their practical disciplines such as meditation, yoga, and the various styles of martial art. One of the most fascinating qualities about the so-called new religions of Japan, which are mostly updated expressions of Buddhism, is their emphasis on personal practice and their no-nonsense, pragmatic attitude. For every fervid preacher of fundamentalist versions of these different world faiths, there are others who are trying to help people uncover — within their own lives — the original vision that brought the tradition to birth. In this connection it is important to recall that Buddha himself was born into an age of religious contention and rival schools of metaphysics. His advice was to accept nothing on the authority of someone else, not even himself, but to test every claim in one's own experience.[43]

43. Harvey Cox, *Fire from Heaven* (Boston: Addison-Wesley, 1995), 309.

## Tantric Buddhism (Naropa Institute)

In our discussion of Tantric Hinduism, enough material was given to provide an understanding of the attraction and emphases of the Tantric tradition. Buddhist as well as Hindu religious leaders have brought the Tantric emphases, originally nurtured in the Himalayas, to America. It is not surprising then to note that mountains are at the center of the Tantric sacred geography. The tradition of esoteric Buddhism was taken to Japan in the ninth century A.D. From Japan and from Tibet it was exported to the United States.

There are a number of American versions of Tantric and Tibetan Buddhism. Elaborate rituals and sexuality are used as a means to enlightenment. Deities are visualized. Such a Buddhism has some parallels with neo-paganism and ceremonial magic.

The largest American school of Tibetan Buddhism is Naropa Institute in Boulder, Colorado. Naropa is not only a center for Buddhist studies but also an accredited university offering undergraduate and graduate degrees. The major intellectual center of Buddhism in the United States, Naropa has invited teachers of several religious traditions to be part of its programs and has attracted writers, poets, psychologists, and artists as teachers and students.

Naropa was founded in 1974 by Chogyam Trungpa Tulku, who attended Oxford University and was trained as a lama. He became the supreme abbot of one of Tibet's strongest Buddhist sects and was called the incarnate lama. After Chinese Communists took over the country, he was forced to flee and sought refuge in India.

Chogyam's Tantric teachings are described as both an intellectual and a practical psychology based on meditation. At one time he had thousands of students. When he died in 1987, he left his movement in the hands of Regent Osel Tendzin. In late 1988 it was revealed that the regent was infected with the AIDS virus, and had been for nearly three years. Although he was sexually active within the community, he had "neither protected his sexual partners nor told them the truth." One young man was infected by the regent, and he in turn infected his girlfriend. The revelation of this tragedy caused a serious rift in the movement. Some members left; others stayed to reevaluate and seek revision of the group. The organization survived this experience. Osel Tendzin died in 1991 while on retreat. Leadership passed to Osel Mukpo, the eldest son of Chogyam, who is a teacher and scholar in his own right.[44]

44. Timothy Miller, *America's Alternative Religions*, 169.

## Mystical Islam and Radical Transformation (Sufism)

In addition to orthodox or dominant Islam there is a mystical, or New Consciousness, Islamic emphasis. In the West this tradition is known as Sufism. Its followers are called Sufis. There are two emphases within Sufism. One groups says that they are only seeking to cultivate immediate communion with Allah. The other moves closer to pantheistic forms of mystical absorption. The goal of Sufism has always been deepened devotion, spiritual transformation, and, ultimately, the interiorization of the basic tenet of Islamic belief, that "there is no God but God" or, in the classic Sufi interpretation, "Only God is the Real; Only God exists."[45]

Sufi scholars see at least three reasons for the rise of the mystical emphasis in Islam. The first factor is the Sufi understanding of the inner life of Muhammad himself. They see Muhammad as a man who knew God intimately, even to moments of trance and rapture in fellowship with God.

A second factor in the emergence of the Sufis was a reaction to the moral laxities, luxuries, and corruption of the Umayyad Caliphate in the Islamic metropolis at Damascus. In fact, the term "Sufism" comes from the Arabic "suf," meaning "wool," and refers to the plain wool gowns worn by the early Sufis ("wool-clad"). Rejecting the luxurious excesses of the Caliphs, the Sufis lived simple, communal, ascetic lives, much like the early Christian monks.

A third factor in the rise of Sufism was discontent with the abstraction, dryness, and legalism of Islamic law and dogma as it developed in the tenth and eleventh centuries A.D.

In 922, Al Hallaj, a Sufi, was tortured and executed in Baghdad for saying, "I am the Real" or "the creative Truth." These statements were regarded as blasphemy since truth and reality are attributes of God alone.

Sufi masters, organized into great Sufi orders, developed special ecstatic techniques for knowing God. One such technique was repetition of the ninety-nine beautiful names of God, aided by prayer beads. Such repetitions helped concentrate the mind and produce an emotional state of swaying and chanting. Another well-known technique was the dervish. Dervish involves the use of rhythmic recitation and rhythmic movements of the body to induce concentration on God and divorcement from the physical world. The dervishes' frenzied dancing is but one example of the music, poetry, and dance accompanying Sufi worship. Spiritual healing is one love duty practiced by the Sufis, but not before they have studied for at least twelve years.

In the West, Sufism has significance beyond its sectarian Islamic origins. Modern Sufi leaders state that Sufi techniques portray the universal

45. Ibid., 249.

process by which humans can attain truth, beauty, and God. The Sufis are thus trying to make their distinctive experience independent and of unconditioned universal validity. This universalistic trend has resulted in the Sufis becoming an important part of the New Age movement in the West.

Many of today's Muslims continue to practice Sufism, but their brotherhoods are usually secret societies keeping mainly to themselves. Sufism attracts a wide following in India, and has large groups of devotees in England and the United States.[46]

The survival and growth of Sufism reveals the inherent weakness within the orthodox Islamic worldview to meet an inner need. The Shariah, or law, does not legislate for the conscience, but confines itself to gathering the faithful around the rites and observances of the Islamic community without troubling the inner life. Sufism addresses that missing dimension.[47]

This emphasis is highlighted in a recent book edited by Seyyed Hossein Nasr, perhaps the most preeminent Muslim scholar in the world today. In *Islamic Spirituality: Manifestations*, the editor defines spirituality as that place in each person which "is open to the transcendent dimension" and where the person "experiences ultimate reality." The book is almost entirely devoted to Sufism, the most experientially intense current in Islam. Sufism has always emphasized the immediate personal union of the soul with God. Sufism has produced some of Islam's finest lyric poets, including Omar Khayyam and Jalal ed-Din Rumi. At a time when the popular press often gives the impression that Islam is little but a nest of terrorists and fanatics, it is important to realize that there are powerful and deeply rooted countertendencies.[48]

From a theological perspective, the Sufis are always in danger of sinking into monism. Monism teaches the identity of the divine and the human. The lack of rational concern easily led into bizarre aberrations and excesses among early Sufis. In contemporary New Age circles, the interest is in more than a knowledge of the history of Sufism. The primary concern is with the secrets of the Sufi masters. How did they alter consciousness? What were their techniques of consciousness raising? How did they attain super-consciousness?

Some of the techniques and insights of Sufism have been brought to the West by one of the most mysterious persons in the area of New Age studies — George Gurdjieff (1872-1949). Born in Russia, near the Persian border, he traveled throughout the Middle and Far East. Many of the techniques which he later taught he learned from the Sufis and Tantric Buddhists.

46. Guiley, *Harper's Encyclopedia*, 581-83.
47. Burnett, *Clash of Worlds*, 113.
48. Cox, *Fire from Heaven*, 308-9.

## GURDJIEFF AND SUFISM

The heart of the teaching of Gurdjieff is related to his techniques of awakening a person's dormant consciousness or potentiality. Gurdjieff called his approach the "Fourth Way." This fourth or highest level can be induced by the experiences of music, dance, and physical labor.

The influence of Gurdjieff continues in the United States. As of late 1994, several of Gurdjieff's own pupils remained actively involved in the work that he began, although responsibility for day-to-day activities has largely devolved into the hands of second-generation followers. In addition to the Gurdjieff foundations in New York, Los Angeles, San Francisco, and other metropolitan areas, a number of smaller Gurdjieff study centers have been located in rural areas. Gurdjieff is now recognized as one of the West's pioneer gurus.[49]

From a Christian perspective, the Gurdjieff movement lacks vertical dimensions. In Calvinist terms, only through God-knowledge can a person gain authentic self-knowledge.

## Western Path to Radical Transformation

We have discussed the transformation emphasis of updated Far Eastern and Middle Eastern traditions as well as the neopagan, ceremonial magic, and witchcraft groups. All of these groups have attempted to recover consciousness paths which they believe are buried in the Western tradition but are half-forgotten.

The third emphasis is found among those groups that are modern Western attempts to work out a path of transformation. Some of them owe debts to the East or to the remote past. In the main, however, they have behind them a Western and modern individual who has walked on the streets of Western cities. The third category is a vast field. One popular book on New Age movements states that there are more than eight thousand ways to "awaken in North America."

We will look at two representative and somewhat dramatic examples of Western secular New Age groups: Scientology and est.

## SCIENTOLOGY

Scientology is a rather unique case. It defies easy definition. Poised on the boundaries of religion, psychology, science, and even magic, it does not fit readily into any of these categories. In the beginning it claimed to be a

49. Timothy Miller, *America's Alternative Religions*, 261.

scientific or psychoanalytic group. For various reasons it now calls itself a religion. Critics see it as a pseudoscience movement rooted in the world of the occult and science fiction.

Lafayette Ronald Hubbard (1911-86) (affectionately known as Elron by his followers) is the founder and central figure of Scientology.

Hubbard's ideas first gained prominence with the publication of his famous book *Dianetics* in 1950. In this book, Hubbard declares that the mind controls the brain. The mind itself has two parts, the analytic and the reactive. The analytic part is similar to Freud's conscious mind. The reactive part is similar to the unconscious. The analytic mind, unless upset, works with precision. Experiences of shock cause engrams (sensory impressions of the event) to be recorded in the reactive or unconscious mind. These records cause mental and mind-body troubles until they are dislodged. Engrams have been compared to psychiatrist Sigmund Freud's repressed desires and psychiatrist Carl G. Jung's complexes.[50]

The patient (called a preclear) can come to a Hubbard-trained therapist, called an auditor. The auditor uses special techniques (commands and questions) to help the patient in looking for forgotten shock incidents. When the patient has confronted and relived the engram (shock memory), the engram is pushed out of the reactive mind. Auditing requires the agency of both human auditor and a machine, the Hubbard Electrometer, or E-Meter. While the auditor functions as a therapist and has been described in recent years as a pastoral counselor, the E-Meter lends the scientific precision of a machine to the proceedings. Similar to a lie detector, the E-Meter's needle registers emotional reaction to particular words called out by the auditor and thus provides clues to underlying sources of engrams lodged in the reactive mind.[51]

Dianetics was primarily secular in its emphases. Hubbard's continuing research led him to teach the existence of the soul, or the Thetan. In *Scientology: The Fundamentals of Thought*, Hubbard states that his greatest contribution to humankind was the isolation, description, and handling of the Thetan. Your Thetan is the real you over against the body, mind, physical universe, or anything else. It is nonphysical and immortal. It has always lived. At your core, you are a fallen immortal god, or Thetan. When the Thetan enters your body it brings with it all the engrams of millions of years of previous existence. Thetans are reincarnated over trillions of years. This means that you must clear out, or erase, the engrams of the past. In earlier days, the goal of Hubbard's movement was to get followers clear of the

---

50. Robert S. Ellwood, Jr., *Religious and Spiritual Groups in Modern America* (Englewood Cliffs, N.J.: Prentice-Hall, 1973), 170; see also Guiley, *Harper's Encyclopedia*, 107.
51. Timothy Miller, *America's Alternative Religions*, 386.

engrams of this life. The new goal is to seek to whisk away the engrams of a million previous lifetimes. If you achieve this new goal, you will be an Operating Thetan. Such a status means you are free of the shackles of this universe and have almost miraculous powers.[52]

According to Scientology, if all people were "clear," the world would be free of drugs, war, pollution, crime, mental illness, and other ills.

## WIDESPREAD ATTRACTION

What type of people does Scientology attract? It seems to be attracting all kinds, from counterculture types, drawn by its radical departure from tradition, to engineers and computer programmers, entertainment personalities, and even Protestant clergy. *Parents* magazine states that many followers are high school graduates; "intrigued with the trappings of science, they are vulnerable to pseudo-science." Still others who come into Scientology are lonely, weak, confused, and emotionally ill.

Scientology has recently given considerable attention to artists, musicians, and theatrical people. Tom Cruise and John Travolta are prominent members. Celebrity centers have been established in key cities. Creativity is said to be part of the total freedom which Scientology releases.

Scientology has also gone to work in prisons. Appealing to the "basic goodness within all people," Scientology's criminon runs events in more than three hundred prisons in thirty-nine states in the United States.

In 1953, Hubbard incorporated the Church of Scientology; and in 1955 he established the Founding Church of Scientology as an unincorporated, independent church. Scientology has since spread throughout the world.

In 1958 the Internal Revenue Service revoked the church's tax-exempt status. Over thirty years later, the church remains in litigation to reinstate it.[53]

From its earliest history, Scientology's claims that it is a religion have been disputed. The movement seldom makes use of traditional theological language or categories except in a very broad sense, if the litigation involving the very question of its religious identity is any indication. Scientology has been involved in endless court cases over its tax-exempt status — sometimes as defendant and sometimes as plaintiff — for most of its history with highly publicized cases in the United States, Australia, Italy, and Canada, and other countries as well.[54]

---

52. Christopher Evans, *Cults of Unreason* (New York: Dell, 1973), 41.
53. Guiley, *Harper's Encyclopedia*, 106-7; cf. also Paul Heelas, *The New Age Movement* (Cambridge, Mass.: Blackwell, 1996), 100.
54. Timothy Miller, *America's Alternative Religions*, 389.

In Germany since 1977, Scientology has been labeled as an exploitative sect which harbors conspiratorial designs, brainwashes followers, and brings them to emotional and financial ruin.

After a trial related to stealing government documents, Scientology began softening its image with an emphasis on its message and Hubbard's prolific writings. While the primary focus of Scientology is on helping individuals become "clear," worship services are held at all churches and missions, and a number of religious holidays are observed. The International headquarters are in Los Angeles.[55]

## EVALUATION OF SCIENTOLOGY

As a religion, Scientology is obviously different from the classical Christian view. It draws from many religions, but perhaps the strongest influence is from Hinayana, or Southern, Buddhism. As in classical Eastern thought, the essential human is seen as innately divine and basically good. Through Scientology techniques inherent divinity can be recovered. The good news of God in Christ coming to humanity's rescue is irrelevant and unnecessary from the Scientology perspective. Humanity is naturally immortal and will live on in countless reincarnations. There is no ultimate standard for right or wrong beyond the cause of upholding and advancing Scientology. Evil is primarily related to anyone misusing or degrading Scientology.

## LESSONS OF "EST," WITH A SMALL "E"

I was told that a man named Werner Erhard had developed the ultimate in New Age insights in "est" (spelled with a small "e"). The master himself was to be in Houston, and I was invited to his guest seminar. Erhard's assistants came out to tell us what est could do for us. Est would expand our experience of aliveness. Aliveness for est is love, health, happiness, and full self-expression. Est will teach you that you are all right just as you are. If you are not all right, then you will learn that it is all right to be not all right.

Erhard was born John Paul Rosenberg in Philadelphia on September 5, 1935, to a Jewish family. In 1959, at age twenty-four, he left his wife and children and went to St. Louis with another woman, Ellen. To avoid being traced by his family, he adopted a pseudonym formed from the names of physicist Werner Heisenberg and West German finance minister (and later chancellor) Ludwig Erhard.

Erhard eventually moved to California, where he worked in various jobs, training and developing executives. He studied Zen, yoga, Scientology,

55. Guiley, *Harper's Encyclopedia*, 108.

Gestalt, Dale Carnegie, Mind Dynamics, and hypnosis. One day while driving on a freeway, he had a transformational experience and soon thereafter quit his job to start est. By 1975 est had a paid staff of 230 plus over six thousand employees.[56]

Erhard himself is by temperament a would-be philosopher and a conceptualist. One university professor calls the est seminar "a crash course in epistemology (the doctrine of knowledge)." Others say est resembles the ideas found in the world-famous Ludwig Wittgenstein's *Philosophical Investigations.* The est program is grounded in philosophical assumptions about reality and the relationship of human beings to the world. It will be helpful to outline some of Erhard's key teachings and ideas.

1. A basic teaching of est is that the world has no meaning or purpose. This idea is similar to that which we have seen in Zen Buddhism. "What is, is" and "What isn't, isn't" are Werner's summaries.

Erhard states that there are only two things in the world, semantics (words) and nothing. Nothing represents the ultimate truth. Semantics is the form of everything and so represents all that appears to exist.

2. A second teaching of est suggests that the mind imposes artificial meanings and purposes on the world. The mind then deceives us into reacting as if reality conforms to these self-imposed "belief systems." We operate on the idea that what we believe is actually so. But this idea is not experiential — it only symbolizes our experience. The mind works with symbols, not direct experience.

Benjamin Whorf, the famous semanticist, states that you have been tricked by your language into a certain way of perceiving reality. We often discard what we perceive that does not fit our language structure. Whorf further suggests that an awareness of the mind's trickery can give you insight. Erhard's teachings are quite similar to the concepts of Whorf on this point.

The est program seeks to teach that every system of meaning imposed by outside sources, such as parents, school, and church, is illusory.

The major part of the exercises (called processes) in the est training seminar seek to dislodge trainees from their belief systems. In an attempt to destroy belief systems, the famous (or infamous) attack or bully approach is used.

When the noise of life has been stopped long enough, you can experience truth, according to est teaching. The truth is: You are. The training allows you to know it with your total being — experientially. This is natural knowing. It is beyond believing, thinking, feeling, sensing, or doing. An enlightened person is one who has learned how to experience the world directly in all its random "suchness." Only what is experienced personally and directly can be true and satisfying.

56. Ibid., 189.

3. The next step in the teaching program is the emphasis on the fact that as an individual you are the cause of your own world.

Although the true reality is our own experience, we still must function in ordinary reality. This involves accepting life exactly as we experience it to be and then acknowledging that we are responsible for the way we experience it. Life works when you choose what you've got.

Once we choose our experience (what we've got), then it becomes impossible to blame others for our experience. It is resistance to what *is* that causes anguish.

If we blame others for a situation, we attribute *cause* to that other person or situation. We then become the *effect* of that person or situation. We have lost control of our own life. But we are responsible for "sourcing" our own life. As a source, each one of us is god in his own universe.

For years, much of our liberal society has told people that whatever is, is not their fault. Their parents were bad or indifferent or overloving. The President (whoever he is) is a bum. Now est says that people created their own experiences and are responsible for themselves. No wonder est hits like a bombshell for many people.

4. The final dramatic step in est is to show the trainee how she can become the author of her own subjective universe of emotions, sensations, and ideas. This is called "getting it." When you get it you understand that others can no longer control you. If everything is illusion, then you are free to choose your illusion. You, therefore, control your world. You are free to transform experience through the prism of your own consciousness. Freedom lies in choosing your illusion. You are god in your own universe.

In order to have this experience or to "get it," est trainees are shown how to create an inner space. Inner space is that space into which a person can retreat and immerse himself in his own consciousness. Once you are in your space, you are taught to construct a little mental room in which you are safe to practice your perfection.[57]

Careful students will recognize Erhard's heavy dependence on Zen Buddhism and its teaching of no soul and the idea that this world is maya, or illusion. Werner comments frequently that Zen is the essential element in est.

Observable is the influence of Mind Dynamics. Mind Dynamics is largely an adaptation of ideas from Scientology and Silva Mind Control.

Werner was so impressed with Psychosynthesis that he went to Italy to visit its founder, Roberto Assagioli. This system uses techniques of imagery to release the person from the boundaries of words.

57. Adam Smith, *Powers of Mind* (New York: Ballantine, 1975), 269, 272, 282, 278, 287; Adelaide Bry, *est* (New York: Avon Books, 1976), 164, 184, 187, 189, 197; Robert A. Hargrove, *est: Making Life Work* (New York: Dell, 1976), 45, 156-57, 184.

Among Western psychologists, Werner has been most influenced by the self-actualization theory of Abraham Maslow and the gestalt therapy of Fritz Perls.

Despite the difficulty in developing acceptable trainers, Erhard talks about having forty million graduates in the United States alone. The name of the est movement was changed to the Forum in the 1980s. The name "Transformational Technologies" is also used.

In her sympathetic book on est, Adelaide Bry cites statements of a number of est graduates who have found est helpful in their religious or theological understanding. A Roman Catholic priest affirms that est gave him the *experience* of what theology had *taught* him. Erhard contends that belief in God is the greatest single barrier to the *experience* of God.[58]

As we have seen, est teaches that experience has no form to it; it is pure substance without form. The est training is planned to search out and destroy all self-concepts in order to relocate the notion of self in the experience beyond conceptual description. This is getting it. What one gets is that there is nothing to get. All perceptions of reality are illusion. There is no objective reality. If everything is illusion, you are free to choose your illusion. You control your world.

For an evangelical Christian, the est viewpoint is not only opposed to the Christian faith and practice, but dangerous. The Christian faith teaches a valued universe. The universe was created by a personal God, who initially proclaimed the universe to be good. Even after the rebellion of humanity, God provided a redemptive plan by which humans could find restoration, forgiveness, and harmony with God and others. The est follower is taught to devalue the universe in contrast to the Christian guidelines. An est trainee must see himself as perfect just as he is. Guilt is an illusion. The need for the cross, resurrection, and second coming of Christ is thus eliminated.[59]

By God's grace, as revealed in Christ, we are accepted and seen as perfect in God's eyes. In our lives we seek with God's help to actualize in our daily walk the righteousness imputed to us by Jesus Christ.

In the est teaching, the usual New Age view of God is evident. Erhard states that there is nothing *but* spirituality. In fact, spirituality is just another name for god, for god is everywhere.

This view is close to the ancient heresy of Pantheism, which identifies god and the world. The Christian theistic view affirms that God created the universe and is immanent in it. But God is more than the universe. He is also transcendent in his power and perfection.

58. Bry, *est*, 209.
59. John P. Newport, *Christ and the New Consciousness* (Nashville: Broadman, 1978), 116.

# DRUGS AND TRANSFORMATION

Natural drugs have been used to induce states of mystical consciousness for centuries. Greek mystery cults as well as religious groups in Siberia and South America have used materials produced from hemp, datura, henbane, and mushroom. Indians in Mexico and the United States have used peyote for the same purpose, and this use in carefully supervised religious services has even been legalized. More recently, synthetic derivatives such as LSD and mescaline have been used for mystical and religious purposes.

John M. Allegro, in his book *Sacred Mushrooms and the Cross*, argues that the stories of the Old Testament and the New Testament reflect a drug and fertility cult that utilized a hallucinogenic mushroom. He even goes so far as to say that the New Testament books were coded initiations into the secrets of the cult. There is little evidence for Allegro's thesis.

## Subjective Science and Drugs

In the 1960s, at Harvard, Timothy Leary and Richard Alpert argued for the place of psychedelics in consciousness raising. Since both Leary and Alpert were at Harvard as scientists, their arguments related to their drug-induced experiences created a discussion in the area of science. Objectivity has commonly been considered essential to the scientific method. We have noted that the monistic worldview held by some recent scientists offers intellectual validation to a subjective approach to life, while devaluing objectivity. Mystical experiences also tend to both produce and progressively intensify a subjective orientation. When this psychospiritual transformation takes place in a scientist, it can profoundly affect his work.

The scientists have accepted pantheism, where nature and God are considered one. Such a view not only makes nature divine, it makes God "natural." The category of the supernatural is ruled out, along with the miraculous. Once this view is adopted, the traditional distinction between science and religion quite easily becomes blurred. Everything, even God, can be explained in terms of laws or principles, and can be approached "scientifically." This is why in Eastern and occult literature it is common to read about the "science of yoga" (or god realization), the "science of soul travel," the "science of karma and reincarnation," and so forth. Even the miracles of Jesus are viewed in a so-called scientific light. He is said to have understood and manipulated nature's more subtle laws.[60]

Typical of mystical teachers, Bhagwan Shree Rajneesh told his followers:

60. Elliot Miller, *Crash Course*, 39.

97

The old religions are based on belief systems. My religion is absolutely scientific. Of course, it is a different science than the science that is being taught in the universities. That is objective science. This is subjective science.[61]

Since New Agers believe that the physical world is really made of consciousness, and that the mind of the individual scientist is part of this universal consciousness, the distinction between subject and object, between "subjective science" and objective science, becomes difficult to define or maintain. Consciousness becomes the final explanation of *all* phenomena, psychic and physical. In such a context the marriage of science and mystical religion would seem inescapable.

Such talk is reminiscent of the controversy that flourished in psychology a quarter century ago. This concerned Harvard professors Timothy Leary and Richard Alpert. (Leary later became the infamous "guru" of the hippie movement. Alpert is now a popular New Age speaker and author also known as Baba Ram Dass.) In 1960, Leary went to Mexico, where he had his first psychedelic experience after ingesting magic mushrooms. He said it took him on a trip through evolution. He proposed systematic drug experiments with psilocybin at Harvard, using graduate students and other volunteers.

From its beginning the drug program was both controversial (among the faculty) and popular (among the students). Participants included the beat intelligentsia, such as Jack Kerouac, Arthur Koestler, Allen Ginsberg, Aldous Huxley, and Neal Cassady, as well as Harvard divinity students. Leary came to see drugs as instant enlightenment for the masses.

In 1962 Leary took LSD for the first time and described it as "the most shattering experience of my life," one which permanently changed him. He and Alpert then introduced LSD into their drug research program. Leary envisioned that society would be transformed and rid of evils if everyone turned on.

The drug research was controversial, and in 1963 Alpert and Leary were fired from Harvard — the first professors to be dismissed from the university in the twentieth century.[62]

Leary and Alpert were not only conducting but *participating* in experiments with chemically induced mystical experiences. Leary insisted that "the subject-object method of research is inadequate for studies of human consciousness." His point was that mystical experiences are so indescribable that they have to be *experienced* to be understood. Thus, competent research on the subject could not be conducted from a nonparticipatory standpoint.

61. "Bhagwan Shree Rajneesh Speaks Again," *The Rajneesh Times,* November 2, 1984, 4-5.

62. Guiley, *Harper's Encyclopedia,* 323, 497.

To Leary and Alpert's colleagues, however, the once-respected researchers' participation in the experiments was transforming them from scientists into mystics (an allegation which the years that followed certainly substantiated). Reporter Dan Wakefield observed at the time:

> The question of who are "qualified researchers" has become increasingly controversial, and charges have been leveled at Leary and Alpert that their own use of the drugs has destroyed their objectivity as scientists. Dr. David C. McClelland, chairman of the Center for Research in Personality and the man who brought Leary and Alpert to Harvard, has said that the more they took the drug "the less they were interested in science." The *Archives of General Psychiatry* editorial warning against the dangers of the drugs noted that some researchers "who became enamored with their mystical hallucinatory state, eventually in their 'mystique' became disqualified as competent investigators."[63]

By 1967 Alpert had become aware of the limitations of psychedelics as a spiritual practice, and traveled to India on a search for Eastern methods of enlightenment. In 1973 Leary was incarcerated for thirty-two months on drug charges. After his release, he lectured widely on the college and New Age conference circuits. He died recently.

## Aldous Huxley, Mysticism, and Drugs

Aldous Huxley was a prominent British author and philosopher. His experimentation with mescaline and LSD had an impact on the psychedelic drug movement of the 1960s. In 1953 he had his first psychedelic experience when he volunteered to take mescaline, the active agent in peyote, in an experiment for a psychologist.

As a result of the experience, Huxley wrote *The Doors of Perception* (1954). He lamented the absence of sacramental drugs in Christianity. He said the mescaline experience "is what Catholic theologians call 'a gratuitous grace,' not necessary to salvation but potentially helpful and to be accepted thankfully, if made available." The essay had a profound impact on the emerging psychedelic drug culture, and served as inspiration for the rock group, the Doors, which took its name from the title.[64]

In *The Perennial Philosophy*, Huxley attempted to show by way of

---

63. Dan Wakefield, "The Hallucinogens: A Reporter's Objective View," in *LSD: The Conscious-Expanding Drug*, ed. David Solomon (New York: Berkeley Medallion, 1966), 60-61.

64. Guiley, *Harper's Encyclopedia*, 272-73.

excerpted quotations that many mystics say identical things. But in his *Doors of Perception* he makes perhaps his strongest theoretical case for the essential sameness of mystical forms. Huxley stipulates a mental function that he calls the "Mind-at-Large." This Mind-at-Large is the human capacity for transcending usual cerebral processes and thereby even the self. An accepted form of self-transcendence is religion, which, however, may not work for everyone. He states, "Ideally, everyone should be able to find self-transcendence in some form of pure or applied religion. In practice it seems unlikely that this hoped for consummation will ever be realized."

But if religious self-transcendence is not attained, it becomes just as legitimate in Huxley's view to use drugs to achieve the same goal. "The urge to transcend self-conscious selfhood is, as I have said, a principal appetite of the soul. When, for whatever reason, men and women fail to transcend themselves by means of worship, good works and spiritual exercises, they are apt to resort to religion's chemical surrogates." In fact, Huxley goes so far as to wish to mandate that thinking people be subjected to a chemical experience of transcendence. As long as some form of transcendence is achieved, the means of bringing it about are irrelevant. Huxley can maintain such a stance only if he believes that all forms of self-transcendence (i.e., mysticism) are inherently the same.[65]

## Castaneda and Drugs

As we noted earlier, as an anthropologist Castaneda decided to study the perspective on reality of a Mexican sorcerer, Don Juan. To do this, he spent years learning the techniques of entering into this different occult mode of seeing life and reality. In order to get into another person's outlook on reality, Castaneda explained, one's own view must be temporarily or permanently broken up. This is a most difficult undertaking. Few Westerners, for various reasons, will attempt such a venture. A guide is needed, and in the case of Castaneda, Don Juan was willing and available.

All of us are acquainted with the visible world. We perceive it through ordinary consciousness or straight thinking. Space is understood as stretched out in three dimensions. The same space cannot be occupied by two bodies at the same time. Time is seen as linear — there is a past, present, and future. Standards of good and evil are accepted.

Beyond the visible world, according to Don Juan, is another world which is called a "separate reality." The particular version of reality which Don

65. Winfried Corduan, *Mysticism: An Evangelical Option?* (Grand Rapids: Zondervan, 1991), 42.

Juan represents is related to animism. It is also known as the sorcery or shamanistic tradition.

Sorcerers, such as Don Juan, are variously called shamans, magicians, or witch doctors. Through a special call and long, strenuous training, the sorcerer learns to control the spirit world, at least to a large extent.

The world is seen as a great unity. Spirit and matter occupy the same continuum. The spiritual distinction between people and animals as made in the Bible is not present.

It is important to have the presence of a guide during early attempts to see a separate reality. In the world of sorcery, one sees only through the help of a person who has already seen it. The guide is analogous to the guru or perfect master in the Hindu-related New Age groups.

The guide must first help you to break the certainty that the world is the way you have been taught. He seeks to help you strip yourself of the explanations and assumptions that shape and limit your vision. After you have been stripped of your limited perspective, the guide shows you the new reality of sorcery.

Natural drugs (psychotropic plants) are valuable for some people as an initiatory vehicle into the separate reality, or new consciousness. As we have seen, the first step in moving into a new reality is bracketing out old views and presuppositions. Castaneda was a tough case, so Don Juan resorted to natural drugs (psychotropic plants) to help him in this initial process of bracketing. Momentarily the drugs wiped out Castaneda's isolated ego.

*The Teachings of Don Juan* describe the way in which natural drugs were used in the initiation. Preparations made from three well-known plants, Peyote cactus, Jimson weed, and a species of mushroom, were ingested under Don Juan's careful control and interpretation. Castaneda stated that the drugs produced in him peculiar states of distorted perception and altered consciousness.

In Castaneda's third and probably most significant book, *Journey to Ixtlan,* a change of viewpoint on drugs is given. He reversed the impression given in *Teachings* and *Separate Reality* that the use of natural drugs was the main method Don Juan intended to use in bringing him to see the separate reality. He stated that Don Juan used psychotropic plants only in the earlier days of his apprenticeship because of his stupidity and bullheadedness. The natural drugs helped to shatter the dogmatic idea that the rational view of reality is the only view. The price Castaneda paid for taking drugs was extensive. The drugs weakened his body, and it took months for him to recuperate.

Don Juan himself does not use natural drugs regularly. He states that when he acts responsibly and properly uses other techniques, drugs are not needed.

Carlos Castaneda was invited to an East Village party in New York City which was attended by such luminaries as Timothy Leary. Under drug

101

influence, Castaneda reported that the partygoers were like silly children indulging in incoherent revelations. He was disgusted with the acid heads. He stated that an authentic sorcerer takes drugs for a different reason than do the acid heads. Drugs are only a means to an end. As ends in themselves, drugs are pathologically regressive and spiritually stultifying. Castaneda further suggested that Timothy Leary was only improvising in his drug-taking from within his Western view and merely rearranging old perspectives. There was no authentic breakthrough for Leary, according to Castaneda.

The negative statements by Carlos Castaneda on drugs came as quite a shock to many of his psychedelic admirers. They thought he would be stoned most of the time. The psychedelic crowd wanted him to tell them to turn on and blow their minds. These drug devotees were further upset when they learned that he does not smoke, drink hard liquor, or even use marijuana. In fact, Castaneda reports that his only drug experiences took place under the careful guidance of Don Juan.[66]

## DRUG MYSTICISM VERSUS CHRISTIAN MYSTICISM

In 1957, the prominent Oxford scholar R. C. Zaehner wrote *Mysticism Sacred and Profane*. In this book he challenged the teaching of Aldous Huxley that there was a positive relationship between drugs and Christian mysticism. Zaehner asserts that it is an absurd arrogance to state that a mescaline drug high is the same as an authentic Christian mystical experience. According to Zaehner, psychedelic experiences may have some similarity to a nontheistic, monistic mysticism. The characteristics of monistic mysticism include cosmic oneness, transcendence of space and time, feelings of well-being, and increased sensory perception of color and sound. This type of mysticism is not in the biblical tradition but, as we have seen, more appropriate to India.

The Christian mystic would say that any mystical absorption restricted to one's self or with nature falls short of biblical mysticism. The idea of a world force or an absolute is not the same as belief in a personal God.

Wayne Oates notes the differences between the Christian's experience of the Holy Spirit and the mystical opening of consciousness through psychedelic drugs. First, the Christian experience of the Holy Spirit arises from a clearly defined community of faith in Jesus Christ as Lord. The Christian experience of the Holy Spirit itself becomes specious and untested when separated from the prior encounter with Christ in his death, burial, and resurrection.

66. Newport, *Christ and the New Consciousness*, 152-56.

The account in the Book of Acts of the creation of the Christian community says it took place through the gift of the Holy Spirit to those who had attested to the resurrection of Christ. In Galatians, freedom from constriction of the law and access to the fruit of the Spirit — love, joy, peace — are brought about by the Spirit as an aftermath of having been crucified with Christ, in spite of which one has new life.

Second, Christians experiencing the Holy Spirit tend to consider it a lifelong journey or pilgrimage. The drug-induced "trips" tend to telescope all eternity into the very "nowness" of a given moment. Then the experience lives in memory until another "trip" is induced. Contrast this drug experience with the long, unremitting pilgrimage of the Apostle Paul *after* receiving the Holy Spirit. The spiritual life in the Holy Spirit is experienced as a "long haul" and not a short "trip." God pours his Holy Spirit into people's spirits, energizing them with ethical power (Rom. 5:5). He has given us a spirit of power, love, and self-control (2 Tim. 1:7).[67]

Thus we see that the Christian calls for the use of criteria to evaluate the results of various kinds of reported mystic or religious experiences. For Christians it is both faith *and* reason. Furthermore, Christianity is rooted in verifiable Christian history.

# PSYCHOLOGICALLY RELATED TRANSFORMATION

W. J. Hanegraaff of the Netherlands contends that it is primarily in America that we have seen New Age's psychologization of religion and sacralization of psychology. This so-called "Psychology and Religion Movement" can be traced from the 1880s to today's Human Potential movement. For the New Age, the "fact" that God can be approached through our own unconscious minds suggests that only a self-imposed, psychological barrier separates us from an immanent divinity. The cultivation of receptivity to the unconscious is thus a spiritually as well as psychologically regenerative act of the whole personality.[68]

## Jung and the Psychological Approach to Transformation

A key background figure in the psychological approaches is Swiss psychiatrist Carl Gustav Jung (1875-1961) and his circle of influence. In fact, Jung

---

67. Wayne Oates, *The Holy Spirit in Five Worlds* (New York: Association, 1968), 26-33.

68. Hanegraaff, *New Age Religion*, 490, 496.

represents a crucial link between traditional esoteric or spiritual worldviews and the New Age movement.

In his early years, Jung became the second-in-command in Sigmund Freud's psychoanalytic movement. In 1913 Jung broke with Freud and established his own movement, called "analytical psychology." Although Freud's importance in the history of psychology has been much greater than Jung's, in recent decades Freud's influence has declined while Jung's has grown. His increasing influence is most noticeable in the broader culture. Best-selling authors who promote Jungian ideas include the late Joseph Campbell *(The Power of Myth)*, Thomas Moore *(The Care of the Soul)*, and Clarissa Pinkola Estes *(Women Who Run with the Wolves)*.

In the judgment of Elliot Miller, prominent New Age critic, no single individual has done more to shape the contemporary New Age movement than Jung. Jung also has won acceptance from many professing Christians, some of whom are popularizers of his ideas, for example, Morton Kelsey and John Sanford.[69]

## Problems with Traditional Christianity

During the critical period described in his autobiography as the time of "Confrontation with the Unconscious" (1913-18), Jung struggled with the tension between traditional Christianity on the one hand and modernity on the other hand. I heard much about Jung and his struggle regarding Christianity as a graduate student at the Universities of Basel and Zurich in the late 1940s.

There is much evidence to support Jung's perspective as related to his lifelong struggle to repudiate traditional Christianity — to free himself from what he saw as its oppressive claims upon his life. Jung, in his mature writings, found traditional Christianity utterly incomprehensible.[70]

In the twentieth century in the West, Jung contended that the Christian myth had collapsed, as evidenced — or so Jung thought — by the tragedy of his father. In his autobiography, Jung, with great poignancy, relates how the religious convictions of his minister father gradually came to steal the joy from his father's life, and may have contributed to its premature end.

Thus we see that Jung's anti-Protestant sentiment stems from his conviction that Protestantism is seldom a "living religion." With its alleged

---

69. Elliot Miller, "The Jung Cult: Origins of a Charismatic Movement," *Christian Research Journal*, Winter 1996, 50.

70. Peter Homans: *Jung in Context: Modernity and the Making of a Psychology* (Chicago: University of Chicago, 1979).

emphasis on blind faith, it does not give us a living experience of a larger reality beyond this world and so cannot minister to our deepest longings and heal us of our deepest distresses. For Jung, Protestantism has become "rationalistic": it has clung to formulas, propositions, and theological dogmas, and it has neglected to open up channels of living contact with the world of spirit. Jung thinks Catholicism is much more a resource of mental health because it has retained a place for mystery, intuition, and symbols.[71]

Jung states that he originally tried to put Christians who had lost their faith back in touch with their traditional religion, but to little avail. The loss of vitality, and of healing power, by the Christian religion meant that for Jung, the God of Western humans had emigrated from His Church. Jung's vision in early puberty of God dropping a gigantic turd on the Basel cathedral was a drastic image of the true state of affairs. But if God had gone into hiding, where was he to be found? Jung discovered him in the catacombs of the psyche known as the region of the unconscious. For Jung, a cataclysmic spiritual shift had taken place, largely missed by Christian theologians, a shift from the God above to the God below.[72]

For Jung, the modern world has become de-spiritualized. The early discoveries of modern science became the foundations of the modern outlook, shaping as they did an entire view of the world. Modern humans "cannot project the divine image any longer" — that is, they are no longer able to believe in the existence of God, as described by the traditional dogmas of the church.

Jung saw two types of people developing in modern culture. First, there was the so-called modern person, who was fully self-conscious, rational, and extroverted, who was oriented to science and the modern state, and who, because he was unconnected with the past, was vulnerable to the unconscious. Second, there was the person who was modern in that he rejected the literalism and authoritarianism of traditional Christianity, but who also was in part traditional, in the sense that he was ready to reinterpret Christian symbols in the light of analytical psychology.

Jung accepted Berger's analysis that it is the essence of modern consciousness to be irrevocably structured by the technological aspects of industrial production. The individual of today transfers the engineering ethos of modern technology and bureaucracy to his personal consciousness and emotional life. This ethos, characterized by mechanicity, reproducibility, and measurability, produces in consciousness the traits of abstraction, functional rationality, and instrumentality. Modern consciousness is therefore capable

71. Robert C. Roberts, *Taking the Word to Heart* (Grand Rapids: Eerdmans, 1993), 107-8.

72. Paul J. Stern, *C. G. Jung: The Haunted Prophet* (New York: Dell, 1976), 32-33.

of a degree of self-analysis and self-abstraction never before achieved. As such it is separated from traditional sources of feeling and meaning — it is, in effect "homeless."

In his biographical reflections and in his major works, Jung shows an acute awareness of the destructive side of religion in general, and, specifically, of the religion into which he was born. According to Jung, Christianity could no longer offer Western humanity sufficient spiritual sustenance. His concern for the spiritual needs of his time led Jung to call for an appreciation and response to the unconscious and symbolic. Psychologically, for Jung, this meant the identification and recognition of those structures and forces within the psyche from which humanity's experience of God both could and has to arise. Jung argues that the God hidden in a person's unconscious becomes incarnate through human consciousness and, in so doing, revitalizes, balances, and enlarges life. In Jung's view, it was the estrangement of human beings from the mythical realm and the subsequent shrinking of their existence to the merely factual that was the major cause of mental illness.[73]

## THE UNCONSCIOUS — JUNG'S BREAK WITH FREUD

At the turn of the century the Swiss Jung and the Viennese Freud were colleagues in the formation of the new science of psychoanalysis, and Freud, nineteen years older, saw Jung as his intellectual heir. Both were committed to advancing a new framework for explaining human behavior, one that pictured humans in terms of the relation between a conscious but fragile ego and the unconscious.

Freud saw the unconscious as a place where the ego puts all its repressed personal past — something like a basement where traumas, unacceptable desires, and unresolved psychological knots of various kinds are stored but active. Although these contents are suppressed, their very unconscious status rules our lives until they are brought forth by the light of psychoanalysis.

In contrast to Freud's "basement" image, Jung proposed a broader view, one that saw the unconscious not just as a garbage bin but more like a mansion with many types of rooms.[74]

As the refuge of the Divine and the abode of symbol and myth, the Jungian unconscious was raised far above the humble station of the Freudian id from which it derived. Whereas Freud imagined the unconscious as a chaos of seething libidinal sexual energies, Jung viewed it as a cosmos, with an intrinsic order and creativity of its own. While Freud saw the unconscious as

---

73. Hanegraaff, *New Age Religion*, 506.
74. William J. Paden, *Interpreting the Sacred: Ways of Viewing Religion* (Boston: Beacon, 1992), 48-49.

a crude storage area for undigested personal trauma, Jung conceived of it as the rich and vast treasure chamber of the archetypes.

Freud took it for granted that consciousness had a greater personal and cultural value than the unconscious. Defining psychoanalysis as an effort to expand the rule of ego (consciousness) at the expense of the id (unconsciousness), he likened analytic work to the arduous reclaiming of arable land from the sea. In Jung's canon, the only appropriate attitude of consciousness vis-à-vis the unconscious is reverence. For Jung, the strife between the unconscious and conscious must be overcome by the "higher copulation" that gives birth to the unity of the self.

At the close of the period of struggle with modernity (1918-21), Jung wrote the first versions of the *Two Essays on Analytical Psychology*, which became a definitive statement of his major ideas, and which outlined the structure of the individuation process. The individuation process became the center of Jung's mature thought.

For Jung, the human psyche, or mind, is really an inhabitant of two distinct worlds, the world of consciousness and the world of the unconscious. These worlds are equally essential to full human life, and neither should be slighted. But as we have seen, the two worlds tend to remain separate.

Jung tends to identify the world of spirit with the unconscious. It is a world of larger meanings that speaks to our need for a significance that goes beyond the physical world. By contrast, the world of consciousness is "down to earth." Jung thought that to be fully human, one had to bring these two worlds together, to live somehow in both of them at the same time.

Jung argues that if we look closely at people's dreams and study the world's mythologies, we find patterns of imagery that cannot be accounted for simply by reference to experiences people have had as individuals. The unconscious already has a structure of its own, independent of our individual histories. Universally across cultures we find recurrent themes that are best accounted for on the supposition that there is an "objective," or "collective," unconscious.[75]

According to Richard Noll, Jung wrote in *The Psychology of the Unconscious* that it may be concluded that the soul possesses in some degree historical strata, the oldest stratum of which would correspond to the unconscious. In the soul there is an impersonal or collective unconscious. By so doing he was shifting his emphasis from a biologically defined unconscious composed of layers of evolutionary experience to a more Platonic unconscious composed of certain symbolic ideas and images. Around 1916 Jung started calling this layer a decidedly pre-Christian layer that has been covered up by centuries of Judeo-Christian sediment. After repudiating the relevance of the Christian

75. Roberts, *Word to Heart*, 114-15.

107

myth in his own life in 1912, Jung advocates deliberately cutting through centuries of strangling Judeo-Christian underbrush to reach the promised land of the "impersonal psyche," a pre-Christian, pagan "land of the Dead," to be revitalized thereby.

These views reveal that Jung was deeply influenced by German Romantic Philosophy of Nature and *Lebensphilosophie* which emphasized the importance of direct experience and intuition over rationality. According to Hanegraaff, Jung's personal religious synthesis, presented by him as scientific psychology, combined esoteric traditions, Romantic *Naturphilosophie*, evolutionist vitalism, "neopagan" solar worship, *volkisch* mythology, and a considerable dose of occultism. Jung's particular genius probably consists less in the originality of his basic worldview than in his remarkable ability to present it to his readers in the terminology of modern psychoanalysis.[76]

## ARCHETYPES

Robert Roberts describes Jung's concept of archetypes which reside in the unconscious. The collective unconscious is formed not of actual images but of forms of images, or themes, that Jung calls "archetypes." According to Jung, archetypes are unlimited in number. They are created by the repetition of situations and experiences engraved upon the psychic constitution. They are not, however, forms of images filled with content, but forms without content. When a situation occurs that corresponds to an archetype, it becomes activated and a compulsiveness appears. God, birth, death, rebirth, power, magic, the sun, the moon, the wind, animals, and the elements are archetypes; as are traits embodied in the Hero, the Sage, the Judge, the Child, the Trickster, and the Earth Mother. Their role in the personality changes as an individual grows and encounters new situations.

Jung said that the existence of archetypes can be proved through dreams, the primary source, as well as through "active imagination," or fantasies, produced by deliberate concentration. He also noted that other sources of archetypal material are found in the fantasies of trance states and in the dreams of children from ages three to five.

Prominent among the Jung archetypes are quasipersonal "figures" that are significant in the development and constitution of the individual psyche. For example, each man has his anima, an archetypal feminine figure that is the unconscious psychic complement of his masculine personality. An exactly analogous remark can be made about the animus present in the unconscious

---

76. Elliot Miller, *Christian Research Journal*, 51. Cf. also Richard Noll, *The Jung Cult* (Princeton: Princeton University, 1994), 86, 269-70; Hanegraaff, *New Age Religion*, 507-8.

of every woman. One pole of our sexuality becomes unconscious and we become sexually one-sided. But the presence of the opposite-sex archetype causes a sense of personal incompleteness such that we find a part of ourselves in members of the opposite sex through projecting on them our unconscious anima or animus. Thus sexual attraction is not just "animal lust" but is part of the quest for psychic wholeness.

Other archetypes are the Wise Old Man, the Hero and the Monster, the Mother, the Maiden, the Child, and the Trickster (a kind of fool-savior). In each case the archetype is a legitimate aspect of the psyche and thus something that needs to be dealt with in the fundamental human project of synthesizing the conscious and the unconscious.

But there is one archetype that has particularly powerful religious and healing significance, and that is the archetype of the Self, symbolized by the mandala — a circle, usually divided into four parts, which recurs often in people's dreams and in the religious symbolism of virtually all cultures. The Self is a representation, in the unconscious, of the whole psyche, both conscious and unconscious. Jung warns us again and again not to confuse the Self with the ego. The ego is the center of consciousness, but the Self is the center of the entire psyche. As such, the Self is itself the synthesis of consciousness and the unconscious — or, better, as an archetype, it is the representation of that synthesis. As the figure of the synthesis of the conscious and the unconscious, the Self archetype represents the psyche as if it were already whole.

Thus an individual can gain wholeness if he can set up some communication with the Self through opening himself to the world of the unconscious.

Jung's "individuation process" is the process of becoming the Self that one already is potentially. As we have seen, the conscious ego is just one aspect of the psyche, a small light in a large, real, and structured darkness. The light and the darkness together are the Self, and human wholeness is achieved when the separation and conflict between these two are overcome, when the two parts are integrated or synthesized into an actual whole in which the conscious ego fully taps the supernatural and mysterious resources of the unconscious.

So the process of becoming a Self, or synthesizing the two dimensions of the psyche, is a process of taking those mental contents that belong to the collective unconscious and personalizing or concretizing or individualizing them, making the infinite finite, as it were, or the eternal temporal.[77]

Jung believed that he had discovered a natural healing process which occurred when traditional dogmas were withdrawn. In the dreams and visions of his patients, especially when they took the form of mandalas (a circle or square containing a central figure), Jung saw a process at work which was

---

77. Roberts, *Word to Heart*, 116-19, 221-22.

remarkably similar to the processes which he believed undergirded the most traditional belief systems. But his theory and techniques brought this process to a higher level of self-consciousness than they had attained under the conditions of traditional faith. The withdrawal of traditional dogmas activated new psychological forces, unknown to the traditional believer, which were then raised to a new level of awareness and integrated into self-consciousness.

Jung also believed that the "homeless" consciousness of the modern person afforded the beginning of the process of individuation. The breakdown of the persona activated the archetypes of the collective unconscious, and called for their assimilation into the conscious ego, thereby broadening the scope of the modern individual's consciousness and alleviating his condition of homelessness. The archetypes might well be called "structures of tradition." As such their existence and the need for their assimilation constituted the dimension of countermodernization in Jung's psychology: they are symbols rooted in the ancient past which, when assimilated, unify modern consciousness and overcome its homeless condition.

The result is the emergence of the Self, the final state of the individuation process. Jung claims that this view of the person is entirely new, being neither simply modern nor simply traditional. According to Noll, self-deification is the same as "individuation" — the therapeutic goal of analytical psychology.

Jungian analysis, explains Noll, is essentially an initiation into a pagan mystery — a means to experience what Jung experienced. It is an occult process in which the opposites of creation supposedly reconcile in the oneness of the god within, and thus the individual becomes psychologically and spiritually whole. As Noll observes: "Jung's familiar psychological theory and method, which are so widely promoted in our culture today, rest on a very early neopagan formulation" — a fact seemingly unknown to thousands of Christian or Jewish Jungians.[78]

## RECLAIMING THE CHRISTIAN TRADITION

From 1921 onward Jung turned his mind back upon the phenomenon of religion, which had vexed him throughout so much of his early life, and interpreted it — or, rather, as Homans explains, reinterpreted it — according to his unique system of psychological ideas, all of which explained in detail the individuation process.

Jung came to see religion potentially as a life-enhancing force. He was deeply impressed by its continuous emergence in myriad forms throughout the history of the human spirit, and gradually he came to locate religion's source in

78. Elliot Miller, *Christian Research Journal*, 52.

the deepest levels of the human unconscious. Keenly aware of its inevitability and of both its creative and destructive power, Jung finally believed that the religious instinct, understood in its widest sense, offered to life its greatest fulfillment. Thus he could write that the improvement of his patients in the second half of life was invariably accompanied by the recovery of a religious sense.

This development in Jung's thought on religion was due to his realization that the possibility of the experience of the supernatural, and so the possibility of religious experience, was grounded in the activation of archetypal forces in the psyche itself. Generally speaking, these forces acted to compensate, expand, and direct the ego toward what he came to call the Self, the archetype of wholeness and the regulating center of the personality. The experience of the reality of the Self emerges from the growing conjunction of the ego and the unconscious in the process Jung terms individuation, which is itself both the direction in which life moves and its goal. Jung also implies that God becomes more conscious of himself through the growing self-consciousness of humans.

For Jung, the unconscious is the place from which comes a person's sense of the divine, and also the source of the movement of human life toward the Self, as consciousness unites with the depths to create a more whole personality. Thus Jung locates the reality of the divine within both nature and humanity, and understands the development of humanity as a process of growing into this awareness.

The state of the Holy Spirit described by Jung involves the unambiguous unity of the ego with the unconscious at the conscious level. If God is mediated through the unconscious, this condition would be one in which the ego is fully pervaded with the sense of God.

Given the fact that religion was a central theme in Jung's mature years, what was his view of it? Did Jung, like Freud, develop a set of interpretive categories by means of which he could "see through" and thereby explain away traditional Christianity? Or did he, in devising his system of unique ideas, conceive of a way to translate traditional Christianity into terminology acceptable to modern humanity, without appreciably altering the traditional doctrines? Liberal and evangelical Christians differ in their answer to this question.

## A SYMPATHETIC CHRISTIAN EVALUATION

Peter Homans of the University of Chicago contends that Jung did not opt for either of these alternatives in an exclusive manner. Rather, his thought on religion is a complex attempt to synthesize the two. By applying the individuation process to traditional Christianity, Jung in effect created a double movement of reduction and retrieval of meaning. In one sense he *was* reductive:

he interpreted the totality of Christian faith in the light of analytical psychology. This psychology became for him the key for "seeing through" the otherwise opaque character of the Christian faith. All the major tenets of Christianity were interpreted as instances of archetypes in the collective unconscious. The individuation process was the lens through which Jung viewed the Christian faith. It was a new set of categories, derived from his research and his contact with Freud, completely foreign to the Christian tradition. Without this psychology, the Christian faith simply did not make any sense. Jung's interpretation of Christianity was in this sense very different from Christianity's own self-interpretation of itself. In this sense his psychology embodied what Paul Ricoeur has called a "hermeneutics of suspicion."

But Jung's psychology contained a second movement, which built upon the first, in which he attempted to retrieve religious meaning from the Christian tradition and incorporate it into his psychological theory of the person. Once the reductive movement had been made — once the psychological meaning of doctrine had been disclosed — then Jung proceeded to clothe these constructs with positive meaning and value. He argued that they were in fact essential if modern humans, uprooted and dissociated from their traditional roots, were ever to re-relate themselves to Christian tradition. Hence he claimed that the archetypes and the individuation process, while not part of the vocabulary of the traditional Christian, nevertheless captured the hidden essence of that tradition. In all this Jung gave expression to an important facet of his personal identity — which existed alongside that of originative psychologist and social critic — that of prophet or re-interpreter of traditional Christianity.

Although Jung repudiated traditional Christianity, he believed that classical Christian experience provided an absolutely essential matrix, or "field," or experiential context out of which the individuation process took its peculiar shape. Thus, for Jung, traditional beliefs in God, Christ, the Trinity, and the Church were all necessary background for the modern individual if he was to come to understand himself in a new way. Traditional Christianity was the indispensable context within which the individuation process could occur. Paradoxically, it was there in order to be put aside. In Jung's mind, analytical psychology evolved out of the Christian tradition, but the end result was just as religious as was the context out of which it emerged.

At the heart of Jung's thought on religion, Homans believed, was his conviction that traditional Christianity and modernity were radically at odds with one another, and he spent much of his life devising a conceptual system which could reconcile the two.[79]

79. Peter Homans, Paper, "C. G. Jung: Christian or Post-Christian Psychologist?", 1-4, 13.

## EVANGELICAL EVALUATION OF JUNG'S APPROACH

Christianity and Judaism are religions of historical revelation. Essential to the Jew's knowledge of God is the story of the liberation from Egypt: for the Jew, God is identified and experienced as the one who delivered the people of Israel from Egyptian bondage. A Jew's knowledge of himself is likewise historical. Who is he most essentially, this individual human being? He is a member of the people that God delivered from Egypt. He belongs in and gets his identity from that historical lineage.

In the same way, the Christian's knowledge of God is definitively related to the story of Christ. The Christian knows God as the Father of Jesus of Nazareth, who was crucified to reconcile the world's sinners to God and was raised by God on the third day. She knows God as the king whose kingdom, inaugurated in the acts of Jesus and furthered in the acts of the apostles and of the disciples in subsequent centuries, will one future day be elaborated before her eyes. She experiences herself as a member of that past, present, and future kingdom, and in this way she belongs not just to this present moment but to the ages of God. This does not exclude her meeting God in the here and now; on the contrary, she could not meet that God in the here and now if she did not know him as the one who has that history.

Jung's religion, by contrast, is one of pure self-exploitation. God is known not by reference to any acts that God may have performed in the past (or any "doctrines" that report and interpret such historical data), but purely by a process in which the individual explores the goings-on within his own psyche. The individual finds God only in the depths of his own being. The first principle of this theology is this: There is nothing in true religion that was not first in the psyche.

For Jung, the ideal is a harmonious or proper relationship with oneself. Thus the term "internalist": virtue is entirely internal to the psyche, and troubles of "relating" all have the form of intrapsychic "conflicts." Insofar as Jungian virtues fit us for relationships with other beings, the relationship is most fundamentally detachment. By contrast, the Christian virtues relate us to other beings — in particular, to other human beings and to God conceived as a being different from us. And the relationship is not detachment but attachment: the double commandment to love God and neighbor sums up the Christian calling to virtue. This relational conception of our well-being, our mental health, is captured in the Christian hope for the kingdom of God, that society in which God is honored as God and our fellow humans are cherished as his children and our sisters and brothers. The centrality of attachment and relation to Christian virtue is also portrayed by the apostle Paul's image of the church as the body of Christ. One can hardly be more "attached" than one is to one's head and other body parts![80]

Jung's description of the particular experience of others as equal to ourselves because of the collective unconscious is quite different from the experience of others as brothers and sisters beloved of a common Parent.

As we have noted, transformation for Jung is the means for reaching higher consciousness or wholeness, "completeness." The method for this in Jungian psychotherapy is to use psychological-psychic techniques to make the unconscious conscious. When the unconscious is made conscious, then greater, or higher, consciousness is said to result. Transformation is thus an ongoing integration, or assimilation, of the unconscious into the personality. Each "successful" archetypal assimilation supposedly makes the unconscious steadily more conscious. Jung believed this produced wholeness, or completeness, which, he stated, few attained.

According to Charles Strohmer, Jung acquired the initial concept of wholeness from a synthesis of gnostic, alchemical, and Eastern-mystical elements, principally the Anthropos figure and the "Self." What this works out to is that Jung's vision of wholeness, or completeness, is a call for a Taoist-style dualism, the balance of yin/yang, feminine/masculine, dark/light, and so forth. Jung's path to completion is therefore a passage to a mystical monism, or holism, the awakening in consciousness of a total Self. This is a clue as to why the process of individuation has become a model for wholeness in the New Age spirituality.[81]

In his controversial book *Answer to Job,* Jung states that by silencing Job's demand for justice with a bullying display of raw power, the biblical Yahweh had exhibited a sovereign disregard for the moral law he had promulgated among human beings. For Jung, in grinding Job into the dust, merely because of Satan's dare, Yahweh had suffered a moral defeat at the hands of his creature. More importantly, Job had given indications of possessing a greater degree of consciousness than Yahweh. He appeared to have recognized the dissociation of Yahweh's nature of which Yahweh himself was unaware.

Yahweh in his omnipotence could afford to remain unconscious. After the Job episode, however, Yahweh came gradually to suspect that his creature might have outstripped him in the matter of self-awareness. According to Jung, Yahweh's realization of this amazing and scandalous state of affairs gave rise to his desire to regenerate himself. Thus the process of God's incarnation in the *Son of Man* was set in motion. In other words, Yahweh's autocratic

---

80. Roberts, *Word to Heart,* 109-10, 123-24.
81. Charles Strohmer, "C. G. Jung: The Fountainhead of Joseph Campbell," *SCP Journal* 9.2 (1990): 39, 40.

excesses vis-à-vis Job, and his discovery of Job's superior consciousness, led directly to his resolve to bring about a state of cordial relations with humans by his becoming flesh in Jesus Christ.

But God's incarnation in Christ was merely a first step, Jung theorized. It was to be followed, sooner or later, by the Christification of many, by God entering into empirical individuals. God's continuing embrace of his creature was eventually going to produce a new race of divine humans. Had not Christ himself with his "You are gods" foretold this triumphant development of humanity?

God's embodiment in human beings, Jung thought, was really the same as the process of individuation. God was just another name for the archetype of the Self, expressive of the same psychic reality. To distinguish between God and the archetype of the Self, and to split hairs about their difference in their nature of being, would only distance human beings from God and might even "prevent God from becoming human." Thus we see that the Jungian God is gathered into the Self and is thus not another being with whom one can enter into a relationship.[82]

Jung's view of religions as grounded in universally possessed archetypes works to show that any particular historical manifestation (Christ, Buddha, Gandhi, etc.) never exhausts the possibilities of expression of the archetype that lies behind the manifestation. Given this model of the genesis of the religious experience, it is not possible to hold any given symbol system or revelation as exhaustive, absolute, or definitive. The Christ therefore is only one personification of an archetypal experience innate to the human psyche. In so extending his understanding of the symbol of Christ, Jung dismisses the uniqueness of Christ as the sole savior of humankind.

Elliot Miller points out that because of Jung's growing importance, the publication of Richard Noll's *The Jung Cult* was an important literary event. It won a prize from the Association of American Publishers as the best book of 1994 on psychology. Noll's most recent book is *The Aryan Christ*. Noll is a clinical psychologist who recently completed a postdoctoral fellowship in the history of science at Harvard University. *The Jung Cult*'s central thesis is that the movement that Jung initiated is much closer in nature to a neopagan (Aryan) cult than the scientific psychiatric discipline that it has always claimed to be. It is not just religious but a religion.

Noll affirms that Jung increasingly guided his movement away from the trappings of a scientific discipline, shaping it instead into a "charismatic movement" or cult of personality built around himself. Jung's true esoteric message was made available mystery-cult style only to initiates who had undergone one hundred hours of analysis and had obtained Jung's personal

82. Roberts, *Word to Heart*, 126.

permission. Since Jung's death it has been passed down to the present generation of initiates by a "body of priest-analysts."[83]

The surprise best-seller of the summer of 1988 was *The Power of Myth* by Joseph Campbell. Campbell draws heavily on Jung. Campbell, like Jung, has diagnosed the modern malady of rootlessness and superficiality. We lack a unified ethos. But Campbell rejects the personal Creator God of the monotheistic tradition. Instead he champions an ineffable, amoral, and impersonal deity.

Although he was more of an academic than a popularizer, Campbell's essential worldview is in basic agreement with that of New Age celebrities like Shirley MacLaine, Werner Erhard, and John Denver: All is one; god is an impersonal and amoral force in which we participate; supernatural revelation and redemption are not needed. Campbell's wide erudition and sophisticated manner may attract those who are less impressed by the metaphysical glitz of a Shirley MacLaine or the rank superstition of "crystal consciousness" or the cosmic hype of the "Harmonic Convergence."

As in the case of Jung, there is little doubt that Campbell's ideological agenda is shaped by personal animus and (probable) early-life resentments. He goes out of his way to toss derision and accusations at Christianity and Christian faith. His on-camera comments in *The Power of the Myth* make it plain that he harbors considerable antagonism toward the Catholic Christianity in which he was raised. One root of his revulsion seems to be an inability to come to terms with his status as a fallen and sinful human being.

By turning the real events of redemptive history into symbols of inner changes, Campbell disarms sin and discounts redemption as well. Campbell's gnostic gospel would have us master the "Christ Archetype" within. If Campbell thinks those are identical, or even compatible, it is no wonder that he can say "Jesus on the cross, Buddha under the tree — these are the same."[84]

## POSSIBLE POSITIVE CONTRIBUTIONS

Strohmer points out that Jung warned against the dangers of dogmatism. He saw religion positively — as a necessity, in fact — and bore witness to the supernatural realm. His theories of personality types, and his elaboration of the universality of symbols, merit further study. His psychology indicates that we are spiritual and not mere machines. It places much more emphasis on

83. Elliot Miller, *Christian Research Journal*, 50.
84. Douglas Groothuis, "Myth and the Power of Joseph Campbell," *SCP Journal* 9.2 (1990), 23, 30.

human responsibility and choice than do models which claim that humans are almost completely determined by preceding events and natural laws.[85]

According to William Paden, in giving some psychological validity to religious symbols, the Jungian translation of religion — unlike the Freudian one — has had the cultural function of creating a kind of alternative religious framework. The gods are alive after all — within the psyche. The interpretive force of this approach, then, has been more reconstructive than destructive.[86]

We have noted that Jungian theology and its corresponding psychology contrast starkly with Christian theology and psychology. Jung's theology is a flat rejection of Christianity's character as a religion of historical revelation, and the character ideal of his psychology, which is internalist, contradicts something fundamental about the Christian virtues — namely, their relational or communal character. Despite these problems, Robert C. Roberts, a Christian psychologist, thinks that Jung has made positive contributions from which Christians can profit.

For example, the Christian psychologist looks for features of human nature and experience that suggest we are made for a relationship with God. Not that we have a divine "side" which needs to be developed, but that we are so constituted as to need God. In our search for features of human nature that suggest our need for God, Jung's studies of the unconscious, of dreams, of schizophrenic imagery, of mythology, and so forth provide rich sources.[87]

Douglas Groothuis suggests that evangelical Christianity need not jettison uncritically Jung's mythic concerns. Christian writers like C. S. Lewis have argued that the world's mythologies present a dim imitation of the redemption made historical through Christ. Mythologies worldwide speak of lost innocence, cosmic conflict, and redemption. In this sense the mythic dimension can be seen as part of general revelation, not in itself a means of salvation, but as pointing beyond itself to what Lewis in *God in the Dock* called "myth become fact," the Incarnation itself.

Thus we can interpret the unconscious as a human organ into which God whispers, ambiguously, things that he makes much clearer in historical revelation and in the doctrines of the church that derive from that revelation. We, of course, do not "deify" the unconscious as Jung does. Rather, Christians have their own ways of interpreting the deliverances of the unconscious and do not need to accept Jungian ones.[88]

85. Strohmer, "C. G. Jung," 142.
86. Paden, *Interpreting the Sacred*, 63-64.
87. Roberts, *Word to Heart*, 129.
88. Ibid., 130-32. cf. also Groothuis, "Myth and Power," 30.

## HUMANISTIC PSYCHOLOGY: MASLOW AND ROGERS

Humanistic psychology, known as Third Force psychology to differentiate it from the First and Second Force psychologies of behaviorism and Freudianism, was a post–World War II creation of psychologists interested in studying psychology scientifically from the perspectives of healthy individuals. It sought to discard behavioristic models based on observations of animal behavior. It is most closely identified with Abraham H. Maslow (1908-70). Trained as an experimental psychologist at the University of Wisconsin, Maslow decided after the start of World War II that he would transform psychology into an instrument for world peace and improvement of the human condition. Maslow was a key figure in the movement from the beginning. He provided an important link between humanistic psychology and psychologies developed in Germany between the two world wars. He frequently acknowledged his intellectual debt to Kurt Goldstein, who first developed a theory of self-actualization.

Maslow believed that all human beings have innate spiritual yearnings to experience the sacred and fulfill themselves to their maximum potential of goodness. Maslow called these yearnings "B-values," the B standing for cognition of Being, or a fully integrated and holistic state.

While human beings do possess inherently pathological natures, which are dealt with in Freud's psychology, they also possess inherently good inner natures, Maslow said. This good inner nature manifests itself as a natural striving for healthy living, honesty, creativity, compassion, unselfishness, and so on. A truly fulfilled and "self-actualized" individual (a term Maslow coined), who was mature, healthy, and filled with a zest for living, is one who has successfully integrated his or her lower, animalistic, "instinctoid" self with his or her higher, god-like self.

The self-actualized individual is happier, healthier, and more creative. Self-actualization is not a transcendence of problems, for all people suffer tragedies, pain, and problems in addition to joy and health. Self-actualization, rather, facilitates the transcendence of the self.

Maslow found that self-actualized people, who cut across the spectrum of society, are more likely to experience B-cognition. They are also more likely to have "peak experiences," the nonreligious equivalent of a mystical experience of sorts. Peak experiences reinforce the holistic outlook and enhance creativity.[89]

Contemporary studies on the human brain have led transpersonal psychologists to assume that it was the left hemisphere of the brain which

89. Guiley, *Harper's Encyclopedia*, 482-83.

was dominant in the Western individual. This hemisphere was the one which was most logical and analytical. The right hemisphere was essentially neglected, and so Westerners were lacking in intuition and mythical awareness. As Mark Cosgrove points out, transpersonal psychologists have therefore argued that people must be educated in an intuitive mode of thought. By having their consciousness altered, people may develop their full potential as persons.[90]

Other leaders of Humanistic Psychology were Carl Rogers and Rollo May. These, in turn, had ties to the Frankfurt School and the existential Continental philosophy developed between the two World Wars. One of Rogers's emphases was his belief in not making diagnoses — a technique known as "client-centered" therapy. The approach stemmed from Rogers's assertion that individuals always hold within themselves the answer to any problem, and therefore the role of the counselor is simply to create the proper environment for the solutions to emerge. This is done by simply reflecting back the client's feelings rather than guiding or directing him or her.

Because, in Rogers's view, human experience is the center and source of meaning, self-realization can be accomplished apart from responsibility to other persons, tradition, or an objective God who makes moral demands. One is responsible only to one's own feelings. Only you can judge your values, Rogers said.[91]

According to Robert Roberts, the Christian emphasis is very different. This life is not supposed to be a setting for the satisfaction of the immediately obvious needs of the "organism"; it is a preparatory school for God's kingdom. So the Christian concept of the true self is as a member of the kingdom of God, in relationships of dependence and love with God and neighbor.[92]

## HUMAN POTENTIAL MOVEMENT

The Human Potential movement mushroomed from these rather clear and simple beginnings in humanistic psychology into a many-branched, diverse phenomenon. Within the parameters of the experiential, anything that could conceivably contribute to human growth, whether scientifically verified or not, was admissible — and was admitted. Growth centers began to spring up either in remote and naturally beautiful areas or in urban centers of population, and as techniques such as yoga were included. It was a short step to understanding

90. Burnett, *Clash of Worlds*, 172.
91. Chandler, *Understanding the New Age*, 156.
92. Roberts, *Word to Heart*, 37-38.

experiences happening in the groups as somehow transpersonal, spiritual, or even mystical.

In addition to Maslow's "peak experiences," the "life force" concept of Wilhelm Reich became popular. Reich (1897-1957) believed that blockages to the development of the human personality were recorded in muscular patterns in the body, forming what he called "character armor." Reich developed a form of physical touch to release the "orgone energy" that permeated the universe. He built orgone accumulators to collect and harness this mysterious cosmic energy. His theories were beginning to link a psychological and philosophical understanding of humanity, and this has become important to the thinking of the New Age.[93]

From the beginning New Thought leaders had also been interested in the flow of force. Whereas in New Thought the flow of power passes from one person to another, the orgone energy of Reich which pervades the natural world is made available to an individual by such techniques as sitting in a box. Mann discusses a similar concept found in yoga known as "prana" and notes, "The basic purpose of yoga is to contact and absorb prana in ever increasing quantities. Certain forms of yoga are specifically directed toward the channeling of energy in a very direct manner. Kundalini yoga, for example, is described in classical texts as 'the Yoga of Psychic Force.'"

The Human Potential movement has become well known because of the popularity of the low-key pop psychology of Transactional Analysis (I'm okay, you're okay) and the many encounter groups begun by Carl Rogers.

## Transpersonal Emphasis and the New Age

Transpersonal psychology, emphasizing, as the name implies, personal experiences transcending the usual range of humanistic investigations, was born out of a new interest in the spiritual dimensions of experience in what had been, as humanistic psychology, a secular movement.

As the Human Potential movement grew, the transpersonal aspect of it received increasing emphasis.

With an emphasis on the ability of each individual to achieve a higher consciousness, the splinter groups interested in transpersonal psychology within the Human Potential movement took a new turn. This approach requires an experiential foundation on the part of the therapist. It includes both Eastern and Western methods such as dream analysis and imagery;

93. Michael Cole et al., *What Is the New Age?* (London: Hodder & Stoughton, 1990), 35.

Eastern meditation and yoga; behavioral medicine; body-work; and the transpersonal experience of altered states of consciousness as a means of achieving higher states.

Experiences that traditional psychiatry would label pathological are being explored in transpersonal psychology for their therapeutic value. Transpersonal psychology is still in its infancy and is still controversial. Critics say it is not sufficiently defined and infringes too much upon religion.[94]

Mystical, peak, and transcendent experiences are described as Cosmic, Mystical, Peak, Religious, Spiritual, Transcendent, Ultimate, Unitive, Expanded, and Heightened. They are also described as Bliss, Buddhi, Ecstasy, Nirvana, Oneness, Rapture, Satori, Supreme Identity, Unity, and Buddha-hood.[95]

Transpersonal ideas have been made popular by psychologist Gerald Janpolsky in his book *Love Is Letting Go of Fear*. John F. Kennedy and Ken Wilber are other leaders in this movement.

Ken Wilber, a leading New Age exponent and figure in transpersonal psychology, traces the stages of psychological growth through fourteen levels which mirror the seven Yogic chakras of Eastern mysticism. At the "most realized state," he maintains, a person experiences higher consciousness — the goal of mystics through the ages, the essence of Maslow's "peak experience," and the apex of transpersonal psychology. At this stage, says Wilber, "we are in touch with the divine; the physical is lost in the spiritual; we become enlightened."[96]

As individual interests branched out, a diversity was born under the rubric "New Age." The New Age movement can be understood as developing broader, more applied versions of the interests of transpersonal psychologists. Even though transpersonal psychologists made a careful effort to remain academically respectable, they attained only a modest acceptance in the academic and psychological circles which had previously rejected humanistic or "Third Force" psychology.[97]

## Evaluation

In an almost paradoxical way, transpersonal psychology postulates a source of outside power without giving up the centrality of the individual self. Universal wisdom is greater than the self yet is contained within the self. By

94. Guiley, *Harper's Encyclopedia*, 484-85.
95. Lewis and Melton, *Perspectives on the New Age*, 43-44.
96. Chandler, *Understanding the New Age*, 157.
97. Lewis and Melton, *Perspectives on the New Age*, 46.

accepting a "divine within," transpersonal psychology has silenced the question of God. It diverts many who need renewal from seeking the true God who could bring healing to their lives.

The Human Potential groups stress human goodness and potential. The "wisdom within" has become a generally accepted alternative to the power Christians find through Christ and the Holy Spirit. An extreme example of the outworkings of the Human Potential movement is the est (Erhard) movement and its derivative groups, such as Lifespring and Forum. I took a course under the founder, Werner Erhard. In his seminars old beliefs are torn down and the supremacy of the self is proclaimed.

In Transpersonal Psychology the ground of all being is consciousness. We gain experience of reality only when all barriers of separateness are broken down. We then move toward higher consciousness, which can be induced by meditation or peak experiences. The goal is that consciousness will return to its original state. The conclusion that consciousness is all-pervading presents a particular view of God. God is no longer an Other out there or transcendent or searching for humanity and communicating to humans through the Holy Spirit, Jesus, or written revelation. In contrast, the biblical view affirms that our fulfillment does not lie in an evolution toward greater consciousness. Rather, our potential is realized through our restored relationship with our Creator. The Christian looks to God's revelation in the Bible, which tells of Jesus.

Russell Chandler points out that elevation of personal growth as the highest good has been sharply criticized on the ground that its assumptions ultimately lead to a psychology of narcissism, asocial irresponsibility, and personal license. Nevertheless, humanistic psychology and transpersonal psychology, the most recent entrant in the human potentials lineup, have made an enormous impact on Western culture. And the New Age script has copied, line for line, their basic tenet: One can realize infinite potential — become enlightened — because personal experience equals reality, and reality can be created by focusing on the self.[98]

## TRANSFORMATION IN THE BIBLICAL TRADITION

Winfried Corduan gives a general definition of a typical mystic: "The mystic believes that there is an absolute and that he or she can enjoy an unmediated link to this absolute in a superrational experience."[99]

98. Chandler, *Understanding the New Age*, 156-57.
99. Corduan, *Mysticism*, 32, 46.

R. C. Zaehner divides mysticism into two categories. The monistic type is exemplified by Hindu and Buddhist mysticism. The individual is here submerged into the impersonal All, or whatever specific name one might give to it. A second type is theistic mysticism. Here the absolute is a personal God and the relationship takes on personal qualities. For example, love for God becomes a dominant theme for Christian mystics.

All groups which emphasize mystical transformation in the biblical tradition would be of the theistic type. In the classical biblical tradition spiritual knowledge and salvation come from personal encounters between the Living God and the Believing Person. The focus is on God outside the self.

Unfortunately, from an evangelical perspective, some persons and groups who call themselves biblical or Christian mystics have been influenced by hellenistic religions and philosophies, especially Gnosticism and Neo-platonism. There is also a connection with the East, where God is seen as beyond the personal. Spirituality is a journey into the interior of the heart. The Christian pilgrimage is pictured as an ascent up the mountain through the cloud of unknowing to a vision of God.

These mystics resymbolize or rename God. New names are given to God, such as the divine darkness, the absolute good, the eternal now, the silent desert, the infinite abyss, the infinite unity, and the ground of being.

Certain persons and groups have compromised the emphases of New Testament mysticism.

## Meister Eckhart

Johannes Eckhart (1260?-?1327) was a Dominican theologian and mystic and founder of "German mysticism." He is known generally as "Meister Eckhart" or simply "Meister" (Master). He is considered the most important medieval German mystic and one of the most important figures in Christian mysticism.

In 1314, Eckhart went to Strasbourg, where he launched his brilliant career as a preacher and teacher. At around 1322 he went to Cologne. On September 26, 1326, Eckhart was formally accused of heresy. He was found guilty of nearly one hundred counts of heresy. His teachings were said to be dangerous to the common people in their own tongue.

Following Eckhart's death, the papal commission dismissed seventy-one of the charges but found that seventeen works, of which Eckhart admitted preaching fifteen, were heretical. Another eleven were questionable. In 1329 Pope John XXII issued a bull condemning the seventeen works. The bull also said that prior to his death, Eckhart had revoked and deplored the twenty-six articles he admitted preaching that might be considered heretical. Therefore the Pope would not excommunicate him posthumously.

123

In the development of mystical doctrine that borders on synthesis between the soul and God, there is special interest in the teachings of Meister Eckhart. He is quoted endlessly as one clear example of the monistic or pantheistic within Christian mysticism.

For example, Eckhart makes a distinction between God and the Godhead. The Godhead is the very essence of God, beyond all categories and characterizations. Eckhart also, with many different expressions, teaches about the union of the soul with God. It is these passages that have caused much controversy on his thought. He speaks of the birth of God in the soul. He asserts, "Henceforth I shall not speak about the soul, for she has lost her name yonder in the oneness of divine essence. There she is no more called soul: she is called infinite being."[100]

Mystical union between God and the soul is achieved in the soul's depths, from which emanates a spark that unites the two.

Another of Eckhart's fundamental concepts, and among the most controversial, was the birth of the Son in the soul. The Father gives birth to the Son in eternity, and so is always giving birth to the Son. God's ground is the same as the soul's ground, so the Father then gives birth to the Son in the soul. The just person, therefore, takes part in the inner life of the Trinity. This concept formed the basis for Eckhart's teachings about the identity of sonship between the just person and the Son of God. In the condemnation of Eckhart, it was considered "suspect of heresy."

Beginning in the nineteenth century, Eckhart was rediscovered, especially by existential philosophers such as Hegel, Fichte, and Heidegger, who were influenced by him. Later Zen Buddhist scholar D. T. Suzuki compared him to Zen masters.

Eckhart's philosophy, which presumes a living cosmology, has found (along with the works of other medieval mystics) new meaning in the Creation Spirituality pioneered by Matthew Fox, which will be discussed later.[101]

Rudolph Otto sets up a very careful comparison between Eckhart and the Hindu mystic Shankara and finds agreement on all major metaphysical points, for example, the conceptions of God, the soul, and salvation. The only major difference Otto sees is in the fact that Eckhart's thought leads to an active morality, whereas Shankara leads to quietism.

Other scholars say that Eckhart uses hyperbolic rhetoric but is not calling for abstractive union with God which would turn the person away from the reality and consciousness of everyday life. Rather, Eckhart used excessive language in order to sell, not a new and different experience, but the validity of the kind of experience accessible even to the humblest Christian.

100. Ibid., 106.
101. Guiley, *Harper's Encyclopedia*, 174-76.

Corduan, an evangelical theologian, has problems with the emphasis of Eckhart that the experience of union with God is premised on proper preparation by meeting God's moral prerequisites for us. Only then can we receive that gracious experience of God's birth in our souls. But from the evangelical standpoint, Eckhart falls short of the New Testament understanding of God's free grace and our justification as a declaration by God based on Christ's righteousness alone, not ours. Thus we see that Eckhart teaches a modest form of mysticism but within a deficient view of grace.[102]

## ST. JOHN OF THE CROSS (1542-91)

John of the Cross was a mystic in sixteenth-century Spain. Together with Teresa of Avila, John spearheaded monastic reform within the Carmelite order based on severe discipline. He advocated mystical union as the pinnacle of Christian experience.

At age thirty-five St. John of the Cross was kidnapped and imprisoned by unreformed Carmelites. He escaped after two years in prison. Shortly after his escape, he wrote *The Ascent of Mount Carmel, The Living Flame of Love,* and his most famous work, *The Dark Night of the Soul.* These works describe the soul's mystical journey toward God.[103]

John is noted for his doctrines of the "ascent" and the "dark night" of the soul. The soul is purified by the "night of the sense," and, becoming detached from outward forms, it subsists in pure faith. Then there is a "night of the spirit," a second purification, usually with intense suffering. Finally, there is union, in "the living flame of love."

John describes this union in terms of spiritual betrothal, where the soul, conceived of as feminine, is married to Christ as the bridegroom. In other places he may say things that sound almost Hindu Vedantic ("The center of the soul is God"), but it is clear that he does not mean to advocate a unity based on a given identity so much as a union brought about as two lovers unite. The two become one. Love motivates the union, and the union should be sought only as the product of the love, not for the ecstasy of the experience.

For John the soul cannot rely on its reason, but must travel by way of faith, which he describes as "as dark as night to the understanding."

According to Winfried Corduan, John of the Cross and Teresa of Avila sought to provide an alternative to a dry and worldly monasticism. Their exuberance is needed at many other times and places — whenever the church has fallen into formalism and superficiality. But in many other ways their descriptions are open to serious questioning. If the experience John advocates

---

102. Corduan, *Mysticism,* 106-9.
103. Guiley, *Harper's Encyclopedia,* 298.

is the culmination of the Christian life, why is this union and the way to achieve it not taught more clearly in the Bible?

For John of the Cross, only the soul that has passed through the preparatory stages and has truly been purged sufficiently of all attachment to the world, receives grace from God. Thus, whatever the nature of the divine bestowal, it is not God's free gift but at best an exceedingly kind reward.[104]

## Matthew Fox and Mysticism

A controversial contemporary exponent of mysticism is the former Dominican priest Matthew Fox of Oakland, California. He has developed Creation Spirituality, a blend of Catholic mysticism, pantheism, feminism, and environmentalism. In addition to similarities to New Age views on the sacredness of nature, Creation Spirituality suggests as an alternative the New Age mystic-science worldview and an evolution of consciousness similar to the view projected by Jesuit Pierre Teilhard de Chardin.[105]

Fox's philosophy began to take shape in the 1960s, when he went to Paris to earn a doctorate in spirituality at the Institute Catholique. In 1977 he founded the Institute in Culture and Creation Spirituality. This is an avant-garde master's degree program at Holy Names College in Oakland, California. Breaking his last formal tie with Roman Catholicism, Fox left the College of the Holy Names in May 1986 to establish a new independent educational institution, the University of Creation Spirituality. Father Fox was expelled from the Dominican Order in 1993. In December 1994, he became an Episcopal priest. His 1983 book *Original Blessing: A Primer in Creation Spirituality* brought him to public attention.

It is Fox's contention that Christianity is static and decadent and cannot survive into the third millennium in its present form. The original, cosmic mysticism of Christ has been suppressed by a patriarchal, moralistic, and human-centered framework that has wreaked severe psychic damage by alienating human beings from the cosmos, the planet, and each other. This alienation has manifested itself in a hatred of women; child and sexual abuse; drug, alcohol, and entertainment addiction; materialism; and, perhaps most important of all, the destruction of Mother Earth.

Creation spirituality celebrates the blessings of God's creation and not the original sin doctrine of the church. It holds that everyone is a mystic, but humanity has lost touch with this transformative power due to the Newtonian-Cartesian mechanistic, dualistic thought of the Enlightenment. According to

104. Corduan, *Mysticism,* 110-12.
105. Chandler, *Understanding the New Age,* 189.

Fox, Creation Spirituality is the oldest tradition in the Bible, espoused by the prophets and by Jesus. It was at the center of the teachings of the Greek church fathers of the fourth and fifth centuries, and of various medieval mystics, most notably Meister Eckhart, Hildegard of Bingen, Julian of Norwich, and Francis of Assisi. Creation Spirituality also is at the core of mystical traditions both East and West.

Creation Spirituality advocates the rebirth of an earthy, ecstatic mysticism that reveres the feminine principle, sexuality, passion, play, prophecy, creativity, and the divine child within, all of which are diametrically opposed to the orthodox Christian mystical tradition of mortification of the senses. Creation Spirituality embraces panentheism, which holds that God is in everything and everything is in God. It advocates a return of body consciousness in worship, that is, movement and dance; if worship is not playful, it loses its transformative power.

In *The Coming of the Cosmic Christ* (1988), Fox articulates his concept of a Cosmic Christ, as opposed to a historical Jesus, who embodies the aforementioned qualities. The appropriate symbol of the Cosmic Christ is Jesus as Mother Earth, who is crucified yet risen daily. Fox says that in order for Christianity to survive, the church must turn from its preoccupation with the historical Jesus and begin a quest for the Cosmic Christ.

The Cosmic Christ is an archetype, and must be reincarnated repeatedly in the mind and imagination before it takes hold as a force. When it does, a paradigm shift will occur in Christianity. Creativity will become the most important moral virtue; there will be a return of folk art as divine creativity is rediscovered within all people. Fox believes it also will bring an age of deep ecumenism.[106]

In *The Cosmic Self,* Ted Peters notes that Fox's teachings sound similar to New Age teachings, from the divine-human identity to ecological unity and social transformation. Yet Fox himself is not happy about classifying his creation-centered spirituality as "New Age." This is because Fox thinks of himself as in league with the liberation theologians of Latin America, with those theologians who are asking the Christian church to identify with the poor and the oppressed peoples of the Third World. New Age practitioners, in contrast, according to Fox, belong to the bourgeoisie of the First World. This is a class distinction. The New Age belongs to the educated middle and upper classes. If Fox were to identify too closely with the New Age, he might lose credibility among his liberationist friends. So to a reporter he complains, "The weakness of the New Age . . . is that it often seems to me to be fundamentalism for the rich. . . . There's a whole money thing in the New Age which really bothers me. That really goes to the heart of the justice issue."[107]

106. Guiley, *Harper's Encyclopedia*, 122-23, 125-26, 128-29.
107. Peters, *The Cosmic Self* (New York: HarperCollins, 1991), 125-26, 128-30.

Peters notes, however, that despite such protestations, the Fox theology clearly overlaps with New Age themes and relies on many of the same resources. His activities are followed closely in the New Age press under the assumption that they share a common lot.

Fox brought criticism from Catholic leaders because he invited Star-hawk, a self-proclaimed witch, to serve on his teaching faculty. In defending this move, Fox dissolves the link between witchcraft and Satanism. He ties witchcraft rather to nature spirituality — to Wicca — and the sense of whole-ness in nature. For Fox, Wicca's view of nature spirituality is a concept that is very close to his concept of the cosmic Christ, namely, that there is a divine sign in everybody.

Theologian Jane Strohl states that goodness is not already in us to the degree that Fox assumes. The overlooked advantage of the fall/redemp-tion theology is that it acknowledges the activity of God's grace. It recognizes that our turning comes as a gift from God, as the first fruit of the redeeming work of Jesus Christ. In sum, by seeking the ground for hope in human creativity, Fox risks missing it; it lies not only in the divine grace of creation but also in the redeeming grace of God bestowed on us in the Easter resurrection.

As we noted earlier, Fox's approach is to state that the traditional fall/redemption spirituality is mistaken and then proceed to blame nearly all the problems of the secular world on this religious vision. He blames Chris-tian theology for the ecological crisis, for the existence of pain and sin, for the "sin of introspective religion," for fear and lack of trust, and even con-sumerism. Peters points out that, for Fox, theology itself is the source of evil. It should follow from this premise, then, that prior to Augustine, who articulated the doctrine of original sin in the fourth century, there did not exist such things as sin, pain, fear, and consumerism. One may wonder, then, why the Hebrew slaves in ancient Egypt cried out for freedom. One wonders how it was that people of the first century — still existing in Fox's alleged created goodness — could ever get around to crucifying the Son of God. The absurdity of the Fox position is that theology ends up creating the fall rather than reporting on a fall that has already happened. Fox constructs a straw theology because fall/redemption theologians equally affirm the essen-tial goodness of the original creation. We all read the same Bible with the Genesis account in which God pronounces all that he created to be "very good."

Peters also critiques Fox's pantheism. Our world and we human beings within it are not extensions of the divine being. Rather, we are creatures. We come from nothing. We have been created out of nothing. We are the result of a gracious and loving act whereby the divine power authored something brand new. The goodness of the creation comes from God's declaring it good because it is an object of the divine love. It does not have to be divine to be good. It is simply because it is God's creation.[108]

Ron Rhodes evaluates Fox from an evangelical perspective. For example, Fox withdraws from his portrait of Jesus the biblical teaching of his uniqueness. Jesus, according to Fox, is merely one of many enlightened individuals who have incarnated the Cosmic Christ. This means that Christianity is only one of many viable options in the smorgasbord of world religions. Rhodes also indicates that Fox superimposes New Age interpretations on numerous biblical texts. In summary, Fox proposes a "cosmic redemption" related to a revival of mysticism rather than the work of the historical Jesus.[109]

## Pentecostal and Charismatic Transformation

According to William McLoughlin, American culture periodically renews itself by what he terms "great awakenings." These are periods of between thirty and forty years when a fundamental reorientation takes place in our belief or value system, ethical norms, and institutional structures. According to McLoughlin, the period 1960-90 saw the beginning of America's Fourth Great Awakening.

The first Great Awakening began near the middle of the eighteenth century with Jonathan Edwards in Northampton, Massachusetts. The revival spread throughout New England and beyond. The second Great Awakening began during the 1790s in New England with scattered revivals, and gathered momentum into the early nineteenth century. What the late Yale historian Sydney Ahlstrom refers to as the most "cataclysmic" outbreaks of religious enthusiasm occurred in Kentucky at the great camp meetings of 1800 and 1801, including the famous meetings at Cane Ridge.

One of the themes developing in the Awakening is the emphasis on the immanence of the divine as opposed to its transcendence. During awakenings God is felt to be present again in the world — in visions, in sacred utterances and revelations, in charismatic leaders, and in the natural environment.[110]

# PENTECOSTAL AND NEW AGE SIMILARITIES

In a recent book *Fire From Heaven: The Rise of Pentecostal Spirituality and the Reshaping of Religion in the Twenty-first Century*, Harvey Cox, of Harvard

108. Ibid., 128-30.
109. Rhodes, *The Counterfeit Christ* (Grand Rapids, Baker, 1990), 222-23.
110. Lewis and Melton, *Perspectives on the New Age*, 190-91.

University, places the ecstatic spirituality of Pentecostalism in the same religious camp as the psycho-spiritual explorations in the Human Potential and New Age movements. "Their psychology is quite similar — a retrieval of primal spirituality," Cox states. "There are a lot of similarities in the way they try to tap into the experience of awe and wonder with visions, healing, dreams and trance. Both have an experiential core."

After recounting the history of modern Pentecostalism and exploring the world growth of the movement, Cox analyzes the social and psychological forces that shape this ongoing religious revival. He points to the similarities between Pentecostalism and many of the mystic and spiritualist manifestations of the so-called New Age movement. Both, Cox says, should be seen as "experiential" forms of religion, which he contrasts to those of a more "fundamentalist" flavor.

According to this map of the religious landscape, the psychology of the worship experience is what matters to Pentecostalism, not differences in religious doctrine.

"In fundamentalism, there is a circling-the-wagons mentality, a sharp delineation of boundaries, along with a rigid, literal reading of the Scripture," Cox says, "There's more flux in Pentecostalism, more of a blurred boundary. Their worship often borders on the chaotic. Fundamentalism is a closing-down; Pentecostalism is an opening-up."

Cox notes that many who gravitate to the New Age movement tend to be white and come from middle- or upper-middle-class backgrounds. "That's not true of Pentecostals. They tend to be from the lower strata," he states. "But here are millions of people, right down the street, who walk off the sidewalk into a Pentecostal church, where something very similar is going on. But it's not packaged as Buddhist, Hindu or New Age philosophy. The interpretation and framework for these experiences is Christian."

Pentecostal practices such as prophecy or speaking in tongues have a lot in common, Cox adds, with New Age channelers or primal therapy workshops offered at Esalen. Regardless of which class these seekers come from or which religion they profess, Cox sees a similar psychological process at work.

Another religion researcher, Phillip Lucas, has interviewed adherents from both the Pentecostal and New Age camps and notes several striking similarities.

Both see the world on the edge of a radical spiritual transformation, whether it is called the "New Age" or the "millennium," the 1,000-year period of blessedness that charismatic and Pentecostals believe will accompany the Second Coming of Christ.

Both stress spiritual and physical healing through the laying on of hands, prayer, crystals, or other techniques outside medical science. Both arose as movements outside the mainline churches but have grown to the extent that they are now subtly changing the beliefs and worship styles of the religious establishment.

Lucas notes that both movements came of age in the chaotic period of the 1960s and 1970s, with its "broken families, normlessness, alienation and focus on self-fulfillment. Both the New Age and the Pentecostal/charismatic movements have attracted large numbers of these people by offering intensive means for self-healing and its subsequent self-empowerment," Lucas notes. "They both offer a taste of the divine, whether through the Holy Spirit or through meditation." Charismatics are distinct from Pentecostals in several ways. Though they embrace a traditionally Christian theology and worldview, they tend to be more open to modern social currents and experimentation in matters of lifestyle, spiritual practice, worship, and self-therapy than classical Pentecostals.

Many Pentecostals object to being lumped into the same category as New Age spiritualists, or take issue with Cox's description of them as "Christian shamanists." "Pentecostals are serious Christians," asserts Vinson Synan, dean of the divinity school at Regent University in Virginia and one of the nation's leading Pentecostal historians. "The average Pentecostal person would call New Age spirituality demonic."

Nevertheless, Synan agrees with Cox that one of the main reasons for the explosive growth of Pentecostalism is its emphasis on personal spiritual experience, its chaotically democratic nature, and its ability to absorb and Christianize such indigenous beliefs as Korean shamanism or African pantheism.

"This is not a rationalist, intellectual, ecclesiastical movement," Synan goes on. "People experience God more than theologize about God. They feel instant deliverance. Alcoholics and drug addicts are delivered — filled with the Holy Spirit. It's pretty heady stuff for poor people to become instant spiritual giants."[111]

Synan's description and evaluation of the Pentecostal movement is undergirded by David Briggs in his description of the "Fervor in Florida." In one of the most spectacular revivals in modern times, charismatic Christians have flocked to a Gulf Coast church in Pensacola, Florida, four nights a week for twenty months. Their goal: to bring about a spiritual awakening in America before the third millennium.

More than 1.5 million people have attended the revivals at Brownsville Assembly of God since it began on Father's Day 1995. People line up as early as 2:30 a.m. to get one of two thousand seats for evening services.

Little noticed by the mainstream secular and religious media, the

111. Don Lattin, "Exploration of Ecstasy," Religious News Service. Cf. also Harvey Cox, *Fire from Heaven*, 299-321.

Brownsville revival has shaken up the Pentecostal/charismatic world with its return to the movement's roots in emotional worship. Hundreds of pastors visit each week in hopes of learning how they, too, might fill their churches with baby boomers.

"I believe America is ripe for revival," maintains evangelist Stephen Hill. "I believe this is turning into an awakening." America has seen other great moments of religious fervor, in the eighteenth and nineteenth centuries. Hill, a 43-year-old former drug addict and leader of the revival, says that this "very well could be" the third or fourth such revival. Hundreds of people lie prostrate, facedown, wailing. Heaven. Hell. Heaven. Hell. Now people are running down the aisles, stepping over the bodies of teenage girls and middle-age men already "slain in the Spirit."

The Assemblies of God, born in the fires of the Pentecostal movement, had come under some criticism that it was becoming too institutional as the denomination grew and entered the religious mainstream. So far the church's leaders in Springfield, Missouri, have embraced Brownsville as a sign of their own commitment to Spirit-led worship.[112]

# PENTECOSTAL AND CHARISMATIC GROWTH

According to Lucas, Pentecostal refers to those American denominations — including the Assemblies of God, the United Pentecostal Church International, the Church of God (Cleveland, Tennessee), the Church of God in Christ, the International Church of the Foursquare Gospel, and the Pentecostal Holiness Church — that were formed at the beginning of the twentieth century as a result of doctrinal and liturgical controversies within the Holiness movement.

These controversies eventually resulted in the emergence of churches that placed primary emphasis on the doctrine of charismatic gifts following a "baptism of the Holy Spirit," and on spontaneity of emotional expression during worship. After slow expansion through their first forty-five years, these churches began growing rapidly during the 1960s.

The term "charismatic" refers to the movement that began in the late 1950s and early 1960s when members of non-Pentecostal denominations began experiencing a Pentecostal-type "baptism of the Holy Spirit." Those experiencing the baptism for the most part did not join classical Pentecostalist churches but rather sought to renew their own denominations from within.

112. David Briggs, "Fervor in Florida," *Fort Worth Star-Telegram*, March 2, 1997, 10D.

This renewal gained national publicity in the 1960s and spread to such mainstream denominations as Roman Catholic, Lutheran, Episcopalian, and Methodist.[113]

For various reasons, time had become ripe for this new emphasis in established churches. During the 1960s the fruits of the Enlightenment finally became the common property of "ordinary" people. On the one hand, this accelerated secularization, and its repudiation stimulated a new quest for spirituality. On the other hand, societies were going through a process of becoming more democratic, as a result of which the autonomy of the individual citizen increased. This autonomy is honored in charismatic celebrations, in which each person has a contribution to make on the basis of his or her gifts. Increasingly during this period, above all in psychology, physics, the philosophy of science and control of the environment, the limits of the one-sided rational Western approach to reality were becoming obvious. This led to a new evaluation of the experience of faith in Pentecostalism, which is in principle holistic. Both were further advanced by the rise of the mass media such as film, radio, and television. Up to the 1960s, the printed word was the principal means of communication, a means which above all appeals to rational and conceptual thought. By contrast, the modern mass media are rich in imagery and appeal to more senses. They also speak not only to the understanding but above all to the feelings.

However, in the charismatic renewal, even more than in the white Pentecostal movement, holistic spirituality has remained predominantly limited to the personal integration of understanding, feeling, and body. In place of a radical reconciliation between people with skins of different colors and different social backgrounds, here we find above all an unprecedented encounter between members of many different churches and groups. Falling away are not so much racial and socio-economic barriers, but church frontiers. Moreover, the rise of the charismatic renewal has given new stimuli to the development of a doctrine of the Holy Spirit.[114]

The Pentecostal and the charismatic movements have mushroomed into the largest Christian movement of the twentieth century. A Gallup Poll taken in 1979 showed that 19 percent, or 29 million adult Americans, identified themselves as "Pentecostal" or "charismatic" Christians. As documented in David Barrett's 1988 report on the movement, there are now over 176 million Pentecostals and 123 million Protestant and Catholic charismatics worldwide. In North America alone, Barrett documents more than 22.5 million Pentecostals and 43.2 million charismatics.

113. Lewis and Melton, *Perspectives on the New Age*, 193.
114. Jean-Jacques Suurmond, *Word and Spirit at Play* (Grand Rapids: Eerdmans, 1995), 15.

In the United States, one-third of those who identify themselves as Pentecostal belong to one of the three hundred or so historically Pentecostal denominations. Most are quite small, yet the two largest, the Church of God in Christ and the Assemblies of God, claim 3.7 million and 2.1 million constituents respectively. The Assemblies of God, which numbers an additional 14 million followers in overseas affiliates, ranks among the strongest, fastest-growing, and proportionately wealthiest denominations in the world.[115]

It is clear that the Pentecostals are still growing rapidly and show no signs of slowing down in the near future. The number of charismatics is also steadily increasing.

## The Teaching of Spiritual Transformation

The Pentecostal/charismatic movement maintains that it has rediscovered invisible realms of sacred power and an ecstatic, emotional experience of this power. This experience occurs generally in its participant-oriented worship, with religious emotions being freely expressed through upraised hands, dancing, and spontaneous shouts of praise.

Lucas points out that, in contrast to the skepticism regarding the supernatural that has prevailed in mainline religious culture, Pentecostals and charismatics believe that the Holy Spirit intervenes directly in their daily lives, performing tangible miracles. These manifestations of divine grace begin with the foundational "baptism of the Holy Spirit," which Pentecostals believe provides them with the same spiritual gifts as were given to the early Christian community. Those who experience one or more of these gifts understand that they have received the "second blessing" and have visible evidence that the Holy Spirit is now intimately at work in their life. These supernatural gifts include the ability to prophesy, to speak in foreign tongues, to interpret these tongues, to sing in the Spirit, to utter words of wisdom, to discern spirit entities, and to exorcise demons. More than one commentator has attributed the popularity of the Pentecostal/charismatic movement to its ability to transcend dry formalism and to mediate continuing encounters with divine power for its adherents.

The literature of the movement articulates its ideas with a striking language of spiritual forces and empowerments. The Pentecostals affirm that the Holy Spirit makes worship come alive, that the Holy Spirit is not the power stored in unused batteries but a live current running through our every action.

There are several ways in which the movement believes that they experience sacred power and contact noncorporeal intelligence. These include

115. Lewis and Melton, *Perspectives on the New Age*, 193-94.

the phenomena termed "speaking in tongues" and "prophecy." Charismatic writer Don Basham describes speaking in tongues as "a form of prayer in which the Christian yields himself to the Holy Spirit and receives from the Spirit a supernatural language with which to praise God." The "tongues" phenomenon is usually unintelligible to listeners, and so a second person is often required who, also inspired by the Holy Spirit, is able to "interpret" the tongues message for the community of believers.

Prophecy is a gift of the Holy Spirit through which a person speaks in the name of God by giving an exhortation, reporting a vision, providing a revelation, or interpreting a glossolalic utterance. This can take place in various contexts, including speaking out at meetings in English with a message for the group, interpreting a vision one has received in private prayer, or interpreting a dream. Like the information "channeled" to New Agers, the primary content of this "gift of the spirit" can be described as messages of encouragement, consolation, correction, and future direction.

Charismatics envision the spiritual realm as inhabited by angels as well as demons, though angels receive far less attention. Some charismatic groups involve the angels to protect their homes and families from harm.

Writers within the movement such as Dave Hunt warn that communication with any entity that has no physical body, other than Jesus and the angels, is a kind of necromancy that can lead to demonic possession.

By calling the ecstatic utterances of their adherents "prophecies of the Holy Spirit," Pentecostals and charismatics can enjoy the community-affirming experience of spontaneous guidances and revelations from the realm of the sacred while remaining within their traditional biblical worldview. Thus glossolalia, or speaking in tongues, and prophesying are methods of intense, immediate encounter with sacred power and of the reception of "further light" and revelation on both personal and cosmological issues from sacred beings.

The Pentecostal/charismatic movement focuses a great deal of attention on the personal healing and transformation of its adherents. The "second blessing," or "baptism of the Holy Spirit," is viewed as the major transformative event in a person's life. One of the charismata is the gift of spiritual healing, which is usually administered through a laying on of hands. (This hands motif is paralleled in the numerous therapies of "healing hands" used in the New Age movement.)

Following the "baptism of the Holy Spirit" in the charismatic movement, great emphasis is placed on personal growth and the realization of one's potential. By the late 1970s, New Age group dynamics, popular psychology, New Thought teachings, and meditation techniques had permeated both modernist and traditionalist segments of the charismatic movement. Interpersonal honesty and nonverbal forms of communication such as handholding, embracing, and massage were encouraged. Ruth Carter Stapleton, a nationally known charismatic, founded her "holovita" retreat center outside Dallas in

1978, where she offered an eclectic mix of spiritual therapies including directed visualizations and meditation. (Visualization techniques are a common staple of New Age self-help therapy.)

Popular New Thought themes such as positive thinking and achieving personal prosperity had gained such adherence in the Pentecostal/charismatic movement by the mid-1980s that conservative Christian leaders were lamenting: "The people are so engaged in making money, subconsciously mammon has become their god until this has clouded, in many places, the real fervor, fire, and New Testament zeal that comes with Pentecostal experience."[116]

We will deal with the health and wealth emphasis in Chapter 9 on business.

Pentecostals and charismatics make direct appeals to the suffering individual self and promise *personal* healing, happiness, and prosperity. The fact that this is done within a traditionally salvationist perspective does not change its actual effect on, and appeal to, the personal self of its adherents.

Clearly this ability to offer to people what they see as an efficacious alternative means to heal and empower body, mind, and soul is the reason for the continued popularity and growth of the movement.

## CELEBRATION AND MUSIC AND PLAY

Jean-Jacques Suurmond, a former Pentecostal and now a Reformed minister in the Netherlands, contends that the essential contribution of Pentecostal spirituality lies in its playful character. This is evident above all from the charismatic celebration, which is not characterized by either order or chaos but by the dynamics of play. Through the gifts of grace (charisms), everyone has a contribution to make — regardless of race, gender, or status.

According to Suurmond, this play of celebration is the play of Word and Spirit, which is summed up in Scripture in the term Wisdom. In and through this Wisdom, God creates the world to be an eternal Sabbath, the kingdom of God. In it the Word represents order (the rules of the game) and the Spirit the dynamism and interchange (the "enthusiasm") which bring the play to life. This playful, creative dynamic is clearly visible in the life and work of Jesus, in which no one was left out of the game.

However, the established church has usually emphasized order (the Word) at the expense of the Spirit. It opted for the status quo without taking much account of the victims of the prevalent system. At the same time, there have always been charismatic countermovements in which the play of Word and Spirit continued and, for example, women, blacks, and the uneducated were welcomed as equals.

116. Ibid., 194, 196-203.

Baptism with Word and Spirit is the experiential dimension of the life of faith and manifests itself in countless charisms. Only through the power of the gifts of grace to bring about openness can the otherness of the neighbor be welcomed as an enrichment. This makes possible the unity in difference that characterizes the community as the body of Christ. The call of the church is in the first place to play this game of Word and Spirit in charismatic celebration. In this way people are equipped to renew the oppressive political and economic order as a guarantee of the eternal sabbath in which death will be dethroned and God will become all in all.[117]

According to Harvey Cox, music (especially jazz) and Pentecostalism belong together. Each first appeared in one of the great polyglot cities of America, jazz in New Orleans and Pentecostalism in Los Angeles. Each was despised and ridiculed at first, but both then went on to become major vehicles through which the Universal Spirit with a distinctly American accent would reach virtually every corner in the world.

Jazz was born in the early years of this century when African rhythms, secondhand American band instruments, and the hymnody of Southern revivalism — both black and white — all met each other in the steamy back streets of New Orleans. The highly complex counterrhythms, scarcely known before in European music, came with the slaves who also brought work songs, field hollers, and circle shouts. Revivalism, with its strong emphasis on ecstatic song, was already the principal religious practice of most African Americans and of most Southern whites as well. The ingredients that were to coalesce into the new jazz music were all there.

It was in the heady environment of New Orleans that jazz, a powerful new fusion of previously disparate musics, emitted its birth shriek. It has never been quiet since.

Pentecostalism draws on the energies of many of these same ancestors. What we now refer to as "the Pentecostal movement" is largely traceable to the revival that took place under the guidance of William Seymour in an abandoned church on Azusa Street in Los Angeles.

Just as white musicians sought out the French Quarter dives where the blacks were playing jazz, and learned to play it too, at Azusa Street, during a period when segregation was on the increase, white people flocked into a revival in what was in fact a black church, and they were welcomed. For the whites the revival was a thrilling demonstration of novel and refreshing ways of worship. For the blacks, of course, there was nothing terribly new about most of the elements.[118]

For Cox, both jazz and Pentecostalism possess an uncanny capacity

117. Suurmond, *Word and Spirit*, 220-22.
118. Cox, *Fire from Heaven*, 143-45.

137

to combine with indigenous cultural features and still retain a recognizable integrity. In fact, jazz has become the first truly universal music in human history.

Pentecostalism has the same uncanny capacity to be at home anywhere. It absorbs spirit possession in the Caribbean, ancestor veneration in Africa, folk healing in Brazil, and shamanism in Korea.

Indeed, Pentecostalism's phenomenal power to embrace and transform almost anything it meets in the cultures to which it travels is one of the qualities that gives it such remarkable energy and creativity. And the same is true for jazz.

Pentecostalism and jazz also resemble each other in one central characteristic: the near abolition of the standard distinction between the composer and the performer, the creator and the interpreter. The key defining quality of jazz is improvisation.

It is the same with Pentecostal worship. The message of the Bible is taught, sung, and celebrated with heartfelt enthusiasm. The basic chords, as it were, are there. But the message is delivered with a free play of Spirit-led embellishment and enactment.

Even speaking in tongues has its equivalent in jazz, or at least some people claim it does. Music historians are now quite certain that both jazz and the type of music called "gospel" have roots in the "moaning" of early African American worship. "Moaning" is the folk term for the chants and hums — without words — that so often accompanied the singing of hymns and spirituals.[119]

According to Cox, on the debit side of the ledger, both jazz and Pentecostalism have had to contend with an endless succession of fakers, overpublicized buffoons, self-promoters, and cynical exploiters. Both have suffered their share of fallen idols. Among the Pentecostal preachers, the lapse from glory has often been tinctured with stories of sex and greed. Among the jazz artists, drugs and liquor have exacted a terrible toll.[120]

The distinguished American composer and critic Virgil Thompson has described jazz as "the most astounding spontaneous musical event to take place anywhere since the Reformation." Some scholars describe Pentecostalism in the same terms — as "the most important event in religious history since the Reformation." Others believe it marks the rebirth of a more catholic, mystical, even medieval spirituality. In any case, it is well to recall that the religious reform that Luther and Calvin set in motion moved across Europe to the tune of a new kind of music. It was the Bach chorales, congregational hymns, and, later, shape-note singing and gospel songs that carried the mes-

119. Ibid., 146-48.
120. Ibid., 150.

sage to the masses. For Cox, in our time as well, music, including jazz, is still bringing people to Jesus.[121]

## COMMON GROUND

According to Phillip Lucas, both the Pentecostal/charismatic and New Age movements represent attempts to bring an experience of sacred power into the daily lives of ordinary people. The actual means of accomplishing this and the theological models for comprehending these experiences may differ, but the underlying theme remains the same. The emphasis in both movements on personal experiences with sacred power, whether through channeling, speaking in tongues, prophesying, meditation, laying on of hands, or exorcism, can be understood as aspects of this characteristic manifestation of a significant awakening.

Second, both of these movements place a strong emphasis on the healing and inner transformation of the wounded, fragmented modern individual through various nonmedical means.

The long-standing revivalistic belief that "God has yet further light to shed upon his revelations" is reflected in each of these movements' privileging of inner voices, visions, and ecstatic utterances over tradition and dogma. Finally, America's pragmatic concern with thisworldly success and material prosperity is strongly reflected in each movement's acceptance of prayer, positive thinking, or visualization as methods for enhancing the individual's spiritual and material conditions.

Charismatics are distinct from Pentecostals in several ways. Though the charismatics embrace a traditionally Christian theology and worldview, they tend to be far more open to modern social currents and experimentation in matters of lifestyle, spiritual practice, worship, and self-therapy than classical Pentecostals.[122]

## ECSTASY

The evidence suggests that the unusual glossolalia, or speaking in tongues, at Corinth is to be understood as a form of ecstasy. But in biblical experience, ecstasy was not permitted to become the norm. The great Hebrew prophets were descended from their ecstatic predecessors. These prophets retained an ecstatic element in their faith, but it was a minor element. With amazing clarity, they spoke the Word of God in their own words. It is unthinkable that Amos would stand on the street corner in Samaria preaching in an

121. Ibid., 156.
122. Lewis and Melton, *Perspectives on the New Age*, 207-8, 210.

unintelligible tongue. This is substantially Paul's attitude toward the situation in Corinth. He acknowledged that the spiritual upheaval which resulted from union with Christ and the gift of the Holy Spirit could manifest itself in unusual ways. Therefore, he would not forbid glossolalia. However, he insisted that the Christian ecstatics should follow the pattern of the Hebrew prophets and outgrow their childish and immature ways for those which were mature and edifying.

Paul's argument was that they should give up their obsession with glossolalia so as to be open to superior gifts of the Spirit. When God's Spirit is present in power while Christians worship, many people sense his presence so intimately that they know joy which borders on or reaches a state of ecstasy. However, people who have essentially the same experience will respond very differently. While some may silently rejoice and breathe prayers of praise and thanksgiving to God, others may weep silently or audibly. Occasionally, a person will lose emotional composure for a moment and literally shout for joy. Others, equally intent in worship, will make no noticeable response, but may describe the experience in calm, rational, and edifying witness to others. From the biblical perspective, we can assume that each one has been in communion with the Spirit.

If this distinction is valid, it may be helpful. None of those described above should expect the others to respond as they do. Nor should there be any effort to produce any of these exact responses since that would discredit the whole experience.

Glossolalia, or tongues, was one response in Corinth to the gift of the Spirit. It should not be forbidden. Yet as Paul indicates, it is not the most desirable response; it should neither be sought nor encouraged. The reported blessings or benefits from glossolalia are really not from glossolalia itself but from the Spirit. Paul believed that the Corinthian emphasis on glossolalia really prevented them from receiving the more excellent benefits and blessing of the Spirit whose gifts are manifold.

## LESSONS TO BE LEARNED

In Corinth, there was apparently a total outgoing of the personality in worship. For them, worship involved emotional expression. There was great variety, spontaneity, and freedom in the worship services. Evidently there was a widespread and heartfelt participation which has been lost in many churches today.

Contemporary psychological knowledge has revealed that the subconscious or unconscious part of humans is very important. A person's ego and consciousness cannot exist in an authentic way cut off from the vast reservoir of psychic reality and power which the church calls the realm of the Spirit. When religion is alive, it brings the individual into vital contact with the Holy Spirit, the creative center of spirituality.

Tongue-speaking suggests that there should be openness and dialogue on the part of ministers and mature Christian leaders. The Christian worker is to be the Spirit's assistant. The spiritually secure worker knows that the Holy Spirit, and not he himself, is the counselor. Small Christian fellowship groups are important. In these groups people can express and verbalize doubts and problems.

There must be no lack of emphasis on the importance of the indwelling of the Holy Spirit in the Christian's life. Excitement and the joy and victory of spiritual presence are needed in this revolutionary time. But the power is for the sake of service and dynamic Christian witness. The experience with God the Holy Spirit does not mean that we shut out the world and delve into each other's depths as do adolescent lovers. Rather, the Spirit is given to us that we might have joy and power in working under God in his redemptive task.

The late John Mackay, president emeritus of Princeton Seminary, is reported to have said, "If it is a choice between the uncouth life of the Pentecostals and the esthetic death of the older churches, I, for one, choose uncouth life."

But why is there a need for this choice? Surely there can be a synthesis on a higher plane than either. That synthesis is found in a rediscovery of authentic Pauline Christianity.


# CRITIQUE

J. I. Packer suggests that we must not only learn from the Pentecostal/charismatic movement but be discriminating and discerning. The charismatic renewal has brought millions of Christians, including many clergy, to a deeper, more exuberant faith in Christ. It has quickened thousands of congregations, invigorating their worship, making love and fellowship blossom among them, increasing their expectancy and enterprise, and giving a stimulus to their evangelism. Charismatic insistence on openness to God has transformed countless lives that previously were not open to him.

However, the pride and folly of triumphalism and the schismatic temper constantly threaten the movement and need to be guarded against. Some things in the renewal are magnificent, but others are not right yet, and the liveliest Christian movements are naturally the objects of Satan's most diligent attention.

Some attitudes about the renewal among Christians not involved in it are not right either, and Satan loves to lure Christians into opposing the work of God. So the word to Christians, both inside and outside the charismatic movement, would seem to be: "Do not put out the Spirit's fire. Test everything. Hold on to the good. Avoid every kind of evil. The grace of our Lord Jesus Christ be with you" (1 Thess. 5:19-22, 28 NIV).

## THE SUPERIORITY OF BIBLICAL SPIRITUALITY

As we have seen, many people are attracted to New Age spirituality. It is our contention that the aspects of New Age spirituality that are half right, that have some validity, can be found in biblical spirituality as well, but there they are lodged in the proper context. Biblical spirituality not only is more adequate rationally and philosophically than New Age spirituality, but it is also more satisfying and richer emotionally and spiritually.[123]

According to David Clark and Norman Geisler, this superiority can be illustrated in several areas.

People want mystery, awe, inspiration, and wonder in their lives. Humans are not satisfied to live sterile, technological, mechanical lives. These people are attracted to New Age spirituality with its mystical and magical claims.

However, Evangelical spirituality also provides an appropriate sense of mystery and awe. The Christian worships the God of creation, whose majesty and sovereignty exalt the mind and lift the heart. Evangelical spirituality offers a loving relationship with the majestic God that far exceeds what New Agers can find in the Age of Aquarius.

In order to heighten a sense of wonder and worship, the New Age movement uses the left-brain, right-brain distinction to downplay the analytical left brain and highlight the intuitive right brain. However, this mystical New Age emphasis is gained at the expense of a very important dimension of human existence — conceptual thought.

Evangelical spirituality preserves both the mystery of an awe-inspiring God and a basic rationality, both of which are important for a balanced life. The gospel of Christ (1 Cor. 15:1-4) provides both the mystery and awe of a majestic and sovereign God who condescends to love us in our need and gives to us the positive sense of human rationality as a gift from that majestic God to his creatures. In Evangelical spirituality there are the resources both for deep spirituality and for deep understanding.

In our technocratic and impersonal world, many people suffer from

123. David K. Clark and Norman L. Geisler, *Apologetics in the New Age: A Christian Critique of Pantheism* (Grand Rapids: Baker, 1990), 232.

low self-esteem. New Age spirituality offers a solution to these negative feelings. The New Age beliefs tell people that we are not just insignificant specks of dust on an unimportant little planet in an out-of-the-way solar system. We are God — we are part of the divine being.

Evangelical spirituality emphasizes the tremendous worth of each person. Because God created each person in his own image, each one is valuable. The Christian truth of human worth is sometimes misunderstood in Christian teaching because of the emphasis on human sinfulness. But the emphases on worth and sin are both true. And Evangelical spirituality, when it is understood in its fullest sense, maintains both worth and sinfulness in proper balance.

In New Age spirituality, the truth of human worth is exalted without the balancing teaching concerning human sinfulness. The New Age teaches the basic divinity of each human person. If we are all God, we are obviously of great value. And this inference is clear to New Agers. This teaching, however, is purchased at a high cost. New Age spirituality is not realistic in its understanding of human evil. It fails to account fully for the basic, self-centered twist of human nature that afflicts all humans. This egocentrism, the sinful nature, is the source and root of specific sinful acts. In fact, New Age spirituality caters to this self-centeredness with its message of God within instead of dealing with the basic root of evil within us. This New Age emphasis on human divinity develops its emphasis on human worth at the cost of presenting an unrealistically optimistic view of human nature.

In contrast, Evangelical spirituality preserves both the worth and the sinfulness of the human person in magnificent balance. Humans are of great worth to God. But humans are sinful and unworthy of God's favor. Nevertheless, God chooses to help humans.

The central Christian symbol, the cross, portrays both human worth and human sinfulness. It demonstrates that we are of great worth to God because God willingly gave the life of his Son to save us from sin and self. It proves that we are unworthy of God's favor and in need of his work on our behalf because God had to give the life of his Son to save us. In the cross we have a message that emphasizes human value in a way far more profound than New Age spirituality. In addition, it avoids the unrealistically optimistic view of humanness that New Age spirituality promotes.

## The Desire for Hope

The fact that many people are attracted to New Age spirituality reveals that people today crave hope. But the New Age promise for hope and transformation lacks substance. Hope without realism is cruel. Clark points out that Evangelical spirituality offers hope for a genuine personal evil and social transformation and cosmic reconciliation which comes not from us but from God. It is in the cross of Christ that the evil we all experience and long to overcome has already been defeated. Through the cross and resurrection, human values are enhanced and human redemption achieved. In Jesus Christ, the living Water, the thirst for peace and hope that drives the New Age will be quenched.[124]

It is in Jesus Christ and Evangelical spirituality that the thirst for transformation which draws many to New Age spirituality can be quenched and satisfied.

124. Ibid., 232-35.

# CHAPTER FIVE

# Spiritism and Channeling vs. Biblical Revelation and Prophecy

Spiritism and channeling are just different words for the same phenomenon, which can be traced to the beginning of all cultures. Spiritism, as it was known then, became popular in the United States in the mid-nineteenth century.

The word *spiritism* refers to the practice of attempting communication with departed human or extra-human intelligences (usually nonphysical) through a human medium. The intent is to receive paranormal information and/or actually to experience metaphysical realities.[1]

The contemporary eruption of spiritism that began in the 1970s is called the "channeling" movement. New Age educator and psychologist Jon Klimo defines it as "the communication of information to or through a physically embodied human being from a source that is said to exist on some other level or dimension of reality than the physical as we know it, and that is not from the normal mind (or self) of the channel."[2]

According to Russell Chandler, channelers "go into a trance state to establish contact with a spirit, an ascended master, an off-planet being, a higher consciousness, or even an evolved animal entity." The channel then receives and reveals the messages and impressions from the "other side." Since the New Age channeling craze hit — with a big assist from actress Shirley Mac-

---

1. Elliot Miller, *A Crash Course on the New Age Movement: Describing and Evaluating a Growing Social Force* (Grand Rapids: Baker, 1989), 141.

2. Jon Klimo, *Channeling: Investigations on Receiving Information from Paranormal Sources* (Los Angeles: Jeremy P. Tarcher, 1987), 2.

Laine — these mediums have multiplied like hobbits. Earthly requests jam the spiritual wave lengths.[3]

Channeling traditionally includes necromancy: communicating with the spirits of departed loved ones in a seance. In the New Age, however, it refers more often to the process whereby a disembodied teacher communicates occult doctrines to a disciple or group of disciples. J. Z. Knight, for example, goes into a trance on stage, and a spirit entity named Ramtha then speaks to the assembled audience through her voice.[4]

Klimo points out that an increasing number of people are now seeking and following the guidance provided through channeling. Accounts of the phenomenon are sweeping the media. Dozens of new books said to be "channeled" are cropping up in bookstores. Millions of readers have been introduced to the phenomenon through Shirley MacLaine's best-selling books featuring her own dramatic experiences with channels.

Thus channeling can be seen as a New Age form of spiritism. Spiritism was common in pagan religions. But spiritism is distinct from biblical revelation and prophecy.

In all fairness, it should be noted that not all New Age leaders are interested in channeling or approve of some of its emphases. In the flood of channeled material which has been published or delivered to "live" audiences in the last two decades, there is much that is trivial, contradictory, and confusing. The authors of much of this material make claims which are difficult or impossible to verify. However, the main channeled documents have a distinctive New Age core and draw heavily from Buddhism, Vedanta, and New Thought, among other traditions. That core emphasizes the creative potential of humans and promises a significant transformation in consciousness. For many New Agers, this material rivals the Scriptures of historical religions in its inspirational and revelational value.[5]

## History of Spiritism and Channeling

Channeling has apparently been an essential part of the human story from its origins. It can be found in all times and across all cultures. Although it takes different forms or names in different lands, this universal, enduring, and controversial phenomenon has permeated history, providing the wellsprings for virtually every spiritual path. For thousands of years, channeling has taught

3. Russell Chandler, *Understanding the New Age* (Dallas: Word, 1991), 66, 67.
4. Ted Peters, *The Cosmic Self* (New York: HarperCollins, 1991), 28.
5. James R. Lewis and J. Gordon Melton, eds., *Perspectives on the New Age* (Albany, N.Y.: State University of New York, 1992), 107-8.

that physical existence is by no means all there is, and that the life of mind and spirit is more vast than most have led themselves to believe. As we will note, channeling has gone through cycles of acceptance and rejection.

## ANCIENT PERIOD

Clinical and research psychologist Robert Masters is a leading authority on the mystical and paranormal in classic Egyptian culture. "Egypt," he reports, "is where, as far as we know, the use of trance in achieving mystical states and talking to the gods really began." He cites the use of "essential statues" as "kinds of teaching machines used by the priests and priestesses to put them into trance where they could see and communicate with the gods."

Under hypnosis, a number of the clients Masters has seen as a therapist have appeared to channel the Egyptian god Sekhmet. Masters notes that the same god that was channeled thousands of years ago may still be channeled today.[6]

Early Chinese history contains reports of communication with disembodied souls through a divining rod that functioned much like the planchette of a modern-day Ouija board. Emperor Wu of the Han dynasty reportedly received material from a deceased princess that became the basis for the legal system of the time.[7]

In Japan, the first written records of trance possession appear in the eighth century A.D. On the grounds of the great national shrine of Ise, one of the temples is dedicated to the spirit of the Sun Goddess in the form she assumes when she enters and mediates information and guidance through people. A number of early empresses were reported to have become divinely possessed, delivering wise and authoritative messages.

Also in the eighth century, the Shingon sect of Shintoism emphasized channeling. The shaman used a wand, shaped like a zigzag of lightning, to call the god's body to descend into the medium. Then the trance voice of the god was reported.

In India, early Hindu history contains a number of descriptions of channeling. To this day, the Hindus believe that with death the human soul moves into a variety of human or animal bodies for additional lifetimes, according to the degree of evolution of that individual spirit. These persons can be channeled. Theosophy leaders H. P. Blavatsky and Alice A. Bailey are just two of many recent teachers who reported having channeled information that echoes this Hindu view of afterlife and reincarnation.

6. Klimo, *Channeling,* 76, 79.
7. J. Gordon Melton, Jerome Clark, and Aidan A. Kelly, *New Age Almanac* (New York: Visible Ink, 1991), 46.

The Greeks saw the human spirit as having its origin in the divine heavens, unencumbered by the constraints of a physical body. As they told it, a kind of fall had led human beings to their earthly predicament. They practiced various Orphic, Dionysian, and Eleusinian mystery rites in an ongoing attempt to seek communication, redemption, and return to that heavenly home. Philosophers Plato, Pythagoras, Heraclitus, and Plotinus held this doctrine.[8]

Some of the leaders of ancient Greece entered into a trance to permit spirits to speak through them. Socrates himself claimed to have a "semidivine" guide who occasionally dissuaded him from a particular course of action. Plato considered prophecy, as practiced by the priestesses at Delphi and Dodona, to be the noblest of arts.[9]

Throughout the British Isles, the Celtic leaders had a reputation for channeling. Animals and plants were said to act as vehicles for messages from the nonphysical realm.

Among the early Babylonian and Assyrian peoples, spirits of the dead, as well as the gods, could be consulted. Revelations were said to come through divinely inspired men, priestesses, and dreams.[10]

## BIBLICAL OPPOSITION AND ALTERNATIVE

With the rise of the biblical belief in only one God, Yahweh, of the Hebrews and Christians, direct contact with the supernatural became suspect unless it was considered to emanate from God through his chosen prophets. All other sources were termed "familiar spirits," and those who consulted with them were considered "defiled." John, whose visions and messages from Christ are reported in Revelation, cautions humankind to beware of false prophets and not to believe every spirit, but to test them to see if they are "of God" (1 John 4:1-3). The biblical religion did not deny the existence of spirits or other nonphysical, nonhuman entities. Rather, it simply forbade the worship of any but the one God.

As we will point out later, the biblical worldview emphasizes the historical revelation of God through verifiable events and inspired interpretations of their meaning and significance. False prophets were those channels who falsely claimed to mediate the voice of the one God. Perhaps some of them were channels whose sources were beings other than the authorized one

8. Klimo, *Channeling*, 81-82
9. Melton, Clark, and Kelly, *New Age Almanac*, 46.
10. Klimo, *Channeling*, 84.

God. The assortment of local gods, spirit guides, higher Selves, and disembodied humans who were not prophets or apostles but served channels were called "familiar spirits." These channels, the humans who conveyed their messages, were called wizards and witches.

Christians strongly disagree with anyone who says that Jesus was merely a channel. Rather, he was God in human form. Nor is his a case of trance mediumship in which the human body was taken over and used by God. In Jesus' case nothing came through an intermediary; the channel and the source were one. The orthodox Christian view does not deny the humanity of Jesus, but rather affirms that he was fully human and fully divine.

The biblical view affirms the nonphysical spiritual presence of the Holy Spirit, who is also part of the one God. Paul, in 1 Corinthians 12-14, outlines the definitive explanation of the individual Christian's relationship to the Spirit, or to the nonphysical realm in general.[11]

## MEDIEVAL PERIOD

During the so-called Dark Ages of Europe, possession appears in the form of spontaneous, or unintentional, channeling. Entities were said to infiltrate the body of a person against his or her will. Many works of art depicted macabre possessing spirits known as incubi and succubi.

There were episodes in which seers and witches, considered to have been possessed by evil spirits, were condemned to burn at the stake. The most famous of these was Joan of Arc, who, in 1424, claimed to have been directed by angels' voices to go to France and assist in liberating it from English siege.

Nostradamus, who claimed to have received prophetic information in the 1500s, was obliged to disguise those messages in cryptic language, which did not prevent their condemnation two centuries later by the Roman Catholic Church.

While the organized medieval church did its best to keep control with its magnificent cathedrals, crusading armies, and inquisitions, this was mostly a time of spiritual anarchy, superstition, and fear.[12]

## EARLY MODERN PERIOD

One of the best-known eighteenth-century European channels was Comte de Saint Germain, also known as Prince Rakoczy of Hungary. Several modern channels claim they are vehicles for his "ascended master" spirit.

After he appeared many times (Sir Francis Bacon was supposed to be

11. Ibid., 85-86, 88-90.
12. Ibid., 90.

his last incarnation), believers claim Saint Germain ascended as master on May 1, 1684. But begging one last chance to show humankind the error of its ways, Saint Germain returned in 1710 as the Comte de St. Germain to the glittering courts of eighteenth-century France and Germany.[13]

## EMANUEL SWEDENBORG

Emanuel Swedenborg (1688-1772) was a respected Swedish scientist with nearly a hundred scientific publications to his credit. He wrote, at age fifty-six, that he began to have extremely vivid and prolonged visions, voices, sojourns, and visitations. Time and again, he reported, angels visited him and took him in his spiritual body into the nonphysical realm, including heaven and hell, giving him guided tours. In the remaining years of his life, using all the analytical care and descriptive prowess of his earlier technical works, he wrote at least sixteen major books on these experiences.[14]

Swedenborg became convinced that he had been designated by God as a spiritual emissary to explore the higher planes and report his findings back to his fellow men and women, who were woefully ignorant of the truth.

He believed that God created humankind to exist simultaneously in the physical, or natural, world and in the spiritual world. The spiritual world belonged to an inner domain. We have lost the ability to recognize and use this inner domain. The inner domain has its own memory, which is what survives after death. This memory includes an eternal record of every thought, emotion, and action accumulated over a lifetime and influences whether the soul goes to heaven or hell.

The Spiritualists of the nineteenth century adopted many of Swedenborg's views. William Blake, Samuel Taylor Coleridge, Ralph Waldo Emerson, and Henry James are among writers who have used Swedenborgian themes.[15]

Even Swedenborg saw the dangers involved in channeling. He cautioned those who might wish to follow his example to exercise discernment: "When spirits begin to speak with man, he must beware lest he believe in anything; for they say almost anything."[16]

From the perspective of biblical Christianity, Swedenborg ignored the warning in the Bible against all forms of spirit contact (Deut. 18:9-12). The

13. Rosemary Ellen Guiley, *Harper's Encyclopedia of Mystical and Paranormal Experiences* (Edison, N.J.: Castle, 1991), 528-29.

14. Klimo, *Channeling*, 93.

15. Guiley, *Harper's Encyclopedia*, 491.

16. Samuel M. Warren, *A Compendium of the Theological Writings of Emmanuel Swedenborg* (New York: Swedenborg Foundation, 1977), 618.

reason Swedenborg ignored God's warning is that he believed "good" spirits had taught him the truth. Yet the "church" Swedenborg founded as a result of these "good" spirits has ever since promoted spiritistic revelation that is contrary to biblical teaching.[17]

## THE MORMONS

In the United States, during the early eighteenth century, Joseph Smith (1805-44) claimed to have channeled material from an angel named Moroni. This experience led him to seek out revelatory tablets he said he found buried in upstate New York and then to lead his people west to the "promised land." The contents of these tablets (which he said were taken away by an angel) and his interpretations of them became *The Book of Mormon* and, along with two other Mormon scriptures, *Doctrine and Covenants* and *The Pearl of Great Price,* became the foundation of the Mormon church, or the Church of Jesus Christ of the Latter-day Saints.

*The Book of Mormon* claims to represent the history of three different groups of people, all of whom allegedly migrated from the Near East to Central and South America. Two of the groups supposedly traveled as far north as Mexico and North America.

These two groups, the Nephites and Mulekites, were semitic, with the most important group being led by Lehi of Jerusalem. His descendants became the Nephites. The main history of *The Book of Mormon* concerns the Nephites.

According to *The Book of Mormon* and other Mormon scriptures, around 600 B.C. the family of Lehi left Jerusalem. By the time of Christ, his descendants had migrated to North America. Earlier, two of Lehi's sons, Nephi and Laman, disputed and the people took sides. This began two quarreling camps named after Lehi's sons: the Nephites and Lamanites. Nephi was a righteous leader, but Laman was not, which had unfortunate consequences for his descendants. Native American Indians are held by Mormons to be descendants of Laman and, along with blacks, their dark skins were considered, at least in the early years, as a sign of a curse by God (1 Nephi 12:23; 2 Nephi 5:21).

When Jesus rose from the dead, he allegedly came and preached to both these peoples, and they were converted. Christ then established the church. Unfortunately, a few centuries later, the Lamanites renounced their faith and were at war with the Nephites.

*The Book of Mormon* teaches that in A.D. 385, during the final battles

17. John Ankerberg and John Weldon, *Cult Watch* (Eugene, Ore.: Harvest House, 1991), 172.

that wiped out the Nephites (around A.D. 380 to 420), some 230,000 Nephites died near the hill Cumorah in New York (Mormon 6:10-15; 8:2). By A.D. 421 all the Nephites had been killed. Only the Lamanites were left. (These were the supposed "Jewish Indians" whom Columbus discovered in 1492.)

Before this time, one Nephite historian-prophet named Mormon (the commander of the Nephites) had gathered all the records of his predecessors. From them he penned an abridged history of his people — allegedly written on gold plates in "reformed Egyptian." This synopsis by Mormon was largely derived from plates written by Nephi (2 Nephi 5:28-31).

Thus Mormon wrote the "history" of his people from about 600 B.C., when they left Jerusalem, to A.D. 385. He entrusted the plates to his son Moroni, who supposedly finished the history and then hid the accounts in the hill Cumorah near Manchester, New York, around A.D. 421. Fourteen hundred years later Joseph Smith was allegedly led to the same hill by the "angel" Moroni (the same Moroni, now a resurrected being) to discover the gold plates on which Mormon had written.

According to Joseph Smith, God had chosen him to retrieve these plates, translate their stories with the accompanying seer stones, and resurrect the church to prepare for the latter days (before the Second Coming).

By use of magical seer stones (called the Urim and Thummim), the young Smith translated the "Egyptian hieroglyphics" (so they claim) of the Jew called Mormon into English — the result being a perfect translation "by the power of God." This translation, named after its author, became known as "the Book of Mormon."

According to Smith, he would put the seer stones in his hat and pull the hat around his face to simulate darkness. Then a character would appear, as if on parchment, accompanied by the English translation. Smith would read the translation to his friend Cowdery, who wrote it down, then another character would appear in the hat. *The Book of Mormon* was published in March 1830. The "angel" Moroni supposedly reclaimed the plates and stones, with many of the plates still sealed.

On May 15, 1829, Smith and Cowdery prayed in the woods for guidance about the sacrament of baptism. Suddenly, a holy messenger, whom they later determined was John the Baptist, appeared and conferred upon them the Priesthood of Aaron: an ordination, lost for centuries, which gave the men authority to preach the gospel of repentance and baptize by immersion. Smith would be First Elder and Cowdery, Second Elder. Each was commanded to baptize and ordain the other. Not long after, the apostles Peter, James, and John appeared, conferring on them the higher Melchizedek Priesthood, allowing them to lay on hands and perform healing miracles. These revelations established a well-defined apostolic priesthood similar to that of the Catholic Church. Smith organized the Mormon Church on April 6, 1830.[18]

Joseph Smith is viewed by the Mormon Church as a true prophet of God in the biblical meaning of that term. Smith, who had been the recipient of numerous visions and supernatural revelations, felt his divine calling in life was unsurpassed. He believed that the entirety of Christendom was in deep ignorance.

In his own words, Smith confessed, "*I have more to boast of than ever any man had.* I am the *only man* who has ever been able to keep *a whole church together* since the days of Adam. . . . Neither Paul, John, Peter, *nor Jesus* ever did it. I boast that *no man ever did such a work as I.*" *Doctrines and Covenants* 135:3 asserts that "Joseph Smith, the Prophet and Seer of the Lord, has done more, save Jesus only, for the salvation of man in this world than any other man that lived in it."

The tenth president of the Church, Joseph Fielding Smith, said bluntly that there was "no salvation without accepting Joseph Smith" and that a man "cannot enter the kingdom of God" if he rejects the truth of Joseph Smith's prophethood. Brigham Young even claimed that for any man to enter heaven, Joseph Smith's *permission* was required, and that Smith reigns in the spirit world today as supremely as God himself does in heaven.[19]

## TERRIKYO AND JAPAN

On the other side of the world, in the final quarter of the nineteenth century, a twenty-eight-year-old Japanese peasant girl was reported to have received divine revelation in a trance state lasting three days. Afterward, Miki Nakayama was honored by those Japanese who followed the Tenrikyo sect as a god-possessed saint. Her sect was an extension of the ancient channeling-oriented Shingon sect, which in turn had branched off from Shintoism. It is interesting to note what Nakayama channeled from "Tenri-O-no-Mikoto," or "God the Parent":

> I am the Creator, the true and real God. I have the Preordination for this Residence. At this time I have appeared in this world in person to save all mankind. I ask to let Me have your Miki as My living Temple. . . . What I think now is spoken through Her mouth. Human is the mouth that speaks, but Divine is the mind that thinks within. Listen attentively to Me! It is because I have borrowed Her mouth, while I have lent My mind to Her.[20]

18. Guiley, *Harper's Encyclopedia*, 103-4.
19. Ankerberg and Weldon, *Cult Watch*, 10-11.
20. Klimo, *Channeling*, 94.

## THE SPIRITUALIST ERA

Except for the contemporary channeling outbreak, there has never been such a period of channeling activity and interest in it as occurred during the mid-nineteenth century under the name *Spiritualism* (usually termed *Spiritism* in Europe). What we now call channeling was called mediumship during the Spiritualist era, and channels were called mediums. The sources being contacted, almost without exception, in the Spiritualist era were considered to be the spirits of deceased human beings. The distinction is maintained by parapsychologist D. Scott Rogo's definition:

> Mediumship is the art of bringing through spirits of the dead specifically to communicate with their relatives. Channeling I define as bringing through some sort of intelligence, the nature undefined, whose purpose is to promote spiritual teachings and philosophical discussion.[21]

The Spiritualist period represented a powerful resurgence of activity and interest in channeling. According to Jon Klimo, by the mid-nineteenth century — the start of the Spiritualist era — there was a loosening of and a turning against the results of the materialistic and rationalistic worldview that had been dominant since the seventeenth-century Enlightenment. This led to a disposition toward transcendental or nonmaterial realities. Klimo also points out that human history is punctuated with both local and global periodic cycles of movement toward the physical realm as the primary reality, or toward inner, or spiritual, superior realities and truths. Spiritualism and the present wave of channeling activity would appear to be two of the most wide-scale moves in this spiritual direction.[22]

## ANDREW JACKSON DAVIS

Andrew Jackson Davis, the person who would come to be called the first prophet of Spiritualism, was born in New York in 1826. Like Joan of Arc before him, he claimed to have received his first channeling while out walking in a field. During these early experiences, he thought he was in communication with the spirits of Galen, the ancient Greek healer, and Swedenborg, who had died fifty years earlier.

Davis's multivolume published work was given the name *The Harmonial Philosophy*. All of the channeled material of this period, including Davis's, describes the basically spiritual rather than physical nature of human beings and of the universe at large. It is rich with descriptions of the afterlife

21. Miller, *Crash Course*, 145.
22. Klimo, *Channeling*, 95.

provided by disembodied human beings said to inhabit it. The majority of the Spiritualist material claims to be detailed private communications from deceased loved ones and relatives, directed at those seeking them out by way of the services of mediums. In 1851 there were an estimated 1,200 mediums in Cincinnati, Ohio, which was a center, as well as hundreds of mediums in other major cities. By 1855, America boasted several thousand mediums and some two million followers. These channelers and their followers became the foundation for an entire century of parapsychological research, or scientific study of the occult, in our country.[23]

## FOX SISTERS

The modern renaissance of widely publicized mediumship or channeling that has been labeled the Spiritualist movement was launched in 1848 in a modest Hydesville, New York, farmhouse belonging to John Fox. Rappings on the wall, presumed to be from an itinerant peddler who had been murdered on the premises and buried under the house, attracted great crowds, eventually giving rise to a transatlantic obsession with contacting "the Other Side."

The press reported the upstate New York occurrences throughout the country and abroad. In November 1849, the first meeting of "Spiritualists" was held in Rochester, New York. Meanwhile, dozens of others claimed to be capable of facilitating coded information by way of physical mediumship, as the Fox sisters did. Seances became common, complete with rappings and table tippings. "Sensitives" (people believed to be naturally endowed with the "gift" of mediumship) would "go into trance" so that people in attendance could make contact with their departed loved ones. "Automatic writing" (in which the medium's hand writes material not originating from his or her conscious mind, as though a spirit were in control) also became popular. Organizations like the Society for Psychical Research in Britain were formed in the interest of verifying the phenomena. Well-known people were drawn to the phenomenon, such as authors James Fenimore Cooper and William Cullen Bryant, plus a host of notable academics, judges, politicians, physicians, and ministers.

As Spiritualism spread, it attracted primarily housebound women into mediumship. Evidently it provided relief from a narrow existence. Mediumship gave these women attention and, most important, freedom: freedom of movement and travel and freedom for outrageous behavior "caused" by the spirits.

Women comprised most of the mediums who took to the lecture circuit and delighted in shocking their audience with deep trance voices and theatrics.

23. Ibid., 96-97; Ankerberg and Weldon, *Cult Watch*, 167.

Some mediums engaged in affairs under the direction of their spirits. Those who bore illegitimate babies sometimes claimed the infants were "spirit babies" produced by consorting with their controls. Others said their controls ordered them to leave their husbands and to counsel other women to divorce their husbands as well.[24]

The years passed and Spiritualist incidents and their investigators numbered in the thousands, including a committee of noted Harvard scientists who engaged in considerable observation and questioning but disagreed on their findings and refused to publish.

The Fox sisters' reputation began to sink, and it was not the outside investigators who did the most damage. Margaret Fox reportedly broke down and confessed to a friend that the sisters had arranged with a Dutch servant girl to hide in the basement and do their rapping for them. Margaret published a letter in the New York *Tribune* in which she severed her ties with Spiritualism and claimed the whole thing had been a fraud. A year later, Margaret completely reversed herself, saying that the initial fraud exposé was done for money, under the influence of anti-Spiritualists. Shortly thereafter, within three years of one another, all three sisters died. But Spiritualism did not die with them. By this time, those who had become convinced of the authenticity of channeling, based on personal investigation, had grown to constitute a small army of dedicated Spiritualists on both sides of the Atlantic.

The Spiritualist movement peaked shortly after World War I. Sociologist Geoffrey K. Nelson attributes the decline to fraud and deception, attacks by traditional churches that branded it as demonic, a hostile press, and insufficient organization, doctrine, and ritual.[25]

Recently the *New York Times* published a story on Lily Dale, a center of Spiritualist activity in New York. The home of the Fox sisters had been moved to Lily Dale and showcased as a Spiritualist museum until it burned in 1955.

## DANIEL DOUGLAS HOME

The most extraordinary of Spiritualist manifestations of this period occurred during seances conducted in the 1850s and 1860s by a Scottish immigrant named Daniel Douglas Home (1833-86). Home engaged in light as well as full-trance channeling. During his sessions, various objects (including a ghostly pair of hands) would reportedly materialize or levitate to the ceiling for private audiences, which included Napoleon II, Prince Metternich, Czar Alexander II, Leo Tolstoy, Alexander Dumas, and Elizabeth Barrett Brown-

24. Guiley, *Harper's Encyclopedia*, 358-59.
25. Klimo, *Channeling*, 99-100.

ing. On one occasion, Home demonstrated the ability to handle live coals unharmed, and an entity spoke through him, declaring, "Mankind ought to have the same power over the material world in which he lives; you little know the power that is in you; had you faith, you could do things you little dream of." His message broadly addressed the nature of evolution and the concept of reincarnation.[26]

## MODERN SPIRITUALISM

The modern Spiritualist churches continue the tradition of this original movement. They often employ many of the outward trappings of Christianity (for example, church services with sermons, evangelical hymns, and so forth) while remaining pantheistic ("everything is a part of God") at their theological core. They also have a strong emphasis on universalism (that is, that there is no hell — everyone will be saved).

Mental mediumistic skills are employed by Spiritualist pastors, who sometimes deliver their sermons in trance. Other main church activities include seances, which usually feature communication with spirits; psychic readings called "spirit greetings" for members; spiritual healing; and the teaching of psychic and mediumistic skills and meditation techniques. Some Spiritualists discourage communication with the dead in favor of contact with highly evolved entities and spiritual masters.

Healing is of particular importance in Spiritualism. Spiritualism considers itself a science because it investigates and classifies spirit phenomena. From a philosophical standpoint, Spiritualism studies the laws of nature of both the physical and spirit worlds, and maintains that mediumship and parapsychology have proved that mediums may obtain information through channels besides the five senses.

Spiritualism enjoys a larger following in Britain, with thousands of churches there, than it does in the United States.[27]

## BISHOP JAMES PIKE AND SPIRITUALISM

Spiritualism became a challenge to the Christian churches in the 1960s when Episcopal Bishop James Pike sought to make contact with his deceased son in a seance. As a confirmed liberal, he was tried by his church for heresy over his denial of Jesus' virgin birth and of the doctrine of the Trinity. He lost his son, Jim Jr., first to the hippie drug culture of Haight-Ashbury, then to suicide. Deeply saddened at the tragedy, Pike went to Cambridge, England, and sought

26. Melton, Clark, and Kelly, *New Age Almanac*, 47-48.
27. Guiley, *Harper's Encyclopedia*, 571.

out medium Ena Twigg. Twigg went into a trance and the voice of Jim Jr. purportedly spoke, referring to his father as "Dad" and speaking of his own failure in life. After returning to the United States, the bishop continued conversations with him through a Santa Barbara medium, George Daisley. Then in 1967 he participated in a dramatic television broadcast in which medium Arthur Ford allegedly brought the voice of Jim Jr. to the viewing public. Jim Jr. brought greetings from many deceased in the Pike family as well as other known clergymen and theologians.

*Newsweek* was sympathetic yet caustic. In its reporting, the national magazine described the seances as unconvincing, noting how Jim time and time again told Pike exactly what a grieving and guilty father wants to hear — that Dad is an OK fellow and in no way responsible for the suicide. Conservatives became hostile and vitriolic. In an attempt to diminish the rising opposition, Pike published a book to express his views, *The Other Side*. It sold seventy-five thousand copies in hardcover and two million in paperback. In its review, *Time* magazine drew out a touch of irony by telling readers to ask themselves why a bishop who had been so skeptical of the received Christian tradition should so readily accept the assurance of asserted spiritualists that there are cats in the afterlife. As for the dead Jim, the *Time* review said he appeared in the book to be so vague and formless as to seem like nothing more than a loving father's wish fulfillment.

With his third wife, Diane Kennedy Pike, the bishop withdrew from the Episcopal church and started a foundation to assist others who find themselves in religious transition.[28]

## MADAME BLAVATSKY AND MODERN CHANNELING

Elliot Miller contends that the founding of Theosophy in the nineteenth century provided the transition toward modern channeling. Instead of transmitting messages from "Uncle Harry" or "George Washington," Madame Blavatsky (1831-1891) began to receive and transcribe spiritual teachings from superhuman "masters," or "mahatmas," allegedly living in the Himalayas. With its evolutionary and hierarchical view of the universe, and its blending of diverse Eastern and Western religious sources, the resulting material (including her two chief works, *Isis Unveiled* and *The Secret Doctrine*) laid the foundation for the modern New Age belief system. In September 1875, Madame Blavatsky and others formed the Theosophical Society.[29]

*The Secret Doctrine*, Blavatsky's most important book, combines a number of ideas drawn from Indian philosophy and the occult, especially ideas

28. Peters, *Cosmic Self,* 29-31.
29. Miller, *Crash Course,* 146.

like monism, karma, and reincarnation. It teaches that all persons participate in a single divine consciousness and that salvation on earth will be accomplished gradually through a further evolution of this consciousness. According to Blavatsky, this evolutionary advance is being guided by a divine plan and paced through a history of what are called "root races." This divine plan is being supervised by perfected individuals called the Masters of the Wisdom, masters who channel this wisdom to humanity through their chosen medium, Mme. Blavatsky.

*The Secret Doctrine* introduced the notion that a "sixth root race" would eventually arise, originating most probably in Southern California, and would develop a new human faculty — called in Sanskrit the buddhi quality — that would enable these people to perceive the truth that everything is God. This sixth root race would then lead the peoples of our planet into a new civilization that would be characterized by brotherhood, love, and peace.

Madame Blavatsky (known as HPB) saw thinkers and writers such as herself as the recipients of thought transference in channeling inspiration from "more evolved spirits," both embodied and disembodied. She saw this as a matter of two sympathetically related minds being "tuned to respond magnetically and electrically."

Although Blavatsky wrote of human masters and beings on other levels of reality, she claimed that *her* guides, responsible for the essential content of her published work, were incarnate spirits. She suggested, however, that they could move in and out of embodiment at will and were as much at home on nonphysical as physical levels of reality.

It should be noted that the Society for Psychical Research studied Madame Blavatsky's claims and did her the honor of dubbing her "one of the most accomplished, ingenious, and interesting imposters of history."[30]

Interest in Theosophy developed rapidly, particularly in higher social circles, as excitement about spiritualism began to decline, and thus a host of imitators appeared on the scene. In 1889 Blavatsky wrote:

> Every bogus swindling society, for commercial purposes, now claims to be guided and directed by "Masters," often supposed to be far higher than ours! . . . Only fourteen years ago, before the Theosophical Society was founded, all the talk was of "Spirits." They were everywhere, in everyone's mouth; and no one by any chance even dreamt of talking about living "Adepts," "Mahatmas," or "Masters."[31]

The influence of Theosophy has been significant. The Theosophical Society is still active and exerts influence through its various spinoffs, including

30. Peters, *Cosmic Self,* 48-49.
31. Miller, *Crash Course,* 146.

the Anthroposophical Society founded by Rudolf Steiner, the teachings of Alice Bailey and Krishnamurti, and groups based on the channeled messages of voices claiming to be "ascended masters," such as the "I AM" Religious Activity and the Church Universal and Triumphant. Like Blavatsky, these groups disparage communication with departed loved ones in favor of contact with entities who are presumed to be more highly evolved than humankind is, and therefore are qualified to act as teachers from higher planes of reality.[32]

### Alice Bailey and the Arcane School

Alice Bailey (1880-1949) was originally an English theosophist who broke from the society in 1920 yet continued her own version of theosophical teachings until nearly mid-century. As founder of the Arcane School, Bailey claims that through her the "Tibetan master Djwhal Khul (D.K.)" wrote twenty-five books between 1919 and 1949. A new cosmology emerged from this "occult" school channeled by Alice Bailey. According to the elaborate scheme taught by Bailey, humankind (and the universe as a whole) is constantly evolving and exists simultaneously on seven levels, these being the physical, the astral, the mental, the buddhic, the nirvanic, the monadic, and the divine.

Another emphasis of Bailey was the coming "reappearance of the Christ" in the form of a new world teacher or era, and the need to prepare for that event by guided meditation. It was, one might say, eschatological Theosophy. Followers of the Alice Bailey tradition meet at every full moon for the work of group meditation.[33]

Bailey also bequeathed to our era "The Great Invocation," a prayer designed to invoke the presence of the combination Maitreya-Christ figure now used by many New Age groups.

### I AM Movement

Another Theosophical offshoot, the I AM religious movement, emphasized the importance of light (a common element in many reports of mystical experience) and added an emphasis upon the spiritual (occult) significance of color. The attention paid to color, especially as experienced in the light of gems, underlies the love of crystals in recent decades.

The "I Am" movement was founded by Guy W. Ballard (1878-1939) and his wife, Edna W. Ballard (1886-1971). Guy Ballard reported that, in 1930, he encountered one of the Theosophical Masters, Saint Germain, on

32. Melton, Clark, and Kelly, *New Age Almanac*, 48-49.
33. Timothy Miller, ed., *America's Alternative Religions* (Albany, N.Y.: State University of New York, 1995), 321.

the slopes of Mount Shasta in California. The experience and teaching are presented in *Unveiled Mysteries* (1934). The I Am activity offers a combination of New Thought-type teaching on the power of mind with Theosophy and colorful accounts of Ascended Masters.[34]

### The Aquarian Gospel of Jesus Christ

In 1907, Levi Dowling published *The Aquarian Gospel of Jesus the Christ,* which purportedly was channeled from the Akashic records (purported cosmic records of all happenings) through Visel, "the Goddess of Wisdom, or the Holy Breath." *The Aquarian Gospel* claims that Jesus studied with the Brahmans and the Buddhist wise men, as well as with a Persian sage, and that he preached to the Athenians before joining a sacred Egyptian brotherhood at Heliopolis. Then he brought back these teachings to Palestine. According to Levi, the reason we normally do not associate such teachings with Jesus is that the established churches with their orthodox theology have conspired to keep his knowledge from the general public. How does this relate to the New Age? It is important because contemporary New Age advocates want to draw the connection between Jesus and the Asian spirituality they promote. The use of Jesus' name just may give Hindu and Buddhist doctrines credibility to Western audiences.[35]

## EDGAR CAYCE AS A CHANNELER

Edgar Cayce is probably the most widely known American channel. By the time of his death in 1945, he had become known to millions as the unassuming, rather colorless gentleman who could lie down, "go to sleep," and "see" into the distant bodies of strangers seeking his diagnosis and advice about their health. Dozens of Cayce books are still in print.

Born in Hopkinsville, Kentucky, in 1877, Cayce began his unusual work around the turn of the century. After he mysteriously lost his voice, a doctor suggested that Cayce learn to hypnotize himself to deal with the symptoms. Between then and his death, some 30,000 case records accumulated of what Cayce said during self-induced trance states. These have been cataloged and made available by the Association for Research and Enlightenment (A.R.E.) in Virginia Beach, Virginia, an organization set up to continue the study and dissemination of Cayce's work.[36]

Cayce's procedure was unique. He was not a medium in the usual sense.

---

34. Ibid., 321.
35. Peters, *Cosmic Self,* 87–88.
36. Klimo, *Channeling,* 113.

He generally did not use an identifiable intermediary "spirit guide" or "entity," but "channeled" from a source he termed the Akashic record. (The Akashic realm, a concept derived from Hinduism through Theosophy, is believed to be a cosmic information record of all that has happened. These records are purported to travel on waves of light.) Also, Cayce's voice remained his own while he channeled. He did, upon occasion, however, relay messages concerning problems with a person's previous incarnations.

Cayce was a simple man and a professing Christian. When he first discovered that he had referred to reincarnation in his readings, he was quite upset. He eventually came to accept this teaching, however. He attempted to use Bible verses to help reconcile himself to the idea that people have more than one lifetime on Earth, and that accountability for one's actions extends from one lifetime to the next.

According to W. J. Hanegraaff, over the years Cayce's conservative Christian beliefs have been increasingly ignored while the esoteric aspects of the material have been emphasized. Although Cayce lived long before the emergence of the New Age movement, the books based on his readings have crucially influenced the development of the New Age. They have been popular at least since the 1960s and have remained so up to the present. Many of the more recent books based on his readings are fully representative of modern New Age thought.

The question remains as to what extent his manner of conveying information can be called channeling. Cayce only occasionally channeled personified sources (notably the archangel Michael). Normally no individual source was identified, but it is widely believed by Cayce's supporters that he in fact tapped into the collective unconscious of humankind. The Cayce phenomenon remains a borderline case with regard to the source of the information. However, Cayce is normally regarded as a channel in the New Age context.[37]

## CHANNELING ENTERS THE NEW AGE

As we have noted, the New Age movement has exploded since the 1970s. Related to this explosion is the extraordinary upswing in public interest in channeling. In the last few years, tens of thousands of people have sought out channels privately or in workshop situations. Millions more have read material or have listened to or viewed tapes said to be channeled.

37. Melton, Clark, and Kelly, *New Age Almanac*, 49. Cf. also W. J. Hanegraaff, *New Age Religion and Western Culture* (Leiden: Brill, 1996), 35-36.

During the late 1960s and 1970s, many were preoccupied with a questioning and a searching for something beyond the material realm, giving rise to what has become known as the New Age movement. Then, to many observers, that era seemed to run its course, and it was back to work in the vineyards of a reality focused on acquiring material things. So what kind of changing cultural climate now allows material like the *Seth* books and *A Course in Miracles* to be received so enthusiastically? Is this a sign of deep and lasting cultural and psychological changes to come or just another passing fad? Considering that channeling, in some form or another, has been with us throughout recorded history and in all cultures, fad doesn't seem to fit the longer-range facts. But why this widespread reemergence of the phenomenon and strong interest in it today? What unmet needs does channeling hold out the promise of fulfilling?

According to New Age psychologist Jon Klimo, the answer may lie in a need for personal meaning in life that cannot be satisfied by material existence alone. Perhaps as a species we can go only so long adhering to a strictly material interpretation of reality. We may be too imaginative and creative to stick for too long to only the facts of the five senses for our basis of ultimate reality. With the current renaissance of channeling activity and interest, we appear to be in the midst of yet another round of experiences that seem to transcend (and, for some, to threaten) the usual sense of reality based on science.[38]

## JANE ROBERTS AND "SETH"

It is generally agreed that the modern era of channeling was born with the appearance in the early 1970s of the first series of books channeled through author Jane Roberts from an entity calling itself "Seth." Seth described itself as "an energy personality essence no longer focused in physical reality." Several of the Seth books became best-sellers, confirming that the concept of communication with intelligences that have no bodily form or other dimensions of consciousness had become immensely popular.

With the writings of Jane Roberts purportedly channeled from Seth, channeling replaced the term mediumship. This was possibly because of the charges of fakery so widely publicized in connection with American spiritualists, and perhaps because the sources contemporary channels typically contact claim to be more evolved than recently deceased relatives. In addition, their message is often more universal in scope.[39]

38. Klimo, *Channeling*, 27-28.
39. Melton, Clark, and Kelly, *New Age Almanac*, 50.

On an early September day in 1963, in her apartment in Elmira, New York, thirty-four-year-old aspiring poet and novelist Jane Roberts first encountered channeling. It was to remain at the center of her life until her death in 1984. As she recalls, it was "as if someone had slipped me an LSD cube on the sly." Having had no more than a couple of fleeting psychic experiences before then, she was overwhelmed by the new phenomenon: "A fantastic avalanche of radical, new ideas burst into my head with tremendous force, as if my skull were some sort of receiving station, turned up to unbearable volume."

Shaken yet inspired by this strange episode, Jane and her painter husband, Robert Butts, decided to embark on a book about developing ESP power. They started by experimenting with the Ouija board. After a few sessions, they were able to receive messages through the board from someone who initially identified himself as "Frank Withers." Soon, however, "Withers" further described himself as a fragment of a larger entity. "I prefer not to be called Frank Withers. You may call me whatever you choose. I call myself Seth. It fits the me of me, the personality more clearly approximating the whole self I am, or am trying to be."[40]

This was the beginning of the teaching career of "Seth." With her husband, Rob, taking verbatim shorthand dictation, twice a week Roberts would go into a trance and allow Seth to expound on metaphysical and physical subjects such as "the nature of physical matter, time, and reality, the god concept, probable universes, health, and reincarnation." Portions of the resulting voluminous "Seth material" were organized into several books, including *The Seth Material* (1970) and *Seth Speaks* (1972). Roberts also channeled a few books from other entities, and wrote a few more herself before she died in 1984.[41]

Throughout her twenty-year career of channeling "Seth," Jane was always questioning the true nature of the phenomenon and whether "Seth" was merely part of her own psyche. On occasion, she deferred to the extraordinary source that "Seth" represented without actually deeming him a separate being.

In the introduction to her second "Seth" book, *Seth Speaks*, Roberts discusses the distinction she made between material emanating from her self and that from beyond, distinctions that call on her sensitivities as a creative writer.

On a few occasions, Roberts channels an entity she later refers to as "Seth Two." It appears that "Seth Two" is a group entity that contains "Seth."

Besides "Seth" and "Seth Two," Roberts also claimed to channel two other sources: the nineteenth-century French impressionist painter Paul Cézanne and the American psychologist and philosopher William James.

40. Klimo, *Channeling*, 29-30.
41. Elliot Miller, *Crash Course*, 147-48.

The main emphasis of the "Seth" literature is that we each create our own reality by our beliefs and desires. We do this as one of many experiencing personalities, each within its own respective level of reality, and each part of a larger reality that is also learning and evolving. This is a common New Age emphasis.[42]

Miller notes that the Seth writings have attracted a readership numbering in the millions. This attraction can be explained by pointing to the exceptional qualities of both Roberts as a medium and the material she channeled.

Unlike the stereotypical medium, Roberts was intellectually engaging, articulate, personally believable, seemingly modest and unambitious when it came to her own personal following, and comparatively objective and non-dogmatic about her experiences with the beyond.

The Seth material itself stands out as perhaps the most intellectually sophisticated and therefore believable of all spiritistic revelations. It has helped many one-time skeptics to accept the plausibility of such phenomena. The Seth books were a milestone because they were produced by Prentice-Hall, a respected general-market publisher. Earlier spirit scribes had mostly been printed by obscure specialty houses. When the Seth venture proved successful, more such writings began to appear from major publishers.[43]

Following the death of Roberts, other channels appeared who claimed to be channeling Seth. The most well-known of them is Thomas Massari, founder of the Seth-Hermes Foundation, who claims to have been channeling Seth since 1972. In recent years a host of new entities have cropped up, all repeating in their own individualized (and usually far less sophisticated) terms the basic message of the Seth material: "You create your own reality." This self-creation concept is a foundational emphasis of the New Age movement that was probably first introduced by Roberts and Seth. According to Hanegraaff, it is hardly an exaggeration to say that Jane Roberts is regarded as the Muhammad of New Age religion, and Seth is its angel Gabriel. Without their metaphysical teamwork, the face of the New Age movement of the 1980s would not have developed as it did.[44]

According to Miller, Seth opened a new chapter in the history of American spiritism. It would soon become common for a disembodied entity to be better known than his or her channel. By means of Seth's popularity the idea of receiving spiritual instruction straight from the Other Side (rather than through some human guru) caught on. This meant that it was no longer

42. Klimo, *Channeling*, 31-34.

43. Brooks Alexander, "Theology from the Twilight Zone," *Christianity Today*, September 18, 1987, 26.

44. Elliot Miller, *Crash Course*, 148. Cf. also Hanegraaff, *New Age Religion*, 126.

necessarily important how spiritually qualified an individual was to teach, since in the case of channels it was believed that a different, far wiser personality was actually doing the thinking. But it should be noted that the person who offered his or her body to the spirit world for such use was still capable of reaping the fame and fortune that often follow spiritual stardom. A new vista of opportunities was opening for the many — particularly since it was not fashionable to believe that channeling was not a "gift" reserved for a select few, but a natural human potentiality that could be awakened and cultivated by all.[45]

This means that contemporary channeling is particularly democratic in character. Unprecedented numbers of individuals of all walks of life and socio-economic backgrounds are engaging in channeling activities and, by extension, increasingly varied populations are being exposed to the phenomenon. This exposure comes through workshops and loosely formed networks that exchange audio- and videotapes, newsletters, and periodicals. A number of channels offer channeling classes, claiming that just about anyone can learn to channel. The popular rejection of the old idea that only a select few (like Blavatsky and Bailey) are chosen as mediums marks a key difference between the contemporary channeling scene and the previous era of Theosophical-style mediumship.[46]

Channeling has gone public. Channels claim to be receiving messages from entities at New Age expositions and fairs, in front of large audiences in hotel ballrooms, and even before the entire nation on television and radio. Although teaching remains their primary function, they now also provide counseling services, answer questions on call-in radio programs, and engage in witty dialogue with television talk show hosts.

There are hundreds of channels. Los Angeles is estimated to have about a thousand channelers. As a result of heavy media exposure in recent times, the names of certain channels and their entities are becoming somewhat recognizable to the American public. It will be helpful to look at three of the most representative channels and their entities, and briefly mention a sampling of other lesser-known but still popular personalities.[47]

## J. Z. KNIGHT AND RAMTHA — KEY INFLUENCE

Undoubtedly the most famous entity is Ramtha, channeled by J. Z. Knight. Knight was born Judith Darlene Hampton on March 16, 1946, in Dexter, New Mexico, the daughter of Helen Printes and Charles Hampton. The

45. Elliot Miller, *Crash Course,* 148-49.
46. Ibid., 149.
47. Ibid.

family was poor and her father was an abusive alcoholic. Thus, Knight moved often in her childhood, living in several towns in Texas and New Mexico. Soon after graduating from high school, she married and settled into life as a housewife. After a divorce, she married J. Mark Burnett. They were living in Tacoma, Washington, in 1977 when Knight allegedly was first contacted by Ramtha.[48]

Knight has a Baptist background and "once claimed she had read the Bible, front to back, at least six times." At some point in her fundamentalist experience, Knight suffered a change of attitude:

> "I saw a lot of people condemned because they wore lipstick or they danced, or things like that," she remembers. Or because they were black, she adds. She loved God and the emphasis on fear dismayed her.
>
> Soon after attending a bristling Baptist revival that thoroughly frightened her, J. Z. had what she believes may have been her first psychic experience.
>
> At an eighth-grade slumber party, she looked out the window to see a huge, pulsating, blood-red object — oddly reminiscent of the preacher's warning that when the devil came, the moon would turn to blood.

Intense though those experiences were, J. Z. doesn't remember any particularly notable occurrences until Ramtha came into her life.[49]

According to Knight's account, she and her husband had been making pyramids, having heard that food placed under a properly aligned pyramid would be dehydrated and preserved. In the midst of their activity, Ramtha appeared. In answer to her question, "Who are you?" he replied, "I am Ramtha, the Enlightened One, and I have come to help you over the ditch." He further explained that "the ditch is limited thought." After a period of confusion, which included the belief that she had been contacted by the devil, Knight found her way to a spiritualist church. There she met Lorraine Graham, who helped her develop an understanding of the initial contact and of making future contact. Ramtha appeared frequently to teach Knight, and she soon emerged as a medium capable of entering a full trance and channeling him. Ramtha worked with her for a year and a half. She held her first public session channeling him on December 17, 1978.[50]

Ramtha claims to be a 35,000-year-old "Lemurian" warrior-king who conquered fabled Atlantis and made his way into India before becoming enlightened and ascending to the higher planes — to be later exalted as the Hindu god Rama. A change occurs in the feminine and seemingly fragile

---

48. Melton, Clark, and Kelly, *New Age Almanac*, 65.
49. Elliot Miller, *Crash Course*, 150.
50. Melton, Clark, and Kelly, *New Age Almanac*, 65-66.

Knight when Ramtha takes over her body. Her movements, expressions, and voice take on a decidedly masculine quality. An unearthly perspective and insight into the lives of complete strangers is demonstrated. A radically different personality consistently comes through, with its own distinctive message, humor, intensity (Ramtha can remain highly animated for hours on end with no sign of fatigue), and particularly distinct speech patterns.[51]

Difficult as Ramtha's delivery may be to follow, in the minds of some it adds support to the notion that the one who is speaking is from a far-distant time, unaccustomed to modern patterns of speech. In a 1986 feature, *Time* magazine described a session Knight conducted: "Her voice, almost preternaturally husky, seemed to take on a gamut of accents from European to Indian as she spouted a relentless stream of imperatives about self-reliance and the god within. "You will receive what you want," she said. "You are masters of your destiny." Every so often she would animatedly cry out to her listeners, "Get it?" to which they would roar back, "Got it!" Many in the audience were weeping or laughing or both.

Ramtha's "teachings" seem to consist of bits and pieces taken from so-called human-potential movements like est and the pop incarnations of Zen Buddhism. The central tenet seems to be a sure crowd pleaser: that everyone is his or her own god. "God the Father lives within each of us," Ramtha says. Nor is Ramtha hung up on morality: there is no right or wrong, he says, just individual reality. Channelers insist that the spirit guides put people in touch with their own innate power to control their destinies.[52]

The theme of "Ramtha's" teaching is that we are like gods; part of God, yet unconscious of this identity. Nonetheless, we create our own realities within which to express ourselves, against which to react, from which to learn, and in which to evolve. This is a view that is virtually identical with the "Seth" teachings as well as with many other channeled materials. And once again, as elsewhere, we are told of great changes that are about to occur on this planet as we move inevitably toward our more spiritual nature.

Until recent years, the only way to experience "Ramtha" was to attend Knight's sessions or to view videotapes of the channeling. Now more than 1,000 hours of video- and audiotapes are available. In 1985 Douglass James Mahr published the first book of selected "Ramtha" channelings, which includes interviews with Knight and her followers. It is called *Voyage to the New World: An Adventure into Unlimitedness.* Since then other books have been published.[53]

51. Elliot Miller, *Crash Course,* 151.
52. Cristina Garcia, "And Now, the 35,000-Year-Old Man," *Time* magazine, December 15, 1986, 36.
53. Klimo, *Channeling,* 43-44.

During the early 1980s, Knight began to give presentations throughout the United States and developed a format of two-day sessions, called "Ramtha Dialogues." Her career was boosted when several movie celebrities — including Shirley MacLaine, Mike Farrell, and Shelley Fabares — attended sessions and gave enthusiastic endorsements of her work. Jess Stearn included a chapter about her in his book *Soul Mates,* and Shirley MacLaine wrote of her in her 1985 book *Dancing in the Light.*

In 1986-87, Knight became the object of public controversy as the national media focused upon her success. She had moved to Yelm, Washington, built an expensive home, and owned an Arabian horse breeding ranch. Some skeptics were concerned that these signs of wealth were obtained with money she earned during her well-attended and relatively expensive public sessions, and from private readings. In addition, many of those attracted to her work had moved to Washington and surrounding states, designated as a safe haven in the face of future earthquakes and other natural disasters predicted by Ramtha for the near future. Some of the moves split families and led to divorces. At least one deprogramming of a Knight follower by people associated with an anti-cult movement has occurred.

Still other controversy has stemmed from advice given by Ramtha to some of his followers to invest in Knight's Arabian horses. Complaints from disgruntled purchasers prompted investigations. As a result, Knight has returned the money of unhappy purchasers.[54]

According to the *New York Times,* Knight's recent divorce litigation with her fifth husband, Jeffrey Knight, has opened a window into the practices of her New Age industry. Jeffrey Knight and other former devotees now say that Ramtha is a sham, and that the channeling sessions that have attracted celebrities such as Shirley MacLaine and Linda Evans are little more than deep-breathing exercises layered with psychic jargon. In the trial, a psychiatrist testifying for Jeffrey Knight called the Ramtha movement a cult.

Outside the courtroom, other critics have described rituals in which blindfolded followers wandered for hours through a maze or were threatened by Knight if they disclosed the inner workings of the ranch. Knight and her attorneys say the allegations are exaggerated or false, motivated by spite. In any event, Knight says she has very little control over how Ramtha may influence people.

From all indications, Knight's Ramtha enterprises continue to flourish despite the courtroom revelations. Her channeling sessions draw people from around the world. These people see Knight as a teacher of a realm which traditional religions cannot explain.

"J. Z. Knight is still the most successful of the New Age channelers,"

54. Melton, Clark ,and Kelly, *New Age Almanac,* 66, 112.

said Dr. J. Gordon Melton, director of the Institute for the Study of American Religion in Santa Barbara, California. "In the New Age world, she is envied for her success. From all outward signs, she still has a large audience."

Many followers, who call themselves "Ramsters," have moved to Yelm, acting on Knight's prophecies that the Pacific Northwest is a safe haven from natural disasters and from space invaders.

Some are extremely angry at Knight. Nancy Barr-Brandon, 50, said she followed the teachings of Ramtha for almost eight years until she decided that Knight was a fraud. That was after she had spent $100,000 at the Ramtha School of Enlightenment and on books, tapes, and survival gear.

The most revealing court testimony has come from Knight's ex-husband, Jeffrey. For most of the last decade, he said, he was under the influence of Ramtha. "I trusted him implicitly," Jeffrey Knight said in court. "He was all-knowing and omnipresent." He no longer believes in Ramtha and says that "mind-control techniques" form the major part of the teachings.

Although some entertainment industry celebrities still praise Knight, the best-known of the New Age proponents, Shirley MacLaine, no longer associates with her.[55]

New Age psychologist Jon Klimo states that whatever the accuracy or inaccuracy of the specific criticisms made about Knight, or about any other channels, past or current, certain questions can be legitimately raised. Could it be that all channels have the potential of burning out or souring? Are the skeptics right in concluding it's all playacting and that the channel is just an act that's gone bad? Is this a channeling-type version of how the American Dream, with all its success and publicity, can contribute to the deterioration of a situation or person?[56]

Channeling advocate Craig Lee is correct when he writes that "many [New Age] people now speculate that whatever [positive] energy came through J. Z. Knight has either shifted, departed or been replaced by a less benign entity."[57]

*Time* magazine points out that some psychologists see the channeling movement as consisting of those who have become disillusioned with organized religion and are seeking something to fill a spiritual void. Others see more ominous, cultlike currents in channeling and dismiss its practitioners as latter-day snake-oil salesmen. "A lot of the stuff is just trite and repeated over and over again," says Carl Rashke, a professor of religion at the University of Denver who has studied the phenomenon. "I'm convinced there is some kind

---

55. "The Worldly and the Spiritual Clash in New Age Divorce," *The New York Times*, p. A1.

56. Klimo, *Channeling*, 44-45.

57. Elliot Miller, *Crash Course*, 152.

of mass hypnosis going on." Observes Reginald Alev, executive director of the Cult Awareness Network in Chicago: "Ramtha reminds me of a ventriloquist's act with one partner missing."[58]

In a later section, we will evaluate the entire channeling process from the biblical perspective.

## KEVIN RYERSON AND SHIRLEY MACLAINE

Kevin Ryerson is the channel/medium made famous by his association with Shirley MacLaine. Ryerson joined a study group sponsored by the Association for Research and Enlightenment and learned meditation. He regularly entered into meditative states. One evening, at a group meeting in 1973 when Ryerson was twenty-one years old, he went into a trance, and a spirit guide, John, spoke through him.

Unlike Ramtha, Lazaris, and others, Ryerson's entities do not claim to be particularly exalted beings, just disembodied spirits in between incarnations, trying to make the earth a better place to live. After all, Ryerson says, they've got to return here. "John" has five entities in all, including an Essene scholar from the time of Jesus; "Tom MacPherson," an Irish pickpocket who lived in Elizabethan times; and "Obadiah," a Haitian herbalist and storyteller who lived 150 years ago.[59]

Ryerson emphasizes that his entities "speak" to help facilitate both individual and collective well-being. "John" comes across as a gentle and wise spiritual presence. In contrast, the highly independent "Tom McPherson" speaks in a strong brogue of his last life in Elizabethan Ireland. Less frequent sources include "Obadiah," a booming West Indian–accented Haitian versed in herbal lore, and sages from ancient Egypt and Japan.[60]

Ryerson's career has been distinguished more by his interest in demonstrating the verifiability and practical value of channeling than by teaching. His entities do teach, though, usually in the context of private consultations, or "readings."

In the early 1980s, Ryerson met Shirley MacLaine and conducted several readings for her. The account of their meeting and early sessions was recorded in MacLaine's book *Out on a Limb* (1983). Ryerson's fame increased even more when he portrayed himself in the 1987 televised version of the book. MacLaine has also mentioned him prominently in her subsequent books, *Dancing in the Light* (1985) and *It's All in the Playing* (1987).[61]

58. Garcia, *Time* magazine, 36.
59. Elliot Miller, *Crash Course*, 155.
60. Klimo, *Channeling*, 46.
61. Melton, Clark, and Kelly, *New Age Almanac*, 96.

As a part of preparing a nationally broadcast television production of her book *Out on a Limb*, MacLaine asked Ryerson if he would play himself as a trance channel in the reenactment of her first session with him. Rather than have Ryerson pretend to portray his own entities in order to follow the script, they had him go into trance, and they asked "John" and "Tom" if they would be able to repeat later in front of the cameras what they had said in the years-earlier situation recounted in the book and TV script. According to Ryerson and MacLaine, what millions saw on television was the real channel playing himself and going into a real trance, and his "real" entities playing themselves!

The content of Ryerson's channeling closely parallels that of other contemporary New Age channeled material. For Klimo it reminds us that, beneath the appearance of the limited physical reality, we are essentially spiritual and immortal in nature, at one at the deepest levels with the universe, or God. From this relationship, we derive our power and our possibilities. Through a kind of cocreation with our Source identity, we can exercise our creative potential and decision-making birthright. We are thus enabled to access the fertile ground of Being to bring forth what we wish for ourselves and for one another on earth, in this lifetime or in any other. Reincarnation is a recurrent theme as well.[62]

## HELEN SCHUCMAN AND *A COURSE IN MIRACLES*

*A Course in Miracles* is a channeled document, nearly 1,200 pages long, transcribed between 1965 and 1973 by Helen Schucman. At the time, Schucman was assistant to the head of the Psychology Department at Presbyterian Hospital in New York City and associate professor of Medical Psychology at Columbia University's College of Physicians and Surgeons. She began to vaguely sense and then clearly hear an inner voice. A trained psychologist, atheist, and disbeliever in the paranormal, she didn't know what to make of it. She told a colleague, "You know that inner voice? It won't leave me alone! It keeps saying, 'This is a course in miracles. Please take notes.'" The initially skeptical Schucman was encouraged by her colleague William Thetford to go ahead and take the notes, using shorthand. During the next seven and a half years, Schucman transcribed a 622-page *Text*, a 478-page *Workbook* containing 365 lessons, and an 88-page *Manual for Teachers* clarifying concepts and terminology used in the previous volumes.[63]

No author's name was given, although the text implies that the source is the biblical Christ, speaking in the first person. Schucman herself said:

62. Klimo, *Channeling*, 45, 47.
63. Melton, Clark, and Kelly, *New Age Almanac*, 53.

Where did the writing come from? Certainly the subject matter itself was the last thing I would have expected to write about, since I knew nothing about the subject. . . . At several points in the writing the Voice itself speaks in no uncertain terms about the Author as Christ, which literally stunned me at the time. . . . I do not understand the process and I certainly do not understand the authorship. It would be pointless for me to attempt an explanation.

New Age sympathizers who knew her give their explanation of the source. Esalen Institute cofounder and author Michael Murphy said: "God knows what she could have regurgitated from the subliminal mind. I don't believe it's Christ. She was raised on that kind of literature. Her father had a metaphysical bookshop. Every single idea has been expressed before. There's nothing new in it."

Close friend and publisher of the *Course*, Judith Skutch said:

Those of us intimately associated with Helen Schucman over a long period of time until her death in 1981 were all aware that Helen's egoic rational mind was incapable of writing this material. I really feel that the part of Helen that was connected to the All received it in a form that was needed for today. This "part" of Helen — and indeed of all of us — is not of the physical. It is our eternal spiritual Self in oneness with the Mind of our Creator, which the course calls the Christ.

Therefore, I see the Christ Spirit as the source of the *Course* with Jesus as the symbol — a spokesperson — a Voice for the message of Love. In her later years Helen certainly shared this belief.

Transpersonal psychologist and author Ken Wilber adds:

Now, I'm not saying that there was not some transcendental insight involved and that Helen probably felt that it was certainly beyond her day-to-day self. I think that's true. But there's much more of Helen in the *Course* than I first thought. She was brought up mystically inclined. Many ideas from the *Course* came from the new thought or metaphysical schools she had been influenced by.[64]

## THE TEACHINGS OF THE *COURSE*

According to Jon Klimo, the 1,200 pages of published material provide an extraordinarily clear attempt to explain the maya, or illusion-like nature, associated with our day-to-day ego, which we are told we mistakenly take to

64. Klimo, *Channeling*, 41-42.

be our true and only self. At the same time, the material pictures the larger spiritual reality within which our true identity resides and within which the ego is only an artificial, transient presence.

*Volume One: Text* has this to say:

> There is nothing outside you. That is what you must ultimately learn, for it is the realization that the Kingdom of Heaven is restored to you. . . . The Kingdom of Heaven is the dwelling place of the Son of God, who left not his father and dwells not apart from him. Heaven is not a place nor a condition. It is merely the awareness of perfect oneness, and the knowledge that there is nothing else; nothing outside this oneness, and nothing else within.

*Volume Two: Workbook for Students* provides 365 exercises, one for each day of the year, each planned around one central idea. The first set of exercises is for "the undoing of the way you see now," and the second set is for the "acquisition of true perceptions."[65]

According to Dean C. Halverson, the ultimate purpose of the *Course* was to help us all gain a new perception of ourselves — the perception that we are sinless sons of God who have never been separated from our Creator. This new perception is essentially what the *Course* means by the term "miracle," which is a matter of the mind and not supernatural intervention, like instantaneous physical healing. Miracles in the *Course* are "examples of right thinking, aligning your perceptions with truth as God created it."

The *Course* chose the terminology of Christianity to convey its message because Christianity has had a great influence on humanity. Unfortunately, so they say, errors have crept into Christianity's teachings — the chief errors being that sin separates us from God and that Jesus' death served as a vicarious atonement for our sin. The Jesus of the *Course* wanted to clear away such misconceptions and, therefore, dictated the truth about Christianity to Schucman.

The worldview of *A Course in Miracles* is a mixture of metaphysical and gnostic elements. It is metaphysical when it portrays God as an abstract and impersonal oneness of Mind. It is gnostic because the reality of the physical creation is denied. God, according to the *Course*, had nothing to do with creating the physical world. It is an illusory projection of the ego, created to escape the judgment that the ego believed God was about to bring against it.[66]

---

65. Ibid., 38-39.
66. Dean C. Halverson, "A Course in Miracles: Seeing Yourself as Sinless," *SCP Journal*, 7.1 (1987), 18, 20.

# REASONS FOR ITS APPEAL

Despite its use of traditional Christian terminology, the popularity of *A Course in Miracles* has been greatest among those who have been disillusioned by organized Christianity, Melton reports. Perhaps this is because it offers Westerners a scripture based on the premises of Eastern religion in a form which is compatible with the historical worldview common to Judeo-Christianity and the modern emphasis on psychology.

The *Course* has been described as a modern form of Christian Science, as a rewrite of the New Testament, and as a Christian version of Vedanta, the ancient Hindu teaching. Author Willis Harman, director of the Institute of Noetic Sciences, has termed it the most important book in the English language.[67]

Klimo suggests that its quiet authority and sound reasoning, presented in an elegantly simple style, have affected a great many people, most of whom seem indifferent to the identity of its source. Most readers seem to feel they have been "spoken to" convincingly by the integrity of the language and the personal meaning it holds for them.

Halverson points out that the *Course* appears to be Christian — at least on the surface. It frequently refers to biblical passages. Its major themes are biblical topics — atonement, salvation, and forgiveness. And the spirit that dictated the *Course* to Helen Schucman claimed to be none other than Jesus himself.

Indeed, some in mainline churches appear to believe the *Course* is Christian. For example, there are a number of churches in California's San Francisco Bay Area where the *Course* is being preached from the pulpit or studied in Sunday school.

One teacher of the *Course* in a church describes it as having been "given as a means of purifying the errors of Christianity, including the belief in separation from God." The *Course* may have been intended to purify the errors of Christianity. What it has accomplished, however, is nothing less than a thorough overhaul.[68]

### *Widespread Dissemination of the* Course

The *Course* was published in 1976 by the Foundation for Inner Peace, headed by parapsychological investigators Robert and Judy Skutch. Over 500,000 sets of the *Course* were sold without the benefit of advertising. The Foundation also offers other books and pamphlets, as well as audio and video cassettes.

67. Melton, Clark, and Kelly, *New Age Almanac*, 54.
68. Halverson, "Course in Miracles," 23.

175

The foundation's publications include material related to the *Course,* such as Gerald Gersham Jampolsky's best-seller *Love Is Letting Go of Fear* and a glossy periodical entitled *New Realities.* The Unity Church has for many years actively advocated the study of the *Course,* and in the fall of 1986 sponsored a national *A Course in Miracles* festival which was held in Honolulu.[69] After only ten years in circulation, the *Course* was being studied by more than three hundred groups formally organized for that purpose, in both rural and urban America.

More recently students of the *Course* are utilizing formal means of promotion. Robert Skutch has written a "biography" of the *Course,* entitled *Journey without Distance* (1984). *New Realities* magazine has devoted its pages to spreading the *Course's* message. A documentary of the story behind the *Course* has been filmed. The Foundation for Inner Peace, sole publisher of the *Course,* has recently put out a less expensive paperback version. The work is being translated into five languages: Spanish, French, Italian, Portuguese, and Hebrew. And Gerald Jampolsky, a popular psychiatrist, has promoted the *Course* in his talks and in two books, entitled *Teach Only Love* (1983) and *Good-Bye to Guilt* (1985).[70]

In recent years Marianne Williamson of San Francisco has been promoting *A Course of Miracles* through her best-selling books, including *Returned to Love,* which is based on the *Course.*

## NEW AGE CRITIQUES OF THE *COURSE*

Many metaphysically inclined students of the *Course* have been puzzled by the author's language, which is reminiscent of the Christian Bible. The seemingly patriarchal cosmology in which God the Father and the Holy Spirit are consistently referred to using the male pronoun, and in which humanity is known as the Sonship, contrasts with the contemporary cultural thrust to reinstate the value of the feminine. Another element in the *Course* which has been difficult for many New Agers to accept is the teaching that the body is but "the instrument the mind made in its efforts to deceive itself."[71]

## EVANGELICAL CRITIQUES OF THE *COURSE*

According to evangelical editor Elliot Miller, despite the fact that the *Course* liberally employs Christian terminology, such terminology is thoroughly re-

---

69. Melton, Clark, and Kelly, *New Age Almanac,* 54.
70. Halverson, "Course in Miracles," 18.
71. Melton, Clark, and Kelly, *New Age Almanac,* 54.

defined, so that the *Course* is in fact no more Christian than any New Age spiritistic tome.[72]

Bob Larson, an evangelical radio commentator, points out that while Christianity is concerned with the forgiveness of sin and communion with God, *A Course in Miracles* boldly proclaims, "It is impossible to think of anything God created that could need forgiveness." Elsewhere, pardon for transgression is referred to as an illusion, a "happy fiction." Ironically, though the *Course* denigrates God's forgiveness, it conversely claims that personal peace is possible when humans forgive others.

In the *Course*, Christ is stripped of his divinity. "The name of Jesus is the name of one who was a man but saw the face of Christ in all his brothers and remembered God." For those Christians who find such comments to border on blasphemy, literature from the Foundation that publishes the books claims that "the *Course* [lends] itself to teaching, parallel to the ongoing teaching of the Holy Spirit."[73]

Halverson notes that even some who believe the *Course* is God's truth acknowledge that the *Course* and Christianity are fundamentally at odds. Kenneth Wapnick, an authoritative interpreter and avid promoter of the *Course*, has plainly stated just that. While teaching a seminar on the *Course*, Kenneth Wapnick commented that if the Bible were considered literally true, then the *Course* would have to be viewed as demonically inspired.

While superficial similarities between the *Course* and Christianity exist, the two belief systems could not be more opposed to one another. The Bible speaks of a sinful humanity that is separated from God and in need of reconciliation through the atoning work of Jesus Christ. The *Course* would dismiss such teaching by saying that its source is not God, but the guilt-ridden, separatistic ego.

For Halverson, anyone who believes the *Course* is compatible with Christianity either does not understand the *Course* or Christianity, or both. For example, God, according to the *Course*, is impersonal oneness, undifferentiated Mind. This concept blurs the distinction between Creator and creation. The meaning the *Course* gives to "creation" is thus not a meaning shared by the Judeo-Christian tradition. In the *Course*, creation is an extension of the oneness that is God. The creation flows from God like a stream flows from a lake or electricity flows from a generator. Creation is an extension of God, indistinguishable in its essence from God's being. This idea of creation as extension provides the *Course* with its version of good news. For, according to the *Course*, the only thing that God has created is the Son of God. In our true selves, we are each a part of the Son of God, or the Sonship. We are,

72. Elliot Miller, *Crash Course*, 147.
73. Bob Larson, *Straight Answers on the New Age* (Nashville: Nelson, 1989), 196.

therefore, eternally secure as extensions of God's Mind. In our true selves, we are one with, and cannot be separated from, God.

The *Course's* solution to the ego's bent toward separation is found in the ability of the Holy Spirit to call us back to our true identity as sinless extensions of God. The Holy Spirit's purpose is to replace our false perception of being alienated from God with the true perception that we have *never* been separated. The *Course* calls this process "accepting the Atonement." "Atonement" itself is used to denote the "undoing," or "correction," of the false belief that we are sinful, guilty, and deserving of punishment. Seeing others as sinless is what the *Course* means by "forgiveness."

Sin, according to the *Course,* is the false belief in separateness, which is unreal. It is this false belief that gives rise to the physical world. It is also this false belief that gives rise to personhood. For to be a person is to be an individual, separate and distinct from others and from God. By affirming separateness as illusory, the *Course* abolishes the value of both the physical world and personhood. Reconciliation with the God of the *Course* means that a person becomes eternally absorbed into a Divine Abstraction.

In contrast, the God of the Bible points out that salvation is not a restored *union* with an impersonal Mind but a restored *communion* with a personal God. The God of the Bible solved the problem of sin, not by obliterating separateness but by restoring a relationship. In the *Course,* the problem is perceptual, the solution impersonal. In the Bible, the problem is relational, the solution interpersonal. The God of the Bible accomplished that reconciliation through Jesus Christ.[74]

*A Course in Miracles* alleges to be the supernatural revelation of a personal, powerful, and controlling psychic "voice," a voice claiming to be Jesus, given through a skeptical and somewhat fearful atheistic research psychologist over a period of almost eight years.[75] But the content of the *Course* forcefully supports the occult and New Age worldview and is intensely anti-biblical.

## LESSER-KNOWN CHANNELERS AND SPIRITUAL ENTITIES

In addition to the three representative contemporary channelers whom we have described and evaluated, there are literally hundreds of other channelers. Some of these call for special attention.

---

74. Halverson, "Course in Miracles," 20-23, 27.
75. "A Course in Miracles: How It Came — What It Is — What It Says" (New York: Foundation for Inner Peace, 1977).

## Elizabeth Clare Prophet and the Church Universal and Triumphant

Elizabeth Prophet is the leader of the Church Universal and Triumphant. She and her husband, Mark, formed the Summit Lighthouse, which evolved into the church she now heads. It has moved several times over the years, first to Colorado Springs, Colorado, in 1966, later to Pasadena and Malibu, California, and most recently to Montana. Elizabeth Prophet took control of the organization in 1973 when her husband died.[76]

The sources channeled by Elizabeth are said to be "ascended masters," spiritually advanced beings no longer residing on the physical plane. Among those most extensively channeled are "Saint Germain"; "Kuthumi," and "Koot Hoomi," also known as "the Master K.H." "The ascended masters," Elizabeth believes, "are contacting mankind today in a very real way. Through the power of the spoken Word, they are reaching . . . all who will hear the true message . . . of the individual Christ Self." The material she supposedly has channeled from them now comprises dozens of volumes.[77]

Prophet affirms belief in Jesus Christ and labels herself a Christian; but it is clearly a gnostic version of Christianity. She contends that in the ancient battle between gnosticism and Christian orthodoxy, the wrong side won. The orthodox Christians, she says, were just seeking power for the clergy, so they repressed the true teachings of Jesus that require no clergy to actualize. She says church leaders hid the mystical sayings of Jesus from the people by excluding them from Scripture. She claims that when church leaders chose which books were to be accepted as Holy Scripture and included in the Bible, they were merely using those choices to consolidate their own power.[78]

The fundamental teachings center on belief that through inner initiations and the use of prayers, mantras, and "decrees" one can realize one's divinity and eventually "ascend" to the ranks of the Masters. Reincarnation is affirmed. The Church Universe Triumphant has engendered much controversy and has identified itself with stalwart American patriotism and with causes generally regarded as politically "right wing."

Since moving to Montana, Elizabeth the Prophet and her church have been under constant attack by anti-cultists and local residents who opposed her plans for developing the property. The development has included a number of bomb shelters erected against a possible nuclear holocaust in the near future. Prophet describes the need to survive the dark transition from the age of Pisces to the dawning of the age of Aquarius. The controversy reached new heights in 1989 when Ed Francis, Prophet's second husband, directed a plan

76. Guiley, *Harper's Encyclopedia*, 12.
77. Klimo, *Channeling*, 56-57.
78. Peters, *Cosmic Self*, 88.

to obtain weapons illegally and store them on the property. Arrested, he served a short jail term for his activity. Since then, devotees have continued to move in, build bomb shelters, and pile up dried food, angering their neighbors.[79]

## BENJAMIN CREME AND MAITREYA

Among internationally known channels, British artist and journalist Benjamin Creme has received particular notoriety for his claim to be a channel for the Christ, whom he refers to as "Maitreya, head of the planet's spiritual hierarchy."

In 1977, Creme was informed in a series of messages that Maitreya had completed and donned his body of manifestation on July 7 and had begun his descent from the Himalayan Retreat of the Masters on July 8. Two months later, Creme began to channel messages from Maitreya in public. He traveled throughout Europe and North America, and in 1979 in London he published a booklet, *The Reappearance of the Christ and the Masters of Wisdom,* which was expanded into a full-length book in 1980. By May 1980, 100 messages from Maitreya had been received and were published as *Messages from Maitreya the Christ.* The next year, Creme founded a magazine entitled *Share International.*

Creme then entered an intense period of traveling to announce the imminent appearance of the Christ (Maitreya) in 1982. As people responded, he established transmission groups and, on April 25, took out full-page ads in seventeen major newspapers worldwide announcing that "The Christ is Now Here" and that his identity would be revealed within the next two months.

That prediction was not fulfilled. Since then Creme has continued to travel and speak about Maitreya's presence and near manifestation. He still expects Maitreya to appear shortly, possibly in a worldwide television broadcast during which he will make his presence known to all peoples. Creme maintains communication with his followers through his magazine, *Share International,* and an organization called the Tara Center, with offices in New York, Los Angeles, Amsterdam, and London.

Melton notes that Creme's statements served as a catalyst in raising the consciousness of the larger Evangelical Christian community toward the emerging New Age movement. Creme's announcement of the appearance of Maitreya, whom he identified with the Christ, was offensive to many Evangelical Christians. A week after Creme's April 25, 1982, newspaper ads, a similar ad appeared in the *Los Angeles Times* condemning Creme as an agent of the Antichrist. Lawyer Constance Cumbey's *Hidden Dangers of the Rainbow* (1983), which became an Evangelical best-seller, drew a picture of the New Age movement as a giant satanic conspiracy built around Creme and the

79. Ibid., 89.

coming Maitreya. The public response to Cumbey's book forced other Evangelical leaders to confront the New Age movement, although many distanced themselves from Cumbey's conspiracy theory. Cumbey's ideas eventually lost their impact, however, as the Maitreya failed to appear.[80]

### Revelations through Birds and Dolphins

Richard Bach is a popular New Age author who is a direct descendant of composer Johann Sebastian Bach and a nephew of metaphysical–New Thought writer Marcus Bach.

*Jonathan Livingston Seagull* was alleged to have been dictated to Richard Bach by an entity that appeared in the form of a bird. Bach claims that he simply wrote down the stream of thoughts and impressions that the entity poured into his mind. The book broke all publishing records since the legendary success of *Gone with the Wind*, and topped the best-seller lists for over two years.[81]

Dolphins are cetaceans, an order of marine mammals that includes whales and porpoises. A New Age mythology has emerged based on the mystical perception of dolphins as a sentient race which may be superior to humankind intellectually and ethically and with which, under certain circumstances, it is possible to communicate. Many New Agers have accepted the contention that dolphins are superior beings with a metaphysical message. One person who alleges such contacts is Joan Ocean of the Hawaii-based Dolphin Connection. The Dolphin Connection's aim is to achieve universal love and harmony through telepathic contact with dolphins, whales, and interstellar beings. Ocean also alleges communications from spirit entities, including the "Arisen Masters" and "The Nine Form Sirius B." The Dolphin Society Church trains persons in out-of-body traveling with dolphin and whale spiritual liberators.

Jerry Doran of Wilmington, California, relates an out-of-body experience in which he encountered "five blue skinned dolphins floating inside [a] starship." The dolphins identified themselves as part of the Stellar Community of Enlightened Ecosystems, which is directing human evolution toward attainment of a "Group Mind which includes the animals and plants of Earth, the Earth itself, the Sun and similar enlightened star systems throughout the Cosmos."[82]

Elliot Miller describes the work of Neville Rowe, a former electrical engineer from Australia, who became one of the first to channel sea mammals.

---

80. Melton, Clark, and Kelly, *New Age Almanac*, 316-17.
81. Alexander, "Theology from the Twilight Zone," 26.
82. Melton, Clark, and Kelly, *New Age Almanac*, 381, 383.

Rowe offers group experiences with the dolphins. He states in an advertisement that:

> The dolphins are highly evolved and loving creatures, eager to assist us to understand our oneness with all life on this Earth. They are more than willing to share their joy with us — to teach us to play![83]

Melton contends that New Age fascination with dolphins stems from a romantic nature mysticism which is expressed in New Agers' concern with ecology and animal rights. Dolphins continue to be a source of speculation and fascination for the New Age community.[84]

### UFOs, Space Aliens, Contactees, and the Channeling of New Age Teaching

The dramatic suicide tragedy in 1997 of the thirty-nine members of the Heaven's Gate cult reminds us that the religious interpretation of UFOs has tended to overwhelm the scientific approach. The alleged visitors from outer space quickly took on the role of space-borne saviors — or became demonic figures.

The modern UFO movement commenced June 24, 1947, when Kenneth Arnold, a civilian pilot from Boise, Idaho, flying over the Cascades in western Washington in search of a lost Marine C-46 transport, reported seeing nine shiny objects in a chain-like formation speeding by at some 1,600 miles per hour. "They flew," Arnold said, "like a saucer would if you skipped it across the water." Here began the modern myth of flying saucers and UFOs. Arnold's account launched a thousand new sightings. Within a few weeks, Roswell, New Mexico, became famous as the site where a spaceship crashed.

Serious believers saw the enigmatic objects as precursors to what for them could be the greatest event in human history: contact with an extraterrestrial race. Furthermore, there were "contactees" among them who claimed that contact had already been made, and by them.

According to Carl Jung, the UFO "visits" have, in a "space age" nurtured on science fiction, played the part once taken by descending gods, angels, saintly apparitions, and heavenly saviors. Mysteriously appearing out of the heavens, they have contacted favored earthlings to deliver messages of warning, hope, or forthcoming apocalypse, and to impart New Age philosophical wisdom. The demonic role is also there, for not all UFO beings are seen as benign.

In one sense, nineteenth-century Spiritualism and twentieth-century UFOism belong in the same category. Both spiritualism and UFOism presuppose an order of spiritually significant beings between the human and

83. Elliot Miller, *Crash Course*, 157-58.
84. Melton, Clark, and Kelly, *New Age Almanac*, 384.

ultimate reality, with which one can have conversational and disciplic relationships. Whether spirits or space brothers, interaction with them opens up a sense of expanded consciousness and cosmic wonder. For both Spiritualism and UFOism, human commerce with the Others begins with the experience of elect individuals. In both, this privileged exchange soon enough becomes the focus of informal "circles" or even minor institutions, in which messages from the invisible friends are transmitted through mediums. However, for interest to be sustained, they need powerful periodic injections of fresh visions or novel messages such as the Heaven's Gate cult provided.[85]

UFOism also has links with "Teaching Spiritualism" and Theosophy. There is the transmitting of instruction from highly advanced spiritual teachers.

One of the first and most famous of those supposedly contacted was George Adamski (1891-1965). Adamski claimed to have seen squadrons of UFOs after the Arnold sighting. Then, in late 1952, he claimed to have met a UFO occupant from Venus, named Orthon, on the Mojave Desert. In a New Zealand lecture, Adamski spoke loftily of Venusian culture and religion, and the aliens' desire to communicate with us, at least "through our minds." Other celebrated UFO contactees of the fifties offered broadly similar stories, claiming visits to different planets.

An early UFO group was Christ Brotherhood, Inc., established in 1956 by Wallace C. Halsey, who in his sleep channeled UFO messages of coming world destruction and the gathering of a saved remnant.[86]

Robert Ellwood points out that by the 1970s UFO groups emerged that fit the common stereotype of a cult. One of the best examples was HIM (Human Individual Metamorphosis), which appeared in California in 1975. HIM was led by a middle-aged man and woman called Bo and Peep, also known as "The Two," who persuaded followers to give up their possessions and follow them into wilderness camps, where they were to be met by UFOs and carried physically to "the level above human." By the late 1990s this Human Individual Metamorphosis group was based in the San Diego area and was called "Heaven's Gate." Sean Wilentz of Princeton states that the most startling difference between today's cults and their early American forerunners is the modern proclivity for mass suicide. In the nineteenth century, believers hoped to hasten the coming of God's kingdom by perfecting human life on Earth; at the end of the twentieth, there is a tendency to want to leave Earth — to be transported (perhaps by UFOs, the modern equivalent of celestial angels) directly to kingdom come.[87]

85. Timothy Miller, *America's Alternative Religions*, 393.

86. Ibid., 395-96.

87. Ibid. Cf. also Sean Wilentz, "Cults: A Long-Standing American Tradition," *Fort Worth Star-Telegram*, April 13, 1997, Section D, 10.

As noted above, early contactees saw the aliens as ultimately friendly and benign. However, by the 1980s and 1990s there was a growing interest in conspiracy theories involving UFOs, government coverups, and even secret and sinister relationships between government agencies, aliens, and abductions.[88]

## "ENCOUNTER THEORY" AND UFOS

The so-called "encounter theory" of extraterrestrial (ET) encounters sees the experience as a psychological projection, perhaps in response to a mass yearning to raise the consciousness of humankind. Many ET encounters fit a pattern of encounters with supernatural and divine beings through history. Furthermore, modern research shows that ET encounters tend to fit a psychological profile called the "encounter-prone personality."[89]

Psychic Ruth Montgomery offers a whole system to explain it all, both the extraterrestrial aliens and the internal psychological experience. Why are they coming to Earth? To help us. To save us. One space being named Rolf has spoken to Ruth through the Guides, declaring: "Ruth, it is vital that you get the message across to others that we are coming in great numbers, not with any intention of harm, but to help rescue earth from pollution and nuclear explosions. We want all to live in harmony."

The bottom line is that Ruth Montgomery sees herself — as do other contactees — as a channel for supraterrestrial teaching. What is the content of this teaching? It is a mixture of Hinduism and gnosticism. The Guides tell Ruth, for example, "that each of us is something of God, and that we are all one. Together we form God, and it is therefore essential that we help each other, so that all may advance together." The teachings revealed by the Guides are quite obviously New Age.

According to Ted Peters, this view suggests that the physical presence of UFOs as a visual phenomenon is less important than their psychological impact, their presence in the dimensions we ordinarily associate with mental telepathy and spiritualism. The space beings live within us.[90]

The encounter theories do not discount the possibility of genuine ET encounters, but may explain why so many have occurred since the middle of the twentieth century and the advent of the threat of nuclear annihilation. However, according to Guiley, there may never be satisfactory answers to the question of whether or not ET encounters are objective or subjective.[91]

UFOs and UFO religions have also produced skeptics. These secular

88. Timothy Miller, *America's Alternative Religions,* 398.
89. Guiley, *Harper's Encyclopedia,* 195.
90. Peters, *Cosmic Self,* 37-38.
91. Guiley, *Harper's Encyclopedia,* 196.

skeptics see UFOism as religion masquerading as science. They perceive it as dangerous because of its promotion of credulity and of authoritarian, even proto-fascist, truth in charismatic contactee figures.[92]

### The Heaven's Gate Cult

Such an evaluation of UFOism leads us to and reminds us of the life and teachings of the founders of the Heaven's Gate cult. Since the mass suicide of the thirty-nine members of the Heaven's Gate cult in March 1997, the media have detailed the life and teaching of Marshall Applewhite and Bonnie Nettles, the founders. The genesis of the cult came in 1972, when Applewhite, then about forty, met a nurse named Bonnie Lu Nettles, then forty-four. The two discovered a mutual interest in astrology and reincarnation and came to the belief that they were the earthly incarnations of aliens. In materials put on the Internet by the Heaven's Gate cult group, we are given a version of what happened: "In the early 1970s, two members of the Kingdom of Heaven (or what some might call two aliens from space) incarnated into two unsuspecting humans in Houston. . . . They consciously recognized that they were sent from space to do a task that had something to do with the Bible."[93]

By 1973 Applewhite and Nettles were convinced they were the Two Witnesses prophesied by the book of Revelation to prepare the way for the kingdom of heaven.

In 1975, Applewhite and Nettles were preaching in Oregon, and they attracted national attention after persuading a group of about twenty people from the tiny coastal town of Waldport to sever all ties to the lives they were leading and make a pilgrimage to the prairie of eastern Colorado, where the group would supposedly rendezvous with a spaceship.

When the spaceship did not appear, the group's Internet materials indicated that they and their followers went into deliberate seclusion for seventeen years, until 1992. Nettles died sometime in the 1980s. In 1994 and 1995, newspaper reports from various cities cite controversial public lectures by the group, then identifying itself as Total Overcomers, in which its followers talked about the coming end of the world and the need for people to live more ascetic lives.

Richard Lacayo points out that astronomical charts may have helped determine the timing of the Heaven's Gate suicides. They apparently began on the weekend of March 22-23, 1997, around the time that the Hale-Bopp comet got ready to make its closest approach to Earth. That weekend also witnessed a full moon and, in parts of the United States, a lunar eclipse. For

92. Timothy Miller, *America's Alternative Religions*, 398.
93. *New York Times*, March 28, 1997, A11.

good measure it included Palm Sunday, the beginning of the Christian Holy Week. Shrouds placed on the corpses were purple, the color of Passiontide, or, for New Agers, the color of those who have passed to a higher plane. The Heaven's Gate philosophy added its astronomical trappings to a core of weirdly adulterated Christianity. Then came a whiff of gnosticism, the old heresy that regarded the body as a burden from which the fretful soul longs to be freed.[94]

In videotaped farewells, the twenty-one women and eighteen men appeared to be happily anticipating the shedding of "their containers" and moving on to a higher "stage" of life. They believed they were going to be taken away by a UFO. They believed the UFO was traveling behind the comet Hale-Bopp, which was passing by the earth.[95]

Peter Jones, in a significant article in *Spiritual Counterfeits Project Newsletter,* contends that the Heaven's Gate group is the herald of a new kind of cult and religious fervor that follows ancient gnosticism in radically despising the world, the human body, and the human condition. The members of Heaven's Gate, he wrote, were prepared for joining the group by the New Age worldview which jettisons absolutes, eliminates guidelines, and sets the mind adrift without moorings.

### UFOs and Computer Technology

It should be noted that for many the search for otherworldly truths is closely bound with earthly technological development. For many, the Internet has a unique ability to lift people out of what Heaven's Gate members called their "human containers." Longtime Internet activist John Perry Barlow, in his Declaration of Independence of Cyberspace, called it the new "home of the mind," with the implied ability to shed the flesh. "It's a millennialist theology," said Phil Agre, a professor of communication at the University of California, San Diego. "Everything will be reconstructed in the image of the order of digital data. Space and the body will be rendered irrelevant, all the powers of the earth will be decimated."[96]

Douglas Groothuis states that because of the influence of strange and sometimes wonderful computer technologies, those not grounded in God's own revelation in Christ and the Scriptures will seek revelations as they can. Apart from God, where better to search than in cyberspace? It is as close as the keyboard and as esoteric as the Internet. Through its massive connectivity

---

94. Richard Lacayo, "The Lure of the Cult," *Time,* April 7, 1997, 46.

95. Mary Otto and Angie Cannon, "Death Seen as Means to Higher State by Cult," *Fort Worth Star-Telegram,* March 28, 1997.

96. Amy Harmon, "Far-out Explanations for Life's Mysteries Increasing in Modern Society," *Dallas Morning News,* April 4, 1997, 46.

it offers a God's-eye vision of endless data through the dimensions of cyber-space. "Our love affair with computers, computer graphics, and computer networks runs deeper than aesthetic fascination and deeper than the play of the senses. We are searching for a home for the mind and heart." As the Jewish philosopher Abraham Heschel has noted, if we will not accept the divine on its terms, we will create fascinating and mystifying surrogates that take on a life of their own, with a seductive appeal that we cannot easily resist. Furthermore, UFOism can be seen as a message of deception.[97]

## EVALUATION OF UFO EXPERIENCES

According to Ellwood, the remarkable twentieth-century UFO experience can be seen as reflecting the hopes and anxieties of a turbulent era. While not often explicitly religious, UFO experience has certainly employed categories from the worlds of myth and religion to make clear its persuasion that we are not alone, that there are modern entities capable of moving among us with supernatural, or virtually supernatural, power to harm and heal, like the de-mons, angels, and saviors of old.[98]

For New Ager David Icke, extraterrestrials are arriving on earth in large numbers to help us "make the giant leap in evolution into the Aquarian Age, where humankind, or those who are evolved enough to meet the chal-lenge, will rise out of the abyss at last. They are here to guide us through tremendously difficult times with love, wisdom, and understanding, and we ignore them and reject what they say to our cost."

New Age author Brad Steiger states that in the last thirty years the extraterrestrials "have been accelerating their interaction with us in preparation for a fast-approaching time of transition and transformation. This period, we have been told, will be a difficult one. For generations our prophets and revelators have been referring to it as The Great Cleansing, Judgment Day, Armageddon. But we have been promised that, after a season of cataclysmic changes on the Earth plane, a New Age consciousness will suffuse the planet. It is to this end that the gods have been utilizing the UFO as a transformative symbol.

But the messages communicated by the alleged extraterrestrials con-sistently go against biblical Christianity. As Ralph Rath puts it, "There is nothing in the UFO phenomena that leads to the belief in the biblical God. There is much in the UFO phenomena, on the other hand, that contradicts the ideas of God as revealed in the biblical worldview.[99]

---

97. Douglas Groothuis, *The Soul in Cyberspace* (Grand Rapids: Baker, 1997), 112.
98. Timothy Miller, *America's Alternative Religions*, 398.
99. Ron Rhodes, *The Culting of America* (Eugene, Ore.: Harvest House, 1994), 190-91, 196.

These channels and entities described above are only a few of many that could be listed. It seems as though there are disembodied voices claiming to be virtually every kind of entity people are capable of believing in.

## AN ANALYSIS OF CHANNELING

Brooks Alexander maintains that we are now in the midst of another major outbreak of spiritism and channeling. The spirits are not only more active than before, but in our biblically illiterate society, they are finding more people who are eager to lend them an ear. An expanding audience not only believes in them, it also believes them. This audience not only accepts their existence, it accepts their guidance as well.[100]

In America millions of followers seek out the channelers for advice or read the literature given by the spirits through their channelers. Some have referred to America's growing interest in channeling as having "epidemic" proportions.

One reason for the growth is that the channelers today are turning to highly sophisticated marketing techniques through radio, television, and videotape. In addition, the endorsement of channeling by famous television and movie stars is making the practice socially acceptable. Examples of stars who have this kind of influence are Shirley MacLaine, Linda Evans (of "Dynasty"), and Michael York (of "Romeo and Juliet").

When Actress Sharon Gless, who played "Cagney" on the hit TV series "Cagney and Lacey," won a 1987 "Emmy" for her role, she told tens of millions in her acceptance speech that her success was due to "Lazaris," a spirit-entity who speaks through medium Jach Pursel.[101]

Elliot Miller maintains that actress Shirley MacLaine has been channeling's most influential friend.[102] She has reverently sat at the feet of many of the major channels, and by her endorsements has catapulted the careers of each. Her own teachings (as presented in her seminars) are derived from these sources and thus are indistinguishable from them.

This influence has come through MacLaine's television programs and lectures. Her spiritual books have sold over five million copies. The *Out on a Limb* miniseries sparked an unprecedented interest in metaphysical subjects, particularly channeling. William Kautz and Melanie Branon predict that the

---

100. Brooks Alexander, *Spirit Channeling,* Downers Grove, IL: InterVaristy, 1988), 14.

101. Ankerberg and Weldon, *Cult Watch,* 167-68.

102. Elliot Miller, *Crash Course,* 159-60.

miniseries will probably go on record as having drawn more public attention to "raising consciousness" in the 1980s than TM (Transcendental Meditation) did in the 1960s. The discoveries she shared have served as a primer in metaphysics for millions.

MacLaine's nationwide two-day seminars called "Connecting with the Higher Self" led fourteen thousand of her admirers into a step-by-step acceptance of the New Age and channeling (using didactic and consciousness-altering methods).

The influence of MacLaine continues through her three-hundred-acre spiritual center in Crestone, Colorado (near Pueblo), funded by proceeds from her seminars. She says one of the purposes for conceiving the center was "so everyone will know there's a place they can go for a really trusted trance channeler."

Alexander points out that to the casual observer, this renewed fascination with spirits and spirit contact seems to have exploded into prominence without warning. The mass media uniformly treated channeling as a fringe phenomenon that swelled to fad status overnight.

But that impression of suddenness is a media-projected illusion. The unnoticed reality is that spiritism has been steadily working its way into the mainstream of American culture for the last twenty years. The reality is that the new spiritism and channeling have moved beyond the weird and the supernatural into the normal and the mundane.[103]

Channeling has become a matter of considerable tracking and study. New retreat centers and workshops are springing up around the country. In both, people are taught how to open their minds and bodies to the spirits to become channels themselves. In these retreat centers and workshops, live teaching sessions are taught by the spirits themselves, motivating people to start study groups, research centers, and magazines devoted solely to the study or development of channeling.

John Ankerberg and John Weldon point out the growing popularity of channeling in the sciences and other disciplines. The spirits are speaking out of their human hosts, giving information which is applied to theories in psychology, to the practice of medicine, to the investigation of parapsychology, to the study of physics, to the application of sociology, and to the development of new ideas in theology, archaeology, and other disciplines. In New York state, spiritism has been used for several years as an adjunct to psychotherapy in some New York community mental health centers.[104]

There is an increasingly visible channeling movement throughout the Western World, including Canada, England, and West Germany. Brazil boasts

103. Alexander, *Spirit Channeling*, 15-16.
104. Ankerberg and Weldon, *Cult Watch*, 168.

over a million channelers or spiritists of various types with tens of millions of followers. Tracy Eaton reports that on the flatlands of central Brazil a place called Vale do Amanhecer is home to more than 10,000 psychics, clairvoyants, and spiritual healers, all trying to commune with the eerie vibrations and energy forces said to inhabit the region. Nearby is the community Chapada dos Guimaraes, home to residents who say they routinely converse with space creatures.[105]

# A SPIRITUAL VOID

The growth of secularism in the United States and Western Europe has resulted in a biblically illiterate "post-Christian" culture. Many who considered themselves Christian had a watered-down, secularized faith. This development meant that a sizable number of people in our Western culture have a secular skepticism toward the Bible, both in its claim to be a special revelation from God and in its depiction of an objective, personal devil.[106]

People from such a secular background have often become acutely aware of a spiritual void within, and are looking for answers. These people have found that meaning in life cannot be found in a material view of reality alone. They desire to know the answers to questions like, "Who am I?" "Why am I here?" and "What happens when I die?" Whether or not they admit it, the thought of life being no more than a few years of pain and pleasure replaced by eternal nonexistence is frightening. People know they are more than the end product of hydrogen atoms and blind chance. They want answers to the ultimate questions about life and death and to the more mundane problems they face in their daily lives. Rather than settling for advice from a mere human, even an "enlightened" human, they believe that through channeling they have found access to a source of wisdom that transcends the human viewpoint. Channeling's ultimate appeal is its claim to connect a person with a realm of reality greater than his or her own. As parapsychologist and channel Alan Vaughan observes: "The thrill, the immediacy, of that contact with another consciousness may be the driving force behind the phenomenal growth of the practice of channeling." Channeling thus provides, from a biblical perspective, a false answer to the modern individual's need for religious experience.

Miller also points out that channeling has become popular because many people are struggling with feelings of low self-esteem, powerlessness,

---

105. Ibid. Cf. also Tracey Eaton, "Out of This World, in Brazil," *Dallas Morning News,* August 17, 1996, 1G.

106. Elliot Miller, *Crash Course,* 161.

and guilt. Channels tell them that as gods they are worthy of self-love and respect, they are powerful beings, and there is nothing for them to feel guilty about.[107]

It is ironic that the New Age movement, which says humans are divine and that all answers are to be found within, has appealed to those who have no religious faith. However, by its current obsession with channeling, it admits that looking within is not sufficient. External help and information are necessary after all.

Channeling also has an appeal because there is big money in channeling. It costs $275 to consult Lazaris at a weekend seminar. Between 600 and 800 people fill each session, which means that Lazaris channels an average of $190,000 for Jach Pursel per weekend of transcendental discourse. Lazaris has a two-year waiting list for private consultations, at $93 per hour. Or you can reach out and touch Lazaris by phone at $53 per half-hour, billed to your Visa or MasterCard account. Audiotapes of Lazaris are available at $20 per set, videotapes at $60. Pursel also sells New Age items and art.

Lazaris/Pursel may seem extreme, but he is by no means unique. It has been estimated that more than a thousand active channels practice in the Los Angeles area alone. Southern California may be "the land of a thousand channels," but it is only a focused version of what is happening in a less concentrated form in other places. For example, Kevin Ryerson charged "$250 per session, [and] has had so many inquiries at his San Francisco office that he is referring business to other channelers."[108]

## Types of Channeling

Channeling can be spontaneous or induced. The channeler has no control over spontaneous channeling, which may involve falling into sudden trance states or lapses of consciousness. Many channelers begin with spontaneous episodes, then learn to control the process and to induce it. Induction methods vary, and include meditation, prayer, self-hypnosis, fasting, chanting, dancing, sleep deprivation, breathing techniques, smoking herbs, or taking hallucinogenic drugs.

By usual definition, all channeling most popularized involves communications to humans from a supposedly nonhuman source through a human medium. However, the manner in which these communications take place varies widely.[109]

107. Ibid., 162.
108. Alexander, *Spirit Channeling*, 10-11.
109. Guiley, *Harper's Encyclopedia*, 89.

## DEEP TRANCE

The kind of channeling most popularized by the media is called full-trance mediumship. The medium, or channel, appears to go unconscious or into trance, and someone or something else appears to occupy the brain and the body and use it for speaking, writing, or moving about. Usually, when a trance channeling session is over and the individual regains normal consciousness, he or she cannot remember anything that occurred during the session.

During the trance sessions, the controlling entity usually has a tone of voice distinctly different from the channel's normal voice; at other times, the voice sounds flat or monotonous, like a robot. Most of the major channels of the last hundred years have been of the trance voice kind.

Full-body, or incarnational, channeling (examples: J. Z. Knight/"Ramtha," Penny Torres/"Mafu") is similar to deep-trance channeling. In this type, the channels fully vacate their bodies and the entities move in.

Some critics see full-body channeling as a conscious creation of Knight, which Torres and others have copied. Miller notes that from the Christian perspective, there is no reason to deny the *possibility* that it is an advanced form of possession, suited to an acceleration of satanic deception in our time.[110]

## LIGHT TRANCE

In light-trance channeling, the individual has partial or full awareness of what is going on in the surrounding environment, as well as within himself or herself, at the time of the channeling. The entity transmitting to or through the channel — operating the vocal cords or writing hand — is said to be a co-dwelling personality, working alongside the channel. Jon Klimo calls it a temporary cohabitation of the seat of consciousness. It involves only a partial "stepping aside," as opposed to what is required for a full trance.[111]

In addition to the voice, the channeler may communicate via automatic writing, a planchette, Ouija board, or similar device. Mental channeling is also accomplished through sleep and dreams.

## VOLUNTARY POSSESSION

In voluntary possession the controlling entity chooses not to force himself upon his or her human instrument. The Christian explanation for this apparent benevolence is that in voluntary possession the entities have elected to

110. Elliot Miller, *Crash Course*, 166.
111. Klimo, *Channeling*, 192.

use the channel as an instrument of mass deception. An enthusiastic channel serves that end better than a debilitated victim of unwanted possession. However, such voluntary relationships at times become involuntary.

## MENTAL AND PHYSICAL CHANNELING

Mediumship falls into two main categories: mental and physical. In *mental* mediumship the medium communicates through inner vision, clairaudience, automatic writing, and automatic speech. *Physical* mediumship is characterized by rappings, apports, levitation, or movement of objects and other paranormal phenomena. Mediums of both types communicate with spirits through one or more entities called "controls," or spirit guides, which usually remain permanently with the medium. In this chapter we are primarily dealing with mental channeling.

In its most liberal interpretation, channeling also includes the processes of imagination, intuition, inspiration, and premonition. Channeling usually occurs as a breakthrough during the process of spiritual development or psychic experimentation. Jane Roberts's interaction with Seth began with a Ouija board, for example, while Jach Pursel, Pat Rodegast, Kevin Ryerson, and others had their breakthroughs after meditation experience.[112]

## EXPLAINING CHANNELING

Various theories have been advanced to explain the channeling phenomenon. The simplest and most basic explanation is that the channeled sources are who — or what — they say they are. Ancient channelers believed they were indeed invoking spirits of the dead, deities, or nature or animal spirits. This view also is held by Spiritualist mediums, who believe they communicate with the dead. This view remains prevalent in societies where channeled information is routinely sought for prophecy, healing, divination, and advice. New Age opinions on the sources are more divided, with some individuals taking channeled sources at their face value and others believing in theories advanced by psychologists.

As we noted earlier, Ken Wilber contends that much of Schucman's work in *A Course in Miracles* flows from her mystical and metaphysical background. Forerunner Alice Bailey said that 85 percent of channeled material comes from the personal subconscious minds of the channels. Many of today's channels would substantially agree. Channel Joey Crinita of Canada believes that channeling is often nothing more than a form of self-hypnosis in which the imagination creates its own characters.[113]

112. Guiley, *Harper's Encyclopedia*, 358, 90.
113. Elliot Miller, *Crash Course*, 167.

Carl Raschke is convinced that most channels, after considerable study in metaphysics and meditation techniques, attain a heightened sensitivity to their own unconscious minds. He also thinks a form of "mass hypnosis" often occurs in group channeling sessions. "A process of collective suggestion and transfer of unconscious content" takes place.[114]

Some channelers believe they are calling upon their own Higher Self, a level of wisdom not normally accessed in waking consciousness. The Higher Self also has been called the "oversoul" and "superconscious."

Other theories related to the channeled-entity-as-self idea hold that human consciousness is far more complex than believed. Thus each individual may actually have multiple consciousnesses of varying levels of sophistication. However, only a few individuals become aware of these and gain access to them.

Ram Dass (also known as Dr. Richard Alpert) is an advocate of channeling who also is a psychologist. But he, too, uses his confusion about the facts as an excuse to avoid the issue of interpretation. Writing about "Emmanuel," an astral-plane entity channeled by Pat Rodegast, Ram Dass says: "From my point of view as a psychologist, I allow for the theoretical possibility that Emmanuel is a deeper part of Pat. In the final analysis, what difference does it really make? What I treasure is the wisdom Emmanuel conveys."[115]

Some New Age analysts, to explain some channeling, accept theories of "dissociation," in which part of the mind splits off from the whole and acts as a separate personality. This approach allows one to acknowledge the sincerity of the channel without having to allow for an otherworldly source.

This explanation is surprising since we would naturally expect channels to insist on the objective reality of their entities. Some do, but as we noted above, others are curiously ambivalent and say that the entities are a higher or deeper part of their subconscious.

Sigmund Freud, the father of psychoanalysis, begrudgingly addressed channeling-type phenomena on occasion. His basic explanation was that channeling-like phenomena must be seen in terms of wish fulfillment and the reemergence of material repressed into the unconscious. He wrote that "what in those days were thought to be evil spirits to us are base and evil wishes, the derivatives of impulses which have been rejected and repressed." A follower of Freud would probably interpret the voices, visions, and expressions of channeling as repressed material unavailable to the conscious mind that seeks ways to get by the gate-guarding mechanism.

Swiss physician/psychoanalyst Carl Gustav Jung broke away from

114. Chandler, *Understanding the New Age*, 73.
115. Alexander, *Spirit Channeling*, 18.

Freud's thinking in order to expand the notion of the unconscious to include nonsexual cognitive and spiritual aspects. Jung wrote that "the psyche is composed of various complexes of psychic material." For Jung, the appearance of communication from nonphysical spirits could be accounted for by these complexes, which become repressed and separated from normal waking consciousness. These complexes might project themselves in a form, he said, which is experienced by the individual as separate from himself.

Jung provided another possible explanation based on what he called the impersonal or collective unconscious. This collective unconscious is composed of primordial images which have always been the basis of human thinking — the whole treasure-house of mythological motifs. Channeling, by this view, might be the individual tapping into the archetypes of this racial memory.

In later life, Jung admitted that he was open to the ideas that all these metapsychic phenomena could be explained better by the theory of spirits than by the qualities and peculiarities of the unconscious. "In each individual case I must of necessity be skeptical, but in the long run I have to admit that the spirit hypothesis yields better results in practice than any other."

However, for followers of Jung, such as Jean Houston, the Seths and the many personal guides are the "projections and creations of the immensity that is personal and collective unconscious."[116]

Some psychologists believe channeling is pathological in origin, and is symptomatic of multiple personality disorder. In multiple personality cases, individuals are host to two or more personalities, each of which has its own identity, memories, beliefs, and history. However, the individual usually has little or no control over the personalities. This could have similar results. For example, Ted Schultz thinks Ramtha's morality is potentially dangerous, because he does not "abhor the act" of murder. Schultz points out that a large number of murderers attribute their actions to the orders of channeled spirits. The famous Son of Sam serial killer of six women, David Berkowitz, claimed he did so at the behest of a six-thousand-year-old entity who spoke to him through his neighbor's dog. Britain's Yorkshire Ripper, killer of thirteen prostitutes in 1975, and Mark David Chapman, the murderer of John Lennon, made similar claims. Although normally harmless, channeling as an expression of our dissociated unconscious mind may, in some instances, lead to destructive consequences.[117]

116. Klimo, *Channeling*, 213-18.
117. Peters, *Cosmic Self*, 34-35.

# THE PARAPSYCHOLOGICAL

In the 1920s, Duke University research psychologist J. B. Rhine and others decided to formalize a new scientific discipline for the study of paranormal phenomena. This new discipline, parapsychology, had as one emphasis the area of extrasensory perception (ESP), which includes all kinds of unusual information reception: telepathy, clairvoyance, precognition, and psychometry. It also studied survival phenomena, including channeling, possession, ghosts and hauntings, reincarnation, and afterlife evidence.

In the super, grand, or general ESP theory, material that could be known by channels in no other way is explained by their having telepathically read the unconscious minds of "distant" individuals who are unknown to everyone involved. In the super ESP model, a database is available which is composed of all living minds. It could include Jung's collective unconscious or the ancient's Akashic records. The adherence of parapsychologists to such a grand ESP explanation for channeling seems to display an inability to make the conceptual leap to the possibility of nonphysical intelligent beings.[118]

## PHYSICS

As noted in Chapter 1, New Agers tend to explain channeling and other New Age teachings along the line of the so-called "New Physics."

However, Melton states that from a scientific point of view, it is difficult to draw the lines between divine revelation, inspiration, possession, multiple personality disorder, and schizophrenia. The current popularity of new channeling poses a challenge to the scientists studying these phenomena. As we noted above, paraphysics and parapsychology are among the new subdisciplines that have developed to investigate paranormal events such as channeling.[119]

## FRAUD, HOAX, GREED

Elliot Miller suggests conscious fraud or greed in the case of highly theatrical channels such as J. Z. Knight. Harmon Bro agrees and states that it is difficult to avoid seeing fraud and greed at work in the high fees for consultations that have built elegant, chandeliered horse stables for the medium (J. Z. Knight), who channels a supposed 30,000-year-old Atlantean warrior. Or there is a suspicion of avarice when a California psychic charges a large fee to produce

118. Klimo, *Channeling*, 247-48.
119. Melton, Clark, and Kelly, *New Age Almanac*, 50.

wisdom direct from the minds of dolphins. Bro also suggests that it is conscious fraud to promote indiscriminately the widely studied *A Course in Miracles* as literally the words of Jesus. Such promotion overlooks the obvious Vedantist, or Hindu, substance of the teaching (which denies the crucifixion and ultimately the reality of sin and evil), far from the New Testament. Such a promotion also robs students of a legitimate and disciplined study of Hindu thought.[120]

In a lengthy article on channelers in *OMNI* magazine, Katharine Lowry tells of spending time with amiable, bearded Jach Pursel, Lazaris's channel, in Beverly Hills. There is the possibility that he is "consciously making this all up. . . . When we talk for an hour alone . . . he is friendly, relaxed, helpful, and seems genuinely modest and kind. But whenever I ask about Lazaris or the mechanics of channeling, his eyes — those windows to the soul — slide this way and that."

Chandler points out that Penny Torres, who channels Mafu, was unabashedly egotistical in her assessment of whether Mafu is a fraud. "What if I am an actress?" she said in a *Life Times* magazine interview. "Those things used to terrify me . . . because I was afraid that there was some part, a subconscious part of me, creating this. My answer to that is that if this is coming from me, then I think that I am absolutely incredible! And I'll take all the credit that they want to give me!"[121]

In other words, channeling can be seen as a particularly pernicious form of self-delusion in which the subconscious mind masquerades as personalities external to the subject.

## CHANNELING AND DEMON POSSESSION

Prominent channeling advocate and psychologist Jon Klimo maintains that those who say that the entities involved in channeling are demons and evil beings are doing harm to the welfare of humanity. Klimo writes, "To the extent to which they [the churches] brand and prohibit channeling as demon worship and consorting with 'unfamiliar spirits,' they will be abdicating what should be their role: to help us reconnect ourselves in our own way with our common Source as underlying Reality." In other words, "to return to the truth of truths . . . that we are God."[122]

But evangelical Christians remember that Satan's primal lie to Adam and Eve was to tell them they could be as God. And contemporary channeling

120. Duncan S. Ferguson, ed., *New Age Spirituality: An Assessment* (Louisville, Ky.: Westminster/John Knox, 1993), 172-73.
121. Chandler, *Understanding the New Age*, 72-73.
122. Ferguson, *New Age Spirituality*, 189.

promotes the active acceptance of a god to replace God. From the biblical perspective, all of humanity is alienated from God as a result of the Fall. We all start with a God-shaped hole in our lives. Channeling tries to fill that hole with something or someone other than God. But the "something else" that replaced God is spiritually harmful. All of this logically suggests that the spirits of channeling are demonic. If a person accepts the basic message of channeling, redemption makes no sense, repentance is irrelevant, and the biblical teaching on salvation has no meaning. That is precisely the dominant message of channeling.[123]

Elliot Miller presents a balanced view of what is involved in channeling in his description of a personal dialogue with Penny Torres and "Mafu." Miller suggests that he did not sense anything directly or essentially supernatural about the *person* (supposedly Mafu) speaking through Torres who was sitting next to him. "On the other hand, I did discern *in* that person a seemingly supernatural ability to twist truth and manipulate the audience."

Elliot's conclusion was that "Mafu" is probably, at best, a dissociated part of Torres's own consciousness and, at worst, her conscious creation. But in any case, through practicing the biblically forbidden art of mediumship, she has become a satanically energized and guided agent of deception. In other words, even if Mafu is unreal, Torres is probably possessed.

Evidently several things are involved in channeling. As many channels are willing to admit, in most if not all cases it is not simply a matter of spirit taking over the channel's body and directly expressing his own words. To varying degrees, the channel's subconscious and/or conscious mind is also involved. Thus the typical "entity" in channeling is partly — but not entirely — an objective reality. He is the combined creation of the channel and a *hidden* spiritual entity, which is in fact *real*.

According to Brooks Alexander and Roberts Burrow, "Real entities do not have to be channeled for real lies to be told and real damage to be done. . . . The runaway popularity of a flagrantly demonic message is cause enough for concern."[124]

## BASIC CONTENT OF CHANNELED TEACHINGS

Suzanne Riordan admits that a survey of the stations on the channeling circuit will reveal quite a bit of static. A bewildering diversity of cosmic voices babble, gossip, and prophesy on every aspect of human and nonhuman life, offering a myriad of (and often mutually contradictory versions of

123. Brooks Alexander. "What Is Spiritism? and Why Are They Saying Those Awful Things About It?" *SCP Journal* 7.1 (1987): 7.
124. Elliot Miller, *Crash Course*, 168-69.

history, theology, and science) and a profusion of clashing — but equally unorthodox — commentaries on current events. In the flood of channeled material which has been published or delivered to "live" audiences in the last two decades, there is much that is trivial, contradictory, and confusing. The authors of much of this material make claims which are difficult or impossible to verify.

However, as we noted in the survey of channelers, the worldview which emerges from these channeled documents has a distinctive and consistent core. Although from different sources, in terms both of their fleshly vehicles and — presumably — of their otherworldly origins, these revelations echo each other in tone and content. Taken as a whole, this body of literature offers an analysis of the human condition and a set of prescriptions designed to assist humanity in discovering its true destiny. The argument is based on certain assumptions about the nature of reality which the authors present from their presumably enhanced perspective. In essence, they seek to convince us that we are not who we think we are and that much of our suffering can be traced to our mistaken identity. Their mission is to "awaken" and "remind" us.[125]

Klimo emphasizes that channeled teachings tend to update that which Aldous Huxley called "perennial philosophy." This is a comprehensive worldview that includes a metaphysic, a psychology, and an ethic. It contrasts sharply with the modern worldview wherein the divine, if it exists at all, is thought to transcend mundane affairs. The consensus from most of the channeled material is that the universe is a multi-dimensional, living Being, which some call God. It is inhabited by aspects of itself — human beings of consciousness — on many or all of its other dimensions besides the physical as we currently experience it. And so we keep hearing messages about, and from, the etheric, astral, mental, causal, and other dimensions of this expanded Nature. Furthermore, according to this channeled wisdom, wherever a being, personality, or entity may be within this cosmological hierarchy, he, she, or it is always in a process of learning for the purpose of evolving into ever-more unity with the one Being that is the source and destiny of all separate beings. Finally, we are told that love reigns over wisdom, light, and pure force or energetic power, as the supreme reality of all creation. We in our "classroom" on earth are pictured as slowly learning to be loving beings who reflect the nature of our Creator. Most versions speak of us as essentially of the same quality or nature as our Creator and thus undying — having many opportunities and contexts for this learning and evolution to take place. Hence the recurrent theme of reincarnation.[126]

125. Lewis and Melton, *Perspectives on the New Age*, 107, 110-11.
126. Klimo, *Channeling*, 151.

Themes emerging from contemporary channelers are:

1. A critique both of modernity and of orthodox religion for denying "the inherent wisdom and goodness of the Self" and for encouraging dependence on external sources of authority.

2. The human flesh-and-blood experience in time and space is but one mode among many of experiencing consciousness.

3. They take for granted the primacy of consciousness over matter and the immanence of the divine — what Willis Harman has called "transcendental monism."[127]

In other words, the self is not limited, there are no boundaries of the self, and you can make your own reality. According to Miller, this doctrine is not unique to channeling. Human potential groups like The Forum (formerly est) and Lifespring are based on it. But the channelers apply it with a new consistency and boldness, taking it to its logical conclusions.

Related to a lack of self-love is our failure to love others. This actually results in an extolling of self-love far above other loves. In addition to self-love, "unconditional love" is emphasized. This means total acceptance: not taking into account anything that is wrong with the one loved. Love is so defined in channeling as to be the antithesis of judgment. When applied to God, this view of love would eliminate ultimate justice from the universe. God is absolutely permissive and accepting — there is no accounting for past sins, no retribution for wrongdoing. Ramtha states that the love of God will allow you to be and do anything you wish and hold you judgeless. God has never judged you or anyone.[128]

4. A prominent theme of the channeled material as a whole is the unfortunate and harmful role which fear plays in human psychology. This fear is due to the fact that humanity has drifted into a deep sleep, severed its connection with its source, and fallen under the "spell of matter" — it has forgotten its origins and identity. Fear can be eliminated by practices designed to lift the spell, to awaken us from the dream, to remind us of our "vastness" and our divinity. To overcome fear and achieve one's potential one must instead *take back* his or her power and become totally autonomous and independent.[129]

5. The alienation of humankind from nature is one of the primary maladies of modern civilization.

6. The tragedy of the modern crisis arose when Judaism and later Christianity unleashed the ego and brought about a situation in which the species came to consider itself apart from the rest of existence. The conscious-

127. Lewis and Melton, *Perspectives on the New Age*, 111.
128. Elliot Miller, *Crash Course*, 170-72.
129. Lewis and Melton, *Perspectives on the New Age*, 111-12.

ness of the species "had to pretend to dislike and disown [its] source." One of the consequences of this orientation, according to this argument, was a polarization of the sexes. Characteristics that were considered female became associated with nature — the source from which humanity wished to distance itself. This resulted in a civilization in which intellect, knowledge, and fact were divorced from intuition, emotion, and revelation and the latter devalued. This divorce has caused a fragmentation in our sense of identity: we distrust and disown part of our own experience. As we distrust Nature, so we distrust our own nature and our very Source as God.[130]

7. The channeled entities agree in affirming that death, as such, is an illusion. What we call death, they say, is merely a transition to a higher plane from which we will probably reincarnate in time, either on earth or elsewhere.

In summary, the channeled sources offer a detailed diagnosis of the ailment which afflicts the modern psyche. It is guilt (self-loathing) and fear. Its origin is the repudiation by an adolescent consciousness of its cosmic parent, the ego's denial of its divine source. The channelers prescription is a reconciliation with Self and Spirit, a "reawakening" from the illusion of separation — a "remembering" of one's own divinity, of one's participation in the Self's wondrous creativity.[131]

## THE PORTRAYAL OF JESUS

According to Ted Peters, the Jesus of the channelers and the New Age is not the historical Jesus who became the Christ for the purpose of saving the human race solely by God's grace. Gone is the belief that the Good Friday cross and the Easter resurrection were historical events in which God did some work, in which God actually took action to defeat the powers of sin, death, or even Karma on our behalf. Gone is the belief that because of what Jesus Christ did we are given the forgiveness of sins and the promise of our own resurrection to eternal life. In short, the Jesus of the new age and channeling is not a savior. He is instead a teacher of mystical truths. Once we learn these mystical truths, then we ourselves can follow the Pelagian path toward enlightenment from our world of darkness, step by step, plane by plane, until we work our way up to the realm of pure light. The historical Christ need not bequeath to us much in the way of gifts of God's grace, because we ourselves, down deep, are already divine. All we need do is raise this divine potential into a divine actuality.[132]

130. Ibid., 114.
131. Ibid., 124.
132. Peters, *Cosmic Self,* 90.

## New Age Teaching on Spiritual Information from the Beyond

Ron Rhodes summarizes the New Age approach to spiritual information from the beyond in four statements:

1. Revelation has come to humanity not only through Jesus Christ but also through the leaders of the other world religions — Buddha, Zoroaster, Krishna, and other metaphysical beings.

2. The revelations that have come from the various teachers teach the same "core truths": all is one (monism), all is God (pantheism), and humanity is God.

3. We must therefore learn from the religious views and practices of all the alleged revealers.

4. Revelations continue to be received today from disembodied humans, "space brothers" (UFOs), and other entities and sources through modern channelers.[133]

# A PERSONAL GOD

According to the biblical worldview, acceptance of a personal revelation from God given to us through particular circumstances of time and space is the only way to reach a saving relationship with the sovereign and personal God and his purposes. For New Age devotees, the teaching that ultimate reality can best be known through particular time and space occurrences is a contradiction and a scandal.

It is a biblical conviction that God entered history in divine acts and raised up and inspired persons to interpret the significance of these acts. In the Old Testament we see the beginning as the living God revealed himself, his will, and his way, in contrast to the nature gods commonly worshiped in ancient times. The continuation and fulfillment of this revelation is seen in the New Testament, where the religions and philosophies of the day were either judged or transformed.

The pagan nations, then and now, sought the absolute or the divine in the material universe alone or in the invisible world. Israel knew that God must be sought elsewhere and in other ways. Israel alone among the nations dared to say that the world is not divine, but that it was created by God.[134]

---

133. Ron Rhodes, *New Age Movement*, Zondervan Guide to Cults and Religious Movements (Grand Rapids: Zondervan, 1995), 40.

134. John P. Newport, *Life's Ultimate Questions* (Dallas: Word, 1989), 10-11.

This concept of revelation led Israel to preserve, to collect, and, ultimately, to write down her historical traditions. The Israelites were the first people to do so in this fashion. Israel's knowledge of God, therefore, led her to an interest in history. This was true because God had chosen the forms of history as the way in which he revealed himself to her.[135]

A primary function of the Bible is to reveal the character and to offer an identity description of an agent, namely God. The Bible does this by recounting the interaction of his deeds and purposes with those of humans in their ever-changing circumstances. These accounts reach their climax in what the Gospels say of the risen, ascended, and ever-present Jesus Christ, whose identity as the divine-human agent is enacted in the stories of Jesus of Nazareth. The climax, however, is logically inseparable from what precedes it. The Jesus of the Gospels is the Son of the God of Abraham, Isaac, and Jacob. The primary focus in the Bible is on how life is to be lived in the realities of this world in the light of God's character — as this is pictured in the stories of Israel and of Jesus.

## THE STORY OF JESUS

Becoming a Christian involves learning the story of Israel and Jesus well enough to interpret and experience oneself in one's world in terms of that story. Biblical religion is above all an external influence that molds and shapes the self and individual experience, rather than an expression of a preexisting self or a preconceptual experience.

The biblical view sees humans as made in God's image, with the capacity to respond to God and live in fellowship with him. However, humans used their freedom to rebel against God and thus are fallen creatures. Nevertheless, they are still responsible; their humanity has not ceased to exist.

The cross of Christ, which provides the key to the whole pattern of biblical events, is a revelation of humanity's rebellious and sinful state. Sin is not just bound up with a person's sensuous nature; it penetrates the inner sanctuary of the spirit. Human beings cannot escape their love of self, and they consequently find themselves prisoners of their own egocentrism.

The dominant biblical teaching about God is that he must be conceived as fully personal. Throughout the Bible there are detailed descriptions of the personal nature of God, including his personal will and purpose in the acts of creation and redemption. The Incarnation is the unique and final disclosure of God's personal nature, as well as the unveiling of the true personal being of humankind.

---

135. G. Ernest Wright, "Archaeology, History and Theology," *Harvard Divinity Bulletin* 28 (April 1964): 85-96.

Creation out of nothing is basic to biblical thought. This doctrine of creation out of nothing draws a sharp distinction between God and the world. It clarifies that the world is not an overflow from God's nature, but distinct from him and made by him. The biblical view thus dismisses pantheism (the belief that God and nature are one). The biblical view of creation stresses God's sovereignty over the physical process and its total dependence upon him. It points to the transcendence of God, which must not be obscured by any view of his immanence.

God has not chosen to disclose the depths and fullness of himself as the end point of a rational argument or in a mystical identification available in unredeemed humanity's subjective depths. Instead, he has chosen to make his final revelation of himself in and through certain particular historical events. These include an exodus of a slave people from Egypt and the vicissitudes of their subsequent history as interpreted through the prophetic consciousness. And his climactic act of disclosure was incarnational — he chose to reveal himself through the life, death, and resurrection of a humble carpenter, Jesus Christ.

In the biblical view, the knowledge of God is further found in obedience to God's personal revelation. The personal self-disclosure of God in revelatory events must be received by men and women in faith, which involves the will as well as the mind and emotions. This response of the whole person is expressed in a person's life and produces changed patterns of living.

Morality from the biblical perspective is empowered and guided by a covenant relationship with a holy and loving God. Ethical decisions are made in relation to the principles found in God's progressive revelation to humankind as recorded in the Bible and centered in Jesus Christ.

## VERIFYING THE BASIC PREMISE

Biblical adherents recognize that in an increasingly pluralistic world, it is important to establish methods of comparing worldviews and ways of undergirding their conviction concerning the superiority of the biblical worldview. Although the biblical worldview cannot be proved in the way that a mathematical equation can be proved, a systematic and consistent approach can present a strong verification of the basic premises of the Christian worldview.

Biblical persons should invite New Age advocates to make an honest inquiry into the Bible. They will encounter a wealth of compelling evidence that the Bible is a special revelation, including scores of historically verifiable miracles (the Exodus of the Jews from Egypt, the Resurrection of Christ), dozens of unambiguously fulfilled prophecies, inspiring teachings which have consistency with the world and humans as we find them, and the person of

Jesus Christ, who endorses the *entirety* of Scripture as God's Word and is himself its fulfillment (Matt. 5:17-19).[136]

The historical and event-centered nature of the Bible indicates the public and coherent nature of the personalities who received key biblical truths — the Old Testament prophets and the New Testament apostles. The prophet was a "public man." His encounter with God was not a private experience withdrawn from contact with workaday things, like that of the mystics and sages of many religions. The pressure of public movements and events upon his spirit was the occasion of the encounters with God which brought compulsion upon him. Furthermore, the inspired truth which the encounter forced upon his mind was public property.

It is true that the encounter with God is often described in terms of what we call "religious experiences." These experiences were sometimes abnormal or at least unusual — such as seeing visions and hearing voices. Most of the prophets were embarrassed by the presence of "false prophets" whose mental processes were not distinguishable psychologically from their own. However, they remained totally convinced that God really had spoken to them.

Two things seem important to note about the validity of the prophetic experience. First, when the prophets said, "I saw the Lord," or "The Lord said unto me," or "The Spirit of the Lord came upon me," the experience to which they refer was an element in the total experience of life which was rational and coherent, forming a logical unity in itself. We can see this quite clearly in prophets such as Isaiah and Jeremiah, whose biographies are in large measure open to us. Their visions and auditions were not aberrations, unrelated to their experience of life as a whole. These were clearly the kind of men of whom it is credible that they did meet with God, whatever psychological form the meeting may have taken.

Second, the personal experience of the prophets was also organically related to the course of the history in which they played a part; it enabled them to give an interpretation of the situation which could stand up to the facts. Also note that the effects which flowed from the prophet's intervention in history were in keeping with its alleged origin in an encounter with God. The prophets made a momentous impact for righteousness, affecting the whole subsequent history of humankind. It is therefore unlikely that the experience which impelled them to speak and act as they did was a delusion, whatever the form in which it may have been embodied. The prophetic experience is related to the events of history itself, inasmuch as the consequences are seen in history.

The coherence and public nature of the experiences of the Old Testament prophets is somewhat similar to the experiences of the New Testament

---

136. Elliot Miller, *Crash Course*, 176.

leaders. For example, note the experiences which determined the New Testament interpretation of events: the appearances of the risen Christ to his followers.

Here again we have strictly firsthand witnesses. For example, the apostle Paul expressly claims to have had an encounter with the risen Christ, and he appeals for corroboration to a large number of other witnesses, whose testimony in a number of cases is indirectly reported in the Gospels and the Acts. When, therefore, Paul speaks of his meeting with Christ, he is not speaking of some private, incommunicable experience, but of an experience which he shared with others — an experience of "public" facts.

It seems clear that the New Testament experience of an encounter with the risen Christ was similar to the prophetic experience in terms of its effect in history. If we question the validity of a reported encounter with the risen Christ, the same tests may be applied. Paul's meeting with Christ is no aberration. We know Paul very intimately from his letters; they reveal a singularly coherent personality. And this coherence depends to a marked degree upon the reality of what we call his conversion.

Paul says he was "arrested" by Christ. Well, he was certainly arrested by something, to great effect. It is noteworthy that the effects of the "arrest" in the whole of his career were in keeping with their alleged cause. Moreover, the remoter effects in history were in keeping with that which the apostles declared to be the starting point of it all. Note the rise of the church — the highly original character of its community life, its astonishing early expansion, and its no less astonishing spiritual and intellectual achievements. The originating event was Paul's meeting with the risen Christ, in whom he saw the glory and salvation of God. It is unlikely, even from a secular perspective, that all of this was based upon a delusion.[137]

## THE FINAL WORD

Jude 3 indicates there are no continuing revelations of foundational, doctrinal truth occurring today: "Contend earnestly for the faith which was once for all delivered to the saints" (NASB). "The faith" refers to "the apostolic teaching and preaching which was regulative upon the Church" (see Acts 6:7; Gal. 1:23; 1 Tim. 4:1). The basic revelatory process was completed after this faith had been delivered. Therefore, there is no need of further basic teachings about the nature of God, the person of Christ, and the way of salvation.

Even if one hypothetically granted that God did wish to reveal additional foundational truths today, any present-day revelation would have

137. C. H. Dodd, *The Bible Today* (Cambridge: Cambridge University, 1962), 101-5.

to be consistent with the previous revelation. The apostle Paul said that "even if we or an angel from heaven should preach a gospel other than the one we preached to you, let him be eternally condemned!" (Gal. 1:8). Any teaching that contradicts previous authoritative teaching from God is an abomination. Paul further spoke of the importance of making sure that new claims to truth be measured against what we know to be true from apostolic teaching. Since channeled "revelations" contradict what we know to be revelation from God (that is, Scripture) for the Christian, they do not qualify as true revelations.[138]

## THE BIBLE AND SPIRITUAL BEINGS

The Bible does affirm the existence of spiritual beings called "angels" and "the spirits of just men made perfect." Some are fallen angels (Satan and demons) and others are unfallen.

Efforts to contact these spirits is prohibited (Deut. 18:10-12). For example, Saul lost his kingdom when, desperate for advice, he asked a medium to bring up the departed prophet Samuel rather than inquiring directly of the Lord (1 Chron. 10:13-14). Furthermore, the Bible points out that real spirits, capable of divulging extraordinary information, can be involved in spiritism (Acts 16:16-19), but it pictures them as deceptive and evil. They are in a different category than the good spirits. The information which the spirits give is a supernaturally sophisticated mixture of truth and error which their followers are incapable of evaluating. This means that they become entrapped in a web of deceit, and suffer moral deterioration from involvement with such evil beings.[139]

According to biblical teaching, departed humans are not available for contact. They are not hovering around in the "great beyond" available for contact with human beings on earth. Departed Christians are in the presence of Christ (Phil. 1:23). Departed unbelievers are in a place of great suffering (Luke 16:19-31), confined until that future day of judgment (Rev. 20:11-15).

## BIBLICAL PROPHECY AND INSPIRATION

In contrast, in biblical prophecy and inspiration God took the initiative in dealing with the human recipients of the revelation. The writers wrote from their own minds and circumstances, but were so moved and superintended by God that what they wrote was exactly what he wanted written. This is

138. Rhodes, *Culting of America*, 44-45.
139. Elliot Miller, *Crash Course*, 143-44.

opposed to channeling, where the personality of the channel moves aside so that another personality can communicate.

Furthermore, the biblical writers emphasized that their revelation was based not on some private, esoteric experience, but on observable historical events (1 John 1:1-3). John, whose contribution to the writing of the New Testament was second only to that of Paul, was talking about what he had seen and heard with his physical eyes and ears, that which could be touched, examined, and witnessed to by others independently. Such a revelation is historical and rational.

Luke and Paul (Acts 9:1-9; 26:24-26) argue that the revelation from God is open to rational investigation because, even though it has a strong subjective side to it, it is objective and public. Paul's vision was not just in his mind. Nor was it just a product of meditation and visualization.

When the disciples saw the resurrected Jesus, they were not visualizing. Thomas, one of the twelve disciples, was not present when the others first saw the risen Lord. When they told him, "We have seen the Lord!" he dismissed it as incredible. "Unless I see the nail marks in his hands and put my finger where the nails were, and put my hand into his side, I will not believe it" (John 20:25). Although Jesus reprimanded Thomas for his doubt, he honored his insistence on the need for verification of a claim of such gigantic proportions, that death had finally been defeated in human history. Therefore Jesus appeared again to his disciples when Thomas was present. And he publicly invited Thomas to verify the claim: "Put your finger here; see my hands. Reach out your hand and put it into my side. Stop doubting and believe" (John 20:27).

In contrast, much channeling is subjective, nonrational visualization. Channeling and visualization are usually experienced as a state of pure consciousness, free from the limitations of the senses and the intellect, or that which is verifiable by these human means.

The Bible teaches that channeling or even prophecy can and must be tested because of the abundance of false prophets. One obvious test is whether its predictive aspects come true (Deut. 18:21-22). Another test is whether the content of a prophet's teaching, in the area of both morals (what is good?) and metaphysics (what is true?), conforms to God's objective revelation in Scripture and nature (Deut. 13:1-4; 1 John 4:1-3).

In contrast, the New Age and occult worldview contends that every spirit is God. Spirit is consciousness; therefore all imagination or visualization is spiritual and divine truth.[140]

---

140. Vishal Mangalwadi, *When the New Age Gets Old* (Downers Grove, Ill.: Inter-Varsity, 1992), 71-75.

## Morality

As we have noted, the New Age emphasis is on humans as being divine, meaning that humans are not bound by moral obligations and should not be held morally accountable or be punished for what they do.

In contrast, the biblical teaching emphasizes that the Holy Spirit is moral and is operative in the world to further the moral work of Jesus and a Holy God. Galatians 5:16-17, 19-24 points out that the power of the Holy Spirit is given primarily to make people holy and to empower them to make their world holy. The Holy Spirit effects moral changes in individuals.

In Luke 4:18-19 Jesus promised the power of the Holy Spirit to his disciples, not for their power or glory, but to make them instruments of God's righteous power, to make them soldiers for God's kingdom. They were to judge their societies by God's yardstick of holiness, to resist evil, and to proclaim justice and rest.[141]

## Demonic Nature of Spiritism and Channeling

In light of its emphasis on the divinity of humans, it is understandable that spiritism and channeling reject the personal moral God revealed in history and in Jesus Christ. It is, as the prophets emphasize, "spiritual adultery" carried to completion. The biblical language that deals with spiritism is negative. Spiritism is called evil, error, folly, falsehood, apostasy, and abomination (see, for example, Deut. 18:9-14 and Rev. 22:15). In the Old Testament, those who indulge in it are considered defiled and deserving of exile or death. In the New Testament, spiritists are identified as opposers of the gospel and enemies of the truth.

For Moses and the prophets, concourse with spirits was a horror and an abomination. Spirits were seen as the driving force behind the false religions in direct conflict and competition with God. The Old Testament unfailingly testifies that all idolatrous worship is demon worship and fellowship with unclean spirits (see Lev. 17:7; Deut. 32:17; 2 Chron. 11:15; Ps. 106:37). Deuteronomy 18:9-14 clearly connects the idolatrous heathen cultures that surround Israel with their spiritism (demonism) and their occult practices, especially divination.

The New Testament reaffirms the Old Testament revelation that the gods of heathen idolatry are demons. In 1 Corinthians 10:19-20 Paul states that there is a spiritual power and reality behind heathen worship, but it is demonic and not the divine power it claims to be. Acts 16:16-18 records Paul's encounter with a pagan oracle — a "slave girl who had a spirit by which she

---

141. Ibid., 80-81.

predicted the future. She earned a great deal of money for her owners by fortune-telling" (v. 16). Paul cast out the spirit with a word of direct command in the name of Jesus Christ. It was a deliverance that her owners did not appreciate, since her demonic bondage had been highly profitable for them (Acts 16:19-24). Paul further states that Satan masquerades as an angel of light, seeking to deceive people (2 Cor. 11:14). In fact, Satan and his fallen angels are actively promoting "doctrines of demons" (doctrines purporting to be the truth but which are in fact lies) (1 Tim. 4:1, NASB). Christians are admonished to "test the spirits" (1 John 4:1).[142]

Further discussion of this subject will be conducted in the chapter on the Satanic and black magic.

## COLLISION OF BIBLICAL AND CHANNELED TEACHINGS

It is clear, after noting the teachings of the channelers and the basic elements of the biblical worldview, that the two views are in collision.

The New Age view teaches that we are divine, perfect, autonomous, and totally self-sufficient. In contrast, the Bible states that we are sinners, accountable to God for our sins, and incapable of saving ourselves (Rom. 3:9-20). The related New Age teaching that we are in need of no savior but ourselves is opposed to the biblical teaching that salvation is through Jesus.

The New Age teaching emphasized by the channelers is self-love. But the Bible states that self-love stands at the root of human problems (see John 12:25; 2 Tim. 3:1-5; Rev. 12:11). One appeal of the New Age is that it combines in its definition of self-love the selfishness that the Bible condemns with the concepts of self-esteem and self-acceptance. Self-esteem and self-love are not necessarily unbiblical if viewed as by-products of a right relationship with Christ.

The New Age channelers equate unconditional love with total non-judgment. In contrast, in the Bible, God perfectly integrates the equally necessary qualities of mercy and justice (Ps. 85:10). The Christian message is not essentially negative and unloving. It does not put us down to keep us down as unworthy sinners. In fact, its purpose is to face us with the truth about ourselves, for only then can we avail ourselves of what Christ has done to raise us forever *above* our sinful condition.

It should be noted that the core New Age/channeling doctrines, "You can be as God," and "You shall not die," were first uttered by the serpent in the Garden of Eden (Gen. 3:4-5). Embraced then, this teaching produced

142. Alexander, *Spirit Channeling*, 23-26; Rhodes, *Culting of America*, 43.

the world's misery. Embraced now, it would make what God has done in Christ to remedy the situation unavailable to those who need the remedy.

Elliot Miller dramatically portrays the possible implications of the acceptance of the channeled New Age teaching. It would eventually lead to a return to a broad acceptance of the amorality, hedonism, social and familial irresponsibility, lack of compassion, and devaluation of human life. These nonbiblical approaches can be found in many, and strongly characterizes some (for example, J. Z. Knight's) channeled teachings. But a larger pattern is becoming discernible. The New Age channeling movement is signaling a return to a superstitious, primitive culture.[143]

Channeled New Age teaching denies the reality of death and its function as judgment. In contrast, the Bible sees God's judgment (either present or impending) as a spur to conscience, which convicts us of our own wrongdoing. It faces us with our need for repentance and redemption. In the midst of that moral and ethical tension, the teaching of God's forgiveness in Christ and his cross is good news indeed, and is easily seen as such.

However, if death is denied and its spur of judgment is left out, then conscience becomes dull and finally dormant. Repentance makes no sense; redemption appears irrelevant; and salvation in Christ seems to have no meaning.[144]

## The Consequences of Conflict

Thus we see that the extent to which a culture accepts spiritism and channeling is crucial. Spiritism represents a people's flight from God. And rejection of God and his revealed way brings God's judgment. The source, message, and effects of the teachings of the channelers are at odds with biblical reality. This leads to God's judgment on us in life today and to the final reckoning called the Last Judgment.

The tragedy is that Jesus Christ can fill the deep void in the lives of New Age followers and bring a sense of purpose, love, and hope. Those of us who have accepted and embraced God's revelation in Christ have not been disappointed, receiving, as he promised, an abundant and purposeful life. We have also found that the "sting of death" has been removed by the historic reality of Christ's own triumph over it, which he has promised to share with those who are his (John 10:25-26; 1 Cor. 15:51-57). All that the channels and entities offer is only a delusion, a dangerous counterfeit of what Jesus permanently gives.[145]

143. Elliot Miller, *Crash Course*, 177-79.
144. Alexander, *Spirit Channeling*, 27.
145. Elliot Miller, *Crash Course*, 181-82.

# CHAPTER SIX

# Magic, Witchcraft, Neopaganism, and the Goddess Movement

A surprising movement of recent times is the growth of paganism, magic, and witchcraft within Western societies. Many thousands of people, both in North America and Europe, are now calling themselves "pagans" or "neopagans" or witches. In general, the neopagans consider themselves part of the general New Age movement despite variances. However, for their inspiration they look to those religions that preceded Christianity and monotheism. They embrace beliefs and practices drawing inspiration from Norse, Greek, Roman, Celtic, and Egyptian religions together with the surviving primal religions of the world.

The neopaganist is obviously in collision with the biblical world. In fact, the general term "neopaganism" covers those modern movements which are based on the conviction that what Christianity has traditionally denounced as idolatry and superstition actually represents a profound and meaningful religious worldview which should be revitalized in our modern world.[1]

In earlier years in the so-called civilized West, people would never apply to themselves terms such as "pagan" and "witch" because these terms were regarded as inferior and uncivilized. By the end of the fourth century the word "pagan" became a derogatory term in Rome, used to refer to the uncivilized.

Today, people are willing to apply these terms to themselves even publicly. Miriam Starhawk, one of the best-known propagandists for Wicca,

---

1. David Burnett, *Clash of Worlds* (Eastbourne: MARC, 1990), 188. Cf. also W. J. Hanegraaff, *New Age Religion and Western Culture* (Leiden: Brill, 1996), 77.

writes and lectures widely about neopaganism and witchcraft. She is on the faculty of the Institute of Spirituality at Holy Name College in Oakland, California. Harvard Divinity School has offered courses on neopaganism and hosted meetings of witches, according to Westmont College sociologist Ron Enroth. Witches are now legally incorporated as recognized churches.

Today, a person can tap into an intricate network of pagans to find festivals, workshops, films, art exhibitions, covens, and circles of friends all determined to revive the "old ways." There are a National Alliance of Pantheists, a Witches League for Public Awareness, and a Pagan Parenting Network.

In Salem, Massachusetts (often called the "Witch City" because of its association with the witch hysteria of 1692 and its promotion of witchcraft today), the local religious leaders association has welcomed a witch to its number. This high priest of the Rosarian Order of Wicca, whose coven is called the Black Rose, now regularly meets with Catholic and Protestant ministers and a Jewish rabbi at the Immaculate Conception Catholic Church to plan activities and discuss issues of faith. The Covenant of Unitarian Universalist Pagans (CUUPS), recognized as an affiliate organization of the Unitarian Universalist Association, is based in Cambridge, Massachusetts.[2]

Margot Adler regards the neopagan movement in the United States as being, in part, a search by uprooted Europeans to find their roots as ancient peoples. Some have looked back to Europe, and others have turned to the ancient religions of North America. A more precise definition would see neopaganism — also referred to as witchcraft, the Craft, Wicca, or the Old Religion — as a fused re-creation of pre-Christian European nature religions and the medieval Western magical tradition.[3]

It should be noted that neopagans do not regard black witches and Satanists as part of their movement. Satanists primarily use biblical terms to develop their anti-Christian rituals. They see Satanism as making the conscious decision to worship an evil power and use one's power only for evil goals. In contrast, neopagans primarily return to ancient pre-Christian traditions for their inspiration.[4] They have no use for the Christian devil, since their religion dates from long before Christianity. Though some neopagans have given up on the word "witch" as too laden with negative connotations, others attempt to reclaim it as a word that rightfully describes a "healer, minister, and wise person."[5]

---

2. Aida Besancon Spencer, Donna F. G. Hailson, Catherine Clark Kroeger, and William David Spencer, *The Goddess Revival* (Grand Rapids: Baker, 1995), 20-21.

3. Burnett, *Clash of Worlds*, 192. Cf. James R. Lewis, ed., *Magical Religion and Modern Witchcraft* (Albany, N.Y.: State University of New York, 1996), 102.

4. Burnett, *Clash of Worlds*, 192.

5. Cynthia Eller, *Living in the Lap of the Goddess* (New York: Crossroad, 1993), 50-51.

## NEOPAGAN/WITCHCRAFT
## MODIFICATIONS OF NEW AGE

According to Aidan Kelly, the neopagan/witchcraft movement in America and other English-speaking nations parallels the New Age movement in some ways, differs sharply from it in others, and overlaps it in some minor ways. Pagans and even witches may or may not be feminists. Many people are drawn to earth-based spiritual traditions, to the celebration of seasonal cycles, and to the awakening of broader dimensions of consciousness without an analysis of the interplay of power and gender. Feminist spirituality, paganism, and witchcraft overlap but are not identical communities. Many feminists draw from goddess traditions of many cultures or prefer to create their own rituals without identifying with any particular tradition. However, Wouter J. Hanegraaff, of the University of Utrecht in the Netherlands, contends that neopaganism is part of the New Age in a general sense but definitely has its own distinctive flavor, which sets it apart from other New Age trends. The neopagan movement should be treated as part of the New Age movement, but should be seen as a special, relatively clearly circumscribed subculture within that movement.[6]

Some New Agers want to avoid the terms "magic" and "witchcraft." New Age bookstores almost never have sections labeled "Magic" or "Witchcraft." Instead, books on magic are shelved with works on spiritual disciplines, such as Yoga; and books on neopagan witchcraft are shelved with books on "Women's Studies."

### NEOPAGAN BELIEFS

Despite similarities, neopagans generally reject a number of typical New Age assumptions about religion. Many New Agers assume, for example, that all religions are ultimately the same. Spirituality is best learned by sitting at the feet of a master teacher or guru, preferably from one of the Eastern religions. New Agers also believe that a new world teacher or messiah will appear to usher in the New Age. In contrast, neopagans generally believe that they are practicing an ancient folk religion, whether as a survival or a revival. Thus, being focused on the pagan religions of the past, they are not particularly interested in a New Age in the future.

Neopagans also generally believe that many religions are radically and irreconcilably different from each other. For them, the "reformed" religions (especially the ones believing in one God) established by Moses, Jesus,

---

6. Aidan A. Kelly, "An Update on Neopagan Witchcraft in America," in *Perspectives on the New Age*, ed. James R. Lewis and J. Gordon Melton (Albany, N.Y.: State University of New York, 1992), 136. Cf. also Hanegraaff, *New Age Relation*, 79.

Muhammad, the Buddha, and similar figures were *not* an improvement over the folk religions they replaced. In fact, they state that if there were a single worldwide religion in the future, it might very well repress human freedom even more than the Roman Catholic Church did in Europe during the "Burning Times." Hence, neopagans are not at all receptive to teachers and teachings from the monotheistic religions nor to any from the East. A possible exception is Hinduism, which is seen (whether accurately or not) as an "un-reformed" polytheism similar to that of the Greco-Roman world. Neopagans tend to be especially interested in the Hindu Tantric traditions, with their sexual emphasis, since these can easily be seen as a type of magic parallel to that developed in the Western occult tradition.

Neopagans generally tend to be extremely antiauthoritarian and so are not at all inclined to accept the personal authority of any guru. The authoritarian structure of the official Gardnerian Witches in America might seem to contradict this view, but this antiauthoritarian emphasis is a reason why there are at least ten times as many Gardnerian-imitating witches as official Gardnerians in the neopagan movement.

Neopagan witches operate with an ethic that forbids them to accept money for initiating anyone or for training anyone in the essential practices of the Craft as a religion. During the last decade, neopagan festivals have grown into national gatherings, often of several thousand people, but they have remained quite inexpensive, since no one is attempting to make a profit from them. Neopagans look upon the "Psychic Fairs" and "New Age Expos" with open contempt. They tend to consider most New Age gurus to be money-hungry frauds who are exploiting the public by charging exorbitant fees for spiritual practices that can be learned for free within a neopagan coven. This attitude does not, of course, encourage New Agers to look kindly upon neopagans.

Nevertheless, some neopagan witches consider themselves members of the New Age movement as well. They see the Craft as contributing to the spiritual growth in the modern world that is leading up to the New Age, whenever and however that might begin.[7]

# HISTORIC PRINCIPLES OF PAGAN WITCHCRAFT

Neopagans speak of reality — both divine and otherwise — as being multiple and diverse. They reject the evolutionary theory popularized in the last century that societies developed from polytheism to monotheism. Neopagans see their movement rooted in pre-Christian European folk religion, or paganism. We

---

7. Kelly, "Neopagan Witchcraft," 138–39.

do not know much about this tradition except that it consisted of a variety of polytheistic nature religions that were practiced openly by most people until Europe was Christianized.

In the contemporary world, the neopagan movement is a leader in emphasizing God's manyness: He is both singular and plural; they are both male and female. For neopagans, a major strength of their movement is its reemphasis of both theological and social pluralism. In primitive societies this polytheistic view is often called animism, nature worship, or spiritism. This is the belief that nature and all the objects of nature are peopled with, and possessed by, living spirits or gods.[8]

## The Primordial Realm and the Gods

The world of magic, neopaganism, and witchcraft is rooted in polytheism. These personal gods are seen as the creators and maintainers of the cosmos. But back of these gods and transcending them is a Primordial Realm. This is a realm of being prior to the gods and above them. The gods are derived from and belong to this Primordial Realm. The religions of India — Brahmanism and, especially, Buddhism — express with unparalleled clarity the idea that the gods are subject to a transcendent order and bound to a system of eternal forces and laws. The gods are thus limited.

Throughout paganism we find good gods and evil gods, equal in their divine rank and power because both types derive independently from the Primordial Realm. The battle between good and evil, between holy and impure, is seen as an everlasting struggle between hostile divine twins.[9]

Since the Primordial Realm contains infinite forces other than and transcending the gods, the influence and dominion of the gods are limited. There are two realms: one of the gods, another of the Primordial Realm. So the gods are portrayed as calling upon the Primordial Realm to surmount their own predestined limitations. Pagans feel themselves subject to and in need of *both* realms. They pray to the gods to enlist their aid. They know, however, that the gods themselves are specific embodiments of the Primordial Realm and that they call upon forces outside themselves. Thus pagans employ magic also, hoping thereby to activate the forces of the Primordial Realm. All of paganism serves as an expression of this basic idea. Only by appreciating this can we understand the unique position of the biblical view in the history of culture.[10]

8. Burnett, *Clash of Worlds*, 194-95.
9. Yehezkel Kaufmann, *The Religion of Israel: From Its Beginnings to the Babylonian Exile* (Chicago: University of Chicago, 1960), 23, 39.
10. Ibid., 23-24.

## Two Kinds of Magic

As we shall see, this primal view with its two levels helps explain two basic types of magic — one calling on the gods and the other relating to the self-operating forces of the Primordial Realm. In the first type of magic, the magician or shaman acts in the name of gods and spirits. He claims that his techniques have been revealed to him by the gods, and he is effective through their power. From this viewpoint, the magician is regarded as a priest who acts with the sanction and help of a potent god.

In the second type, magic appears in a "pure" form in rites that have no connection with the will of the gods. Rather, they are viewed as automatically effective or even capable of coercing the gods to do the will of the practitioner. It is this ever-present assumption of a realm of forces apart from the gods that makes pagan religion, even in its highest manifestations, amenable to belief in magic.

The distinctive mark of all pagan rituals is that they are not directed toward the will of the gods alone. They call upon the Primordial Realm of self-operating forces that is independent of the gods. The gods themselves need and utilize this Primordial Realm for their own benefit. The two types of magic can be illustrated in the religions of Egypt and Babylon.

Egypt was permeated with magical beliefs. It developed an enormous literature on the subject and an extensive manufacture of magical objects. Magic was called upon at every turn in life. The gods practiced magic in their own right. Egyptian magicians merely imitated them. This meant that the mana, or power, that inheres in the gods and their names is but part of a universal power which the gods themselves require and know how to use for their own benefit. Magic is thus an autonomous force that is operative even in the life of the gods. It is no wonder, then, that the Egyptian magician can threaten the gods, and, if necessary, compel them to do his will.

Babylonian magic displays the same pattern. In some primitive tribes this high god or Primordial Realm does not receive as much attention as does the need to propitiate and placate a multitude of far more immanent spirits or gods.[11]

## MANA, FORCE, POWER

Another basic concept of primitive, or primal, religions is the belief in mana. Stephen Neill believes that mana, which he refers to as "force" or "power," is the key to understanding the logic of the primitive. Mana is believed to act either for the benefit or for the harm of humankind. It thus becomes of utmost

11. Ibid., 40-41.

importance for human beings to possess and control mana. This means that its pursuit is the chief ingredient in the tribal religions. The effort to control mana is the basis of superstition, magic, faith in charms, amulets, and talismans. Because they claim to control mana, shamans or medicine men are revered and have controlling power among peoples who practice primitive religion.

The power of belief in mana is inconceivably great and is almost impossible to wipe out. Witness the many superstitions by which even Christian people in today's enlightened society are dominated. We see a carryover of mana in a belief in or fear of an impersonal power which can influence and control human life — whether a black cat, a lucky pocket piece, or some more "religious" object.

## THE EARTH MOTHER GODDESS

The earth is seen as possessing a life of its own and, therefore, requiring profound reverence. This devotion is given to the Earth Mother goddess, who may be called Gaia, Freyja, The Lady, or some other title. The Earth Mother goddess is often worshiped in the threefold form of maiden, mother, and old crone. This concern for the earth has also led to a common concern with ecology.

Starhawk states that two core principles of goddess religion are immanence and interconnection. Immanence means that the goddess and the gods are embodiments. Each one is a manifestation of the living being of earth. This means that nature, culture, and life itself in all their diversity are sacred. Interconnection is the understanding that all being is interrelated. We are linked with all of the cosmos as parts of one living organism. What affects one of us affects us all.[12]

Laurie Cabot, who is known as the "Official Witch of Massachusetts," echoes, in her *Power of the Witch*, a similar theology: the witches' belief in their "oneness with the source of all life, the Great Mother," their position as "co-creators of the universe," and the interconnectedness of nature. Since "religion is about creation," Cabot writes, "religion should be about the earth."

In its various incarnations we have, in the pagan and Wiccan religions of the earth, systems that elevate nature to living consciousness, declare its Oneness with humanity, and pull it altogether as an idea — a goddess.[13]

---

12. Miriam Starhawk, *The Spiral Dance: A Rebirth of the Ancient Religion of the Great Goddess* (New York: HarperCollins, 1989), 10.

13. Spencer, *Goddess Revival*, 26-27.

## Central Focus of the Feminine

The great mother goddess is a central concept of neopaganism, although the male horned god is recognized. The feminine nature of reality is stressed to counter the long-held emphasis upon masculinity. Goddess feminists have many complaints about Christianity and Judaism. Nelle Morton writes: "Women had no cosmic advocate in any of the five major patriarchal religions of the world." They charge that the God of the Bible is a white, male sky god who is warlike, intolerant, and dominating. God is remote, unreal, not powerful, and impersonal. Christianity is ascetic, body-denying, life-denying. Divine experience has no sexual dimension. Rather than a burden for neopagans, life in the body is viewed as good, and physical pleasure is a blessing that should be sought rather than avoided.

Charlene Spretnak writes: "Christianity, Judaism, Islam, and Hinduism all combine male godheads with proscriptions against women as temptress, as unclean, as evil." Women are deeply hurt. They feel bad about themselves, their bodies, power, will, and heritage. They feel their creativity is not encouraged. They blame Judaism and Christianity and, instead, are creating a goddess in their own image.[14]

## Ritual and "Out-of-Body" Experiences

A common feature is the manipulation of the world by means of rituals. Neopagans claim that by the use of these rituals, a person comes to a deeper experience of power as he or she comes in tune with the earth and other powers. Ritual uses props and words to calm and focus the mind in order that the universe/goddess may be made aware of the needs and wants of the practitioner. Most pagans strongly emphasize that while the items used in spells or in magic, such as candles, colored cloth, herbs, and incense, are facilitators of magic, the real magic lies in one's own focus and intentions. Props are used to help create an atmosphere, and in some instances represent a kind of sacrifice to deities being called upon, as a payment for their attention and concern.[15]

In *The Spiral Dance* Starhawk describes in detail the rituals used in neopagan seasonal festivals.

Growing importance is given to "out-of-body" experiences, especially in shamanistic groups. These experiences can give knowledge and power.

14. Ibid., 176. Cf. also Lewis, ed., *Magical Religion*, 3.
15. Timothy Miller, ed., *America's Alternative Religions* (Albany, N.Y.: State University of New York, 1995), 342.

## Nontraditional Magic and Witchcraft

### Africa

John Cooper points out that for over two hundred years the United States has been influenced by religious and magical ideas from Africa, the Caribbean, and Asia. The practice of slavery brought West African practices to the Caribbean islands and then to the Deep South. Many Latin American ideas and practices came into the United States from Mexico.

The Yoruba tribal religion is the common background of Santeria, Macumba, Candomble, Lucumi, Santuario, and Palo Mayombe. This influence has multiplied in the United States since the Mariel boat lifts of 1980. All African background groups have a common element in ritual sacrifices, called "matanza." Blood offerings are the most important feature for all these groups. Animals sacrificed mainly include chickens, goats, and turtles.[16]

### Mayan Magic

Lectures on a recent study tour into the Mayan area of Central America alerted me to the similarity of the Mayan view and the African view brought to the Caribbean and the United States with slave trade. According to both views, harmony and power are achieved through taboos, the fire ceremony, and other rituals. The powers of the nature gods are enlisted through sacrifices and magic. Taboos and rituals protect order and harmony. Time has no future focus. In their book *A Forest of Kings*, Linda Schele and David Freidel have portrayed this Mayan view in a dramatic form. With the deciphering of the Mayan writing system, we now better understand the Mayan view.

For the Mayans, the continued well-being of the universe required the active participation of the human community through magic and ritual. As maize, or corn, cannot seed itself without the intervention of human beings, so the cosmos required sacrificial blood to maintain life. Mayan life was filled with endless magical rituals which seem bizarre and shocking to us. However, to the Mayans, they embodied the highest concepts of spiritual devotion.

The world the Mayans experienced manifested itself in two complementary dimensions. One dimension was the world in which they lived out their lives. The other was the abode of the gods, ancestors, and other supernatural beings. This manner of understanding reality is still true for many of the contemporary descendants of the ancient Mayans.

16. John Charles Cooper, *The Black Mask: Satanism in America Today* (Old Tappan, N.J.: Revell, 1990), 70-71.

These two planes of existence were inextricably locked together. The actions and interactions of otherworldly beings influenced the fate of this world, bringing disease or health, disaster or victory, life or death, prosperity or misfortune into the lives of human beings. But the denizens of the otherworld were also dependent upon the deeds of the living for their continued well-being. Only the living could provide the nourishment required by both the inhabitants of the otherworld and the souls who would be reborn there as the ancestors. The kings were, above all, divine shamans who operated in both dimensions. Through the power of their ritual performance they kept the two worlds in balance, thus bringing prosperity to their domains. As we will see, this notion is opposed to the biblical view.

### Brazil

Though statistically the world's largest Roman Catholic nation, Brazil may also be home to the globe's richest variety of magical religious cults. Nobody knows how many such sects there are, but they include the wildly popular Macumba movement, which incorporates a good deal of voodoo, and the more sophisticated Umbanda, which draws on voodoo, Roman Catholicism, and local Indian religions. On a lecture tour in Brazil, I attended Umbanda services. Pictures and statues of both Roman Catholic Christians and African gods were on the walls.

Further evidence of the popularity of the Macumba cult abounds in Rio de Janeiro and other Brazilian cities. Such offerings as lighted candles with ribbons around them, partially smoked cigars, bottles of sugar-cane liquor, and chickens with their throats slit are placed regularly at sites along the road in one of Rio's fashionable districts.

The biggest surprise awaiting the visitor to Brazil is the spell that magic and spiritism have cast over the country. Their origin goes back to the African slaves who were imported in the middle of the sixteenth century to work on the sugar plantations. Today 15 percent of the population are Africans, and two of the most popular spiritistic cults — Macumba and Umbanda — are clearly Afro-Brazilian.

The popularity of magic spiritistic cults in Brazil has been variously explained. Some trace it to the hunger for transcendence many churches are failing to satisfy. Others point to the desire for physical healing, personal blessing, or business success that spiritism promises. The many educated people who have embraced spiritism say they appreciate its offer of a complete worldview, without too many embarrassing ethical demands. Some even claim that spiritism is the logical completion of Judaism, Christianity, and Islam.

Magic spiritism presents one of the biggest challenges to the biblical view in Brazil. There are said to be about half a million active mediums and shamans, 15 million professed members, and, according to some, a fringe following of up to 50 million, nearly half the population of the country.

## Native American Magic

According to Catherine Albanese, the American Indians saw the world peopled with other-than-human persons, often of mysterious powers and dispositions. Not all of what we call nature was identified by the Indians in personal terms, but the presence of persons animating "nature" radically grounded their nature religion.[17]

Fascination with tribal cultures is often captured in the term "shamanism." The shaman is described as one who can transform both the seen and the unseen, who can journey to other realms, who experiences trances and visions and can predict the future, and who can move between this world and a less substantial — though ultimately more "real" — world for the benefit of others as well as for herself. It is not a description that is markedly different from that of the nineteenth-century spiritualists, but it conjures up a different set of associations, which exert a greater appeal to late twentieth-century feminists. Rather than the crystal balls, gypsies, and darkened rooms of spiritualism, shamanism is associated with ritual masks, tribal peoples, and ecstatic dancing under the open sky.

The shamans, magicians, and seers worked out of their sense of *correspondence* with natural forms. They were leaders in communication with other-than-human persons who dwelled in nature. The shamans were sharers in the mysterious power that made things happen. From this point of view, what we call magic and miracle were simply cases of like effecting like or of part affecting whole. Since everything was, in fact, part of everything else, it followed that one piece of the world could act powerfully on another, effecting change and transformation. With correspondence as the controlling metaphor, they sought their own versions of mastery and control through magic.

### INFLUENCE ON MODERN FEMINISM

According to Cynthia Eller, the most popular source for feminist religious borrowing over the last decade has been Native American religions. At feminist spirituality workshops and retreats, one is as likely to run across the symbols and rituals of Native American religions as those of Wicca. A key figure in the growing connection between women and Native American

17. Catherine L. Albanese, *Nature Religion in America: From the Algonkian Indians to the New Age* (Chicago: University of Chicago, 1990), 20, 24-25.

religions is Lynn Andrews. In 1981, Andrews adopted a Native American mentor and began a series of books lauding the Native American connection to nature. These books also revealed the existence of a secret sorority of spiritual women from tribal cultures.

The title "medicine woman," like "witch" before it, has now found its way into the spiritual feminist vocabulary (though it lacks the common currency in the feminist movement as a whole that "witch" has enjoyed).

Those spiritual feminists who adopt Native American religions (or pieces of them) are mostly European-American women, but there is a core of Native American women who act as teachers and leaders and grant a certain legitimacy to the project.

Spiritual feminist interest is focused less on living Native American cultures and more on what is reported about pre-conquest Native American cultures. Just as spiritual feminists are drawn to Eastern goddesses as remnants of an earlier matriarchal, goddess-worshiping culture, they are drawn to Native American mythology and culture as remnants of a more recent matriarchy.

Other Native Americans and spiritual feminists stress that in addition to the prominent place given to women in Native American religions and cultures, it is also important to recognize that these religions developed on American soil and were not imported from other lands as were Christianity, Judaism, Buddhism, Islam, and even witchcraft, whose roots are European. Thus feminists claim that Native Americans "live close to the land," they respect women and women's special powers, and they are held to be living fragments of a global culture that was nonsexist.[18]

## Magic and Witchcraft

Magic is the attempt to manipulate or command natural, paranormal, or supernatural forces for private, selfish, or evil purposes. A key idea of magical beliefs, of which witchcraft is a form, is that unseen Powers and a Primordial Realm exist. By performing the right kind of ritual, these powers or this power can be contacted and forced to assist. Magic, therefore, is the attempt by a practitioner to manipulate universal forces. It should be noted that neopaganism is different from traditional magic in that the magical worldview is *purposely adopted* as a reaction to the "disenchanted" world of the modern "scientific" worldview.[19]

18. Eller, *Lap of the Goddess*, 69-72.
19. John P. Newport, *Demons, Demons, Demons: A Christian Guide through the Murky Maze of the Occult* (Nashville: Broadman, 1972), 35; cf. G. B. Gardner, *The Meaning of Witchcraft* (London: Aquarian, 1959), 23; cf. also Hanegraaff, *New Age Religion*, 84.

Anton LaVey and P. E. I. Bonewits see magic as completely natural, utilizing emotional energy and manipulating universal forces. Incidentally, Bonewits was the first person to get a doctorate in magic at the University of California at Berkeley.

Sybil Leek sees magic as a religious exercise of paranormal or psychic powers. She wrote a book entitled *Cast Your Own Spell — The Complete Art of Witchcraft*. One psychologist has compared magic to experimental parapsychology findings regarding "psi," which he defines as a general term used to identify personal factors or processes in nature that transcend accepted laws and that are nonphysical. He cites evidence to suggest that some aspects of magical practice involve psi.[20]

Aleister Crowley, the so-called Great Beast, sees magic as a manipulation of supernatural forces. The devil is the magician's god. The magician gets power by worshiping the devil and doing his will. Demon hosts can be dominated by a daring magician using rituals and symbols.

## WHITE MAGIC

White magic seeks to manipulate universal forces for helpful purposes. Some suggest that the medieval Catholic Church took over white magic. In any case, Constantine, the first Christian emperor, tolerated it. Goddess devotees and spiritual feminists offer two theories that limit magic's power to do evil, while leaving it free to do good. The first theory is that the universe has a preference for the good and will reward magical attempts to enhance life, and frustrate magical attempts to harm it.

A second, more popular, theory of magic that retains greater power while still restricting magic's ability to do evil is "karma." The term is borrowed from Hinduism, though the concept, according to mainstream neopagans, is found in their tradition at least as far back as medieval witchcraft. The doctrine of karma for the spiritual feminist offers a measure of protection against the potential abusive power of magic, since those who seek to harm spiritual feminists magically will find their evil intentions cast back on themselves. They will suffer and, one can hope, will learn not to use magic for malicious purposes.[21]

## BLACK MAGIC

Black magic seeks to utilize universal forces for evil purposes. Constantine executed black magicians. Spiritual feminists who practice negative magic are,

20. Lewis, ed., *Magical Religion*, 58-59.
21. Woods, *Occult Revolution*, 129.

it seems, women who have been victims of a large amount of abuse in their lives. Safety, they say, comes only in self-defense, in being prepared to retaliate against those who would do them harm.

## NEUTRAL MAGIC

Neutral magic involves itself with neutral forces of nature such as ESP, telepathy, and clairvoyance.

The principle of controlling and manipulating power is basic to all three forms of magic. It is an art. It has a hierarchy of degrees or grades.

## PRINCIPLES OF MAGIC

Scholars in the area of magic, such as Richard Cavendish in *The Black Arts*, outline three basic principles of magic.

### Macrocosm and Microcosm

One principle is "As above, so below; and as below, so above." It is also called the principle of macrocosm and microcosm. Humans are seen as a miniature copy of the total universe and as a miniature replica of God. This means that a man or woman can mystically expand himself or herself and control some of God's power and the universe's power. Based upon the theme of interconnectedness, but going beyond it, magic involves the recognition that each part of the interconnected whole affects every other part. Given this model, many pagans believe that magic can be used to gain insight from, as well as to influence, other aspects of the interconnected whole.

Magical rituals, spells, and sex are seen as important vehicles to control cosmic powers. If a drive is powerful in humans, it is powerful in the universe. Hence the magical importance of sex, and the reason why magical groups often have a naked girl on the altar in their meetings. A magician or shaman is reputed to know the techniques of controlling cosmic power. This is behind the hold shamans or witch doctors around the world have on people.

### Like Produces Like

A second principle of magic is based on the principle of analogy, or "like produces like." This is the presupposition of sympathetic, imitative, and contagion magic. Ceremonies are performed that imitate the desired end. Seashells are old. Rub your forehead with a powdered seashell and, by analogy, you will live a long life. Salt is anti-demonic. Throw it over your shoulder,

225

and it will keep off the devil. The Moonies (Unification Church members) use holy salt.

In voodoo, sticking pins in a doll resembling an enemy is said to cause the enemy's death. If you carry a piece of a strong person's clothing, you will gain something of that person's vital force. This is the mana idea of the primitives. In 1932, after the outlaw John Dillinger was killed, a woman tried to soak up his blood to preserve his vital force.

### Intensity of Will

A third principle of magic is related to the intensity of the magician's will. Magic is the art of causing change to occur in conformity with will. The intensity of a magician's will is even more important than the ritual used in the magic ceremonies.

Sympathetic and contagion magic are closely related to the sacramental rituals which are observed in all the world religions. These sacramental practices can easily cross the border back into magical superstition. Examples include crossing oneself in times of danger, wearing medals for protection, or burning blessing candles.

The main vehicle or source of ceremonial magic in the West is the late medieval and early modern European books called *The Grimoires*. These books tell how to evoke and bind demons, or even planetary gods, to the magician's will, and how to perform various minor rites of magic. The magicians also use what they call the Sixth and Seventh Books of Moses.

The tradition of *The Grimoires* uses techniques similar to those of the Hellenistic Greek and Egyptian magic papyri and Babylonian magic. They adopt, however, Hebrew names and Christian invocations.

Legend assigns *The Grimoires* both to King Solomon and to Pope Honorius. The tradition affirms that in his old age Solomon built a temple for his foreign wives. He had a magic lamp in the temple. After his reign, Jerusalem turned into a magico-religious chaos.

Hanegraaff points out that neopaganism is a continuation of nineteenth-century occultist ritual magic, which in turn has its historical roots in the hermetic revival of the sixteenth century. Renaissance magic is indisputably fundamental to the ceremonial magic of nineteenth-century occultism and has thus provided the historical conditions for the emergence of its contemporary descendant, New Age neopaganism. This "magic" is understood as referring to a "participatory" holistic *worldview* which reunites the spiritual and the material dimensions. Alchemy can be seen as a form of magic. The alchemical process was believed to take place simultaneously both on the material and the spiritual levels. With reference to New Age religion, it may be argued that traditional alchemy is relevant primarily because of its influence on the work of Carl Gustav Jung, the most popularly influential interpreter of alchemy of this century.[22]

## RITUALS AND CEREMONIES

Starhawk contends that ritual serves a magical function in stimulating an awareness of the hidden side of reality and awakening long-forgotten powers of the human mind. Starhawk further maintains that magical rituals are used to create states of ecstasy, of union with the Divine, as well as to achieve material results such as healings.[23]

The basic unit of pagan worship is the coven (for witches), grove, or circle (for most other pagan groups). It consists of ten to twenty members headed by a priest or priestess. They meet twice monthly (at the full and new moons) and on the eight pagan holidays. The seasonal rituals are quite important, as Starhawk spells out in *The Spiral Dance*.[24]

Pagans prefer to gather out-of-doors where sky, moon, stars, earth, trees, birds, and animals form nature's "temple." A secluded hilltop, clearing, or private garden are the preferred spots. There are a growing number of nature sanctuaries: land permanently dedicated to be used only for worship of nature deities. These are not open to the general public, but can be used by visiting neopagans and friends who have been properly vouched for.

There are temples — buildings dedicated for use as places of worship in which there is a weekly liturgy (usually on Friday or Saturday night, rather than Sunday morning) to which anyone can come simply by walking in. This is considered a radical innovation, and not necessarily a welcome one, by many in the Craft.

Normally, the esbat, or worship, of a coven is utterly private. In order even to hear that an esbat is going to occur, you need to know members of a coven well enough that you could be considered for membership yourself. Even then you could be invited to an esbat only with the permission of the coven's reigning elders.

Some Sabbats are more public. Such a Sabbat might be held in a rented hall or out in a park, and friends would be invited to it. But these "open" Sabbats are not advertised, and to be invited to one, you must already be in contact with the sponsoring network. Similarly, the national festivals are not advertised except through the network of neopagan publications, which are normally available only by subscription, though a few are beginning to be sold through bookstores.[25]

22. Hanegraaff, *New Age Religion*, 85, 394-95.
23. Lewis, ed., *Magical Religion*, 58.
24. Dave Bass, "Drawing Down the Moon," *Christianity Today*, April 29, 1991, 16.
25. Kelly, "Neopagan Witchcraft," 144-45.

In any event, the neopagan temples seem, even more than the festivals, to be creating a neopagan laity: people who consider themselves to be members of the religion, but not clergy, and who therefore do not call themselves witches. To the members of the neopagan movement, a witch is a neopagan clergyperson. They do not use the word "witch" with any other meaning.[26]

A typical pagan "service" might include these elements, although there is considerable room for variation:

1. Creation of a sacred space, the circle. This is seen as a place between this world and the Other where the worshiper communes with the gods.

2. Invocation of gods and spirits. Worshipers invite them into the circle, and thereby into fellowship with the participants. This is called "drawing down the moon."

The central act of ceremonial magic is the calling up of a god. This god is generally one of the pagan gods of Egypt, Babylon, or Greece, or one of the "demons" mentioned in the old *Grimoires*. Some magicians claim that they truly see a shadowy figure appear in the magic nine-foot ritual circle. Others say they call up the veiled wisdom and splendor of the unconscious.

The basic steps in the ceremony involve purification of the magician by fasting, sexual continence, and purification of the magical implements. There is the utilization of incense, herbs, and repeated incantations and commands until the god or spirit appears. This is called "summoning."

3. Evocation of "magical" forces. The worshiper seeks to master these forms and use them for some willed purpose. In an actual ceremony, the presence of the pagan god is called up through gestures and manipulation of instruments and uttering words of command from the old *Grimoires*. The "receiver" shakes and becomes transformed with the appearance of the god.

According to Starhawk, the drum brings together the energy of a group and is especially important for unifying a large group. Rhythm alters consciousness. A drumbeat can induce a trance or arouse worshipers to a dancing frenzy. It helps a circle get loose and wild and provides the pulse of the ritual. The drum lets those involved hear the heartbeat of the earth.

4. Opening of the circle. Here the circle becomes simple space again. After the ceremony, the deity must be dismissed, or serious psychic effects will follow. It is claimed that the magic rite gives wisdom, assurance of immortality, a feeling of wonder, and a sense of power.

To become part of such a group often requires diligent work and research. The potential member must first make contact with a present member, be approved, and then go through a period of initiation (generally a year and a day). Depending on the type of circle, from three to as many as ten "levels" of participation are attainable as one achieves various states of "gnosis,"

26. Bass, "Drawing Down the Moon," 16.

or knowledge. The rule for organization is to stay small, local, and decentralized. Each grove, or circle, is autonomous. There is, however, a "friendly affinity" between circles, and considerable consensus on matters of worship, belief, and lifestyle.[27]

# AN OVERVIEW OF NEOPAGANISM

The *goal* of the neopagan is much more ambitious than to reclaim in a literal fashion the old gods from the misty past. They believe that a mature neopagan worldview can appeal to twenty-first century people. And they are willing to draw from divergent streams of thought to make a persuasive case.

1. At the center of neopagan philosophy is a thorough *critique* of the Judeo-Christian faith. Tom Williams, priest of the Church of All Worlds, puts it like this: "Someday people may speak of the last two thousand years as 'The Christian Interlude.'"

2. Neopaganism claims to have an inherent respect for *nature*. Her gods embody nature. Neopagans worship the natural.

Even though Neopaganism considers itself to be a nature religion, its regard for nature is much more akin to romanticism than to ancient paganism. It is far easier to be romantic about cows if you do not own any. Neopaganism appears to be a religion of city people and of what Spectorsky labeled "exurbanites": people who have moved from the city out into the country for noneconomic reasons.

3. Neopagans claim to be in line with modern *scientific* developments. They attempt to buttress their worldview by integrating concepts from the sciences into their apologetic, especially from physics, biology, and psychology.

They find in one version of Big Bang cosmology — that the universe goes through endless cycles of expansion and contraction — support for their cyclical view of history.

4. Neopagans have adopted and adapted a form of the Gaia Hypothesis. Gaia was the Greeks' Mother Earth Goddess and as such serves as a symbol of one who watches over her brood. They attribute consciousness to the planet, which is seen as a complex, single organism analogous to a human with a brain and nervous system. If any part of the biosystem becomes imbalanced, then "Gaia" works to bring the system back to homeostasis. The neopagans point to a form of scientific neopaganism which has taken shape among a group of intellectuals called the Princeton Gnosis.

This ecological emphasis has led more and more persons to speak out

27. Kelly, "Neopagan Witchcraft," 151.

as identified Witches on questions of public policy related to ecology. There are also indications that the neopagans in some areas are beginning to forge a political alliance with the Greens and are beginning to exert more influence on Democratic Party platforms.

5. Neopagans stress ritual and symbol. They claim that the ritual of "drawing down the moon," for instance, transforms the priest/priestess and those in the circle so that they participate in the presence and power of the gods or goddesses they invoke.

Not unrelated to ritual and symbol is neopaganism's attempt to *resacralize* the world. The human passions are meant to be celebrated and indulged. The human appetites — for pleasure, goodness, sex, power, wealth — are good. Evil becomes that which inhibits the actualization of our full potential in any given area. Kelly also suggests that the neopagan community is one of the only spiritual communities that is exploring humor, joy, abandonment, even silliness and outrageousness as valid parts of spiritual experience.

6. Another characteristic of neopaganism is its affirmation of *fate*. There is no escape from the wheel of fate but to reach the center, the still point. Innocence and guilt also dissolve in such a view. There is no fall of humankind; rather, we are justified as we live out our lives in harmony with our fate. We acquire innocence apart from any objective redemption or morality. Just as the cosmos, in the act of becoming, is innocent, so we, as we participate in and obey the process of becoming, are innocent.

7. Dave Bass suggests that a number of neopagan thinkers are heralding the imminent death of Christianity and the dawn of a new age. They see their movement as able to pull together the scattered fragments of Western culture, religion, and philosophy into a *coherent* worldview.[28]

## ACADEMIC INTEREST IN MAGIC AND WITCHCRAFT

### Castaneda and Don Juan

A major doorway into the world of magic and witchcraft for the academic community has been opened by a transplanted Peruvian, Carlos Castaneda. While an anthropology student, Castaneda claims to have been apprenticed to Don Juan, a Yaqui Indian sorcerer or magician.

Castaneda's twelve years of reported field work with Don Juan eventually formed the basis for more than a half dozen books, which have sold hundreds of thousands of copies and made Castaneda a wealthy man. The work with Don Juan also led to M.A. and Ph.D. degrees from UCLA and to international recognition.

28. Bass, "Drawing Down the Moon," 17-19.

From the beginning, Castaneda and his work have been controversial. By the time *Journey to Ixtlan* was published in 1972, criticism was rampant about the authenticity of the conversations with Don Juan since it was doubted that Don Juan ever lived. Anthropologists contended that Don Juan did not reflect the true Yaqui Indian way of life. A Mexican ethnologist stated that he felt that Castaneda's works have a very high percentage of imagination. Others say that Don Juan may be a composite Indian.

Castaneda himself contends that the books are in his own words but that they are true reflections of an objective person's teachings. In any case, Castaneda's books unfold, with clarity and narrative power, the world of the shaman in a way unmatched in other anthropological studies. These books are dramatic presentations of the age-old techniques of sorcery, drugs, magic, and witchcraft. Even if they are partly fiction, these writings provide us with material to understand and evaluate magic and witchcraft.

### Basic Teachings

In his works, Castaneda suggests a number of teachings related to magic and witchcraft.

1. There is a separate occult world of reality which is accessible to the rational Western individual through certain ancient mind-altering techniques. Beyond the visible world, according to Don Juan, is another world which is called a "separate reality." The particular version of reality which Don Juan represents is related to animism. It is also known as the sorcery or shamanistic tradition. It is the general view of life that underlies primitive or so-called pagan or primal religions. The only way to survive in life is to learn how to placate, or "buy off," the evil spirits and get the help of the good spirits.

Sorcerers, such as Don Juan, are variously called shamans, magicians, or witch doctors. Through a special call and long, strenuous training, the sorcerer learns to control the spirit world, at least to a large extent. The heart of magic is the discovery of how to manipulate the universal powers or forces of the universe. The sorcerer is theoretically an expert in the "power" field. The world is seen as a great unity. Spirit and matter occupy the same continuum.

2. It is important to have the presence of a *guide* during early attempts to "see" a separate reality. In the world of sorcery, one "sees" only through the help of a person who has already seen it. The guide is analogous to the guru, or Perfect Master, in the Hindu-related New Consciousness groups.

3. Natural drugs (psychotropic plants) are valuable for some people as an initiatory vehicle into the "separate reality," or "new consciousness."

4. The full use of magical power can only be acquired with the help of an ally, or a spirit entity.

5. The final purpose of taking an apprenticeship is the ancient desire to know and to learn how to control the mysterious forces of the universe. One who really knows and can manipulate the universal forces is called a "warrior."[29]

The significance of Castaneda is his appeal to the academic world and to university students. He helped to break the generally accepted idea that humans are primarily rational creatures.

## THE HARNER RESEARCH AND METHOD

Professor Michael Harner has done much to popularize magic and witchcraft. Harner is a well-known anthropologist who has been visiting professor at Columbia and Yale Universities.

As part of his fieldwork from 1956 to 1957 and again from 1960 to 1961, Harner experimented with shamanic practice in the Jivaro and Conibo cultures of South America. His Indian guides gave Harner strong (and dangerous) medicinal plant substances to induce the shamanic state, and Harner became seriously ill in the process. In 1980, Harner's *Way of the Shaman* appeared, with its programmatic subtitle *A Guide to Power and Healing*. There was some material about Jivaro, Conibo, and other traditional forms of shamanism in the book, but more about neoshamanic practice among contemporary Americans.

Included in the so-called Harner Method is an emphasis on sonic driving, or drumming, as a practical technique for shamanic journeying. According to Harner, the shaman stands in the middle, "between ordinary reality and nonordinary reality," a "'power-broker' in the sense of manipulating spiritual power to help people, to put them into a healthy equilibrium." The unconscious mind of the shaman's patient, under the influence of sonic driving, is "programmed" by the ritual to activate the body's immune system against disease.

The shaman described by Harner follows a stock of simple instructions and techniques, journeying to lower, middle, and upper worlds, meeting power animals and teachers, learning what to avoid and what to carry back as wisdom and knowledge gained. For Harner, the enlightenment of shamanism is the ability to light up what others perceive as darkness, and thereby to see and to journey on behalf of a humanity that is perilously close to losing its spiritual connectedness with all its relatives, the plants and animals of this good earth.

In recent years, Harner's Foundation for Shamanic Studies has grown

---

29. John P. Newport, *Christ and the New Consciousness* (Nashville: Broadman, 1978), 148-60.

more and more to emphasize the presence of shamanism in human cultures throughout the world, even as it has grown to rely increasingly on the tape recorder to supply its sonic drive.[30]

Thus we see that Harner's Central American shamanistic teachings are quite similar to the Wiccan, or witchcraft, worldview. In fact, Harner's shamanistic workshops have been a considerable source of stimulus to the neopagan movement in the States. His drumming tapes to accompany shamanic trance journeys are now available commercially.[31]

Aidan Kelly suggests that emphases such as those of Harner on mystical experiences and altered states of consciousness (ESP, clairvoyance, out-of-body experiences, and religious ecstasy) are being neglected by mainstream churches. This means that the various magical religions, which train people how to use and benefit from such abilities and experiences, and of which the neopagan witches are now the most important and fastest-growing, are thus being left a clear field to walk away with whatever prizes there are to be won.[32]

A new trend in magic is to adapt materials from Tibetan Buddhistic magic with its elaborate oriental rituals.

## KEY LEADERS OF MODERN WITCHCRAFT AND NEOPAGANISM

### Margaret Murray

Witchcraft and ritual magic were first given a pseudoscientific standing through the theories of anthropologist Margaret Murray in her book *The Witch Cult in Western Europe*. Murray put forward the theory that the witches of Western Europe were the lingering adherents of a once general pagan religion that has been displaced, though not completely, by Christianity.

Brooks Alexander contends that Murray's work, despite its inaccuracies, was an important preparation for the later rise of neopaganism. Her theories set off a wave of enthusiasm for things ancient, native, and pagan that is still with us and still gathering strength. Her scholarship may have been bogus, but its results are very real.[33]

---

30. Catherine L. Albanese, "The Magical Staff: Quantum Healing in the New Age," 82-83.

31. Burnett, *Clash of Worlds*, 192.

32. Kelly, "Neopagan Witchcraft," 150.

33. Brooks Alexander, *SCP Journal* 16.3 (1991): 30-31.

### Marija Gimbutas

In more recent years, archaeologist Marija Gimbutas has been active in reviving praise for a supposed prepatriarchal civilization in which, she claims, matristic, goddess-worshiping cultures held nature in higher esteem and thus lived in greater harmony with the environment. Some scholars have challenged her conclusions on the existence of a goddess religion in Neolithic Europe with its roots in the Paleolithic. Her work — along with that of others — has been influential enough to spark a trend.

### Gerald B. Gardner

Gerald B. Gardner (1884-1964) was the chief figure in the new-witchcraft revival. Gardner knew Margaret Murray — she wrote an introduction to his first book. By Gardner's own account, he ran across a surviving coven of the "Old Religion" almost by accident. Gardner met "Old Dorothy" Clutterbuck. According to Gardner, "Old Dorothy" turned out to be the leader of a secretive, surviving coven of the "Old Religion." In 1939 she initiated him into what she called "Wicca."

For Gardner, witchcraft was a peaceful, happy nature religion. Witches met in covens, led by a priestess. They worshiped two principal deities, the god of forests and what lies beyond, and the great Triple Goddess of fertility and rebirth. They focused primarily on the Goddess. They celebrated the eight ancient pagan festivals of Europe and sought to attune themselves to nature. Their communal rituals involved dancing, nudity, chanting, and meditation. All these forms are still common among neopagans today.[34]

### Raymond Buckland

Gardner was effective in recruiting converts, and some of them helped to spread the craft beyond the British Isles, to both Europe and America. One of Gardner's initiates was Raymond Buckland. Buckland imported Gardner's witchcraft to the United States and, with his wife Rosemary as High Priestess, founded the New York coven in Bayside, Long Island. Buckland's coven initiated others, who in turn began their own covens and initiated still others.[35]

The official Gardnerian witches in America maintain a strict apostolic succession of high priestesses who can trace their lineage back to Lady Rowen (Rosemary Buckland). All the other traditions of neopagan witchcraft in America were begun as an imitation of the Gardnerians.

34. Eller, *Lap of the Goddess*, 51.
35. Alexander, *SCP Journal*, 34-35.

Kelly estimates that there are about 3,000 covens in America and about 300,000 practicing neopagans.

The neopagan movement has evolved far enough that the need for formal seminary training is beginning to be felt fairly widely. For one thing, many Wiccans would like to serve as chaplains in prisons, hospitals, and the military, but find that that route is closed to them as long as they lack the normal academic credentials that Protestant ministers usually have. At least two Wiccan seminaries have been founded during the last decade, one in New Hampshire, another in Wisconsin.

Much professional training of neopagan witches takes place at Unitarian seminaries. In 1991, there were three Wiccan priestesses at the Harvard Divinity School and at least a dozen of pagan persuasion at the Graduate Theological Union at Berkeley, California. According to Adler, the Unitarian Church remains the only place where pagans and women involved with Goddess religion can enter organized ministry.

After surveying a broad spectrum of evaluations of Gardner's work, Brooks Alexander concludes that Gardner harbored anti-Christian sentiments that moved and shaped his work. Anti-Christianity has been a consistent element of paganism since the time of Christ. It has clearly been a dominant theme within the modern witchcraft revival.

## THE GODDESS-FEMINIST MOVEMENT

### Prebiblical

Robert Graves is an English poet, essayist, and novelist. Graves's influence on the formation of the Goddess movement comes from his 1948 publication *The White Goddess*, subtitled *A Historical Grammar of Poetic Myth*.

According to Graves, there was an original universal goddess religion which was overthrown and suppressed by an emerging patriarchal culture that was violent, warlike, and hostile to nature. The last four thousand years of human history, therefore, represent a steady spiritual decline from that original, prepatriarchal golden age.

In his concluding chapter, Graves pronounced the failure and irrelevance of what he called "Father-god worship," in which he included Christianity. He believed that the time was coming when humanity would be ripe for the goddess's return.[36]

36. Ibid., 31-32.

*Miriam Starhawk*

Miriam Starhawk points out that "The Goddess," the whole, has no genitalia (or is all genitalia). But she prefers using a female-gendered word for a number of reasons. One is simply that, at this time in history, she thinks that we still subconsciously perceive a word of neutral gender as male. The word *Goddess* breaks our expectations and reminds us that we are talking about something different from the patriarchal Godfather.

The female image of a goddess also reminds us that what we call sacred is immanent in the world. The sacred is perceivable through the body, through the senses, through real contact with real things, and through metaphors that are body based.[37]

## REIMAGING THE SACRED

Although it is closely related and could be seen as part of the neopagan group, the Goddess movement has some unique emphases. I attended a conference conducted by the Isthmus Institute in Dallas, Texas, with the theme "The Goddess Returns." The announcement brochure stated that in mainstream Judaism, Christianity, and Islam, the masculine has held the singular and dominant sway. For thousands of years, men in Western culture have benefited psychologically and spiritually from this self-reflective portrayal of the Divine as masculine and from biblical stories representing men and their relationship to a patriarchal God.

It was pointed out that many religious writings (including the Bible) picture women as even more fallen than men, more fleshly, more trapped in matter. Thus, women are not only more susceptible to sin; they are objects of temptation as well, for they pull men down into matter — into the nonsacred. In addition, the established traditions have reserved positions of spiritual leadership for men and have defined spiritual leadership in ways that are hierarchical and excluding. A primary task of the goddess movement is the reimaging of the sacred. It is the Goddess who is the primary vehicle in this enterprise, for not only does her indwelling presence restore life to the universe, but she infuses it with the particular qualities of the feminine which have been lost to universal consciousness through the dominance of patriarchal religion and mechanistic science.

The work of UCLA archaeologist Marija Gimbutas was featured at the Isthmus Institute's conference held in Dallas, Texas, in 1991. Gimbutas has resurrected ancient images of womanhood and the Goddess which she claims are over 100,000 years old. They portray a world in which women held

37. Starhawk, *The Spiral Dance,* 229.

equal power with men. In this world, for a period lasting from 100,000 to 600,000 years, a united sexuality and spirituality were represented by the body of the Great Mother, with her sacred vulva as the source of life. The masculine gods, making their entrance only six thousand or seven thousand years ago, moved into a preeminence which split the body from the soul, emphasizing intellect over instinct and dominance over cooperation, and subjugating the feminine to an inferior role.

According to *Greek Politics: The Global Promise* by Fritjof Capra and Charlene Spretnak, only a female goddess from the East can deliver humanity from the authoritarianism of the oppressive patriarchal style of religion that has dominated in the West.

A large number of radical feminists who ardently desire an expression for their spiritual selves have gravitated to witches' covens over the last several decades. Here they find a model more readily identifiable with their aspirations. Whether she is called one of the names of the ancient past (Artemis, Astarte, Mélusine, Aphrodite, Diana, Brigit) or just Great Goddess or Great Mother, she can supposedly imbue the worshiper with a sense of power and control over life.

According to this feminist way of thinking, Christianity is too bound by patriarchal structures to be of any use to women. The church's long tradition, founded on the reputedly oppressive writings of Paul, Peter, and a male-dominated Israel, is too monolithic to be changed. It must be replaced.

## UNITARIAN UNIVERSALISM

Lesley Phillips, in a conference at the American Academy of Religion, stated that historically the institutional Unitarian Universalism denomination developed with the Christian, and more recently the Judeo-Christian, tradition. In recent years, it has also begun to acknowledge its debts to the theological traditions of the East. As Unitarian Universalism continues to mature as a religious movement, the neopagan path needs to be recognized as another stream that is part of our radical religious pluralism.

At this same conference, material was passed out with testimonies from various members of the Unitarian Universalist Church. One said, "I am very excited to learn about pagan-identified UU's. Please send me information about . . . how to start a chapter in our own congregation." Another person exclaimed, "I am glad to finally find a word to describe my beliefs — pagan!"

Recently, among the Unitarian churches, the Covenant of Unitarian Universalist Pagans has been formed, which serves as a forum for interested people to meet and explore pagan ritual within the Unitarian Church. In 1990 there were sixty chapters throughout the United States.

## POST-CHRISTIAN FEMINISTS

According to Daphne Hampson, the person who first gave voice to the conclusion that feminism and Christianity were never going to be reconcilable, was Mary Daly in her book *Beyond God the Father*, published in 1973. A well-trained Catholic theologian and professor at Boston College, Daly was invited in 1971 to be the first woman preacher in Harvard Memorial Church. Her sermon topic was "The Women's Movement: An Exodus Community." She ended her sermon by walking out of the church in protest against it, and inviting the other women present to do likewise. She defended this exodus in her sermon, saying: "We cannot really belong to institutional religion as it exists. It isn't good enough to be token preachers. . . . Singing sexist hymns, praying to a male god breaks our spirit, makes us less than human. The crushing weight of this tradition, of this power structure, tells us that we do not even exist."[38]

For Daly, the unalienated, almost "pure," female-identified Being emerges as the standard or measure against which alienation on the particular level of concrete existence is defined. She has an almost vicious discussion of the "painted bird." This type of woman is a cosmeticized token and totally unreal agent of patriarchy whose purpose is to undermine natural, authentic women. Daly wants to separate the real women from the "fembots" and "totalled women" who participate in maintaining their own servitude. According to Daly, "the painted bird functions in the anti-process of double-crossing her sisters, polluting them with poisonous paint." In traditional theological terminology, it might be said that such "painted bird" women are damned, alienated from salvation, steeped in the sinfulness of collaborating with patriarchal evil.

Of course, for Daly, the ultimate enemy is maleness and patriarchy.

Women's hope for wholeness and authenticity is contingent on the negation of the male, both within the female self and in external phallicist social forms, described by Daly in terms such as "phallocracy," "cockocracy," "boreocracy," "sadosociety," "Vapor State," "jockdom," "Daddydom," and so on.[39]

## ACHTEMEIER'S CRITIQUE

Truth regarding the nature of God or ultimate reality is the ultimate source of contention between Christians and feminists. Elizabeth Achtemeier identifies one critical issue as the feminist refusal to differentiate Creator from creation:

38. Eller, *Lap of the Goddess*, 47.
39. Marsha Aileen Hewitt, *Critical Theory of Religion* (Minneapolis: Fortress, 1995), 133-36.

As soon as God is called female, the images of birth, of suckling, of carrying in the womb, and, most importantly, the identification of the deity with life in all things become inevitable, and the Bible's careful and consistent distinction between Creator and Creation is blurred and lost.

This distinction is critical when one places the male imagery in the Bible in the context of the surrounding cultures that practiced fertility rites and goddess worship. God reveals himself in the Old Testament to the Israelites so that they might be set apart for God and that God might be revealed in their midst. He claimed to be the true God in the midst of pagan idols.

For God to reveal himself in primarily female metaphor in that ancient context would result in a misconception about his nature. God is neither male nor female (Num. 23:19). He is spirit (John 4:24).[40]

## THE RADICAL FEMINIST DEPARTURE FROM CHRISTIANITY

In 1994, I participated in a summer study program at the University of St. Andrews in Scotland. One of the speakers was Daphne Hampson, lecturer in Systematic Theology at the University of St. Andrews. She was introduced as one of Europe's finest feminist theologians with a doctorate from both Oxford and Harvard. One of her books, *Theology and Feminism,* is described as a story of how a once-Christian woman followed her intellect and passion for justice out of Christianity and began to reconceptualize God.

Hampson contends that the feminist challenge strikes at the heart of Christianity. She states that she can no longer live with the Christian myth and interpret the world through that pair of spectacles.

And so Hampson states that she is post-Christian because Christianity (and not Islam) is the historical context within which her religious sensibilities were formed and because she does not believe that God could be related in a particular way to a particular age or to one particular person, Jesus Christ, or to Israel and the Christian church. And so her career is devoted to finding a way to conceptualize God which is independent of the Christian myth, a myth she says is neither tenable nor ethical.[41]

40. Carl E. Braaten and Robert W. Jensen, eds., *Reclaiming the Bible for the Church* (Grand Rapids: Eerdmans, 1995); and Elizabeth Achtemeier, *Nature, God, and Pulpit* (Grand Rapids: Eerdmans, 1992).

41. Daphne Hampson, *Theology and Feminism* (Oxford: Blackwell, 1990), 42, 171.

# THE CHRISTIAN FEMINIST USE OF THE BIBLE

In this section, we will consider two Christian feminists of a liberal disposition who affirm that they will remain in the Christian tradition and attempt to throw a bridge between the past biblical revelation and the present feminist and domination crisis. They must, as Christians, make reference to the past. But they seek also to have a religion which is in tune with the world in which we live.

## THE "GOLDEN THREAD"

These feminists use what Hampson calls the "golden thread, two-stage" approach. In this approach a leading motif is lifted out of the past and applied in another situation.[42]

Utilizing the golden thread approach (the golden thread being justification by faith), Martin Luther names the Epistle to James (which appears to speak of justification by works) an "epistle of straw."

The Golden Thread approach has also been applied to the various (apparently conflicting) New Testament verses which have to do with the status of women. For those who use this approach it seems clear that the Galatians passage (that there is neither Jew nor Greek, bond nor free, male nor female) was of the essence of Christianity. Other passages were to be judged mistaken or subordinate in terms of this criterion. In this passage, one may well argue, Paul broke through to the ultimate implications of the Christian message. It is a passage in which he is concerned with the nature of life in Christ.

By contrast, in the Corinthians passage in which Paul speaks of male headship, and in which it is said that women should be silent, he is concerned with a practical situation which has arisen, a situation in which the church, still insecure in a pagan world, was likely to cause scandal if it departed too far from social convention — and his concern is that it should not unnecessarily put itself in jeopardy. One might further say that Paul would surely want to be judged in terms of the highest that he knew. Furthermore, one may argue that the subordination of women in the church reflected the cultural conditioning of people in the first century. By contrast, the principle of human equality is a fundamental implication of the gospel.

The advantage of a golden thread approach is that it provides a way of moving between the past and the very different circumstances of the present. It allows a translation process to be undertaken, while the underlying theme (that, for example, of human liberation) remains constant.

42. Ibid., 22.

240

The problem with such an approach is that if one's starting point is "what are the Scriptures fundamentally about?" it is possible for others to contend that some other theme is "fundamental" to the Scriptures. Thus opponents of the ordination of women might plausibly say that fundamental to the Scriptures is male headship. A conservative could adduce in support of this contention that in Scripture God is overwhelmingly conceptualized by using male metaphors; that God came in Christ, a male human person; and that he chose men alone to head the church (if one thinks that the calling of the twelve bears a relation to the constitution of the church). Thus a debate or dispute can arise about the dominating thrust of the Bible.[43]

## USE OF THE BIBLE FOR FEMALE LIBERATION

There are many facets to Rosemary Redford Ruether's golden thread approach. Ruether is a prominent theologian. Her interest in the transformation of family structures extends far beyond the freeing of women from domestic chores that is a precondition for the development of their full capacities. She writes, "A genuine change in the pattern of parenting must be understood, not as a slight adjustment toward males 'helping' females with childcare, but a fundamental reconstruction of the primary roots of culture, transforming the gender imaging of child-parent relations and the movement into adulthood for both males and females."[44]

Unlike Mary Daly, Ruether states that it is important that societies "develop an adequately affirmative role for men, one that gives men prestige parallel to that of women but prevents their assuming aggressive dominance over women."

Another critique by Ruether of feminist Goddess spirituality theories relates to the feminist treatment of history and archaeological dates, concluding that, "However good feminine values may seem for us today, to project them on an ancient Neolithic people and to presume that these must have been their values and their understanding of both 'woman' and 'nature,' on the grounds that they had a 'goddess-domination' culture and society, is very questionable."

Ruether also critiques feminist views that elevate femininity as a repository of values superior to those associated with masculinity. What Ruether suggests is that feminism develop a full humanist perspective and corresponding politics which affirms that "all humans possess a full and equivalent human nature and personhood, as male and female."

Despite her critiques of Goddess spirituality, Ruether contends that

43. Ibid., 26-28.
44. Hewitt, *Critical Theory*, 181-84.

the liberation of women is a necessary precondition of human liberation. Ruether defines the "basic principle" of feminist theology as the affirmation and the promotion of the full humanity of women. When consciously embraced, this critical principle opens possibilities for right relations between men and women and with the divine. The struggle against sexism is not just a struggle to promote the full equality of women; it is also a process of "humaniz[ing] the world" because sexism cannot be challenged without the "dethronement of the cultural universe" that distorts both female and male humanity.

The indivisible connection between feminism and humanism is the basis on which Ruether criticizes separatist tendencies in the so-called radical feminism of thinkers like Mary Daly, whose concept of the male as "generically evil" is dehumanizing both to men and to women.[45]

Thus we see that Ruether engages in a deconstructive and reconstructive critique of Christianity that seeks to reclaim and refashion its emancipatory impulses in the context of women's current condition and needs.

## ELISABETH SCHÜSSLER FIORENZA AND THE MARGINALIZED

Widely known and respected, Elisabeth Schüssler Fiorenza is professor of Scripture and Interpretation at Harvard Divinity School. She sees the Bible as both redemptive and liberating. This viewpoint informs the feminist critical hermeneutics and liberation theology of Fiorenza.[46]

In contrast to both fundamentalist and liberal scientific theology, Fiorenza calls for reading the Bible in the community of faith, from the social position of the poor and marginalized. The purpose of such biblical interpretation is not primarily to seek information about the past but to interpret daily life in the global village with the help of the biblical God of justice and salvation. She sees the Bible as portraying a vision of a world freed from the structural sin of patriarchal domination. Such a biblical reading aims to give dignity and value to the life of exploited women in whose struggles and survival the presence and image of God can be experienced in our midst. For Fiorenza, the Bible does not restrict salvation to the soul but it also aims to inspire Christians to engage in the struggle for transforming patriarchal structures of domination.[47]

Feminist interpretation holds that masculine supremacy is socially constructed rather than innate or ordained by God.

45. Ibid., 201-2.
46. Ibid., 162.
47. Rebecca S. Chopp and Mark Lewis Taylor, eds., *Reconstructing Christian Theology* (Minneapolis: Fortress, 1994), 86-87.

For Fiorenza, the historical project of women's liberation is the very condition of the possibility for "the emancipation of the Christian community from patriarchal structures and male-biased mind-sets" that allows the gospel to "become again a 'power for the salvation' of women as well as men." Christianity will either consciously embrace and promote the liberation of women and all subjugated peoples, or it will wither away of its own historical irrelevance.[48]

The primary ritual at a 1993 Re-Imagining Conference was the pervasive invocation of "Sophia, Divine Wisdom." The conference, held in Minneapolis, was funded and supported by twenty ecclesiastical organizations, including the Presbyterian Church (U.S.A.), the United Methodist Church, the Evangelical Lutheran Church in America (ELCA), the American Baptist Convention (ABC), the United Church of Christ, and four religious communities of Roman Catholics. More than two thousand — mostly women — were in attendance.

The furor caused by the conference exceeded in magnitude anything in the memory of mainline Christianity.

The main criticisms of the conference were with theological problems related to the worship programs. A particularly problematic aspect of the reimagining rituals was the pervasive invocation of "Sophia, Divine Wisdom." Recent biblical and theological scholarship has recovered elements of the Old Testament wisdom tradition that have been too often ignored, including the personification of wisdom in several significant passages from Proverbs. An emerging appreciation of the New Testament's use of the wisdom motif has enriched our understanding of biblical Christology. However, reimagining rituals failed to assist worshipers to understand the connection between Old Testament wisdom motifs and God's self-disclosure in Jesus Christ. The New Testament proclaims "Christ the power of God and the wisdom of God" (1 Cor. 1:24), not wisdom as a divine manifestation apart from Jesus Christ.

Wisdom and Sophia became an alternative employed in distinction from the triune God. Such was clearly the case in the "Ritual of the Spirit of Re-Imagining," in which a corporate prayer concludes with the words "through the power and guidance of the spirit of wisdom whom we name Sophia." Here, Sophia is not merely the Greek word for wisdom, but a name invoked within a formulation that serves as an alternative to the living tradition of the church catholic which prays "through Jesus Christ." In the Lord's Supper, the apostolic biblical prayer forms give thankful praise to God for God's gracious acts, recalling the acts of salvation in Jesus Christ, and calling upon the Holy Spirit; but "Sophia" was the one to whom thanks and praise were offered.

48. Hewitt, *Critical Theory*, 169-70.

Sophia was blessed, thanked, celebrated, and praised in language properly reserved for expressing the grace of our Lord Jesus Christ, the love of God, and the communion of the Holy Spirit.[49]

The triune God of Bible and creed was roundly circumvented. The audience was directed to pantheism over transcendence, to a spirituality of creation. Even more than pantheism, however, a rampant syncretism characterized reimagining. The audience was invited to supply its own names for God: divine ancestor, mother God, lover, alpha and omega, fire of love, she who is eternal, Sophia, earth mother, spirit woman, cosmic maxim, ninjan, womb of creation, prime mover, and yin and yang. Jesus Christ was not named.

There was a decisive shift away from a salvation procured for us by the work of God in Jesus Christ to a salvation potential within creation. The doctrine of redemption, with its call for repentance and promise of transformation of self and society, was supplanted by a theology of immanence in which the distinction between God and the world was blurred or eliminated.

No prayer was addressed to Jesus, and none ended in his name. The cross and atonement were likewise subjected to derision and dismissed as sanctions for violence and oppression.

Reimagining's theology of immanence came to most explicit elaboration in sexual imagery. That motif pervaded reimagining at every level. It was most apparent in the default apology for lesbianism, homosexuality, transgenderism, and bisexuality that characterized reimagining. Not a few speakers identified themselves as lesbian.

An appeal for consensual sexual acts followed in consort with the affirmation of lesbianism. "Imagine sex among friends as the norm," affirmed Mary Hunt, "young people learning to make friends rather than to date. Imagine valuing genital sexual interaction in terms of whether or how it fosters friendship and pleasure. . . . Pleasure is our birthright."[50]

## EVANGELICAL CRITIQUES

In contrast, in his essay in *Reclaiming the Bible for the Church*, Karl Donfried of Smith College affirms that

> marriage is linked with the procreative power of and responsibility to the Creator God. In fact, marriage represents the complementariness of male

---

49. Joseph D. Small and John P. Burgess, "Evaluating 'Re-Imagining,'" *Christian Century*, April 6, 1994, 342-43.

50. James R. Edwards, "Earthquake in the Mainline," *Christianity Today*, November 14, 1994, 39-41, 43.

and female, and marriage is the only arena for the expression of sexual desire, a desire that is powerful and often unpredictable. Consistent with this reading of Scripture, the Ramsey colloquium urges that marriage is a place where, in a singular manner, our waywardness begins to be healed and our fear of commitment overcome, where we may learn to place another person's needs rather than our own desires at the center of life.

In fact, for Donfried,

there is not one biblical text that contradicts Paul's negative evaluation of homosexuality. In the Bible, homosexuality is repeatedly declared to be a path that deviates from God's creational intentionality. Today's cultural situation is not new: Paul unwaveringly speaks against a culture with a radically divergent sexual ethic.[51]

Conservative groups in the Methodist and Presbyterian churches affirmed that the conference applauded heresy, celebrated blasphemy, and applauded heretical speakers.

Thomas Oden, well-known Methodist theologian of Drew Seminary, evaluates Sophia worship and theology in his autobiographical book, *Requiem*. Oden sees the rise of Sophia worship and teaching by ultra-feminists as an occasion to restudy and reclaim the classic consensual biblical worldview.[52]

Elizabeth Achtemeier of the Union Presbyterian Seminary, in Richmond, Virginia, states that

the radical feminists among us — and I emphasize the word "radical," because we must always distinguish between feminism as fairness and radical feminism as ideology — have abandoned any thought of an authoritative canon and replaced it with reliance on their own subjective experiences, shared in their communities called Women-church.[53]

Recently, in Mexico City, I met a woman from San Francisco who has established a new denomination called "Women's Church."

## EVANGELICALISM AND THE PATRIARCHAL CRISIS

As we have noted, for some feminists such as Mary Daly and Daphne Hampson, the Christian faith is too patriarchal to meet the needs of twentieth-century women and culture. For some so-called liberal or moderate Christian feminists, such as Rosemary Ruether and Elizabeth Fiorenza, to meet the

51. Braaten and Jenson, eds., *Reclaiming the Bible*, 40-41.
52. Thomas C. Oden, *Requiem* (Nashville: Abingdon, 1995), 146.
53. Braaten and Jenson, eds., *Reclaiming the Bible*, 121.

contemporary crisis of women, the biblical faith must be reinterpreted and reconstructed. On the other hand, there are evangelical scholars, both female and male, who find a more balanced approach to the so-called patriarchal crisis in the Bible. They see the biblical faith, when properly interpreted, as liberating for women and all marginalized groups.

The evangelical stance affirms that both men and women are made in the image of God without embracing in any way a perception of God as some sort of androgynous oddity, as a god/dess, as an archetype, or as a pantheistic oneness that encompasses each human being. Instead, according to Donna Hailson, evangelicals affirm that the Bible furnishes a worldview that meets human needs with its clear expression of:

- the triunity of the one God, the personal God, the eternal, nonslumbering, nonchanging, nonillusory God who created the world and is not contained by creation;
- the sinfulness of all human beings through the fall of Adam and Eve and individual choice;
- the only means of salvation — repentance from sin and acceptance of Christ Jesus as Savior and Lord;
- the partnership of men and women in the priesthood of all believers;
- the call of each redeemed person to incarnate and share the gospel of Christ.[54]

Aida Besancon Spencer, a professor at Gordon-Conwell Seminary, maintains that biblical Christianity has been misrepresented, misunderstood, or misinterpreted by many goddess worshipers. Their picture of God is rarely interpreted from the Bible itself. Rather, it is an archetypal stereotype projected onto the Bible. They portray God as impersonal, abstract, uninterested, detached, and a power-over. Metaphors are treated literally. Artificial divisions are made between God's immanence and transcendence. God has no paradox or intimate concern. The patriarchal stereotype is assumed to be an accurate projection of God.

Any constructive concepts in the Goddess movements are in reality imitations of biblical concepts. In the biblical text we find strong exhortations for peace, service, care of nature, equality, harmony, wisdom, light, visions, diversity in oneness, concern for the oppressed, power, healing, courage, a right process, immediacy, truth, compassion, freedom, and an interdependence between humanity and creation. Why then is the biblical God often pictured as violent, hierarchical, destructive, and repressive? The core of the criticism and the core of the defense lie with the nature of God. Again and again the

54. Spencer, *Goddess Revival*, 36-37.

God of the Bible is wrongly described in the goddess literature as the male warrior God (Yahweh).

Spencer points out that the God of the Bible is distinct from all other entities and is unique. We humans, too, are distinct from God. Only a very superficial reader of the Bible can conclude that God is impersonal, abstract, uninteresting, and detached. Although God is unique, God is also dynamic, surprising us humans and making us marvel. The idea of inner empowerment and social change is modeled by this God who has great power but uses that power for others who need empowerment and change. That is compassion, taking one's power and using it for others. We see no hierarchy in the Trinity, nor hierarchy in the humans God created.

As we have noted, goddess devotees say that they reject the patriarchal God of the Bible — his sex, his warlike nature, his religious intolerance, his destruction of peoples of other religions. "If God in 'his' heaven is a father ruling 'his' people, then it is in the 'nature' of things and according to divine plan and the order of the universe that society be male-dominated." Spencer points out that the Bible highlights that God became human in Jesus. That Jesus was male is also true, but that fact should never be said to reflect God's sexuality. We can only guess why Jesus became a male rather than a female. Possibly, he symbolized the male Passover lamb. Possibly he wanted to be more mobile in a traditional ancient society. (No woman could have taught in the male-only synagogue classes.) Nevertheless, Jesus' maleness was a limitation imposed on the incarnate God, not a reflection of God's essence.

The Bible, which claims to record reliable accounts of God's self-revelation, attests that God, in addition to revealing himself in the incarnation, can be known in a multiplicity of ways: through actions, descriptive adjectives, and metaphorical language. Even in the incarnation, Jesus continually pointed to his actions and used adjectives and metaphors for self-description (for example, John 10:37-38).

Aida Spencer, a biblical language specialist, points out that language and human "bodyness" do provide some limitations to God's self-revelation. However, metaphor and language are accurate only insofar as they are not stretched beyond their intentions. God uses a great variety of metaphors, only one of which is "father." Every metaphor must be studied for its analogies and disanalogies. "Lord" teaches us that because God is so good, God should be always obeyed. "Father" is part of a constellation of connotations, the everyday parent, the all-powerful idealized Parent, and the intimate but powerful ruler. Ultimately, when referring to God, "he" in Hebrew or Greek is not masculine but rather genderless, since "masculine" gender is simply an androgynous pronoun or noun. It should also be noted that the "masculine," "feminine," and "neuter" genera all symbolize different qualities about God. God is powerful, personal, forceful, causing results, one, and diverse.

Some goddess advocates suggest that the portrayal of God as transcendent should be abandoned: "In this time of global ecological crisis, it is important that human beings abandon a paradigm of the divine as above nature, existing eternally whether the natural universe lives or dies; rather let us return to the earlier reverence for all nature as sacred." Starhawk proposes the Goddess as "a living religion of immanence." On the other hand, Donald G. Bloesch has developed in an abstract manner what many people actually feel, that even though God is both transcendent and immanent, God "is primarily and originally transcendent and secondarily and derivatively immanent."

## BALANCE BETWEEN GOD'S IMMANENCE AND TRANSCENDENCE

Some people overemphasize God's transcendence through the metaphor of father, degenerating into picturing an absent, tyrannical sovereign father. In reaction, other people overemphasize God's immanence through the metaphor of mother, arriving at a present, caring, but also capricious, mother. The biblical answer is to embrace both transcendence and immanence in our conception of God because God is not we, yet God is in us. Immanence indicates the nearness or presence or indwelling of God in the creation, God sustaining and preserving creation generally and, more particularly, energizing the wills of believers. But God is also transcendent. God is in the world but also other than the world.[55]

Millard Erickson describes both the excesses and the implications of the two doctrines: "If we emphasize immanence too much, we may identify everything that happens as God's will and working." If we emphasize transcendence too much, "we may expect God to work miracles at all times," "we may tend to mistreat the creation, forgetting that he himself is present and active there," and "we may depreciate the value of what non-Christians do."[56]

According to Spencer, we as humans cannot have the power to love, to be united, to be mature and pure, without having a generous God who is other than we but close to us. Because God is transcendent, God can be immanent. Both immanence and transcendence are concepts of power and love, because Christians do not worship two gods but one God. This biblical view does not call for hierarchical dualism as the goddess people claim.[57]

55. Ibid., 80-81, 91-93, 101, 103, 126, 131-33, 190.
56. Millard J. Erickson, *Introducing Christian Doctrine* (Grand Rapids: Baker, 1992), 76-77.
57. Spencer, *Goddess Revival,* 149.

## THE DIGNITY AND EQUALITY OF WOMEN

In fact, as Carl Henry, a prominent evangelical theologian, states, the role and status of women in biblical doctrine and in the Christian community differ tellingly from those in pagan lands untouched by Christian ideals, or where ancient nonbiblical religions control society. Persons who emphasize the frequently misinterpreted and misunderstood Pauline passages on "subordination" (1 Cor. 11:3-5) and "silence" (1 Tim. 2:11-12) often obscure the fact that the apostle is actually a champion of women's progress in a world where their rights and dignity were routinely ignored, and overlook the dramatic gains that Christianity signaled for feminine fortunes.

While Greco-Roman society emphasized the duty of wives toward husbands, it disregarded reciprocal duties of husbands to wives. Plato held a somewhat higher view of women than did Aristotle, but it was Aristotle's severe limitation of feminine activities that prevailed. Roman law gave women no choice in the matter of marriage and provided no significant safeguards against its dissolution.

The apostle Paul, by contrast, stressed the dignity of women and their equality with men, and emphasized reciprocal responsibilities of husbands and wives. At a time when women were condemned to menial tasks, and intellectual pursuits were reserved for only upper-class males, it is remarkable that the Apostle — in the very passage in which he excludes women from teaching in public church assembles, probably because of lack of education, stipulates that they are to "learn in silence," that is, they are to be taught (1 Tim. 2:11; 1 Cor. 14:35).

In a society in which women were not considered learners, Paul's emphasis on the education of Gentile female believers is noteworthy. Greek women not only did not share in the education given to men but were confined to their own apartments. Paul nowhere teaches that women may not pray or prophesy in church meetings. While Islam later permitted upper-class women to study poetry and science and even to become teachers, their seclusion in the harem worked against such education. But in the early Christian movement women were welcomed into roles of leadership. The daughters of Philip, for example, were prophetesses (Acts 21:9); women served as deaconesses (note Phoebe in Rom. 16:1-3); Priscilla labored for the gospel alongside Aquila (in four of six mentions of them Paul gives Priscilla's name first). Paul commended the women who "laboured with me in the gospel" (Phil. 4:3, KJV).[58]

---

58. Carl Henry, "The Bible and the Dignity of Women," in *God, Revelation and Authority*, vol. 4 (Waco: Word Books, 1979), 514-15.

## AN EVANGELICAL APPROACH TO
## WOMEN AND CHURCH LEADERSHIP

One particularly controversial area of biblical interpretation for evangelicals is related to the place of women in ordained Christian ministry and church leadership. This subject was one area of discussion at an evangelical conference on biblical interpretation held at Ridgecrest, North Carolina, in 1988. This conference on interpretation was necessitated because a previous conference on biblical inerrancy revealed that the primary crux of disagreement among evangelical leaders was not on devotion to the full inspiration and normativity of the Scriptures, but on the interpretation of Scripture.

In my own pilgrimage, I relived the difference between an abstract affirmation of an infallible Bible and an interpretation of its meaning in regard to women's leadership and ordination. While a student at Southern Baptist Seminary in Louisville, Kentucky, I was asked to be pastor of a rural church in eastern Kentucky. The first question the pulpit committee asked was whether or not I believed in the infallible Bible. I said, "Yes." This was not a difficult answer since I came from the Springfield, Missouri, area, which is one of the fundamentalist headquarters of the country and the location of the Baptist New Testament Bible College which Jerry Falwell attended, as well as of the Assemblies of God schools. I came to find out, however, that the Kentucky church's interpretation of infallibility was different from that which I had been taught in Missouri. In this Kentucky church, women could not vote in church business meetings, they could not teach a male over five, they could not pray in public, they could not sing a solo, they could not sit on the same side of the church as their husbands, and they could not worship unless their heads were covered.

I found that the perspective in Kentucky was very different from my experience in Buffalo, Missouri. My grandmother was the daughter of a pioneer physician. He died in an epidemic in Kansas, and his last wish was that his daughter be sent back to Wisconsin to receive a college education. Her mother remarried and moved to Missouri. After her college education in Wisconsin, my grandmother returned to Missouri and was one of the few college-educated women in a small town of less than a thousand people. She was a devout and informed Christian. It seemed appropriate for her to take a leadership role in the church. Her husband, my grandfather, had a limited education. He encouraged her leadership role. She spoke in the church, she prayed in the church, she taught Bible studies for both men and women, and was perhaps the key woman in the growth and development of the church. Later, this background was to help me understand Paul's teaching about women's leadership in 1 Timothy 2.

## WOMEN AS MINISTERS

Aida Spencer points out that contemporary historians have shown that Christian female leadership goes back many years, long before twentieth-century feminists. For example, Janette Hassey in her study "Evangelical Women in Public Ministry around the Turn of the Century, No Time for Silence," notes how many fundamentalist or evangelical individuals and organizations supported women in ministry.

A. B. Simpson, the founder of the Christian and Missionary Alliance, called the Holy Spirit "our Mother God" and included women on the executive board committee, employed them as Bible professors, and supported female evangelists and branch officers (the early Christian and Missionary Alliance equivalent of a local minister). She also shows how Dwight L. Moody worked together with a number of women preachers. At the turn of the century, female graduates of Moody Bible Institute "openly served as pastors, evangelists, pulpit supply preachers, Bible teachers, and even in the ordained ministry." Gordon Bible and Missionary Training School in its earliest years had an equal number of male and female professors.

Katherine C. Bushnell had her study "God's Word to Women" published in 1919. It showed that if the Bible is treated as "inspired, infallible, and inviolable" then one must conclude that "the teaching that woman must perpetually 'keep silence' in the Church, be obedient to her husband, and never presume to teach or preach, because Eve sinned, blights the doctrine of the atonement, and robs Christ of glory, in that His death atoned for all sin, including Eve's of course." Five years later, Judson Press celebrated one hundred years of Bible distribution by publishing Helen Barrett Montgomery's *The New Testament in Modern English* in which she translates, as one example, Romans 16:1-2: "our sister Phoebe, who is a minister of the church of Cenchreae. . . . For she herself has been made an overseer to many people, including myself."[59]

## ALTERNATIVE APPROACHES BY CONSERVATIVE LEADERS

The problem of women's leadership roles in the church is still of continuing concern in conservative circles. J. I. Packer, of Regent College in Vancouver, the accepted intellectual leader of the inerrantist movement at that time, was a keynote speaker at the Southern Baptist National Biblical Interpretation Conference. He spoke on the interpretation of the Bible related to women in ministry.

59. Spencer, *Goddess Revival*, 180-81.

In his address, Packer said, "I do not believe that any New Testament passage could be quoted as forbidding the people of God or anyone else to put a woman into the pastor's role. I think we ought to see the task as having two facets. One is that all the gifts God has given are given to be used. If in the Christian community a woman has a gift, that gift was meant to be used. That's what God gave it for."

However, Packer continued, the clue that we ought to be following is that women's ministry be a womanly ministry. It will have a maternal rather than a paternal cast, because women are women and they are not men in disguise. We ought to be working toward a consensus whereby women who may be on the church staff working full time in that kind of activity see their role as a true fulfillment of their womanly, maternal nature in Christian ministry. Later, in 1991, Packer concluded "that it is unwise to make women presbyters, by which he means the senior leader of a congregation." He contended that:

> Presbyters are set apart for a role of authoritative pastoral leadership. But this role is for manly men rather than womanly women, according to the creation pattern that redemption restores. Paternal pastoral oversight, which is the essence of the presbyterial role, is not a task for which women are naturally fitted by their maker.

Packer's view is that a woman's best service in ministry would be in partnership with a male leader rather than as sole pastor. He opposes ordination for women on the basis of its actually "decreasing the possibilities of women's ministry in the churches."

Other speakers included Walter Kaiser in the Old Testament area, and Grant Osborne in the New Testament field, both from Trinity Evangelical Divinity School. The theological speaker was Robert Johnston, now of Fuller Seminary. All of the addresses were published in the book on the proceedings of this conference entitled *Biblical Interpretation: Proceedings of the Conference on Biblical Interpretation.*

Walter Kaiser, dean of Trinity Evangelical Divinity School at the time, said that he did not think that 1 Timothy 2 excluded educated, mature, and doctrinally sound women from ministry. For Kaiser, Paul restricted women from teaching or exercising authority because they had not learned. Paul's imperative is to let women learn. Kaiser affirmed, "I think the whole concept is that man was shaped, walked, and talked with God in the garden, had the advantage of being instructed, but the woman was tricked. She was deceived. Therefore, once women have been taught, and once the gift has been recognized, then they can have ministry."

Kaiser said the faculty of Trinity Evangelical Dininity School was divided on the place of women in ministry. The seminary had some women teaching in the School of Theology, but there was some disagreement among the constituency and the faculty. The Evangelical Free Church, of which he is a member, is also divided on this subject. Kaiser contended, however, that a consensus of evangelical scholarship tended to see the passage in 1 Timothy as referring to women who had been seduced by the heretics described in 1 Timothy 3.

Robert Johnston mentioned that oftentimes we forget that the Bible states that a man should leave his family and join the woman in marriage as opposed to the opposite approach. Why would the author of Genesis make that statement? One possibility, according to Johnston, was to make sure that we do not misread his intention in terms of a creational ordering in which the male, being first, has priority and authority, but rather that the two, who are different and yet one, enjoy co-relationship and mutuality. So to make sure the pattern of first-second is not seen as the point of the text in Genesis 2:24, the author has a second-first arrangement.

Johnston went on to say that from the earliest days of the current discussion about women in ministry, which began in more liberal churches more than twenty years ago, the question of the role of women within the congregation and the home has been recognized as largely a question of the interpretation of relevant biblical passages. The real question, at least for most Christians, is: Which of these views, the hierarchical or the egalitarian — or perhaps a synthesis of the two — has a clear grounding in Scripture? Both sides of the debate ground their positions in Scripture, yet they reach opposite conclusions.[60]

All of the leaders mentioned above emphasized that each biblical text must be treated within its full unit of meaning and in light of the total biblical canon. The literary form of a passage must be understood if it is to be adequately interpreted. The historical concept of a passage helps the interpreter understand both the function and the meaning that a text had in its own day. The immediate context of a passage should be considered before one looks at parallel texts. The author's explicit intention, methodology, theology, and practice, as understood in other biblical texts, can provide helpful interpretive clues. The Bible has an overarching consistency despite its seemingly different teaching in particular situations. Interpretations of given texts can be productively correlated with wider biblical attitudes, statements, themes, and descriptions. Interpreters of Scripture should seek the help of other devout scholars so that insights can be shared, humility fostered, and biases of culture and theological tradition overcome.

Furthermore, interpreters should be aware of progressive understand-

---

60. *Proceedings of the Conference on Biblical Interpretation* (Nashville: Broadman, 1988), 211-14.

ing. This is different from ongoing revelation. Theological controversy and new cultural situations cause us to restudy the implications of the Bible for our day. This does not mean that culture determines our interpretation of the biblical text. However, culture can serve us by being the occasion for renewed reflection and debate. New implications of the text may come to light. We need to give ourselves to continued prayerful reading, study, and discussion of the Scripture so that further clarity can be gained.

To utilize the correct principles of biblical interpretation, Johnston maintained that we must look at the book of Acts, Philippians, Romans 16, the emphasis of the ministry of Jesus, as well as dealing with the 1 Corinthians 11 and 14 passages and the 1 Timothy 2 passage to understand the biblical teaching on women in the ministry. For example, we need to read 1 Timothy 2 in the light of the total biblical emphasis to understand the place of women in the early church.

## ORDINATION OF WOMEN: EVANGELICAL DIFFERENCES

The fact that there is disagreement was clearly demonstrated at a meeting of the Evangelical Theological Society. I walked into the book exhibit. Two large tables were in the middle of the room. One was manned by the Council on Biblical Manhood and Womanhood. The other was for a group known as Christians for Biblical Equality. As I would visit one table, people from the other would tap me on the shoulder and tell me to be sure to come to their exhibit because *they* represented an authentic interpretation of the Bible concerning women in ministry. This disagreement seemed especially interesting since one of the requirements for anyone wanting to join the Theological Society is to affirm the inerrancy of the Bible.

It was also interesting to note the background of the leaders of the respective groups listed on the brochures handed out. The more conservative group, "Biblical Manhood and Womanhood," listed professors from conservative seminaries such as Trinity, Westminster, and Mid-America. The group "Christians for Biblical Equality" listed faculty members from the same schools and, in addition, people from conservative schools such as Wheaton, Bethel, Trinity, Gordon, and Fuller. I was somewhat surprised to see Roger Nicole on the more moderate Biblical Equality Council because he is known as one of the most conservative theologians in the United States. This points out that there is disagreement on the women in ministry issue among some of the most widely recognized scholars constituting the conservative movement in America.

In recent years, the *Christianity Today* Institute presented a symposium in which Kenneth Kantzer, Walter Kaiser, and Bruce Waltke expressed their opinions on women in ministry. Kantzer and Kaiser were more sympathetic, while Waltke, of Westminster Seminary, questioned the biblical approval of women in ministry.[61]

At a philosophy conference at Wheaton College I heard Carol Westphal, who has been lauded as one of Wheaton's outstanding graduates. She had come to Wheaton from Grand Rapids Bible College in Michigan and had achieved an outstanding academic and leadership position. As a woman from a very conservative background, she gave her testimony about how she struggled with the biblical material until finally she worked through it and believed that her call to ministry would allow her to be ordained in the Reformed Church in America.

Prior to the 1990 decision by the Christian Reformed Church to allow women to be ordained, Claire Wolterstorff, the wife of Nicholas Wolterstorff of Calvin College and Yale University, joined the Episcopal Church so that she could be ordained. Since then the denomination has ordained a few women to the ministry. It is also interesting that in the tenth General Assembly of the Evangelical Presbyterian Church in the United States in 1990, Andrew Jumper said that in his opinion, any denomination that denies women a role in leadership of the church will be pushed aside by the stream of history.

I have noted that in the discussions among evangelicals there was confusion about the place of ordination in the biblical concept of ministry. The New Testament says relatively little about ordination. It clearly indicates, however, that the early church had a varied and faithful ministry and emphasizes that all of God's people are gifted by the Holy Spirit for the purpose of edifying or building up one another. We see this emphasis in 1 Corinthians 12 and 14, Romans 12, Ephesians 4, and 1 Peter 4. Any person could exercise ministry or service who was called and gifted by God and affirmed by the body of Christ, the church. Some were set apart in leadership positions. Some were assigned specific tasks. But the differences among ministers were not distinctions of kind. Eventually, certain types of affirmation were combined with certain functions of ministry to produce our current understanding of ordination.

Grant Osborne of Trinity Evangelical Divinity School argued at the 1988 Biblical Interpretation Conference in North Carolina and in an article given to those attending that there are no biblical obstacles to the ordination of women in Western society where teaching and speaking in the church no longer have the implications they did in the first century. The teacher today is viewed as one who shares his or her knowledge rather than as an authoritative giant whose every statement is "ex cathedra." The same is true of the pastor-teacher. The pastor is no longer seen as a hierarchical, or command, person but as occupying a servant role.

61. "Shared Leadership," *Christianity Today*, October 3, 1986, 12-15.

However, Osborne and Kantzer say that women should not force the issue. It is one thing to say that Western society no longer has such cultural restrictions, but quite another to conclude that women should everywhere take pulpits. There are pockets of conservative thinking where such a move would not serve the cause of Christ. The proclamation of the gospel is the overriding principle of the scriptural lifestyle. Any actions that interfere with this should be abandoned. Also, in such instances, the "weaker" brother principle would seem to make such a movement ill-advised. Instead, women should work within the cultural mores to change the situation in ways the culture can accept. Even here, however, the stress should not be just on changing the culture but on magnifying Christ. That is the preeminent biblical maxim.

In a *Christianity Today* symposium, Bruce Waltke defended the leadership role of the male but added the term "servant-leadership." Male leadership must not be self-serving. Raymond C. Ortlund, Jr., of Trinity Evangelical Divinity School likewise holds that male headship means that in the "partnership of two spiritually equal human beings, man and woman, the man bears the primary responsibility to lead the partnership in a God-glorifying direction."[62]

In that same symposium, Kantzer pointed out that most of the new churches in America which have been so successful, not only here but in their worldwide missionary approach, have made provisions for women to assume positions of leadership. Kantzer contended that the total impact of the Scriptures provides a conclusive case against taking either 1 Timothy 2 or 1 Corinthians 14 as prohibitions against women in Christian leadership. The Bible simply cannot be construed as universally forbidding women to teach the church or teach men.

In their recent book *Women in the Church*, Stanley J. Grenz and Denise Muir Kjesbo make a detailed and comprehensive contribution to the theology of women in ministry. For Grenz, the foundational premise of the traditional position seems to be that there is a hierarchy of male over female within the creation order itself. Their book, he states, "deals with this issue, and in it we think the egalitarian position of evangelical feminism is the better of the two."

According to evangelical leader Rebecca Merrill Groothuis,

evangelical feminism consists of the effort to teach and implement the fundamental principle of the biblical equality of all human beings before God. According to this principle, there is no moral or theological justifi-

62. Raymond C. Ortlund, Jr., *Gender, Worth and Equality* (Wheaton, Ill.: CBMW, 1990), 7.

cation for permanently granting or denying status, privilege, or prerogative solely on the basis of a person's race, class, or gender. This is one of the differences the new covenant makes, as Galatians 3:26-28 points out.

Evangelical feminism disagrees with the traditionalist belief that the Bible teaches a universal spiritual principle of female subordination to male authority within the church and the home. Rather, the appropriate outworking of the biblical ideal of equality is for women to have equal opportunity with men for ministry in the church, and shared authority and mutual submission with their husbands in the home.

None of this has anything to do with the unpleasant and downright immoral ideas that so many people associate with the term "feminism."

For Groothuis "there is no insidious, underlying, secularizing agenda to evangelical feminism." Rather,

a viable and biblically consistent theology of sexuality must be firmly grounded in the biblical teachings concerning the creation of both man and woman as equally imaging God, the priesthood of all believers, and Christ as the one mediator between God and humanity. The implications of these fundamental theological principles rule out any universal hierarchies or cosmic principles of male supremacy.[63]

As a senior statesman of the Inerrantist Movement, and as a conservative leader, both as former editor of *Christianity Today* and as dean at Trinity Evangelical Divinity School, Kantzer states that though "all things are lawful, not all things are expedient." Sometimes for the sake of the weaker brother, we must forgo using legitimate freedoms. Christians have often practiced such self-restraint, especially in missionary efforts where cultural customs must be respected. In order not to offend others who are convinced (mistakenly, he believes) that the Bible forbids women to teach, in certain situations we must choose not to ordain women for the sake of the gospel.

This does not mean, Kantzer affirms, that we set aside our concern for the status of women in the church. If anything, we must intensify our efforts to bring others to a proper understanding of Scripture. We do this with grace and sensitivity. However, Kantzer goes on to say that we are seeing an increasing number of highly gifted and well-trained women seeking to use their gifts to minister in the church. His answer is that if the Scripture does not forbid, ordain them and encourage them to teach in the church. Unfortunately, however, we do not live in an ideal world where simple answers are the best. We live with the baggage of history.

63. Rebecca Merrill Groothuis, *The Feminist Bogeywoman* (Grand Rapids: Baker, 1995), 3, 32.

Kantzer points out that American women are among the most liberated women in the world. Many Christian women (as well as men) sincerely believe that this new-found freedom will destroy the home and damage the Christian nurture of our young. Others, like Bruce Waltke, are convinced that the Bible flatly prohibits women from teaching men. Still others, including Kantzer's wife, argue that for cultural reasons a woman ought not to be given senior roles in teaching and in the leadership of the church. Despite this, Kantzer believes that we must encourage women in their exercise of God-given gifts. Where necessary, we must urge them to seek avenues that are less disturbing to the peace of the church. As women exercise their gifts and confirm their divine call to ministry, the church profits. We thus will be driven to reexamine our interpretation of the Bible to see if its seemingly universal prohibition of women teachers and leaders is not more derived from ancient prejudices than from the biblical text.

Kantzer continues by stating that our failure to utilize women's skills becomes more and more irrational in the light of the accomplishments of women in society around us. Throughout society, women are proving that they have the ability to teach and to lead. Margaret Thatcher could instruct and guide millions of citizens, men and women alike, throughout Great Britain and the Commonwealth. However, even if she possessed a vital Christian experience, she could not be a deacon or minister in many of our evangelical churches. And the church is the loser. The church loses because it is not availing itself of tremendous gifts, but it also loses because increasingly it is turning some of our finest women away from a church that they see not as the body of Christ where we all are one in the Lord, but as a male preserve which selfishly clings to worldly power in the name of Christ.

# AN EVANGELICAL
# COMPLEMENTARITY APPROACH

In 1992, *Christianity Today* published a helpful article, "Breaking the Gender Impasse," by R. Paul Stevens, dean at Regent College in Vancouver, British Columbia. He calls for a position of complementarity regarding the seemingly diverse teachings on women in ministry. He believes that this approach will help provide a clue to the resolution of the bind in which Scripture seemingly places those who are conservative Christians. He contends that it is more faithful to biblical theology, and more fruitful for biblical worship, for men and women to serve together in partnership. He also claims this would more fully reflect God's glory. We should allow men and women in all their sexual distinctiveness to share completely as partners in ministry rather than to institutionalize gender-restricted roles.

Stevens states that the failure to equip the church for such partnership has been disastrous. Men who serve in public ministry often seem to develop an unnatural femininity in order to encompass fully the ministry of a church. Some women who have successfully broken into the male world of public ministry have succeeded only by adopting a masculine bearing. Is it not better for men to be men and women to be women in ministry and leadership? What is needed is a ministry that prizes the shared contribution of both sexes. The whole is more than the sum of the parts. This is also true in marriage. Each helps the other more completely resemble and express the image of God himself.

The deepest issues of our life in Christ resist reduction to manageable ideas or stereotypical roles. The biblical teaching is often ambiguous in just these areas. Hence, we find ourselves living with tensions individually, maritally, and in the church. These tensions can generate friction and frustration. Or they can be resolved by an artificial choice to live out only one side of the biblical witness. Alternatively, the tension can be embraced by joining in partnership or complementarity.[64] In any case, the American Association of Theological Schools in 1972 reported that 89 percent of the nation's 66,000 seminary students were men. By fall 1995, 32.8 percent of seminary students were women.

# THE BIBLICAL RESPONSE TO MAGIC, WITCHCRAFT, AND NEOPAGANISM

## The Old Testament Struggle against Magic and Witchcraft

For more than four hundred years, the Hebrews lived in Egypt, far from the land promised to Abraham. Those centuries took a spiritual as well as a physical toll. The people had no Scriptures, only a few oral traditions passed down from the time of the patriarchs. Devotion to the God of their forefather Joseph had largely been forsaken for the worship of the gods of other nations.

It should be noted that the incident of the golden calf related in Exodus 32:1-6 suggests that fertility cults may have been part of Hebrew religious life in Egypt. Even though the Hebrews were miraculously delivered from slavery and led toward Canaan, many of the people had a limited understanding of the God of Abraham, Isaac, and Jacob. When the Hebrews arrived at Mount Horeb, their worldview and lifestyle differed little from that of the surrounding

---

64. R. Paul Stevens, "Breaking the Gender Gap," *Christianity Today*, January 13, 1992, 28-31.

nations. Their culture was essentially pagan. It is interesting to note that today many Egyptian gods and goddesses are worshiped. The "ankh," the ancient Egyptian symbol of eternal life, is worn; people wear their names spelled out in hieroglyphics on cartouche pendants; some sit under and contemplate the pyramid. And Isis, especially, is receiving great attention in Wiccan circles and in cults that bear her name.

Moses faced a difficult task. His people needed a radically different worldview as a basis for a proper understanding of God and his purposes. They also needed a new perspective to restructure their attitudes toward the created order. The primary concern of the biblical texts was to affirm the radical difference between a worldview in which many gods were worshiped and the one god, or monotheistic, view. All the surrounding worldviews identified the major aspects of the world and life with their various gods and goddesses.

Genesis is radically opposed to this pagan worlview. It counters with a firm affirmation that there is only one God, that this God is not identified with or contained by any region of nature, that the pagan gods and goddesses are not divinities at all but rather creations of the one true God, and that the worship of any of these false divinities is idolatry.[65]

Thus we see that the basic biblical view is that God and his kingdom are supreme. There is no realm above or beside him to limit his absolute sovereignty. He is utterly distinct from, and other than, the world. God is subject to no laws, no compulsions, no powers that transcend him. He is, in short, nonmythological. This is the essence of the biblical view and that which sets it apart from the pagan view and magic.

This biblical view is not a product of intellectual speculation or of mystical meditation, in the Greek or Indian manner. It first appeared as a revelation from God himself. Over the course of centuries, this new idea pervaded every aspect of the creativity of biblical people. However, it was a perpetual struggle to eradicate all traces of the pagan view. For centuries, Israel's ancestors lived among peoples of Semitic and mixed stock who worshiped more than one god. The cultures of Canaan, Babylonia, and Egypt colored Israelite thought profoundly.[66]

Anderson points out that at the time when the Bible was written people struggled with the question "Is the meaning of human life disclosed in his relation to divine powers within nature or in his relation to the Lord of history?" This fundamental question was not answered overnight. In Canaanite religion, for example, Israel's faith met the challenge, but it took

---

65. Conrad Hyers, *The Meaning of Creation: Genesis and Modern Science* (Atlanta: John Knox, 1998), 150-56.

66. Kaufmann, *Religion of Israel*, 60-61, 63.

many generations for the true strength and uniqueness of the Mosaic faith to be seen. For example, Israel had to recast Canaanite motifs. Thus the ancient pagan myths were fundamentally transmuted by the biblical view.

Solomon came close to succumbing to the pagan view and calling for people to worship foreign gods or even himself. But under the leadership of the prophet Elijah, Israel relearned the lesson that had been impressed upon her memory in the period of Moses and Joshua: that Yahweh participates in the historical struggle. Yahweh had rescued his people from the tyranny of an Egyptian king whose pretensions to absolute power were hidden behind the glorious facade of a state religion. Israel's covenant accented Yahweh's uncompromising "jealous" demand for absolute allegiance.

But it was difficult to maintain faithfulness to the biblical tradition in the cultural cross currents of Canaan, where the gods of the Fertile Crescent made an irresistible claim upon people's lives. The tendency of popular religion was toward tolerance and compromise — the very attitudes that were encouraged during the reign of Solomon. Had not this pursuit of their devices and desires been rebuked and arrested by the prophets, Israel's distinctive faith would have fallen into oblivion along with the religions of the Fertile Crescent. Yahweh himself acted to stir up the revolutionary ferment, even to the point of raising up adversaries against Solomon (1 Kings 11:14, 23).[67]

## The New Testament Rejection of Magic and Witchcraft

In the New Testament period, magic was seen as a method of manipulating good and evil spirits to lend help or bring harm. Magical formulas could be used for such things as attracting a lover or winning a chariot race. Black magic, or sorcery, involved summoning spirits to accomplish all kinds of evil deeds. Curses could be placed, competitors subdued, and enemies restrained.

Magic was an important part of the official religions in the New Testament period, though in many cases not a sanctioned part. For example, the cult of Artemis in Ephesus did not have an official magician. Nevertheless, this goddess was invoked in magical formulas. Many of the people who worshiped Artemis also practiced magic. Amulets and charms were commonly used for protective magic. It was believed the injurious work of malevolent evil spirits could be repelled with an effective amulet.[68]

In the book of Acts, Luke records four separate instances involving

---

67. Bernhard W. Anderson, *Understanding the Old Testament* (Englewood Cliffs, N.J.: Prentice-Hall, 1957), 151-53.

68. Clinton E. Arnold, *Powers of Darkness* (Downers Grove, Ill.: InterVarsity, 1992), 21-22.

the use of magic. In three of these instances Luke directly connects magic with the work of Satan or his demons. Luke also gives us an account of a situation involving magic during Paul's ministry at Ephesus (Acts 19:13-20). It reinforces the impression that Ephesus was a center of magical practices during the first century. In this instance, after their conversion, numerous people brought out their books of magical formulas and incantations and burned them. The combined value of the books was estimated by Luke to be as much as 50,000 days' wages.

Artemis was the patron deity of Ephesus; and her temple, the great Artemisium, was considered one of the Seven Wonders of the Ancient World. We are given an important picture of the passionate devotion that Artemis inspired in Acts 19. Worship of the goddess was widely spread throughout the Mediterranean world. Indeed, one writer maintained that in private devotions Artemis of Ephesus was the most widely worshiped deity in the Mediterranean world. Though she had a bizarre stiff form, covered with many breasts, her adherents maintained that the configuration had a peculiar sanctity.

Human sacrifice, especially to Artemis, was still being practiced at the beginning of the Christian era. The famous temple of Diana (Roman name for Artemis) at Aricia was presided over by a priest-king who was in fact a runaway slave who had gained his position by killing his predecessor. In the second century A.D. Scymnus Chius mentioned human sacrifice as still being used to propitiate the goddess. Tatian (A.D. 110-172) announced that after he had been initiated into the mysteries and studied the various rites, he discovered that near Rome Artemis was worshiped with the slaughter of men.

The shrine of the Ephesian Artemis was said to have been founded by the female Amazons, who brought to Ephesus a statue of the Tauropolian Artemis. One of the epithets applied to the Amazons was "manslaying." In keeping with this tradition, Amazons were not allowed to marry until they had slain a man of the enemy. During the classical age, four enormous statues of Amazons stood in the temple of Artemis of Ephesus; and for centuries after Christ, the Amazons were commemorated yearly in a marvelous dance at Ephesus. In Ephesus women also assumed the role of the man-slaying Amazons who had founded the cult of Artemis of Ephesus. The dance may have contained a simulated attack on males, especially as the dances were performed with spears.[69]

In my many visits to Ephesus, I am always besieged by hawkers trying to sell statues of Diana.

This account in the book of Acts is very important for understanding the social and religious situation of the early Christian churches. Luke gives

---

69. Spencer, Hailson, Kroeger, and Spencer, *Goddess Revival*, 60-61.

the distinct impression that those who were burning their magical texts were already Christians. He observes, "Many of those who believed now came and openly confessed their evil deeds. A number who had practiced sorcery brought their scrolls together and burned them publicly" (Acts 19:18-19a). It underlines the temptation faced by early believers to return to their former practices — in particular, magic.

It should be remembered that the widespread community inaugurated by Alexander the Great over the three centuries before Christ would forever alter the course of history. In fact, historians commonly refer to the next three centuries following his reign as the Hellenistic age.

Not only did Greek become the universal language, but Greek culture was also spread throughout Middle Eastern and Oriental countries. The influence worked both ways, however, especially with regard to religion. Gods and goddesses worshiped in the Orient were transplanted in Greek and Roman lands. The spiritual and religious ideas of the East proved exceedingly attractive to the West. By the New Testament era an incredible mixture of deities was being worshiped in the cities of the Mediterranean world.

Corinth is a good example of the influence of magic in Greece. There is literary and archaeological evidence for the worship of many of the traditional Greek deities — Apollo, Athena, Aphrodite, Dionysus, Asclepius, Demeter, Kore, Poseidon, and Zeus — dating to the time of Paul's ministry in that city. In addition, there is evidence that two originally Egyptian deities, Isis and Sarapis, had become quite popular among the Corinthians.

During Paul's ministry, the practice of combining several religions into one, called syncretism, was reaching new heights. Hellenistic Greeks were not compelled to render exclusive allegiance to their ancestral gods. They could now also worship Persian, Syrian, Egyptian, or Asian gods.

For example, a magical rite was related to the Asian female deity known as Cybele. The best-known part of her rite is an event called the *taurobolium*. In this rite the initiate descends into an underground pit, which is partially covered with a series of wooden lattices. Walking out onto the latticework, the priests of Cybele would slaughter a young bull and allow its blood to pour through the openings of the wood, drenching the initiate in the pit below. Franz Cumont contends that there was even a materialistic concept of a transfer of strength to the initiate. It was contended that the new access to this deity's cosmic power, symbolized by the blood of the bull, provided magical benefits.[70]

---

70. Arnold, *Powers of Darkness*, 31-33, 36-40.

# The Centrality of the Kingdom of God

## OLD TESTAMENT EMPHASIS

Yehezkel Kaufmann contends that the biblical view which opposes magic is understandable only as the outcome of the profound change brought about by the monotheistic idea. Belief in the gods ended; all divinity became concentrated in the domain of Yahweh. In the popular consciousness, magic was comprehended as a form of human wisdom. It was idolatrous precisely because it was godless or sought to control gods. Magic represented human rebellion against God. The Bible does not condemn wisdom and science at large (for they are divine gifts to humans). However, it does ban the occult science of magic that enables humans to work wonders without recourse to God, thus feeding their ambition "to become like God."

In the Bible we do have wonders and signs performed by God's chosen messengers. But in the biblical view, the wonders glorify God and his kingdom mission. Any so-called "magical" actions merely provide the setting for the revelation of God's power and the authentication of his messengers. Whatever Moses or Aaron perform with their staffs is at the bidding of Yahweh who effects the wonders.

The biblical laws banning magic, and all references to magic in Israel, view it as a product of heathen or foreign influence. All the stories concerning Israelite men of God and prophets support the view that magic was alien to native Israelite creativity. In Israel, magic was not present in the form we know it elsewhere. What magic was practiced was under foreign influence, a matter of ignorant superstition, not an expression of biblical religion.[71]

## NEW TESTAMENT EMPHASIS

From a more positive perspective, the biblical view is quite clear that the "age to come" has dawned in Jesus Christ, and the kingdom of God has come with power. The powers of the kingdom were already at work in the lives of the early Christians. The death, resurrection, and ascension of Christ had released those powers, and the Spirit of Christ was operating in the Christian fellowship as an earnest or down payment of their future inheritance. Thus the kingdom of God was both present and future. The "age to come" is that realm of divine, redeeming existence, that sovereign rule of the triune God, that heavenly form of existence which has come in and through Christ. The blessings of the new age have reached back to those who are in Christ. Meanwhile, the world and humankind as a whole remain in the grip of the old age.

71. Kaufmann, *Religion of Israel*, 83-84, 86-87.

The church, as God's new creation in Christ, is not to be equated with the kingdom. The kingdom is to be thought of as the reign of God. The church, by contrast, is a realm of God, the people who are under his rule. The kingdom is the rule of God, whereas the church is the human community under that rule.

## Kingdom Men and Feminism

A kingdom-centered person is not egocentric as are people involved in magic. Agape, outgoing, unselfish love, is central. The Christian gospel gives particular attention to the suffering and the oppressed.

The kingdom person reflects the love of Christ within marriage. Sexuality has a new dimension as the expression of personal love between husband and wife.

Kingdom men, in the past few decades, have begun to understand how women have been victimized by the generations that have gone before and how they have been victimized by what they have inherited in their relationships with men. As men have addressed feminism, many of them have discovered that they cannot respond to women's demands for justice, equality, and opportunity without exploring radical redefinitions of how manhood and maleness are understood and lived out.

Out of men's confusion and anger in response to women's demands, and out of men's desire to take women's demands seriously, has sprung up a new field of psycho-sociology called "Men's Studies." Suddenly, a whole library of works exists in the field, which makes for fascinating reading. These men take feminism seriously and try to figure out who they have been, who they are now, what they need, and how they understand themselves. They seek ways to continue to claim all that is good about maleness and masculinity without perpetuating violence against women.

Of course, there is disagreement about how kingdom persons are to respond to the demands of the feminist movement. For example, we see within the church the beginnings of a broader use of inclusive language, new theologies of feminism and liberation, and greater opportunities for ministry to and by women. Some men within the church are trying to change in order to grant women the equality, justice, and opportunity that they demand. But women's demands are sometimes refused in the church. Pope John Paul II has announced that he will never approve of the ordination of women. As we have noted earlier, many Protestant denominations, such as the Episcopalians and Baptists, are divided concerning the ordination of women. Inclusive language continues to meet significant opposition at the national conventions of Protestant denominations and in the new Vatican catechism.

Some critics would call this whole affair the war between the sexes, a war between men and women. That characterization seems terribly unfair, for many men take women's issues very seriously, just as more and more women are becoming sensitive to men's issues and taking them seriously. This is not a war between men and women. It is a war between women and women-sensitive men against more traditionalist men and women. The war began outside the religious community but has spilled over into it.

Kingdom men and women should care deeply about each other, fellow beings with whom we share God's creation. It is only through the whole community's working together that there is any hope for the success of God's kingdom. The Bible speaks often of how men and women complement each other; without each other, each is incomplete. As a result of discussions on sexual roles, many men are learning new ways of valuing the needs and aspirations of their spouses and making a greater commitment to shared parenting.[72]

## THE SECULAR MEN'S MOVEMENT

Kingdom men will evaluate critically the men's movement represented by Richard Bly's *Iron John* view that contemporary American men need to connect with the primitive and isolationist myths buried deep inside ourselves. Of course those myths are there, and we cannot be authentic until we confront and heal them. But this confrontation is only one part of the struggle to create the new Adam.

William Spencer suggests that much of the current thinking of the new men's movement can be summarized by the work of psychoanalyst Robert Moore and mythologist Douglas Gillette. Moore states that he has discovered that men have lost touch with their masculinity. His view is that patriarchy and reactive feminist criticism have served unwittingly as dual causes of this condition, both being attacks "on masculinity in its fullness as well as femininity in its fullness":

> What they were missing was an adequate connection to the deep and instinctual masculine energies, the potentials of natural masculinity. They were being blocked from connection to these potentials by patriarchy itself, and by the feminist critique upon what little masculinity they could still hold onto for themselves.

One contribution of their work is that Moore and Gillette distinguish masculinity from patriarchy: "In our view, patriarchy is not the expression of deep and rooted masculinity, for truly deep and rooted masculinity is not

---

72. Philip Culbertson, *New Adam: The Future of Male Spirituality* (Minneapolis: Fortress, 1992), 4-6.

abusive. Patriarchy is the expression of the immature masculine." Patriarchy expresses what the authors call "Boy psychology," whose "sadomasochistic" characteristics are "abusive and violent acting-out behaviors against others, both men and women; passivity and weakness, the inability to act effectively and creatively in one's own life and to engender life and creativity in others (both men and women) and, often, an oscillation between the two — abuse/weakness, weakness/abuse." This Boy psychology causes the immature to attack women and mature men, for it is a Peter Pan complex that fears growing and refuses to let others grow. "Man psychology is always the opposite. It is nurturing and generative, not wounding and destructive." The emphasis on masculinity champions mature attitudes and practices, among which it numbers monogamy as a "product of a man's own deep rootedness and centeredness." It also puts a premium on true humility.[73]

## EVANGELICAL CRITIQUES

Although there are positive facets in their work, evangelical Christians question much in Moore and Gillette's *The King Within*. For example, they state that the early Christians transformed Jesus into the archetype of the King. Never having known the man, they vested in him the structures and dynamics of the King-Gods from their non-Hebraic heritages. These statements are similar to comments made by the Jesus Seminar.

Moore and Gillette point out that many early Christians came from religious backgrounds that included the sacred-king traditions of ancient Egypt, Greece, and Rome, as well as Hermetic influences, the Mystery religions, and the Persian religions of Zoroastrianism and Mithraism. The myths of these various faiths were replete with King-Gods, even where actual sacred kings were a thing of the distant past.

Jesus was soon considered God incarnate, born of a mortal woman divinely impregnated. Like Osiris in the Egyptian myths, he had been slain by his evil brother, called Satan by the early Christians. Again like Osiris, Jesus Christ had then been resurrected and had become the ruler of the dead. After his sacrifice, Jesus did just what the ancient pharaohs had done, ascending into the heavens and becoming one with the high God.

As William Spencer points out, since Moore and Gillette read the biblical accounts as mythical stories, they also adopt the prevalent pagan mythologies of our time in opposition to biblical revelation:

> It seems that in prepatriarchal times, the earth as Mother was seen as the primary source of fertility. But as patriarchal cultures rose to ascendancy,

73. Spencer, *Goddess Revival*, 40-41.

the emphasis shifted from the feminine as the source of fertility to the masculine. . . . Our Jewish, Christian, and Moslem God today is never seen as being in creative partnership with a Goddess. He is viewed as male, and as the sole source of creativity and generativity. He is the sole source of fertility and blessing. Many of our modern beliefs come from the beliefs of the ancient patriarchies.[74]

Thus, they would contend that the Judeo-Christian God is a patriarchal product. Patriarchy, as we know from their work, is seen as an immature state hostile to maturity.

In *Fire in the Belly,* Sam Keen, another leader of the men's movement, agrees with this mythological view, adding a currently popular slant, "Feminists who argue that goddess-worship historically preceded the notion of God as father are certainly correct." Keen portrays this popular view of a conflict between a new patriarchal deity and a previous matriarchal one as a kind of divine family squabble with human sexuality as the ultimate loser.

Keen states, "Being a jealous God, He ordered His followers to worship no other deities. . . . Yahweh, in the manner of oriental kings, thus dethroned and demeaned the Great Mother. Beelzebub (formerly god of the phallus) was proclaimed a devil. . . . Nature was not to be trusted. Nor were women. In effect, the Judeo-Christian God cast the phallus and the vulva out of the sanctuary and reduced nature to a backdrop against which God's redemptive drama was being played out on the stage of history."

"This God, who stands above the fatedness of nature, commands men to stand above nature and society and woman and take charge of his own destiny. Without the historical introduction of the notion of a transcendent God who ordered his subjects to name the animals and to have dominion over the earth, neither individualism nor empirical science and technology would have developed," since "life in the garden of the goddess was harmonious but the spirit of history called for man to stand up and take charge."

Instead of following the Genesis account with man and woman created and called together to worship the one God reflected in both creatures and till and nurture the ground together, Keen and his colleagues envision sexual dualism at war on earth and in heaven.

All three of the men's movement authors agree with the teaching of Joseph Campbell, who in *The Masks of Eternity* claimed, "All of these symbols in mythology refer to you." This is a theological teaching that can only empty into one conclusion: "You are God in your deepest identity. You are one with the transcendent."

74. Ibid., 43–47.

According to William Spencer, if our God is simply a reflection of each of us, no male can escape worshiping a masculine deity, and no female can escape worshiping a feminine one. God is limited here by our genders. However, if one considers Scripture as the divine revelation of the one true, all-good God in whom there is no shadow of turning, these men's movement interpretations are contrary to biblical teaching.

When one cuts oneself off from the revelation of the God of the Bible, one must turn elsewhere. Sam Keen opts for adapting "Eastern religious practice," drawn from "Zen Buddhism and the more mystical forms of Hinduism" with "the martial arts — judo, kung fu, akido" as "meditations" to "discover our true identity and participate in ultimate reality. He concludes his book by upholding the ideal of Buddhism, not Christianity. Only the otherworldliness of Eastern religion can help him escape the masculine captivity of his view of God.

Robert Bly concludes that as "women have taken on the task of lifting Sophia and Kali up again, . . . our job is to lift up Dionysius, Hermes, and the Zeus energy." He would have us reintroduce dead pagan deities to our self-images.

Psychotherapist Robert Moore goes even a step further, counseling therapeutic worship of female and male deities, prescribing therapy to one counselee, for example, to seek "the Goddess in her many forms." He commends another young man to overcome his timidity with women by praying to Eros, the Greek god of love. A procession of crystals, pyramids, incense, candles, and similar invocations to other gods and goddesses (as archetypal representations) are also recommended.

Spencer suggests that this approach must have been going on in ancient Corinth as countless temples lined the pathway to the acropolis and jostled for attention in the marketplace.[75]

For the authors mentioned above who have influenced the secular men's movement, God functions inversely as a reflection of the image of fallen humanity. They forget the full dangers of the paganism from which the world was so gladly freed by God's love in Christ. It is the contention of classical Christianity that the truly good God in the true Jesus displays wholeness, an unfallen ideal alive in this world for men and women in equal measure. Christ's full selfless, giving example of steadfast love and firm truth is the one on which all Christians should model themselves.[76]

75. Ibid., 48, 51-53.
76. Ibid., 54-55.

# THE CHRISTIAN MEN'S MOVEMENT

Philip Culbertson suggests, as a Christian alternative to the secular men's movement and Iron John approach, an emphasis on creativity, dignity, the value of a nurturing response, and the importance of being connected to those who share with us God's redemption and good creation. The New Adam is birthed among companions in emotion and spirituality who seek together a way to be masculine without perpetuating violence either toward women or toward men. With a rereading of the Bible, Christian men will find values to which they will be committed: compassion, integrity, flexibility, humility, mercy, patience, fidelity, generosity, cooperation, intellectual honesty, and dependence on others who are within the Christian community of men.[77]

Edward Gilbreath points out that Promise Keepers and other groups in the Christian men's movement have arisen against the backdrop of a waning secular men's movement. The late eighties and early nineties saw white baby boomers displaying a deep interest in the perplexing puzzle of being a man in America. Sociologists and journalists described the movement as a phenomenon that sought to get men in touch with themselves. The movement's books were high on the best-seller lists, and men lined up to attend seminars and run around bare-chested during tribal-oriented "Wild Man" weekends. Others saw it as a way for men to be both vulnerable and aggressive without being lambasted for wimpiness or insensitivity.

Although the secular movement did identify men's problems, it did not appear to offer dynamic and constructive solutions and empowerment. As Stu Weber states, "You can only go so far with myths and tribal lore. Eventually, you've got to get to the Genesis spring, which is a Judeo-Christian foundation." One speaker at a Promise Keepers meeting, Gary Oliver, believes that the Industrial Revolution is at the heart of the present dilemma. "It changed the meaning of manhood in America," he explains. "Men left their homes and farms to work in factories and offices. Through much of our history, child rearing was shared by men and women. With industrialization, child rearing became a 'feminine thing.' Boys no longer had their father's physical presence as a model and a source for their ideals and identity."

Oliver adds that industrialization accelerated the pace of living, creating a major social shift from stability and community to insecurity and detachment. "I think this process caused men to lose touch with what it means to be a husband, a father, a friend — and a person."

The results can be seen at every hand. The expectation that men be the prime breadwinners in our society has driven them to correlate their self-worth with their earnings. And cultural images of John Wayne and Arnold

77. Culbertson, *New Adam*, 161-67.

Schwarzenegger taint perceptions of what a "real man" is, often leading men to buy into the strong and silent approach to life. All of this has led to men who are disconnected from their families and themselves.

And yet, as men try to overcome this legacy of the "silent approach" and emotional aloofness, they are faced with conflicting expectations. On the one hand, they are told — whether directly or implicitly — to be gentle and compassionate. On the other hand, the message urges acting strong and taking responsibility. Men must somehow navigate between being lions and lambs.[78]

As an Evangelical movement, Promise Keepers seeks a biblical model of what it means to be a Christian man. What is the biblical model? According to theologian Lewis Smedes, "Men's and women's roles may be situationally different and have different forms of expression, but the Bible is mainly interested in the moral and spiritual qualities of a human being." Smedes, who recently retired from Fuller Theological Seminary, suggests that following Christ is a gender-neutral calling: "That which is important about Jesus being a model is not his modeling of maleness but his modeling of humanity."

Promise Keepers has already entered into the tricky task of showing that feminine virtues and masculine virtues need not be in conflict in the lives of Christian men.

Founded in 1990 by Bill McCartney, who subsequently resigned as coach of the University of Colorado football team, Promise Keepers began as a local fellowship of men joining for prayer, fasting, and mutual encouragement. The core group of 72 has since mushroomed into a national phenomenon, rocketing from 4,200 in 1991 to a national rally in Boulder, Colorado, of 52,000 in 1993 to a combined total of 234,000 during the summer of 1994, the first year of the conference's expansion to regional sites. In October 1997, a rally in Washington, D.C., called "Stand in the Gap," filled the Capitol Mall with men from across the nation.

## Women and Promise Keepers

As one would imagine, from the beginning Promise Keepers has been an object of suspicion for many women — feminist and otherwise — who are certain that a meeting of so many Christian men can only be about one thing: keeping women in their place.

Promise Keepers president Randy Phillips says he understands the distrust that many women have toward his organization. "I think there are a lot of women inside and outside the church who have been victims of the

78. Edward Gilbreath, "Manhood's Great Awakening," *Christianity Today*, February 6, 1995, 25-26.

misuse of male authority, and it has brought a lot of pain and wariness." Phillips suggests that Promise Keepers not ask men to go back home with an iron fist. "We're asking them to go back on their knees, with a spirit of service and respect for their wives and families." In fact, many Christian wives have been praising Promise Keepers for its work in bringing men back into the life of the church. Many of the men admitted that their wives had made them attend a Promise Keepers' conference. Some women still wonder if the tone of the conferences carries a subtle and generally unspoken promotion of male hierarchy in the church.

## Emphases, Questions, and Contributions

Realizing the frailty of any organized movement, Promise Keepers has maintained its commitment to build up the local church through empowering pastors. Founder McCartney has made it an ongoing aim to restore the office of the pastor to one of respect and proper authority. The organization has also sought to strengthen local churches through encouraging the formation of small groups of men for fellowship and accountability.

Gilbreath raises another question. If the problems Promise Keepers seeks to combat arise from the Industrial Revolution, a massive structural shift in our society, then, ultimately, any solution to those problems must address structural as well as individual issues. The epidemic of fatherlessness is in part a consequence of massive social change. Racism is an institutional evil as well as a matter of individual wrongdoing. Will Promise Keepers itself eventually branch out to develop public policy arms to support the goal of structural change? For instance, advocating flex-time programs for working fathers or racial-awareness initiatives for young men might be logical extensions of the organization's current objectives.

As a movement, Promise Keepers has promise: a flexible leadership not concerned with building an empire, a commitment to communicating the basics, a holistic vision for men — encouraging them to be servants at home, at church, and in their community — and a desire to see things happen at the grassroots level.

If our culture continues in its current state of moral chaos, and if Promise Keepers' ultimate promises of stable homes, unified communities, and stronger churches begin to be realized, America at large may find that promise-keeping is not just about evangelical religion or male leadership but about truth, responsibility, and agape love — concepts that find their true fruition in the Christian faith.[79]

79. Ibid., 22, 24, 26, 28.

## Evangelical Women's Groups as Counterparts

Stephen Arterburn, an evangelical Protestant businessman and co-founder of New Life Clinics, stated that he "had seen what the men's conferences such as Promise Keepers had done. I wanted to see if we could do something to meet women's needs." Women of Faith–Joyful Journey meetings is the result, with some 150,000 women expected to meet in conferences in thirteen cities in 1997 alone. A conference in the Rose Bowl entitled "Chosen Women: Daughters of the King" projects an attendance of 80,000. Other groups which have formed recently include Heritage Keepers and Keys for Abundant Living.[80]

# THE URGENT ROLE OF THE KINGDOM PERSON

In magic, people seek to be God and determine for themselves what is good and what is evil. The kingdom person walks a narrow road. On the right there is the threat of slavery to the forces exhibited in nature worship, witchcraft, shamanism, magic, and distorted religion. On the left is the threat of the anarchy of autonomous secular life that too often steps in when the power of nature and pagan religious forces is broken. Without a kingdom-centered person and perspective, technology and a lifestyle that is freed from pagan nature-worship can be harmful.

As we have seen, witchcraft and magic are primarily related to the human desire to understand and control the universal forces. Both white and black magic are related to power. The lack of moral content in magic and sorcery, apart from a crude hedonism, should be a point of great concern.

The Bible recognizes the danger of the occult world. Since the time that God's people moved into Canaan (land of many sorcerers and much magic), the prophets, Jesus Christ, and biblical leaders have opposed magic.

Wayne Oates points out that insights related to magic, instead of being brought into a consecrated relationship to God, are more and more used as a means of self-aggrandizement and cleverness and even harm. They are used in a manner that attempts to take over God's place in the scheme of things.[81]

The Bible's answer to magic and witchcraft is dynamic devotion to the Kingdom of God. This is the way of joy, fulfillment, and service. This is what humans, created in the image of God, are made for.

---

80. "Promise Keepers Counterpart Burgeon," *Christianity Today*, March 3, 1997, 62; Gustave Niebuhr, "Lay Women of Faith Seek Joy on a Journey," *New York Times*, January 27, 1997, A8.
81. Wayne Oates, *The Psychology of Religion* (Waco: Word, 1973), 154.

# CHAPTER SEVEN

# *Ecology and the New Age*

Most people agree that our planet is in trouble. The earth's geological features and animal and plant life are routinely sacrificed on the altars of corporate profit and the public's ever-expanding hunger for consumable goods.

The ecological outlook informs us that the natural world is not a moldable material for the imprint of human purposes. To the contrary, the natural world is comprised of fragile networks of interrelationships between organism and environment. The capacity and willingness of human beings to disrupt these networks has become dramatically evident in recent years.

The Cold War specter of nuclear war and the fear of nuclear power plant accidents have destroyed all smug confidence about the beneficial effects of human efforts to harness the forces of nature. Ecological sciences make clear that human needs cannot be served without attention to the well-regulated functioning of wider biosystems. Human life is part of larger patterns and is therefore dependent upon them.[1]

Evangelical ethicist Ebbie Smith states, "After surveying the literature and observing the facts, I have concluded that we do indeed face an ecological crisis. The land, air, and water have been assaulted by the intended and unintended actions of humans, corporations, nations, and multinational groups. Christians, like all other humans, must be knowledgeable of the threat, apprehensive of its outcome, concerned about its results, and active in the efforts to protect God's creation."

Another evangelical, John Stott, states that the greatest threat to

1. Rebecca S. Chopp and Mark Lewis Taylor, eds., *Reconstructing Christian Theology* (Minneapolis: Fortress, 1994), 99-100.

274

humankind and the environment is not war but rather peacetime peril — namely, the plundering of the earth's natural resources by human folly and greed.[2]

Social scientists tell us that the religious and worldview beliefs people hold often have a marked influence on their overall outlook. We will examine the relation of the New Age and biblical worldviews to the ecological crisis and suggest a possible solution.

But first we must understand the beliefs, values, and survival rules that have guided expectations and behavior in the Industrial Era. These beliefs and values include an expectation of unlimited material progress and ever-growing consumption; faith in science and technology to solve all problems; goals of efficiency, growth, and productivity; mastery of nature; and competition and individualism.

Willis Harman, who identified these Industrial Age beliefs, says they have led to environmental degradation, resource depletion, loss of meaningful work roles, inequitable distribution, and ineffective control of technology.[3]

Prior to the Industrial Age many people held a mechanistic view of nature. In the seventeenth and eighteenth centuries this view was one factor in the growth of exploitative attitudes. Isaac Newton and his followers said that nature is constituted by impersonal masses and forces which operate according to definite laws. Newton himself thought of nature as a complex machine designed by God, but his more secular successors had no scruples about exploiting it. If nature is a machine, it has no inherent rights or interests, and we need not hesitate to manipulate and use it.

Moreover, the Newtonian worldview perpetuated a sharp separation of humanity from the nonhuman world. It was claimed that apart from the human mind, the world consists of particles in motion. Newton accepted the Cartesian dualism of mind and matter. Descartes asserted that animals are machines without minds or feelings. He emphasized practical knowledge that would make us "the lords and masters of nature," and he thought that our unique rationality justified such sovereignty. Others gave greater prominence to the control of nature. Francis Bacon, another philosopher of this period, said that the goal of science is the conquest of nature, for "knowledge is power." "Let the human race recover the right over nature which belongs to it by divine bequest." Bacon's *New Atlantis* called for a state-funded research establishment and a scientific elite through which humanity's rightful supremacy would be systematically extended.

2. John R. Stott, *Decisive Issues Facing Christians Today* (Old Tappon, N.J.: Revell, 1990), 121.

3. Ian Barbour, *Ethics in an Age of Technology* (New York: HarperCollins, 1993), 258.

In the emerging industrial technology of the eighteenth century, domination over nature was increasingly achieved in practice as well as in theory. To the leaders of the Industrial Revolution, the environment was primarily a source of raw materials. In the new capitalism, private ownership of resources fostered the treatment of the natural world as a source of commercial profit. Along with rising standards of living came increasing burdens on the environment. Ever since antiquity, deforestation, overgrazing, and soil erosion have been occurring; but the technologies that developed in the last two centuries produced pollution and consumed natural resources at unprecedented rates. Mechanistic science, industrial technology, and capitalist economics — along with certain themes in the Christian tradition that separated this world from the world to come — all encouraged domination over nature.[4]

# THE ECOLOGICAL CRISIS:
## MODERNISM AND BIBLICAL INFLUENCE

Edward Goldsmith, a prominent ecologist, states that people are rapidly destroying the natural world on which they depend for their very survival. The basic problem is that our society is committed to economic development — a process which by its very nature must systematically increase the impact of our economic activities on an environment ever less capable of sustaining them, and ever more deeply degraded by them.

Even the academic world has viewed this critical problem with indifference. Its acknowledged role is to provide governments and society at large with knowledge that serves the public interest and maximizes the general welfare. But how can it achieve this task if it systematically ignores the fatal process that is rendering our planet ever less habitable and, unchecked, must inevitably lead to the extinction of countless species — including our own?

The worldview which today's academics share with everybody else in our society — including our political leaders — can be called modernism. The first fundamental tenet of this worldview is that our welfare — and our real wealth — is derived from the man-made world. This means, in effect, that it is the product of science, technology and industry, and of the economic development that these make possible. Not surprisingly, a country's wealth is measured by its per capita Gross National Product (GNP), which provides a rough measure of its ability to provide its citizens with all such man-made commodities, a principle faithfully reflected in modern economics.

4. Ibid., 57-58.

For economists trained in these ideas, natural benefits — those provided by the normal workings of biospheric processes, that assure the stability of our climate, the fertility of our soil, the replenishment of our water supplies, and the integrity and cohesion of our families and communities — are not regarded as benefits at all.

The second fundamental tenet of the worldview of modernism, according to Goldsmith, follows quite logically from the first. It is that to maximize all benefits and hence our welfare and our wealth, we must maximize economic development — a process we identify with progress. It is blasphemous to suggest that economic development, rather than solving our problems, is the main cause of these problems. Scientists will lift up their hands in horror if it is suggested that the terrible social and environmental destruction we are witnessing today is a result of economic development. Instead, it will be imputed to deficiencies or difficulties in its implementation — government interference, corruption among local officials, or freak economic or climatic conditions. Malnutrition and famine are also attributed to archaic agricultural practices and, in particular, to low inputs of fertilizer.

Our problems, whether unemployment, crime, delinquency, drug addiction, alcoholism, pollution, resource depletion, global deforestation, or global warming, can be solved by economic development. Each of these problems is interpreted in a way that rationalizes policies we have already decided to adopt: those that make the greatest contribution to economic development and hence best satisfy the requirements of the corporations and institutions that dominate our society. In other words, rather than interpreting our problems as the inevitable consequence of economic development or progress, we interpret them as providing evidence that economic development has not proceeded far enough or fast enough. Modern industrialism has drawn us into a veritable chain reaction which leads to ever greater social and environmental destruction.[5]

A number of authors have claimed that the biblical idea of dominion over nature was the main historical root of environmentally destructive attitudes in the West. In a widely quoted article, Lynn White described the separation of humanity and nature in biblical thought. Holding that ideas and attitudes are significant influences in history, White concluded that Christianity "bears a huge burden of guilt" for the environmental crisis because it has been so anthropocentric and arrogant toward nature. White, a medieval historian, presented a paper at a meeting of the American Association for the Advancement of Science in December 1966. His paper blasted the Christian belief system for justifying the rape of nature in the name of our "God-given

5. Edward Goldsmith, "Toward the Worldview of Ecology: Not Business as Usual," *Noetic Sciences Review* 27 (1993): 53.

dominion." It was published the following March in *Science* magazine, and was titled "The Historic Roots of Our Ecologic Crisis."

According to White, Christianity, especially in its Western form, is the most anthropocentric religion the world has seen. In absolute contrast to ancient paganism and Asia's religions, it not only established a dualism of humans and nature but also insisted that it is God's will that humans exploit nature for their proper ends. By destroying pagan respect and devotion to nature and animals, Christianity made it possible to exploit nature in a mood of indifference to the feelings of natural objects.

Christianity bears a huge burden of guilt. More science and more technology are not going to get us out of the present ecological crisis until we find a new religion. The ecological crisis will continue to worsen until we reject the Christian axiom that nature has no reason for existence except to serve humans.

White's arguments took twenty years to become headline news, but they provided the "turning point" in the way Americans look at natural resource management. Today, thirty years after the fact, their influence extends to the bashing of Columbus that we saw on the 500th anniversary of his voyage. Columbus, with his Christian worldview and missionary zeal, is blamed for every ill that now besets the Western world — including our environmental crisis. But according to White, the real villain behind Columbus is the Christian doctrine of creation.[6]

Millard Erickson summarizes the indictment against Christianity in four charges:

- The call to have dominion over the earth, found in Genesis 1:28, entails treating the earth as being important only to support the good of the human being. This then leads to the exploitation and rape of the earth.
- Christianity has condoned modern science and technology's exploitation of the earth.
- Christianity has promoted a dualism, according to which the natural or the physical or the secular is of less value, or even is negative in character, compared with the spiritual or the otherworldly.
- Belief in the Second Coming, which will usher in Christ's complete and perfect reign, effectively removes any reason for us to be concerned about ecology.[7]

Catherine Keller of Drew Theological Seminary amplifies the critique of certain types of Christian eschatology, those views on the final events of

6. Barbour, *Ethics in an Age of Technology*, 74-75.
7. Richard D. Land and Louis A. Moore, eds., *The Earth is the Lord's* (Nashville: Broadman, 1992), 36-37.

the world, in regard to the ecological crisis. For Keller, Christian eschatology often gathers under its wings that array of doctrinal symbolics which has drawn interest away from the earth, from natural conditions, and from human life in time and space. With the apocalyptic emphasis upon the new heaven and earth, the new creation comes about by the supernatural intervention of the omnipotent God. Serious concern with the natural world indicates within this eschatological framework a materialism that obstructs faith. There is no need for endlessly renewable resources if the earth is coming to an end anyway. Thus it happens that, according to Keller, the neofundamentalist teaching of the rapture out of this world, just as the going gets bad, followed by a supernatural new creation, claimed much public attention, especially in the 1980s and 1990s. This was precisely the time of the most wildly extravagant development of the throwaway consumer culture.

When salvation means removal from the earth to a heavenly home, then our earthly home is abandoned to the assaults of those whose ultimate concern is neither heaven nor earth, but the power and wealth of their particular households.[8]

# ECOLOGICAL INDICTMENT OF GREEK AND ROMAN THOUGHT

Scholars have noted that White has ignored sources other than Christianity of exploitative attitudes in Western culture. For example, Greek and Roman thought also had great influence on the West. Plato and Aristotle portrayed a gulf between humans and all other beings based on the unique human capacity for reason. Aristotle stated that other creatures are devoid of the contemplative activity in which humans are most akin to God; plant and animal life exists solely for the sake of human life. Cicero, drawing upon Stoic writings, insisted that we have no obligation to respect animals because they are not rational beings. To the Neoplatonists of the early Christian era, the eternal forms are embodied only imperfectly in the world of nature. To the Gnostics and Manichaeans, nature is the realm of evil from which the human soul seeks to escape.

Greek and Roman views are indeed extraordinarily diverse; some pantheistic authors were more appreciative of the natural world. But the classical sources that were taken up in the early church, the Middle Ages, and subsequent Western thought seem to have stressed the differences between humankind and nature and the inferiority of nature.

8. Chopp and Taylor, *Reconstructing Christian Theology*, 329-32.

Other critics of White's exclusive concentration on Christian thought say that later institutions such as industrial capitalism were the main determinants of environmentally destructive behavior. It could be argued that those institutions were themselves in part the outcome of Christian assumptions, but some authors maintain that economic forces are the main determinants of social change and that White overemphasized the role of ideas in history. Moreover, extensive environmental damage occurred in non-Christian countries at many periods of history. White seems to have oversimplified a complex historical phenomenon.[9]

Carolyn Merchant calls the modernist industrial approach to the human-nature relationship egocentric. It is the dominant Western worldview — where reality is always seen as how we human beings can maintain our separateness and dominance over the rest of creation.[10]

# BIBLICAL COMPROMISE WITH GREEK THOUGHT

Historians generally agree with Ian Barbour that the very mixed record of Christian thought in the medieval and Reformation periods has been amply documented. Biblical themes were combined with dualistic ideas from late Greek thought. Biblical theology was systematized, but also altered, by the philosophical categories used in Catholic theological writings, and then in Protestant theology. The doctrine of creation ensured that nature was never ignored in theology or ethics, but it was considered subordinate to the doctrine of redemption. Most theologians assumed that humanity would be saved from nature, not in and with nature. The created order was too often viewed as the stage or background for the drama of redemption, not as part of that drama. Only in recent decades have attempts been made to develop a more affirmative theology of nature and a biblically grounded and ecologically informed environmental ethics.[11]

Brooks Alexander, an evangelical Christian scholar, agrees that the Bible had given Western culture the idea of humanity ruling nature, and "working" nature for human benefit. Secularism retained those biblical ideas but rejected their biblical foundation. The rule of nature *under God* turned into the sheer domination of nature *under humans*. The demands of stewardship were replaced by the demands of the marketplace. New technologies

---

9. Barbour, *Ethics in an Age of Technology*, 75.
10. Alan S. Miller, *Gaia Connections* (Lanham, Md.: Rowman and Littlefield, 1991), 25.
11. Barbour, *Ethics in an Age of Technology*, 77.

vastly increased our powers of dominion, and in our new pragmatic freedom we embarked on the systematic rape of nature with a clear conscience. Over time, our eco-abuse took its toll. We reaped a crop of plenty for the present, but we also sowed a crop of trouble for the future.

Alexander further points out that the trouble that we planted has matured. Today, our legacy of exploitation troubles us all. In particular, it troubles the churches in the form of confusion, uncertainty, and guilt. Many Christians have been led to believe that their religion is responsible for all the eco-crises — real and imagined — that intrude on our attention today.

In response to those accusations, many liberal and mainline Christian churches, Catholics included, have put the agenda of the environmental movement — as distinguished from the interests of the environment — at the head of their priorities. According to Alexander, since they don't understand the authentic biblical basis of environmentalism, they don't understand that in many cases they have alloyed their Christianity with incompatible beliefs.[12]

# THE NEW AGE SOLUTION TO THE ECOLOGICAL CRISIS

## THE GAIA CONCEPT

From earliest times, certain groups have had an awareness of the delicately balanced and interconnected relationships between all things and living beings on the planet — not only with each other but with Mother Earth herself. Beginning in the 1960s a new awareness of the earth developed. Thomas Berry, a historian and Catholic priest, calls this new awareness the "ecological age," an age that reflects the interdependence of all living and nonliving systems of the earth.

As we will note later in detail, the "Gaia hypothesis" — that the earth is a self-regulating organism — was put forward in the early 1970s by James E. Lovelock, a British scientist. The name Gaia, after the Greek Earth Mother goddess, was proposed to Lovelock by novelist William Golding.

The concept was largely unnoticed until Lovelock's 1979 book *Gaia: A New Look at Life on Earth* caught people's attention.

According to the Gaia hypothesis, humankind is part of a complex organismic biosphere. People, along with all other life forms on the planet,

12. Michael Coffman and Brooks Alexander, "Eco-Religion and Cultural Change," *SCP Journal*, 17.3 (1992): 19.

make an integral contribution to Gaia's homeostasis, which in turn makes life possible.[13]

## A PRIMITIVE VERSION OF GAIA

Edward Goldsmith, a prominent ecologist, identifies the Gaia hypothesis, or ecology worldview, with those primal peoples who practiced a Gaian religion, or a religion of the earth. It seems certain that most primal societies at one time practiced such a religion and hence were imbued with the worldview of ecology. It is only in this way that we can explain their great stability, the fact that such societies could thrive for as long as they did without destroying the natural world on which they depended for their welfare and indeed for their survival.

These primal peoples understood, as Donald Hughes notes, that "hunger, ill-health, erosion, poverty and general ruin" were only different forms "that the Earth's revenge could take for the terrible mistreatment meted out to her by man" — punishments for having turned from what was called "The Way" in pursuit of the anti-Way. The only cure for these ills, therefore, was to treat the earth with greater care, which meant to return to the Way of Mother Earth.[14]

According to Theodore Roszak, in the case of the mothering earth soul concept, we are dealing with one of the oldest experiences of humankind, the spontaneous sense of dread and wonder primitive humans once felt in the presence of the earth's majestic power. When there were no more than the first few representatives of a timid, scurrying new species in the world, these early humans must have greeted the immense creativity of nature with an awe that has since been lost to all but the poetic minority in the modern world. The earth goes so powerfully and competently about her work, bringing forth the crops, ushering in the seasons, nurturing the many species that find their home in her vast body. She can, of course, also be a menacing giant; that, too, is remembered in myth and folklore. Many of the oldest rituals are acts of propitiation offered to a sometimes fierce and punishing divinity, an earth who can be an angry mother as well as a bountiful one.[15]

13. Rosemary Ellen Guiley, *Harper's Encyclopedia of Mystical and Paranormal Experience* (Edison, N.J.: Castle, 1991), 447-49.

14. Goldsmith, "Toward the Worldview of Ecology," 59.

15. Theodore Roszak, *The Voice of the Earth* (New York: Simon & Schuster, 1992), 137.

## FAR EASTERN VIEW OF GAIA

### *Taoism*

According to Ian Barbour, Taoism in China portrays the world as an organic, interconnected system. Nothing exists in isolation; the parts of the whole are interpenetrating and interfused. Every particular being is a manifestation of the Tao, the nameless unity that exists before differentiation into multiplicity. Humanity is part of a wider cosmic order. To achieve a harmonious relationship to the natural world, we must respect it and adjust to its demands. The path to the recovery of harmony and wholeness is surrender, tranquillity, nonattachment, the ability to "let things be." The love of nature in traditional China is evident in its poetry and painting (especially of trees, mountains, and landscapes). But even agriculture and land management were represented as cooperation with nature rather than as conquest.

The Taoist term *wu wei* does not mean inaction but rather action that is in harmony with the true nature of things. By adapting to natural processes the maximum effect is achieved with minimum effort. Humanity and nature are intimately linked, and there is an ontological equality among all the manifestations of the Tao. But reality is dynamic rather than static, and there is a creative spontaneity in the world. Yin and yang are complementary and opposing principles, yet they are united in a larger whole. The black and white portions of the famous yin/yang symbol are interlocking and flowing, but together they form a perfect circle.

Joseph Needham's monumental study, titled *Science and Civilization in China*, shows that the Taoists' holistic assumptions did not hinder the development of science and technology. Their goal was harmonious adaptation rather than dominion, and humans were thought of as part of nature. The Taoists were not against technology but said that intervention in nature must respect the totality of life. Chinese medicine was also holistic and sought the achievement of balance and harmony.

There were, of course, diverse strands in Chinese history. The same culture that produced Taoist nature mysticism and holism also accepted Confucian principles of hierarchical orders. Moreover, there are gaps between the ideals and the practices of every culture. Behavior is the product of social and economic forces and institutional structures as well as beliefs. Environmental destruction was by no means absent from classical China. For instance, wood was in great demand for building, for fuel, and for charcoal for metallurgy; deforestation resulted in widespread soil erosion.

The changes in attitudes in China during the twentieth century have been mainly the result of Western influences. Chinese communism shares the

Marxist assumption that nature is an object of conquest. Mao Tse-tung called for "a war against nature."[16]

### Zen Buddhism

Zen Buddhism arose first in China from the confluence of Taoism and Mahayana Buddhism and then developed further in Japan. Here, too, human kinship with nature was stressed. According to Zen, the merging of self and other is known in immediate experience. Intuition and personal awareness, not analytic rationality or conceptual abstraction, reveal the unity of subject and object. In the Zen tradition, nature is to be contemplated and appreciated rather than mastered. Humankind should act on nature with restraint, bringing out the latent beauty and power of the natural world.

These aesthetic elements in the Zen outlook found many expressions of Japanese culture, such as flower arrangement, the tea ceremony, and the garden. All the wabi arts value gracefulness, serenity, tranquillity, simplicity, and aesthetic balance. In the short poems known as haiku, events in nature typically provide moments of insight into the beauty, harmony, and dynamic flow of reality. The path of spiritual awareness, it is held, can liberate a person from the obsessive drives of the ego and from preoccupation with material possessions. The goal is nonattachment and freedom from control by our desires. Barbour contends that the Buddhist ethic thus encourages humility, simplicity, and frugality, as well as compassion and service.[17]

## DECLINE OF NATURE PRESERVATION IN JAPAN

In Japan, there have been many religious traditions, including several forms of Buddhism. The indigenous Shinto heritage affirmed the sacredness of the cosmos and the continuum between humanity and nature. But the industrialization of modern Japan arose largely from the impact of the West. The attitudes engendered have remained in considerable tension with traditional views of nature. The postwar period saw the single-minded pursuit of rapid industrial development, and by 1965 Japan was the most polluted nation in the world.

Environmental legislation in Japan has dealt primarily with threats to human health and has done little to preserve wildlife or scenic beauty. In fact, Japan's actions have been highly destructive of endangered species, whether in killing whales at sea or in obtaining lumber from the Amazon basin, and in international negotiations Japan has strenuously opposed environmental

16. Barbour, *Ethics in an Age of Technology,* 72-74.
17. Ibid.

restrictions. One might take this as evidence that economic considerations dominate modern industrial nations or as evidence that Buddhism is a minor force amidst the secularism of contemporary Japan.

Barbour contends that we have much to learn from Taoism and Zen, especially about meditation and respect for the natural world, both of which have been neglected in the West. But most Westerners are not familiar with these religions. Furthermore, Eastern traditions have had less to say about social justice.[18]

## WESTERN "HARMONY WITH NATURE" GROUPS

In the West, many voices called for harmony with nature. Barbour notes that the romantic literature of the late eighteenth and early nineteenth centuries was in part a reaction to the view of nature fostered by Newtonian science and the Industrial Revolution. For William Blake, William Wordsworth, and Wolfgang Goethe, nature was not an impersonal machine but an organic process with which humanity is united. God is not the remote watchmaker but a vital force immanent in the natural world. Not rational analysis, but feeling and imagination are the highest human capacities. Intuition grasps the unity of organic wholes, the interrelatedness of life. In natural settings a person may find a healing power, a sacramental presence, an experience of peace and joy. Other romantic writers extolled wild, sublime, untouched landscapes, forests, and rivers. They idealized the "noble savage" uncorrupted by civilization, and they exalted the "natural" and the "primitive."

The Transcendentalists in New England referred in similar terms to the presence of the sacred in the realm of nature. Henry Thoreau held that nature is a source of inspiration, vitality, and spiritual renewal; it can teach us humility and simplicity. "In Wildness is the preservation of the World," he wrote.

Thoreau criticized the frantic pursuit of progress and affluence, the growth of technological industrialism, and the pressures of an impersonal urban life. His year and a half of living alone at Walden Pond made him more aware of the interrelationships among creatures and the natural stability upset by humans; in solitude he found serenity and peace. Unspoiled nature was for him both a symbol of qualities that he valued (freedom, courage, and vitality) and a setting that would bring out these qualities in us. But he did not advocate giving up civilization. He sought a simplification of life and an alternation and balance between life with nature and civilization.

In the twentieth century, Rachel Carson's writings combined scientific knowledge with a sense of spiritual unity with nature reminiscent of Roman-

18. Ibid., 72-74.

ticism. In her influential book *Silent Spring* (1962), the call for an ecological conscience was tied to scientific studies of the effects of pesticides on bird populations. By the early 1970s a large number of popular writings were delineating with increasing urgency the effects of a variety of pesticides, phosphates, nitrates, lead, mercury, radioactive wastes, and air pollutants. The word "ecology" had entered the public vocabuary.[19]

## MODERN DEVELOPMENT OF GAIA

In the mid-1960s, chemist James Lovelock found himself part of a team at the Jet Propulsion Laboratory whose assignment was to search for life on Mars. While the lab was committed to carrying out this project by way of robotic landing craft, Lovelock came to the conclusion that this was not necessary. Life could be detected remotely and far more cheaply by long-range scrutiny of the planetary atmosphere, whether on Mars or on any other planet. This thesis was connected with Lovelock's earlier invention of a technique called electron capture detection, which was able to identify faint traces of specified chemical substances. This bit of technology was to have a significant though unforeseen political result. It allowed Lovelock to document the existence of faint toxic residues in the environment that could be traced back to the widespread use of agricultural pesticides. This discovery was the basis of Rachel Carson's research in *Silent Spring*, the book usually credited with launching the environmental movement. From the outset, Lovelock's work was freighted with ecological significance.

Lovelock's assignment quickly flowered into an ambitious hypothesis regarding the relationship of atmosphere to biosphere. His contention was that living things, once they appeared on our planet, took charge of the global environment in a creative way. They became full-fledged partners in the shaping of the earth, its rocks and water and soil. At that time, the orthodox view in the earth sciences was that life was a passive dependent riding the planet, just fortunate enough to find a niche and survive. While it was recognized that biological systems might alter their immediate ecosystem in ways that produced significant local effects, such changes were not prominently regarded as globally significant, nor were they measured on a time scale that comprehended the whole of geological history. Lovelock's hypothesis was a departure. It held that all species in the planetary biomass act symbiotically to enhance the total life-giving potentiality of the planet. The goal of life is global homeostasis, and toward this end it transforms the planet into what might be viewed as a single regulating organism.[20]

19. Ibid., 58-60.
20. Roszak, *Voice of the Earth*, 144-45.

Thus the Gaia hypothesis proposes that all living things and the chemical and physical environment in which they live work together like the parts of one vast organism. Ultimately, Lovelock says, this "composite organism" manipulates the air, the land, and the sea to generate the conditions most suited to supporting life.

"Life and its environment," Lovelock explains, "constitute a single entity, which regulates physical conditions in order to keep the environment at a comfortable state for the organisms themselves."

Teamwork between the physical world and the life it bears is responsible for the richly diverse living earth. It is Gaia that has kept global temperatures from rising high enough or dropping low enough to destroy all life. It is Gaia itself that has sustained the atmosphere and the oceans so that they are suitable for living organisms. In other words, the "Gaia Hypothesis postulates that the planet Earth is a living creature, that the Earth's climate and surface environment are controlled by the plants, animals, and microorganisms that inhabit it. That taken as a whole, the planet behaves not as an inanimate sphere of rock and soil . . . but more as a biological superorganism — a planetary body — that adjusts and regulates itself."

This, in essence, is the hypothesis that Lovelock and his close collaborator Lynn Margulis, a microbiologist, were to call "Gaia." The idea significantly modifies the central Darwinian paradigm of modern biology. Competition — natural selection at the species level — becomes much less important than the overall integration of living things within a symbiotic global network. The basic unit of evolutionary survival becomes the biomass as a whole, which may select species for their capacity to enhance the livability of the planet.

Lovelock introduced the Gaia hypothesis to the general public in 1979 through his work *Gaia: A New Look at Life on Earth* and, while it and other writings of Lovelock and Margulis have sparked much scientific debate, the scholarly attention has also lent an air of validity to the spiritual descendants of the theory.[21]

## REJECTION OF THE NEO-DARWINIAN VIEW

Lovelock and Margulis are convinced that as studies supporting Gaia grow in number, the competitive neo-Darwinian paradigm will begin to crumble. In its place will be a more holistic view of nature in which competition is supplanted by cooperation. The living earth will be seen as an integrated system in which organisms and the environment co-evolve. Furthermore, according to Jane Bosveld, Lovelock is quite at ease with his role as "freelance scientist." With no position in academe, he says, he has the freedom to think

21. Ibid., 146.

and do science in his own way. His laboratory, for instance, is in his home, Coombe Mill, a small mud-and-straw cottage set in the Thomas Hardy countryside of southwestern England. But in a larger sense his lab is not contained within the walls of his small house or even in his thirty acres of meadowland and woods, which he helped to plant. It stretches beyond the moor, the mysterious circle of Stonehenge, and the stony coasts of Cornwall. It spans the Atlantic Ocean, the deserts of Africa, the towering Andes, the Great Barrier Reef. Lovelock's laboratory is the living earth in all its multifarious incarnations. It is Gaia, and he will not allow her to be dismissed without a fight.[22]

## CRITIQUES OF GAIA

Gaia has been a suspicious character since Lovelock and Margulis first introduced her to the scientific community. For one thing, Gaia is a big hypothesis, an attempt to synthesize several disciplines — always a risky enterprise in the highly territorial academic world. But more provocatively, the theory is saturated with purposeful and human implications. If there is one signal that will raise the collective hackles (and the guard) of professional science, it is any hint of intentionality. The great commandment of the guild is: "Thou shalt not endow nature with goals, purposes, sentience, values," except where human beings are concerned.

Yet in Gaia we have a hypothesis that, for all its mathematical precision, seems bent on smuggling a barely disguised version of the anima mundi, or mothering earth, concept back into polite scientific society. The effort has met strong opposition. In a typical response, one critic characterized Gaia as "pseudoscientific myth-making," an "almost medieval" idea that rings of "obscurantism, wishful thinking, and mysticism." The hypothesis does echo elements of mysticism and medieval thought. For that very reason no one proved to be more uneasy with this seeming indiscretion than Lovelock and Margulis themselves. Challenged or stung by the criticism of his colleagues, Lovelock sought to find some chance-based, nonintentional mechanism to explain the actions of Gaia. The effort was an understandable bid to stay in the good graces of the scientific community.

Lovelock suggested that the name Gaia was chosen merely as a device for communicating with the lay public without the need to employ "precise but esoteric language." Lovelock tells us that if he had not fancifully called his hypothesis Gaia, he might have come up with something like "Biocybernetic Universal System Tendency" — a title whose acronym (BUST) preserves a certain motherly connotation.

22. Jane Bosveld, "Life According to Gaia," *OMNI*, 3.

Despite these disclaimers, not even Lovelock and Margulis could possibly make sense of their own theory, let alone communicate it to anybody else, without reference to goals, purposes, and intentions. Nothing that is taken to be "self-regulating" can be freed of these attributes. Gaia seen as an active intelligence is emphatically not a metaphor. She is the very substance of the idea.[23]

## NEW AGE IMPLICATIONS OF GAIA

Goldsmith contends that the constituents of the living world are not here to provide us humans with short-term material benefits but rather to contribute in all sorts of sophisticated ways to maintaining the critical order and stability of the biosphere. In reality, there is no way in which they can be adequately replaced by human artifacts, however elaborate they might appear to us.

Not surprisingly, even after 150 years of industrial development, the vast bulk of the services required to keep our planet functioning are still provided by the self-regulating processes of the biosphere. No more than a minute fraction of essential self-regulating biospheric functions can be taken over — very inadequately, at that — by the externally regulated, technospheric institutions and corporations of our modern world.[24]

Indeed, a spate of current studies have reinforced the Gaia position. Most of the studies have come from earth systems scientists who are discovering strong links between the activity of living things and the physical environment. One body of research, for example, indicates that without life, global temperatures would be much higher than they are today. New York University researcher Tyler Volk and his colleague David Schartzman, who spearheaded the research, examined single-celled ocean organisms that make calcium carbonate shells and deposit them at the bottom of the sea. The shells absorb carbon, effectively removing it from the atmosphere and burying it in the ocean. Removing carbon from the atmosphere cools the earth, creating conditions favorable to life.

Other research by Volk examines microorganisms that create soil by eating away at rock. Without all the soil to absorb carbon from the atmosphere, the earth might conceivably be as much as 80°F (45°C) warmer than it is today. "Under those circumstances," says Volk, the planet might be "uninhabitable for all but the most primitive microbes."[25]

---

23. Roszak, *Voice of the Earth*, 146-47, 150-51, 155.
24. Goldsmith, "Toward the Worldview of Ecology," 54.
25. Bosveld, "Life According to Gaia," 2.

## GAIA, NEOPAGANISM, AND RADICAL FEMINISM

Andrew Dobson, an environmental writer and lecturer in policies at the University of Keele, identifies a virtually deified Nature as the religion of environmentalism today: "Spirituality ghosts Green politics; Green politics is a filling of the spiritual vacuum at the center of late-industrial society, and the land itself is the cathedral at which we are urged to worship."[26]

Many contingents march under the banner of Gaia. Among these are groups that are prepared to embrace Gaia as the rebirth of paganism in our time; others take her as a basis for nature mysticism; others see her as an ally in the development of ecofeminism. The pronouncements and activities of these followers may be a long way from anything a practicing scientist had in mind. Yet here are those who have given the hypothesis, or at least their understanding of it, much emotional and moral force.

The Gaia idea that the earth is a conscious, living organism has been enlarged by theosophist Alice Bailey, David Spangler, and other New Age leaders in describing the sun and the planets as conscious, divine, or semi-divine beings. Our solar system is an actual Body governed by the "Solar Logos," who lives in the sun and who is the entity we refer to when we talk of "God." However, the Solar Logos and his body — the Solar System — is in turn just part of a larger galactic body which possesses a greater and more encompassing consciousness. The earth, while being part of the Solar Body, is itself the body of the "Earth Logos." The theosophical Earth Logos is usually reinterpreted as female and identified with "the Goddess," and "Gaia" is used as an appropriate name to address her. These theosophical cosmic visions are strongly reminiscent of science fiction.[27]

Otter and Morning Glory G'Zell, of *Green Egg Magazine,* describe themselves as priest and priestess of Gaia. The Boston Museum of Science sells books and magazines focusing on Gaia. A group of women have come together on an island in the Pacific Northwest, now called Gaia Island. On the island, one meets such artists as Diane Snow Austin, whose song "The Goddess Walks Again" has a rousing pop hit style.

Evangelical scholars such as Donna Hailson maintain that Lovelock and others who have called for the development of a new theology more compatible with contemporary views of reality as now offered by the sciences have in reality called for a return to the old paganism. For Margaret Brearley, this emphasis on divinity located only within deified Creation and within humanity's deified unconscious is essentially paganism.[28]

26. Coffman and Alexander, "Eco-Religion and Cultural Change," 21.
27. Roszak, *Voice of the Earth,* 156; see also W. J. Hanegraaff, *New Age Religion and Western Culture* (Leiden: Brill, 1996), 157.
28. Aida Besancon Spencer, *The Goddess Revival* (Grand Rapids: Baker, 1995), 29.

While Lovelock has not endorsed the many poetic and religious extensions that have grown up around Gaia, he has in later writings somewhat mellowed toward those who take these liberties. He describes his own outlook as a "positive agnosticism" that prefers to keep the hypothesis modest and "manageable." Though he cannot see Gaia as having awareness, he admits to finding it "satisfying" that the theory has found a spiritual as well as a scientific reading. According to Tal Brooke, Lovelock has a statue of Gaia in his garden at Cornwall and is a member of Lindisfarne, the New Age group headquartered at the Episcopal Cathedral of Saint John the Divine in New York City. He revealed his deeper convictions in an interview in *Orion Nature Quarterly:* "Gaia is Mother Earth. Gaia is immortal. She is the eternal source of life. She is surely a virgin. She does not need to reproduce herself as she is immortal. She is certainly the mother of us all, including Jesus."[29]

Theodore Roszak contends that there may be more to these developments than he recognizes. A hypothesis that contends that the great biofeedback system of planet earth acts upon all its cargo of life in ways that seek homeostasis must at some point weigh the possibility that Gaian politics, including its ecofeminist and mystic "extremes," is among the ways such action finds expression in our species. The poetic license and religious fervor of these efforts may even be among the planet's most effective means of self-defense — more effective than the cold edge of mathematics or the weight of fact. Gaia was, after all, born of wonder and ecstasy.

On the other hand, Roszak indicates that what may have been overlooked by the Gaians in their often sentimental depiction of the Goddess is the dark side of the matriarchal tradition. Not all Earth Mothers are endowed with lovingkindness and mercy; some, like Kali and Hecate, are hard, often chastising parents. Sekhmet, the terrible lion-headed goddess of Egypt, once sought to devour the entire human race for its disobedience. Lovelock has warned of that. Gaia is, in his view, "stern and tough, always keeping the world warm and comfortable for those who obey the rules, but ruthless in her destruction of those who transgress."

If so, in her brute determination to defend the variety and quantity of life she carries, Gaia may at some point decide that this so-clever human species is too troublesome a hazard to maintain. The adjustment she may then see fit to make will be far from gentle.[30]

---

29. Ibid., 27-28.
30. Roszak, *Voice of the Earth*, 157-59.

## Deep Ecology

Rejecting both resource management and environmental stewardship are those adhering to what has been termed "deep ecology." They blame the present crisis on human domination of nature. They say human manipulation of nature is not a solution, it's the problem.

According to Brooks Alexander, deep ecology is one of the most extreme of the Gaia-based ideologies. It is the most radical as well as the most mystical form of environmentalism today. Deep ecology

> rejects the "dominant worldview" that nature and its species exist to serve humans; it affirms the "intrinsic value" of other species apart from human purposes; it encourages a direct spiritual relation to nature; it rejects consumerism in favor of voluntary simplicity; it calls for a decrease in the human population of the earth; it advocates direct action at the grassroots level to resist or repair the environmental damage done by industrialism.

The term "deep ecology" originated in 1973. It was coined by Norwegian philosopher Arne Naess in his article "The Shallow and the Deep, Long Range Ecology Movements: A Summary." Naess was frustrated that the ecology movements could do little more than nibble away at the symptoms of our eco-crisis because they wouldn't ask the "big questions."

To Naess, the piecemeal, troubleshooting approach was "shallow ecology," and he saw it as condemned forever to being reactive, defensive, and inadequate. Deep ecology, on the other hand, embraces a "deeper" outlook that includes the interests of nonhuman life. It also asks and answers "deeper" questions in a way that amounts to a worldview. In 1982, Naess put the worldview issue up front:

> We (deep ecologists) ask which society, which education, which religion, is beneficial for all life on the planet as a whole, and then we ask further what we need to do in order to make the necessary changes. We are not limited to a scientific approach; we have an obligation to verbalize a total view.

The basic idea is that there is no bifurcation in reality between the human and the nonhuman realms. To the extent that we perceive boundaries, we fall short of deep ecological consciousness. The meaning of this insight is twofold. First, it means that humankind is not unique, distinct, or special; at best, we are just one brick in a very large building. Second, it ultimately means that all distinctions are unreal. There are, finally, no gaps or grades in the "great chain of being," there is just a single, seamless, process of "being-ness" that encompasses everything from God to rocks.

When the intuition of deep ecology is described in that way, it sounds a great deal like the "oneness" mysticism of Eastern/occult enlightenment. The other name for the mystical insight is "cosmic consciousness."[31]

An important emphasis in deep ecology is biocentric equality. Biocentric equality means that all things in the biosphere have an equal right to live and blossom and to reach their own individual forms of unfolding and self-realization within the larger Self-realization. This basic intuition is that all organisms and entities in the ecosphere, as parts of the interrelated whole, are equal in intrinsic worth. In practical terms, that means that human beings have the same value as camels, trees, turtles, felas, and microbes — neither more nor less.

In 1984, Arne Naess and George Sessions formulated eight "Basic Principles" of deep ecology. The "Basic Principles" acknowledge that deep ecologists are trying to change "basic economic, technological, and ideological structures." The basic principles of deep ecology are as follows:

1. The well-being and flourishing of human and nonhuman life on earth have value in themselves. These values are independent of the usefulness of the nonhuman world for human purposes.

2. Richness and diversity of life forms contribute to the realization of these values and are also values in themselves.

3. Humans have no right to reduce this richness and diversity except to satisfy vital needs.

4. The flourishing of human life and cultures is compatible with a substantial decrease of the human population. The flourishing of nonhuman life requires such a decrease.

5. Present human interference with the nonhuman world is excessive, and the situation is rapidly worsening.

6. Policies must therefore be changed. These policies affect basic economic, technological, and ideological structures. The resulting state of affairs will be deeply different from the present.

7. The ideological change is mainly that of appreciating life quality rather than adhering to an increasingly higher standard of living. There will be a profound awareness of the difference between big and great.

8. Those who subscribe to the foregoing points have an obligation directly or indirectly to try to implement the necessary changes.

Points 4 and 8 lead to a form of militant mysticism that is revolutionary and elitist. From its base in mystical zealotry, it pursues a self-assigned and self-defined mandate to reduce human impact in general, and human numbers in particular. Earth First! and animal rights activities have become notorious for their acts of disruption, destruction, and sabotage carried out in the name of opposing "abuses" of nature — especially related to logging and animal

31. Brooks Alexander, "Deep Ecology," *SCP Journal* 16.1 (1991): 8-9.

experiments. Deep ecology is a principled rejection of the mainline ideology of environmentalism, and proposes a revolt against it, both theoretically and in practical terms.[32]

## A Radical Critique of Moderate Ecology

As already noted, deep ecologists oppose the "resource management" school of thought. In their view, the "old-fashioned, Sierra-Club, conservation-minded, politically oriented, reformist, 'shallow ecology' — or environmental-ism — is only a Band-aid approach to a mortal disease."

In the long run, deep ecologists say environmental destruction must be reversed, not just slowed down. And for that, a more profound change of values is required — a radical change in humanity's understanding of itself and what its place is in nature.

Brooks Alexander notes that a "revolution in self-understanding" is what deep ecology is all about, and it seeks to leave behind (or overturn) not only "resource management" theories, but all forms of the "stewardship" ap-proach as well. Even those forms of stewardship that come clothed in "Gaian" terminology are suspect at best.[33]

## Ecofeminism and Gaia

Gaia was seen as the mother or grandmother of Zeus, the head Greek god. The rule of Zeus was dependent on the approval and consent of Gaia. The priority of the female principle in the Gaia concept may partly explain why the Gaian theory finds a sympathetic audience among feminist writers wishing to reimage our understanding of God and creation according to feminine characteristics. In fact, ecofeminism can be defined as that movement which establishes the connection between the oppression of women and the oppres-sion of nature.[34]

Alan Miller notes that throughout history, men have dominated both women and nature. The traditional social norms of most societies and the normative stability of economic system functioning have required the formal subjugation of both feminine and earthly values. Woman has been confined (with modest changes only in quite recent times) to certain carefully defined

32. Ibid., 11-13.
33. Ibid., 14-15.
34. Celia Deane Drummond, "God and Gaia: Myth or Reality?" *Theology*, July/August 1992, 281.

roles in much the same fashion that the intrinsic values of nature have been carefully obscured by both philosophers and social planners in order that the formal "use-value" of each may be maximized. Theologian Rosemary Reuther notes that "Women simply cannot be persons within the present system of work and family, and they can only rise to liberated personhood by the most radical and fundamental reshaping of the entire human environment in a way that redefines the very nature of work, family, and the institutional expressions of social relations."[35]

Feminist theologian and writer Anne Primavesi waxes eloquent about the importance of the Gaia concept. She rejoices that James Lovelock has named the earth creature Gaia: this living planet on which the living things, the air, the oceans, and the rocks all combine in one.

According to Primavesi, ecofeminists see in the present ecological crisis the possibility of the use of an ecological paradigm resulting in a more inclusive vision of the world. By its very nature this paradigm is a force for change. It is gaining ground at a time of crisis in the life of the planet, the very moment at which paradigm shifts occur by necessity. The hierarchical paradigm that places men over women and over nature which prevails in much of Western culture is now seen as inadequate by a post-Einsteinian scientific consciousness.

It is possible, therefore, for ecofeminists to question the very basic assumptions about the nature of human nature, about human gender relations and their effects on the nonhuman world. They also draw conclusions about the relationship between these matters and how we behave as organisms embedded in the systemic creature Earth. They do this through radical critiques of the prevailing gender hierarchies, which assume that men, by nature, have rights and power over women and the nonhuman world. A feminist critique is a consistent recognition of the limits of hierarchical patterns of thought, of the way in which our culture has been and still is dominated by the questions posed and answers given by male "scientific" consciousness.[36]

Tracing his personal mental evolution, nuclear physicist Fritjof Capra wrote that his engagement with feminism and its radical critiques of society transformed his entire perception of social and culture change. He realized that the full power of male dominance is extremely difficult to grasp because it is omnipresent. It has influenced our most basic ideas about human nature and about our relationship to the universe, for "man's" nature and "his" relationship are taken as normal. But then patriarchy, as Capra remarks, had never been challenged until recently, and its preconceptions and structures are as yet only barely touched by feminist critiques.

35. Miller, *Gaia Connections*, 20-21.
36. Anne Primavesi, *From Apocalypse to Genesis* (Minneapolis: Fortress, 1991), 13, 37-40.

A quick browse through a "Women's Studies" section in a library will give more than enough proof that attributions of "mindlessness" against women are part of our history. Why else were they denied the right to higher education, the right to vote, the right to their own property on marriage, the right to maintenance and/or custody of their children on divorce, and all the other manifestations of lack of moral and ethical consideration only slowly being legislated out of existence? The women of Liechtenstein in Europe were fully enfranchised only in 1984.

But, says G. Bateson, this lack of moral and ethical consideration shows itself in the exploitation of the environment. Ecofeminists say that what is true for nature is true for women, and vice versa. If you have no moral or ethical relationship with nature and you have an advanced technology, then poisonous by-products which bring about the death of nature cause you no qualms. If you say you have a moral or ethical approach to women and then, for instance, use advanced technology on their reproductive organs with no more qualms than if they were battery hens or hybrid apple trees, then you must grant the ecofeminists their case. "Earthly" bodies are there to produce and reproduce under the control of men. In such a hierarchical society, women are "lower" than men and nature "lower" than women, which leaves both subject to male control, "objectified" for experiment in the name of science.

Ecofeminism makes connections between such fragmentation of male and female sensibility within human relationships and attitudes to nature. It connects the exclusion of female perception and experience from patriarchal culture with rigid and unchanging structures of control over the natural world. It connects patterns of male domination of woman with those in which science and technology are bound to a conception of absolute mastery over matter. It insists on the inclusion of women's perceptions as corrective to a solely male, and therefore partial, view of the systemic creature world. It relates natural ecosystems with human ones consistently and sensitively.[37]

## Natural Kinship of Gaia and Feminism

Ecofeminism stresses the connection between woman and nature on the grounds that nature, in our distanced, masculine-scientific culture, has also been made "other," something essentially different from the dominant human male who has an unlimited right to exploit "mother" earth.

For both men and women working in ecology, there comes a change in our perception of nature when, by consistently linking women's history of oppression with the history of the environment, we affirm the natural kinship

37. Ibid., 40-42.

between feminism and ecology. Then we realize that in our readings of environmental crises we will compound the errors if we do not keep faith with the ecological paradigm, starting with our own lives and finding there the deepest manifestation of nature-hating: our collusion with male-dominated structures. We belong to a society in which women, identified with nature, have been objectified and subordinated. The attitudes we bring to nature in our ecological work will reflect this, especially in an unwillingness to accord it autonomy or value in its own right. By becoming aware of patterns of domination in our own lives, we learn to connect these patterns with the domination of nonhuman nature. This is the first step outside the common perception of ourselves as discrete static beings who must control others and the environment in order to survive. It is the first step toward an ecological society and sensibility.[38]

Karen Warren has set forth four main points:

1. There are important connections between the oppression and exploitation of women and the oppression and exploitation of nature.
2. An understanding of the nature of these connections is necessary to any adequate understanding of the double oppression of women and of nature.
3. All feminist theory and practice must include an ecological perspective.
4. Any solution to ecological problems must include a feminist perspective.[39]

In other words, feminists are pointing to the connections between the exploitation of nature and the exploitation of women. They note the dichotomies prevalent in Western culture: spirit/nature, mind/body, reason/emotion, objectivity/subjectivity, and domination/submission. In our culture the first term in each of these pairs has been identified with men, the second term with women. The technological and economic institutions that have harmed the environment have been run almost exclusively by men. A patriarchal society values power, competition, and control more than nurture, cooperation, and reciprocity. Women are said to be more aware of the connectedness of life; they tend to reject hierarchical ordering and to welcome diversity in society and nature. These feminist authors hold that women and environmentalists can make common cause in seeking liberation from the conceptual dualisms and the societal structures of domination that have harmed both women and nature.[40]

38. Ibid., 36-37, 42-43.
39. Miller, *Gaia Connections*, 22-23.
40. Barbour, *Ethics in an Age of Technology*, 59.

But ecofeminism wants to go beyond deep ecology. It agrees with deep ecology in rejecting both of the mainline ideologies (resource management and stewardship). However, eco-feminists reject deep ecology as well, because it fails to get at the "real" root of the problem, which is "patriarchy." In fact, some eco-feminists see deep ecology as another classic, male-centered, patriarchal distortion, and hence a part of the problem. The deep ecologist's desire to break out of "human centeredness" and to identify with the larger whole is interpreted by eco-feminists as the familiar masculine urge to transcend the concrete world of particular problems such as male domination in preference for something more enduring and abstract.

Ecofeminists also think that deep ecology's emphasis on population reduction betrays the long-standing patriarchal desire to dominate the female reproductive process. In the final feminist analysis, men are just deficient, and they create their mental/emotional games to compensate for that fact: Isolated from others and from nature, the alienated male ego invents deep ecology as another desperate attempt to become reattached to the world.[41]

## Reimaging the Sacred

According to Brooks Alexander, ecofeminism extends generic feminism's hostility to males and maleness into a new area of public concern — the environment. Here is one more evil we can charge to the masculine factor. As our media chant a rising chorus of environmental anxiety, ecology becomes a point of entry to the mind of the public at large. Ecomania becomes a vehicle for propagating feminist ideology to a wider audience than would otherwise be receptive to it.[42]

Even though some feminists see the ecofeminists as strident, feminist leaders in general see the necessity of reimaging the sacred. It is the Goddess who is seen as the primary vehicle in this enterprise, for not only does her indwelling presence restore life to the universe, but she infuses it with the particular qualities of the feminine which have been lost to universal consciousness through the dominance of patriarchal religion and mechanistic science. The Goddess emerges in two major manifestations: the Goddess in history, which refers to the goddesses of ancient matriarchies, a concept often used in conjunction with political issues; and the Goddess within, a reference to the indwelling of the divine within the human, particularly the feminine, psyche.

At one level, the Goddess is the One that unites the many. But, very

41. Alexander, "Deep Ecology," 9.
42. Ibid.

quickly, the multiple nature of the Goddess emerges. She has innumerable manifestations and functions. She makes sacred the earth and nature, natural functions, female body functions, and the interior of the human, particularly the female, psyche.

## Ecology and the Sacred as Immanent and Feminine

However they reimage the sacred and whatever sources they draw upon to do so, New Age interpreters of feminist spirituality understand the sacred as immanent within the natural world, the body, and the psyche. To perceive the divine as immanent counteracts the fear that we are alone in a lifeless universe leading lives that are meaningless in any cosmic sense. Immanence, likewise, implies that the sacred aspect of reality is accessible. We may find the divine within ourselves, within each other, and within nature.

In his nontechnical writings, physicist David Bohm speaks in terms of the values that emerge from a more holistic way of thinking about the universe. He maintains that the way we envision the world is a crucial factor in our consciousness and being. If we respond intuitively and imaginatively to an understanding of the world and feel at one with it, we are more likely to feel "genuine love" for the world than a desire to manipulate it. "We will want to care for it, as we would for anyone who is close to us and therefore enfolded in us as an inseparable part."[43]

Miriam Starhawk, a feminist witch, insists that an ecofeminist spirituality must be "earth-based." Feminist spirituality makes the claim that however the sacred or the transcendent is defined, its home is the earth and the body.

For Starhawk and other Goddess advocates, the Goddess is not just a symbol for nature, but is nature. This is the reason why Starhawk makes immanence the core of her theology, defining it as "the awareness of the world and everything in it as alive, dynamic, interdependent, interacting, and infused with moving energies: a living being, a weaving dance." She suggests that this is the wisdom of tribal culture around the world, "that the sacred is found here, where we are, immanent in the world." As the earth, the cosmos, and everything in it, the Goddess is also present in human beings (at least in women; men's status is less sure). Such a view, that the divine is in everything, is usually termed "pantheism," and spiritual feminists are happy to claim the term.

43. Mary Farrell Bednarowski, "The New Age Movement and Feminist Spirituality: Overlapping Conversations at the End of the Century," a paper presented at the Fifth International Conference on New Religions, The Institute for the Study of American Religion, May 16-17, 1991, 7-10, 15.

The view that the earth is a living being is extremely common among spiritual feminists, along with the view that this being is somehow female. The earth is feminine, they argue, because it shares characteristics in common with women: qualities of nurturing, creating, sustaining, giving birth. As Jeannine Garawitz says, "Women give birth in their wombs and the earth births trees, mountains, nature."[44]

Spiritual feminists use the goddess title more literally than Lovelock does: for them the earth is the living body of the goddess. This is graphically illustrated in a drawing by M. Lynn Shiavi titled "Only Goddess Can Make a Tree." The drawing shows a pair of breast-shaped hills, one of which is topped with a nipple, the other with a nipple from which grows a tree.

Because the goddess is portrayed as an immanent deity, one who is in nature and inseparable from it, it is not transparently clear how she could have created it. And indeed, creation stories play a less important role in feminist spirituality than they do in many other religions, especially the biblical religion.

## Capra's Science, Feminism, and Ecology

Following up on the thought of Lovelock, but going beyond it, Capra, the well-known physicist, emphasizes that the earth is a sentient being, a surrogate God. Capra sees the answer to the ecological crisis in this hypothesis. His argument, though sophisticated and backed by great detail, is in fact quite simple: men have exploited the earth because they have considered it to be non-living and therefore inferior to themselves. Capra says: "Our attitudes will be very different when we realize that the environment is not only alive but also mindful, like ourselves." His reasoning is that if an attitude of religious awe toward Mother Earth as a goddess replaces the desire to dominate nature, then there is a greater chance we will give better care to the planet.

According to Vishal Mangalwadi, to be fair to Capra, we have to give him credit for admitting honestly that in presenting feminist spirituality as a basis for ecological reform he is not offering scientific truth, but a myth. In a lengthy interview with Mike McGrath entitled "Zen and the Art of Changing the World," Capra admits candidly:

> At the beginning, I still thought, well the Old Physics — the Newtonian worldview — has influenced medicine and economics and everything, so now let's build a new set of sciences patterned after the New Physics. Then I changed my way of thinking, shifting away from physics as the

44. Cynthia Eller, *Living in the Lap of the Goddess* (New York: Crossroad, 1993), 136-38.

model for other sciences, and as the source of our metaphors about reality. . . . The new 'paradigm' or the new vision of reality is an ecological vision.

Simply paraphrased, Capra is saying that in earlier times life and society were built on what was thought to be the truth about the universe. But now the mechanistic worldview has been shown to be untrue. At first Capra thought the New Physics (or his mystical interpretation of it, expounded in his book *The Tao of Physics*) could provide an alternative intellectual basis for building life and society. Upon realizing the new physics cannot be such a basis, he has given up attempts to build life on that truth and now builds life on what appears ecological.

Capra's book *The Turning Point,* which has become the springboard for a film, *Mindwalk,* has become something of a manifesto for the New Age movement and a source of inspiration for the feminist spirituality of theologians such as Matthew Fox. It contains, among other things, Capra's ecological vision. Besides the proposal that feminist spirituality be developed for the sake of ecology, Capra also discusses two other aspects of the ecological problem. The first, which receives major attention, is our modern secular outlook, a view that has been shaped by the teachings of René Descartes and Isaac Newton. This outlook views the universe, human beings, and society as machines. This worldview, Capra thinks, is at the root of all our problems. Therefore, the book issues a call to turn the present culture away from this mechanistic outlook to a holistic worldview based on the General Systems Theory.

The second cause of the ecological crisis which Capra identifies is the "human" problem. Capra's worldview, however, does not permit him to identify it as a moral problem. It therefore receives no more than a few passing references.[45]

## New Age Religious Adaptation of Gaia

When Lovelock first proposed Gaia (named after the Greek goddess of the earth), the most positive response came from New Age types and "ecofreaks," who grabbed onto the idea with religious fervor. Here at last, some thought, was a scientific theory that implied a purposeful order, even consciousness, in nature.

Stewart Chevre points out that New Age quickly incorporated Gaia worship into its system of spiritual beliefs and practices. The feminist and

45. Vishal Mangalwadi, *When the New Age Gets Old* (Downers Grove, Ill.: Inter-Varsity, 1991), 133-34, 137.

ecologically based spiritualities (witchcraft, goddess worship, ecofeminism, paganism, and other earth worship groups) have become strong supporters of the mystical, quasireligious Gaia. Earth spirituality, in particular, is quickly becoming equated with Gaia worship to the applause of most New Age leaders.

While environmental scientists busy themselves with the formulation of mathematical and computer-simulated models of Gaian ecosystems, New Age writers are going in entirely different directions. They concern themselves with Gaia as religion. Their self-proclaimed task is to describe the psychology, spirituality, and political and social implications of the goddess. Many of these writers dismiss the scientific version of Gaia as too narrow, rationalistic, and mechanistic. Nevertheless, they enjoy the benefits of name recognition and the notoriety resulting from Gaia's increasing scientific credibility. Gaia the goddess has greatly benefited from the great attention paid to Gaia the scientific hypothesis — this in spite of the fact that many scientists completely reject the spiritual aspects of Gaia theory.[46]

## REJECTING CHRISTIANITY FOR ECOLOGICAL SURVIVAL

Although Lovelock gives lip service to some aspects of the Christian church, he believes that orthodox Christianity, properly understood, is a distortion of the purest form of religious truth. To recover our true spiritual nature, Lovelock believes we need to return to ancient forms of goddess and earth spirituality — with a modern form of Gaia worship. Lovelock would like us to believe that Gaia created humankind and that it was Gaia who gave birth to Jesus Christ.

In the closing pages of his book *The Ages of Gaia — A Biography of the Living Earth,* Lovelock's attitude toward Christianity becomes quite apparent. How have we arrived at our present precarious position in history? According to Lovelock, it is because we no longer practice the rites of the ancients, when "the Earth was worshipped as a goddess and believed to be alive."

Lovelock believes that humankind must immediately return to the worship of the earth goddess if we are to save ourselves from destruction. He does his best to convince us that it is the worldview rooted in the Judeo-Christian concept of God that destroyed "the peaceful, artful, Goddess-oriented culture in old Europe" and is responsible for all present woes. Unless we rid ourselves of the biblical conception of God and replace it with the fundamentally pagan worldview centered in Gaian-Earth worship and goddess spirituality we are surely doomed, declares Lovelock.[47]

46. Stewart Chevre, "The Gaia Hypothesis: Science, Mythology, and the Desecration of God," *SCP Journal* 16.1 (1991): 28-29.
47. Ibid., 29-30.

## The Findhorn Community

Vishal Mangalwadi, a Hindu Christian author, contends that concern with ecology and the Gaia hypothesis leads in some cases to a reincarnation of animism. An example of such a development is found in the Findhorn Community. This group, one of the early centers of the New Age movement, was founded in northern rural Scotland in 1965 by Eileen Caddy, Peter Caddy, and Dorothy Maclean. Already in place as the movement emerged in the early 1970s, Findhorn was seen as embodying its principal ideas of transformation. New Age leaders, especially in the United States, looked to the community for guidance and from it the movement's major theoretician, David Spangler, emerged.

Maclean, Findhorn leader and also a channel, made contact with the devas — nature spirits said to be associated with various plant or landscape features — which the three leaders came to view as angelic archetypical forces. The first contact was made with a pea deva. Maclean was told that the garden would succeed as they cooperated with the devas by seeking their advice and gaining their permission to rearrange the landscape. Some, like the pea deva, were specific to a species, while others, like the landscape deva, relate to more general aspects of the garden itself.[48]

The Findhorn community, situated at Moray Firth, Scotland, where the soil is poor and the weather is unfavorable to agriculture, has had remarkable success in growing forty-pound cabbages and sixty-pound broccoli with the alleged help of devas, or nature spirits. However, as David Spangler, an ex-spokesman of Findhorn saw it, the magic of Findhorn was not primarily about ecology but a religious transformation of humankind. "The myth of Findhorn," he says, is the "rebirth of an emerging culture into a totally new consciousness . . . to see the true divine nature of the planet."

How can one see the divine nature of the planet? It is not a question of a conceptual shift from a materialistic philosophy to a spiritual one. Findhorn advocates our "identification" with these spirit beings in order to see the "true nature" of nature.

According to Mangalwadi, in the case of Findhorn, doing ecology means seeking "nature spirits" — or even being identified with or possessed by them.[49]

48. J. Gordon Melton, *New Age Almanac* (Detroit: Visible Ink, 1991), 401.
49. Mangalwadi, *When the New Age Gets Old,* 130.

## Psychic Mysticism as the Ecological Solution

England's best-known psychic healer, Matthew Manning, led more than two thousand people in a healing session at the closing session of the "Festival for Body, Mind and Spirit" held in London in 1990. It is not enough, he taught, to heal individuals when our planet itself is sick. It is also impossible to heal the environment in England while the industrial activities on the continent contribute to the pollution in the English Channel, the North Sea, and England. The globe itself has to be healed, he said. And that, Manning said, calls for everyone to send out the healing vibrations of their united psychic energies to envelop the globe.

Those attending closed their eyes and "visualized" harmonious, healthy vibrations going out of the hall, beyond London, beyond England, beyond Europe, to cover the whole earth. According to Manning, if the universe is a process in the divine mind of humankind, then our psychic energy is certainly enough to restore the ecobalance. Because New Age thought does not make a distinction between consciousness, physical energy, and matter, it sees the heart of our environmental problem in terms of a disturbance in the earth's psyche.

According to David Icke, as reported in his book *The Truth Vibrations,* the main problem of the earth is that "She is feeling unloved. . . . The dark energy forms that our aggression, anger, fear and resentment have created are the most destructive contribution we have made to the planet's decline. . . . The Earth is a living being with feeling and emotions. . . . Strange weather patterns we have experienced in every part of the world are the result of the Earth-Spirit suffering the effects of, particularly, emotional pressures. She is becoming confused. This is making her lose control and the nature order of the planet is failing."[50]

If the ecological problem is a psychic problem, the solution lies in sending positive psychic vibrations to the earth — especially through its ley-lines and psychic centers. The idea of the earth's leylines corresponds roughly to the Chinese idea behind acupuncture, that the chi, or life-energy, flows through certain meridians in the human body. The idea that there are psychic points on the earth corresponds to the Hindu tantric notion that the human body has certain psychic pulse points.

Thus, in order to meet the ecological crisis, New Age psychics attempt to find the earth's psychic points and transmit their psychic energy to them.

50. Ibid., 130-31.

## Ecology Assumptions and the Natural World

Ecofeminist philosopher Carolyn Merchant summarizes the New Age's eco-centric approach to the natural world. She emphasizes that, while human beings do have special characteristics distinguishing and to some degree setting them apart from the other animals, they are nevertheless interdependently involved with the global ecosystem. The metaphysical base, as we have noted, is the organic or holistic paradigm.

- everything is connected to everything else;
- the whole is far greater than the sum of the parts;
- the world is active and alive: internal causation;
- the primacy of change and ongoing process is always affirmed; and
- the unity of mind/body, matter/spirit, people/nature is nondualistic.[51]

According to Merchant, ecocentric exponents are Taoism, Buddhism, Native American philosophy, Thoreau, Gary Snyder, Theodore Roszak and "right brain" analysis, Aldo Leopold, Rachel Carson, Fritjof Capra, political ecology, deep ecology, and feminism.

# CRITIQUES OF THE GAIA HYPOTHESIS ABOUT NATURE

## Scientific Critiques

A sizable majority of the scientific community dismissed the Gaia hypothesis as being, at best, untestable and, at worst, poetic nonsense. Gaia's most outspoken critics were and continue to be Neo-Darwinists, evolutionary biologists who have blended Darwin's theory with studies of modern genetics. Neo-Darwinists see the world not as a sphere of cooperation, but rather as a jungle of organisms battling one another in a fight for survival. Organisms evolve, say Neo-Darwinists, when a genetic mutation makes the organism a better competitor and thus better at passing along its genes to the next generation.

Doolittle, a molecular biologist at Dalhousie University in Nova Scotia, may sum up the majority opinion when he says, "I get irritated at what I think is fuzzy thinking." There's certainly no malice in Doolittle's judgment. He considers Margulis, the co-creator of the Gaia Hypothesis, a good friend and a first-rate biologist. But he disagrees with her assertions about Gaia and symbiosis.

51. Miller, *Gaia Connections,* 25, 28.

Like most biologists, Doolittle questions the role of cooperation in evolution. The evolutionary process, he says, could not accommodate the kind of global cooperation necessary in Gaia. "Natural selection," he says, "only favors an organism that has a mutation that allows it to make more of itself. It does not favor organisms that behave themselves in a global sense." Moreover, Doolittle argues, organisms that unite in a symbiotic union do so because they gain some advantage from it. "It is really just selfishness," he says. "Cooperative efforts can evolve out of symbiosis, but the driving force is not cooperation."

Other scientists question what they see as Gaia's basic premise — that life manipulates the oceans and atmosphere to benefit itself. "Any change in the atmosphere and the oceans might be positive for some species and negative for others," says Harvard geochemist Heinrich Holland. "Who is Gaia optimizing the planet for? The theory sounds something like a post-Christian view of reality, in which the hand of God, renamed Gaia, controls the fate of the earth."[52]

Celia Deane-Drummond states that Gaia is very difficult to test, and if untestable it cannot really be taken seriously as science. If the life of the earth as a living system contains the regulatory device, how can we begin to test such a mechanism when it must involve inter-species communication from microbes to humankind?

According to Drummond, for those who support the Gaia hypothesis, it is not just a way of interpreting stable mechanisms operating at the global level, but a new approach to scientific investigation that deliberately directs its attention to the whole planet as the final destination of scientific inquiry. Physiology has always concerned itself with regulatory steps at the whole organism level, but in the past it has tended to direct itself toward explanations at the cellular and molecular biochemical level. It is the impossibility of testing the interactions between all the facets of nature that makes Gaia more like a scientific myth. The concrete observations which show constant atmospheric conditions over long periods can be explained in terms of thermodynamics. Once we admit this, the idea of Gaia as "living" begins to fade. Its persistence among a small group of dedicated biologists owes much to their quasireligious attitude to nature.[53]

## Psychological Critiques

According to Coffman and Alexander, the New Age ecological view is psychologically damaging. It rejects the human nature we were born with, but cannot replace it with anything new. It proclaims humanity reprobate, but

52. Bosveld, "Life According to Gaia," 2.
53. Drummond, "God and Gaia," 279-80.

cannot absolve or redeem us. It condemns us for being human, but can only offer mysticism as an escape hatch. Since mysticism is a minority option at best, this New Age view implicitly condemns most people to permanent moral despair. Furthermore, by making the environment the centerpiece of Christian attention and action, this new emphasis shifts the basis of the Christian faith. We achieve peace with God by attaining peace with divinized Nature, that is, by assuming our appropriate status as one equal element of Nature among many. In its extreme forms, ecotheology can lead us to "exchange the truth of God for a lie, and worship and serve created things rather than the Creator" (Rom. 1:25).[54]

The approach of the Gaian hypothesis projects long periods of relatively little change "punctuated" by short bursts of drastic change while the earth approaches a new steady state. There is no guarantee that human life will be part of the next "stable state" of the earth, since according to Lovelock's theory the priority is the persistence of life, rather than human life. If we interpret Gaia according to Craik's dissipative theory, even life itself, in theory, could be under threat, since the next stable state depends on energy flow.

## Gaia's Pessimism and Inconsistency with New Age Teaching

The theological problem of the Gaia hypothesis is that it not only seems to remove the special place of humankind in creation, but it is also essentially pessimistic. Gaia does not have a "moral" responsibility to preserve humankind. Pedler suggests that Gaia is a "revolutionary" who is "neither cruel, moral, nor immoral. It cares nothing for the continuance of the human race and can design the death of man, woman, or child as and when appropriate. It possesses ancient wisdom, is wholly integrated into its purpose, and cannot be defeated, but only joined." Hence Pedler remarks that Gaia is the most dangerous and determined opponent ever to face us. The harsh tone of Tennyson/Darwin's nature "red in tooth and claw" seems relatively mild compared with the threat of the world organism turned against us.

In fact, according to Aida Spencer, Lovelock's scientific version of Gaia paganism is almost fatalistic. Since, he states, pollution is natural, cleaning the environment is a routine, automatic operation of homeostasis or Gaia. Human pollution will not probably endanger the life of Gaia as a whole, even though it may destroy the human species itself. Humans are simply one part of a pattern. The whole pattern has more importance than any one part.[55]

Once more nature as malevolent seems to have surfaced in the con-

54. Coffman and Alexander, "Eco-Religion and Cultural Change," 20, 22.
55. Spencer, *Goddess Revival*, 188.

sciousness of twentieth-century humankind. The New Age movement has welcomed the idea in Gaian theory that diversity is an aspect of unity, and believes that Gaia is a scientific basis for New Age ideology. However, it has failed to recognize the inconsistency of Gaian thought with the New Age affirmation of human potential and individual self-improvement. The uncritical adoption of Gaian theory seems to depend on the mythical aspect of its theory, rather than its basis in science. In other words, it seems more likely that the implicit attraction of Gaia for New Age thinkers is in its religious connotations associated with ancient Greek myth than in its value as science.

## GAIA CONFLICTS

Once we believe the Gaia view that the earth has the power of a single living organism to set the future for its component parts, it becomes difficult to affirm belief in a loving Creator God who became incarnate in humanity. A trinitarian approach to the relationship between God and creation prevents Gaia from assuming too great an importance over against a scientific hypothesis. The truth of the interconnectedness of all parts of creation that Gaia emphasizes in the wake of disillusionment with reductionistic science can best be expressed theologically since it is outside the boundary of accessibility to scientific method. The service of theology to science becomes a reminder of the unity of all creation expressed in the doctrine of the immanence of God the Holy Spirit.

The reversion to a view of the world which, logically, leads to a fearful and fateful attitude to human existence denies the Christian hope in the future. Rather, in the words of Celia Drummond, like the Darwinian theory of evolutionism which outgrew its place in the nineteenth century, Gaia needs to be "tamed" if she is not going to become "too big for her boots." The spurious links between Gaia and mysticism are unhelpful both from the perspective of scientists, who then tend to reject Gaia altogether, and from the perspective of some theologians, who revert to a form of pantheism under the guise of innovative Gaia science.[56]

# Ecological Neglect, An Admission

According to both James Nash and Loren Wilkinson, Christianity does bear part of the burden of guilt for the ecological crisis. It is not satisfactory to draw a neat distinction between Christianity and Christendom, between the faith itself and perversions of it by its practitioners. That distinction may be

56. Drummond, "God and Gaia," 282-83.

formally or logically true, but it is unconvincing when applied to history. We cannot so easily distinguish between the faith and its professed followers. The fact is that Christianity — as interpreted and affirmed by billions of its adherents over the centuries and in official practice and Bible interpretation — has not been, as a whole, ecologically sensitive.

Ecological concerns have rarely been a prominent, let alone a dominant, feature in Christian theory and practice. That is true in both the so-called Eastern and Western churches, though less so in the former. In the mainstream Christian traditions in the West, Protestant and Catholic, the ecosphere has generally not been perceived as theologically and ethically important.

For most theologians — Augustine to Luther, Aquinas to Barth, and most of the others in between and before and after — the theological focus has been on sin and salvation, the fall and redemption, the divine-human relationship over against the biophysical world as a whole.

There has tended to be a dualism between the material and spiritual in different degrees in most historical strains of Christian thought and practice — a dualism that has tended to neglect or negate nature.

Paul Santmire goes so far as to state: "In the nineteenth and early twentieth centuries, Protestant theology by and large washed its hands of nature . . . and thereby gave the spirit of modern industrialism its 'de facto' permission — sometimes its 'de jure' encouragement — to work its will on nature." This same description is applicable to Roman Catholic and Orthodox emphases.[57]

## Oversimplification and Exaggeration

James Nash points out that New Age statements tend to reduce the explanation of the complex ecological crisis to a single cause. They also exaggerate the authority of Christianity in cultures and minimize the fact that non-Christian cultures also have been environmental despoilers. In addition, they overlook the number of dissenting opinions in Christian history and underestimate the potential for ecological reform in Christianity.

Examples of ecological sensitivity can be found among the early medieval Celtic saints. The legends of these Irish monks are filled with accounts of mutual affection and service between saints and animals. In the monastic communities of Europe, their practices were remembered, celebrated, and imitated — including the stories of their affectionate relationship with non-human creatures. Their sacramental sense of the natural world as the place of

57. James A. Nash, *Loving Nature: Ecological Integrity and Christian Responsibility* (Nashville: Abingdon, 1991), 72-74.

divine presence and revelation ran deep; their appreciation of that world as the creation of God was intense.

Francis of Assisi is frequently treated as a nearly isolated example of ecological responsibility in a sea of Christian exploitation of nature. Though sometimes innovative, his expressions and actions were "some of the grandest and most explicit manifestations and elaborations of common presuppositions" of his time.

Francis genuinely loved the Creator, the creation, and its creatures, and he expressed that love with extravagant friendship, compassion, tenderness, kindness, and even sacrifice.

Francis's integrated affinities did not stop with the animal world; they were inclusive and cosmos centered. The sun, moon, water, fire, plants, and rocks were greeted as siblings because he shared with them a common Source. His affinities with nature are understood not as an alien addition to the gospel, but rather as an appropriate and even essential extension of it.

Members of the Evangelical movement in England in the latter part of the eighteenth century, especially Quakers and Methodists, were in the forefront of the struggle against cruelty to animals.[58]

In 1992, Vice President Al Gore published a book entitled *Earth in the Balance: Ecology and the Human Spirit.* As indicated by the book's subtitle — *Ecology and the Human Spirit* — Gore believes that the current ecological crisis is actually a *spiritual* problem. Gore writes: "The more deeply I search for the roots of the global environmental crisis, the more I am convinced that it is an outer manifestation of an inner crisis that is, for lack of a better word, spiritual." In an interview with *Christianity Today,* Gore said, "The foundation of all of my work on the environment is my faith in Jesus Christ." However, as Ron Rhodes points out, Gore also finds concern for the environment in most of the world religions, including the Mother Earth religions.[59]

This list is only a sample of the substream of Christian ecological consciousness, which appears throughout Christian-influenced cultures. It provides significant evidence against the charge that Christianity has always been historically or is inherently an anti-ecological faith.

## Ecological Disasters in Other Faiths

Ecological crises are not peculiar to Christian-influenced cultures. Non-Christian cultures have also caused severe or irreparable harm to their ecosys-

58. Ibid., 74, 83-87.
59. Ron Rhodes, *The Culting of America* (Eugene, Ore.: Harvest House, 1994), 147-48.

tems. Ecological mismanagement is not the property of areas of Christian influence, nor exclusively of modern technology. Over-grazing, deforestation, and similar errors of sufficient magnitude to destroy civilizations (and ecosystems) have been committed by Egyptians, Assyrians, Romans, North Africans, Persians, Indians, Aztecs, and Buddhists. Thomas Derr adds: "We are simply being gullible when we take at face value the advertisement for the ecological harmony of non-Western cultures." Historically, for instance, there seems to be an "intractable ambiguity" about the ecological norms and practices of Native American cultures and religions.

The near-universality of ecological problems suggests that the roots of the crisis are not just in theological affirmations themselves, but also in human character.[60]


# THE CHRISTIAN RESPONSE

## A Commitment to Reformation and Renewal

Classic Christianity assumes enduring fidelity to the intentions of faith in the central affirmations found in the apostolic witnesses in Scripture. But Christianity is not otherwise bound to its past — to its various interpretations in its history. It stands ready to correct the corruptions of the past.

Historically, the Christian faith has shown a remarkable capacity for flexibility, for extensions of the applications of its doctrines, and for reinterpretations based on new insights into Scripture.

Christian groups have also used elements from the cultures in which they were embedded to express their understanding of the Christian faith. The Patristic theologians, for example, utilized aspects of the metaphysics and often the mythologies of their milieus to communicate the gospel.

In other words, the Christian churches have had a history of and a capacity for self-reformation. "Always Reforming" was a Protestant motto in the post-Reformation period. New light, new truth is always breaking forth from the Scriptures through the Holy Spirit. The Spirit cannot be closeted. This capacity for change means that the Christian churches can and should reinterpret their main themes to develop a solid, theological grounding for an ecological ethic. That development is a refutation of the New Age ecological complaint against Christianity.

James Nash contends that the Christian churches do not need a new worldview (such as the New Age view) to undergird worthy ecological integ-

60. Nash, *Loving Nature*, 88-89, 91.

rity. Christianity should not abandon its key biblical doctrines. Ecological responsibility does not require the abandonment or replacement of Christianity's main theological themes. "New" or "radical" or "imported" theologies are not necessary.[61]

Rather, Christianity should extend and reinterpret these main biblical themes in ways that preserve their historic identity and are consistent with ecological data. The important point is that Christian theology can remain loyal to the intentions of faith in the historic affirmations of the biblical faith while developing a genuinely ecological theology. In fact, in reaction to eco-feminist critique of Judeo-Christianity, many new books on the care of the earth have been published, such as Richard D. Land and Louis A. Moore, eds., *The Earth Is the Lord's: Christians and the Environment* (Nashville: Broadman, 1992) and Shannon Jung, *We Are Home: A Spirituality of the Environment* (New York: Paulist, 1993). Berit Kjos suggests many ecological family projects in *Under the Spell of Mother Earth* (Wheaton: Victor, 1993).[62]

## Christianity's Answer to the Ecological Crisis

James Nash, executive director of the Center for Theology and Public Policy, affirms that classical biblical doctrines have the potential to become an indestructibly firm foundation for ecological integrity. The basic doctrines contain all things necessary for such integrity. Indeed, nothing short of that integrity is compatible with authentic representations of the Christian faith. It is important and should be helpful to point out the ecological affirmations embedded in representative doctrines of the biblical faith. A "creation theology" is insufficient as an ecological grounding; other doctrinal foundations need to be included.[63]

Nash provides a helpful summary of the main theological supports for Christian ecological ethics and action:

1. The Christian teachings of God as Creator, Spirit, and Redeemer imply that the whole creation and all its creatures are valued and loved by God. Divine valuations appear to be centered on the cosmos and on nature, not just simply on people. Since loyalty to God entails loyalty to God's values, Christians are called to practice "earth love." All life forms have intrinsic value and are to be treated with appropriate care and concern.

61. Ibid., 91-94.
62. Spencer, *Goddess Revival*, 264.
63. Nash, *Loving Nature*, 93-94.

2. The biblical faith teaches that no element of the biophysical world is divine; nothing in nature, therefore, is to be worshiped. However, since God created all creatures and things, they are to be treated as sacred subjects and objects. They are to be used reverently and respectfully insofar as necessary, and otherwise to be left untouched.

3. The Christian teaching recognizes a rational and moral order of interdependence and a God-centered kinship of all creation. Humans are interrelated parts and products of nature. Moral responsibilities for the necessary use of the biophysical world are shaped and limited by these relationships.

4. Humans are unique and made in God's image and have "natural" rights to use biophysical goods as resources to satisfy human needs and fulfill our cultural potential. However, we also have moral responsibilities to use these resources frugally, fairly, and prudently in respect for our co-created animal kin.

5. According to biblical teaching, the biophysical world has an interim goodness in experience and an ultimate goodness in hope. It is not to be despised, rejected, or transcended, either spiritually or materially.

6. Human dominion or stewardship is not a sanction for the exploitation of nature, but a judgment on such exploitation. As a dimension of the image of God, dominion is responsible representation, reflecting the divine love, including justice, in all relationships with humanity and the rest of the biophysical world. Dominion involves protecting this planet (and every other planet) from human abuse.

7. From the biblical perspective, all forms of ecological negligence or undue harm — from pollution to profligate consumption — are expressions of sin.

8. The biblical faith notes causal connections between ecological disorders and human violations of the ecological covenant. Christians can thus understand God as exercising ecological judgments against ecological sins to call the human community to ecological repentance.

9. In the broad biblical context, ecological responsibility should be seen as an inherent part of the ministry of the church, which is called to re-present God's ministry of love to all creation and to be a sign of God's reign of love. The church, therefore, is called upon to be a model of ecological ministries to the world. The ministry entails frugality, equity, and humility.

10. According to Nash, an urgent and difficult task in the development of a Christian ecological ethic is an adequate interpretation of Christian love in an ecological context. This emphasis is essential because love is the integrating center of the whole of Christian faith and ethics. This ecological love must recognize the uniqueness of humans made

in God's image. Thus Christians affirm that human values are primary. However, we should deny any claim that only humans have value. Other creatures also have intrinsic value — for themselves and for God — which warrants respect from human beings. Thus, Christian love makes serious ethical demands upon human beings in ecological interactions.

11. Christian responses to ecological problems should be developed in the light of biblical commitments to justice. Justice is a prominent theme in the originating source of Christian norms. While justice is a prominent theme in the Old Testament, it is also clearly visible in the New. Justice is not an option for Christians, but a moral imperative. The Lover of Justice sets no boundaries on justice. The gospel we are called to incarnate relates to all creatures in all situations.[64]

In emphasizing ecological justice, Kathryn Tanner, a professor of theology at Yale, points out that more factors than usual will have to be taken into account when considering environmental issues. Questions of human justice, for example, will have to be included. Thus, North American worries about the destruction of Brazilian rain forests cannot be acted upon without considering the plight of the Brazilian underclasses who have been encouraged to farm there as one of their only hopes for economic advancement. The challenge to be concerned about the preservation of rain forests should therefore lead to questions concerning national and global economies in relation to the income and survival of the Brazilian underclass. Furthermore, the decisions reached will often remain agonizing. In some cases, the well-being of both the human and nonhuman cannot be achieved at once.

According to Tanner, Christians in our time have been brought to a new understanding of the environmental movement. Environmental concerns have historically been disassociated from concerns about justice issues. But for Christians, concerns for environmental well-being, on the one hand, and sensitivity to issues of human justice, on the other, should not be alternatives. Christians, because of their own distinctive starting point in beliefs about God and the world, can encourage a perspective that combines worries about the environment and a just society within a single focus of moral concern. They can help to support a movement of ecological justice.[65]

Catherine Keller, of Drew Theological Seminary, believes that a responsible Christian eschatology is an ecological eschatology. It motivates work — preaching, teaching, modeling, organizing, politics, prayer — to save our planet. It inspires and challenges the caretaking, biblically referred

64. Nash, *Loving Nature*, 137-39, 149-51, 163-66.
65. Chopp and Taylor, *Reconstructing Christian Theology*, 120-22.

to as stewardship, to which we, the human component of creation, are called. Keller calls for a recycled eschatology, an ecoeschatology. This emphasis roots eschatology in the ongoing (albeit so far hideously neglected and thwarted) call of stewardship for the groaning creation. This particular dimension of an eschatological ethic is clear and is revealed to us now in a way that it could not have been during the biblical periods, when nature still laid claim to a certain ferocious inexhaustibility. Indeed, as earthbound Christians, we may indeed embrace a utopian realism. We are bound to the rhythms of earth and its indelible history, but nonetheless still "bound for the promised land" — a promising place (and time) that is the final healing of this one.[66]

Rebecca McLeod of Yale, in lectures at Wheaton College, said that evangelicals believe that the ecological movement — as it is understood by many — poses a profound threat to their central view of God. For many religious environmentalists, there was an urgency "to test" their particular faith to see how it fared in light of the new revelation of the ecological crisis. If environmentalists needed to make revisions, they usually were inclined to abandon religious purity rather than a so-called scientific understanding of the religion of ecology. Many newly converted environmentalists expressed a willingness or an openness to explore and, if necessary, modify or reject traditional tenets of their religion or their faith altogether. Evangelicals or others who were not willing to alter their own religious beliefs were concerned that perhaps their fellow believers might be tempted to capitulate. There was, therefore, at least the impression that even among religiously or spiritually devout people, the science of ecology threatened religion.

In particular, the aggregate, unifying, interconnecting marrow of ecology tended to grow into some type of pantheism, according to many religious environmentalists. For example, according to biologist David Barash, "remarkable parallels exist between ecology and Zen Buddhism." Zen rejected the Western dichotomies between intellect and emotion, God and creation, spirit and flesh, sin and redemption, humans and nature. In fact, Barash concluded: "The very study of ecology . . . is the elaboration of Zen's nondualistic thinking." It was the *perception* of this phenomenon that deeply concerned evangelicals. Their traditional Judeo-Christian, monotheistic theology was under attack.

Evangelicals noted that some environmentalists found ancient paganism and some Eastern religious paganism to be more desirable from the ecological perspective than the Judeo-Christian Yahweh. Arnold Toynbee, for instance, found that his education in Latin and pre-Christian Greek literature influenced his perspective far more than his Christian upbringing. For him,

66. Ibid., 328, 343.

the Greek gods Dionysus, Demeter, Zeus, and Poseidon were reasserting their power because they demonstrated that humans "cannot pollute soil, air, and water with impunity." Therefore, the solution to ecological crisis for Toynbee meant "reverting from the worldview of monotheism to the worldview of pantheism, which [was] older and was once universal."

The harmonic, "less-aggressive" trends that some environmentalists found helpful included a number of traditions that were often blended into some kind of pantheistic appreciation of the environment. These included, among other groups, Zen Buddhism, Hinduism, Confucianism, Taoism, Yoga, Shinto, the ancient Greek cults, and various American Indian religions.[67]

# A THEOLOGY OF CREATION

Evangelicals were somewhat forced to explore and develop a "theology of creation." Lynn White and others had charged that the Judeo-Christian tradition put all its emphasis on humans and none on nature. Another factor prompting them to make known their stand on creation was the link between the belief that everything, plants and humans, is God (pantheism) and the science of ecology as it was developing in the environmental movement. For some evangelicals this meant becoming vocal about the importance of nature in the biblical view. For others, it meant bringing practice into line with existing doctrines. For most it meant that there was more than enough room for clarification on the subject. But for all evangelicals, the situation produced nothing short of a mandate to speak out clearly on the position of conservative Christianity on the environment.[68]

One of the earliest and most prominent evangelical writers on religion and the environment was Francis A. Schaeffer. In his 1970 *Pollution and the Death of Man*, Schaeffer argued against both the White thesis and pantheism in general. Schaeffer agreed with White that Christendom had not been as ecologically sensitive as it should have been, but disagreed with him about why. Schaeffer contended that it was not because Scripture advocated an exploitative mandate, but because the church had failed to live up to its true biblical calling as laid down in Genesis. Thus evangelical scholars — true to their orthodoxy — wanted to maintain scriptural integrity and purity by positioning any blame on tainted human efforts. So they called for a rediscovery

67. Rebecca L. M. McCleod, "A Peculiar People and Pantheism: Evangelicals and the Rise of Religious Environmentalism, 1960s-1970s," Wheaton College, April 1, 1995, 5, 8-12.

68. Ibid., 16.

of creation theology. Schaeffer commented that the concept of creation was "the beginning of the Christian view of nature." In the beginning was God. He was there before anything else, including the origin of time. God created everything by speaking it into existence. He did not begin with some organic matter or solution floating around the universe. He made the world and its universe out of nothing — *creatio ex nihilo*. Contrary to pantheistic belief, the cosmos was not an extension of the creator or a part of anything else. It was God's unique creation.[69]

Lynn White contended that according to the Christian doctrine of creation, only God was sacred. Thus God remained transcendent over nature, which allowed humans to regard it as insignificant. Evangelical writers affirmed God's deity and transcendence, but rejected the notion that his attributes led to careless treatment of his creation. On the contrary, they argued that the environment should be treated reverently precisely because God made it. They did not think that the environment had to share God's nature in order for it to be regarded with dignity. More than anything else, a high view of God's transcendence countered any kind of pantheism.

Not only was creation distinct from God's essence, it was good. Susan Power Bratton, an evangelical biologist then working for the National Park Service, pointed to God's favorable pronouncement on creation as evidence that God himself did not belittle the natural order. For example, six times in the first chapter of Genesis after God had made something new, he "saw that it was good." Five of these times occurred before God made Adam. Thus God deemed creation good, independent of humans.

Evangelicals continued their development of a theology of creation by exploring God's relationship with the natural order. They said that God entered into a personal and covenantal relationship with the cosmos at creation and maintained it throughout history. For evangelicals, God was the source of the unity of the system, and all creation depended on him. Colossians 1:17 declares that God "is before all things, and in him all things hold together." Schaeffer observed, therefore, that the Judeo-Christian God was different from any other god. He was personal, infinite, and able to hold the universe lovingly in his hands.

Based on the flood account, evangelicals concluded that God cared for the natural order since he provided for its salvation along with humanity's. Moreover, God entered into a covenant with it. As part of creation, it was on a par with humans. The rainbow was a sign of this covenant. God did not simply create the environment at the beginning of time and then ignore it. He continues to care for it and all its creatures.

69. Ibid., 16, 17; see also Francis A. Schaeffer, *Pollution and the Death of Man — The Christian View of Ecology* (Wheaton, Ill.: Tyndale, 1970), 47-61.

Evangelicals also quote biblical passages which demonstrate God's concern for animals (Ps. 104:21; 148; Prov. 12:10; Matt. 10:29; Luke 12:6; 15).[70]

Richard T. Wright, a professor at Gordon College, has identified himself as a Christian and a biologist. He notes that Psalm 104 was crucial for indicating how nature related to God. The psalmist described the totality of the environment as the clothing of God. It was God's glory, and it covered him with splendor and majesty. The psalmist wrote, "Let the glory of the LORD endure forever." Others concurred with Wright that there could hardly have been a stronger environmental admonition in Scripture. The environment needs protection because it is God's splendid panoply, his covering. Like God, it should last forever.

## Creation and the Fall

Wright provides the setting for the human aspect of the biblical drama documented in Genesis, as it is related to ecology. By Word and Wisdom, God created the heavens and the earth and populated them with an amazing array of living creatures. Although all of creation glorifies God and was declared by him to be good, God made one species — humankind — in his image, and gave them dominion — rulership — over the rest of creation. This dominion included the responsibility to develop a culture ("subdue the earth") and to care for the creation as his representatives — stewardship. But the first people — Adam and Eve — were led by Satan into sin; they rebelled against God. Doubting God's word to them, they asserted their freedom and reached for forbidden knowledge.

This rebellion, described in Genesis, brought profound consequences: sin would continue to plague us and deeply mar our ability to image God, and through our sin the rest of creation would be affected. In particular, our sin alienated us from God, from our fellow human beings, and from the rest of the created order. We speak of the world as a "fallen world," and rightfully assign to the Fall all of the misery, pain, and suffering that continue to afflict our race. Most of this is traced directly to the effects of sin on the way in which we have carried out the cultural mandate. Not only are individuals sinful, but the very structures of society have incorporated the results of human sin.

---

70. McLeod, "A Peculiar People and Pantheism," 17-18, 21, 23-24; see also Schaeffer, *Pollution and the Death of Man*, 57.

## Redemption as Reformation and Healing

The good news is that God has not abandoned his works of creation. The Bible speaks to us of God's redemptive concern for humankind, and this concern extends to all of creation. The redemptive word of his Son, Jesus Christ, makes possible the reconciliation of the relationships broken by the Fall. That which was broken can be made whole. God invites us as individuals to come over to his side — to be reconciled. And as his stewards, we are privileged to participate in redeeming the creation.

This redemptive task has two major dimensions: a reforming work and a healing work. The culture must be reformed — brought into conformity to God's law; and the creation must be healed — restored to ecological wholeness. When Jesus came, he announced the arrival of the Kingdom of God. God's Kingdom is under way, and the reforming and healing work we are called to is identified as Kingdom work.

Finally, as we trace the flow of time into the future, the Bible speaks of a time when peace will reign and justice will prevail, a future when the creation will be purified of its corruption. At this time, the Kingdom of God will reveal itself in its final and intended manifestation, and the creation will be whole.[71]

## Ecological Stewardship

Roger Olson emphasizes that the earliest Christians understood the resurrection of Jesus Christ as the down payment on the final and complete liberation of all creation from its bondage to decay and of the perfect transformation of the cosmos into God's kingdom of glory in which God will be "all in all." A recovery of this dimension of the resurrection can contribute to an enriching of evangelical concern for and involvement in the stewardship of nature.

Unfortunately, many recent theological works on Christian ecology ignore or downplay a strong biblical and resurrection foundation. Some borrow on pagan images such as the "Mother Goddess" myth, or seek their biblical-theological foundation in the doctrine of creation rather than the model of the new creation anticipated in Jesus' bodily resurrection.

Rosemary Ruether's *God and Gaia* represents an ecofeminist theology of earth healing which totally ignores the resurrection and practically deifies nature. It is of little help to evangelical pastors or laypeople who wish to develop a sound biblical view of ecology.

71. Richard T. Wright, *Biology through the Eyes of Faith* (New York: HarperCollins, 1989), 251-52.

For Olson, what is needed is a biblically informed systematic theology of nature aimed at a Christian ecological stewardship which brings together in intimate interdependence the themes of resurrection, liberation, eschatology, and ecology.[72]

The apostle Paul brings together important biblical themes related to ecology. In summary, Paul teaches in Romans 1:18-20 that God may be known experientially from God's creation, not only from inanimate nature, but also from animate nature, humans, birds, four-footed animals, and reptiles. Although creation is fallen, Paul still stresses the clarity of God's self-revelation. Therefore, God's "everlasting" (not temporary) power and divinity can be seen thoroughly when contemplated by receptive wills. Nevertheless, special revelation is still indispensable. Because of the testimony of creation, humans are left with the bad news that they are accountable for their impiety to God. They have no defense. Therefore, Gentiles and Jews alike need to hear the good news that they may become righteous through faith in Jesus the Messiah, proclaimed by the prophets of old and by believers in face-to-face proclamations.[73]

For Paul, the natural universe is "creation" and therefore God's. God is its author and sustainer. However, something has gone terribly wrong with God's creation. It has been subjected to futility by coming into bondage to decay. Paul's theology of the "fall" is not limited to the human story but widens to encompass all of natural created reality. In his description of fallen creation, described in Romans 8:19-24, Paul compares the universe to a prisoner serving a life sentence and yearning with every fiber of its being for deliverance, and to a woman in birth pangs looking forward to the new life to come forth from the struggle.

A part of the fallenness of nature is its *openness* to being raped by humans. The actual rape of nature by humans is another shackle added to its imprisonment and another cause for its groaning.

Of course, the final liberation of nature involves a transformation to a hardly imaginable new corporeal existence analogous to Jesus' bodily existence after his resurrection. Meanwhile, as in a Christian's personal life, the resurrection of Jesus and the work of the Holy Spirit have implications for the present. They form the ethical ground and basis for a future-oriented ethic of environmental stewardship or "earth-keeping."[74]

In light of Paul's theology of promised cosmic liberation in Romans 8, Christians must recognize nature as part of God's redemptive plan and

---

72. Roger E. Olson, "Resurrection, Cosmic Liberation, and Christian Earth Keeping," in *Ex Auditu* (Allison Park, Pa.: Pickwick, 1994), 123, 125.

73. Spencer, *Goddess Revival,* 161.

74. Olson, "Resurrection, Cosmic Liberation," 126.

action, and proclamation and social action must extend in that direction under correct spiritual and theological principles.

According to Barbara Reid, professor of New Testament Studies at the Catholic Theological Union and a Grand Rapids Dominican, in Romans 8:18-30 Paul says not only that the person of faith will be transformed but also that "creation itself will be set free from its bondage to decay and will obtain the freedom of the glory of the children of God" (8:21). Paul ascribes to creation the same ends and desires as human creatures. As humanity waits (8:23, 25) in hope (8:24-25), groaning for the fullness of redemption (8:23), so creation awaits (8:19) in hope (8:20), groaning (8:22) to be set free (8:21).[75]

## The Importance of Sacrifice and Suffering

Thomas Berry, a prominent Christian ecologist, states that the reshaping of all aspects of our existence for the Ecozoic Age cannot occur without our willingness to accept sacrifice. "Sacrifice is the idea that whatever is achieved has a price," he explains. According to Reid, here is where New Testament theology can make a significant contribution to the Ecozoic Age. The sacrifice of the life of Christ on the cross for the life of all is the essence of the Christian message. Central to Paul is the theology of the cross. Although Paul's language is different from Berry's, the thought of the smaller self being sacrificed to the larger self can be seen in a number of Pauline texts, such as Philippians 2:3-11 and 2 Corinthians 8:9.

For survival into the Ecozoic Age, we must resonate with Paul, who says in 1 Corinthians 1:18, "the message about the cross is foolishness to those who are perishing, but to us who are being saved it is the power of God." If we do not strengthen our inner capacity to act in the sacrificial mode, the alternative, says Berry, is a destructive mode in which we attempt to overcome the limits and rhythms and conditions of the planet with technology.[76]

The proper direction for the Christian is realistic identification with nature in its suffering. Peter Stuhlmacher has pointed in this direction: "In the midst of the ecological crisis, it is [the Christian] task to prevent God's creation from being completely victimized by civilization or from being deified by the apostles of nature who are hostile to civilization."

Karl Heim states that if we do not transpose the power of the risen Christ into action, then we live in an illusion. Our confession of the Risen One is not genuine if it does not immediately and naturally place us in an

---

75. Richard N. Fragomeni and John T. Pawlikowski, eds., *The Ecological Challenge* (Collegeville, Minn.: Liturgical, 1994), 21.

76. Ibid., 22-23.

attitude of responsibility for the terrestrial reality in which we find ourselves according to God's ordinance.

Not only does the resurrection affirm life on earth (nature), but it also forbids any shallow optimism. The earth and nature must be transformed. In the ultimate and final end, God must redeem nature supernaturally. Just as the Kingdom of God among men and women cannot happen merely by social engineering, so the new earth cannot appear merely through ecological activism. However, the resurrection provides the hope that sustains fervent effort to approximate the new, liberated creation which lies in the future.

Liberation is God's activity, and its approximation in anticipation is delegated to us. That leads Christians to ecological concern and practice under the dynamics of the resurrection as an empowering force. What shape might this resurrection-based action take? First, the church must seek to raise Christian consciousness about the groaning of creation and its need for liberation. Second, the church must become a "community of light" in the midst of a darkening of nature. The church needs to hold up a prophetic example and show society that the body of Christ cares about the future of nature. Third, the church must make concrete and specific proposals for a better future for nature.[77]

## Redeeming the Creation

Dominion over creation is the delegated responsibility to rule as God's image bearers. Creation continues to belong to its Creator, and the concept of stewardship captures well the proper relationship of humankind to the rest of the natural order. An implication of this task is that as God's stewards we are responsible for the welfare of creation. We are to serve and preserve it — and love it — even while we make use of it for our culture-building purposes.

Many people today are seeking and finding firm knowledge of the workings of natural ecosystems and the ways that human activities interact with those systems. In fact, most of the essential information is already in our grasp. Yet the human population continues to expand, and the pollutants continue to be poured out on the land and into the air and the water.

A missing factor is provided by the biblical worldview. This factor is a dynamic vision of humankind as steward over the rest of the natural order. Radical biblical stewardship elevates stewardly action over political and economic concerns. The global world economy, based as it is on profit-making and not on justice or stewardship, has become dominant. Economist Bob Goudzwaard has called the ideology of economic growth one of the dominant gods of our time — we have worshiped at its feet, and it has betrayed us.

77. Olson, "Resurrection, Cosmic Liberation," 130-32.

Richard Wright reiterates that the Kingdom of God will come. God has acted in history to redeem his creation. Although that redemption will not be complete until the return of Christ, we as God's people have the responsibility to act as God's agents in demonstrating what the Kingdom is like and, to the extent possible, bringing the Kingdom to reality in this world. Our work is a reforming task; the Fall has corrupted both human culture and the created world, and both are in need of the healing word of *shalom*, the restoration of wholeness.[78]

## The Biblical Ecological Challenge

Thus we see that Bible-honoring evangelicals have developed or can develop a systematic theology of creation. In doing so, they reaffirm Christianity's ability to engender environmental sensitivity. In the process they are gaining confidence in their position. Not only was Lynn White inaccurate and pantheism untenable, but evangelicals believe that only Christianity provides the correct view of God, humans, and nature. Ultimately, only from a biblical metaphysic can one properly understand and participate in all of reality, which includes nature, culture, and the divine. Hopefully this evangelical view will be understandable and compelling to Christians and non-Christians alike. According to Steven Bouma-Prediger, given both the crisis of our age and the demands of biblical faith, Christians must enthusiastically and vigorously act in ways that are in harmony with a Christian ecological theology. Many technological competencies are available to those who are committed to being good stewards of the earth. Beneath the competencies will lie some deep understanding of the world. The Christian understanding is the ideal one; it teaches us neither to deify the planet nor to defile it, but to care for it responsibly.[79]

Compared with the New Age and secular worldviews, the biblical worldview with its holistic teachings and its dynamic vision of Christian stewardship provides a divinely revealed theoretical and practical ecological vision for the present and for the future.

---

78. Wright, *Biology through the Eyes of Faith*, 260-62, 264-65.

79. McCleod, "A Peculiar People and Pantheism," 24; see also Steven Bouma-Prediger, *The Greening of Theology* (Atlanta: Scholars Press, 1995), 301-2; and Fisher Humphreys, "All Creatures of Our God and King," *The Theological Educator*, Spring 1995, 58.

# CHAPTER EIGHT

# *Health and the New Age Worldview*

The New Age view on health is dominated, if not controlled, by a consistent and systematic form of spirituality that is radically opposed to biblical Christianity. This does not mean that holistic medicine can be dismissed by the Christian community or that the movement's answers to all the complex questions concerning illness, health, and health care can simply be discarded. Nevertheless, like a compass, a holistic approach does help sort out insights that are contrary to the biblical worldview.

Biblical Christians agree that physical health involves a unity of body, mind, and spirit.

The broader term "holistic health" refers to a wide range of alternative approaches to health care which emphasize spiritual and psychological as well as the physical dimensions of personal health. People who promote holistic health see it as a corrective response to traditional, or allopathic, medicine's major focus on the physical aspects of health.[1]

## DENIAL OF GOD AS CREATOR AND HEALER

The primary trait of a New Age–oriented approach to health and healing is its denial of God as Creator and healer. In the New Age worldview, God is not necessarily a person, and God is not separate from humanity and the universe. The authority shift — from without to within — is related to New

1. Hank Hanegraaff, *SCP Journal*, August 1978, 15.

Age "selfism." Healing comes from within, from one's own body — as spiritual energy.

The matter of modality, or specific healing techniques, is more complicated. Most New Age health techniques are filled with subtle and complex spiritual implications which derive from the humanistic, occult, or religious worldviews of their originators. Most of them are designed to produce novel states of consciousness which are interpreted to the patient in ways that seem to validate the worldview of the originator. To the extent that these considerations are ignored or remain unanalyzed, they are capable of eroding the intellectual and experiential foundations of Christian faith. As a practical matter the "accompanying New Age philosophical system" will usually be conveyed by the person who administers the treatment.

It is generally accepted that none of the Eastern or occult healing techniques are "neutral" in themselves, even when ostensibly divorced from overt philosophical statements. The metaphysical framework from which they emerge is so pervasive and encompassing that every detail of practice is intricately related to elements of the underlying belief system. As a result, the technique taken as a whole will carry overtones and implications of the metaphysical system from which it is derived, even if that system is not explicitly discussed.

In other words, the religious point of view embodied in the New Age health movement is an integral part of the occult/mystical worldview that is making its way into every aspect of our cultural consciousness. It is not a fad. It will not go away. And it is fundamentally hostile to biblical Christianity.

Former New Age health leader Randall N. Baer contends that the New Age health movement has been making steady, vigorous inroads into mainstream society. From more obviously metaphysically oriented health practices to mainstream health care, the field of holistic health has been a primary carrier of Westernized occultism and Eastern philosophies into American culture. This trend has been steady over the last two decades and shows no sign of letup.[2]

# PUBLIC FUNDS FOR NEW AGE TEACHING

An important part of the New Age health movement's strategy is based on an effort to bend the structures of government and public policy in its behalf — to enlist the state in the propagation of its religious vision for humanity.

2. Ibid., 15-17; see also Paul Heelas, *The New Age Movement* (Cambridge, Mass.: Blackwell, 1996), 82. Randall N. Baer, *Inside the New Age Nightmare* (Lafayette, La.: Huntington, 1989), 20-21.

Public funding is already being sought — and obtained — for teaching New Age concepts to various audiences, professional and otherwise. This policy raises serious constitutional problems in terms of separation of church and state.

According to Paul Reisser, holistic health is, in essence, the banner under which the New Age consciousness is making its move into the realm of health and medicine. Indeed, the holistic health movement does not appear nearly as concerned with changing the way medicine is practiced as it is with changing the fundamental orientation of people toward themselves, the universe, and especially the supernatural realm.[3]

The disillusionment of Baer with New Age emphases led him to accept the biblical worldview. From his inside view, he states that, in general, biblical Christianity is dismissed by New Agers as a limited, exclusivistic, narrow-minded relic of an age now past. Little serious consideration is given by New Agers to the profound theological differences that stand between them and Christianity. They repudiate Christianity as antiquated and limited and so distorted as to merit little-to-no serious, open-minded thought or investigation. In fact, J. Randolph Price, New Age writer and primary inspirer and organizer of numerous large-scale World Peace Meditation events, asserts that those who deny "the divinity of all men" (in other words, humans are gods) are of the "Antichrist."

Following this line of reasoning, Price is saying that those who oppose the coming "New World Order" — those Christians, Jews, and others who resist this thinking — are by definition of a "lower vibratory rate" and thereby are blocking the fullness of the New Age from happening.[4]

For most of human history, the diagnosis and treatment of bodily malfunctions have belonged to the realm of the supernatural. Indeed, if a history of the world's medicine were to give equal time to each century of the last five thousand years, most of it would be a Who's Who of mystics, faith healers, gurus, and shamans (the medicine man/priest of primitive societies). Only in the recent past has the study of the human body been separated somewhat from a supernatural overlay.

---

3. Paul C. Reisser, *The Holistic Healers* (Downers Grove, Ill.: InterVarsity Press, 1983), 12-13.

4. Baer, *Inside the New Age Nightmare,* 169.

# THE SCIENTIFIC METHOD

What we call the scientific method, that process of observing, hypothesizing, experimenting, and revising old ideas with new evidence, gained ground slowly but eventually became preeminent in Western civilization as the primary approach to health and disease. Since the seventeenth century, Western medicine has been based on the Cartesian philosophy of dualism — the separation of mind and body. The Cartesian split between science and religion led medicine down the path of gaining knowledge by observation and experiment and the treatment of symptoms. With the rise of medical faculties at European and American universities, the view of illness as a strictly biophysical defect gradually took hold. The application of scientific, or allegedly scientific, methods to the diagnosis and treatment of diseases forced the spiritual dimensions of healing more and more to the periphery. This approach to health science tended to see the human body primarily as a biological mechanism. Thus diseases were considered to be physical changes in the biological organism resulting from an intrusion of germs, or the breakdown of the body-machine due to cold, fatigue, or the lack of proper food.[5]

David Fetcho states that we tend to regard our bodies in much the same way we regard our automobiles. The body is good for only two things: pleasure and productivity. This view relates to the heart of the predicament of the medical establishment in the West today. As the average person has come to regard his or her body as an alien "instrument," the worth of which is in utility or pleasure, so he or she has come to gauge the "health" of the body according to whether or not it works or feels good. When the body malfunctions, its illness is most likely regarded in isolation from the total circumstance of the patient's life, which may in fact be contributing to the dysfunction.

For example, a person suffering from intense headaches and failing eyesight may be unable or unwilling to make the connection between his ailments and the fact that he works in a noisy factory at a high-pressure job which he basically hates. Because society is managed mainly by technical experts, both the suffering person and the physician already share an implicit understanding of what must be done. The patient must be "fixed" (or at least the symptoms of his ailment obscured) so that he can resume his normal routine without discomfort. He will probably be given a tranquilizing drug to round off the edges of his experience at work and to make him better able to cope at home. The remedy prescribed and accepted addresses the problem only at the symptomatic level in a mechanistic fashion. Only in the most severe case will the physician advise the patient to quit his dehumanizing job

5. Harvey Cox, *Fire from Heaven* (Reading, Mass.: Addison-Wesley, 1995), 108.

or take an extended vacation. Both the patient and the physician have had their view of human life conditioned by the technocratic society. Their presuppositions about what constitutes adequate health care are defined in advance. The person must be kept on the job. "Life," thus defined, must go on.[6]

The broad picture for most Americans, until recently, has been to seek a sophisticated complex of trained professionals and institutions — what we call the health care system. This is the familiar world of doctors and hospitals, of X-rays, drugs, and surgery, the product of the scientific advances of the last few hundred years. The successes of this system are indisputable, and, at least until recently, its physicians and technologists enjoyed almost godlike status in society.

The unintended result of the wrenching apart of healing and spirituality was that the human body came to be thought of as an object of analysis and observation. Led by the scientific community, people lost sight of the patient as "self," to say nothing of the patient as "spirit." Any mutual exchange between the healer and the healed almost disappeared as the physician became increasingly powerful and the sick person was defined as feeble and incapable. As the medical establishment tightened its monopoly on diagnosis and prescription, it also expanded the area under its control. Soon aspects of human life related to health problems that had once had a personal dimension were "medicalized."[7]

## ALTERNATIVE MEDICINE
## OPENS DOOR FOR NEW AGE

Claudia Wallis contends that the growth of alternative medicine, now a $27-billion-a-year industry, is more than just an American flirtation with exotic New Age thinking. It reflects a gnawing dissatisfaction with conventional, or allopathic, medicine. For all its brilliant achievements — the polio vaccine, penicillin, transplant surgery — conventional medicine has some serious weak spots, not the least of which is the endless waiting in paper gowns for doctors who view you as a sore back, an inoperable tumor, or a cardiac case rather than a person. "The problem with modern medicine is that it is only pathology oriented, and practitioners don't take the time to communicate with their patients," says Stephan Rechtschaffen, a medical doctor who uses a preventive approach to healing at the Omega Institute for Holistic Studies in Rhinebeck, New York. "People are fed up with the old answers. They are

---

6. David Fetcho, "Holistic Health; the Sensual Machine; and Thou," *SCP Journal*, August 1978, 7.

7. Cox, *Fire from Heaven*, 108.

beginning to realize that illness does not just drop out of the sky and hit them over the head. Health is an ongoing process."

"Doctors are trained to use drugs and surgery," says internist Dean Ornish of the University of California at San Francisco, who pioneered research into the use of diet, exercise, and meditation to reverse heart disease. Doctors tend to downplay interactions of mind and body. That a patient's state of mind doesn't matter to bacteria is the thinking of conventional medicine. So whether the patient is optimistic or anxiety ridden is of little practical concern. In any case, doctors are often too rushed to find out.[8]

Thus we see that Western medicine is confronted with a new challenge. During the last few years a movement has been growing which argues that the health care system has lost touch with the human soul and spirit. Beginning in the 1960s, the broad humanistic movement and various scientific researches have provided impetus for integration of so-called alternative and conventional medicines. This movement seeks to restore that broken relationship in the everyday practice of medicine. Its leaders call not simply for an overhaul of the way in which medicine is practiced, but for nothing less than a radical revision of the underlying thinking about health and disease. This revision, it is said, includes reuniting modern medicine with its mystical traditions as well as opening it to paranormal phenomena. These and other factors have opened the door for the New Age approach to health.[9]

## TRADITIONAL CHRISTIANITY NEGLECTS ITS HOLISTIC ROOTS

David Maberg contends that the evangelical church has abdicated its healing function. In many instances, the conservative Christian movement disengaged itself from many aspects of the external world, including social and political concerns. It withdrew into a stance that was much more interior and individualistic. Christianity began to define its resolution of the human condition exclusively in terms of the transcendent, the afterlife, and the inner life. The primary focus of salvation became the intellectual and/or emotional, and became external only in the area of personal morality.

This withdrawal happened in the last half of the nineteenth century and was partly a response to the attack on the credibility of orthodox biblical belief by the combined forces of rationalism, science, and liberal theology.

8. Claudia Wallis, "Why New Age Medicine Is Catching On," *Time,* November 1, 1991, 68-69.
9. Reisser, *Holistic Healers,* 10.

Orthodox Christians were very much under siege in those days and felt that an abstract and subjective definition of Christianity would be more defensible. In fact, the shortcomings of traditional medicine and those of conventional Christianity may be more closely related than they appear to be. Medicine abandoned the spiritual dimensions of care because its material successes led doctors to think that all health problems could be solved in a more mechanical way. At the same time, Christians withdrew their attention from the physical and social realms because they half-believed the presumptuous claim that rationalistic science was now lord of the visible world. But it took both of these factors to provide the opening in our collective consciousness that the New Age movement, in the last few years, has been able to enter.

## Mainline Protestant Neglect

On the other hand, mainline Protestantism has emphasized social responsibility, but it has done so almost from a position of despair — based on the conviction that God doesn't intervene directly in human affairs. Miracles are allegorical, and humans are really on their own. If *we* don't solve the problem, nobody will. Anyone who accepts this outlook is left with no awareness whatsoever that there is a God who really exists in the personal sense, who cares about him, and who might want to heal him. That kind of thinking is relegated to the realm of myth or psychological symbolism.

## Fundamentalist Neglect

The idea that God doesn't intervene is ironically echoed by some schools of conservative and fundamentalist theology. Some Christians are convinced that everything came to a screeching halt when John finished the book of Revelation, and that God has declined to intervene in the physical realm since then.

A certain brand of fundamentalism is saying almost the same thing as liberal theology: "God healed physically back then, but he doesn't do that anymore. We're all done with that now."

Brooks Alexander notes that there is a danger in overreacting to the emptiness of liberal theology. You can get a kind of pendulum effect, and Morton Kelsey and others have fallen into that trap in trying to fill the void with psychic phenomena, occult techniques, anything that will produce visible results — including, occasionally, the Holy Spirit.

A different kind of pendulum effect is seen in the viewpoint that most if not all illness is sent from God, and it is therefore wrong to attempt healing.

Surely this attitude is both negative and out of touch with Scripture. That attitude was very commonly held before the advance of scientific medicine, when there was little one could do for most illnesses. It still survives today, however. The underlying idea is that God sends illness as chastisement, to build up patience, or to lead a person to repentance. Suffering becomes a virtue, and anyone who is sick needs to find out what is wrong in his life and get it straight — then things will improve.

Of course, there are passages in the Bible which indicate that God *does* sometimes send disease to further his purposes. Furthermore, even a sickness that is not sent by God may be redeemed by him and used for a person's betterment. At the same time, it is a serious mistake to generalize that concept to cover all illness. Some people benefit from suffering and some do not. In some cases God's purpose in the illness is simply that it be healed "in order that the words of God might be displayed." Even in conservative circles, there has been a reluctance, not so much to pray for people to be healed in a broad psychological sense, but to believe that God might actually do something and intervene in a miraculous way. Because of these attitudes, calling the minister or chaplain to a patient's bedside in case of a serious illness is often seen as the equivalent of having a mortician come in and sign the person up for a gravesite and a coffin.[10]

# CONTRASTING APPROACHES REQUIRE CAUTION

Discerning biblical advocates are cautious about discrediting everything the New Age health movement is saying. Although New Agers often abuse medical, psychological, and spiritual truths in support of a false religious position, due recognition should be given to the truths they are abusing. These abused truths should be "recovered" and revalued within the context of a biblical understanding of reality.

The biblical view would accept the fact that by common grace, various groups and religions, Eastern and Western, primitive and sophisticated, have received truths related to health. For example, Kenneth Cooper, widely acclaimed Christian health specialist, finds help in the work of Herbert Benson, who has drawn widely from Eastern philosophies such as Transcendental Meditation. I was present when Benson introduced the Maharishi Mahish Yogi, the founder of T.M., at a major address in Houston, Texas, in 1973. According to Cooper, Benson, a professor at Harvard Medical School, has identified what he calls the "Faith Factor" in physical and emotional healing.

10. Brooks Alexander, *SCP Journal,* August 1978, 34-35.

In his *Beyond the Relaxation Response,* he defines this Faith Factor as a means of natural healing that is made possible by the interaction of two forces:

1. a strong personal belief system that accepts the importance of caring for the body, and
2. the practice of prayer and meditation as part of those beliefs.

Cooper states that as a Christian and a physician he finds the research conducted by Benson to be quite encouraging because he believes it makes sense that a deep faith, enhanced by a life of prayer and meditation, would have a positive influence on the way our God-given bodies function and heal.[11]

It is the Christian contention that these helpful insights from many cultures are crystallized, historicized, and fulfilled in the biblical view.

# DISCERNMENT IS KEY

The key issue is one of discernment, and that is really a spiritual gift, according to the apostle Paul. Assuming some discernment, however, there are a number of things of importance. One, of course, is the obvious: the need for caring — the need a sick person has to feel cared for. Unfortunately, many holistic proponents exalt this emotional factor of care to a status which is unrealistic, to the point that the power of love becomes more important than the actual treatment. The logical extension of that is to say that loving quackery is better than emotionally neutral competence.[12]

Advocates of the biblical worldview agree that it may be possible to neutralize or even revalue certain New Age health techniques by thoroughly grasping their philosophical derivations, analyzing those derivations carefully, and then replacing them with a framework of biblical understanding. This would be a delicate and difficult undertaking because few New Age health techniques address themselves strictly to the health of the person without adding a metaphysical orientation.[13]

Paul Reisser points out that there are organizations which disseminate information without a New Age slant, such as the network of Wholistic Health Centers founded in the Midwest by Granger Westberg. Traditional Western medicine is used but integrated into a much broader scope of care.

11. Kenneth H. Cooper, *It's Better to Believe* (Nashville: Thomas Nelson, 1995), 28.

12. Alexander, *SCP Journal*, 36.

13. Ibid.

New Age Health mysticism and occultism are not used. Westberg has been developing what he calls the "parish nurse" program. The way it works is that nurses and doctors and other health professionals in a given congregation come together and formulate their own philosophy of health in the church setting. Then they plan ways to meet the needs of their congregation through programs that complement — not replace — the normal care given by physicians, clinics, and hospitals. Whatever is done integrates physical well-being with emotional health, and medicine with prayer. Westberg calls it "wholism," and by it he intends to treat each person wholistically in a way that combines body, soul, and spirit.[14]

Kenneth Cooper has become internationally famous for his work in projecting preventive medicine and wellness in a biblical context. His philosophy and Christian convictions are dramatically presented in his 1995 book entitled *It's Better to Believe*. Cooper has been honored by *The Times* of London as one of seventy-five people who have contributed the most to the health and welfare of humankind during the twentieth century. In 1993 he was recognized by the national medical community with both the $50,000 Health-trac Foundation Prize for Improving Health and the C. Everett Koop Award for "his distinguished advocacy of health and wellness." To develop his work, he founded the Cooper Institute for Aerobics Research in 1970, focusing on clinical research into the relationship between health and living habits. His fourteen books have sold more than 30 million copies in forty-one languages and in Braille. At age eighteen, Cooper says, he thought that he had a call from God to be a medical missionary to China. Today, he realizes that he is a medical missionary who has taken his fitness and wellness crusade not only to China but to every continent.[15]

I owe a personal debt of gratitude to Kenneth Cooper and his program. During a treadmill stress test in 1981 that was part of a routine annual physical examination at Cooper Clinic, doctors learned that my heart's blood vessels were seriously clogged. I needed triple bypass surgery, which I had. To prevent further heart disease, I also needed to begin a radical new lifestyle, which I continue to this day. The results have been revolutionary.

Another encouraging recent development has been the participation of hospitals, many of which are related to Christian churches, in promoting wellness.

It is obvious that the dimensions of mind and spirit have been too isolated from the body, which is too often looked at as merely a biochemical machine.

---

14. Reisser, *Holistic Healers,* 140; see also Ted Peters, *The Cosmic Self* (New York: HarperCollins, 1991), 23-24.

15. Carolyn Poirot, "Aerobics," *Fort Worth Star Telegram*, December 27, 1993, 3.

It is unfortunate that, at least for the time being, the word "holistic" has been captured by those who are convinced that the New Age metaphysical view holds the key to health and wholeness.

It is time for advocates of the biblical view of health to walk through the open door of opportunity and call for the total health care so crucial to human well-being.[16]

# HISTORICAL ORIGINS OF HOLISTIC HEALTH SYSTEMS

Holistic health is a cross-cultural and historical synthesis, a descendant of powerful ancient medical and philosophical traditions. Holistic health has reunited the common assumptions of the great naturalistic medical systems of the Old World — the Asian, Ayurvedic, and Hippocratic traditions. The holistic health tradition is derived from thousands of years of naturalistic medicine — medical systems based primarily on the balance of metaphysical forces (elements and life forces). Continuity is maintained by the dispersed, decentralized nature of the practitioners.[17]

The holistic health movement is not simply a group of people favoring one health care system over the prevailing one, but an ideological community actively pursuing a desired future.

## EAST ASIAN THERAPIES

There is an impressive range of therapies that use assumptions and techniques derived from East Asian medicine. Some practices are truly cross-cultural imports. The individuals in such practices are practitioners from Taiwan, Japan, or Korea. They use "pure" forms of acupuncture (using needles to stimulate the acupuncture meridians), moxibustion (use of burning mugwort on the meridian points), and tonic and curative herbalism.

Asian-American or Asian practitioners are only the tip of the iceberg. The overwhelming majority of the practitioners of traditional Asian medicine are Euro-American students who are two or three generations removed from the original Asian therapist. They may use classical techniques, often jointly with martial arts or an Asian-American religion.

Whatever the variations, the techniques mentioned are based on a set

16. Reisser, *Holistic Healers,* 13.
17. J. A. English-Lueck, *Health in the New Age* (Albuquerque, N.M.: University of New Mexico, 1990), 9.

of common assumptions. They all acknowledge the basic premise that energy flow is the basis of organic function. This energy is a pervasive environmental constant. It is absorbed into living entities and is the vital force. In human beings the energy enters through food and breath and is ultimately transformed into chen ch'i. Chen ch'i nourishes and defends the body and provides for reproduction. The ch'i travels along paths of "least resistance" in the body. Each of these "energy freeways" is a meridian and each is named after an organ in the human body.

Imbalance is the source of disease. Balance, longevity, and clear thinking are the clearly articulated goals of Asian-American medicine. Here as elsewhere in New Age thinking, we find a partnership between modern Western and ancient Asian thought. This approach reflects eighth-century Shankara and the ancient Upanishadic teachings of Brahmanism wherein one's true self is designated Atman. The Atman is never born and never dies. It is changeless, beyond time, permanent, and eternal. It does not die when the body dies. In fact, for one who has true knowledge, the Atman is equivalent to and identical with Brahman, the all, the totality of reality. Life's goal, according to Hinduism, is to come to this awareness. It is our task as human beings to become aware of this metaphysical power, this unifying reality that lies within us. Those who have joined the New Age are in touch with their higher self and are vigorously pursuing deeper awareness of it. This leads to the notion of the divine spark, which we find in most New Age programs. Once we come to know the divine potential that lies within us, we find ourselves caught up in the gloriousness of expanded creativity and genuine happiness and health. Ramtha teaches: "You are God, I am God."

Attitude change, meditation, and physical and spiritual exercise are significant tools of holistic therapy. Because of the unity of mind and body in this approach, "physical therapies" are intertwined with Taoist, Buddhist, or Confucianist philosophical-meditation centers and martial arts. T'ai chi ch'uan, a martial art, is prescribed as a "meridian tonic" by some acupuncturists.[18]

## AYURVEDIC MEDICAL PRACTICES

Ayurvedic medicine is India's classical, naturalistic medical system. It has had profound historical influence on the East Asian and Hippocratic traditions. Unlike its East Asian kin, Ayurvedic medicine is rarely practiced in a "culturally pure" form in the United States.

In spite of these variations, the Ayurvedic practices retain many of the basic assumptions of classical Indian medicine. This includes the manipulation of elemental energy, a focus on reincarnation, and personal evolution toward

18. Ibid., 34-40; see also Peters, *The Cosmic Self,* 66-67.

a divine state. Vital force, or prana, in imbalance is the basis of all disease and, flowing properly, is the source of all well-being.

The energy exists on an ethereal plane. Once it enters, it cycles through the body in a series of chakras. The chakras are envisioned as nodes of rotating energy; they are associated with the elements, colors, and diverse virtues.

The basic tenets of Ayurvedic medicine are intimately linked with Hinduism. They reflect some of the biases that have evolved hand in hand with the hierarchical social structure of India. Karma, learning to fit into one's inborn place in the scheme of things, is the basis of imbalance and disease. In the classical Indian system, the high status of priests and male human beings in general was reinforced by these ideas.

Although usually the realm of psychic healers, Mediterranean and European astrology is used to diagnose potential "areas of weakness," which can then be manipulated according to Ayurvedic principles.[19]

## HIPPOCRATIC MEDICINE

Asia was hardly the only continent to conceive a holistic medical tradition. Hippocratic medicine, which originated on the Greek island of Kos, also focused on elemental energy, and the equilibrium of natural and internal forces as the source of well-being. Illness was conceived, once again, as the result of the imbalance of these forces. Naturalistic medical systems are rooted in the concept that natural forces in balance will produce health and wholeness.

There were three hundred healing centers in Greece, but the most famous were in Kos and Epidaurus. Originally founded as worship centers, they later sought to cure patients and teach medicine. Priests worked in these healing centers. They used sacrifices, baths, sleep cures, dreams, fasts, and exorcism.

For a number of years I have taken study groups to Kos. There we visit the Asclepeion, a healing center developed in the fifth century B.C. by Hippocrates, who is generally recognized as the "father" of what is now called modern, or scientific, medicine. People came from all over the ancient world to bring gifts and to seek healing at this center. Hippocrates was not only a practical physician but also a theoretical teacher, researcher, and writer. He studied the various medical methods of his day. But he went beyond others, carefully studying the human body and its various systems and the laws relating to its well-being. He was called to fight epidemics all over the Greek world. The Hippocratic oath is still taken by physicians today.

In the field of holistic health, most of the basic therapeutic techniques such as dietary change, herbal medicine, and physical manipulation are ancient Hippocratic approaches. The idea that the body, if kept in harmony, will be

19. English-Lueck, *Health in the New Age,* 42-45.

well is the key concept in chiropractic as well as in twentieth-century bodywork therapies and Rolfing.

Thus we see that the various techniques used by contemporary holistic health workers are the products of geographically diverse origins and creative syntheses, linked by common symbolic concerns. Holistic health is brought together by both symbols and networking. By understanding the assumptions, causative models, and diagnostic and therapeutic practices used, we can extract elements of the symbolic, philosophical, and religious systems behind them. Long before the dawn of Aquarian consciousness in the 1960s, the techniques and assumptions existed.[20]

## Contemporary Origin of Holistic and New Age Approaches to Health

The term "new age," without the capital letters, has been a favorite phrase in American history since at least the time of the American Revolution. Use of the term acquired a special self-consciousness in the Theosophical movement of the late nineteenth century. Then, in the late 1960s and early 1970s, with ties to occult and metaphysical movements as part of its prehistory, the New Age movement began.

One way in which the New Age approach congealed was through a series of English "light" groups, made up of individuals who came together to "channel" spiritual light to the world and to discuss Theosophical writings about the advent of a New Age. Light groups spread from England to this country, and by the early seventies they were part of an international network that expected the imminent arrival of a New Age.

Meanwhile, by 1971, the *East-West Journal,* begun that year in Boston under macrobiotic auspices, became a vehicle for the spread of New Age ideas. Changes in the American immigration law likewise facilitated the influx of Eastern teachers and teachings, while at the same time a holistic health movement began to gain momentum, and Native American spirituality became increasingly attractive. In this climate, many Americans — after the decade of the sixties and the Vietnam War era — seemed less spiritually certain of themselves and more open to a new syncretism of East-West teachings.[21]

The term "holism" was coined from the Greek *holos,* "whole," in 1926 by Jan Smuts, a student of biology and the first prime minister of South

20. Ibid., 47-49, 61.
21. James R. Lewis and J. Gordon Melton, *Perspectives on the New Age* (Albany, N.Y.: State University of New York, 1992), 18-21.

Africa, in his book *Holism and Evolution*. Several decades later Smuts's holistic perspective on biological evolution was expanded by psychologist Abraham H. Maslow and others in defining human nature and developing psychologies of health and transcendence that treat the human being as a whole organism and not a collection of parts.

The humanistic movement, coupled with a revival of interest in Eastern philosophy, brought renewed interest to holistic health in the 1960s.

The movement grew, at first quietly and without mainstream media attention, through a mostly informal network of communication. Bulletin boards in natural-food stores, yoga centers, and alternative healing clinics; word-of-mouth messages from chiropractors and massage therapists; local directories of people, goods, and services; multiplying numbers of small, often newsprint, periodicals — all helped to announce the New Age. Teachers appeared, and seminars and weekend workshops flourished. Movement leaders began to attract followings, and New Agers increasingly found one another.

# DOMINANT THEMES IN NEW AGE HEALTH

## Transformation through Healing

As noted in Chapter 4, a primary emphasis of the New Age movement is the experience of transformation. According to Ted Peters, the New Agers are diligently seeking a profound personal transformation from an old, unacceptable life to a new, exciting future. One prominent model for that transformation is healing, which has given rise to what is possibly the largest identifiable segment of the New Age movement.[22]

During the 1970s, the New Age movement and the holistic health movement merged until now it is difficult, if not impossible, for an observer to draw a line between them. It is apparent that New Age spokespersons claim that the holistic health movement is a major component of their movement. In turn, many holistic health practitioners look to New Agers for public support and as the clientele upon whom they practice their profession.[23]

### Basic Holistic Themes

Randall Baer, a former New Age health leader, says, "From my own experience, over 70 percent of holistic health professionals have an underlying New

22. Peters, *The Cosmic Self,* 20-22.
23. J. Gordon Melton, *New Age Almanac* (Detroit: Visible Ink, 1991), 174.

Age-based philosophy. Many who have New Age roots do not advertise as such."[24]

Paul and Teri Reisser and John Weldon, in *The Holistic Healers*, have listed a number of dominant themes in the holistic approach to medicine. A number of these emphases have been utilized or adapted by New Age leaders. Although the authors, two of whom are medical doctors, are sympathetic to some of the emphases of holistic medicine, they believe that from a medical perspective there are flaws in holistic medicine. They are especially critical of the theological and philosophical background of some of the holistic teachings. However, there are positive aspects of the holistic approach that can be taken out of the New Age context and utilized in the biblical context. Accepting the truth in some of these holistic emphases does not make a person automatically a disciple of the New Age movement.

Following are the major holistic themes or precepts:

1. The whole is greater than the sum of its parts. This is a helpful emphasis on the interrelatedness of body, mind, and spirit.

2. Health, or "wellness," is more than an absence of disease. In other words, health or wellness is also a *positive* state of growth in self-realization.

3. Individuals are ultimately responsible for their own health or disease. Traditional medicine's dependency monopoly must be broken. We must actively pursue our own health.

4. Natural forms of healing are preferable to drugs and surgery. An emphasis is placed on changes in diet, lifestyle, and attitude.

5. Some methods of promoting health are more innately holistic than others. Technique, or methodology, is one of the most controversial areas in holistic medicine. Some of the more popular techniques emphasized are acupuncture, biofeedback, chiropractic and osteopathy, homeopathy, iridology, massage and bodywork therapies, Eastern meditation techniques, visualization or guided imagery to diagnose and heal illnesses, self-hypnosis, oriental martial arts, and nutritional therapies. Psychic diagnosis and psychic healing are also becoming more popular.

From the Far East comes an interest in mystical practices which promise a fuller and healthier sex life. These practices include various forms of Tantric Yoga. Another favorite New Age cure for the misfortunes of the body is Therapeutic Touch. Some American healers have gone to the Philippines to study how the people there use hands to connect them to the healing source. There is also an interest in psychic surgery.

Bernie Siegel, a surgeon who teaches at Yale, has written a new bestseller entitled *Love, Medicine and Miracles*. After years of treating cancer

24. Randall N. Baer, *Inside the New Age Nightmare* (Lafayette, La.: Huntington, 1989), 154.

patients he believes that all disease is related to a lack of love or to love that is only conditional. This lack exhausts the immune system and creates a physical vulnerability for diseases such as cancer.

6. Health implies evolution. As we have seen, the New Age movement is permeated with messianic and evolutionary anticipations. Holistic health is seen as one manifestation of this evolutionary development. This emphasis will be developed in Chapter 13 on the New Age approach to history.

7. An understanding that energy — not matter — is the key to health. To increase the flow of healing energy we must attune ourselves to the universal source and realize our unity with all things. In his well-known book *Space, Time and Medicine,* Larry Dossey has emphasized this approach. This idea is closely akin to the Hindu concept of God as impersonal, universal energy. This energy has been called prana, kundalini (Hinduism), mana (Primitives) and Ch'i (Taoism).

8. Death is the final stage of growth. According to the New Age movement, death is a transition to another state of consciousness or an illusion. Hope for this easy transition or glorious evolution has been sparked by the work of Raymond Moody and Elisabeth Kübler-Ross. They tell of the adventures of people who were clinically "dead" and later revived. They report that the "life beyond" is an evolution to a state of glory and beauty.

Other New Age leaders contend that because all is one, individuals cannot die. This means that the notion of individual death is absurd. We must abandon the concept of death and its specter of fierce suffering and the inexorable decline of life.

9. The thinking and practices of many ancient civilizations are a rich source for healthy living. The Chinese and Hindu cultures are especially helpful. The Bible is noticeably avoided.

10. Holistic health practices must be incorporated into the fabric of society through public policy. Capra, for example, contends that health education and health policy should follow the holistic model.

As we have noted, it is difficult to define the New Age movement and its approach to health. It is not represented by any single organization, group, or type of practice, and it is continually being reshaped by its adherents. These include physicians and scientists with impressive credentials, chiropractors and osteopaths, psychologists and sociologists, healers and mystics, nurses and laypeople, as well as an odd assortment of health "practitioners" whose ideas and techniques have varying degrees of credibility.[25]

25. Reisser, *Holistic Healers,* 11, 14-32.

## PROMOTING HOLISTIC AND NEW AGE HEALTH

Organizations which promote or practice holistic health (by their own definition) range from storefront operations to associations with impressive budgets and conference schedules. The book *Wholistic Dimensions in Healing* by Leslie Kaslof lists eight major holistic organizations in the United States and Canada.

It is impossible to estimate the total number of holistic practitioners and patients at the present time, but the movement obviously has tremendous influence. Articles on the New Medicine or "universal energy" at times appear in such supermarket checkout staples as *Cosmopolitan* or *House and Garden*. Courses on "yoga and health" are routine offerings at neighborhood recreational centers. Lawmakers are lobbied on holistic health as they grapple with health-care legislation. The California Assembly's Health Committee, for example, has considered whether alternative health care is more cost-effective than conventional medicine.

A different issue, especially in California, is the legal status of some forms of alternative practice. Holistic health is, in essence, the banner under which the New Consciousness is making its move into the realm of health and medicine. Indeed, the holistic health movement does not appear nearly as concerned with changing the way medicine is practiced as it is with changing the fundamental orientation of people toward themselves, the universe, and especially the supernatural realm.[26]

The Public Broadcasting System presented a five-part series in October 1993, entitled "Healing and the Mind." Bill Moyers edited a companion book with the same name. PBS has also presented a series featuring Deepak Chopra, a New Age exponent.

## MAJOR CONCEPTS OF NEW AGE HEALTH

The stuff of reality, according to New Agers, is mind — or consciousness. This New Age view is not a new concept. For the last century, several "mind science" groups, such as Christian Science, Religious Science, and Science of Mind, have been setting forth similar teachings. For instance, Mary Baker Eddy, in the Christian Science textbook *Science and Health*, taught that the material world was unreal, an "error" created and maintained by our collective "mortal mind."[27]

26. Ibid., 11-13.
27. Karen Hoyt, *The New Age Rage* (Old Tappan, N.J.: Revell, 1987), 61, 81-83.

We now give a broader statement of the New Age view. The concept that "all is one," all is energy, and all is consciousness is foundational to the New Age. According to Douglas Groothuis of Denver Seminary, this concept "permeates the movement in all its various manifestations including holistic health." This broad view includes the idea that the purpose of life is to become aware of our divine nature. Since we are all emanations of one reality, the New Age view states that there is no need for forgiveness or salvation. Instead, individuals need enlightenment to understand their own divinity. (Illumination, self-realization, and at-one-ment are examples of terms equivalent to enlightenment.)

As Vishal Mangalwadi has pointed out, the only consistent New Age therapy is the belief that there is no therapy, because self, the only thing that is real, cannot be sick. The *Course in Miracles* sums it up in this way: "Nothing real can be threatened. Nothing unreal exists." As noted in Chapter 5, Helen Schucman reportedly channeled Jesus to give us *A Course in Miracles*. This *Course* prescribes a step-by-step method to enable readers to begin to see disease as illusion and thereby find self-healing. The "Teachers Manual" of the course states:

> There can be no order of difficulty in healing . . . because all sickness is illusion.
>     Healing involves an understanding of what the illusion of sickness is for.
>
> The acceptance of sickness as a decision of the mind . . . is the basis for healing. And this is so for healing in all forms. A patient decides that this is so, and he recovers. If he decides against recovery, he will not be healed. Who is the physician? Only the mind of the patient himself. . . . Special agents, or therapists, seem to be ministering to him, yet they but give form to his own choice. He chooses them in order to bring tangible form to his desires. And it is this they do, and nothing else. They are not actually needed at all. The patient could merely rise up without their aid and say, "I have no use for this." There is no form of sickness that would not be cured at once.
>
> What is the single requisite for this shift in perception? It is simply this: the recognition that sickness is of the mind, and has nothing to do with the body. What does this recognition "cost"? It costs the whole world you see.[28]

It is not difficult to understand the power of this teaching. On this view, the inactive sugar pills of a homeopath heal us not because he has given us anything potent, but because our disease is in fact an illusion.

28. Vishal Mangalwadi, *When the New Age Gets Old* (Downers Grove, Ill.: Inter-Varsity, 1992), 212-16.

# REEMPHASIS ON ENERGY AND HEALING

In recent years the term "energy" has become central in the New Age movement. In New Age health, it appears under a variety of names such as universal life energy, vital forces, Ch'i, prana, bioplasma, para-electricity, and animal magnetism. We are told that, regardless of its name, this energy pervades everything in the universe, unites each individual to the cosmos, and is the doorway to untapped human potential. It is at the root of all healing, all psychic abilities, all so-called miraculous occurrences. It is what religions have called God.[29]

In fact, as we have noted, the idea of a pervasive life energy is very old. It has been called by many names over the centuries.

New Age health has utilized some basic ideas about universal energy out of the systems which promote it.

Universal energy, for example, is said to be the basic fabric of everything, seen or unseen, in the universe. Here the New Age health has appropriated for its own use the fundamental statement of the atomic age: $E = mc^2$. Einstein's famous equation, in simple terms, says that matter can be converted into energy and vice versa. What we see as material objects (whether living or inanimate) are actually nothing more than congealed energy. Human beings are but one manifestation of universal energy. It does not merely flow through us; it defines us. Traditional medicine, therefore, is portrayed as mechanistic, old-fashioned, and pre-Einsteinian because it treats the body as a material entity. The New Age approach, on the other hand, provides us with new ways to heal because it views the body as energy and manipulates energy to change the body.

A well-known osteopathic physician, Irvin Oyle, states that "the idea of the identity of energy and matter has enormous implications for all the healing professions. It gives us a theoretical basis from which to consider therapeutic methods such as acupuncture which purport to restore normal bodily states by manipulating the flow of cosmic energy." Oyle further states that by manipulating consciousness through meditation and by contacting inner guides, one can change energy and thus change matter, producing physical healing.

A correlative statement about energy is that disease results from a blockage or imbalance in the natural flow of universal energy through the body. The ancient Chinese described an elaborate system of channels through which energy circulates. According to Hindu thought, energy, known as prana, flows through a series of psychic centers called chakras, which can be activated through meditation. D. D. Palmer, the founder of chiropractic, called universal

29. Reisser, *Holistic Healers*, 33-36.

energy the Innate and claimed that its flow through the nervous system could be blocked by spinal misalignments called subluxations.

In Polynesian culture universal energy is called mana and is the force used by Polynesian shamans (known as kahunas) in the practice of "white" and "black" magic. The primitive, or kahuna, system is overtly spiritistic and leaves the doors of consciousness wide open for contact with nonphysical entities. Some kahunas have stated that spirits of the dead make contact with the higher self to assist in psychic feats and healing, or to manipulate mana (for good or ill) in others.[30]

# THE ENERGY CONCEPT IN AYURVEDIC MEDICINE

Deepak Chopra, a medical doctor from New Delhi, India, established the American Association of Ayurvedic Medicine. In 1992 he was appointed to the National Institutes of Health ad hoc panel on alternative medicine. His books *Creating Health, Return of the Rishi, Quantum Healing, Perfect Health,* and *Unconditional Life* have been translated into more than twenty-five languages. A more recent book is *Ageless Body, Timeless Mind.* He is featured in this chapter because he became a luminary in medical circles when his book *Ageless Body, Timeless Mind* hit the best-seller list in 1993 and stayed there for many weeks. Also published that year were *The Path to Love* and *The Higher Self.*[31] His initial core of followers came from the Transcendental Meditation movement since he was a former associate of the Maharishi Mahesh Yogi, but the number of his proponents grew as alternative and New Age health practices became more accepted. In 1989 the Mahesh Yogi awarded Chopra a title translatable as "Lord of Immortality."[32]

# THE SUPERSTITION OF MATERIALISM

According to the ancient Indian philosophy of Ayurveda, one of the reasons people grow old, age, and die is that they see other people growing old, aging, and dying. What we see we become because we have this superstition that seeing is believing. For Chopra, seeing is not believing. Rather, such a view

30. Ibid., 36-37, 42, 44.
31. Deepak Chopra, "Timeless Mind, Ageless Body," *Noetic Sciences Review,* Winter 1993, 16-17.
32. David Jeremiah, *Invasion of Other Gods* (Dallas: Word, 1995), 116.

is just a superstition, a superstition of materialism. An endocrinologist, Chopra has operated his own Ayurveda clinic.

According to Chopra, the superstition of materialism comes about because we trust our senses. And yet even with common sense we know that, if anything, sensory experience is the least reliable test of reality. After all, my senses tell me that the earth is flat. Nobody believes that anymore. My senses tell me that the ground I'm standing on is stationary, and yet I know it's spinning at dizzying speeds.

But the superstition of materialism is pervasive. We've been stuck with it for the last three hundred years. We think of ourselves as encapsulated egos, enmeshed in bags of flesh and bone, confined to prisons of space, time, and causation squeezed into volumes of bodies and spans of lifetimes. We think of the human body basically as a physical machine that has learned how to think. Consciousness becomes the by-product of matter.

All of Western scientific research has been based on this model of the human body until recently. Science has held that if you can understand the mechanisms of disease on the level of matter, then you should be able to get rid of disease. If you can understand, for example, how bacteria multiply and if you interfere by using the appropriate antibiotic, then you shouldn't have infections anymore.

Granted that understanding the mechanisms of disease can be important in eliminating illness, it really does nothing to help us deal with the origins of health. Chopra contends that in the very act of treating illness, we sow the seeds for illness in the future. The number one drug addiction in the world is not street drugs but medicine legally prescribed by physicians. It is estimated that in this country 80 percent of the population swallow a medically prescribed chemical every 24 hours.

For Chopra, something is wrong with our current model of the human body. The reality is that the body is not a frozen anatomical structure, but literally a river of intelligence and information and energy that's constantly renewing itself every second of its existence. The origins of health have to do with understanding one's own spiritual nature — the essence of life itself. We are not physical machines that have learned how to think. Rather, we are thoughts (and impulses, consciousness, feelings, emotions, desires, and dreams) that have learned how to create physical bodies.

Chopra insists that this view of reality is not just an interesting, esoteric, philosophical speculation based on Eastern mysticism. This view holds that the body is actually the objective experience of consciousness. But the two are inseparably one. The body is a field of ideas. When you say "My heart is heavy with sadness," your heart is literally loaded with fat chemicals. When you say "I'm bursting with joy," your skin is loaded with endorphins, interleukins, and interferons, which are powerful immunobody regulators and powerful anti-cancer drugs.

Disease continues because through conditioning we generate the same impulses of energy and information, the same behavioral practices that result in the same space/time events and the same biochemistry, and ultimately the same disease-infested life experiences. But it shouldn't have to be like that, according to Chopra.[33]

# THE PRIORITY OF CONSCIOUSNESS

For Chopra, our bodies are fields of ideas, but, even more important, our experience of time and space is similarly self-engendered. For example, people think that there is such a thing as external time, although no physicist has ever proved within an experiment the existence of the flow of time. We have never experienced the flow of time — all we have experienced is the flow of thoughts or ideas. We can experience timelessness when we experience unity consciousness, in which we have the knowledge somewhere deep inside us that humans are not only made up of the same stuff, but that we may be the same being in different disguises. The beauty of the mountain can be an experience of timelessness because we and the mountain become one. The observer, the process of observation, and that which was being observed became one. In that moment we escape time-bound awareness and enter timeless awareness, which is the realm of eternity, which is true reality.

Chopra contends that all spiritual traditions teach that somewhere deep inside you is some animating force that makes your body alive. This animating force is called the soul or the spirit or the self or consciousness — this is what creates the mind and the body, and this is who you really are. We are not in the body, the body is in us; we are not in the mind, the mind is in us; we are not in the world, the world is in us. The human body and the human brain are just a set of instruments that take what is universal, unbounded and infinite, and trap it into a local space/time perceptual artifact.

The spirit is a real force. It is very powerful, and only when we touch that spiritual core of awareness can we be healed.

Deep inside you, even on the level of the cells, is the holographic memory of every experience you have. You and I are different because we have had different experiences. Every experience you have or ever have had is recorded in the very cells of your body.

To go even beyond that, there is the memory of wholeness, the true

33. Chopra, "Timeless Mind, Ageless Body," 17.

memory of the experiencer — because you and I are not the experience, we are the experiencer behind the experience. If we can find the experiencer in the midst of every experience, then we escape the tyranny of time-bound awareness. As we go into the joy of timeless awareness, the world becomes magical and different and healing takes place.[34]

Catherine Albanese indicates that for Chopra, healing means journeying into the realm of nonmatter in which the subtle forces transmute into material substance. Here, as in the mental journeys of Andrew Jackson Davis, mind and imagination assume control over the life of matter. The healing shaman, whether self or other, travels to the place of primal energy from which the blueprint for organic life is thought to come. Thus, the consciousness of an individual has a creative role in healing. Neurochemical events in the brain's life tell Chopra of the subtle process by which immaterial thoughts of fear are translated into the material substance of disease. For Chopra, mental power becomes the invisible fluid that magnetizes belief into bodily change. The fusion of matter and spirit functions to empower the mind to alter form and substance. In sum, Chopra's mind is at once mind as slayer and mind as healer.[35]

# EVALUATION OF CHOPRA ON HEALING

Therapists credit Ayurveda with subduing such problems as chronic migraine headaches and with eliminating pains that have no identifiable cause. Chopra says that when someone quickly improves or overcomes a chronic illness through Ayurveda therapy, that person has triggered his body's own healing response and cured the condition. As we have seen, his basic tenet is that the mind and body are not separate entities.

Says Chopra, "As soon as you lose your attachment to your disease, the sooner the disease also seems to go away." It's your responsibility: do you choose to have your disease, or do you not? Make up your mind!

Chopra is eager to claim 100 percent cure rates for some disorders, such as mild hypertension and migraine headaches. For more serious disorders, including coronary artery disease, he claims Ayurveda practitioners are able to free as many as 50 to 60 percent of their patients of the symptoms. Though he says he cooperates with his patients' other therapies, such as chemotherapy, his tendency is to move away from such treatments.

As we have noted, the charismatic figure behind Ayurveda is Maharishi

34. Ibid., 20-21.
35. Lewis and Melton, *Perspectives on the New Age,* 77.

Yogi, the founder of the Transcendental Meditation movement. Chopra recognizes that he is a disciple of the Yogi, whom he describes as "one of the greatest living sages." For his part, the Maharishi considers Ayurveda so beneficial that it is a major factor in his global campaign to create a disease-free society in every country. He has singled Chopra out to deliver the special Ayurveda techniques to the West.

David Sneed notes that here we see the intense Eastern, or New Age, religious emphasis, this time disguised as "nouveau medicine" for the rich and famous.

Sneed, an osteopathic physician, does not argue with the Ayurveda slogan, "sound body, sound mind." And some therapies, including a low-fat diet, are helpful. The problem is that there is another side to the slogan. If we accept the idea that positive thinking can cure an illness, we have to accept also that if one isn't cured, that person must have had negative thoughts. Sick people suffer enough misery from their illnesses. They shouldn't also be made to bear all the blame for having the illness. That would be cruel enough if it were a proven fact. That it is an unsubstantiated theory makes it worse.[36]

In a June 1996 *Time* magazine cover story, David Van Biema lists four medical doctors who have advocated alternative or New Age medical strategies. He wrote that Andrew Weil and Larry Dossey seek to relate theories of the spirit to Western science. Bernie Siegel is more consciously inspirational. And psychiatrist Brian Weiss champions reincarnation therapy.

Chopra, he wrote, combines the appeal of the various categories of New Age healing. He is an endocrinologist, a synthesizer of Indian medicine and quantum physics, a writer of great passion, and a propagator of magic and mysticism.[37]

But his words speak for themselves. I recently received a sales pitch from Chopra for one of his books, *The Higher Self.* Here's the letter.

> Dear Friend:
>
> You *are* your own reality.
>
> You create it; you carry it around with you; and, most importantly, you project it onto everyone else and everything else you encounter.
>
> But the traditional Western notion of reality is much too limiting for a true realization of life. If you are to understand yourself and the world around you properly, you need to expand your boundaries of reality — of time, space and matter
>
> Once you've done this, you can align the energy of your physical body

36. David Sneed and Sharon Sneed, *The Hidden Agenda* (Nashville: Nelson, 1991), 80-82.

37. David Van Biema, "Healing of the Soul," *Time*, June 24, 1996, 66-67.

with the energy of the universe. In doing this, you tap into an infinite reservoir of intelligence.

This is the Higher Self. The "you" inside of you. The living force that knows why you are here on earth, what you need and how to get it.

Your spiritual needs for love, compassion, meaningfulness, total acceptance and inner peace are not impossible goals for the future. Find your Higher Self and these needs will be fulfilled spontaneously. You will become a peaceful, harmonious and whole person at last.

So come with me to a new reality where all is love and lightness, bliss and unbelievable beauty. Accept THE HIGHER SELF for 30 days free!

It was signed, Deepak Chopra, M.D.

# METHODS OF ACTIVATING AND CHANNELING HEALING ENERGY

Marilyn Ferguson is one of the major theoreticians of the New Age movement. Five years of observation on the changes in society led to the 1980 publication of Ferguson's *The Aquarian Conspiracy*. The book, which quickly became a best-seller, has been accepted more than any other book as a consensus statement of the New Age perspective. Ferguson contends that many of the methods and persons channeling universal energy serve primarily as an intermediate step by undermining faith in rationalism. A healer is ministering in much the same way as a doctor, doing something to the patient.[38] New Age healers are seen as possessing some real healing powers, even though, somewhat paradoxically, they call their healing method "self-healing" by their patients.

In any case, New Age healing is seen by the average person as activated or channeled by a healer with a method. Nearly all therapies of the New Age health movement presume to direct universal energy by one method or another, either by direct physical contact or by some form of invisible transfer from healer to patient.

## Acupuncture and Acupressure

In traditional Chinese medicine, the proper function of the body (not to mention the mind and spirit) hinges on the proper flow of "life energy," or

---

38. Mangalwadi, *When the New Age Gets Old*, 209-11.

Chi'i, through the body. Chi'i supposedly circulates through twelve pairs of invisible channels called meridians, most of which are identified with organs such as the liver and heart.

If the flow becomes sluggish or blocked, you might develop symptoms or overt disease. While the diagnosis is based partly on your history and general appearance, it depends most of all on the radial (wrist) pulses. With proper training — and much patience — the Chinese therapist can presumably assess all twelve meridians by feeling six positions at each wrist. If the flow of Ch'i needs to be improved, the therapist stimulates specific points on the skin, either by needling or by applying finger pressure.

The basic tenets of the system are found in Chinese medicine's original text, *The Yellow Emperor's Classic of Internal Medicine,* which consists largely of long discourses on philosophy and Taoist metaphysics.

The idea that Ch'i flows through your body in defined channels comes from Taoism, and it is now deeply tied, in contemporary New Age spirituality, to the belief that this universal energy is what Western religions have traditionally called God.[39]

According to the New England School of Acupuncture, social, political, religious, and spiritual forces worked together to evolve into what we know today as acupuncture. Religion is a heavy element. In their classes the major philosophies of Confucianism, Taoism, Monism, Legalism, and Yin/Yang theory are all examined.

Paul Reisser, a physician, states that the only by-product of ancient Chinese medicine which has been reasonably validated is the treatment of chronic pain with counter-stimulation therapy, using either needles or electrical pulses. Controlled study of other uses is limited. According to Reisser, energy therapists, whether they realize it or not, are carrying out a form of religious practice and conditioning their patients to accept its teachings. The Taoist philosophy supports a system whose basic message is that "all is one."[40]

In the United States, the rich and famous have touted its virtues: Actress Jaclyn Smith had whiplash. James Garner had pain in his knee. Robert Wagner wanted to quit smoking. Merv Griffin was exhausted. What did they do? Each went to see Zion Yu, Hollywood's leading acupuncturist. Yu jokes he has needled more people than Don Rickles and Rona Barrett combined.

It is not just the celebrity circuit that is turned on to acupuncture. It has become a respectable research topic in Western universities and medical centers. Many aspects of Chinese medicine, including acupuncture, address problems that Western doctors often have difficulty treating. While the efficacy of those traditional treatments is still unproven, the Chinese system may

39. Hoyt, *The New Age Rage,* 68-69.
40. Reisser, *Holistic Healers,* 92.

offer clues to areas Western science is just beginning to explore. The impact of thoughts and emotions on physical health, an integral part of Chinese medicine, is being taken more seriously by Western researchers. However, as we have noted, classical acupuncture carries its metaphysical baggage, involving the practice of ancient pagan medicine tied to Taoism, and is deliberately or inadvertently involved with psychic healing.[41]

## Chiropractic, Applied Kinesiology, and Touch for Health

Paul Reisser points out that an interesting phenomenon has been the blending of the uniquely American invention, chiropractic, with the techniques of the ancient Chinese, producing an entirely new discipline with some interesting variations. Chiropractic was developed during the later 1800s by magnetic healer D. D. Palmer, who had come to the conclusion that most (if not all) bodily ailments arose from deficiencies in the transmission of vital nerve energy from the spinal cord. These blockages were said to occur because of misalignments, or subluxations, of the vertebral column, and could be corrected by appropriate manipulations.

One major concern in chiropractic has always been to correct improper posture and muscle tightness or spasm, since these can pull the spine out of proper alignment. In the early 1960s, practitioner George Goodheart came to the conclusion that muscle spasm was not so much a problem as was muscle weakness, which would cause normal muscles on the opposite side of the body to appear (or become) tight. The crucial issue was thus finding the weak muscles and somehow strengthening them. Goodheart appropriated standard muscle-testing techniques from physical therapy texts and combined them with Chinese concepts of energy flow, eventually producing in 1954-71 the *Applied Kinesiology Research Manuals.* His ideas were popularized by Pasadena chiropractor John Thie as Touch for Health, "a new approach to restoring our natural energies."

Touch for Health has become the most popular form in which applied kinesiology has been packaged for widespread consumption. The crux of Touch for Health is the flow of Ch'i — flowing through meridians, just as the ancients claimed — bringing health when in balance, and disorder when blocked or drained. The new approach is the effect of Ch'i imbalances on specific muscles, which provides a convenient way to diagnose or treat. Thie makes clear his adoption of Eastern metaphysics. When asked, "What exactly are the energies you balance and unblock in your work?" Thie replied:

41. Jeremiah, *Invasion of Other Gods,* 122; see also *Consumer Reports,* January 1994, 59.

They are the energies of the universe, taking form in the individual. To really understand this, we must remember that we are all one with the universe, with the universal energy. When this energy is highly concentrated, we call it "matter," and our bodies are that matter. Therefore, our bodies are literally this universal energy, in some of its various forms.

According to this, the universe is energy. We are energy. We are one.[42]

Many chiropractors disavow any use of "energy balancing." They emphasize spinal manipulation for the treatment of lower back pain. Several authoritative studies have confirmed that chiropractic-style spinal manipulation is effective for the treatment of lower-back pain. Such positive findings come despite the fact that no one is entirely sure how chiropractic manipulation works. Practitioners assert that they are correcting spinal "subluxations," which they describe as misalignments of vertebrae that result in pressure and damage to the spinal cord. Because nerves from the cord connect to every organ and body part, such misalignments, they say, can cause problems in the feet, hands, and internal organs as well as in the back.

Chiropractors point out that they spend at least four years studying the subtleties of the spine, including exhaustive courses in anatomy, pathology, biochemistry, and microbiology, and are, in fact, more knowledgeable than many medical doctors about this region of the body.

According to Andrew Purvis, whatever the benefits of manipulation and massage, many chiropractors admit that at least some of their success stems from their attentive manner and holistic approach to disease. Practitioners tend to discuss a patient's entire lifestyle, emphasizing stress reduction, a healthful diet, exercise, and maybe even a change in work habits. Patients love it, especially after experiencing the sometimes narrow approach of medical specialists, who may thoroughly examine a body part without a hint of interest in the human being.[43]

## Crystals and Flower Essence

New Age crystal healing claims that the healing power of crystals is due to their unique ability to harmonize the physical body with the etheric fields from which spiritual energy ultimately emanates. Gemstones, Robert Fuller notes, are selected because of the resonance between their properties and one's personal "vibrations." Furthermore, crystal healing is seen as part of a continuum that graduates into healing with liquid essences of flowers and gemstones and then into more traditional forms of homeopathy.

42. Reisser, *Holistic Healers*, 80-82.
43. Ibid., 83; see also Andrew Purvis, "Is There a Method to Manipulation?" *Time*, September 23, 1991, 60-61.

When a flower essence or gem elixir is ingested or used as a salve, it follows a specific path through the physical and subtle bodies. They initially are assimilated into the circulatory system. . . . The remedy settles midway between the circulatory and nervous systems. An electromagnetic current is created here by the polarity of these two systems. . . . These two systems contain quartz-like properties and an electromagnetic current. The blood cells, especially the red and white blood cells, contain more quartz-like properties, and the nervous system contains an electromagnetic current. The life force and consciousness use these properties to enter and stimulate the physical body. This intricate process ends in a balanced distribution of various energies at correct frequencies, which stimulates the discharge of toxicity to create health.[44]

John Weldon and John Ankerberg, in contrast, see New Age crystal healing as a minor variation upon an ancient occultic theme: that of working with objects called talismans and amulets having supposed supernatural powers. Throughout history, these items have been associated with the spirit world, and because of this, are believed to possess magical abilities. This is why metaphysical traditions of every type, East and West, use these magical stones in their occult work. In native American healing, the shaman utilizes the crystal as a method of both diagnosis and treatment; the crystal is believed to be a vehicle through which the healing spirits work.

Because spirits were believed to indwell and to work through these stones, healing properties were naturally assigned to them.

Although most crystal healers believe that the crystals themselves contain magical powers, Ankerberg and Weldon claim that the truth is that the crystals have no power and are merely vehicles through which spirits may choose to work. Wherever we look in modern New Age crystal healing, we discover that the real power in crystals comes from the spirit world, not the crystal itself. This is proven by the fact that after spirit contact is made, the crystals are no longer needed. Several crystal healers affirm that crystals are merely devices for attracting the spirits who supply the real power. Even when the crystals are dispensed with, the occult power remains.[45]

## Therapeutic Touch and Nursing

The fastest-growing alternative nursing practice is called Therapeutic Touch. Nurses who practice the treatment keep their hands about two inches above

44. Lewis and Melton, *Perspectives on the New Age*, 79.
45. John Ankerberg and John Weldon, *Can You Trust Your Doctor?* (Brentwood, Tenn.: Wolgemuth & Hyatt, 1991), 244-47.

their patients. Its appeal is in being noninvasive, nontoxic, and useful for pain reduction and the promotion of healing.

By 1996, about 100,000 American nurses had been trained in the technique. Today, more than 80 nursing schools in America and 70 foreign schools are teaching some form of Therapeutic Touch.[46]

Yet, despite many testimonials and diverse applications, Therapeutic Touch has garnered an outspoken chorus of critics. Some researchers allege Therapeutic Touch is medical quackery, while others, including some conservative Christians, have labeled it a New Age religious practice inappropriate for use in health care.

The developer of Therapeutic Touch is Dolores Krieger, a registered nurse with a doctoral degree who has taught this technique primarily to nurses. Her class at New York University, entitled "Frontiers in Nursing: The Actualization of Potential for Therapeutic Human Field Interaction," has been attended by hundreds of nurses as part of their master's or doctoral programs. Continuing Education courses nationwide have trained thousands of other health professionals in similar techniques.[47]

In her book *The Therapeutic Touch,* Krieger describes how she became acquainted with the idea of healing through touch while studying the approach of Hungarian healer Oskar Estebany. While a colonel in the Hungarian cavalry, Estebany had discovered by accident an ability to heal animals and humans through the laying on of hands.[48]

A New York research team, made up of a physician and a self-proclaimed clairvoyant and healer named Dora Kuntz, conducted a study of the effects of the direct laying-on-of-hands treatment of Estebany. Krieger joined the team and chose a biochemical measure for healer-energy influence, that of blood hemoglobin levels in nineteen medically referred subjects. The three researchers felt that hemoglobin, which is integral to the body's functioning, would be affected by such a healing energy.

So impressed was Krieger by the results of the studies involving this psychic that she decided to see if a nonpsychic such as she with no natural "healing ability" could learn to do what Estebany did in the experiment. Krieger claims that she discovered not only how to feel the energy flow, but to channel it as well. She began teaching Therapeutic Touch in 1975.[49]

46. Joe Maxwell, "Nursing's New Age?" *Christianity Today,* February 5, 1996.
47. Reisser, *Holistic Healers,* 44-45.
48. Ibid.
49. Sneed and Sneed, *The Hidden Agenda,* 172.

## Basic Method and Process

Therapeutic Touch is described as a four-step process.

Step one is called *centering*, a meditative process of becoming quiet and relaxed, developing a state of inner equilibrium.

Step two is *assessment*, scanning the patient's energy fields with the hands seeking to perceive blockages of the energy flow. This perception, and its interpretation, are not meant to be equivalent to standard medical diagnosis. The perception works at a very direct, perhaps primitive, level.

Step three involves *unruffling the field*, the process of decongesting the energy flow. When the healer perceives a sense of pressure while scanning the body, he or she is said to be bumping against stagnant energy. The cure is to sweep the energy downward with the hands, thus paving the way for the transfer of energy in the next step.

Step four, the *transfer of energy*, moves energy from the healer to the patient or from one place to another within the body of the patient. In Krieger's approach, the healer uses the sensations felt in the hands in step two as a guide for treatment. An area which feels hot needs to be cooled, a cool area warmed, an area of tingling quieted, and so forth. These changes are brought about as the healer creates the desired feeling (cool in place of warm) in his or her mind and then directs this image through the hands.[50]

## Evaluation of Therapeutic Touch

Some analysts of the treatment contend that scientific evidence supporting Therapeutic Touch methods are in short supply, and that until the "Does it work?" issue is resolved, Therapeutic Touch should be avoided.

According to Arlene Miller, nursing professor at Messiah College in Grantham, Pennsylvania, additional research indicates that the "placebo effect" may be the cause of patient improvement after Therapeutic Touch, meaning that the patient's expectations of improvement, not the therapy itself, brought about physiological changes.[51]

According to Reisser, Therapeutic Touch epitomizes the thrust of almost every therapy based on universal energy. A mystical concept is extracted from Eastern philosophy, sanitized in Western scientific trappings, and then taught to members of the helping professions who are looking for new ways to relieve suffering. Krieger began with an emphasis on healing, then emphasizes psychic communication and the drawing of mandalas (complex visual

50. Reisser, *Holistic Healers*, 46-47.
51. Maxwell, "Nursing's New Age?" 96-97.

patterns used for meditation). The healing emphasis and the religious message are inseparable. The approach is made to appear scientific by a core of mystical physicists who believe they have found a unifying connection between Eastern mysticism, especially Advaita Vedantic Hinduism, Mahayana Buddhism, and Taoism, and modern quantum mechanics. (Fritjof Capra's *The Tao of Physics* is a notable example of this thinking.)

The crucial question is not just whether objective (or subjective) healings actually take place, but what they mean. In the area of universal energy the interpretation proceeds from the spiritual precepts of the New Age movement.[52]

## Mind Therapies

In recent years a number of books, some written by physicians, have promoted the belief that the mind can indeed heal the body. The public has responded by making several of these books best-sellers. The idea that the mind and body are connected goes back thousands of years. Hypnosis, meditation, biofeedback — all these have been applied with some success to conditions many consider somewhat psychosomatic in nature. Asthmatics have found relief through relaxation exercises. Hypertensive patients have lowered their blood pressure. Migraine sufferers have controlled their headaches. The difference is that now some insist that mind power techniques are equally meaningful for such conditions as cancer. Berne Siegel, the Drs. Simonton, and AIDS counselor Louise L. Hay are well-known professionals who are promoting the gospel of the healing power of the mind.

In Chapter 2 we told of the claims of Christian Science. Other groups also exalt the mind in the healing process. The United Church of Religious Science (Science of Mind), founded by Ernest Holmes, teaches that "man controls the course of his life, his success or failure, his health or sickness, his happiness, boredom, or misery, by mental processes which function according to a universal law. Apply the principles of this law, and you can control it all."[53]

## Norman Cousins — The Will for Wellness

In the 1960s, scientific research began providing evidence of the mind-body link. One product of that research, psychoneuroimmunology, explores the

---

52. Reisser, *Holistic Healers*, 47.
53. Sneed and Sneed, *The Hidden Agenda*, , 115, 124-25.

collaboration between the mind, the brain, the body's self-protection mechanisms, and the immune system.[54]

Author Norman Cousins, after a demanding schedule in Leningrad and Moscow when he was editor of *The Saturday Review*, found himself in what he called a state of "adrenal exhaustion." Later he claimed it was a precondition of his supposedly "progressive, incurable" collagen disease (which turned out to be ankylosing spondylitis) which attacked his connective tissue. He was told he had six months to live.

Cousins did not accept the verdict. He decided to take responsibility for his treatment, in large measure, into his own hands. He based his plan on the ideas that positive emotions have a positive effect on body chemistry, that pain is affected by attitude, and that Vitamin C helps to oxygenate the blood.

Cousins watched old television shows of *Candid Camera* and movies by the Marx brothers. He found that ten minutes of a good belly laugh acted as a natural anesthetic, and he could sleep. A nurse read him humorous stories. He took massive intravenous doses of Vitamin C in the form of ascorbic acid. Dramatic improvement followed within eight days. He had been so ill that it still took many months before almost total recovery took place, with essentially full mobility and no twinges of pain in the joints from sudden movement. He lived for twenty-six more years. His 1983 book *The Healing Heart* has reportedly helped many people.[55]

In his writing, Cousins tells of some conclusions which he reached.

1. "The will to live is not a theoretical abstraction, but a physiologic reality with therapeutic characteristics." Cousins says you can actually change the physiology of your body. A thought can change the rate at which your heart beats. It can change your pulse or your immune system or your white blood count.
2. "My doctor knew that his biggest job was to encourage the patient's will to live and to mobilize all the natural resources of the body and mind to combat disease." Actually, Dr. Cousins acted as his own doctor. He is the one who prescribed the vitamin C and the movies. He placed himself at complete rest. And it was he himself who came to the conclusion that encouraging his body's natural resources was his biggest job.
3. "Since I didn't accept the verdict, I wasn't trapped in the cycle of fear, depression, and panic that frequently accompany a supposedly incurable illness." What Cousins did was to take physical action.

54. Rosemary Ellen Guiley, *Harper's Encyclopedia of Mystical and Paranormal Experience* (Edison, N.J.: Castle, 1991), 51.
55. Duncan S. Ferguson, *New Age Spirituality* (Louisville, Ky.: Westminster/John Knox, 1993), 155.

Cousins's basic message is that each person needs to take responsibility for maintaining health and even, if possible, to participate in treatment plans if ill. This is one of the helpful concepts emphasized by New Age health care. His story is a clear example of why the alternative and New Age health movement appeals to so many people.

According to Daniel Sneed, the problem comes when alternative practices lead the patient away from scientifically proven medicine. Furthermore, all the ramifications of the possible impact on the physical body, the mental self, and the spiritual soul need to be considered, both by those recommending the treatment and by those taking it.[56] It is important to note that Cousins made it abundantly clear that he deeply respected traditional medical skill in diagnosis, clinical evidence, and the systematic thought of the scientific method.

## CREATIVE VISUALIZATION

### Basic Concept

Creative visualization — the systematic use of mental imagery to achieve desired ends — is used for two purposes: one, to put oneself into a positive state of mind so that social and economic objectives can be realized in one's personal life, and two, to heal oneself of a dangerous illness or at least alleviate its symptoms. Practitioners of this methodology meditate on literal or symbolic images important in one way or another to their hopes and lives. The visualizing of light, and "sending" this light in the imagination to places, things, or persons that need healing (including ourselves), is a common practice in New Age religion. Many variations are possible, for instance visualizing oneself inside a bubble of light, as protection against negative energies or for enhancing one's rate of spiritual vibration.

On a fundamental level, visualization is little more than a variation of the notion of "positive thinking" and Aristotle's idea of the mental image as a motivating force in human behavior. However, New Age writers such as Melita Denning and Osborne Phillips see visualization as a powerful metaphysical force. In *The Llewellyn Practice Guide to Creative Visualization* (1980) they write, "Truly, by the power of this spiritual source of imaging channeled through the conscious and unconscious levels of your own psyche, the action takes place on the corresponding levels of the external universe, to bring about the presentation to you on the earthly level of what you have imaged. That is WHY you can truly affirm that what you visualize IS YOURS NOW. Astrally it is YOURS, because you have implanted it in astral reality;

56. Sneed and Sneed, *The Hidden Agenda*, 117-18.

mentally and spiritually it is YOURS, because you are activating those levels by means of your own mental and spiritual force so that what you create astrally shall be REALIZED materially."[57]

Within the New Age movement the practice of creative visualization is usually identified with Shakti Gawain, who got her start working on the staff of Ken Keyes's Living Love Center in Berkeley, California, in the 1970s. Her workshops led to the writing of her book *Creative Visualization* (1979).

It is this second use of creative visualization in healing that is said to produce empirically measurable results and that has generated the most attention and controversy outside self-help and occult circles.

In *Creative Visualization,* Shakti Gawain presides over a familiar universe in which the physical world is an energy phenomenon. "The scientific world is beginning to discover what metaphysical and spiritual teachers have known for centuries. Our physical universe is not really composed of any 'matter' at all; its basic component is a kind of force or essence which we can call energy." The things that "appear to be solid and separate" on "finer . . . atomic and subatomic levels" are "smaller and smaller particles within particles, which eventually turn out to be just pure energy." As important, "the energy is vibrating at different rates of speed," and so has "different qualities." "Thought is a relatively fine, light form of energy and therefore very quick and easy to change." On the other hand, "matter is relatively dense, compact energy, and therefore slower to move and change." In this world of faster and slower vibrating energy, magnetic law reigns supreme: "energy of a certain quality or vibration tends to attract energy of a similar quality and vibration." From this perspective, an idea becomes a "blueprint" that "creates an image of the form, which then magnetizes and guides the physical energy to flow into that form and eventually manifests it on the physical plane."

Given the theoretical frame, Gawain's general direction seems clear, according to Catherine Albanese. She acknowledges that "we always attract into our lives whatever we think about the most, believe in most strongly, expect on the deepest levels, and/or imagine most vividly." Disciplined technique is at hand to reprogram the mind at these strongest, deepest levels. But for Gawain, this means more than a simple assertion of will over imagination. Rather, it is a process she describes as akin to learning to sail in the current of a river, at once moving with the flow and guiding.

Thus, creative visualization properly performed requires contacting a "higher self" and "coming from 'source.'" And "source," Gawain declares, "means the supply of infinite love, wisdom, and energy in the universe. . . . Source may mean God, or the universal mind, or the oneness of all, or your true essence." In sum, Gawain is prescribing an inward journey, a voyage to

57. Melton, *New Age Almanac,* 202-3.

the self to unlock its dormant powers of reconfiguration. In so doing, Gawain is recommending a New Age form of shamanism. In fact, in her book *Creative Visualization*, Gawain likens visualization to "magic" in the highest sense of the word. Positive energy attracts more positive energy.[58]

The concept of creative visualization has been popularized in the West through various writings, such as the many books by Norman Vincent Peale, a Methodist minister. Peale's initial book on the subject, *The Power of Positive Thinking* (1952), advises a combination of prayer, faith in God, a positive frame of mind, and affirmations, words, or phrases that trigger positive forces. For example, "I am beautiful and loved" and "I am successful" are affirmations. When repeated, written down, and contemplated, affirmations become part of consciousness.[59]

Tantric Buddhism in particular makes extensive use of vivid and complex imagery. Through yoga concentration exercises, the adept trains himself or herself to visualize shapes and colors, then progresses to more complex imagery of Tibetan letters, deities, and mandalas. Ritual dramas are projected through imagery that attains a dreamlike state, which the adept controls at will. The visualization demonstrates the illusory nature of the material plane, and that the physical body is created by the mind.[60]

## The Simontons and the Cure of Cancer

The most publicized — and dramatic — work on the medical implications of imaging was done by physician O. Carl Simonton and then-wife and psychologist Stephanie Matthews-Simonton. Matthews-Simonton was familiar with visualization through her study of highly motivated, highly successful individuals — many of whom, she found, practiced positive imaging. Simonton had already noted informally that patients who had an optimistic outlook generally responded more successfully to treatment. The couple decided to see whether the technique could help cancer patients Simonton was treating at the University of Oregon Medical School. They taught visualization techniques to 159 patients who had been diagnosed as suffering from incurable, malignant cancer; none of the patients was given more than a year to live. Four years later 63 were still alive; 14 no longer had cancer in their bodies, and 12 had shrinking tumors. The patients who died had lived an average of 1½ times longer than patients in a nonvisualizing control group. All of the patients continued to receive conventional medical treatment during the experiment.

58. Lewis and Melton, *Perspectives on the New Age*, 80-81.
59. Guiley, *Harper's Encyclopedia*, 125.
60. Ibid., 283.

Reflecting on this and other experiences, Simonton has concluded that active and positive participation can influence the onset of the disease, the outcome of treatment, and the subsequent quality of life. Simonton also believes that positive or negative expectations can play a significant role in determining an outcome. A negative expectation will prevent the possibility of disappointment, Simonton says, but it may also contribute to a negative outcome that was not inevitable.

Paul Reisser criticizes the Simontons for encouraging patients to locate an inner guide. The meditative techniques for procuring the services of a guide, as described by the Simontons and many others, are strikingly similar to the old occult practice of contacting a familiar spirit. Both inner guides and familiar spirits are often said to appear in the form of friendly animals or humans who give advice and counsel upon request. At worst, this may begin to transform patients into spirit mediums. At best, it assumes that one's subconscious is an infallible fountain of wisdom, a naive and shaky presupposition for sorting out life's problems.[61]

## The Christian Faith Movement

The founding father of the Faith movement that is related to the Christian Charismatic emphasis is commonly held to be Kenneth Erwin Hagin, the man termed by *Charisma* magazine "the granddaddy of the Faith teachers" and "the father of the Faith movement." Hagin's teachings on faith, healing, and prosperity have been foundational for almost every major minister of the Faith movement. Even the older leaders of the Faith movement such as Kenneth Copeland readily admit that Hagin's teaching and leadership were the key both to their own success, and that of the movement.[62]

However, D. R. McConnell has given strong evidence that the modern Faith movement is philosophically and religiously based on the teachings of E. W. Kenyon. The roots of Kenyon's theology may be traced to his personal background in the metaphysical groups, specifically New Thought and Christian Science. In 1891, he attended the Emerson School of Oratory, an institution that has been described by its own historians as permeated with New Thought metaphysics, and whose founder, Charles Emerson, died a member of the Christian Science mother church in Boston. Kenyon's friends verify that he was well read in metaphysics, in the writings of Ralph Waldo Emerson, and in New England Transcendentalism. His friends also verify that Kenyon openly confessed the influence of metaphysical thought upon his own theology.

61. Reisser, *Holistic Healers*, 126.
62. D. R. McConnell, *A Different Gospel* (Peabody, Mass.: Hendrickson, 1988), 3-4.

Evidently Kenyon attempted to forge a synthesis of metaphysical and evangelical thought in order to help the traditional church provide for its members the missing spiritual element that he thought caused many to defect to the cults. The resultant Faith theology is a strange mixture of biblical fundamentalism and New Thought metaphysics.[63]

Although Kenyon authored the teachings on which the Faith movement is based, Kenneth Hagin is the man who fashioned these teachings into the fastest-growing movement in charismatic Christendom. He is universally recognized in the movement as both a teacher and a prophet. Because of Hagin's success in the ministry, Kenyon's teachings have become the foundational principles of the Faith movement. Moreover, because of the success of the Faith movement, Kenyon's teachings are also now widely accepted throughout much of the independent charismatic movement.[64]

## Healing in the Spiritual Atonement

The doctrine of healing in the modern Faith movement is based on its understanding of the atonement of Christ. In the Faith theology, the purpose of the atonement is as much to provide healing of disease as it is forgiveness of sin. On the basis of passages such as Isaiah 53:4, Matthew 8:17, and 1 Peter 2:24, Kenyon and Hagin insist that Christ has provided complete physical healing from all sickness. But unlike classical Pentecostals, Faith teachers believe that diseases are healed by Christ's *spiritual* atonement in hell, not his physical death on the cross. Christ had to suffer spiritually in hell to provide healing because all diseases are but a physical effect of a spiritual cause.

### FORERUNNERS: NEW THOUGHT AND UNITY

The idea that all disease is a physical manifestation of something spiritual in origin comes directly from the metaphysical tradition. The founding father of New Thought, P. P. Quimby, defines sickness completely in terms of spiritual causes. The spiritual causality of disease, indeed, of all life, is a central dogma of New Thought metaphysics. Several startling parallels can be drawn between Faith theology and New Thought. Both systems of thought deny that disease has any physical or organic causes, teaching instead that disease is entirely the physical effect of a spiritual cause. Both systems teach that since disease is spiritual, the highest form of healing must be spiritual as well. This exclusively

63. Ibid., 185-86.
64. Ibid., 57, 67.

spiritual understanding of disease, on which Kenyon's doctrine of healing rests, is derived from his background in New Thought.[65]

The mental healing practice of Phineas Parkhurst Quimby (1802-66) of Belfast, Maine, sparked new ideas regarding the power of the mind. Quimby, a skilled clockmaker, had been exposed to hypnosis. He began to believe that sickness was the result of erroneous thinking and a cure could be effected by changing one's own belief system. He eventually dropped hypnosis as a therapeutic tool and began speaking directly with the patient about linking the individual's spiritual nature with divine spirit. Quimby's pioneering ventures had a unique impact on the "mind cure" movement which would later evolve into New Thought.

The Unity School of Christianity cofounded by the Fillmores in 1886 is the most prominent of New Thought movements today. Myrtle Fillmore (1845-1931) suffered from tuberculosis and had been slowly healed over a period of two years by affirming the "Truth principle": "I am a child of God, and therefore I do not inherit sickness," spoken in a lecture by E. B. Weeks in 1886. Statements like this are believed to have restorative or healing power when used daily with the positive power of faith as the underlying dynamic. Consequently, Unity traces its roots to Myrtle's healing process. In 1891, the Fillmores were ordained by Hopkins as Christian Science (New Thought) ministers and their movement officially became known as Unity.[66]

## "Faith Fact" and Physical Healing

The Faith teachers assert the New Thought metaphysical dogma that sickness is always caused by unbelief and sin. They claim that God has done all that he is going to do to provide healing and it is up to the believer to appropriate the perfect healing that is in the atonement. The believer who fails to do so has only himself to blame. He has failed not only himself, but also God.

One sure way a believer can become sick is by uttering a negative confession. A "negative confession" is any mental or verbal acknowledgment of the presence of disease in one's body. The verbal acknowledgment of a disease gives Satan the "right" to inflict it. In the Faith movement, the truly mature rarely even admit they are ill, much less talk about it.

In the Faith movement, the believer is instructed that healing is an accomplished "faith fact," but that it is not instantaneously manifested as a physical fact in the believer's body. During the interlude between the confes-

---

65. Ibid., 149-50.

66. Timothy Miller, ed., *America's Alternative Religions* (Albany, N.Y: State University of New York, 1995), 325, 327.

sion of healing and its manifestation, the believer might encounter "symptoms" of a disease. These symptoms are not the disease itself. The disease itself was laid on Jesus when he died spiritually. Any symptoms of illness are spiritual decoys with which Satan is attempting to trick the believer into making a negative confession, thereby forfeiting his healing.

The New Thought understanding of symptoms is slightly different from Christian Science and is the more direct source of the Faith theology. For the most part, New Thought writers do not deny the reality of physical matter as in Christian Science. Instead, they assert that the higher reality of spiritual truth can overcome any reality perceived by the physical senses. But in practice, New Thought writers recommend the same denial of physical symptoms practiced by Christian Science. Like New Thought, Faith theology in *theory* does not deny the reality of physical matter. In *practice,* however, Faith theology engages in the same sort of denial of physical symptoms advocated by both New Thought and Christian Science. Faith teachers may have a more sophisticated set of biblical proof-texts to justify the practice of denial, but the source of the practice itself is decidedly occultic.[67]

## Medicine as a "Crutch"

The attitude of the Faith teachers toward the medical profession also has strong parallels in the New Thought groups. On the one hand, Faith teachers warn their followers not to get off medication until their faith is strong enough to handle it. On the other hand, by precept and example, they implicitly challenge their followers to abstain from medication whenever possible.

Fred Price, a Faith movement healer, depicts medicine as a "crutch" upon which the immature believer relies: "If you need a crutch or something to help you get along, then praise God, hobble along until you get your faith moving to the point that you don't need a crutch."

Faith theology's position on medical science is based on its New Thought metaphysical understanding of physical symptoms. Medicine is a *physical* science. The whole science of medicine is based on the ability to detect, diagnose, and prescribe treatment of disease and its symptoms. Because Faith teachers believe that disease is *spiritual,* or *metaphysical,* in origin, they must, by definition, also consider the physical science of medicine an inferior means of healing. Faith theology of healing is based not on the ability to detect physical symptoms, but to deny them. The physical symptoms are not real. They will become real, however, if the believer acknowl-

67. McConnell, *A Different Gospel,* 151-54.

edges their existence and fails to apply the principles of spiritual healing. Only people who do not know how to believe God for spiritual healing resort to medical science.[68]

## Biblical Evaluation of New Thought,
## Faith Movement Doctrine of Healing

According to McConnell, because of its New Thought metaphysical background, Faith theology has transformed healing, a biblical practice of long standing in the church, into a cultic obsession. Healing is, indeed, a gift of the Holy Spirit (1 Cor. 14:9). The church has been commissioned to pray for the sick (James 5:14-15). These spiritual experiences and ministries are the heritage of the people of God. This heritage is not, however, the gospel itself. Christianity is not primarily a healing cult, and the gospel is not a metaphysical formula for divine health and wealth. Faith theology's inordinate emphasis on healing is a gross exaggeration of the biblical doctrine and distorts the centrality of Christ and the gospel.

For the Faith movement, healing is not a sovereign miracle bestowed by a merciful God. Healing is a cause-and-effect formula that works every time the Christian applies it in "faith."

Christians must neither deny healing nor simplify it into "steps" or "principles" or "formulas" to which God must respond. To quote Professor Gordon Fee, "God *must* do nothing!" God does, indeed, respond to faith, but he does not always respond with healing. Just as in all areas of prayer, we must exercise faith under the lordship of Christ. His lordship demands that we abandon ourselves to his will.

The Bible teaches that believers will not be entirely free from bodily suffering until the return of Christ and the general resurrection. Kenyon and Hagin's thesis that believers can be fully redeemed from bodily suffering in this life directly contradicts Pauline teaching on bodily redemption. Although through the Holy Spirit we have the "firstfruits" of redemption, even believers "groan" in hope of bodily redemption. Along with the rest of creation, we, too, must "with perseverance wait eagerly for it" (Rom. 8:24-25).

The apostle Paul certainly had need of a personal physician, for he himself was also subject to illness. For our purposes, it is not necessary to know the exact nature of Paul's illness, but the fact that he was ill is hardly in question and is enough to cast serious doubt upon Faith teachers' claim that a believer can and should always manifest perfect health.

68. Ibid., 155.

Moreover, one cannot help but wonder how Paul's bodily illness would have been received today among charismatics. Would charismatics "despise" and "loathe" his illness as an indication of his immature faith?

One of the most dangerous practices encouraged by Faith teachers, both by precept and example, is denial. Because of its background in the metaphysical healing cults, Faith theology instructs believers to deny any physical symptom of illness. Such denial is dangerous. In diseases such as cancer, where early detection is directly proportional to cure rates, it is not only dangerous, it can be deadly. In more serious diseases in which symptoms persist and worsen, the practice of denial can result in a progression of the disease beyond the point at which medical science can help. In some cases, the symptoms are denied to such an extent that a serious illness becomes a deadly one.

Another practice common in the Faith movement is the refusal to seek medical care for illnesses. However, the more moderate faith healers of the Healing Revival, such as Oral Roberts and Kathryn Kuhlman, consistently warned their followers not to reject medicine. Indeed, whenever possible, Roberts and Kuhlman always made it a practice to verify claimed healings with doctors.

The most consistent reports of abuse caused by Faith doctrine of healing involve the treatment of those in the movement with chronic and/or terminal illnesses. Basically, Faith churches have little or no concept of pastoral care for the chronically and terminally ill believer. The time when a dying believer needs a word of encouragement is when he receives a sermonette on the failure of his faith. The time when he needs the support of a sensitive, supportive body of believers is when he is ostracized and isolated as though he was himself infectious.[69]

Douglas Groothuis indicates that holistic health practices are not easy to evaluate. Social critic Ivan Illich emphasizes the detrimental effects of the radical monopoly in health care that has been achieved by traditional medical doctors. I heard him give a dramatic lecture at Baylor University Medical School on this subject. He pointed out that the medical monopoly has not only economic but psychological consequences. He contends that we should utilize alternative holistic approaches and question many established medical practices and philosophies.

69. Ibid., 158-66.

## Lessons in the New Age Approach to Health

Glen Olds, well-known educator, philosopher, and clergyman, suggests lessons we can learn from the New Age approach to health:

1. Never seek to imprison a living God in any dead word, symbol, tradition, or orthodoxy.
2. Be prepared to acknowledge that surprise is the counterpart of God's amazing grace, which is too abundant and unfathomable to be captured finally or fully by any age or system.
3. Objectivity in knowledge or reality does not mean finality, but only dependability.
4. The discipline, public verifiability, and universality of intent in the sciences is an important instrument of knowledge, including theological. New and richer methods of knowing must be forged with comparable dependability to accommodate a wider and richer access to reality than we are now prepared to accept.
5. Organized religion and traditional faith need perpetual challenge and change to remain fresh and resilient. Personal renewal is at the root of that change, which it should reflect and accommodate.
6. If New Age is seen as a conspiracy, Christians should correct it with a wider, better grasp of the biblical worldview.[70]

There are other lessons to be learned from dialogue with alternative medical and New Age health leaders. For example, many New Age health leaders encourage us to take primary responsibility for our own health, to involve ourselves in treatment decisions, and to change unhealthy lifestyles if necessary. Avoiding the role of passive observer is essential. Also important is the healer's attitude toward the patient; a doctor who projects a sense of unconcerned hopelessness or detached disinterest is much less effective than one who is sincerely concerned and intimately involved in the patient's life. There is no better example of a compassionate healer than Jesus Christ (Matt. 15:30-31).[71]

Obviously we do not want to give up valuable aspects of traditional medicine, but we should be open to new emphases. We should treat people as whole beings. The spiritual dimensions of healing should not be avoided. We should remember that our entire life and lifestyle contribute to our health. We are more than machines and should be treated as such. It should be noted that some alternative treatments have experienced enough quantifiable results to warrant serious investigation. Moreover, there have been a number of speculative

70. Ferguson, *New Age Spirituality,* 74-76.
71. Stewart Chevre, "Visualization, Guided Imagery, and the Holistic Health Movement," *SCP Journal* 9.3 (1990): 26-27.

but sound scientific studies indicating that *something* is going on. Acupuncture is just one example of a therapy once considered bizarre that may indeed have some scientific basis. Doctors and clinicians know that acupuncture can provide at least short-term relief for a wide range of pains, either by releasing endorphins — naturally produced, morphine-like substances — or by inhibiting the transmission of pain impulses through the nerves.

Relaxation techniques like meditation and biofeedback — which teach patients to control heart rate, blood pressure, temperature, and other involuntary functions through concentration — have also given respectability to alternative medicine, and are routinely taught to patients and medical students. Although chiropractic clearly has its drawbacks (notably its stubborn insistence that spinal misalignments cause or underlie most ailments, including those far afield from the backbone), its use of vertebral manipulation has proved useful not only in treating acute low-back pain and other muscular and neurological problems but also in comforting patients who appreciate the deft way skilled chiropractors use their hands. Many medical doctors today are more open-minded, but most feel strongly that alternative methods need more thorough testing and caution patients not to abandon traditional treatment.[72]

Lisa Woodside points out that New Age techniques for health have a common denominator of decreasing stress, quieting the mind, and increasing concentration. Thus, these practices agree with the concept of pursuing physical health through good psychic health.

The New Age concept of health and illness maintains that a person's health is a matter of complex interaction among biological, psychological, and social determinants. This more holistic approach to health is compatible with New Age thought with its practices of seeking physical, psychological and spiritual health.

H. H. Bro states that if the body is an instrument to be played with and for others, not just a lump to be prodded and distracted and medicated, then the New Age preoccupation with holistic health is appropriate and a real challenge to churches.[73]

## Weaknesses and Dangers of New Age Health Teachings

New Age health teachings have been critically evaluated by New Age sympathizers, doctors, evangelical cult critics, philosophers, and theologians. Representative examples of the critiques by each group should be helpful.

72. Reisser, *Holistic Healers*, 13; see also John Langone, "Challenging the Mainstream," *Time*, Fall 1996, 42-43.
73. Ferguson, *New Age Spirituality*, 159-60, 186, 208.

## Critiques by New Age Sympathizers

Matthew Fox, ex-priest and spokesman for Creation-centered Spirituality, notes a basic New Age weakness that has implications for health:

The New Age movement tends to be self-centered and anti-institutional. While some persons are called to leave our institutions and begin new ones and some are called to begin the new within the old structures, nevertheless we cannot turn our back on the reality of our species' need for some structure and institutionalization. We will not change civilization without a concerted effort to bring along our institutions, kicking and screaming if necessary, into the new millennium. This is part of one's commitment to incarnation, to matter, to the body, to the political and economic realities of life. It, along with suffering, is part of our being grounded.[74]

Glen Olds, educator and philosopher, lists problematic metaphysical underpinnings for the New Age movement which relate to health.

- Though knowing may be anchored by self-consciousness, objective reality is not always or necessarily constituted by it. The perils of this perspective intrude in a wide range of New Age perspectives. In reaching for full correction to the scientific neutralization, or even nullifying the role of mind in objective reality, the movement frequently overreacts to make mind the sole constituent of reality. The end of this route is to swallow up reality in a self-conscious ingestion of all reality reduced to its self-authenticating encounter. The mode of the beyond is not necessarily the same as within!
- The second liability flows from the first, a mistaken reductionism to self-centered subjectivity. Much criticism has been directed to the New Age's self-serving, self-seeking, and selectively narcissistic roots. It mistakes the window for the world, and perverts what we look *through* to what we look *at*.
- Ironically, the early sense of the New Age that the secular had been stripped of anything sacred turns into the *rejection of anything transcendental* that might give it meaning. In saving the near and immediate from oblivion and loss of value, it commits the fallacy of inversion, claiming that only the *immanent* has meaning. Losing any cosmic sources for vindication of value or calling as a higher and other referent for consciousness, the movement surrenders any objective source of authentication for its own claims to truth.
- Much of the movement is vulnerable to an enduring dilemma of all

74. Ibid., 211.

pantheism. If God is all and in all, how can meaningful distinctions be made within or between elements of reality or preferences, for choice or action? Why should any form of life be given up for any other? And why, if all mirror the Divine, should one value perspective, or person, be used to arbitrate the truth of any other?

- A searching Christian critique of the New Age is that it has no clear theory of sin or evil, and overlooks the human propensity to perversion. As a corrective to a fatalistic materialism, it goes too far in neglect of limitation, power, alienation, and violence.
- As the New Age matures, as all movements tend to do, it is inclined to make a new orthodoxy out of its revolt against the old orthodoxies. One often sees this trend as a movement beginning outside the church and opposed to the church, then turning into a new church or churches with their own tenacious orthodoxy.[75]

## Red Flag Approach

David Sneed, D.O., lists a number of red flags to guide persons in evaluating or following New Age health practitioners.

- An unscientific approach. Ask yourself: Is this therapy within the scientific mainstream?
- Claims to manipulate energy or use psychic power.
- Attempts to make you alone or the "power within" responsible for your health. Watch out for a practitioner who insists that it is the placebo response of your own "inner physician" that heals you.
- Claims that the therapy is a cure-all.
- The practitioner's qualifications are questionable.[76]

## Philosophical and Theological Critiques

James Sire, well-known evangelical scholar and editor, and Paul Reisser, M.D., note basic philosophical and theological critiques that are related to the New Age health movement.

---

75. Ibid., 71-74.
76. Sneed and Sneed, *The Hidden Agenda*, 62-64, 66, 70.

## Closed Universe

A basic difficulty with the New Age worldview is its notion of a closed universe — the absence of a transcendent God. Such a situation makes ethics impossible, for either there is no value at all in the external universe (pure naturalism) or God is inseparable from all its activities and at the level of the cosmos distinctions between good and evil disappear.[77]

## Return to Animism

Second, major difficulty in the New Age worldview comes with what it borrows from animism — a host of demi-gods, demons, and guardians who inhabit the separate reality or the inner spaces of the mind. Call them projections of the psyche or spirits of another order of reality. Either way they haunt the new world of the new person and must be placated by rituals or controlled by incantation. The New Age movement has reopened a door closed since Christianity drove out the dominance of the demons and generally took a dim view of excessive interest in the affairs of Satan's kingdom of fallen angels. Now they are back through the New Age worldview.

The Bible contains no model for enlisting fallen angels in the plans of humans. It does contain warnings against enlisting the aid of spirits of "other gods." One of the earliest and clearest is in Deuteronomy 18:9-14. The New Testament likewise enjoins divination and recounts many instances of demon possession. But it is also clear — and this is most important — that Jesus had complete control over them. It is in this that Christians have hope (Rom. 8:31-39; Col. 2:15).

## No Basis for Truth

A third major difficulty with the New Age is its understanding of the nature of reality and the nature of truth. New Age leaders normally accept the languages of all systems of reality — the languages of sorcery and science, of witchcraft and philosophy, of drug experience and waking reality, and they understand them all to be equally valid descriptions of reality. So there is little critique of anyone's ideas or of anyone's experience. Every system is equally valid; it must only pass the test of experience, and experience is private.

Taken to its logical conclusion, this notion leads to a knowledge vacuum. For one can never know what really is. He can only know what he

77. James W. Sire, *The Universe Next Door* (Downers Grove, Ill.: InterVarsity, 1976), 197-98.

experiences. The flip side is that the self is kingpin — god if you will — and reality is what any god takes it to be or makes it to be.

We are caught in an impasse. The issue is primary: either the self is god and the new consciousness is a readout of the implications of that, or the self is not god and thus is subject to the existence of things other than itself. To the self that opts for its own godhead, there is no argument. Theoretically such a self accepts as real only what it decides to accept. But if we are not the unity-giver (god), who or what is? If we answer that the cosmos is the unity-giver, we end in naturalism.

## No Understanding of Spiritual Conflict

A biblical review clearly teaches the existence of a supernatural realm with which human beings may interact. But in contrast to the picture painted by the New Age view, the Bible consistently declares the psychic realm in whatever guise to be off-limits for humans.

Eastern mysticism and the New Consciousness declare that the categories of good and evil are based only on our limited understanding of the universe. There are no absolutes, but only the ebb and flow of the Tao, the cycles of yin and yang, the polarities of the same unity, the light and dark sides of the Force.

The biblical view, on the other hand, describes a spiritual rebellion against the Creator which eventually contaminated humankind and continues to this day. This warfare is never presented as a symbol of humanity's struggle with itself, but as a direct confrontation between opposing personalities (Isa. 45:5; 14:13-14).

The apostle Paul, highly educated in the Old Testament and well aware of the mysticism of his day, wrote to the church in Ephesus: "Our struggle is not against flesh and blood, but against the rulers, against the authorities, against the power of this dark world and against the spiritual forces of evil in the heavenly realms" (Eph. 6:12). The Old Testament gives a consistent condemnation of practices designed to gather knowledge from invisible sources and to exercise spiritual power apart from God (Deut. 18:10-12; Isa. 8:19). The Bible describes such behavior as spiritual prostitution, fruitless consorting with God's invisible adversaries.

The New Testament elaborates on this theme by raising the issue of spiritual deception. Jesus spoke quite bluntly about the activities of demons, and all four Gospels describe confrontations with them in vivid detail. Jesus predicted that, prior to his return to earth, "false Christs and false prophets will appear and perform great signs and miracles to deceive even the elect — if that were possible" (Matt. 24:24).

Paul, who not only established numerous congregations but constantly battled against their infiltration by false teachers, characterized his adversaries as "false prophets, deceitful workmen, masquerading as apostles of Christ. And no wonder, for Satan himself masquerades as an angel of light" (2 Cor. 11:13-14).

These and other passages describe the invisible enemy of God and humanity as capable of producing impressive and inspiring displays which are deliberately misleading. This casts an uneasy shadow on psychic diagnosis and healing. If one accepts the Old and New Testaments as authoritative, then one cannot assume that an insight gained from an unseen intelligence is necessarily true, nor that a supernatural healing comes from God.

If healing signs and wonders are consistently accompanied by metaphysical messages which contradict the core of biblical teaching — humanity's estrangement from God, God's rescue through the Messiah, and the need for individual repentance and submission to God's authority — then whatever physical benefit results from the healing may be offset by a far more profound spiritual consequence. Jesus never minced words on the relative importance of physical and spiritual well-being: "What good will it be for a man if he gains the whole world, yet forfeits his soul?" (Matt. 16:26).

Especially in making judgments in the area of psychic healing, a person's belief system is involved. One will either discount healing claims as unlikely or impossible, accept them as evidence of new dimensions of human potential, or view them as a skirmish in an invisible war.[78]

# THE BIBLICAL WORLDVIEW AND HEALTH

The emphasis of this study has been on the collision between the New Age and biblical views. There has also been an effort toward dialogue, evaluation, and transformation. The teachings of the Bible have been used as a basis for critiquing the New Age health movement and warning of the hazards of tampering with the psychic realm. It would not be appropriate to conclude a study of health without outlining the biblical vision of health and its guidance for approaching the person who is ill, for preventing illness, and for creating the kind of balanced, enriched life which is the essence of wellness.

78. Sire, *The Universe Next Door*, 199-203; Hoyt, *The New Age Rage*, 89-90; Reisser, *Holistic Healers*, 129-32.

## Health Principles of the Biblical Worldview

Paul Reisser, a Christian physician who coedited the book *Holistic Healers,* lists the following biblical teaching as related to the general health area:

1. The Bible declares the significance of humans as individuals created and loved by a sovereign God (Ps. 139:1-3, 13-14). The very basis for caring for ourselves and each other is this awareness of our worth, our importance as individuals. There is ultimately no more secure basis for self-esteem than a working knowledge of this personal recognition of the Creator.

2. The biblical view orients us to the fallenness of humanity and the biological world. Even if we treat our bodies impeccably, they still eventually wear out and die. Unavoidable accidents, injuries, infections, and genetic mistakes happen in the lives of the wise and foolish alike (Rom. 8:22-23).

This teaching not only helps us deal both with annoyances and catastrophes, but it also helps us understand that achieving anything of value — including good health — is an uphill struggle. Without deliberate effort and maintenance, muscles become weak, fat accumulates, teeth decay, marriages crumble, and the mind stagnates. Once we have realized that this tendency toward deterioration in ourselves and disorder in our relationships is a universal pattern in the fallen world, we can avoid wallowing in self-pity and get on with constructive activity.

3. The Bible makes it clear that we have a personal responsibility for excellence in our physical condition, our thinking, our behavior, and our relationships. Paul wrote that the body is "meant . . . for the Lord, and the Lord for the body" (1 Cor. 6:13). For the believer in Christ the issue is not only that of God's ownership of our lives, but the very presence of the risen Christ and the Holy Spirit in the believer. This puts a new perspective on our conduct. Paul used this fact as a powerful argument against sexual promiscuity (1 Cor. 6:15, 18-20). Furthermore, there is no more helpful statement on examining what we allow to enter and dwell in our minds than the exhortation that "whatever is right, whatever is pure, whatever is lovely, whatever is admirable — if anything is excellent or praiseworthy — think about such things" (Phil. 4:8).

4. The Bible also reminds us of our limitations. Though wisdom and health are much to be desired, they are not ends in themselves. Apart from being rightly related to God, they are not of crucial importance (Eccl. 12:13).[79]

---

79. Reisser, *Holistic Healers,* 142-45.

## BIBLICAL ENCOURAGEMENT FOR
## BOTH ILLNESS AND HEALTH

For the ill, according to Reisser, there are words of comfort: affliction will ultimately end, and while present it can be an occasion both for learning compassion and gaining inner strength. Paul wrote to the Corinthian church that "the Father of compassion . . . comforts us in all our troubles, so that we can comfort those in any trouble with the comfort we ourselves have received from God" (2 Cor. 1:3-4). In addition to the harassment and indignities which he suffered at the hands of his adversaries, Paul also endured a "thorn in the flesh," which many interpreters believe was a physical ailment. God's response to his repeated prayers that the suffering be relieved was this: "My grace is sufficient for you, for my power is made perfect in weakness" (2 Cor. 12:8).

In terms of prevention of illness, the Bible provides guidelines for temperate behavior. Indeed, if humans would begin to follow biblical standards, there would be a revolution of health. There would be an end to the physical deterioration, violence, and accidents which result from alcohol abuse. Self-destruction from illicit drug use would cease. The current epidemic of sexually transmitted disease would come to an end. The incalculable physical and social effects of anxiety, hatred, loneliness, and disrupted relationships would largely disappear.[80]

In addition, there would be a widespread dedication to proper diet and physical exercise. In fact, Kenneth Cooper affirms that your Christian faith can become the key you've been seeking to unlock the doorway to better fitness. Cooper states that a raft of recent scientific studies has established that having deep personal convictions and values can do wonders for almost every aspect of your physical and emotional well-being. He lists some specific enhancements to health that have been linked to firm, inner commitments to moral principles, social values, God, or even oneself: less depression, smoking, and alcohol abuse; healthier mothers and babies; protection from colon and rectal cancer; improved coping with breast cancer; a healthier emotional balance; reduced levels of stress; lower blood pressure and a healthier cardiovascular system; stronger marriages ties; overcoming poor eating habits — including overeating that leads to obesity.[81]

The need for a correlation of Christian faith and proper diet came home to me as I drove through Siloam Springs, Arkansas, which is known as a small city with a large segment of strong conservative Christian citizens and as the home of the conservative Christian John Brown University. First, I noted a large display board on the highway affirming that "Jesus is Lord in

80. Ibid., 146.
81. Cooper, *It's Better to Believe*, 8.

Siloam Springs, Arkansas." Second, I stopped to eat at the Western Sizzler cafe. In the adjacent booth were two extremely overweight women and an overweight teenager. They were deeply engrossed in talk about a revival in their church and their dedication to Christ. At the same time they were eating three plates each of fried chicken and french fries. Evidently, for them, there was little correlation between their devout Christian faith and the care of the human body. Unfortunately, such an attitude exists among many professing Christians. Ray Furr of the Southern Baptist Annuity Board recently was quoted in a newspaper story, titled "Baptist's Battle of the Bulge," as saying that he finds it extremely difficult to listen to a minister who is physically out of condition. It's like a doctor who smokes.

On a positive note, for those who desire wellness, the Bible emphasizes the emotional and physical health that is provided by living under the control of the Holy Spirit. "But the fruit of the Spirit is love, joy, peace, patience, kindness, goodness, faithfulness, gentleness and self-control" (Gal. 5:22). The by-product of continuously communicating our needs and desires to God is an inner tranquillity "which transcends all understanding" (Phil. 4:7). The teachings of Jesus on worry are familiar but have been forgotten by a society in which anxiety seems to have become a national state of mind (Matt. 6:25-27). Furthermore, we should remember that the Holy Spirit renews our inner being day by day (2 Cor. 4:16; Eph. 3:16). Although our bodies will remain mortal during this life, limited healings and physical blessings are available now. Preliminary healing can flow through Christian workers and Christian communities. Prayer for the sick and the laying on of hands have value. In Romans 8:11 the promise of life to our mortal bodies primarily refers to the new body in the new era, but there is promise here and now of some preliminary healing and quickening.

Christians do pray for the sick. In James 5:14-16, the early church is portrayed as being in prayer, and this prayer became a channel of healing. As those who are ill are accepted and undergirded and loved and prayed for in the Christian group, guilt, isolation, and loneliness are dispelled. In a Spirit-filled church of power, illness-producing factors are faced, shared, and dissolved. Leslie Weatherhead, prominent British minister and Yale lecturer, has found that the laying on of hands is also a means whereby the power of the Holy Spirit flows through the hands into the personality of the afflicted. Anointing with oil is generally thought of as a form of dedication and a symbolic ceremony. Some ministers, however, such as Leslie Weatherhead, contend that the oil on the forehead enables the power to flow more powerfully through the hands to the person who is ill. As was noted in the discussion of Therapeutic Touch, the emphasis of Weatherhead on the laying on of hands is disputed.

The close alliance of the apostle Paul and the beloved physician Luke causes one to realize that every advance in medicine can be accepted as a gift of God. But surely Spirit-filled leaders would never want the medical profession to become a crutch for spiritual laziness. Pills should be secondary in attempts to heal a spiritually rooted maladjustment.

If excesses, glorification of the individual, exhibitionism, sensationalism, and overemphasis on the physical are avoided, much good can come through Christian healers. This healing can take place in connection with visitation in the home and hospital. It can involve a ministry of intercession. It will involve close cooperation with the medical profession and psychologists. Many denominational hospitals are a partial, if not a full, expression of Christian healing concern. This healing emphasis could also utilize small healing sessions where hands are laid on, oil is employed, and specific prayer is offered. In these sessions and in many other ways lives are straightened out, emotions are released, guilty souls blessed, and bodies given at least a preliminary healing.

Above all, the sick person should be oriented to the idea that health is a by-product. Physical healing comes as a by-product of full surrender to Christ and active devotion to his larger redemptive purpose. The Christian's greatest encouragement is the fact that one day the Holy Spirit will transform his body of flesh into a new spiritual body which will know no pain (1 Cor. 15:44).

Beyond physical and emotional health, God offers hope and the security of knowing our ultimate destination if we will abandon our willfulness and submit to his gospel and authority. Furthermore, in exchange for the stagnation and despair which stems from preoccupation with self, God offers the fulfilling satisfaction of being his steward and representative on earth and participating in helping to change the lives of others.

The Bible realistically points out that the world "groans" and is fallen. This means that we are not offered any guarantee of freedom from illness, adversity, and danger during our stay on earth. We are promised that, if we have accepted God's pardon for our fallenness and rebellion — the pardon which is available only because Jesus Christ suffered and died in our place — our final destiny will include that freedom and much more in the new heavens. In the meantime, we are offered the ultimate resource — God himself — for making the most of our lives, regardless of circumstances. Writing from prison, the apostle Paul declared:

> I know what it is to be in need, and I know what it is to have plenty. I have learned the secret of being content in any and every situation, whether well fed or hungry, whether living in plenty or in want. I can do everything through him who gives me strength. (Phil. 4:12-13)

We would agree with Reisser that the Bible has the most adequate definition of healing and wholeness — in time and eternity.[82]

---

82. Reisser, *Holistic Healers*, 146.

## Firefighting versus Prevention in Medicine

Paul Reisser openly acknowledges that the traditional system of medical education still trains new physicians primarily to be firefighters. Medical students, interns, and residents are geared from day one to derive great satisfaction from discovering pathology (or taking a look at that which someone else has found). Any interest which the doctor in training might have in exploring the patient's attitudes and emotions will usually be buried under an uncivilized schedule and lack of sleep. Reisser notes that most physicians are not, in fact, unfeeling technicians with a search-and-destroy mentality which dehumanizes patients. However, the vast majority do find firefighting more interesting, challenging, and rewarding than trying to influence their patients' long-term behavior. Most patients unknowingly reinforce this preference by expressing requests (subtle or otherwise) that something be done to them or for them — and the sooner the better.

A more troublesome situation is the young adult who complains of fatigue, headaches, and episodes of dizziness over a period of several months. Evaluating such symptoms can frustrate patient and physician alike because all too often a small fortune is spent on time-consuming exams, X-rays and laboratory tests which reveal no abnormalities. An awkward moment then arrives when the doctor announces, "I can't find anything wrong with you." The patient responds, "Then why do I feel so lousy all the time?" The answer is that there are probably a lot of reasons, which may include bad eating habits, poor self-image, boredom, frustrations with children, job dissatisfaction, lack of exercise, and a troubled marriage.

Unfortunately, tackling such issues is no small project. The disease-oriented physician may reach for the prescription pad and supply a drug to dull the anxiety level or ship the patient to a psychiatrist, while muttering to himself that he'd prefer taking care of people who are "really sick." (Unfortunately, the patient in front of him probably will be really sick before long.)

Even if the patient welcomes the reassurance that no serious pathology is apparent, bringing about meaningful changes in habits and attitudes may prove to be a formidable task. The doctor can describe the risks of smoking in sickening detail or rhapsodize on the benefits of quitting, but he or she cannot follow the patients around to extinguish their cigarettes.[83]

---

83. Ibid., 136-38.

## Discernment Relating to Worldview

Above all, the holistic health movement has served as a platform for disseminating the worldview of the New Age and promoting various kinds of occultism as an approach to health.

Those who seek to prevent lifestyle-related illness and promote wellness without embroiling themselves in Eastern mysticism and occultism should be encouraged, however, to know that a growing number of resources are available to them. As we noted earlier, sophisticated programs in wholeperson care have been developed by such persons and organizations as Granger Westberg, Wholistic Health Centers, and Kenneth Cooper.

Another encouraging recent development has been the participation of hospitals, many of which are related to Christian churches, in promoting wellness. Health promotion has also been initiated in business settings. Many corporations promote physical fitness among employees.

## Need for Discipline and Concern for the Person

According to Reisser, for doctor and patient alike, perhaps the greatest obstacle to improving health is what Eugene H. Peterson describes as the "assumption that anything worthwhile can be acquired at once." We forget too quickly that meaningful changes in lifestyle require "long obedience": hundreds of small decisions made over a period of months and years. Most of these entail some degree of self-discipline or temporary self-denial, commodities which are rarely prized in an "instant society." If it feels good, do it" has become a cliche, and too many of us continue to build our lives on the shifting sand of momentary feelings. Indeed, most of the plagues of the 1990s — including coronary disease, obesity, chemical dependency, and sexually transmitted disease — are but the end point of day-to-day choices based on transient emotions.

In summary, Reisser admits that most of the delivery systems and patients of Western medicine's practitioners remain fixated on crisis care. As a society we seem more interested in putting out fires than in preventing them. We hope for technological solutions to our health problems while paying scant attention to the daily decisions which truly influence health. This behavior is on a collision course with its own price tag.[84]

Human beings are very complex, and health and illness are affected by thousands of variables. For this reason, controlled studies are extremely important in determining whether a therapy is safe and effective. The long and laborious methods of Western medical research are not a clever scheme to

84. Ibid., 139-42.

keep alternative therapies out of the mainstream. They have evolved because it is so difficult to acquire reliable knowledge, and because reputable scientific institutions have a commitment (even if imperfectly kept) to protect people from worthless or harmful treatments.[85]

Christians, including physicians, should be especially discerning in all areas related to the New Age worldview. We should beware of the dangers and limitations of psychic diagnosis and healing. We should also be careful about therapies which claim to manipulate life energies and are at odds with known biological mechanisms. It is especially important to develop a clearly defined, biblically based worldview and use this in a discerning way in the area of health practices.

# REAPPLYING THE BIBLICAL WORLDVIEW TO HEALING

James P. Wind of the Religious Division of the Lily Endowment makes a strong case for reapplying the biblical worldview in the ministry of healing. The challenge facing those who wish to heal according to the biblical worldview in our age is how to help people move from isolated experiences of suffering with strangers into communities where the multidimensional healing of the gospel can occur. This task is a complex one since it involves welcoming the Creator's good gifts through modern medicine as well as resisting powerful temptations to reduce healing to physical cure. It implies a complex stance in which Christians and the church welcome and, at the same time, criticize medicine's gifts. A special kind of hospitality needs to be developed in our parishes and congregations, one that makes room for sufferers and curers within a much larger and deeper understanding of healing.

A large part of the challenge facing the church is the need to heal our own traditions. Although our various denominations and congregations have been extraordinary innovators in the arts of healing, we have also participated far too willingly in the fragmentation of healing. Whereas we have handed bodies to physicians and minds to therapists, we have withheld only souls for a kind of spiritual care. Following the biblical view, Christians need to start a fresh argument with the world about what real healing is. At the same time, we need to set human experience in a larger biblical context in which God's gifts of health and salvation can be encountered in fresh, life-giving ways.[86]

85. Hoyt, *The New Age Rage*, 66-67.
86. James P. Wind, "A Case for Theology in the Ministry of Healing," *Interpretation*, 155-56.

But let us return to the more limited personal emphasis. In a Brooks Alexander interview, the Christian physician admitted that it is impossible to deal with a patient without some hint of one's personal values, especially if one is doing the kind of medicine that is concerned with the "whole person." "If a patient has some problem which seems to have a definite spiritual component, there is not any reason why a doctor should be prevented from sharing his convictions, assuming it is not done in a pushy or manipulative way. It is not a simple question at all, but as Christians we are called upon to defend and explain our hope gently and in an intelligible manner when we are asked or as the opportunity arises."[87]

This statement appropriately points out that we should go beyond dialogue and evaluation to confession and incarnation of our biblical faith and the hoped-for Christian transformation, healing, and health.

87. Brooks Alexander, *SCP Journal*, August 1978, 37.

# CHAPTER NINE

# The World of Business

Poverty and prosperity are simply a matter of belief. God has given us more than we could ever need or want. Resources are unlimited. Those who are poor or lacking in some way simply see themselves that way, and the world fulfills their belief. All you have to do to overcome poverty is change your belief. Think that you are prosperous and enjoying God's abundance, and the world rewards you by giving you prosperity.

At least that's the thinking of one segment of the New Age. They call it "prosperity consciousness." Poverty or prosperity is all a matter of individual consciousness, these New Agers say.

During the early nineteenth century, a major person in the development of prosperity consciousness was writer Ralph Waldo Emerson. Emerson was the major advocate of self-culture, the development of one's mind or capacities through one's own efforts. Having left traditional Christianity behind, Emerson developed a philosophy (Transcendentalism) built around the existence of the Oversoul, a universal spirit/spiritual energy which he said pervades existence. Human life finds meaning as it lives in harmony with the Oversoul. Self-culture is one means of living in harmony. The rewards of a vigorous life of self-culture, according to Emerson, are usually wealth and prosperity.

## METAPHYSICAL WRITERS

During the early decades of the twentieth century, numerous metaphysical writers picked up on the prosperity theme. Richard Ingalese clearly presented the basic approach to wealth in his classic text *The History and Power of Mind* (1902). In introducing his readers to "The Law of Opulence," he emphasized the necessity of being in tune with certain "truths." First, there must be an acceptance that everything one might want already exists in the Divine Mind. Second, the Divine Mind owns everything and gives possessions only as a temporary loan. Third, as the world is run by law, so Divine Mind distributes things to people according to law, in this case the law of opulence. The law of opulence then works on the principle of demand. The individual must earnestly want, picture clearly in the mind, and demand from the Divine Mind to receive a specific item. If the law of opulence is followed, the Divine Mind will supply accordingly, although to all appearances the desire will have been fulfilled by ordinary, if seemingly miraculous, means.

Charles Fillmore, the founder of the Unity School of Christianity, exerted a leadership role in the metaphysical community for forty years before the stock market crash and had frequently written on prosperity themes. In the face of a severe test for the school he headed and the followers who were living in trying economic conditions, his book on *Prosperity* became a reaffirmation of faith in the themes of prosperity consciousness.[1]

Napoleon Hill was probably the single most important person in the developing tradition of prosperity consciousness. Operating out of a primarily secular background, Hill assumed all of the common religious metaphysical beliefs, but stated them in blunt, businesslike fashion. Prayer for prosperity became *Think and Grow Rich,* the title of his 1937 classic. Authors of a recent biography of Hill state that it sold 20 million copies over the next fifty years. Politician Newt Gingrich lists it among the books that most influenced him.

Hill claimed to have learned the secrets of those who had accumulated a fortune in twentieth-century America and to have reduced that information to a set of simple rules. The rules generally follow the outlines of prosperity consciousness.

A unique idea developed by Hill was the Master Mind group. He advised people searching for wealth to regularly meet with a group of other people on a similar quest. By sharing knowledge, listening as others told of success in reaching goals, and enjoying the spirit of harmony between people united around the same purpose, the sessions served to continually motivate and encourage each individual member of the group. This group was backed by a wealthy disciple, insurance executive W. Clement Stone, who made the Master books required reading for his agents.[2]

---

1. J. Gordon Melton, *New Age Almanac* (Detroit: Visible Ink, 1991), 429-32.
2. Michael J. Ritt, Jr., and Kirk Landers, *A Lifetime of Riches* (New York: Dutton, 1997).

## New Age Prosperity Consciousness

In the 1960s prosperity consciousness, which had been somewhat neglected in the metaphysical movement, was revived within the New Thought movement by students of Hill and Fillmore, and from there passed into the New Age movement. The New Age prosperity teachings follow closely the prosperity consciousness teachings which have been passed through New Thought for a century. The teachings emphasize individual responsibility for one's state of relative poverty or abundance. People either choose to think of themselves as poor or develop an image of themselves as abundantly endowed. Most people, according to Terry Cole-Whitaker, choose to regard themselves as victims of circumstances.

All prosperity teachers believe that, in the end, it is one's consciousness, rather than hard work, native intelligence, or luck, that determines one's lot in life. Thus, according to proponents of prosperity consciousness, to move from poverty to opulence requires some significant changes in an individual's self-image.

First, there must be the assumption that every person can have all that he or she wants without taking anything from anyone else. This assumption is based on the belief that resources are unlimited, which assuages any guilt at having more than others.

Second, wealth is a matter of inner mind-set rather than inherited outer circumstances. One chooses one's position in life, and most people, quite early in life, unconsciously choose that of their parents and the people with whom they grew up. However, once one assumes the position of a person deserving all of the abundance of life, and knows that it is possible to receive it, then it is simply a matter of learning the metaphysical techniques of acquiring wealth, which are numerous, and working at it.

It has been observed that many people who have been attracted to the New Age movement are upwardly mobile young adults. Prosperity consciousness fits directly into their lifestyle and has become a meaningful adjunct to their business and professional lives, either as people moving up in a corporation or as founders of their own businesses. Those in sales will quickly discover that they are being taught a form of prosperity consciousness as part of their company's sales motivation training.[3]


## Human Potential Seminars Leading to the New Age

The business world picked up on this thinking, seeing it as a way to increase productivity, creativity, and profits. American businesses had noted that one

3. Melton, *New Age Almanac*, 432-33.

of the ingredients of Japan's business success was the shared vision, values, and traditions of its workforce. They needed some way to instill those common values in American workers. They also desired a powerful group experience that could change employees' thinking and values along common lines beneficial to the corporation.

Enter the human potential movement, which is quite accomplished at producing such group experiences. Thus, the nation's leading businesses began inviting such seminars as "Transformational Technologies" (Werner Erhard's development), Lifespring, and Summit Workshops to help change their "corporate cultures." Through what has come to be known as "organization development," New Age humanistic psychology has penetrated into the very soul of corporate America.[4]

## Erhard and Business

"The gospel according to Erhard," or est, is seen as a philosophically distilled version of Eastern mysticism and human potential psychology packaged in a high-pressure group situation. The essence is that we all create our own reality (right and wrong do not exist); we are responsible to no one but ourselves; we become effective not by thinking but by being, and we have limitless potential. This is taught not in a lecture format of critical discussion and evaluation, but in sessions in which trainees are jolted by a kind of New Age marathon shock therapy.[5]

The New Age Marx, according to Carl Raschke, was probably Michael Murphy, the architect of Esalen. He influenced the thinking of the sixties. But history waited for a "Lenin" with supreme organizational talents, an appetite for glory and power, and a paucity of scruples for the actual "movement" to be born.

The New Age found its Lenin in the very salesman-turned-psychobabble, specialist-turned-management consultant to whom his legions of trainees refer affectionately as "Werner." Werner Erhard "Americanized" the earlier version of Oriental-style Maslowian esotericism developed by Esalen and made a mass of true believers out of it, according to Raschke.[6]

It is hard to imagine that people paid big money to be sequestered in

---

4. Elliot Miller, *A Crash Course in the New Age Movement* (Grand Rapids: Baker, 1989), 99-100.

5. Douglas Groothuis, *Confronting the New Age* (Downers Grove, Ill.: InterVarsity, 1988), 154.

6. Carl Raschke, "Business as Usual: The New Age Rage and Corporate America," *SCP Journal* 9.1 (1989), 23.

a room, deprived of food and sleep, told when and if they could go to the bathroom, and broken emotionally, all in the name of self-improvement! I should know; I enrolled in a seminar led by Werner Erhard himself.

Noted "estians" included celebrities like John Denver, Yoko Ono, Joanne Woodward, Cher, Polly Bergen, Norman Lear, Judy Collins, and Diana Ross, plus corporate and professional leaders of such prestigious institutions as MIT, the American Management Association, Harvard Business School, and Stanford Business School, all of whom sat at the feet of Erhard.

## The Forum, Transformational Technologies, and Related Groups

When that style of group teaching began to fall into disrepute, it was given a facelift and a new name. Such regrouping has become a consistent pattern. Out of est came The Forum, and from that has come a franchise called Transformational Technologies. Although names changed and techniques have been made more palatable for the business community, the underlying belief system is still the same.[7]

In 1985, Erhard started the Forum with the business world as its target audience. His strategy may have slightly changed since the days of est, but his worldview has not. The Forum is for Erhard the entry point into business for the New Age.

Because the Forum's ostentatious approach may alienate some, its basic teaching is being channeled through another Erhard enterprise, Transformational Technologies, Inc. TTI is a management consulting company started in 1984 that has sold intensive (and expensive) seminars to large corporations such as TRW and municipalities such as the City of Chicago, as well as to entrepreneurial firms. Erhard used his well-developed network of est graduates — many of whom sit at elevated positions on the corporate ladder — to establish the venture, setting up in less than two years 47 franchises which are experiencing rapid growth. Each franchise — preferring to be called a "TTI affiliate" — has the right to package Erhardian ideas for various clients in exchange for an initial outlay of $20,000 and 8 percent of the gross income over the first five years. Erhard is a controversial figure whose notoriety could bar him from many large corporations. But his protégés carry no such baggage.[8]

Human potential seminars sponsored by the Pacific Institute — originally called "New Age Thinking" — "have attracted hundreds of high-paying clients like ABC-TV, NASA, Eastman Kodak, John Fluke Manufacturing, People's National Bank, McDonald Corporation, AT&T, IBM, the U.S.

---

7. David Jeremiah, *Invasion of Other Gods* (Dallas: Word, 1995), 135.
8. Groothuis, *Confronting the New Age*, 153, 155-56.

Army, General Motors Corporation, and most of the nation's top one hundred corporate giants — plus many foreign clients." Although the Pacific Institute's seminars are less occult oriented than some, their main emphasis is on self-actualization through visualization and affirmation.

The Inner Game is a human potential approach to achieving higher physical and mental performance in sports and in life. Founded in 1979, Inner Game Limited was originated by Tim Gallwey, who said that "the opponent in one's head may be more daunting than the one on the other side of the net." Gallwey is the author of such volumes as *The Inner Game of Tennis, Inner Skiing,* and *The Inner Game of Golf.* He now applies these principles to business training.[9]

## Human Potential Seminars

Even Stanford Business School offers a course on how to use New Age metaphysical teaching to increase their creativity in a business setting. The professor of the course, Michael Ray, has put his teachings into a book titled *Creativity in Business.* In it he gives meditation techniques, yoga exercises, and specific instructions on how to contact a personal "Spirit Guide."

*Creativity in Business* is a clear example of how the American business community is becoming more and more receptive to using New Age practices to increase productivity and efficiency. In July 1986 officials from IBM, AT&T, and General Motors met in New Mexico to discuss how metaphysics, the occult, and Hindu mysticism could possibly aid businessmen in an increasingly competitive marketplace.

According to Glenn Rupert, it is estimated that American corporations collectively spend about $4 billion per year on New Age seminars. Some seminars are more "religious" than others. Two of the most prominent, Lifespring and Transformational Technologies, are similar to est, a self-help seminar of the seventies. Like their predecessor, they maintain a secular appearance. However, many underlying religious beliefs do show through.[10]

## John-Roger and Insight Seminars

From Rupert's perspective, a more obvious example of a "New Age" training seminar is Insight Seminars, part of the Movement for Spiritual Inner Aware-

9. Paul Heelas, *The New Age Movement* (Cambridge, Mass.: Blackwell, 1996), 72.
10. James R. Lewis and J. Gordon Melton, eds., *Perspectives on the New Age* (Albany, N.Y.: State University of New York, 1992), 127-28.

ness. The California-based MSIA (pronounced "Messiah") was founded by John-Roger (Hinkins) in the early seventies. John-Roger is the self-proclaimed carrier of Mystical Traveller Consciousness, a spiritual entity that has purportedly come in many incarnations to bring humans closer to their divine potential. MSIA is a New Age organization which launched Insight Seminars in 1978.

Immediately preceding the first Insight meeting, John-Roger called together a group of ministers to tell them of a meeting in Hawaii from which he had just returned. It was a "four-day meeting up on a high mountain peak . . . called through the Traveller Consciousness. . . ." It was attended by "the spiritual hierarchy of the planet," which included Jesus, Krishna, and other "ascended masters." In fact, he claimed that he left the earth after an operation, and a spiritual entity, "John the Beloved," entered his body. From that time on, Roger D. Hinkins became John-Roger.

Since its inception, Insight Seminars has grown considerably. It has now been split into Insight I, II, and III. Each level progresses further into John-Roger's mystical teachings. To date, well over fifty thousand people have participated in Insight training. Philip Lippincott, president and CEO of the former Scott Paper, was so captivated by John-Roger's teachings that he offered the insight training to all employees at company expense. Some other companies which have sent employees include Lockheed, McDonnell Douglas, Chemical Bank, and the U.S. Social Security Administration.

*Fortune* magazine reported that MSIA has been boosted by Barbra Streisand, Leigh Taylor-Young, and Arianna Staffinopoulos Huffington, the latter capping a brilliant social career in London and New York by writing a best-seller and marrying Texas millionaire and California politician Michael Huffington. "She promoted MSIA by writing about it and introducing John-Roger to her friends," *Fortune* noted.[11]

## TM, Ron Hubbard, and Scientology

The New Age involvement in business began in earnest with the "counter-culture" and its evangelists, who made a point of packaging the Ancient Wisdom for modern consumption. In particular, Maharishi Mahesh Yogi's Transcendental Meditation (TM) set the pace for today's New Age approach to business when it came up with the earliest systematic plan to penetrate the business community with its technique. Another important influence has been L. Ron Hubbard's Scientology, which preceded TM by a decade and a half.

11. Jeremiah, *Invasion of Other Gods*, 131, 136.

Hubbard was a pioneer in the process of secularizing the Eastern/occult worldview. After years of studying occultism and Eastern religions, Hubbard demythologized their philosophies and Westernized their cultural styles. He stripped away the saffron robes, the gongs, and the intoned mantras, replacing them with business suits, electronic gadgetry, and the jargon of self-improvement. But he retained all the core themes and values of the Eastern/occult worldview.

Hubbard was among the first to realize that in a largely secular culture "ultimate concerns" could be addressed "scientifically" and "therapeutically" rather than from a traditional "religious" standpoint. Hubbard's genius is that he was the first to combine commerce, enlightenment, and electronics into a unified system of franchised high "techgnosis."[12]

The Church of Scientology oversees two organizations which train corporate employees: WISE and Sterling Management. WISE is a non-profit organization which claims to have Volkswagen as a customer. Sterling Management is a fledgling consulting firm which so far has served only smaller companies.

In 1987 employees of Megaplex, an Atlanta answering service, were encouraged to attend a Scientology seminar at company expense. According to one employee, the seminar began as a normal management course, but soon it plunged deep into the doctrines of Scientology.

Paul Heelas, a British sociologist, states that it is safe to assume that *at least* five million people have taken the business-related seminars of est-like organizations since the early 1970s.[13]

## Basic Emphases and Techniques of New Age Prosperity Programs

Briefly stated, the New Age movement promotes a "personal transformation" of spirit (usually referred to as consciousness) through the use of certain techniques, often called psychotechnologies. The movement suggests that humankind has the ability and capacity fully to self-actualize (sometimes called reaching enlightenment or inner-wisdom, the higher self) and that this is the goal of transformation. Inherent in the movement is the Eastern philosophical view of monism, the belief that there is no distinction between matter and spirit and that, therefore, humanity is connected and individuals are extensions or manifestations of that whole.

Because humanity's true destination is the realization that humankind is divine, the movement promotes techniques that accelerate this transforming process.

12. Brooks Alexander, "Not Built in a Day," *SCP Journal* 9.1 (1989): 15.
13. Heelas, *New Age Movement*, 111-12.

Among these techniques are a number that are being used with greater frequency in business.[14] Reasons cited for the use of various techniques usually bypass the main result — transformation. Among the reasons are the following:

- Meditative techniques are used as part of a stress management strategy. Techniques recommended for their stress reduction value include: transcendental meditation, self-hypnosis, guided imagery, yoga, and centering.
- Some techniques are used to enhance the creativity of the intuitive process: guided imagery, visualization, Silva mind control, dianetics, and focusing.

New Age themes are interwoven in the best-seller *Reinventing the Corporation* (1985), co-authored by John Naisbitt of *Megatrends* (1982) fame. In commenting that intuition is becoming "increasingly valuable in the new information society precisely because there is so much data," Naisbett — who himself meditates, consults a psychic, and believes in reincarnation — notes that "in a test at Neward College of Engineering, eleven of twelve company presidents who had doubled sales in the previous four years scored abnormally high in precognition [psychically predicting the future]." He also adds that Peter Senge "notes that successful entrepreneurs score well above average on tests of intuitive ability such as precognition and remote viewing."

Bob LoPinto, a broker with E. F. Hutton in 1986 who has been faithfully meditating since age sixteen, credited his success as the top broker in his group to his meditation. He said that Transcendental Meditation "really does develop your intuition and creativity. Those two things really help you compete against everyone else."[15]

- Certain techniques enhance self-regulation. Techniques that assist in self-regulation include biofeedback, hypnosis, self-hypnosis, and affirmation.
- Other techniques are used to encourage employees to accept a greater share of responsibility for themselves and their company. These include est (now called The Forum or Transformation Technologies), Lifespring, DMA, actualizations, and other human potential seminar programs.
- Some techniques — namely, suggestology and visualization — are used to promote accelerated learning. Others — such as neurolinguistic programming — are used to improve interpersonal skills.

14. Richard Watring, "New Age Training in Business," *Eternity* magazine, February 1995, 30.
15. Groothuis, *Confronting the New Age*, 158-59.

These goals are not bad, in and of themselves. The possible danger is in the techniques used to achieve them.[16]

## Problems with New Age Prosperity Techniques

In order for the techniques to be of value, the individual must adopt a new view (often called a paradigm shift) which underlies the change being sought. For this reason, one sees increasing acceptance of beliefs in reincarnation, karma, monism (or pantheism), synchronicity (the belief in the interconnectedness of all life), New Age metaphysics (the belief that the mind has the power to influence forces within the universe which can change material reality), cosmic unity, paranormal phenomena, and out-of-body experiences.

New Age training techniques are not "value neutral," asserts Ron Zemke, senior editor of *Training*. "Rather, they are techniques inherently geared toward getting people to adopt New Age paradigms. The problem is that the values with which they are imbued are Eastern philosophical views of a pantheistic, non-Christian nature. Techniques that depend on protocols that command the learners to project themselves into some "other" reality and then to experience themselves as being one with all things, including God, are hardly neutral. They certainly are not neutral to Christians whose faith rests on the concept of God as an entity outside themselves.[17]

Biblical Christians see this new view as heretical. Richard Watring states that the underlying view of reality and of the nature of human beings in the New Age movement stands in direct contrast to the primary tenets of orthodox Christianity.[18]

### THE DANGER OF HYPNOTIC INDUCTION

Most techniques used in seminars are either tantamount to hypnotic induction or render the individual more highly suggestible to hypnotic induction. Most people know what hypnosis is. Very few know that affirmation, suggestology, neurolinguistic programming, some forms of guided imagery, est, and est-type human potential seminars employ some of the same dynamics as hypnosis.

Kevin Garvey spoke to this issue in his letter to *Training and Development Journal*. "The training attacks the conscious intellect while barraging

16. Watring, *Eternity* magazine, 31.
17. Ralph Rath, *The New Age: A Christian Critique* (South Bend: Greenlawn, 1990), 240-41.
18. Watring, *Eternity* magazine, 32.

the unconscious with suggestive and outright command." Most people are not aware that hypnosis can be induced without relaxation suggestion.

Even techniques that do not qualify as hypnotic induction may ultimately facilitate the same result. Most meditative techniques (chanting, repeating a mantra, and other spiritual exercises) increase the level of "alpha" rhythms in the brain. People who are in an alpha state are substantially more suggestible than those who are not. Further, when people use certain meditative exercises, they often experience the loss of self-identifying awareness and believe that they are experiencing a oneness with a wider consciousness, often called cosmic or unitary consciousness. If this experience is reached while a person is in this heightened state of suggestibility, the person is more susceptible to influence than if he or she was in a normal waking state.[19]

Margaret Singer of the University of California, Berkeley, said that training based on New Age principles is essentially the updating of age-old techniques of social and psychological "influence" designed to create "deployable" people. The result is that the majority of trainees experience varying degrees of alienation and "anomie," or personal unrest, because they were urged to give up old norms, goals, and ideals.

Richard Watring, of Chicago, personnel director for Budget Rent-a-Car, warned that these New Age seminars employ techniques which alter the consciousness of those who come under their influence without first getting their informed consent.[20]

### Visualization and Imagination

In *Creative Visualization*, New Age writer Shakti Gawain teaches that we can bring into existence whatever we visualize, since "we create our own reality" and are not limited by any fixed, objective order of creation. This is New Age teaching. We can tap into unlimited potential by visualizing whatever we desire.

According to Douglas Groothuis, Christians have erred in two directions concerning visualization and imagination. One group has uncritically accepted much New Age teaching, viewing the imagination as almost unfallen and unlimited. The other group is so critical of New Age and Christian abuses of the imagination that it entirely rules out the imagination, declaring it to be the devil's playground and thus falling into a quarantine or taboo mentality. Yet there is a middle course, and it can be navigated by considering the following:

First of all, is that the imagination, like all our mental faculties, is

19. Ibid., 31.
20. Rath, *The New Age*, 238-40.

affected by the Fall. Even if we are being transformed by the renewing of our minds (Rom. 12:2), our minds will not be perfected until we see Perfection face to face (1 Cor. 13:12; 1 John 3:1-3). New Age visualizers deny the Fall and venture off into the deep of the imagination with no sure rudder, compass, map, or fixed stars to guide them.

Second, visualization and imagination themselves, once demystified, should be seen as natural human faculties which are not intrinsically evil. All people visualize and imagine to varying degrees. Some often think "in pictures." Jesus himself appealed to the imagination when relating his many parables, fictitious stories aimed at conveying objective truth. Much of biblical literature evokes vivid images. Consider, for example, the many images of the book of Revelation. These do not negate factual content; rather, this type of biblical writing engages both the rational and imaginative faculties.

Third, it needs to be clarified that the many visions given in the Bible are not the same as visualizations. A vision is objectively given by God for a specific purpose: to foretell the future (as with Daniel), to call a prophet (as with Ezekiel), or for some other God-directed reason. Visualization, on the other hand, is the result of human will activating the imagination. Visualizing a certain scene is not the same as receiving a vision sent by God. The one is created by a person's thought process. The other is divinely introduced.

We must also realize that the psychological conjuring practice of visualization may, under certain conditions, open one up to counterfeit Christs, "angels of light" (2 Cor. 11:14), who are the enemies of God and humanity. An elaborate visualization exercise could induce an altered state of consciousness quite amenable to demonic insurgents. Shakti Gawain, for instance, says that "creative visualization" can easily introduce one to "spirit guides," the likes of which would be thrilled to meet us.

Fourth, although the Bible sometimes uses visually evocative language, we need not vividly visualize Jesus to have faith in him. Faith does not depend on how good we are at visualizing, but rather on the sure promises of God which we lay hold of by a reasonable faith. Paul's emphasis is that "faith comes from hearing the message, and the message is heard through the word of Christ" (Rom. 10:17).

Fifth, another problem concerning visualization is that it can become a kind of magic, a way of manipulating reality through mind power. New Agers grant to the imagination a divine power beyond that of finite creatures. In his imagination, the fallen person sees himself as god and creator.

A positive use of the imagination is to encourage physical healing. This natural interaction of mind and body is not to be confused with the New Age claim that we "create our own reality" through "mind over matter."

Colin Brown notes that "the Lord's Prayer and other prayers of Jesus have a completely different orientation than magic. Magic is concerned with the control of the supernatural by techniques to further one's own ends. Jesus' concern was to do the will of the Father and to teach men to submit their whole lives to that will."[21]

## THE DANGER OF ENCOURAGING SPIRITISM

Many of the techniques being promoted involve encountering a person's "inner wisdom" or "higher self" or "master teacher." This entity encountered through Silva Mind Control and some forms of guided imagery and visualization is often described as simply the personification of one's own psyche or subconscious. But what if it is not? If there really is a spiritual realm, then it is possible that the entities which are encountered are not really part of our self, but some other self. If so, then the promoters of these techniques are really promoting a form of spiritism.

Even more frightening is the fact that some programs and leaders, including Willis Harman, are encouraging "channeling" as a means toward higher creativity. What used to be considered mediumship or occult correspondence is now promoted as a benign technique for transformation and human potential.

In his book *Higher Creativity*, Harman downplays the issue of whether or not the source of "illumination" is the self or is apart from the self. He writes, "The fruits of the channeling phenomenon can come to be appreciated and used to the benefit of human kind — leaving open the issue of the ultimate nature of the channeling source."[22]

## Danger of Legal Liabilities

Richard Watring foresees serious liability damages being awarded to persons who suffer psychological harm as a result of New Age techniques. Some psychologists and sociologists consider many New Age techniques to be a form of mind control. Already, many individuals have sued a number of human potential or "new religious" movements for psychological harm.[23] Glenn Rupert maintains that New Age business seminars have caused some people to be psychologically harmed, and many have successfully sued these training organizations and their employers, especially if attendance was required. Seminars based on distinctly religious doctrines may infringe upon the First Amendment rights of an employee required to attend.[24]

21. Groothuis, *Confronting the New Age*, 180-85.
22. Watring, *Eternity* magazine, 31-32.
23. Ibid.
24. Lewis and Melton, *Perspectives on the New Age*, 135.

James Baumgartel, an inspector at the Puget Sound Shipyard in Bremerton, Washington, filed a formal Equal Employment Opportunity Class Complaint of Religious Discrimination against the shipyard. His argument is that his First Amendment rights were violated when he was forced to attend training programs using guided visualizations, meditation, and other techniques that he alleges "can change a person's view of reality and religious beliefs."[25]

According to Herbert Rosedale, the question of employee rights comes into play only if a program is mandatory. A common and relevant observation, however, is that managerial participants in New Age programs, like others committed to alleged revealed truths, are often seized with missionary zeal and do not take rebuffs lightly.

The anti-discrimination law applies to those instances when participation in New Age programs violates an employee's religious beliefs. Under that law, the employer is obligated to make reasonable accommodation to the employee's religious beliefs.[26]

# CHRISTIAN ADAPTATIONS
# OF NEW AGE TEACHINGS

Christian Positive Thinking refers to a number of movements or philosophies advocated by those who claim the teachings are Christian. These teachings sometimes incorporate human potential psychology and stress the powers of the mind. Their goal is to get people to believe in a new power. They claim this power will provide success, happiness, and abundance in life and even allow some to perform miracles. Their emphasis is on such conscious methods as exercising one's "faith" to develop a new outlook on life. Usually, faith is seen as a force or power that can be used to change one's environment (bringing financial or other success) or change other people (as in physical healing). As a by-product, such success will bring self-esteem and self-worth, changing the person who uses that power. Many teach that exercising such a faith can even influence divine laws and force God to act on one's behalf.

Representative persons stressing the powers of the mind, "faith," or Positive Thinking include: Robert Schuller — "Possibility Thinking"; Clement Stone — "Positive Mental Attitude"; Norman Vincent Peale —

---

25. Groothuis, *Confronting the New Age*, 161-62.
26. Herbert L. Rosedale, "New Age, Business, and the Law," *SCP Journal* 9.1 (1989): 27.

Positive Thinking; Oral Roberts — "Seed-Faith" principles; Kenneth Hagin and Kenneth Copeland — "Word-Faith" teaching; Robert Tilton — "Success in Life"; Mike Velarde of the Philippines — El Shaddai; Paul Yonggi Cho — health and prosperity; and Charles Capps and many others — "Positive Confession." Positive Confession, Prosperity Thinking, Theology of Success Movement, and "name it and claim it" are all terms used to describe those stressing the powers of faith as a force to influence the environment or God.[27]

## The Modern Faith Movement, the Charismatic Revival, and Prosperity Consciousness

The doctrine of prosperity has come to be "the most important new idea of the charismatic revival," according to David Harrell. In his book *All Things Are Possible*, Harrell says that the doctrine of prosperity has "almost supplanted the earlier emphasis on healing." In its infancy, the Faith movement was known for its radical emphasis upon healing. Today, prosperity is the goal. Promises of material prosperity and financial success are undoubtedly a major source of motivation for many who join the movement.

For years, teachings on prosperity have characterized the ministry of faith-healing evangelists. Much of it was egocentric. It centers on the personality of the evangelist and the welfare of the evangelist and his or her ministry. This type of teaching promises success and prosperity from God to those who give to the evangelist's ministry. The pressing financial needs of the evangelists forces a greater emphasis on the need for giving and, with it, God's promise to bless the cheerful giver.[28]

Some, such as A. A. Allen, were blatant in their portrait of God as specializing in financial miracles. He spellbound his audiences with an account that God once answered his prayer to meet a $410 printing bill by turning the one-dollar bills he had into twenty-dollar bills. Allen's explanation was a clear pronouncement of the prosperity doctrine that would begin to flourish in the charismatic congregations of the 1960s.[29]

---

27. John Ankerberg and John Weldon, *Cult Watch* (Eugene, Ore.: Harvest House, 1991), 305-6; see also *New York Times*, April 11, 1997.

28. D. R. McConnell, *A Different Gospel* (Peabody, Mass.: Hendrickson, 1988), 170-71.

29. Harold B. Smith, *Pentecostals from the Inside Out* (Wheaton, Ill.: Victor, 1990), 69-70.

## Kenneth Hagin and Kenneth Copeland

In the modern Faith movement, Kenneth Hagin and Kenneth Copeland emphasize cosmic teaching on prosperity. This type of teaching promises success and prosperity from God to those who know the spiritual laws of the universe that govern financial prosperity. It is cosmic because it centers on the universal principles of prosperity that God has set up in the cosmos. Although there were cosmic teachings on prosperity in the post–World War II Healing Revival, the vast majority were of the egocentric variety and promised success and finances only to those who supported the evangelist's ministry.

One of the best-known practitioners of this new "health-and-wealth gospel" is Kenneth Hagin. He explains it in a book aptly titled *Redeemed from Poverty, Sickness and Death.* The idea is that through the crucifixion of Christ, Christians have inherited all the promises God made to Abraham, and these include both spiritual and material well-being. The only problem is that Christians have too little faith to appropriate what is rightly theirs. What they need to do is state that claim loud and clear. This so-called "name it and claim it" view, or Positive Confession theology, has become very popular — and very controversial — in Pentecostal circles.

In 1990 an Assemblies of God professor at the denomination's Southeastern College in Lakeland, Florida, published a strong condemnation of the "health-and-wealth gospel" as a serious deviation from the Christian gospel. He traced its roots to such cultic sources as New Thought, a nineteenth-century mind-healing movement. He also correctly added that it owed much to the "Positive Thinking" philosophy of the late Norman Vincent Peale and to the upbeat religious boosterism that televangelist Robert Schuller teaches from his Crystal Cathedral. Still, few Pentecostals will deny that despite such critiques, the gospel of health and wealth has many adherents among their people and their ministers.[30]

In 1962, Hagin launched his own evangelistic association. After moving his headquarters in 1966 to Tulsa, Oklahoma, his ministry finally began a meteoric rise. Riding the crest of the fast-growing charismatic movement, he became, by the early 1980s, one of the nation's best-known evangelists. His daily radio program was carried on 180 stations in the United States and Canada; his monthly *Word of Faith* magazine enjoyed a circulation of 200,000; his $20 million Rhema Bible Training Center enrolled almost 2,000 students. Out of a total of 10,000 graduates of Rhema, a thousand remained affiliated with Hagin through membership in the Rhema Ministerial Association, an organization that granted them ordination to the ministry.

30. Harvey Cox, *Fire from Heaven* (Reading, Mass.: Addison-Wesley, 1995), 271-72.

More important, Hagin's ministry sponsored other faith teachers. By the late 1980s, Kenneth and Gloria Copeland, Fred Price, Charles Capps, Robert Tilton, and a host of others were citing similar themes and enjoying remarkable success.[31]

A quotation from Kenneth Copeland is typical of the cosmic view of prosperity taught in the Faith movement.

> We must understand that there are laws governing every single thing in existence. Nothing is by accident. There are laws of the world of the spirit and there are laws of the world of the natural. . . . We need to realize that the spiritual world and its laws are more powerful than the physical world and its laws. Spiritual laws gave birth to physical laws. The world and the physical forces governing it were created by the power of faith — a spiritual force. . . . It is this force of faith which makes the laws of the spirit world function. . . . This same rule is true in prosperity. There are certain laws governing prosperity in God's Word. Faith causes them to function. . . . The success formulas in the Word of God produce results when used as directed.[32]

## The Idea of Cosmic Prosperity

The modern Faith movement's idea of the law of cosmic prosperity originated largely in the late nineteenth and early twentieth centuries with E. W. Kenyon. Kenyon appropriated many of his ideas from Ralph Waldo Emerson and New England Transcendentalism and from Charles Fillmore and the Unity School of Christianity.

The metaphysical cults, particularly New Thought and the Unity School of Christianity, were the first to propagate the idea that God will make rich all those who know "the laws of prosperity" which govern the universe. Through Kenyon, this cultic belief entered the Faith movement. It was expanded by Hagin and the other Faith teachers to a degree which even Kenyon would never have approved.

Kenyon preached prosperity; he did not condone materialism or greed. He wrote that biblical prosperity "is not the prosperity of the senses, which thinks gold and political favor are prosperity." Biblical prosperity, he taught, is ultimately the presence of God himself. Although all of the basic concepts on prosperity are present in his writings, Kenyon defined prosperity in terms of deliverance from poverty and the power to deliver others.[33]

31. Smith, *Pentecostals from the Inside Out*, 72.
32. McConnell, *A Different Gospel*, 171.
33. Ibid., 182-83, 174-75.

## Unity and Charles Fillmore

One of the major attractions of the Unity School of Christianity has always been its teaching on prosperity. In his book *Prosperity,* Charles Fillmore, the founder of Unity, insists that Unity's "law of prosperity has been proved time and time again. All men who have prospered have used the law, for there is no other way." Long before Copeland claimed to have "discovered" the laws of prosperity, Fillmore wrote that "everything is governed by law" and "there is a law that governs the manifestation of supply." Just like Copeland, Fillmore claims that to operate the law of prosperity, one must first understand it; second, one must have faith in it; and third, one must apply it to one's needs.

Thus, the prosperity of both the metaphysical cults and Faith theology is based on knowing how to manipulate spiritual laws rather than on personal trust in the provision of a sovereign God. The metaphysical cults and Faith theology both teach that these laws are set in motion by positive mental attitudes and positive confession.[34]

## Ralph Waldo Trine

Another New Thought prosperity advocate is Ralph Waldo Trine. Like Copeland, Trine teaches that there are "laws" in the universe that govern prosperity and that faith is the key to operating these laws. Both Trine and Copeland teach that faith is the "law of success," which imparts the power to create prosperous circumstances.

Trine attributes the confession of prosperity to "occult power." He believes that "thought is a force, and it has occult power of unknown proportions when rightly used and wisely directed." This usage of occult powers is, of course, a practice that Faith teachers would publicly reject. Nevertheless, Faith teachers must come to grips with the fact that those who began the practices of positive mental attitudes and positive confession attributed their ability to acquire riches to psychic and occultic power.

For example, Trine advocates the occultic practice of visualization as a means to become prosperous. He instructs his followers in the art of visualizing prosperity through mental suggestion and verbal affirmation. We should note that the practice of visualization had its origins in the occult and Eastern religions. While there may well be some harmless uses of visualization, its origins are decidedly non-Christian. To the degree that Faith teachers recommend faith-visualization and discipline of the mind to obtain prosperity, they are introducing an alien and, perhaps, occult practice as a substitute for biblical faith.[35]

34. Ibid., 172-73.
35. Ibid., 173-74.

Acknowledging that some of the Faith movement's teachings are biblical, one major charismatic critic charged: "The sad truth is that the cultic, not the biblical, elements of the Faith theology are the very elements that distinguish it the most, cause its amazing growth, and occupy center stage in the Faith movement."

Hagin takes issue with the charge that Faith theology is essentially New Thought metaphysics. Admitting that some New Age movements, like Positive Thinking, work because they apply biblical principles, he nonetheless dismisses the argument by saying that "just because they have discovered some principles that sound a whole lot like what we're saying, it doesn't mean our teaching is the same as New Age."[36]

### Recent Developments and Changes

The modern Faith movement has gone far beyond Kenyon's original doctrine of prosperity. Whereas Kenyon interpreted prosperity in terms of the believer's fundamental needs, many modern Faith teachers claim that God wants to grant every desire as well. Hagin teaches that God not only wants to deliver believers from poverty, "He wants His children to eat the best, He wants them to wear the best clothing, He wants them to drive the best cars, and He wants them to have the best of everything." Nothing is too good for the "King's kids." As children of royalty, believers are to live in a manner befitting their exalted station in Christ. In the doctrine of prosperity there is a noticeable absence of any distinction between a believer's needs and his desires.[37]

Though not an explicit proponent of Faith theology himself, Oral Roberts nevertheless bordered on many of its theological precepts throughout his ministry. Yet even Roberts's considerable prestige has not been enough to protect the Faith movement from criticism. While some believe that Faith teachers have moderated their more extreme positions, others express their doubts. The result is a continuing debate over the merits and dangers of the movement.[38]

## Charismatics, "Health and Wealth," and Dominion Theology

Dominion Theology is based on a particular reading of the first chapter of the biblical book of Genesis in which God, having created Adam and Eve, says to them:

36. Smith, *Pentecostals from the Inside Out*, 73-75.
37. McConnell, *A Different Gospel*, 175.
38. Smith, *Pentecostals from the Inside Out*, 76.

Be fruitful and multiply, and fill the earth and subdue it; and have dominion over the fish of the sea and over the birds of the air and over every
living thing that moves upon the face of the earth. (Gen. 1:27)

According to this reading, "every living thing" means not only animals
but institutions; and since — as Health and Wealth theology teaches —
Christians have inherited all these Old Testament mandates, this clearly means
that Christians (Pat Robertson would add religious Jews) should rule on earth.
They should "take dominion" over all the institutions and run them until
Christ comes again, which might be soon but could be a very long time.

Pat Robertson is a Baptist, and was an ordained minister in that
denomination before resigning his position to seek the Republican nomination
for president in 1988. But he clearly belongs to what is sometimes referred
to as the "Pentecostal charismatic movement," that amorphous grouping of
Pentecostal churches and congregations — some in the established denominations and some independent — that encourage a Pentecostal style. Robertson's following among members of Pentecostal churches is considerable. He
is a well-known exponent of one version of Dominion Theology, believing
that Christians are called upon to try to assume positions of power wherever
they can in order to build a more righteous and God-fearing society.

In a 1991 article in a journal called *Church and State*, Fred Clarkson
quotes Robertson as saying: "One day, if we read the Bible correctly, we will
rule and reign along with our sovereign, Jesus Christ. So this is a kingdom
institution to teach people how they may enter into the privilege they have
as God's representatives on earth."

In his book on the "New World Order," Robertson vigorously defended
his belief that only those "who believe in Judeo-Christian values" are qualified
to rule.[39]

## Charismatic Interest in Dominion Theology

Harvey Cox, a Harvard Divinity School professor and a recognized religious
analyst, states that at first he was puzzled about how so many Pentecostals,
whose battle cry for years was the imminent return of Christ, could have fallen
in love with dominion theology. Then he discovered what some historians of
the movement think the answer is. These historians believe that the turning
point came with the "Latter Rain" movement of the 1950s. The leaders of
this movement were so convinced that the Spirit was at work in their spectacular displays of healings and prophecies that they believed a worldwide

39. Cox, *Fire from Heaven*, 288-91.

revival was at hand. They quietly set aside the idea that Jesus would return soon, which, according to George Hawkins, one of Latter Rain's leaders, may once have "served a useful purpose" but was really "a false hope." In 1948 Hawkin wrote these words, which are remarkably prophetic of present-day Kingdom Now theology:

> We are entering into the Kingdom Age in a sense now, for the Kingdom is being formed in us and when it is completed . . . all judicial as well as religious authority will be vested in the church of Christ.

According to Cox, the Latter Rain revival laid the theological groundwork for what has now become the Kingdom Now movement with its passionate activism and its intention to reestablish civil society along biblically mandated lines. There also appears to be correlation with Dominion Theology and the "Health and Wealth" and prosperity emphases in charismatic circles.[40]

## A Belief in Going "First Class"

The fundamental fault with the gospel of prosperity lies in one central affirmation: God wills the financial prosperity of every one of his children; therefore, for a Christian to be in poverty is to be outside God's intended will — it is to be living a Satan-defeated life. Usually related to this affirmation is a second. Because we are God's children, we should always go first class — we should have the biggest and the best. This alone brings glory to God.

These claims are not biblical, no matter how much they might be wrapped in biblical garb. The basic problem involves questions of scriptural interpretation, which is obvious even to a layperson.

The most distressing thing about the prosperity evangelists' use of Scripture, according to Gordon Fee of Regent College in Vancouver, is the subjective and arbitrary way they interpret texts. The plain meaning of a text is what prosperity advocates promise to deliver. But that is precisely what is not given.

Plain meaning has to do with the author's original intent, with what would have been plain to those originally addressed.

Take, for example, a basic Scripture verse used by this movement: "Beloved [Gaius], I wish above all things that thou mayest prosper and be in health, even as thy soul prospereth" (3 John 2, KJV). This verse has been cited as support that it is God's will that all Christians be wealthy and healthy. But is this what the text actually says?

40. Ibid., 293-94.

The Greek word translated "prosper" in the King James Version means "to go well with someone." This wish for "things to go well" and for "good health" was the standard form of greeting in a personal letter of antiquity — just as a friend today may say, "I pray this letter finds you all well." To extend John's wish for Gaius's welfare to material prosperity for all Christians is totally foreign to the original meaning. John could not have intended that, nor could Gaius have so understood it. It is plainly not the plain meaning of the text.

"Abundant life" in John 10:10, another important text of this movement, also has nothing to do with material abundance. "Life" or "eternal life" in John's Gospel is the equivalent of the "Kingdom of God." It literally means the "life of the Age to Come." It is the life that God has in and of himself; and it is his gift to believers in the present age. The Greek word *perisson*, translated "more abundantly" in the King James Version, means simply that believers are to enjoy this gift of life "to the full" (NIV). Material abundance is not implied either in "life" or "to the full." Such an idea is foreign to the context of John 10 as well as to the whole teaching of Jesus.

In the biblical view, wealth and possessions have no inherent value for the people of God. Granted, often in the Old Testament — but never in the New Testament — possessions are frequently related to a life of obedience. But even there they are seen to have the double danger of removing the eye from trusting in God and of coming to possess the possessor. Poverty, however, is not seen as better. God has revealed himself as the one who pleads the cause of the poor, but he is not thereby blessing poverty. Rather, he is revealing his mercy and justice on behalf of those who are oppressed.

This liberating biblical attitude toward possessions is emphasized in the New Testament. According to Jesus, the good news of the Kingdom frees us from preoccupation with material concerns (Matt. 6:33). With his own coming, the Kingdom has been inaugurated — even though it has yet to be fully consummated. The time of God's rule is now; the future with its new values is already at work in the present.

The standard of the Kingdom is sufficiency; surplus is called into question. The person with two tunics should share with the one who has none (Luke 3:11). Indeed, unshared wealth is contrary to the Kingdom as good news for the poor. Precisely because possessions have no inherent value, the one who has possessions can freely share with the needy.

It is these Kingdom values that are reflected in the early chapters of Acts. The early church was the new community — the new people of God. Hence, no one considered anything owned to be his or her own possession. The coming of the Spirit that marked the beginning of the new order had freed them from the need of possessing. In the Kingdom, prosperity is simply of no value. How then could it be God's will for all his children?

## HUMAN CENTERED, NOT GOD CENTERED

Finally, the theology of the gospel of prosperity is sub-Christian at several points. First, the cult of prosperity offers a human-centered, rather than God-centered, theology. Even though one is regularly told that it is to God's own glory that we should prosper, the appeal is always made to our own selfishness and sense of well-being.

Second, this gospel presents a false theology of giving. Throughout Scripture, God loves, gives, and forgives unconditionally — no strings attached. The human response to divine grace is gratitude, which expresses itself in similar unconditional love, giving, and forgiving. The cult of prosperity, on the other hand, tells us that we are to give in order to get. Giving to the Lord and to the poor, we are told, guarantees our own prosperity.

Third, such an Americanized perversion of the gospel tends to reinforce a way of life and an economic system that repeatedly oppress the poor — the very thing that the prophetic message denounces so forcefully.

The best antidote to the disease of the gospel of prosperity is a healthy dose of biblical theology. One writer summed it up with: "Any gospel that will not 'sell' as well among believers in Ouagadougou, Upper Volta, as in Orange County, California, is not the Gospel of our Lord Jesus Christ."[41]

## THE DIFFERENCE BETWEEN "NEED" AND "WANT"

What is a "need"? And when does a "want" become a "need"?

D. R. McConnell, who is affiliated with the Free University of Amsterdam, contends that the distorted view of prosperity in Faith theology centers on its definition of "need." The doctrine of prosperity fails to make a distinction between a need and a want, and a want and a lust. Under normal circumstances, God has promised to meet every legitimate need. He has also stated his desire to fulfill many of our wants. But nowhere has God given any indication that he would ever cater to our lusts. The only "promise" that God has made with regard to our lusts is his promise to crucify them (Rom. 6:1-4; 8:12-13; Gal. 5:16-24).

The Faith doctrine of prosperity is a direct contradiction of Paul's teaching and lifestyle, which did not always reflect "perfect health," "prosperity," and "abundance." He often "suffered need" and knew lack. Many Faith teachers have claimed — usually, off the record — that if Paul knew what the Faith movement knows today, his poverty and sufferings would not have been necessary.

41. Gordon D. Fee, "The Disease of the Health & Wealth 'Gospels,'" *SCP Newsletter,* Spring 1985, 19-20.

The Corinthians misunderstood Paul for the same reason that many modern Faith teachers do today. They did not understand that the cross of Christ was the foundation of both Paul's theology and his life. For Paul, the cross crucified the totality of the believer's existence. This includes both the believer's life and his lust for the things of the world. To believe in the cross meant the death of the believer's claims on his own life. To believe in the cross meant the death of the believer's claims on God through the law. To believe in the cross was to deliver the totality of one's existence to him who delivered himself up for us.

It is also evident from Galatians that Paul did not conceive of Jesus' cross in terms of its worldly benefits. He realized that identification with the cross of Jesus entailed the crucifixion of the believer's relation to the world and its lusts.

The other apostles also clearly taught that to believe in Jesus demanded renunciation of this world's lusts. Those who would teach that the purpose of the cross was to bestow worldly prosperity on believers should heed again the words of the crucified Messiah: "If anyone wishes to come after me, let him deny himself, and take up his cross, and follow me" (Mark 8:34).

According to McConnell, this prosperity mind-set contradicts the cross in at least three ways. First, it subverts the demand of the cross for self-denial. Second, the doctrine of prosperity reduces God to a means to an end. God becomes the means whereby prosperity is attained. Third, the mind-set of prosperity is focused on the things of this world as the sign of God's approval and the means of God's blessing.[42]

## MONEY, PROSPERITY, AND THE BIBLE

What, then, is the correct biblical attitude toward money and prosperity? Gordon Fee, the Pentecostal scholar who has written extensively on prosperity doctrine, cites two extreme viewpoints that one should avoid in relation to wealth. The first is rejection. In this viewpoint, the believer rejects all prosperity in the belief that money is inherently evil. The second extreme is that of accommodation. In this viewpoint, the believer accommodates himself to worldly cultural values with little or no thought of the demands of Jesus and his cross or regarding the tremendous economic disparity in the world today.

The prosperity doctrine is based on a very selective set of biblical texts, the majority of which are from the Old Testament. It can be held only by excluding countless other passages of the Bible which address the subject of wealth and poverty.[43]

42. McConnell, *A Different Gospel,* 176-80.
43. Ibid., 181.

# GUIDELINES FOR BUSINESS

In the Bible, ethical obligation is motivated not by the search for self-realization or social coherence, but by human response to the sovereignty of God. The whole of a person's life is to be presented in service to God as a "living sacrifice" (Rom. 12:1). The context of ethical obligation is in relationship to God. Apart from this relationship there is no biblical ethic.

In the Old Testament story, the activity of God in his righteousness is the origin of human responsibility and freedom and therefore of morality. More specifically, God's actions in delivering his people out of slavery resulted in a covenant people who gladly served him and reflected his character as grateful servants.

It is important to emphasize that God's acts in history provided the *motivation* for Israel's obedience and thus for human conduct. The acts of God in history provide not only the motivation but also the *pattern* for human conduct. God teaches his people how they should serve him in the present through the remembrance of what he has done for them in the past. In other words, God's people know what "justice" is, not by contemplating some abstract norm of justice, but by remembering how God delivered his people from oppression and bondage.

Hence it is significant that Micah, after summarizing "the saving acts of the LORD," focusing primarily on the Exodus (Mic. 6:3-5), says: "He has showed you, O man, what is good; and what does the LORD require of you but to do justice, and to love kindness, and to walk humbly with your God?" (Mic. 6:8). In the relationship of the covenant, the human task is nothing less than "imitation of God."[44]

## A New Type of Obedience and Law

Because of the covenant, the Israelite attained a new understanding of his work and of his use of earthly goods.

Since Israel had been redeemed from slavery in Egypt, the righteousness of God in the law was seen to be especially solicitous of the poor and the weak in society: "If you do afflict them, and they cry out to me, I will surely hear their cry" (Exod. 22:22).

The Israelite attitude toward earthly goods is determined by this new theology. Property belongs to God, who gives it to his people as a loan (cf.

44. John P. Newport, *Life's Ultimate Questions* (Dallas: Word, 1989), 480-81; see also Bernhard W. Anderson, "The Biblical Ethic of Obedience," *The Christian Scholar,* 39.1 (March 1956): 66.

Lev. 25:23). There is no such thing as a natural and private right to the exploitation of property.

## THE PROPHETS OF ISRAEL
## (EMPHASES OF THE PROPHETS OF ISRAEL)

The prophets of ancient Israel lived in a world very different from ours, yet they lived, as we do, in times of national crisis and international conflict.

The prophets' commitment to *justice* was rooted in a belief in the fundamental equality of all persons before God. Speaking in the name of a God of justice, Amos denounced the inequalities of his day: "For three transgressions of Israel, and for four, I will not revoke the punishment; because they sell the righteous for silver, and the needy for a pair of shoes — they that trample the head of the poor into the dust of the earth, and turn aside the way of the afflicted. . . . But let justice roll down like waters, and righteousness like an everflowing stream" (Amos 2:6 and 5:24). The biblical God is identified with the dispossessed and portrayed as Redeemer and Liberator.

The prophetic view of a *created order* that is inclusive in space and time is also relevant today. The whole creation is part of God's purpose. Because all forms of life are within God's plan, we are accountable for the way we treat them. *Stewardship* of nature is more typical of the Bible than *dominion* over nature, though it was often ignored in subsequent Western history. Moreover, the prophets used an extended time scale because they believed that God's purposes extend into the future. We have obligations to posterity and to a God who spans the generations.

# Human Fulfillment

A broad view of human fulfillment is expressed in the biblical literature. The good life is identified not with material possessions but with personal existence in community. The prophets upheld the dignity of the individual and the importance of interpersonal relationships. They portrayed harmony with God and neighbor as the goal of life. They recognized the dangers of both poverty and affluence. They saw the harmful consequences of affluence — for the rich as well as for the poor. Jesus, in turn, stressed the importance of feeding the hungry, but he also said that "man does not live by bread alone," and he vividly pictured the dangers of wealth.

Over the ensuing centuries, Christian groups preserved the ideals of *simplicity* and *community*. The Reformation and then the Puritan movement upheld frugality and simplicity and were critical of "the luxuries of the rich." Today, in an overconsumptive society, we need both a rejection of the dominant materialism and a positive witness to the priority of the personal and the quality of life of the community. New lifestyles should arise from a *new vision of the good life,* a focus on the sources of satisfaction that are not resource consumptive.

The Bible also offers a distinctive view of *persons in community* that avoids both collectivism and individualism. The local church remains a unique opportunity for personal interaction and mutual support. At its best it can be a community of forgiveness, celebration, and common search for both personal and social renewal, starting with the renewal of the church itself.

Finally, the Hebrew prophets brought a double message of judgment and hope. On the one hand, they spoke of God's *judgment* on human greed. They saw military defeat and national catastrophe as forms of divine judgment on the materialism, idolatry, and injustice of national life. The prophets were realistic about human sinfulness and aware of the misuse of economic and political power concentrated in the hands of a group or a nation. Their first word was a call to repentance and humility. Today such humility would be an antidote to the Promethean pride to which industrial nations are prone. The starting point would have to be repentance for our complicity in structures of power, greed, and injustice.

The other side of the prophetic message is *hope.* Beyond judgment and repentance is the prospect of reconciliation and redemption. Reconciliation is restoration of wholeness, the overcoming of alienation from God, from other persons, and from nature. Redemption is creative renewal and response to God's redemptive activity. The ultimate symbol of hope is the vision of a future Kingdom of peace and community.[45]

## New Testament Overview

In the New Testament, the activity of God culminating in Jesus Christ is the origin of an enlarged teaching about human responsibility, freedom, and human morality.

The message of Jesus brought to a climax the Old Testament motif of the kingship of God. Jesus proclaimed that God is King and that he is now beginning to inaugurate his kingdom in history. Hence people were called to serve the King — not in submission to an overwhelming assertion of power, but in gratitude for his grace and forgiving love.

The New Testament then goes on to show how the moral life the Christian is called to is created and sustained by dependence on Christ as

45. Ian Barbour, *Ethics in an Age of Technology* (San Francisco: HarperCollins, 1993), 261-63.

Lord. The Christian who acknowledges Christ's lordship is to possess the same mind and the same obedience demonstrated by Christ. The result is that such a Christian will act in love and without strife or vainglory. Instead of looking only to his or her own affairs, such a Christian will be humbly concerned with the lot of others.

The moral obedience of the Christians was also the expression of the Spirit's working. The sacrifices of the wealthy Christians in Acts, for instance, were the result of the work of the Spirit in the church.[46]

## UNITING GOSPEL AND LAW

The New Testament has a paradoxical position with regard to law. On the one hand, it states clearly that the law is of God and is to be obeyed as his will laid before us. Jesus himself said that his purpose was not to destroy the law but to fulfill it.

On the other hand, the freedom of Jesus in dealing with questions of law is evident. Paul taught, moreover, that the Christian has liberty in Christ and is no longer "under the law" (see Rom. 6:14; Gal. 3:24-25; 5:18). These would appear to set the law aside as the less important focus of the Christian's attention.

Nevertheless, Paul knew that so long as Christ's followers are ambiguously placed as citizens of heaven in a world very much under the sway of the old order, there must be some kind of law. This fact can be seen in the following emphases.

- Without some law and order, life in a community of imperfect Christians and vast numbers of unbelievers is not possible. This fact was probably one reason why Paul enjoined obedience to the Roman authorities.
- Law elicits a knowledge of wrongdoing. That is, the law brings to us indirectly a realization of our own sinfulness and helplessness in the face of evil.
- Even for the committed Christian, fully conscious of his Christian liberty, law still provides useful guidance as to the best use of his freedom. We can still learn a good deal about the Christian style of life from the law of Moses if that law is studied in the light of Christ's coming and in the spirit of Christ.[47]

46. Newport, *Life's Ultimate Questions*, 485; see also Ninian Smart, *Worldviews: Crosscultural Explorations of Human Beliefs* (New York: Scribner, 1983), 115.

47. Newport, *Life's Ultimate Questions*, 485-86; see also William Lillie, *Studies in New Testament Ethics* (Philadelphia: Westminster, 1961), 73-75.

## The "Already–Not Yet" Kingdom

The community life of the New Testament church reflected a two-sided situation. On the one hand, it exhibited the ethics of a kingdom which had been foretold by the prophets and had actually dawned in Christ. On the other hand, it tells of the ethical life and decisions of a small, nonpolitical group which understood itself to be living in the interval before the second coming of Christ. It is this expectation of a future consummation which gives the New Testament its urgency and intensity.

We in the twentieth century are still living in that interim period, the period after the kingdom has come in Christ but before it has come in its final power and glory.

Christian ethics today, therefore, has its place precisely in the field of tension between the old and the new aeons. Christian ethics and morality are not for the old alone, nor for the new alone, but for the time between the old and new. This "already–not yet" kingdom emphasis undergirds intense moral responsibility.[48]

## Human Responsibility and Freedom under the Covenant

In the biblical view, every situation in which human beings find themselves has some margin of freedom of decision and responsibility. Humans possess a will which may be conditioned by external factors of nature and society and distorted by sin, but humans still have some freedom for decisions. And along with decision-making freedom comes real responsibility. Such a responsible freedom is presupposed by key biblical words such as *sin, repentance, forgiveness, love,* and *covenant.*

The love-and-revealed-principles approach finds in the Bible, especially in the New Testament, guidelines for the kinds of moral action that are appropriate for a Christian.

The Bible specifies moral principles in a preliminary way in the Ten Commandments. These fundamental commandments reflect the moral character of God. The Psalms and the prophets give more moral principles. In addition, the prophets are helpful examples of the application of God's principles to specific moral problems of a particular time. For example, we can get general guidance from a book like Amos.

The Sermon on the Mount is the New Testament statement of the ideals of God's will, which with God's help we can seek to approximate.[49]

---

48. Newport, *Life's Ultimate Questions,* 487; see also Helmut Thielicke, *Theological Ethics,* Vol. 1: *Foundations* (Grand Rapids: Eerdmans, 1966), 43.

49. Newport, *Life's Ultimate Questions,* 511; see also Carl F. H. Henry, *Christian Personal Ethics* (Grand Rapids: Eerdmans, 1957), 24, 26.

## The Christological Focus

The love-and-revealed-principles approach holds that it is important to see the progressive nature of revelation from the Old Testament to the New Testament with its center in Christ. It must be remembered that the New Testament is the ethical center of gravity of the Bible and, therefore, that whatever is said in the Old Testament must be evaluated from the perspective of the New Testament.

More specifically, the love-and-revealed-principles approach utilizes a christological interpretation of Scripture in determining biblical norms.

Since they focus on Christ as the ultimate, or final, criterion, ethical statements of the Old Testament as well as incidents with proposed ethical content are not to be accepted at face value. If they contradict the ethics suggested by the life of the Son of God, they are considered not binding on Christians. That part of the Old Testament which can be binding to Christians must pass the christological test — it must not contradict Christ's teachings or his example.

In conflict situations, Christians are never called to compromise their faith. However, they may be called upon to fall back temporarily from the ideal in order to be obedient to the interpretation of God's will in that particular situation. While obedience to the divine commandment is always good and never evil, in a conflict situation it may involve us in acts that fall short of the goal toward which God beckons us.[50]

## DOING GOD'S WILL

As any practicing Christian is aware, morals and ethics involve more than just determining what is right and wrong. Biblical ethics involves *doing* what is right, not just *knowing* what is right. A key moral and ethical issue, then, is how Christians can be empowered to follow Christian morals and ethics.

Three things are important: a vital union with Christ, prayer and Bible study, and supportive church fellowship.

## Rewards and Consequences

Although the primary motive for the Christian's ethical acts is gratitude to Christ, the Christian is also encouraged by God's promise of the ultimate success of his kingdom and the promise of spiritual reward.

50. Newport, *Life's Ultimate Questions*, 512, 514; see also Donald G. Bloesch, *Freedom for Obedience: Evangelical Ethics in Contemporary Times* (San Francisco: Harper, 1987), 250, 252, 279; and Bernard L. Ramm, *The Right, the Good and the Happy* (Waco: Word, 1971), 69-71.

Our Lord had no scruples about encouraging his disciples in ways of good by the assurance that their rewards would be great in heaven. There is a practical realism in this teaching which takes us as we are — creatures who are motivated by the anticipation of rewards and the fear of consequences. In the biblical concept of judgment, the vindication of goodness is always included.

## Christian Ethics and Business

To some, Christian ethics seems to be an arbitrary set of rules imposed by a remote God for no very good reason. To others, it seems that Christian morality is unrelated to reality — a set of norms imposed on the Christian for no reason than that God says so. If this is true, then the unbeliever would be right in feeling no obligation to follow Christian moral standards.

Advocates of creation ethics, however, believe that their approach shows us how and why Christian ethics should apply to *all* human beings.

According to creation ethics, God's will creates and defines the good (for he alone is the measure of good). However, because he is both the Creator and the providential Ruler of this world, God commands only what corresponds both to humanity's God-given moral sense and to the good or benefit of humankind.

The contention of creation ethics is that the observance of Christian ethics is in the long run, and in the community as a whole, for our own good. Creation ethics holds that in following the Christian way we are enabled to live as near as possible to the way in which we function best or the way we were created to live.[51]

### TRUTHFULNESS AND HONESTY IN BUSINESS
### AND LIFE IN GENERAL

The creation approach to ethics is associated with the concept of divinely given structures that are a part of God's creation. One of these structures is truthfulness and honesty.

Ephesians 4:25-30 provides an example of this created structure. Here we are told that everyone is to "speak the truth with his neighbor" (with non-Christian as well as Christian). Two reasons are given for this admonition. The first is that "we are members one of another" — part of a social commu-

---

51. Newport, *Life's Ultimate Questions*, 498-500; see also Oliver Barclay, "The Nature of Christian Morality," in Bryce Kaye and Gordon Wenham, eds., *Law, Morality and the Bible* (Downers Grove, Ill.: InterVarsity, 1978), 125, 129-33.

nity whose solidarity is undermined by lies. The second is that not being truthful would "grieve the Holy Spirit of God."

Creation ethicists point out that practical experience clearly undergirds the creation ideal in this instance. A school, a family, or a wider community in which truthfulness cannot be assumed is, as we all know, impoverished. At best, it is extremely inconvenient, destroys good personal relationships, and wastes a lot of time and effort.

### Stealing

We are to refrain from stealing — both for social reasons and because of our relationship to God. Whether we like it or not, we are in a society, and stealing injures all social relationships. It is perhaps possible to have a society that does not respect honesty, but it would be a sadly deprived community. God has made us "members one of another" and intends that we respect that fact of creation.

## Creation Ethics Are Universal

The creation approach maintains that on serious examination over a period of time, the Christian approach to morality can be shown to be extraordinarily fitting to the way things really are. Far from being alien, or arbitrary, Christian ethics are exactly fitted to the creation as we find it. In this sense they correspond to what is truly natural — not necessarily to what people like to do or find it "natural" to do.

This explains why many aspects of Christian ethics are also held by other religions and philosophies. This is logical if they are a result of a right understanding of human society and can be seen to be so to a considerable extent by any wise person. Any rational reflection on humanity and society produces some of the same "obvious" points: there must be a basic morality; it must include qualities such as justice, truth, and respect for life.

According to creation ethics, the Christian can recommend these moral teachings without reference to revelation, but he can go much further on the basis of revelation. He knows that they are commanded, but he can also recommend them in terms of an understanding of the world and of humans as they are and are intended to be.

413

## Biblical Call for Conversion
## (Renewal, Creativity, and Prophetic Activity)

The biblical vision of human conduct outlined above calls all aspects of cultures, including the business world, to conversion. Jane Collier, a lecturer at Cambridge University, divides the process of conversion into two stages, the importance of a believing community and the call for intellectual and moral conversion.

The effectiveness with which the biblical view is presented depends on the mission and witness of the believing community in our culture. The church is the community of persons who keep the biblical view alive as an inspiration in daily living. In order to transmit that inspiration to others, it needs to be sensitive to cultural needs for healing and wholeness, and to the needs of persons for faith and hope in their lives. It must also remember that whereas on the one hand it is a pilgrim church, it is also a human institution which itself stands in need of conversion or renewal. If they are to be effective as signs of the presence of God in the world, the established and free churches must engineer their own structures of critique in order to identify their failures in relation to witnessing in the areas of business and culture.

There is an essential role for a prophetic voice to be exercised in our society by those who hear the word of God and reflect on it. The prophetic voice is not merely a critical voice, it is also the voice which gives hope and encouragement to those who pray that God's Kingdom may be established "in our lifetime and in our days. . . ." People need to see and hear "signs of the Kingdom" in their own culture and language.[52]

## INTELLECTUAL AND MORAL CONVERSION

The call to conversion is addressed to all, believers and non-believers alike. It is addressed to business leaders, and is articulated as a requirement first that they reassess the value of what they do in the light of the contribution it makes to human welfare and, second, that they seek new ways of "doing economics."

We have all, at one time or another, been persuaded to believe, to value, and to practice what is deemed culturally acceptable. As business leaders — or as practitioners of other disciplines — we are caught in a climate of opinion where doubt is expressed about the wisdom and relevance of what we do. We exist in a situation where our livelihood, our research, and, in the end, our thought is ideologically pressured and politically manipulated. It is all too easy

52. Hugh Montefiore, ed., *The Gospel and Contemporary Culture* (London: Mowbray, 1992), 125, 126.

to flow with the tide. We may do so for purely practical or pragmatic reasons. We may not realize the extent to which we succumb to cultural conditioning.

What is needed is an "intellectual conversion" by which we come to know that we are capable of knowing, judging, and criticizing the way knowledge is produced. Such a stance will involve challenging New Age ideologies. It will generate a practical concern for the fate and quality of social life.

Conversion is not only intellectual, it is moral. The biblical view challenges all who live as "economic agents" to open their eyes to the gulf between the values of the biblical view and the values of secular economics.[53]

## THE BIBLICAL APPROACH TO BUSINESS

So we see that the contemporary business culture is being greatly influenced by the New Age. Many people have problems with the New Age view. They may sense its inadequacies, but they cannot provide an alternative because they lack a biblical foundation.

The New Age view which sees economic activity as "the pursuit of self-enrichment," for ever greater monetary possessions, even at the "expense of others," which characterizes much of our culture, conflicts with the biblical norms of justice, love, community, and kindness.

The Bible understands economic activity as stewardship. The purpose of this stewardship is twofold: it must responsibly nurture what belongs to the Master (a restatement of the original cultural mandate), and it must do so for the service of those who live on the estate (the whole human race, in that the whole creation is our Master's estate). There is no room in this understanding of economic life for individualism, greed, self-interest, exploitation, or the idolatry of profits.[54]

## A Changing Marketplace

It is obvious that new trends in business indicate that workers, managers, and corporations are changing in many ways. For example, more women are entering the workforce, more workers are content with less than full-time employment, and workers seem to be valuing the quality of their work and their life as a whole more highly than they do their salary or prestige.

In our changing society, some of the emphases of New Age seminars and theory are acceptable and should be conserved. Douglas Groothuis, a

53. Ibid., 126.
54. Brian J. Walsh and J. Richard Middleton, *The Transforming Vision: Shaping a Christian Worldview* (Downers Grove, Ill.: InterVarsity, 1984), 156-57.

Denver Seminary professor, points to increased worker ownership and responsibility, a holistic concern for business, and the importance of a vision for
business.[55]

The New Age contention is that both the secular and biblical views do
not work for business or in anything else. For them, the New Age is the answer.

Groothuis agrees with G. K. Chesterton, who said that "the Christian
ideal has not been tried and found wanting. It has rather been found difficult;
and left untried."

Groothuis lists five Christian ethical considerations that constitute a
Christian business philosophy.

- A Godward Orientation. The biblical prohibition of idols (Exod.
  20:34; Jer. 16:20) cautions us not to treat profit, prestige, and power
  as ends in themselves.
- The Standard of Stewardship. John Stott outlines a biblical view of
  work: "Work is the expenditure of energy (manual or mental or both)
  in the service of others, which brings fulfillment to the worker, benefit
  to the community, and glory to God."
- The Value of the Person. By claiming that humans share the divine
  image, Christianity values people as responsible moral agents. For
  business this means not treating people as merely means to a better
  business, but as valuable in themselves. Although the profit motivation
  is not intrinsically immoral (the Bible affirms the value of private
  property and industry), the Bible condemns a profit domination that
  sacrifices the values of employees (or consumers) for the sake of greed.
- Honesty. Christian ethics affirms truthfulness as essential to moral
  integrity. "Speaking the truth in love" (Eph. 4:15) means straight talk
  to employees, no deception in advertising or merchandising, and no
  illegalities (in taxes or elsewhere).
- Thrift. In a credit-happy society, we should remember that biblical
  ethics restricts large, long-term debt. Proverbs warns that "the borrower
  is servant to the lender" (Prov. 22:7), and Paul teaches that we should
  "let no debt remain outstanding except the continuing debt to love one
  another" (Rom. 13:8). This indicates that the modern convention of
  massive, long-term debt is less than wise and should be avoided whenever possible. The application of this biblical principle minimizes
  economic risk and focuses on the gradual development of businesses
  that grow according to real assets, not according to exorbitant financial
  liabilities.[56]

55. Groothuis, *Confronting the New Age,* 167.
56. Ibid., 167-70.

We have given severe critiques of the underlying philosophy of most New Age emphases in regard to business. This criticism is important. In the business world — as everywhere else — our strategy should be to conserve what is good, to reject and separate from the unredeemable, and to transform all we can.

We have sought to give guidelines for a Christian approach to business. The development of such alternatives calls for an informed Christian activism at both the theoretical and practical levels.

## Conclusion

The Christian community is God's crucial means of empowering people. Our communal obedience to God's norms in all areas of life is a light to the world. The Christian community should foster a responsible economic lifestyle which radically breaks with the narcissistic consumerism that surrounds it.

"Worship" is what makes the Christian community Christian. As Christians worship, serve, and pray to God, they set the pattern for their whole life, a life different from the dominant culture, from the world. Rather than conforming to the world, Christians are transformed by God. Their worship is not limited to liturgical activities; it is a giving of their whole life to God as a sacrificial offering (this is the point of Rom. 12:1-2).[57]

Here, then, is the essence of Christian witness in a society that is increasingly being influenced by the New Age — not only in the area of business but everywhere.

---

57. Walsh and Middleton, *The Transforming Vision*, 161.

# CHAPTER TEN

# *Education*

All would agree that education is important in today's world. The crucial question is which worldview — secular humanist, New Age, or biblical — is most adequate for education, life, and thought. The question must be seen in historical and contemporary contexts and then an answer can be proposed.

After the Protestant Reformation in the sixteenth century against the medieval church, the reforms established separate state churches in various European nations. Civil power was used to enforce support and membership in the state church. In Geneva, Switzerland, for example, worship was enforced by law.

England had an especially difficult time with the problem of religious fanaticism during the seventeenth century. In the religious conflicts of the Cromwellian period there were fanatics who were anxious to secure a monopoly for their particular version of the Christian faith. But there were some Christian groups, including some Independents, Levellers, Baptists, and moderate Anglicans, who called for religious humility without giving up cherished religious convictions. The most notable spokesman for this group was John Milton.

During these struggles, many fled to Holland and later to New England seeking religious liberty. It was ironic indeed that the leaders of the Massachusetts Bay Colony had no sooner reached the shores of New England than they began to persecute those who did not agree with their version of the Christian faith and would not join the established church. Those persecuted included the Quakers and Baptists.

The Puritans began their life in New England with a vision of the church, state, and the school as partners, dominated by Christian saints. Later, in light of the realities of life in New England, they compromised with a development which they called the Half-Way Covenant. This modification allowed them to admit people to church membership who made only a general or more cursory profession of Christianity. Some compromise was necessary, for they allowed only civil and school privileges for those who were church members in the established church of the Massachusetts Bay colony.[1]

## Roger Williams and Religious Liberty

Finally, in the name of high religion, some of the colonists in America established a secular state which would give no religion an official status. Roger Williams, the leader, a pious evangelical Christian and founder of the Baptist Church in Providence, Rhode Island, in 1639, saw that this new country would never fulfill its purpose unless religious liberty was established.

In the early seventeenth century Roger Williams rejected the Puritan teaching that America was to be developed as an exclusive covenant Christian community. He did this because he saw that such an approach would grant one particular religious group exclusive political power over the government and the schools.

In rejecting the Puritan exclusive covenant concept, Williams called for religious liberty. Civil power was necessary, but it should exert influence only in civil matters. The religious communities were important but were restricted from directly controlling civil powers. Furthermore, civil powers should not seek to control religious groups. Quaker William Penn was soon to establish Pennsylvania, following what was seen then as a radical tradition of religious liberty and religious pluralism.[2]

The Puritans raised many questions about the dangers of religious liberty. For example, how could America's moral and spiritual calling and sense of destiny be maintained in such a pluralistic society? Furthermore, how could this varied community retain its sense of unity and destiny?

## Civil Religion

The approach of civil religion was created by Thomas Jefferson and his fellow Enlightenment leaders. Their proposal reached out to both the exponents of religious and moral destiny and the champions of religious liberty.

1. Robert D. Linder, "Religion and the American Dream: A Study in Confusion and Tension," *Mennonite Life* 38.4 (December 1983): 17ff.
2. Ibid., 18.

This vision took the form of civil, or public, religion. It saw the state using consensus religious sentiments, concepts, and symbols for its own purposes.

The Enlightenment leaders, Jefferson and James Madison, supported this approach because it was general enough to include the majority of Americans. It also provided the moral glue for the country. The religious leaders supported this approach because it had religious and biblical undertones.[3]

As late as 1899 President William McKinley referred to civil religion in annexing the Philippines. McKinley said that it was America's destiny and duty to bring civilization and light — democratic civilization and biblical teachings — to the poor Filipinos. And who can forget Woodrow Wilson's vision of the United States as a nation of moral destiny?[4]

## Development of Cultural Pluralism

Religious liberty prepared the way for cultural pluralism. Near the end of the nineteenth century new immigrants from non-Protestant, or even non-believing, backgrounds flowed into the United States. When I was in school at Harvard University, we lived in Cambridge, Massachusetts. The paradox of Cambridge vividly reminded me of what happened to the United States in the latter part of the nineteenth century. Cambridge was the seat of the original Puritan emphasis on theocracy. But in the area where we lived, some two or three blocks from Harvard, both the community and the public schools were dominated by Italians, Poles, and African Americans. My daughter, born in Mississippi, often recalls her cultural shock in the public school in our Cambridge neighborhood.

In addition to the flow of diverse types of immigrants, there were other secularizing forces associated with Darwin, urbanization, industrialization, and John Dewey. In more recent years, we have seen an influx of Hispanics and East Asians.

# SECULAR HUMANISM

Jacques Maritain, a prominent French philosopher, contends that humanism, which focuses on the worth and centrality of humans, has its roots in the

---

3. Robert N. Bellah, "Civil Religion in America," *Daedalus* 96 (Winter 1967): 1-21.

4. Charles S. Olcott, *The Life of William McKinley* (New York: Houghton Mifflin, 1916), 2:109-11.

Judeo-Christian tradition. Much of the Western humanist tradition has been theistic in a broad sense, with a general concept of one God. Even Renaissance humanism, although revolting against the authority of the church and the otherworldliness of religion, was rooted in theism. By the nineteenth century, humanism moved more toward the direction of scientific humanism and deism. There was a belief in God as a giver of laws but not active in the universe. In the twentieth century, humanism has become increasingly secular, scientific, and naturalistic.[5]

A summary of the perspective of secular humanism can be found in the *Humanist Manifestos I* (1933) and *II* (1973). These manifestos state that Secular Humanism is committed to human values. Carl Sagan opened the public television series "Cosmos" with the statement: "The cosmos is all that is or ever was or ever will be." Humans are part of nature. For the humanists, there is no supernatural or cosmic guarantee of human values. Traditional dogmatic or authoritarian religions are seen as performing a disservice to humankind. Promises of immortal salvation are illusory and harmful.[6]

Perhaps the most influential American secular humanist in the twentieth century was John Dewey of Columbia University. He called his philosophy "humanistic naturalism." Early in his career Dewey acquired a profound suspicion of everything that "smacked" of metaphysics, transcendentalism, and the eternal. He felt, for example, that institutional Christianity erected a barrier between humans and nature with its distinctions between the spiritual and the worldly, the eternal and the temporal, the hereafter and the here-and-now. He became convinced that every affirmation of the transcendent and supernatural involved a separation from and a depreciation of earthly life.[7]

In his later writings Dewey contended that the whole question about the ultimate principle of order and nature is a meaningless one. Accepting naturalism, Dewey eliminated religious questions as meaningless according to his adopted pattern of biological inquiry and evolutionary interests. One aspect of the human situation, the biological, was taken as the clue to the whole. Dewey brought humans into the scope of evolutionary explanation and thus sealed them in the circle of natural beings. Humans thus find their self-realization along lines similar to that of the lower organisms. Dewey would admit nothing which transcends the concrete human experience. He had no room for the supernatural or the transcendent.[8]

5. Jacques Maritain, *True Humanism* (London: Geoffrey Bles, 1941), vii-87.

6. *Humanist Manifestos*, vols. 1 and 2 (Buffalo: Prometheus, 1973).

7. John Blewett, ed., *John Dewey: His Thought and Influence* (New York: Fordham University, 1960), 14-17.

8. John Dewey, *Reconstruction in Philosophy* (New York: Holt, 1920), 169.

The result of pragmatism and other secular philosphies was that the old original Protestant center was greatly diminished. If studied at all in the secular and state universities, religion was examined in a phenomenological, or descriptive, way. I experienced this approach to the study of the Bible and religion while I was professor at Rice University. Religion was part of the required humanities option and was taught by professors of Roman Catholic, Jewish, Buddhist, Christian Science, Protestant, and Evangelical backgrounds. Many of the former church-related colleges which were earlier insulated from these trends have followed suit in order to appear adequately professional, pluralistic, and up-to-date.

## SECULAR HUMANISM AND THE NEW AGE VIEW

As already noted, secular humanism has defined itself in opposition to the supernaturalism and "irrationality" of all religions. But it actually operates on the basis of assumptions compatible with the aims of Eastern spirituality and later New Age concepts. According to Brooks Alexander, an evangelical author and editor of *SCP Journal*, Swami Vivekananda, for instance, states that "Buddhists and Jains do not depend on God; [they seek] to evolve a God out of man." This approach is similar to that of secular humanism, which regards humanity as the source of meaning and value in life.

New Age philosophy, including certain forms of Eastern spirituality, also takes humanity as the source and center of meaning. But it defines humankind as a manifestation of deity and thereby inflates it to cosmic dimensions. A personal transcendent God is excluded.

Secular humanism and cosmic humanism, or Eastern spirituality, can be seen as connected beliefs. This merging of the two has spawned a new wave of movements which are combinations of the secular and the spiritual. These groups include human potential groups; self-actualization, humanistic and transpersonal psychologies; new therapies and religious groups which believe in a god within. Cosmic humanism includes specific groups such as est (Erhard Seminar Training), Lifespring, and Scientology.

Alexander suggests that the New Age worldview (related to Eastern spirituality) has thus become prominent in the United States as it attempts to infuse and spiritualize secularism. In fact, as we have seen, the New Age view is infiltrating American culture in a wide variety of fields from public school, health care, and physical-fitness programs to the areas of financial success and executive efficiency.[9]

9. Brooks Alexander, "The Rise of Cosmic Humanism: What Is Religion?", *SCP Journal*, Winter 1981-82, 1-6.

## Understanding New Age

The New Age concept of education begins with the assumption that all is one, a view called monism. Monism is the notion that God or Ultimate Reality or Infinite Consciousness merely expanded itself to become the universe and all that exists. There is no difference between God and creation, a belief known as pantheism. New Age advocates often use impersonal terms such as "life force," Mind, Power, Energy, Being, the Inner Self, Awareness, or Consciousness to describe their understanding of God.

Another aspect of the New Age worldview holds that human beings are divine. This assumption follows from the first one: since all is one and all is God, humanity is inherently divine. In other words, the true self is divine. The goal of all New Age techniques is to change the thinking of humans so that they will know that they are divine. Since humans are divine, they have unlimited power and knowledge that can be tapped through various New Age techniques and practices.

The New Age worldview holds that humanity's problem is ignorance of the oneness of all and, consequently, their own divinity. The solution to the human problem is to discover humanity's true nature: divinity. All people must change their thinking, transform their consciousness, realize their own divinity, and create their own reality. This can be accomplished through techniques such as meditation, channeling, guided imagery, visualization, yoga, and chanting.

A basic thrust of the New Age approach is summed up in the New Age phrase "Create your own reality." Since there are no absolutes, all religions must be true and, therefore, ultimately one. No religion has all truth; there are many truths, often spoken of as "realities" by New Age teachers such as actress Shirley MacLaine.

Another emphasis is on direct and intuitive experience as the way to ultimate truth.[10]

Elliot Miller, editor of the *Christian Research Journal*, points out that in the New Age approach to education it is the teacher's responsibility to "unbury" or awaken within each child this sleeping Self (variously called "God within," "Inner Self," "Higher Self," "Inner Wisdom," "Infinite Potential," and so on). This goal is the cornerstone of all transpersonal education. It is believed that each student already has all knowledge and wisdom. He or she needs only to be taught (through meditation, guided imagery, and so forth) how to tap into it.[11]

10. Gary Leazer, "The New Age Movement and Education," *Light*, Summer 1992, 5-6.

11. Elliot Miller, *A Crash Course on the New Age Movement* (Grand Rapids: Baker, 1989), 96-97.

According to Jack Canfield and Paula Klimek, New Age education has arrived, and "more and more teachers are exposing children to ways of contacting their inner wisdom and higher selves." An influx of spiritual teachings from the East, combined with a new psychological perspective in the West, has resulted in a fresh look at the learning process. People everywhere are looking for a new vision, a new approach, a new paradigm of life. A new vision is beginning to manifest itself.

Thus, holistic, transpersonal education views the student as engaged in an integral process of unfolding under the direction of his/her higher self. This process is perceived as taking place in a universe that is also constantly evolving: each of us is seen as an important part of the larger planetary and universal evolution of consciousness. There are endless pointers: "Children of all ages love physical exercise and seem to be particularly fascinated with yoga: they move easily into all sorts of contortions." There are numerous books on yoga for children. Centering becomes the more acceptable word for meditation. "Relaxation and centering exercises are a fundamental process for New Age education, because they provide a space for listening to the voice within."[12]

## NEW AGE EDUCATION PRACTICES AND TERMS

Beverly Galyean is known as the chief architect of confluent education. She has described it as a holistic approach using thinking, the five senses, feeling, and intuition. "Once we begin to see that we are all God, that we all have the attributes of God, then I think the whole purpose of human life is to reown the Godlikeness within us; the perfect love, the perfect wisdom, the perfect understanding, the perfect intelligence, and when we do that, we create back to that old, that essential oneness which is consciousness."

Galyean developed three federally funded education programs for the Los Angeles Public Schools — using guided imagery and meditation.[13] These education programs prepare teachers of all grade levels to use transpersonal "confluent education" techniques. Galyean suggests techniques to help students contact and learn from the source of wisdom, love, and intelligence within us — often called the "higher self" — God, universal wisdom or spirit, conscience. This is done through the symbolic use of light, such as the sun, the sky, mountaintops, wise persons, golden liquid energy, and the colors white, gold, purple, and violet. Teachers who are deeply spiritual and who feel comfortable working with their own spiritual development may choose to

12. Tal Brooke, "Education: Capturing Hearts and Minds for a New World," *SCP Journal* 16.4 (1992): 21-22.
13. Russell Chandler, *Understanding the New Age* (Dallas: Word, 1991), 136.

offer spiritually oriented meditations to their students. This is done when there is an explicit sense of appropriateness established between the teacher and the students, parents, school personnel, and community.[14]

### Guided Imagery and Visualization

Guided imagery and visualization exercises are based on the New Age assumption that every person already has all knowledge and wisdom. Guided imagery and visualization are used to draw out this hidden knowledge and wisdom. Canfield states: "We believe that guided imagery is a key to finding out what is in the consciousness of New Age children. . . . Children are so close to spirit if we only allow room for their process to emerge. . . . The only requirement is to provide a space and an environment where these beautiful young spirits can open up and allow their wisdom to be seen."[15]

Deborah Rozeman's *Meditating with Children* made its way into a California school district. One visualization Rozeman recommends is this: "Meditate and go into the Source within, and in that One Source feel that you are One with everyone else's Light, Intelligence, Love, and Power. . . . Chant 'Om' softly to fill the whole circle and the whole room with your experience of the Source within."[16]

### Right-Brain Learning

Many educators say that the right brain governs human creative and intuitive abilities. The right-brain/left-brain distinction is not New Age as such, but New Agers have appropriated the distinction to justify bringing "right-brain learning techniques" into the classroom. These include meditation, yoga, guided imagery, chanting, mandalas (visual symbols used as aids to meditation), and games involving fantasy and role playing. Children are being led into mystical and psychic experiences (including encounters with spirit guides called "Wise Ones") on the premise that this will develop their intuitive abilities and thus provide a more balanced, holistic, or "whole-brained" education as opposed to strictly left-brain (objective) learning.[17]

There is still controversy over the scientific evidence that the brain's two hemispheres can be split into two tidy sections, one the center of creativity and the other the center of logical thinking.

14. Miller, *Crash Course*, 97.

15. Brooke, "Education: Capturing Hearts and Minds," 22.

16. Ron Rhodes, *New Age Movement*, Zondervan Guide to Cults and Religious Movements (Grand Rapids: Zondervan, 1995), 22.

17. Miller, *Crash Course*, 95.

## Values Clarification

Values Clarification was formulated in the mid-1960s by social scientists Louis E. Baths, Merrill Harman, Sidney B. Simon, and others. This method plays a pivotal role in both humanistic and transpersonal education. Holding that values emerge from within and therefore should not be imposed from without (a view compatible both with basic humanism and "Inner Wisdom"), it attempts to help students discover and clarify their own values. It has been widely implemented in public schools under the pretext that it is an appropriate approach to values in a pluralistic society since it does not seek to impose any particular value system on the children. The underlying assumption is that there are no absolute truths or values.

However, Richard A. Baer, Jr., contends that on a deeper level the claim to neutrality is entirely misleading. At this more basic level, the originators of Values Clarification simply assume that their own subjective theory of values is correct. If parents object to their children using pot or engaging in pre-marital sex, the theory behind Values Clarification makes it appropriate for the child to respond, "But that's just YOUR value judgment. Don't force it on me."[18]

In fact, in the April 1989 *Journal of the American Family Association*, W. R. Coulson, one of the early proponents of value-free education, said he owed parents an apology. "Youthful experimentation with sex, alcohol, marijuana and a variety of other drugs — whatever is popular at the time — has been shown to follow affective, value-free education quite predictably; we now know that after these classes, students become more prone to give in to temptation than if they had never been enrolled." He pointed out that a leading tobacco company is contributing substantially to the support of several value-free educational programs.

Thus we see that the word "values" — rather than ethics or morals — carries with it the assumption that right and wrong are something we choose, as we would choose what clothes to wear. The purpose of the process is not to discover an objective system of moral absolutes, but to create a subjective set of values to clarify our value options — in other words, what is right and wrong for me. The clarification of our "sense of values" replaces the quest for true goodness; feeling replaces right; preference replaces virtue. The only thing prohibited by the Values Clarification method is a recognition of and respect for the objective, universal, and absolute moral law of God. Immature, subjective impulses can be "clarified," thus obscuring objective verities.[19]

18. Ibid., 98.
19. Ralph Rath, *The New Age: A Christian Critique* (South Bend, Ind.: Greenlawn Press, 1990), 203; Douglas Groothuis, *Confronting the New Age* (Downers Grove, Ill.: InterVarsity, 1988), 132-33.

### Global Education

Global education refers to educating students to think of themselves as global citizens in keeping with the New Age political agenda. Global education includes such ideas as religious syncretism (in which all religions are essentially one) and the need for one world government. Ron Rhodes points out that global education is a prominent aspect of education among New Agers.

Globalism in education is obviously rooted in the monistic ("all is one") and pantheistic ("all is God") worldview of the New Age movement. In his book on global education, *New Genesis: Shaping a Global Spirituality*, Robert Muller says:

> On a universal scale, humankind is seeking no less than its reunion with the "divine," its transcendence into ever higher forms of life. Hindus call our earth Brahma, or God, for they rightly see no difference between our earth and the divine. This ancient simple truth is slowly dawning again upon humanity . . . as we are about to enter our cosmic age and to become what we were always meant to be: the planet of God.[20]

## RELIGIOUS PRACTICES

If an educational program contains yoga, meditation, or talk of the "Inner Self" and "Wise Ones," its religious nature can be easily demonstrated to any open-minded individual. Elliot Miller points out that it is important to understand that something can also be religious (or at least metaphysical, and thus in the same "personal faith" category as religion) without employing traditionally religious practices or terminology (for instance, prayer, meditation, or reference to "God" or "salvation").

The Supreme Court has affirmed that one of the primary characteristics of a religion is that it adheres to and promotes "underlying theories" concerning such "ultimate realities" as the nature and place of human beings in the universe. Virtually all transpersonal/humanistic programs operate from such metaphysical assumptions. Thus it can be argued that even those programs that use only Values Clarification are religious in nature.[21]

## A FORM OF INDOCTRINATION

Since the New Age approach to education follows a religious worldview — that of pantheism or monism — it is a form of religious indoctrination and violates

20. Rhodes, *New Age Movement*, 23; see also Ron Rhodes, *The Culting of America* (Eugene, Ore.: Harvest House, 1994), 156.
21. Miller, *Crash Course*, 103-4.

the constitutional prohibition against government promotion of any particular religion. Of even more concern for Christians is the fact that the religion the New Age promotes is incompatible with Christianity at virtually every point.

The religious premises of New Age educational programs are usually buried in secular rhetoric, a practice that is often intentional. As New Age leader Dick Sutphen candidly says: "One of the biggest advantages we have as New Agers is, once the occult, metaphysical, and New Age terminology is removed, we have concepts and techniques that are very acceptable to the general public [and] open the New Age door to millions who normally would not be receptive."

Even if a program's religious premises are concealed, they are there, and the program remains a tool of religious indoctrination. Thus it is important, according to Erick Buehrer, vice president of Citizens for Excellence in Education, and Robert Burrows, to go through the primary source material of a program with these questions in mind: What are the program's explicit or implied premises about ultimate reality or God, about the nature of humanity (particularly human consciousness), and about the solution to the human predicament?

Specific techniques, without any teaching attached, can themselves serve as vehicles for indoctrination when they are closely associated with a particular religious tradition. For example, getting students to sit in full lotus position and meditate for relaxation will make them receptive to Eastern mysticism or New Age spirituality in a way that watching tropical fish, another proven relaxant, would never do.[22]

### Positive Reinforcement, Not Discipline

A weakness of the New Age program of education is its heavy reliance on education and "positive reinforcement" for correcting social problems and crime without the discipline and punitive measures that the biblical view believes human nature requires.

It should be clear, then, that wherever else the New Age and the biblical view may be compatible, they differ radically over the human moral condition. And the very nature of political and educational structures is being determined by such an assumption. (For example, influenced by the biblical view of humanity's egoism and fallenness, the U.S. Constitution's system of checks and balances has helped maintain a framework of freedom within a framework of order and restraint for over two hundred years.)[23]

22. Eric Buehrer with Robert Burrows, "Challenging the New Age in Education," *SCP Newsletter* 14.2 (1989): 3-4.
23. Miller, *Crash Course*, 114.

## EVALUATING THE NEW AGE APPROACH

According to Douglas Groothuis, an evangelical scholar at Denver Seminary, Christians do not need to adopt a simplistic "quarantine" or "taboo" mentality in critiquing New Age involvement in education. A few elements of the New Age approach should be conserved.[24]

Elliot Miller, another evangelical scholar, points out that the biblical view has room for agreement with the New Age approach to humanness. Rejecting views of some secularists and materialists who reduce human beings to the level of complex machines or incurable savages, the New Agers celebrate humanity's higher qualities: his capacities for a certain type of spirituality and rationality as well as deep feeling, creativity, and meaningful relationships.

This humanism translates into a concern about the dehumanizing effects of our modern technocracy. New Agers often argue that materialistic values, and the uncontrolled industrialization and urban growth they produce, are robbing us of life's greater riches while depleting our natural resources and wreaking ecological havoc. They call for a turning away from consumer values to a lifestyle of "simple living and high thinking."

The New Age view also argues that growth should be limited to an "appropriate" or "human" scale that protects the personal dimensions of life and keeps society manageable.

While the biblical view makes God, rather than human beings, the measure of all things, in the sense of valuing humanness the biblical view is "humanistic." In fact, in this sense it is more humanistic than both New Age and secular humanism, since neither the impersonal New Age god nor the impersonal secular universe can lend ultimate validation and worth to human personality. In addition, the biblical view confirms humans' sense of their own dignity and uniqueness by showing that their distinctive personal qualities reflect the very likeness of God.

The biblical view takes issue, however, with the New Age view of humanness with respect to the extent to which it is carried out. The New Age view goes beyond appreciation and respect for humanity to adoration and worship: an idolatry of the image of God in human beings. The biblical view affirms that our distinctiveness and unique humanness, as great as it is, pales before that infinite and perfect Being from whom it is derived. God is the one to whom worship is directed. God's personal realities — holy and loving — are worth celebrating! [25]

Most people in the more sophisticated facets of the New Age movement are sincerely concerned about salvaging the world, and much that they are calling

24. Groothuis, *Confronting the New Age,* 141.
25. Miller, *Crash Course,* 120-21.

for is compatible with biblical values. But from the biblical perspective, the kind of enlightened society they desire could never be realized apart from a radical transformation of human nature — as they themselves recognize. The biblical view offers such a transformation in the "new birth." In contrast, the New Age view advocates instead a "psychic birth," a quickening of spiritual consciousness and power apart from Christ's atonement and the regenerating work of the Holy Spirit. From the biblical perspective, this New Age approach results in a sense of peace and wholeness that fails to touch the dynamic, sometimes inscrutable, operation of the sinful nature. Such psychic "transformation" opens up possibilities for a more refined, even apocalyptic, kind of evil to emerge.

The sense of "transcending" normal consciousness and connecting with "Universal Mind" can produce such self-assurance that the need to check one's beliefs for truthfulness or one's actions for morality can easily be forgotten. In fact, many conclude that they have gone beyond what they call the "illusory duality" of good and evil.

It should also be noted that the altered states of consciousness of New Agers do not long remain separate from the beliefs and practices of the occult.[26]

# THE IMPORTANCE OF THE PUBLIC SCHOOL

For those who have the perspective not only of American history but of the history of the world, the importance of the public school is crucial. Some say that the concept of a free, universal, nonsectarian public school is one of the noblest contributions of the United States to the world. As an agent for maintaining the American community, the public school theoretically magnifies the aspects of our life which we hold in common. It is the school for democracy.

It is true that in the early years Protestants sometimes used pressure in the public schools against Roman Catholics and Jews. That situation has greatly improved. It is also true that in many areas public schools were used to evade facing our racial diversity. But it is now in the public schools that we learn to live with people of different faiths and backgrounds.

In *The Disuniting of America* Arthur Schlesinger contends that the genius of America is that it has forged a single nation from peoples of remarkably diverse racial, religious, and ethnic origins.

The United States has worked thus far because it has given ethnically diverse peoples compelling reasons to see themselves as part of the same

26. Ibid., 133-34.

nation. According to Schlesinger, our public schools in particular have been the great instrument of assimilation and the great means of forming an American identity.[27]

## SECULARIZATION OF EDUCATION

The culture-forming power of education is especially noteworthy in light of the United States's system of compulsory education. Tax-supported schools choose curricula through a bureaucracy of vying interests: those of the federal government, school boards, teachers, other interest groups, and, often least influential, the parents.

Douglas Groothuis contends that the educational community, whether intentionally or not, fosters a non-Christian or anti-traditional mind-set. Through the considerable influence of the educational philosophy of John Dewey and others, a non-Christian worldview has permeated modern public educational thinking.

The actual content of public school textbooks reveals a dearth of Christian morality and positive references to traditional American religious life.

In 1985, Paul Vitz conducted a federally funded, systematic study of the content of public school textbooks through the National Institute of Education. His conclusion was simply that textbooks have been censored. "Religion, traditional family values, and conservative political and economic positions have been reliably excluded from the children's textbooks." He found this to be the case at all educational levels from grade one through high school. America's substantial Christian heritage is overwhelmingly edited out. And if the Pilgrims happen to make a rare guest appearance, their Christian orientation is omitted.[28]

## OPENNESS OF THE PUBLIC SCHOOL TO THE NEW AGE

Although openly hostile to the influence of traditional Christian viewpoints, schools are often open to New Age viewpoints posing as nonreligious psychological practices. As I have already mentioned, New Age activist Dick Sutphen makes the point that "One of the biggest advantages we have as New Agers is, once the occult, metaphysical and New Age terminology is removed, we have concepts and techniques that are very acceptable to the general public."

Jack Canfield and Paula Klimek advise their fellow educators how to

---

27. Arthur J. Schlesinger, Jr., *The Disuniting of America* (New York: Norton, 1992), 11.

28. Groothuis, *Confronting the New Age*, 130-31, 142.

present 'centering' — a form of Eastern meditation — in the classroom: "Centering can also be extended into work with meditation in the classroom."

According to Groothuis, many educators who proudly wear the label of "progressive" greet with open arms New Age practices, while pushing away "old age" traditions as outmoded relics.[29]

Earle Ellis, a prominent evangelical scholar, contends that a religion of secular and New Age humanism is clearly established in the public schools with its explicit exclusion of God, its naturalistic interpretation of meanings and values, and its relativizing of contrary worldviews and value systems. Such a school may affirm that honesty is the best policy, but it must forbid the Ten Commandments to hang upon the wall. With its secular humanistic framework it teaches implicitly or explicitly that human beings are the measure of all things; and, while it can laud liberty or democracy as important values, it cannot, as Thomas Jefferson did, present them as gifts "endowed by [the] Creator." Thus, we see not a realization of a state neutrality but rather the establishment of a religion of secular humanism. This results in a quasi-monopoly on tax funds given to one kind of educational structure, the secular-humanist and New Age public school.[30]

## PROBLEMS WITH TEACHING RELIGION IN PUBLIC SCHOOLS

In dealing with religion in the public schools, Christians face several problems of principle. First, a tax-funded public education can never, in our pluralistic society, be fully Christian in content or method.

Second, how fair is a mandatory public education system that violates the beliefs of so many taxpayers? How can any curriculum fairly represent and please all the members of a pluralistic society? Christians object to New Age influences in the schools and are concerned that Christianity be fairly presented. New Agers object to whatever denies their viewpoint. Yet both New Agers and Christians must pay taxes to support these schools, whether they send their children there or not.

Third, some have attempted to answer the question of fairness in the curriculum by appealing to some "neutral" core of educational materials that would be both educationally appropriate and personally inoffensive. Yet no such neutrality exists. Curricula can vary in terms of fairness and accuracy, but every curriculum is written by human beings whose worldviews affect their work. As we have noted, excluding Christianity from textbooks is not a neutral

29. Ibid., 142-43.
30. E. Earle Ellis, "If Only a Secularist Religion Is Taught," *Wall Street Journal*, March 27, 1984, 34.

presentation of American history. Likewise, presenting all religions as equal is not a neutral presentation because it negates Christ's exclusive claim. Neutrality is impossible.[31]

## Christian Schools and Home Schooling

Responding to the perceived threats from the secularization of public schools, fundamentalist and conservative Christians in the United States have opened their own schools. Their goal is to restore religious and parental authority, provide quality education, and protect children from the evils of drugs, sex, violence, and lack of discipline. Aside from the fundamentalist emphasis on the Bible, creationism, patriarchal values, and a denigration of secular humanism in general, the curriculum teaches the same subjects as the secular schools. The methods, however, include corporal punishment and traditional and standardized teaching principles. Evangelical schools draw their students from most socioeconomic groups, but particularly from white, middle-class families.[32]

According to Susan Rose, a consultant for the Fundamentalisms and Society project, in the creation of Christian schools we see neither total rejection of secular processes nor total acceptance of traditional, patriarchal, evangelical ways. Although Christian schools stress the values of the traditional patriarchal family and the "natural" submission of women, because of their size and curriculum the schools tend not to segregate boys from girls, nor do they offer them different curricula.

A number of studies in Christian schools suggest that their students are well behaved, obedient, and well mannered, without being overly pious. Students tend to express political and attitudinal beliefs similar to those of their families, and to spend a good deal of their time with "Christian" friends.

In terms of organizational impact, Christian schools have contributed to the momentum of the New Christian Right. Evangelical parents enroll their children in Christian schools believing that their authority and role as parents are reinforced, even though they do not necessarily gain greater control over their children's education. Evangelical teachers say they are able to express their beliefs and values more freely and to form more intimate relationships with their students. Many evangelical pastors also serve as school principals, increasing the influence they have on their flock. With mutually reinforcing

31. Groothuis, *Confronting the New Age*, 143-44.
32. Martin E. Marty and R. Scott Appleby, eds., *Fundamentalisms and Society: Reclaiming the Sciences, the Family, and Education* (Chicago: University of Chicago, 1993), 326-27.

institutions based on consensus and dedicated to similar goals, one finds more consistent results in socializing children.

It appears that the growth of the Christian school movement has plateaued but that Christian schools will remain a viable option for educating children in the United States for some time to come. Some suggest that we may be seeing a convergence of public and Christian schooling. If this is the case, and the public schools continue to move right of center, with an emphasis on the "neutrality" of the "basics," and increasingly approach "accountability" through standardized programs, then evangelical parents may become less dissatisfied with public education and less willing to bear the costs of Christian schooling. However, this would not affect those Christian school parents whose prime motivation is to have their children go to school in an explicitly Christian environment.[33] Home schooling remains a desired option for many fundamentalist and conservative families.

## THE VOUCHER APPROACH

One group of conservative leaders, calling themselves the Third Millennium, is pushing for underwriting private schools with tax funds. They have called for a comprehensive policy of parental choice in education. Calling parents the "primary educators of their children," these leaders insist that "the state and other institutions should be supportive of [parents'] exercise of that responsibility." Although the group's manifesto stops short of using the word "vouchers," the implication is clear. They want the government to set policies "that enable parents to effectively exercise their right and responsibility to choose the schooling that they consider best for their children." In other words, they want tax money for parochial and other private religious schools.

Rob Boston states that all the pro-voucher activity, including the formation of state groups, is simply a renewed push by the Roman Catholic hierarchy for taxpayer subsidies for Catholic schools.

Support for vouchers also is becoming a litmus test for political hopefuls seeking Religious Right support.

A number of state governors are also advocating a voucher system for private schools, among them George W. Bush, Jr., of Texas.

Critics contend that the voucher plan would hurt the disadvantaged and give no accountability on how the money would be spent. "Under voucher plans, no private school would be required to accept poor, academically disadvantaged students from the inner city. Parochial and other private

33. Ibid., 478-80.

schools would receive funding from taxpayers but not be accountable to them at all."[34]

John Leland and the Virginia Baptists struggled against the "Assessment Bill," which allowed the collection by the civil government of a religious tax which was then to be distributed to the churches according to designations by taxpayers. The Virginia Baptists saw in the Assessment Bill a threat to religious liberty.

The temptation to compromise is great, especially when such compromise would secure money for financially struggling private schools and mandate public religious exercises as hedges against societal immorality.

## PRAYER AMENDMENT

In early years, "separation of church and state" and secular emphases had led to a virtual ban on prayer in public schools. Immediately after the 1994 election, Republican leaders proposed a constitutional amendment for prayer in the public schools, stimulating controversy in Congress and across the country.

While recognizing the wide support for school prayer as well as the social problems among young people, many people still oppose a constitutional amendment. Several religious groups even held a news conference announcing their opposition.

The proposed amendment would generally protect voluntary school prayer and religious liberty. The draft's wording clearly articulates a principle of government neutrality toward religion and explicitly restores student religious expression in public schools.

Ronald Flowers of Texas Christian University points out that the main argument against the amendment is that it attempts to restore what has never been taken away. According to Flowers, there is nothing now to prevent students from praying, silently or aloud, alone or in groups, in public schools. Of course, it is implicit that prayers may not be disruptive of the educational process or abusive of classmates, but that is a matter of school decorum, not constitutional law, he explains.

It is generally accepted that descriptive courses on religion can be taught in the public schools. In that teaching, schools should not take sides in religious disputes or suggest that one religious tradition is superior to others. Teaching should not be done in a way that undermines a student's sense of citizenship if the student does not conform to a prescribed religious norm.

In awareness of the limits to the responsibilities and resources of public

34. Rob Boston, "Parochial Gambit," *Church and State* 47.8 (September 1994): 4-6, 9, 11.

education, the American participation creed calls for religiously motivated people to involve themselves in a constructive way in public school programs. Parents in religious homes should encourage their children to become teachers and leaders in the schools.

According to Flowers, if the American creed is to survive and prosper, Christian people must restudy the implications of their flight from the public schools. In fact, they must ask if the Christian private school program is a proper stewardship of their funds and energy. Even more serious questions should be asked about home-study programs. Instead of turning from the public schools, many thoughtful Christians are becoming involved as teachers and administrators in the public schools as part of their Christian stewardship.[35]

## "Transforming the System"

Some Christian parents are unable to afford or don't have access to good Christian schools, and sometimes home schooling is a practical impossibility. Other parents who have their children in Christian schools may still want to work toward better education in the public schools. In these cases, suggests Groothuis, the transformation theme is called into action — although public education is usually considered less than ideal for conservative Christians.[36]

### TWO APPROACHES

The more extreme or theocratic groups argue that conservative Christians should infiltrate public schools and seek to control them. Certain specially suited Christians, they believe, should pray and work tirelessly to obtain teaching and school board and even administrative posts within public education.

More moderate conservative groups take a less strident approach. They monitor and critique curriculum and required school literature and programs such as outcome-based education and some sex education courses. They also sponsor programs such as Christian literature distribution by students, flagpole prayers, equal access clubs, and student-initiated prayers. In addition, they nominate school board members and attend board meetings.

In the March 31, 1994, manifesto "Evangelicals and Catholics Together: The Christian Mission in the Third Millennium," conservative leaders

35. Ronald B. Flowers, "Who Says Kids Can't Pray in Schools?", *Texas Christian University Magazine*, March 1995, 4-5.
36. Groothuis, *Confronting the New Age*, 144.

called on public schools to add religious content. Public schools, the statement said, should "transmit to coming generations our cultural heritage, which is inseparable from the formative influence of religion, especially Judaism and Christianity." Calling for schools to "cultivate the morality of honesty, law observance, work, caring, chastity, mutual respect between sexes and readiness for marriage, parenthood and family," manifesto signers asserted, "We reject the claim that, in any or all of these areas, 'tolerance' requires the promotion of moral equivalence between the normative and the deviant."

## COMMON CHARACTER QUALITIES

Because of the importance of the public schools in maintaining the unique American creed of a common culture that is at the same time multicultural, other religious leaders advocate teaching in the public schools those character qualities that are common to faith communities and other groups.

The recent book by William Bennett, *Book of Virtues,* reminds us of the success of the Modern McGuffey Readers formulated by Ullen W. Leavell, professor of education and director of the McGuffey Reading Clinic at the University of Virginia, Charlottesville, Virginia. In the 1950s the Texas school system adopted the McGuffey Readers as required books, and our children used them.

The moral and human-relations themes most emphasized in the Modern McGuffey Readers of the Golden Rule Series include cooperation, courage, fairness, friendliness, honesty, kindness, patriotism, perseverance, responsibility, reverence, and unselfishness.

Other leaders advocate that Christian and other faith groups explore the possibilities of utilizing and critiquing the recent Character Education movement which is today being used to teach character development to millions of American children in the nation's public schools.

Character education represents an effort to teach moral behavior to primary and secondary school students in a time perceived to be morally rudderless and to be without such teaching in local communities or in the home. Across the country, teachers are confronting children with moral dilemmas and asking them to think and talk. The felt need for this kind of education is so deep and widespread that it has spurred a movement that has attracted support from such nationally known leaders and celebrities as Barbara Jordan, Barbara Bush, Marian Wright Edelman, Jesse Jackson, Tom Selleck, and Nathan Glazer.

The main concern of this camp is that public schools not become centers of a cultural war between those on the right who believe that character education must incorporate religion and those on the left who do not want religious teaching included at all.

437

The American Civil Liberties Union is leery of the character education approach on the grounds that it will provide opportunities for people to impose religious views. On the right, meanwhile, organizations such as Concerned Women of America and Citizens for Excellence in Education are hostile to character education because they believe that public education cannot be trusted with moral issues — that in its insistent secularity it will wind up being anti-church.

Thus, while few religious organizations have taken a formal stand on character education, most are opposed in general to the notion of schools getting involved in what has traditionally been the province of church and family.

## A JOINT STATEMENT OF CURRENT LAW

In April 1995, thirty-five organizations as liberal as the American Civil Liberties Union and as conservative as the Christian Legal Society signed a six-page accord outlining what religious activity is permissible in public schools. It is an 18-point statement entitled "Religion in the Public Schools: A Joint Statement of Current Law."

Such a consensus statement of church-state issues in public schools was possible largely because the document focuses not on what the law should be but on what current law is. A clear assessment of existing laws, the representatives of these organizations believe, will go a long way toward combating the caricatures, exaggerations, and alarmist portrayals common to both liberals and conservatives. In practical terms, it should keep confused and skittish public school superintendents and principals from infringing on the right of students who legally express their faith.

Civil liberties organizations value the statement because, in their view, it dispels the notion that God has been outlawed in public schools. According to the statement, students may pray in informal settings, individually, or in groups, "audibly or silently, subject to the same rules of order as applied to other speech in these locations."

Students may "express their religious beliefs in the form of reports, homework, and artwork." Also, "students have the right to speak to, and attempt to persuade, their peers about religious topics just as they do with regard to political topics, though such efforts must steer free of religious 'harassment.'"

The significance of clear statements of what is permissible outweighs concerns about the document's ambiguities. "It is nothing short of extraordinary that Jewish groups, the ACLU, and others would concede that students have the right to evangelize."[37]

37. Randy Frame, "Access Endorses Religion in Public Schools," *Christianity Today*, May 15, 1995, 45-46.

## FAITH COMMUNITIES AND CHARACTER DEVELOPMENT

As a supplement to the work of public schools, some religious leaders point out emphases and programs of faith communities which undergird character development.

### Faith Emphasis

Ron Rhodes suggests that parents can learn about and exercise their rights as parents in relation to public schools. For example, they can become familiar with *The Protection of Pupil Rights (Hatch) Amendment,* which says that public school instructional materials can be inspected by parents. They can also become familiar with the "equal protection" clause of the Fourteenth Amendment, which affirms that New Age educators have no more right to promote their beliefs in school than do Christians. Parents can equip their children to recognize spiritual deception. They can go over important New Age buzzwords like "meditation," "centering," "visualization," "guided imagery," "higher self," and "globalism." They can thus warn their children *in advance* of the problems and dangers of these practices and ideas.

Parents can also keep abreast of what their children are doing in school. They can talk with their children about what they are learning. Parents should scan through children's textbooks and watch for any religious or anti-Christian elements. It is also wise and helpful to volunteer in the child's classroom as often as possible. By doing this, parents can provide much-needed assistance, establish a positive relationship with the teacher and the school, and observe firsthand a child's learning environment.[38]

## Group and Faith Communities

There is a renewed emphasis on the importance of faith communities (such as churches and synagogues) in character education. This concern has been spurred in part by teen pregnancies, alcohol and drug abuse, and the power that gangs have in influencing young people. Various programs already are working, such as "Parents as Volunteers," "Friends of the Schools," and "mentoring" efforts, all of which can be correlated with the public schools.

38. Rhodes, *The Culting of America,* 156-57.

# THE BIBLICAL VIEW OF EDUCATION

The biblical view of education has certain assumptions and priorities. It brings to education the perspective of eternity and divine revelation. The biblical worldview affirms the reality of God, the incarnation of the divine within the structure of the world and of history, and the primacy of the spiritual dimension of life. Qualities of love, forgiveness, and holiness, springing from a genuine and sustained following of Christ, have a creative impact wherever they occur. They lift the educational experience into something profoundly meaningful.

Despite mistakes and distortion of interpretation and application in the past, the biblical worldview comes back to affirm that each individual is made in the image of God. The gift of reason, although it is found in its rudiments within the animal kingdom, is, in its articulated and conscious form, a special characteristic of humanity whereby we resemble God and are made in his image. Education, therefore, must encourage the power of reasoning.

Another unique characteristic of humanity is our power of reasonable choice. This is our ability to decide for ourselves. This is another aspect of the image of God in which we are made. An appropriate view of education encourages us to make responsible use of this freedom. In other words, there should be no division between education properly understood and the Christian faith.

This biblical emphasis upon choice and freedom implies that the biblical worldview is to be presented in a context of religious freedom. Christians must be cautious in the way in which they present Christian truth claims. This obviously does not mean failing to say anything at all, which merely allows a different form of indoctrination to take place. It means expressing Christian beliefs in a way that invites honest and genuine reflection without assuming what the outcome might be. Such openness of approach to promote dialogue is in keeping with the teaching methods of Jesus himself.

## Principles and Practices Based on the Bible

British scholar Hugh Montefiore suggests that despite our Christian critique of the Enlightenment, in many ways we are indebted to the Enlightenment. None of us would wish to turn back to the age of superstition. However, many people involved in education who are under the influence of the Enlightenment understand an appeal to reason to be in fact an appeal to a particular form of rationality which takes its origin in the Enlightenment. It presupposes that the unaided reason is the sole means of true knowledge.

The Christian faith has a long tradition of a different type of rationality. It presupposes a belief in human reason purified and assisted by revelation and in particular by the final self-revelation of God in Jesus Christ culminating in his death and resurrection. We believe that this Christian structure of rationality enables us to have some degree of understanding about our relationship with God. Its framework of discourse allows us to have a coherent view of God's world which we believe to correspond to the real world around us. This is made possible because there is a corresponding structure in reality itself which enables us to understand it in this way.

This means that a choice must be made between the worldview of the Enlightenment and the New Age and that of the Bible. As Lesslie Newbigin has said, "A true opposition is not between reason and revelation as sources of criteria of truth. It is between two uses to which reason is put." A choice must be made between the Christian tradition of rationality and that of secular humanism and the New Age worldview. The basis of choice between these views should be a judgment about which worldview with its accompanying form of rationality is most adequate.

The credentials of the biblical view based on divine revelation must be adequate for belief. Such a faith must be adequate to an individual's personal experience and at the same time do justice to the religious experience of adherents of other faiths. It must cohere within a structure of rationality in a way which corresponds to the truth as it is perceived. In a historical religion such as Christianity, interpretation of divine revelation must be seen to rest upon an adequate historical base. This is one reason why distinguished evangelical scholars such as N. T. Wright are projecting a vigorous critique of the "Jesus Seminar." Furthermore, it must measure up to fundamental human needs. It must also go along with our understanding of the physical universe as well as with our understanding of the psychological and sociological aspects of humanity.

According to the continuing Christian tradition, Christians believe that their faith is adequate in terms of these criteria. In fact, Christians believe that the Christian faith provides a more adequate basis for life and thought than a New Age or secular worldview which regards the world as lacking ultimate purpose and values other than those which individuals may ascribe to it.[39]

## OPENNESS TO DIALOGUE AND EVALUATION

In an increasingly pluralistic world it is important to establish methods of comparing worldviews and ways of strengthening our conviction regarding

39. Hugh Montefiore, *The Gospel and Contemporary Culture* (London: Mowbray, 1992), 9-10.

the superiority of the biblical worldview. There must be an openness to looking at the criteria for establishing the validity of a worldview. Admittedly factors other than rational arguments are important in leading people to build their lives around certain worldviews. These factors, however, should not displace sound reasoning. Christians must decide their worldview by faith and by reason. Through the centuries notable leaders have done just that, establishing the superiority of the biblical worldview in their own particular context.

The biblical worldview cannot be proved in a way that a mathematical equation can be proved. But there are rational tests that are helpful. We can begin by applying the test of coherence to the Christian worldview, placing major assumptions of the biblical view side by side to note how they cohere and avoid contradiction. The Christian insists that biblical assumptions are coherent because they are rooted in the rationality of God and his creation.

A worldview must also be comprehensive and creative. Although the biblical worldview cannot be perfectly verified, it does explain in a comprehensive and satisfying way the facets of life and experience. In addition, existentially or experientially it brings satisfaction and fulfillment.

A worldview must not do violence to the empirical propositions of science and common sense within their own limits — working according to their own experimental methods. In other words, according to British philosopher Dorothy Emmet, no worldview or metaphysical theory can be sustained which does not respect empirical propositions in their own sphere. But an adequate worldview can set these patterns in a wider context of interpretative theory without distorting their essential character and thus give us a synoptic vision. I have sought to demonstrate how this can be done in a number of areas such as psychology, history, and natural science in my book *Life's Ultimate Questions — A Contemporary Philosophy of Religion.*[40]

An example of Christian willingness to have elements in the Christian view discussed is their belief in a moral world. This is not a crude notion of sin and retribution. But as Dietrich Bonhoeffer said: "The world is simply ordered in such a way that a profound respect for absolute laws and human rights is also the best means of self-preservation"; in other words, self-preservation demands respect for morality or, put in the negative, disregard for biblical morality brings its own penalty.

Historical examples of morality operating in this way are not hard to find. Herbert Butterfield points to the catastrophic end of Hitlerite Germany as a penalty for Prussian militarism.

---

40. John P. Newport, "The Biblical World-view and Church-Related Colleges," *The Southern Baptist Educator,* August 1989, 31; see also John P. Newport, *Life's Ultimate Questions* (Dallas: Word, 1989), 31-32; and Dorothy M. Emmet, *The Nature of Metaphysical Thinking* (London: Macmillan, 1953), 200.

Christians say there is evidence of the Christian doctrine of providence and grace operating in history. Again and again, human disasters have been redeemed by becoming a base for something better.

Christians also affirm that the Christian understanding of history comprehends both the good and the bad. It recognizes that the nonrational and irrational are inherent in humankind. It starts not with humans as they ought to be, but as they are; it allows for — even expects — evil as well as glory from a flawed humanity.

Not only does the Christian view understand women and men both as individuals and in society, comprehensively and realistically, but it also believes that something has been done about, rather than just done for, them and their follies, and is being done, and will be done. The Christian understanding of history, while it is the least optimistic, does offer the greatest hope.

The Christian understanding of history does not merely require blind faith, like most other groups. It gives historical grounds for faith. It stands or falls by the historical facts of the life, death, and resurrection of Jesus Christ. In consequence, the commitment the Christian view requires is more than intellectual preference; it is a faith based on historical and rational grounds.[41]

The biblical view does not attempt any escape from our material world. We cannot climb out of our bodies into some purely conceptual state of reason. The human condition is inescapably material, particular, fallible, and finite. Any knowledge which seeks to evade this fact ceases to be human knowledge and so is not knowledge at all. This is a negative note we must sound in the face not only of Greek and Enlightenment rationalism but also in the light of the New Age approach in which humans seek to be God. The positive note of the Christian view is that culture can be developed according to the promise inherent in our createdness. This promise says that creation embodies the rationality given to it by its Maker and Redeemer, whose spirit liberates the human mind to discover what is and what is to be.

## THE IMPORTANCE OF RELIGIOUS HUMILITY

The Christian conviction that there is a revealed word of God outside our existence calling us to acceptance and obedience is fully compatible with acknowledging that we as Christians along with the rest of humanity could be mistaken in our religious interpretations. In fact, we sometimes find ourselves in the presence of evidence so compelling that we must give up some convictions that we had earlier thought were part of the revealed word from outside our existence. At a certain point, for instance, it was no longer per-

---

41. Montefiore, *Gospel and Contemporary Culture*, 33, 36-37.

missible for Christians to believe that they were religiously obligated to hold to the old geocentric theory of the universe.[42]

In summary, the biblical worldview and the Christian gospel are not to be identified with the interpretations of Scripture offered by some Christian leaders, although the gospel is certain to be found within the pages of Scripture. The gospel is God's gracious action in creating the world, and in re-creating men and women and restoring them to a loving relationship with himself.

The biblical worldview tells of God's saving activity within human history, foreshadowed in the writings of the Old Testament, fully embodied in the event of Christ, particularly in his death and resurrection. It is the acceptance of Christ as the Way, the Truth, and the Life. The gospel is our means of access through Christ to God's Kingdom. It is the good news that God has freed us to be our true selves. It is the power of God to renew lives in the strength of his spirit and to weld people together in a true community.

So the biblical worldview and the gospel are for society and educational institutions as well as for individuals. Society itself needs renewal, redemption, and reconciliation. Since the presuppositions of contemporary culture are opposed in many ways to the biblical worldview, it is hardly surprising that we find ourselves living in an increasingly frustrated and unsatisfied society. It is our challenge to proclaim and teach and incarnate this gospel in a way that is appropriate for those of us who are finite and sinful even though we have known the inauguration of God's final redemptive act in Jesus Christ and in the biblical worldview.[43]

## THE IMPORTANCE OF SHARING THE BIBLICAL WORLDVIEW

For almost thirty years, I have spent my Thanksgiving holidays with international students at various conferences across the country. I point out that one reason we can have conferences where all viewpoints are discussed is that we do not fear truth. Any worldview, or philosophy of religion, which is based on truth and reality and not just on inheritance or establishment, should prosper in a context of openness and testing.

At these international student conferences, we talk about the basic problems of humans. Of course there are the immediate problems of ignorance, war, and starvation. But in a more basic sense, the students almost always agree that the lives and programs of humankind are related to selfishness, egocentricity, hate, greed, lust, and pride. We then discuss ways in which various countries, ideologies, and religions deal with these problems. During

---

42. Paul A. Marshall, Sander Griffioen, and Richard J. Mouw, eds., *Stained Glass: Worldviews and Social Science* (Lanham, Md.: University Press of America, 1989), 77-78.

43. Montefiore, *Gospel and Contemporary Culture*, 10-11.

these discussions I have an opportunity to trace the story of the American vision and tell of its origins. I share with them my conviction about the place which the Judeo-Christian tradition has in the American vision. Although I apologize for the fact that we have often distorted this tradition and have not lived up to its ideals, I share with them how much it means to me personally.

Because we are finite and believe in religious freedom, I point out that I would not try to use political, economic, or psychological pressure to force them to accept this view which means so much to me. However, I tell them that I think it is important for them to understand this Judeo-Christian view because it plays an important part in the background of the American vision. In fact, this view undergirds the humanist belief in the worth and dignity of persons. It provides a motivation for education as well as scientific research. It justifies and sustains a visionary and noble humanitarian program. In addition, it gives an answer to the longings for the ultimate meaning of individual life and the cosmic process.

# CHAPTER ELEVEN

# Science

Interest in science, including the New Age and biblical approaches to it, has come to the forefront in recent times. The Public Broadcasting Service series on science, based on Carl Sagan's book *Cosmos,* became the most-watched series of its type in the history of American public television. Carl Sagan's untimely death in 1996 and the response to the movie *Contact* in 1997 have continued the public interest in science.

In his book *The Demon-Haunted World: Science as a Candle in the Dark,* Sagan lists pseudoscience, superstition, New Age beliefs, and fundamentalist Christianity as four aspects of the demonic which must be exorcised from the human mind and spirit.

An evaluation of both the New Age and biblical views of science is necessary in order to arrive at a constructive approach to the relation of science and religion — from a biblical perspective.

## Development of Science

### EARLY GREEK APPROACH

Philosophers of science point out that one method in their area develops its view of science by starting with broader theories of knowledge. It looks outside the practice of science itself to general views about human knowing. On this basis it constructs an idealized view of science. Thus it earns the designation "external philosophy of science." External philosophy of science uses its ideal view of science to evaluate actual scientific work. It tends not to use actual scientific work to prompt an understanding of scientific methods.[1]

Aristotle's philosophy held that the human mind, in seeking to understand the world, operates with an antecedent set of ideas and concepts that have little basis in experimental observation and testing. Aristotle developed his concept of science in the *Posterior Analytics*. But his discussion took little account of the work he actually did as a practicing biologist. In spite of Aristotle's genius, this approach is flawed. His categories of teleology (purpose) did not in general lend themselves to theories that could be tested by further experiment. We shall see that Galileo deliberately set aside all questions of purpose and "final cause," and introduced a totally different kind of concept for the interpretation of nature.[2]

## THE PTOLEMAIC DEVELOPMENT

In the middle of the second century A.D., Ptolemaic astronomy, with its concept of the sun, moon, and planets orbiting around the earth, became the dominant scientific worldview. In contrast to Aristotelian philosophy (which held that the orbits of bodies in the heavenly realms should be perfect), Ptolemy had found that the moon's orbit was indeed irregular. Consequently, a deep rift within Aristotelian philosophy developed between the projected intelligible patterns of the cosmos and the actual observable data of human experience. Christianity's adopting the Ptolemaic concept of the earth as the center of the universe in order to assert the church's authority over all spheres of life only added to the problems the church was to face later on.

When the Ptolemaic, earth-centered theories on the universe gave way to the Copernican, sun-centered, or heliocentric, worldview, the result in Christian theology was that God, who could no longer be seen as simply dwelling above the earth in heaven, began to lose his reference point in the universe.[3]

## FROM COPERNICUS TO MODERN SCIENCE

An early attack on Aristotle's system of thought was made by astronomer Nicolaus Copernicus in 1543, with the publication of *On the Revolutions of the Heavenly Spheres*. Next came Johann Kepler (1571-1630), Galileo (1564-

---

1. David K. Clark, *Dialogical Apologetics* (Grand Rapids: Baker, 1993), 55.
2. Ibid., 55; see also Ian G. Barbour, *Issues in Science and Religion* (Englewood Cliffs, N.J.: Prentice-Hall, 1966), 18.
3. Yandall Woodfin, *With All Your Mind: A Christian Philosophy* (Nashville: Abingdon, 1980), 180-81.

1643), and Sir Isaac Newton (1642-1727). The discoveries of these four men in astronomy and physics — and especially their methods of investigation — established a new kind of science based on a foundation of mathematics and experimentation rather than preset ideas and principles.

The Ptolemaic scheme, in which the sun and planets were assumed to revolve around the earth, had required more and more amendments, adding wheels within wheels, in order to agree with the astronomical data available. These additions were cumbersome and arbitrary. The Copernican model, in which the planets and the earth revolve around the sun, agreed with observations and was much simpler mathematically.

## GALILEO'S EXPERIMENTATION

It was in the work of Galileo that Kepler's mathematical approach was combined with an emphasis on experimentation. Galileo has rightly been called the father of modern science, for in his work the distinctive features of the new methodology first found clear formulas and positive results. The theories and explanations of earlier thought gave way to "descriptive explanation."

## NEWTONIAN PHYSICS

Sir Isaac Newton completed the revolution in science and the alliance of mathematics and experimentation which Galileo had pioneered. Newton's approach strengthened the use of observation and experimentation to gain knowledge. He was even more insistent than Galileo that the scientist's task is descriptive, and that premature speculation must be avoided. The world was seen as an intricate machine following unchangeable laws, with every detail precisely predictable. Here was the basis for the philosophies of determinism (everything is determined by natural laws or preceding events) and materialism (a belief that reality is limited to physical matter) which later generations were to develop. Newton himself believed that the world-machine was designed by an intelligent creator and expressed his purpose.[4]

Newton's physics and its corresponding philosophy of science served to increase humans' confidence in their ability to understand and master the material, observable world. In other words, Newton understood the universe in terms of predictable mechanical laws set in the context of "absolute space and time." The realm of the divine or spiritual became less and less knowable, significant, and necessary.

---

4. Barbour, *Issues in Science and Religion*, 23, 26, 34-36.

## BACON'S INDUCTIVISM

Related to the Copernican revolution was perhaps the earliest modern philosophy of science, the inductivism associated with Francis Bacon (1561-1626). Bacon held that scientists form hypotheses by observing the patterns that arise from the data. The scientist begins with a tabula rasa (his mind is a blank slate) and allows the facts to form a preliminary thesis. Next he tests this thesis against other observations to see if it holds generally.

As we will see, inductivism fails to describe science adequately, for it sees the mind as passive. In science, as in other fields, the human mind does not passively receive knowledge but actively seeks it.[5]

## THE DEVELOPMENT OF "SCIENTISM"

The end result of this progression is a "God who is reduced to invisibility, intangibility, and exclusiveness" and thus "hardly differs from being no God." With God and the spiritual realm reduced to nothingness, and a newfound humanistic confidence in science and scientific methodology, modern science was left to develop on its own under the assumption that the material realm is all there is to reality.

Theories developed that tried to explain human life with the same laws of nature that govern animals and nonliving objects. The result was the French Enlightenment of the eighteenth century with its deterministic, materialistic, and atheistic philosophies.[6]

Ian Barbour describes scientism's exalted view of this scientific method. "Science starts from reproducible public data. Theories are formulated and their implications are tested against experimental observations. Additional criteria of coherence, comprehensiveness, and fruitfulness influence choice among theories. Religious beliefs are not acceptable, in this view, because religion lacks such public data, such experimental testing, and such criteria of evaluation. Science alone is objective, open-minded, universal, cumulative, and progressive. Religious traditions, by contrast, are said to be subjective, closed-minded, parochial, uncritical, and resistant to change."[7]

To label a position as nonscientific (or, by implication, irrational) just because it does not correspond to the more modern scientific or materialistic view of the world is not justifiable. Nicholas Rescher, in his book *The Limits of Science*, states, "The theorist who maintains that science is the be-all and

5. Clark, *Dialogical Apologetics*, 56, 75.

6. Hans Schwarz, "God's Place in a Space Age," *Zygon* 21 (September 1986): 355.

7. Ian G. Barbour, *Religion in an Age of Science* (San Francisco: HarperCollins, 1990), 1:5.

end-all — that what is not in science textbooks is not worth knowing — is an ideologist with a peculiar and distorted doctrine of his own. For him, science is no longer a sector of the cognitive enterprise but an all-inclusive world-view. This is the doctrine not of science but of scientism. To take this stance is not to celebrate science but to distort it."[8]

## Einstein Starts Revolution in Science

Scientific thinking of our last three centuries has been characterized by atomism, mechanism, and objectivism. The result is fragmentation — reality is assumed to be composed of separate atomic objects functioning according to mechanical laws, externally related to one another as subjects and objects. Newton's scientifically understood world is seen as a sort of cosmic cuckoo clock. God wound up the cosmic mechanism at the beginning, and it has been running like clockwork ever since.

Big changes in the Newtonian worldview came during the first quarter of the twentieth century. Albert Einstein's theory of relativity destroyed the framework of absolute space and time.[9]

When Albert Einstein set forth his theory of relativity, the limitations of Newton's mechanical theories became apparent. As New Age critic Douglas Groothuis explains it, "relativity ushered Newton's view of time and space out of the scientific back door. Space and time were no longer viewed as distinct and absolute."

The emergence of an Einsteinian cosmology, or view of the universe (in particular the development of relativity theory and atomic physics), radically altered the classical mechanistic conceptions of Newtonian physics. Space and time can no longer be viewed as absolutes; instead, both are linked together in a four-dimensional space-time continuum that makes the ideal of objective observation impossible.

Scientists also discovered that matter behaves in a wave-like manner, and electromagnetic waves (like light) have particle-like properties. These findings directly led to quantum physics. Quantum physics involves the idea that matter — at the atomic and subatomic levels — absorbs heat and light energy and emits light energy discontinuously in bursts called "energy packets" (quanta).

Quantum physics has also discovered that the "barrier" between the observer (experimental apparatus) and the observed (subatomic particles) is

8. J. P. Moreland, *Christianity and the Nature of Science* (Grand Rapids: Baker, 1989), 103-4.

9. Ted Peters, *The Cosmic Self* (New York: HarperCollins, 1991), 136-37.

broken down; the very act of observing has an effect on that which is observed. Quantum physics has broken down the imaginary barrier that was thought to exist between the instrument and the object; to some degree the instrument and the object are always interrelated.[10]

## Holistic Approaches to Science

Since the 1960s, philosophers of science have emphasized contextual, sociological, and even psychological factors in the formation of scientific theory. Perhaps the best known of the new philosophies of science is Thomas Kuhn's. In writing *The Structure of Scientific Revolutions,* Kuhn caused a revolution. Kuhn saw science as choosing among competing theories under the influence of sociological factors and the guidance of certain approaches to knowledge.

Kuhn's central concept is the paradigm, the ordered set of beliefs, values, and methods shared by a particular community. A paradigm tells its adherents what to believe about the world and how to communicate their beliefs. It is a self-contained holistic perspective, a total view of things, not just an unorganized accumulation of facts.

Kuhn saw the history of science as a story of the rise and fall of competing paradigms. All science operates in the context of a paradigm — that is, the reigning complex of beliefs, values, and methods. Most of the time, scientists work to extend and defend the current paradigm.

But the elaboration of a paradigm inevitably uncovers anomalies, rogue observations that contradict the predicted results of the paradigm. Anomalies, like proverbial square pegs in round holes, do not fit the theory. If the anomalies continue to mount and stubbornly resist interpretation, they erode confidence in the paradigm and throw science into a phase called a crisis state.

In a crisis state, scientific discipline breaks down, and unanimous support for the reigning paradigm crumbles. Then, in order to explain the data, scientists will propose a new paradigm, complete with a new set of assumptions and rules. If the new paradigm handles the anomalies more successfully, it may replace the old and become the new guide. This shift is called a scientific revolution.

We have noted key paradigm shifts in the history of science. Among Kuhn's examples are Copernican astronomy, Newtonian physics, Lavoisier's discovery of oxygen, and Einstein's relativity.[11]

---

10. Ron Rhodes, *New Age Movement,* Zondervan Guide to Cults and Religious Movements (Grand Rapids: Zondervan, 1995), 17-18.

11. Clark, *Dialogical Apologetics,* 62-64; see also Thomas S. Kuhn, *The Structure of Scientific Revolutions,* 2nd ed. (Chicago: University of Chicago, 1970), 1, 24, 175, 182-85.

# USING SCIENCE TO PROMOTE THE NEW AGE

New Age leaders contend that science and technology have become scientism and barren materialism. However, the more sophisticated New Age leaders affirm that new developments in physics call for a monistic (all is one) worldview. As noted in Chapter 1, the New Age movement is an extremely large, loosely structured network of organizations and individuals bound together by common values (based on mysticism and monism — the worldview that "all is one") and a common vision (a coming "new age" of peace and mass enlightenment, the "Age of Aquarius").

Indeed, for New Age leaders, the New Physics offers powerful leverage in a culture where science is seen as the ultimate criterion of truth. According to Marilyn Ferguson,

> Abraham Maslow (the "father of the human potential movement") observed that although our visionary artists and mystics may be correct in their insights they can never make the whole of mankind sure. "Science," he wrote, "is the only way we have of shoving truth down the reluctant throat."[12]

## The Quantum Theory of Physics

As is well known, the quantum theory of physics disrupted the Newtonian worldview of science. The first feature of quantum theory is that it sees atomic particles, such as electrons, as things that cannot be described simply by using concepts such as location, velocity, or size. Thought of as particles, they travel from one location to another without traversing the distance in between. They move discontinuously. They do not appear to function at all like the material objects we understand at the level of common sense. Thus, understanding them as particles of matter can be misleading. It is helpful to understand them also as waves or wavicles.

Quantum theory also recognizes that no apparent structure of efficient causation belongs to individual subatomic events. We must study them in groups, in quanta. Individual subatomic events are not predictable. Individually they do not even seem to be causally determined. This is "indeterminacy" in physics.

Scientists also affirm that subatomic experiments demonstrate nonlocal relationships between electrons. This seems to indicate an intimate interconnection between particles not dependent on actual spatial contact.

---

12. Elliot Miller, *A Crash Course on the New Age Movement* (Grand Rapids: Baker, 1989), 38.

In summary, quantum theory takes us away from a material notion of matter and a closed link of efficient causation, away from a strictly mechanistic picture of the world, away from the world of Descartes and Newton. University of California physicist and popular New Age author Fritjof Capra describes the significance of these new perspectives:

> The first three decades of our century changed the situation in physics radically. Two separate developments — that of relativity theory and atomic physics — shattered all the principal concepts of the Newtonian worldview: the notion of absolute space and time, the elementary solid particles, the strictly causal nature of physical phenomena, and the ideal of an objective description of nature.[13]

Theoretical physicist David Bohm speaks of an "implicate" or "unfolded" order of "unbroken wholeness" that binds all things together in unceasing fluctuation. We must move from a fragmented viewpoint to one that encompasses the whole. In Bohm's emphasis on undivided wholeness, the observing instrument is not separated from what is observed.[14]

## Capra's Identification of Modern Physics and Eastern Mysticism and New Age Views

In an interview, Capra traced his path of thinking to his final beliefs. "I grew up as a Catholic and then turned away from Catholicism for various reasons. I became very interested in Eastern religion and found very striking parallels between the theories of modern science, particularly physics (which is my field), and the basic ideas in Hinduism, Buddhism, and Taoism. This discovery also went hand in hand with a strong personal transformation. I had always been a spiritual person. I came from a spiritual family. And so I turned toward Eastern spirituality and over the years worked out a personal spiritual path that is actually influenced by all three traditions — Taoism, Buddhism, and Hinduism.[15]

### THE CONCEPT "ALL IS ONE"

For Capra, we are at the "turning point." As Capra makes the turn from the modern to the postmodern vision, he ties modern physics with ancient mys-

---

13. Peters, *Cosmic Self,* 137-39.
14. Douglas R. Groothuis, *Unmasking the New Age* (Downers Grove, Ill.: Inter-Varsity, 1986), 97.
15. Fritjof Capra and David Steindl-Rast, *Belonging to the Universe* (New York: HarperCollins, 1991), 3.

ticism. Capra believes that because we cannot cut up the universe into "independently existing smaller units," we must see its "basic oneness."

This "all is one" concept, according to Capra, is what the Eastern mystics have been holding for thousands of years. In Capra's very popular and influential book *The Tao of Physics*, he finds parallels between the new physics and the mystics. By setting statements by physicists next to those of Buddhist, Taoist, and Hindu mystics and their Scriptures, he finds mutually supportive testimony for the oneness of all things, the unity of opposites (complementarity), the relativity of space and time, and the ever-changing nature of reality.

## PARADOX IN KNOWLEDGE

In *The Tao of Physics*, Capra develops his view of the unity of physics and Eastern mysticism by setting forth certain parallels. According to Capra, both physics and Asian religions recognize the limitations of human thought and language. Paradoxes in physics, such as the wave/particle duality, are reminiscent of the yin/yang polarity in Chinese Taoism, which portrays the unity of apparent opposites. Physicist Bohm places the yin/yang symbol at the center of his coat of arms. Zen Buddhism asks us to meditate on "koans," the famous paradoxical sayings to which there is no rational solution.

## WHOLENESS OF REALITY AND UNITY OF ALL THINGS

The "wholeness of reality" is another theme Capra finds in both West and East. Quantum physics points to the unity and interconnectedness of all events. Particles are local disturbances in interpenetrating fields. In relativity, space and time form a unified whole, and matter-energy is identified with the curvature of space. Eastern thought likewise presents the unity of all things and speaks of the experience of undifferentiated oneness encountered in the depth of meditation. There is one ultimate reality, referred to as Brahman in India and Tao in China, with which the individual is merged. The new physics says that the observer and the observed are inseparable, much as the mystic tradition envisages the union of subject and object.

## EXISTENCE AS TIMELESS AND IN CEASELESS MOTION

Both physics and Eastern thought are said to see the world as dynamic and ever-changing. Particles are patterns of vibration that are continually being created and destroyed. Matter appears as energy, and energy appears as matter. Asian religions hold that life is transitory; all existence is impermanent and in ceaseless motion. The dance of Shiva is an image of the cosmic dance of form and energy. But in both fields there is also an underlying timeless realm.

Capra maintains that in relativity, space-time is timeless; the eternal now of mystical experience is also timeless. In contrast, biblical thought understands a God who is intimately involved in the here and now, the temporality of the world.[16]

## THE PRIORITY OF HUMAN CONSCIOUSNESS

Werner Heisenburg's uncertainty principle asserts that when observing, we affect what is observed. There is no strict subject-object split or dualism. We do not simply observe the universe, we participate in it.

Capra says that "in Eastern mysticism [the] universal interwovenness always includes the human observer and his or her consciousness, and this is also true in atomic physics." He explains it with: "The electron does not have objective properties independent of my mind."

According to Fred Alan Wolf, in his book *Taking the Quantum Leap*, "Everything depends on you. You create the whole universe; you are the 'you-niverse.'" Thus, consciousness is thrust into the metaphysical driver's seat. According to this view, rather than recording reality, we determine it. The result is that for many New Age thinkers, all knowledge is potentially contained in consciousness. Thus, if consciousness "creates reality" and the whole is contained in the parts, the reality and prerogatives of the godhead are within us.[17]

## Using Physics to Explain the Paranormal

According to Marilyn Ferguson, the idea of "all is one" provides the scientific model to explain the paranormal, or psychic, realm. Despite the fact that many criticize the scientific integrity of the paranormal, it has become a passion for millions, even for national governments. Both the former Soviet Union and the United States governments funded parapsychological research relating to military intelligence and espionage. Various other national governments have subsidized research on telepathy, clairvoyance, and psychokinesis.[18] Thus, New Age protagonists seek legitimization by linking parapsychology, right/left brain models, ESP, and the like to scientific respectability. Robert Ellwood notes that New Agers make a "desperate attempt" to assert human autonomy in a world that seems to be totally dominated by science and technology.[19]

16. Barbour, *Religion in an Age of Science*, 118-19, 121.
17. Groothuis, *Unmasking the New Age*, 98-99; see also Fred Alan Wolf, *Taking the Quantum Leap* (San Francisco: Harper & Row, 1981), 63.
18. Groothuis, *Unmasking the New Age*, 99-100.
19. Russell Chandler, *Understanding the New Age* (Dallas: Word, 1991), 163-64.

## Computers and Occult Claims

According to Brooks Alexander, a senior editor of *SCP Journal,* there are preemptive spiritual connections in the labyrinths of computer networks. Contemporary theophobes believe in a kind of "cyber-supernaturalism." Some cyber-enthusiasts speak of the Internet as a "global mind" — created and operated by human beings but animated by a higher collective consciousness. Others claim that Virtual Reality (VR) opens a "portal to transcendence," creating a new nonspatial world of infinite freedom that exists in and through our interactions in cyberspace.

Modern technoculture is itself seen as a form of "instrumental gnosticism" — a kind of delusionary "knowledge" about reality that is mediated to us through the instruments of mass communication.

Original gnosticism required dedication and hard work to condition the mind for enlightenment, but computers promise to make that kind of mental discipline obsolete. Some scientists believe that with the aid of computers and neurophysiology, "enlightenment" can be produced without any effort — or even any intent! — on the part of the "enlightenee."

According to Alexander, computers empower every aspect of human nature without exception, and they do so with breathtaking speed and breadth of effect. Because rejection of the personal Creator God has become a built-in part of human nature since the Fall, we can unerringly predict that the computer revolution will greatly increase the number and power of available ways to flee from the presence of God — with particular emphasis on the more radical ways, such as technomagic and digital spiritism.

In the estimate of Alexander, the "fleeing from God" delusions flourishing in cyberspace will become extremely strong. They will also become extremely powerful, both socially and politically — at least within the context of the collective consent that sustains them. Those who don't consent to the computer delusion will be marginalized at best, since computers will increasingly dominate human life, and the computer "knowledge of all reality" delusion will increasingly dominate many of the computer elite.

But no matter how strong the power of computer technologies may be in human terms, in God's terms it remains impotent in the face of "actual reality." According to Alexander, we should not forget that through his sovereignty, God has some serious options available for upsetting our possible wrongful use of computer technology.[20]

20. Brooks Alexander, "Virtuality and Theophobia," *SCP Journal* 20 (1996): 34-36, 38.

## Denying Objective Reality

There are definite weaknesses to the New Age approach to science. One issue is the question of objective reality. If you cannot assume that reality is to some extent independent of observation, then science is not possible. If there is no reality, then my description of the results of an experiment would say nothing about what might happen in your reality. Richard Bube, professor at Stanford University, states that authentic science is committed to the existence of objective reality. A knowledge of this reality must indeed be personal knowledge, but this does not imply that it is therefore *just* subjective knowledge. Authentic scientists must believe in some objective reality.[21]

Christians maintain that the biblical teaching about a personal creator God explains the consistency that science finds. It also explains the objectivity we sense in reality.

Glen Olds, an educator, philosopher, and minister who is sympathetic with some correctives provided by the New Age, points out that though knowing may be anchored by self-consciousness, objective reality is not always or necessarily constituted by it. The perils of this perspective intrude in a wide range of New Age perspectives. In reaching for full correction to the tendency of traditional science to seek to neutralize the mind in research, or even nullifying the role of mind in relation to objective reality, the New Age movement frequently overreacts to make mind the sole constituent of reality. The end of this route is to swallow up reality in a self-conscious ingestion of all reality reduced to self-authenticating encounter. The mode of that which is beyond the mind is not necessarily the same as within![22]

## Overlooking Prior Beliefs and Values

The New Age view tends to minimize or overlook the fact that the worldview of a scientist affects that scientist's studies and their results. Capra admits to his Eastern-monistic bias after summarizing the new physics in *The Turning Point*:

> My presentation of modern physics . . . has been influenced by my personal beliefs and allegiances. I have emphasized certain concepts and theories that are not yet accepted by the majority of physicists, but that I consider significant philosophically, of great importance for the other sciences and for our culture as a whole.[23]

21. Karen Hoyt, *The New Age Rage* (Old Tappan, N.J.: Revell, 1987), 82-83.
22. Duncan S. Ferguson, ed., *New Age Spirituality: An Assessment* (Louisville, Ky.: Westminster/John Knox, 1993), 71-72.
23. Groothuis, *Unmasking the New Age*, 103.

457

In his earlier book *The Tao of Physics,* Capra began by reporting a profound mystical experience that affected his later integration of physics and mysticism. Thus we can say that Capra's views stem at least in part from a "visionary experience" he had while he sat on a beach meditating — and which he acknowledged was primed by psychedelic herbs: "I suddenly became aware of my whole environment as being engaged in a gigantic cosmic dance. . . . I 'saw' cascades of energy coming down from outer space, in which particles were created and destroyed in rhythmic pulses: I 'saw' the atoms of the elements and those of my body participating in this cosmic dance of energy, I felt its rhythm and 'heard' its sound, and at that moment I knew that this was the Dance of Shiva, the Lord of Dancers worshipped by the Hindus."[24]

Christian philosopher Arthur Holmes of Wheaton College states that a value-free or absolutely objective science is impossible because "science itself is a human enterprise dependent on beliefs and values — even on the worldviews — that scientists themselves bring to science rather than simply drawing them from their work." Furthermore, Thomas Kuhn in *The Structure of Scientific Revolutions* has argued that revolutions in scientific theories, which he calls "paradigm shifts," often result from psychological and sociological influence more than from observation, experience, and logic. Holmes's warning is not to suggest total skepticism but rather to consider carefully scientific claims in their overall context.[25]

The New Age approach tends to minimize the limitations of the scientific method. It ignores the possibility of multiple levels of reality.

Advocates of the biblical worldview affirm that scientists are not dealing with ultimate reality but are dealing with a lower reality. Ian Barbour, professor emeritus at Carleton College, points out that the primary significance of the new physics lies not in its disclosure of the fundamental nature of reality but in the recognition of the limitations of science. Reality can be viewed from several levels, but each level has its own limitation as well as its own terminology. For example, theologians Karl Heim and T. F. Torrance have shown the importance of seeing reality as being made up of many layers or dimensions, a portion of which is outside the scope of human existence or experience.

God can be conceived in such a way that he exists in a dimension of reality that is beyond human comprehension. While embracing all of our available possibilities in space and time, God would also embrace possibilities that are not available to humans in our present dimension. God is thus seen as being present in our own space-time reality (immanence) while at the same time maintaining

24. Chandler, *Understanding the New Age,* 169-70.
25. Groothuis, *Unmasking the New Age,* 103.

superiority over it (transcendence).[26] The quality and intelligibility of God's presence are affirmed in the incarnation of Christ. Thus while the Incarnation does not mean that God is limited by space and time, it asserts the reality of space and time for God in the actuality of his relations with us.[27]

Science is able to explain the workings of physical reality but is not adequate nor was it ever intended to explain all of reality. If we accept the definition of science as the "empirical and theoretical inquiry into natural processes and relationships," it is barred from making comprehensive and indisputable pronouncements about ultimate reality. Science informs a worldview but cannot, by itself, create one. As Arthur Holmes says, "To extrapolate from what is empirically observable to everything that is involves a logical non sequitur."[28]

The New Age wrongly identifies its scientific theory with "reality out there." University of Chicago professor Langdon Gilkey, in *Nature, Reality and the Sacred,* charges that leading scientists, particularly cosmologists, carry out their work with total indifference to the revolutions that have occurred in philosophy, which now focuses on the ambiguities, partialness, social conditioning, and finitude of human knowing, including scientific theorizing. Gilkey finds scientists Heinz Pagels, Frank Tipler, Steven Weinberg, Richard Dawkins, Carl Sagan, and others to be guilty of arrogant assertions: that science can resolve fully "its own deepest puzzles"; that it is without presuppositions; that science adjudicates its claims on no other basis than mathematics and logic, with no presuppositions of a historical, sociological, psychological, or metaphysical sort; and that it claims there is an identity between scientific theories and "reality out there."[29]

## Minimizing Sin and the Fall

An important Christian critique of the New Age is that it has no clear theory of sin or evil and overlooks the human propensity to perversion. As a corrective to a fatalistic materialism, it goes too far in its neglect of limitation, power, alienation, and violence. The New Age view maximizes the idea that "all is one" and thus tends to ignore the ever-present reality of sin and the Fall.

Adam's fall is an important part of the biblical worldview. Adam is

26. Schwarz, "God's Place in a Space Age," 365-66.
27. Thomas F. Torrance, *Space, Time and Incarnation* (New York: Oxford University Press, 1969), 67.
28. Arthur F. Holmes, *Contours of a World View* (Grand Rapids: Eerdmans, 1983), 41, 44.
29. Philip Hefner, "Theology and Science Approach the Third Millennium," *Journal of the NABPR: Perspectives in Religious Studies* 22.1 (Spring 1995): 68.

portrayed as both an actual individual and a representative of humanity. Adam's story is Everyman's journey from innocence to responsibility for sin. Sin is compounded both by egocentricity and disobedience to God. Self-centeredness and turning from God are two sides of the same act. The biblical account goes on to portray the experience of anxiety, evasiveness, and guilt. To these facets of individual sin, other biblical passages, especially in the Prophets, add the communal dimension of social injustice (for example, Amos 1–4). Failure to love God and neighbor is seen as inseparable from excessive self-love.

Modern theologians continue to express these biblical ideas of sin and the Fall in contemporary terms. Reinhold Niebuhr says that we inherit sinful social structures that perpetuate themselves in injustice and oppression. Every group tends to absolutize and center on itself, blind to the rationalization of its self-interest. Niebuhr also describes the anxiety and insecurity that lead individuals to try to deny their limitations.[30]

For Stanley Jaki, not only does the influence of Christ bring to bear upon science the perspective of creation out of nothing, a fully ordered universe, and cosmic purpose, but it also enables scientists to overcome the effects of original sin and brings service to humanity, moral scrupulousness, and intellectual honesty into science as well.[31]

## The Paranormal

New Ager Mary Coddington observes that for centuries people of genius have tried to harness the mysterious paranormal force and enlist it to the aid of science. Thus far it has remained out of grasp, eluding its would-be captors with an almost capricious tenacity and always escaping definition. However, the realities of the paranormal do conform to biblical theism's supernatural/natural distinction, which depicts the energy source behind occultism as both nonphysical and personal and therefore unmeasurable (in any direct sense) and unpredictable.

This inability to explain psychic phenomena in physical terms results in many conversions to the New Age worldview. Researchers, unwilling to part with their antisupernatural bias even after encountering the paranormal, resort to pantheism, the belief that God and nature are one. This allows for a "natural" (though nonphysical) explanation. In this way they feel they can retain a "scientific" frame of mind.[32]

30. Barbour, *Religion in an Age of Science*, 206.
31. Stanley Jaki, *The Savior of Science* (Washington, D.C.: Regnery Gateway, 1988), 195.
32. Miller, *Crash Course*, 48.

Apollo 14 astronaut Edgar D. Mitchell states that "there are no un-natural or supernatural phenomena, only very large gaps in our knowledge of what is natural. We should strive to fill those gaps of ignorance." In 1973, Mitchell founded the Institute of Noetic Sciences in Sausalito, California, to investigate PSI, which is shorthand for phenomena that escape traditional scientific definitions, including telepathy, clairvoyance (broadly referred to as ESP), precognition, and PK (psychokinesis).[33]

Parapsychology — which achieved some respectability in 1969 when the American Association for the Advancement of Science made the Para-psychological Association a full member organization — is still a marginal science. Problems of validation persist, while disclosures of deceptions, shoddy and ignorant research, and failed predictions have sidelined much of parapsy-chology in the eyes of the mainstream scientific community. To those who already believe in the paranormal, scientific evidence is unnecessary.[34]

According to Groothuis, if the paranormal world is exploited without the protection and guidance of Christ, what began as a fascinating exploration may end as psychic violence. Despite the scientific respectability oftentimes given to the paranormal, apart from the lordship of Christ it becomes the occultism prohibited throughout the Bible. It is the search for power in the wrong places. The traditional shaman returns in scientific guise, presenting his erroneous concepts.[35]

Elliot Miller points out that throughout the Bible we find the super-natural realms capable of interaction with our natural world. However, because of willful rebellion against God, humans and some of the angels are morally fallen. Therefore, as a protection to humans, the communion that they are capable of is forbidden (for example, see 1 Cor. 10:20). Thus the entire range of occult practices is prohibited (Deut. 18:9-14). Included in that prohibition are passive, trancelike states of consciousness, which increase our susceptibility to demonic influence. We find this prohibition chiefly in biblical condemna-tions of mediumistic trances, but the same spiritual dangers can be shown to accompany other altered states of consciousness as well.

The Bible does not deny the human need for communion with the spiritual realm, but it must be met in the manner that God prescribes:

> And when they say to you, "Consult the mediums and the spiritists who whisper and mutter," should not a people consult their God? . . . To the law and to the testimony! If they do not speak according to this word, it is because they have no dawn. (Isa. 8:19-20)

---

33. Chandler, *Understanding the New Age*, 164.
34. Ibid., 165.
35. Groothuis, *Unmasking the New Age*, 109.

For the biblical worldview, Scripture ("the law and the testimony") is the historically reliable, objective criterion whereby the nature and value of spiritual experience must be determined.[36]

According to James Sire, the New Age worldview has reopened a door closed since Christianity drove the demons from the woods, desacralized the natural world, and generally took a dim view of any excessive interest in the affairs of Satan's kingdom of fallen angels. For Sire, the demonic has returned, parading as the paranormal, knocking on university dorm doors, sneaking around psychology laboratories, and chilling the spines of Ouija players.[37]

# UNIQUENESS OF THE BIBLICAL VIEW OF SCIENCE

According to Douglas Groothuis, the biblical worldview does not endorse a mechanistic cosmology. The God of the Bible is not a deistic clockmaker totally removed from creation who just keeps things running. The universe is created and unified by Christ, who is the Logos, or Word of God. God directs and coordinates the richness of the cosmic drama without being completely merged with it. The unity and harmony of creation are products of God's governance. This view is upheld by Stanley L. Jaki, a Hungarian-born Benedictine priest and scientist. In fact, Jaki defends the thesis that the hope of any scientific enterprise stems from the significance of Christ:

> The alertness within a genuine Christian milieu to the danger of toying with pantheism served the proper understanding of the universe in a measure still not sufficiently esteemed by historians of science. Christ's rejection of pantheism was, historically speaking, the first manifestation of the saving grace which the Christian doctrine of salvation in and through Jesus of Nazareth, the Son of the Living God, provided for science.[38]

Dutch theologian Abraham Kuyper stresses this point by saying, "There is on earth no life, energy, law, atom, or element except that the Almighty and Omnipresent God [who] quickens and supports that life from moment to moment, causes that energy to work, and enforces that law."[39]

Although humans are enlightened by the Logos, we are still finite and not required to untie every scientific knot. We appreciate any cosmology which

36. Miller, *Crash Course*, 46.
37. Groothuis, *Unmasking the New Age*, 109.
38. Jaki, *Savior of Science*, 20.
39. Groothuis, *Unmasking the New Age*, 106.

talks about the unity and interconnection of creation. The biblical worldview pictures a God who sustains and unifies creation without violating the created integrity of distinct entities. The biblical view is holistic, covering all, without being monistic, the belief that all is one, one ultimate substance. The general systems theory (which combines physics, biology, and other sciences in a unified worldview) is widely held. If this theory is removed from a pantheistic background, it can be used for a Christian cosmology which can provide a model for how the processes of providence work. In summary, the biblical worldview affirms one God as the ultimate reality. However, there is a distinction between God and the created order. The created order is not sufficient unto itself. Even if we conceive of it as a whole, as a totality of finite reality, we must recognize that we can then in principle conceive of something outside, or beyond, it.[40]

## ANCIENT CHINESE, HINDU, AND GREEK SCIENCE

Studies in the origin and development of modern science have led historians to ask why the brilliant intellectual powers of the ancient Chinese, Indians, Egyptians, and Greeks, in spite of their achievements both in observation and in pure speculation, never brought forth the dynamic science of the modern era. It has been very plausibly argued that the decisive factor is to be found in the biblical vision of the world as both rational (capable of being comprehended by the mind) and contingent (finite, limited, and filled with mystery).

On the one hand, the enterprise of science would be impossible if there were no principle of rationality in the universe. Without a passionate faith in the ultimate rationality of the world, science would falter, stagnate, and die. However, faith in the rationality of the universe would not sustain science without belief that there is a certain contingent or surprise quality in the universe.

Indian metaphysics has been totally committed to the rationality of the universe, but has understood it as necessary being, that is, part of the eternal cycle of evolution and involution. The universe and humankind are emanations of the Hindu concept of an ultimately impersonal god, not the creation of a personal God. The ultimate secrets of the universe are therefore to be discovered within the recesses of the human soul where it makes direct contact with the cosmic soul, not through observation and experiment. Therefore science, in the sense in which it has developed in our culture, is not impossible, but it is unnecessary.

Scientific thought in Greek circles was controlled by the idea of perfect numbers and perfect circles or by the concept of the purposeful organism. There was no need for observation and experiment. The same was true of the

40. Peters, *Cosmic Self,* 159.

great cultures of ancient China and Egypt. Consequently, in spite of the brilliant intellectual powers of these great civilizations, science in the modern sense did not develop.[41]

## BIBLICAL VIEW — A PARTNER WITH SCIENCE

Such lines of evidence show that Christianity was more of a senior partner of the new science than its enemy. The biblical revelation portrays a God who is consistent in character and orderly in creative activity. Furthermore, the important concept of the flexibility and open-structured order of nature has a biblical source (Isa. 42:5-7; 51:9-11).

Unexpected twists and turns take place in the course of scientific research. The Protestant Reformation made an important contribution to the new science. On the continent of Europe, the Reformers had a generally positive view of science as they knew it in its beginning stage. John Calvin, for example, saw astronomy as useful and as an art that unfolded the wisdom of God. The doctrinal thought-forms of the Reformers, such as the love of nature, the glory of God, the welfare of humanity, and the priesthood of all believers, were congenial as background for a science that used experiments to prove its theories. Nevertheless, both John Calvin and Martin Luther were concerned that concentration on science might divert attention from the Creator and give people the impression that natural processes are outside God's control.[42]

In *Toward a Theology of Nature*, German theologian Wolfhart Pannenberg maintains that scientific field theory opens up to the theological concept of God's Spirit as the source of all reality. As field theories unveil concepts of causality which are of the "whole-part" or "downward causality" type, they also reveal and clarify how God exercises causality in nature. The eschatologically energized field constituted by the continuum of universal history is the largest field of all, in which all else exists, and in which God may indeed exercise this causality and action.[43]

The biblical worldview affirms the discipline, public verifiability, and universality of intent in the sciences as important instruments of knowledge, including theological knowledge. We must be open to new and richer methods of increasing our knowledge in order to gain a wider and richer access to reality that we are not now even prepared to accept.[44]

---

41. Lesslie Newbigin, *Foolishness to the Greeks: The Gospel and Western Culture* (Grand Rapids: Eerdmans, 1986), 70.

42. Charles E. Hummel, *The Galileo Connection* (Downers Grove, Ill.: InterVarsity, 1986), 160; see also R. Hooykaas, *Religion and the Rise of Modern Science*, 135-60.

43. Hefner, "Theology and Science,"73.

44. Ferguson, *New Age Spirituality*, 75.

## Focus on the Immanent

According to Glen Olds, it is ironic that the early sense of the New Age that the secular had been stripped of anything sacred turned into the rejection of anything transcendental that might give it meaning. In saving the near and immediate from oblivion and loss of value, the New Age view commits the fallacy of inversion, claiming that only the immanent has meaning. Losing any cosmic sources or vindication of value or calling as a higher and other referent for consciousness, the New Age movement surrenders any objective source of authentication for its own claims to truth.[45]

For the New Age view, the wholeness of the cosmos, by being conceived of as ultimate and infinite, is inadvertently equated with God by transcending in itself all the subwholes within it. Ted Peters suggests that it is in principle possible to solve the problem of the relationship between the one and the many without recourse to the Christian God. A monism would do, and it is monism that is attracting New Age devotees. Monism is the view that the plurality of things in the phenomenal world is ultimately part of a single reality. Parmenides and Heraclitus provide us with examples. In more recent times monism has become attractive as a tool for overcoming the dualism of mind and body because one can simply suggest a more primary reality of which both mind and body are modes. This seems to be what is attracting some scientists and their New Age followers.

However, according to Peters, the problem with monism in all its forms is that it denies the Christian belief in a radical distinction between God and the creation. The distinction functions to affirm divine ultimacy. Although God is present in the world, the being of God transcends the world, the whole world. This means, among other things, that the creature can never become totally divine. Although God as Trinity does participate in creation through the incarnation in Jesus Christ and through the work of the Holy Spirit, that which has been created will remain the created and finite.[46]

## Biblical View of Creation

The distinction between God and the creation has two by-products in the biblical worldview. First, God is not thought of as simply a craftsperson who molds and shapes and directs already existent world stuff. Rather, God creates ex nihilo, out of nothing. He summons the universe into existence. Had he not, there would be only God.

45. Ibid., 72.
46. Peters, *Cosmic Self,* 159-60.

Second, the created realm is entirely dependent on God as the source and power of its continued existence. We have become part of the universe not by some natural right, but only by the grace of God. Life is a gift. The proper response is to be thankful.

Furthermore, the biblical worldview contends that God's created reality is historical and that such things as creativity and irreversible change occur within history. The biblical worldview makes room for a comprehensive view of the category of history. Both nature and humans are historical. Nature is not timeless. The natural realm is historical and hence subject to newness and to irreversible changes.[47]

## The Future and God's Purpose

Munich theologian Wolfhart Pannenberg contends that the essence of all things is yet to be determined. It will not be determined until the final future of God's purpose. The meaning we find in the present is dependent upon the biblical faith in defining the final future that we will find in God.[48]

Ted Peters, a professor at Pacific Lutheran Seminary, points out that all events are moving ahead to meet a common future, a common future that is the reality of God. No whole exists at present. What do exist are separate subjects and objects and the uncertainty in human knowing. Fragmentation and brokenness also really do exist in our world, and no amount of thinking wholistically or saying that "all is one" will make them go away. In fact, if we were to convert our minds to engage only in "all is one" thinking, and if the fragmentation and brokenness persisted, then our thoughts would be illusory. We would be naive.

Instead, what we need to do is to think in a wholistic way, utilizing the biblical categories of hope and expectation. We need to be realistic about the divisions and destructive forces in our world while looking forward to a future that has healing and fulfilling power. Once this hope and vision are clear, then that future healing can have an impact on present brokenness. This is how our future orientation based on the promises in the revelation of the creating and redeeming God works in the biblical view.

According to Peters, there is some value in the wholistic insight of New Age thinking. But to remain realistic, it must be consistent with the Christian doctrine of Creation and the Fall. Christians believe that God is the creator of the world. God creates continually and will not finish the divine creative work until his plan is fulfilled in the eschaton, or last days.

47. Ibid., 160-61.
48. Wolfhart Pannenberg, *Theology and the Philosophy of Science* (Philadelphia: Westminster, 1976), 310.

In other words, God creates from the future, not the past. The first thing God did for the world was to give it a future. Without a future, the world would be nothing. Despite the Fall, God gave humankind and nature a future by opening up the possibility of their becoming something they never had been before and by supplying them with the power to change. This is something we experience constantly. Moment by moment, God is giving us a future. He is giving nature a future. Creation is not merely an event that happened once, a long time ago. Creation is continuing. It is going on right now.

God's creative activity is a pull from the future. God's creative activity within nature and history derives from his redemptive work of drawing fallen yet free and contingent beings toward his planned future, with an emphasis on wholeness.[49]

# CONCLUSION: COMPLEMENTARY APPROACH

The biblical worldview, properly understood, is the best worldview for the proper development of science. In fact, a distinguished group of Christian scholars, including David Clark, D. M. MacKay, T. F. Torrance, Richard Bube, and Charles Hummel, suggest that the biblical and scientific descriptions are to be seen as complementary perspectives — different kinds of maps for the same terrain. Their respective limitations are not a matter of territory, but of purpose and methodology. Each partial view of science serves its intended purpose and should be appreciated for the specific contribution it makes to our lives. According to Bube and Hummel, the biblical and scientific perspectives on nature and science can mutually benefit from interacting with each other as allies with complementary approaches.[50]

Biblical thinking is more like the humanities than science is, but both scientific and religious thinking are rational exercises performed by humans. According to David Clark, despite important differences in the object of study and the method of thought, parallels in thinking processes do exist between biblical and scientific scholars.

In one sense, the biblical worldview is like a web of beliefs, or a scientific paradigm, or a point of view. Of course, states Clark, the biblical view is much more than a web of ideas. It guides believers' personal living, not just their professional research. As a result, some may want to redraw the line between the biblical worldview and scientific paradigms. The former gives values for

49. Peters, *Cosmic Self*, 165-66.
50. John P. Newport, *Life's Ultimate Questions* (Dallas: Word, 1989), 152.

living; the latter describes the world. But scientific points of view do guide living. Scientific points of view explaining the mechanisms of pollution, for instance, may describe a real world, but they also direct daily living. Surely different sorts of webs, including scientific ones, can both be about the world and function to guide life.

The broad theistic point of view has hard-core and auxiliary hypotheses. Its hard core includes beliefs that a creator God exists, that humans are the creatures of this God, and that humans' lives and destinies are wrapped up with their creator. The distinctly Christian theistic point of view adds to this core the belief in Jesus Christ as the Son of God and the one through whom any person can come into a saving and fulfilling relation with the Creator. These are nonnegotiables.

Clark points out that many auxiliary hypotheses with varying degrees of probability flesh out this fundamental biblical vision. Christians adjust these outer belt beliefs to new evidence in order to protect the hard core. Suppose, for example, that *how* God creates is part of the protective belt while *that* God creates is part of the hard core. Under the influence of geology and biology, theists have clearly altered their views on the precise nature of God's creative activity. Some may see this as making concessions to the enemy. But in fact, according to Clark, this maneuver protects the hard core even while it allows the biblical vision to incorporate more data about the world. In this way it brings progress.[51]

Those Christian scholars who hold this complementary approach stress that, in our scientific age, it is especially important that both science and religion recognize their limitations of purpose and method.

The Bible reveals the who and why of the universe, the Creator, and his purposes for nature and for humanity. The biblical message, meant for all cultures and generations, is communicated in the everyday language of sense perception, not in the language of mathematics, which is the primary language with which science represents the how of natural events.[52]

Similarly, science needs to seek to free itself from positivistic, one-dimensional philosophical presuppositions and acknowledge the limitations of its method. Lesslie Newbigin says that the methodological elimination of final causes from the study of nature by science has been immensely fruitful on certain levels and for limited purposes. However, the attempt to explain all that exists solely in terms of secondary causes at secondary levels or dimensions is not appropriate from the standpoint of logic and the evidence available concerning human nature and activity.

With the ultimate explanation of things found in the creating, sus-

51. Clark, *Dialogical Apologetics*, 71, 73.
52. Hummel, *Galileo Connection*, 264.

taining, judging, and redeeming work of a personal God, science can be the servant of humanity, not its master. In turn, biblical studies, freed from futile attempts at dealing with technical science, can focus on the broader issues of using science (and technology) for the good of humanity and the environment.[53]

In the last analysis, says David Livingston, a biblical approach to science must be both confessional and critical. It must encourage us to confess our commitment both to the Bible and science, to the God of creation, and to the creation itself. The biblical approach to science must call for both the Christian theologian and the scientist to be humble and self-critical before the Creator, his creation, and his inspired revelation to humankind.[54]

53. Newbigin, *Foolishness,* 93-94; see also Hummel, *Galileo Connection,* 264-65.
54. Mark A. Noll and David F. Wells, eds., *Christian Faith and Practice in the Modern World* (Grand Rapids: Eerdmans, 1988), 262.

# CHAPTER TWELVE

# The Arts

"The arts" constitute an important facet of any given worldview. By "the arts," I refer to that part of life which expresses itself in the creative, the imaginative, and the dramatic. This, of course, includes the traditional "fine arts," such as music, painting, literature, sculpture, and architecture. It obviously includes the "lively arts," such as drama and ballet. And in our day it definitely includes the "popular arts," such as movies, television, and radio.

The arts give direct access to the distinctive tone, concerns, and feelings of a given worldview. For this reason, it is important to know both the New Age and the biblical views of the arts as a basis for dialogue and possible transformation.

## NEW AGE APPROACH TO VISUAL ART

To understand the developments of New Age art in our time, it is helpful to recall the break with traditional religious art that took place in the Romantic period. German theologian and philosopher Friedrich Schleiermacher gave theological impetus to highly subjective religious forms with his Romantic insistence that inner piety is more important than outer forms. "Indeed," argues Robert Rosenblum in *Modern Painting and the Northern Romantic Tradition: Friedrich to Rothko*, "Schleiermacher's theological search for divinity outside the trappings of the Church lies at the core of many a Romantic artist's dilemma. The problem was how to express experiences of the spiritual, of the transcendental, without having recourse to such traditional themes as the

Adoration, the Crucifixion, the Resurrection, the Ascension, whose vitality, in the Age of Enlightenment, was constantly being sapped."

Rosenblum, an art historian, was among the first scholars to assert that abstract art, far from representing a neat break with representational art, is actually part of a Romantic tradition reflected in the work of northern European artists like Caspar David Friedrich and Joseph M. Turner, who infused landscape paintings with a "sense of divinity." Abstract artists faced the same problem as the earlier Romantics. This problem was how to find, in a secular world, a convincing means of expressing those religious experiences that, before the Romantics, had been channeled into the traditional themes of Christian art. According to art historian Charlotte Douglas, the shift to abstract art in the early twentieth century was prompted by a need for new dimensions of consciousness, forms suited "to serve as a passport to and report from" the so-called higher realms.

Chief among the new religious movements capturing the imagination of those early twentieth-century artists who turned to abstract forms was Theosophy. The founder of the Theosophical Society, Helena Petrovna Blavatsky, was a reputed mystic who professed to teach the "natural truth" underlying all religions. Her system, based on Eastern philosophy, was billed as a "spiritual science." According to historian Sydney Ahlstrom, the society, founded in New York in 1875, attracted some 40,000 members in forty-three countries in the next five decades under Blavatsky and her successor, Annie Wood Besant.

Esoteric cousins of Theosophy that attracted artists include Rosicrucianism, Alchemy, Tantrism, Cabalism, and Hermeticism. The writings of psychiatrist Carl Jung, who was himself interested in alchemy, parapsychology, and the occult, were favorites of some artists. Others favored Jacob Boehme, the sixteenth-century Lutheran shoemaker who combined Neoplatonism, the Jewish Cabala and Hermetic writings, and the Bible in explaining his experiences of God. Still other artists made use of symbols from medieval legends, Hinduism, Zen Buddhism, the religion of American Indians, the teachings of G. I. Gurdjieff, and the works of medieval mystics such as Meister Eckhart, John of Ruysbroeck, and Richard Rolle.

An important art exhibition, "The Spiritual in Art: Abstract Painting 1890-1985," was on display recently in Los Angeles and Chicago. The thesis that Theosophy and other types of occult and mystical thought have influenced abstract artists is supplemented in the show by 125 books by theosophers, philosophers, and mystics whose images and ideas also appear in the tradition of abstract art.[1]

1. Pamela Schaeffer, "Spirituality in Abstract Art," *The Christian Century*, September 30, 1987, 819-20.

# REPRESENTATIVE ABSTRACT NEW AGE ARTISTS

The argument of the Abstract Painting Exhibition begins with four artists generally viewed as pioneer abstractionists, all of whom are shown to have been steeped in occult spiritual concerns and the New Age view.

### Mondrian

Piet Mondrian, the Dutch painter best known for his abstract gridwork of interlocking perpendicular black lines and enclosing squares of red and yellow, was an avid reader of Theosophy. Mondrian once said that he learned everything he knew from Madame Blavatsky. He joined the Dutch Theosophical Society in 1889, about the same time that his work began its gradual evolution toward the abstract.

Mondrian's preoccupation was with the tension between vertical and horizontal and was depicted in the haunting abstract cruciform patterns that would become his trademark. According to Mondrian's own notebooks, the patterns represent the spiritual struggle toward unity of cosmic dualities and the religious symmetry undergirding the material universe. A strong believer in the theosophical doctrine of human evolution from a lower, materialistic stage toward spirituality and higher insight, Mondrian wrote that the hallmark of the New Age would be the "new man" who "can live only in the atmosphere of the universal."

### Kandinsky

The religious themes implicit in the paintings of Wassily Kandinsky are made explicit in *Concerning the Spiritual in Art,* a small book he wrote in 1910, the year he did his first abstract painting. Kandinsky was versed in Theosophy, and felt that abstraction was the best means available to artists for depicting an unseen realm. With near-messianic fervor, Kandinsky announced that the type of painting he envisioned would advance the new "spiritual epoch." In his book he describes the spiritual realm as a triangle in upward motion. At its apex stands a person whose vision points the way; within are artists, who are "prophets," providing "spiritual food."

Kandinsky's immersion in spiritual texts clearly seems to have established his rationale for abstraction. Kandinsky's paintings were very much a product of his close reading of theosophical and anthroposophical writings by New Age leaders Madame Blavatsky and Rudolf Steiner in which he reflected the New Age emphasis on "all is one."[2]

2. Maurice Tuchman, *The Spiritual in Art: Abstract Painting 1890-1985* (New York: Abbeville, 1986), 35.

*Kupka and Malevitch*

Two other pioneer abstract artists, Frantisek Kupka, a Czech, and Kasimir Malevich, a Russian whose paintings, exhibited in 1914 and 1915, featured a series of squares on plain backgrounds, were also avid readers of Theosophy and other metaphysical works. Kupka studied Greek, German, and Oriental philosophy along with a variety of theosophical texts. Douglas writes that the aesthetics of Malevich and his circle "resulted [in] a unified world view that encompassed all dichotomies; for them science and Eastern mystical ideas were seamlessly joined in a conceptual continuum, and knowledge of the world might be obtained by beginning at any point." This is classical New Age teaching.

Strong evidence for the thesis that the artworks are intricately linked to reflections on the New Age spiritual realm is in the illustrations of texts known to have influenced abstract artists. Robert Fludd's *Urtiusque cosmi* (History of Both Worlds, 1617), Henry Cornelius Agrippa's *Three Books of Occult Philosophy* (1651), *The Works of Jacob Boehme* (1764), Edwin D. Babbitt's *Principles of Light and Color* (1878), Charles W. Leadbeater's *Man Visible and Invisible* (1903), and Claude Bragdon's *Primer of Higher Space* (1913) contain rich illustrations of visions of nonmaterial realities. For example, Bragdon uses a spiral to suggest the upward evolution of consciousness, and Fludd's work contains a series of strikingly beautiful mandalas intended to convey the mystical concept that the universe is a single, living substance.[3]

## THE INFLUENCE OF OCCULT MYSTICISM

The works of Marsden Hartley (1877-1943), an early American abstractionist who was influenced by mystics and Mexican cultures, combined symbols from various forms of the occult. The use of American Indian pictography by Jackson Pollock and others indicates the interest in the 1930s and '40s in the occult spirituality of Indian culture.[4]

Jackson Pollock grew up in the Western states, and his interaction with Native American art and culture began early in life. In 1923, when Pollock was eleven, he, his brothers, and their friends explored the Indian ruins (cliff dwellings and mounds) north of their home near Phoenix. Pollock, Gottleib, and other painters incorporated ancient Native American art into a modern Abstract Expressionism.[5]

---

3. Schaeffer, "Spirituality in Abstract Art," 821.
4. Ibid.
5. Tuchman, *The Spiritual in Art*, 281, 293.

Later in the twentieth century, some artists turned to more radical abstraction. Viewing the pictures in the Los Angeles exhibition book is a fascinating study of some of the purer abstract works — such as the rich, dark, imageless canvases of Barnett Newman and Mark Rothko. Masters of that tradition, sometimes called the *via negativa*, choose words like nothingness, darkness, and obscurity to symbolize the wholly other Absolute.[6]

Barnett Newman was convinced that primitive art gave the modern individual a deeper sense of the primordial roots of the unconscious mind and that understanding and even adapting primitive art values would create a more universal art in the present.[7]

Newman's and Rothko's somber, borderless canvases suggest deep silence and infinite void, yet somehow, too, evoke a sense of presence and mystery. Newman, an American who died in 1970, made no attempt to hide his spiritual interests. In 1943 he wrote, "The painter is concerned . . . with the presentation into the world of mystery. His imagination is therefore attempting to dig into metaphysical secrets. To that extent, his art is concerned with the sublime. It is a religious art which through symbols will catch the basic truth of life."[8]

# BIBLICAL AND SOCIOLOGICAL EVALUATION

The Christian sees many difficulties with the New Age spirituality taught and reflected in the work of these abstract artists.

Scrutiny of the artists' sources reveals a deep immersion in multiple forms of Neoplatonic spirituality — a spiritual pursuit that has accompanied Christianity from the time of Irenaeus, who thundered against the gnostics in the second century, to the present, a time in which conservative Christians view the occult as opposed to the biblical view. One is reminded of the apostle Paul's admonition to "test the spirits."

However, seeing the connection between abstract art and New age spiritual exploration contributes to a better understanding of the growth of the New Age view taking place in our culture. Though these quests are alien to the biblical view, they are rooted in intellectual and spiritual currents which arose more than a century ago and continue to grow.

6. Schaeffer, "Spirituality in Abstract Art," 821.
7. Tuchman, *The Spiritual in Art*, 275.
8. Schaeffer, "Spirituality in Abstract Art," 821-22.

## Non-abstract Forms

In addition to abstract painting, artists involved in the New Age movement have produced other kinds of painting. The nondualistic, or monistic, dimension of existence, seen as underlying all of life, reverberates powerfully in New Age art and architecture.

"New Age art is an attempt to create a safe, fantasized environment, with its friendly animals like unicorns, trees, landscapes and castles," says Karen Hoyt, a psychologist and artist who has studied and written about the New Age movement.

Gilbert Williams, considered to be a quintessential Visionary painter, exemplifies these themes in canvases filled with the subjective imagery of transcendence: moons and temples, goddesses and gateways, groves and guardians, lakes and light "beings" shining with bright color and intricacy.

In similar fashion, New Age architecture is "art for the people": "It has to do with earth-sheltering homes, solar-powered homes, and hand-built homes." The new wave concerns itself with log homes and Buckminster Fuller's geodesic domes. The latest in technology, in energy-aware physics, is being combined with the pervasive belief that homes are to live in, that they should be comfortable, that even if a wood-burning stove spoils "the line of a wall," it can be tolerated.

New Age artist Sharon Skolnick, who is fond of painting surreal images within images of San Francisco scenes, sums it up well: "Making art for me is a day trip into my primal self and the collective selves where we all join in a kind of divine molecular dance-prayer."[9]

# MUSIC

According to Gordon Melton, the term "New Age music" does not refer to any specific genre of music; rather, it refers to music that is used therapeutically or for other New Age (and inherently nonmusical) purposes. It has been defined as "music to create an environment with" in the catalog of Unity Records, an early major distributor of New Age music.

The concept of New Age music arose as professional musicians and composers became members of the New Age movement and began devoting their musical talents to the service of the movement. At first their efforts were shunned by the music industry, largely because what they were doing made very little sense in traditional musical terms. These musicians therefore set up

9. Russell Chandler, *Understanding the New Age* (Dallas: Word, 1991), 142-43.

their own small recording and distributing businesses and began selling their music directly to the public. When it became clear that a large market demanded their music (annual sales are now around $100 million), the major recording companies leaped upon this new bandwagon and began commissioning and promoting New Age music with great enthusiasm.[10]

"New Age" has now become a standard section in music stores, but it can contain almost any kind of music, since every conceivable type of music has by now been claimed as being New Age. That is, "New Age music" is a marketing slogan, not a musical category. As *Billboard* magazine observed in November 1987, "New Age music may be the most startling successful non-defined music ever to hit the public consciousness."

There is a religious philosophy, however, that is associated with the sounds that are heard in classical New Age music. "In the beginning was the Word, the sound of the mighty Aum, the first vibration: creator and sustainer of the universe," writes Joanne Crandall in *Self-Transformation through Music*. An underlying principle of the New Age movement is that everything has a vibration, and that this vibration is the divine energy of Aum that holds the universe together. True New Age music is produced by someone who is in touch with the great Aum or Om — someone who has tapped into this vibration and has thus assimilated a higher consciousness into the music. The listener then will also be lifted into a higher consciousness, which can bring about healing and self-actualization.[11] The tape *The Eternal One* has been described as: "The OM is all sound and silence throughout time.... It invokes the ALL that is otherwise inexpressible, and it is the highest spiritual sound on the earth. And now, using the latest in electronic technology, we have synthesized various pitches from human voices, and all intoning the OM together at the prescribed vibrations. In the background is an almost subliminal sounding choir."[12]

## MEDITATIVE-MYSTICAL NEW AGE MUSIC

Although New Age music includes any and all genres, its major use is as background music for meditation or for achieving some sort of altered state of consciousness. To be useful for meditation the music must be fairly consistent in dynamics and texture since sudden loud chords would tend to jolt a meditator out of his or her trance. Less obviously, abrupt changes of key, and the beginnings and endings of recognizable melodies, have the same

---

10. J. Gordon Melton, *New Age Almanac* (Detroit: Visible Ink, 1991), 71.
11. Ruth Tucker, *Another Gospel* (Academie Books, 1989), 350-51.
12. Douglas Groothuis, *Confronting the New Age* (Downers Grove, Ill.: InterVarsity, 1988), 192.

undesirable effect. For this reason, music designed to enhance a meditative trance tends to lack most of the characteristics that make traditional music interesting, such as complex textures, contrasts in dynamics, and melody itself. Music for meditation can seem quite boring if listened to in an ordinary state of mind.

In New Age music, intent is more important than form. It may be acoustic, electronic, or both. It can contain elements of classical patterns or exude free-form ambient explorations. True New Age music, as distinguished from the more commercial variety, is composed to affect the listener's consciousness.

Steven Bergman, who promotes New Age music, says, "Most of us benefit from love music that calms us, nurtures us, and inspires us. It plays a fundamental role in the transition to a new age. We want to spread this vibrant energy form as far as we can."

Steven Halpern, an innovator in New Age music with over thirty albums to his credit, has produced many albums that clearly integrate Eastern mystical practices with his music. His "Spectrum Suite" is designed to enable listeners to focus on each of the seven chakras (energy centers) in their bodies, which he thinks correspond to seven separate colors and sounds. Halpern says, "When the seventh and final selection begins, keynote B, focus your attention at the crown of your head. Visualize a violet color there and welcome the energy of divine consciousness." Halpern's orientation and intent for his music are clear: "The term spiritual connotes that which is eternal and that which is most in tune and in harmony with the universal God-force that we know by so many different names. In my work, I seek to align myself with that force, and to uplift the life energies of the performer and listener in order to bring them into closer attunement with their own God-Self."

Kitaro, a popular Japanese New Age performer and composer, has sold more than eight million copies of his seventeen albums. His cover art and song titles reveal the influence of Oriental mysticism on his work. Rick Ingrasci comments that Kitaro's *The Light of the Spirit* (1987) album is a means "through which Kitaro says he strives to express the universal ideas about human existence, nature, and the cosmos. . . . Kitaro . . . calls himself a 'musician of the new culture.' He considers his music part of his spiritual path and sees his role as that of a cultural change agent, helping others gain a fresh outlook on the world."

This type of meditative/mystical music is an example of "inner harmony New Age music," according to an explanatory advertisement by the Valley of the Sun New Age label (which is owned by the prominent New Age seminar leader and lecture tape distributor Dick Sutphen). Such music is described as "gentle, flowing, sustained environmental music without tension or resolve" which supposedly has been "scientifically proven to produce dramatic changes of consciousness" and is "ideal for altered-state-of-consciousness work." Some of the tapes of this music also contain subliminal messages thought to break into the unconscious mind to alter one's thoughts and entire life.[13]

## PROGRESSIVE NEW AGE MUSIC

Sutphen describes progressive New Age music as "mellow, but high energy music that usually combines acoustical and electronic instruments" for a "stimulating, but not distracting effect." Vangelis's *Chariots of Fire* soundtrack, he says, fits this category. Much of modern jazz-rock fusion, music which may or may not be composed and performed by people with a New Age worldview, might also fit this classification.[14]

## EASTERN NEW AGE MUSIC

True to their New Age Eastern roots, some New Age groups have also produced nonmusical commodities such as the "Tibetan Tantric Choir" and Tibetan prayer chants based on the supposed magic of spiritual sexual energy.[15]

In 1964, Tony Scott recorded "Music for Zen Meditation." In the years that followed, this "impressionistic" music became popular in California, but it was not sold nationally until the 1980s.

An exuberant and colorful school of meditation music has arisen among the followers of the Bhagwan Shri Rajneesh. The best known of the Rajneesh musicians is Swami Chaitanya (Georg Deuter), who recorded his early albums at Poona, India, then at Rajneeshpuram in Oregon. His first album, *Aum*, mixed acoustic instruments, synthesizers, and the sounds of the sea.

Two anonymous albums released by the Rajneesh community are popular. The first of these, *Nataraj*, begins with forty minutes of a meditation dance of total frenzy in which the unconscious mind is encouraged to take over completely. It continues with twenty minutes of stillness and calm, and concludes with five minutes of "celebration and joy." The other, *Nadabrahma*, is designed to accompany a specific Tibetan meditation technique.[16]

## MUSIC RELATED TO NATURE

There is a wide variety in style of New Age music, but very often it is dreamy music associated with nature. Typical would be that of Paul Winter, who, on his saxophone, accompanies the sounds of humpback whales, timber wolves,

13. Ibid., 191-93.
14. Ibid., 193.
15. Bob Larson, *Straight Answers on the New Age* (Nashville: Nelson, 1989), 168.
16. Melton, *New Age Almanac*, 74.

and eagles — letting them "create" the melody. Other New Age music features the sounds of waterfalls, ocean waves, and crickets.[17]

This music is part of a complex cultural trend, and appeals to a growing cross-section of Americans that extends far beyond the core of identifiable New Agers. It includes the sounds of plant vibrations, animal and nature noises, Celtic harps, gourd-shaped sitars, tunable tabla drums, drone-generating tambouras, and digital synthesizers. It can even be produced by a sheet of steel balanced on a balloon submerged in water.

Many New Age music superstars, such as Japanese synthesist-composer Mansanori Takahashi, consider their music to be part of their spiritual path and a means to express New Age values and shape culture.[18]

Records, cassettes, and CDs are often obtained through such non-traditional outlets as health food stores, metaphysical bookshops, and meditation centers.

## Evaluation of New Age Music

Douglas Groothuis, a professor at Denver Seminary, states that to reject categorically all music labeled "New Age" would be to fall prey to the taboo and quarantine mentalities. Much of what gets labeled as "New Age" is in the category of "progressive" New Age music — for the most part relaxing, instrumental music written and performed by people who do not necessarily have a New Age worldview. This style of music can be acceptable for Christians if they find it aesthetically pleasing and edifying. It does not seem to pose the spiritual threat that the meditative/mystical New Age music does.

Much of what is called New Age music does not fall philosophically or theologically into the New Age movement. "New Age" is a popular designation. It sells records. Most music called New Age really consists of light instrumentals and natural sounds like that of the surf.

Critics call New Age music "yuppie Muzak," "aural wallpaper," and "audio valium." Those who like it say it echoes the ambience of natural environments, helps them relax and meditate, or elicits a joy that energizes and brightens them.

A certain percentage of New Age music is composed with the deliberate design to alter consciousness, or to give the listener a pantheistic mystical experience, or to open up the individual to the influence of demonic spirits. From the biblical perspective, this New Age music can be dangerous,

17. Tucker, *Another Gospel*, 351.
18. Chandler, *Understanding the New Age*, 139-40.

and it may be difficult to differentiate between the simply mellow New Age music and the hard-core pantheistic New Age music.

However, to accept and utilize categorically all music labeled "New Age" would be to fall prey to the ostrich or chameleon mentalities. Much of New Age music is inspired by a pantheistic, monistic, and spiritistic worldview which is revealed in the music both instrumentally and vocally. Many New Age musicians and writers see their genre as a tool to advance the New Age agenda. Stephen Hill, director of the New Age radio program "Hearts of Space," heard on 220 stations, comments that "many of the artists are very sincerely and fully committed to New Age ideas and ways of life."[19]

"It is generally recognized that the New Age musicians indulge in various forms of occult meditation and cosmic awareness philosophies," writes radio talk show host Bob Larson. "Some of them freely admit using trance channeling as a source of inspiration. Consequently, a biblical perspective could define some of the music as satanically inspired."

True New Age music, then, is theologically wrong in its roots as well as in the effects it hopes to achieve. "Genuine New Age music is written to alter personal reality and expose one to his supposed inner divine nature," Larson explains. "In this sense, it is a kind of musical yoga. Serious New Age composers actually believe they can vibrate the body's psychic energy centers to awaken and transform the spiritual awareness of the human spirit."

The Christian should use his or her biblical critique in regard to New Age music. Much of it is harmless and simply relaxing. Some of it, however, promotes nonbiblical concepts.[20]

Groothuis reminds us of the words of the apostle Paul: "Let the word of Christ dwell in you richly as you teach and admonish one another with all wisdom, and as you sing psalms, hymns and spiritual songs with gratitude in your hearts to God" (Col. 3:16). Music intended to flip us into a mystical state of mind does not seem to fit these qualifications.

We need to recognize that God can use non-Christians to create beautiful music that edifies as well as delights. Also, music may affect different people differently, and we should allow for these differences in our practices. At the same time, some matters are clear. No Christian, for example, should listen to true New Age music such as *The Eternal OM* because to do so would be similar to entering into a pagan religious practice (see 1 Cor. 10:18-22). All meditative or mystically oriented New Age music should be viewed with suspicion.

In all things the Christian's goal should be to "take captive every

19. Groothuis, *Confronting the New Age*, 194.
20. Ralph Rath, *The New Age: A Christian Critique* (South Bend, Ind.: Greenlawn, 1990), 259-61.

thought to make it obedient to Christ" (2 Cor. 10:5). Only then can Christians confront the issues raised by New Age music with an authentic Christian discernment.[21]

## Music and Worship

Music and visual arts have traditionally been seen as aids to worship. The whole history of excellent music, including that of the present, is ours to use and enjoy.

The Christian musician, like his Christian colleagues in the other arts, is responsible to live and work in accord with the biblical, God-centered worldview. The Christian is to spend his life knowing that the words "Jesus saves" mean that nothing is beyond the scrutiny of redemption. Witness is not complete unless it demonstrates that every creaturely gift, including music, should be expressed in a way which reflects the Christian perspective or at least does not contradict it.

Today we are inundated by an unprecedented quantity of music, literature, films, and art. In music the market overflows with anthems, folk music, cantatas, and that unscrupulous aggregate of pseudo-rock-folk-pop called "Christian contemporary." Among these, the ratio of quantity to quality is appalling. And it is all supposed to support a so-called radicalizing gospel. The Christian artist must examine the practice of borrowing from secular art and music in the light of a distance between the church and secular culture. Most musicians confront an unprecedented proliferation of musical styles from both within and outside Western culture.[22]

The concept of music as "act-of" and "aid-to" pertains to witness as much as it does to worship. For if art is used primarily for its associative powers and perceived only as a tool by which people can be moved, we must then ask, to what extent can art and music carry an extrinsic message, and to what extent does the message subordinate the medium? There is a difference between the concept of medium as a carrier and medium as a message. The ideal situation is when both "media" agree.

Unfortunately, this is not always the case with those who stress mass communication in the spread of the gospel. If communication is described as the success with which a maximum audience is attracted and held to get a message across, and if art forms are the supporting means (the carriers surrounding the "word"), then the blunt question must be asked: "Given today's preference for shallow entertainment and instant pleasure, how does the

21. Groothuis, *Confronting the New Age*, 195.
22. Tucker, *Another Gospel*, 410-11.

church reconcile the use of media, including music of certain secular types, with an authentic Christian gospel?" According to Leland Ryken, music, viewed as a carrier, tends to be reduced to a format equated with entertainment. The greater the exposure desired, the lower the common denominator. So oftentimes the distance increases between the radical authenticity of the Christian message and the vulgarity of the means used to communicate it.

This is a peril, because in the very presentation of Christianity, a union of evangelical truth and inappropriate means of communication may result. Christian witness may play into the hands of the very secular culture it sets itself against. Thus the Christian new creation message and the secular non-Christian culture may be confused. This is the ultimate consequence of a series of mistakes issuing from an honest desire to save souls without fully understanding the complete integrity that must mark any activity done in the name of the sovereign God. After all, it is God who saves souls, not a fawning musical "package."[23]

The biblical worldview calls for a dynamic, vigorous, and passionate approach to music and the arts. By contrast, a Greek or New Age approach stresses a more abstract and withdrawn approach. The Greek idea is that since material reality is logically and ontologically dependent on formal or conceptual reality, true and great art must be that which most nearly mirrors the perfect and unchanging abstract forms and the relationship among their qualities. This interpretation would suggest that it is only by focusing on the formal qualities of a work of art which reflect eternal forms that we can ascertain its true worth.[24]

For the biblical view, on the other hand, the beautiful is that which fulfills purpose. "How beautiful are the feet of those who preach good news" (Rom. 10:15). Purpose implies power and authority and movement. Therefore the biblical view finds beauty in that which lives and moves and exudes power and authority. Furthermore, it is not primarily the form which mediates or supports the experience of beauty as for Plato, but the sensations of light, voice, sound, tone, smell, and taste.[25]

The commandment against making images meant that, for the Hebrews, there was to be no portrayal of God through sculpture or painting. The Hebrews did not even make visual images of God in their imagination. The images of God which the Hebrews held in their mind were mobile, dynamic,

23. Leland Ryken, *The Christian Imagination* (Grand Rapids: Baker, 1981), 410-12.

24. Jerry H. Gill, *Faith in Dialogue: A Christian Apologetic* (Waco: Word, 1985), 81-82.

25. Thorlief Boman, *Hebrew Thought Compared with Greek* (Philadelphia: Westminster, 1960), 92.

and auditory. Their concept of God had to do with God's dynamic qualities, not his image.

These Hebrew emphases on the dynamic and concrete give us a clue as to the art forms which are most compatible with the biblical worldview. The sermon, music, and drama are surely more basic than static visual forms such as painting and sculpture.

An emphasis on dynamic yet controlled spontaneity in worship is congenial with the biblical emphasis. At the Wailing Wall in Jerusalem, the Hebrews never stop moving as they pray. This emphasis is also congenial with the creation of a more dynamic context for worship in terms of lighting, worship, and space for movement.

## Implications of the Biblical View

Since the sermon and drama and music have been mentioned as uniquely effective art forms for a biblical worldview, it is interesting to note the way in which the Hebrew speaker used language. He sought to awaken feelings and passions in the listeners. He used language to challenge listeners to do something in obedience to God's will. It was by doing the right thing that the Hebrew learned the truth. We continue today to emphasize that we know God as we keep his commandments.

Music also helps to reach the will by touching the emotions.

For the Hebrews, God was interested primarily in time. He created in time and acted in time. Time for the Hebrews is a container for God's revealing events. God revealed himself when he acted in time and history. Paul said, "In the fullness of time, God sent Christ." The Hebrews gave special attention to the peculiarity of events — and what is time but the stream of events?

Danish philosopher Søren Kierkegaard has recovered for us the essentially Hebraic idea that to be a true Christian means to leap across the centuries in order to become contemporaneous with Jesus and his disciples and then, in that situation, make a decision for Christ as the Son of God.

The context of Greek, Eastern, and New Age thought and of much Christian thought which follows Greek and New Age thought is the "upward and downward" emphasis. The salvation principle is that of ascent to union with God.

The motif of the Bible is that of "journey and return" after the redemptive pattern of the Prodigal Son. It is the context of human revolt against God, of God's redemptive love plan, and of human response and return.

Instead of mystical withdrawal into otherworldly absorption, the biblical movement is one of redemptive experience with God in the context of history. In the Bible the purpose of the great religious experiences was not just seeking mystical union with God, but also securing knowledge of one's vocation.[26]

Evangelical groups have come to power and influence in American religious life. This means that they have the responsibility to understand and create and utilize new and constructive art forms under the guidance of the biblical worldview. The power and value of the arts call for conservative Christians to give up their fear of the arts.

If there is ever a truly authentic church music, it will come through a relocation of priorities in a flow of excellence celebrated creatively, by faith, as worship. Church music can then be the place where excellence is born and where it is continuously welcome. We need never invert our priorities and violate our artistic integrity or principles for Jesus' sake. The gospel is too great for this kind of compromise. In reconciling the world to God, our Lord Jesus Christ did not compromise his integrity to gain maximum results. And he is the true model for a redeemed musician or artist.[27] Christians must be sure their music truly reflects the revealed biblical and trinitarian gospel.

## MOVIES, TV, AND THE COMPUTER

The New Age is very strong in the entertainment field. There are many more popular movies with New Age themes than there are with Christian themes. Actress and author Shirley MacLaine produced a TV miniseries with a New Age theme which was very popular.

Science fiction has been a major factor in the spread of New Age consciousness into American culture, especially science fiction cinema. Nowhere is that spread of new consciousness more easily demonstrated than in the *Star Wars* saga.

"May the force be with you." Almost everybody knows what that means. This is a catchphrase the good guys used in the tremendously popular *Star Wars* movies. The underlying theology was pure New Age. There is no Creator God, no objective rules of right and wrong. There is simply this blind force which can be used by good people for good, and bad people for bad.

This force can be tapped into by suspending reason and using instinct. In the finale of the first movie, *Star Wars,* for example, Luke Skywalker was able to shoot his proton torpedo into a small opening in the Death Star only after he shut his eyes and let the force guide him.

26. Will Herberg, *Judaism and Modern Man* (New York: Farrar, Straus & Young, 1951), 203-4.
27. Tucker, *Another Gospel,* 412-14.

In the second movie, *The Empire Strikes Back*, we were introduced to Yoda, who is essentially a yogi. He taught Skywalker that he could create reality — such as lifting a plane — simply by thinking. In the final movie, *Return of the Jedi*, Darth Vader became a good guy by turning to the light side of the force instead of the dark side. This is all New Age.[28]

As creator of this celluloid epic, George Lucas has inherited the Promethean mantle worn by such science fiction demigods as H. G. Wells, John W. Campbell, Robert A. Heinlein, and Arthur C. Clarke — all of whom sought to replace the Western Judeo-Christian worldview with a more "scientific" definition of God. To the biblically discerning, it should come as no surprise that those more scientific definitions usually smack of Eastern mysticism and occult metaphysics and, specifically in the case of *Star Wars*, Manichaean pantheism. In a near-death experience in 1962, Lucas affirmed that he found the Force.[29]

The Force is pantheistic, "all is one," because the supreme reality (the two basic and opposing principles of the cosmos) is identified with the forces and workings of nature. In other words, the cosmos is equated with God. That is idolatry.

## BIBLICAL EVALUATION OF *STAR WARS*

As the apostle Paul details in Romans, the belief system of *Star Wars* breaks the first commandment because it results in worship of the creation rather than the Creator (Rom. 1:16-32). The biblical God is not dualistic. He is a person who is absolutely transcendent over what he has made: he created the cosmos *ex nihilo*, out of nothing. Even though God is not part of what he has made, he dwells within it. We can have access to him partially through his general revelation of himself in the created order and savingly through his prophetic revelation as recorded in Scripture. But ultimately we have access to him through his son Jesus Christ, our redeemer. God is a transcendent God but also the God who is there — at all times, for anyone who will repent of rebellion and respond to his redemptive plan.[30]

## *E.T.* AND *CLOSE ENCOUNTERS*

Another theme in contemporary movies common to the New Age is that of a more highly evolved race from outer space visiting us to improve our lives.

28. Rath, *New Age*, 254.
29. Woodrow Nichols, "Celluloid Prometheus: The Transcendentalism of George Lucas," *SCP Newsletter* 10.5 (Winter 1984-85): 9.
30. Ibid., 10.

*E.T.* and *Close Encounters of the Third Kind* are two movies with this theme that were very popular. This concept presupposes that humans can evolve into a higher type of existence. These outer-space beings have evolved further than we humans have, and the implication is given that, with luck, we can evolve further, too. E.T. was so evolved, in fact, that he could heal people and resurrect himself from the dead. No hint is given in these movies that there is a Supreme Being, a God who created the extraterrestrials as well as the humans.[31]

## Children's Movies

Douglas Groothuis found an unabashed New Age theme in the children's movie *The Dark Crystal,* produced by Jim Henson, the creator of the Muppets. "It is essentially a fairy tale of monism," wrote Groothuis. "All is one; ultimate reality is beyond good and evil."[32]

## Controversy

The extremely controversial movie *The Last Temptation of Christ* depicted Jesus as a confused wimp who doubted his messiahship and struggled with lustful temptations. Russell Chandler, religion editor of the *Los Angeles Times,* saw a New Age influence in the movie, which was based on Nikos Kazantzakis's 1955 novel. "Everything's a part of God," the tormented Christ declares in the movie in a decidedly pantheistic context. Chandler continued his analysis:

> On the introduction page of the script is this quotation from Kazantzakis: "It is not God who will save us — it is [we] who will save God, by battling, by creating and transmuting matter into spirit." In the prologue to his novel, Kazantzakis speaks of the "yearning . . . of man to attain God, or more exactly, to return to God and identify himself with him."

## Satanism

Satanism also is very rampant in the entertainment field. At a time when polls reveal that two-thirds of Americans do not believe a personal devil exists, teenagers and others are flocking to movies about Satan and demonic possession. Note the movie ads in your daily paper. If you are living in a city with

31. Rath, *New Age,* 255-256.
32. Groothuis, *Unmasking,* 19.

more than one or two movie theaters, there is a very good chance that you will find ads for several movies that deal with demonic influence. Take the first *Ghostbusters* movie, for example. This was a raucous comedy, but the demonic and occultic aspects were treated seriously.[33]

## TELEVISION

The New Age has also become part of television series. A *Charlie's Angels* show talked about the energy fields of the chakras. Shirley MacLaine's mini-series also had a New Age theme.

# Computer Technologies

Computers are doing more than just collecting, processing, and saving information. They are playing a key role in orchestrating experience. Michael Deering, head of a research team at Sun Micro Systems, a California computer company, recently claimed that "You can duplicate any human emotion or re-create any human experience with technology." Timothy Leary, who became famous for his 1960s use of the drug LSD, is now a spokesman for digital technology. The computer has replaced his faith in LSD as a way of transforming conciousness. The New Age now offers things like Mystic Vision's "Virtual Reality Experiences," promising an "enlightening adventure through the divine levels of the Celestial Kingdom," and Mind Explorer's equipment, which, it is promised, serves to ensure that "the brainwave state is gently transformed from everyday 'beta' through 'alpha' to meditative 'theta.'"

As researchers work to perfect supercomputers that will be 200 million times faster than today's home computers and single electron chips that will perform calculations, plans are also being made to insert silicon chips into people's heads so they can plug directly into the information highway.

British sociologist Paul Heelas anticipates computerized resources taking participants out of their egos. Digitalized music, computer-generated light and vision displays, virtual reality equipment — along with the use of experience-determinate drugs — are utilized to transform people into a New Age mystical experience.

According to Joshua Quittner in his article "Life and Death on the Web," the Heaven's Gate cult of San Diego left its fingerprints all over cyberspace: in postings broadcast to dozens of newsgroups, in recruitment

33. Rath, *New Age*, 249-50, 257-58.

chats with teenagers, and in Web sites designed for rich clients. Here was obsession, delusion, and mass suicide played out in multimedia and hypertext — a horror, finally, best observed online.

The Heaven's Gate Web site was perhaps the most elaborate suicide note in history. From the blinking "RED ALERT" headline of its celestial home page to its computer-generated painting of a resident of the kingdom of heaven, the site served up five megabytes of soul-chilling information. Hundreds of pages of millennialist writings, including transcripts of videotapes and the full text of a book called *Heaven's Gate*, laid out the cult's history and cosmology. One posting sent from a *heavensgate.com* e-mail address was "spammed" to dozens of Usenet newsgroups. "Time to die for God?" it began. "Whether we like it or not, the Armageddon — the Mother of Holy Wars — has begun, and it will not cease until the plowing under is completed." Quittner sees computer Web pages being used to suck people into a suicide cult.[34]

## Power of the Media

According to Larry Poland, president of Mastermedia International, probably in no other generation has such a small contingent of people had such enormous influence in shaping a culture's definitions of truth and error, right and wrong, purity and impurity — even reality and unreality — as does the media establishment in America today.

Furthermore, in his book *Four Arguments for the Elimination of Television*, Jerry Mander cites research that indicates that the interaction between the television screen and the viewer is such that it frequently bypasses the viewer's consciousness. Not only do the media get their content past the guard and into the minds of Christians through subconscious communication, but they are also relentless and persuasive instructors in paganism at the conscious level. The media have become an all-pervasive, powerful, and pagan influence in our society and in the church. The danger for the media-immersed Christian is that he or she unconsciously begins to tolerate and then to embrace the values of the media, which are commonly at odds with those of the typical American and deeply opposed to biblical values.[35]

34. Paul Heelas, *The New Age Movement* (Cambridge, Mass.: Blackwell, 1996), 217-18; and Joshua Quittner, "Life and Death on the Web," *Time*, April 7, 1997, 47.

35. D. A. Carson and John D. Woodbridge, eds., *God and Culture* (Grand Rapids: Eerdmans, 1993), 261, 268-70.

# Three Ways to Deal with the Media

Poland suggests three methods of dealing with the media as a community of largely pagan, or secular, people — using public pressure, creating a Christian media industry, and having a strong Christian presence in the secular media.

Poland's definition of "media" focuses on the community of people who control and operate the media, not on instruments, technologies, or even messages. People are behind the media; therefore, a change in the values of the people who run the industry would result in dramatic changes in the content, values, messages, styles, and responsibility taken by various segments of the media.

### Public Pressure

The first stratagem is the mobilization of an aggressive national protest to hold the media leadership accountable for what they do, to raise a standard of righteousness in society and in the media, and to pressure the media to change their content in the direction of this standard. A host of political and moral action groups and organizations have already chosen this approach.

While Poland believes that there is a clear biblical mandate for proclaiming God's law and "seasoning" society with the salt of Christian values, he also believes that, by themselves, these efforts will fail.

### Christian Media

A second stratagem is that of establishing a "Christian media industry" to harness the potential power of the technology for kingdom objectives and to compete with the secular media power structure with redemptive motivations and products. However, while there is biblical admonition to proclaim the good news by every means possible, these Christian media organizations have not made a significant dent in the power, values, or content of the secular media establishment, which continues to hold a virtual monopoly. By some media trade estimates, all of Christian television reaches less than 4 percent of the nation's television viewers, and these are largely within the Christian fold. Similar statistics could probably be gathered for the Christian radio, music, and book-selling industries.

Furthermore, according to Poland, the elite of the Christian media have often perpetuated such strange, irrelevant, or subculturally distinctive stereotypes of Christianity that nationally they have been more the object of ridicule than of serious consideration or influence. Add to this the exploitable corruption of a handful of Christian media leaders, and it becomes clear that this strategy is not going to have a significant impact. Charles Colson, a

Christian evangelical writer, states that much of the electronic church has given in to the prevailing moods of the culture it purportedly exists to confront.[36]

The third method, and the one Poland contends is more central to the biblical mandate (and consequently more effective), is building up a powerful Christian presence within the secular media establishment. This, he suggests, must be accomplished through

1. the mobilization of specific prayer for media leaders;
2. the evangelism of media professionals at every level of media influence;
3. the discipleship of existing Christian professionals in media to equip them for a more powerful witness and a more redemptive use of their media skills;
4. the networking, support, and mobilization of committed believers in media for significant spiritual impact; and
5. the penetration of the media power structure by trained, committed Christian professionals.

Poland says the church's mandate in dealing with the media is the same as it has been with all other hostile groups, from Roman polytheists to intellectual Greek philosophers — to proclaim the good news in the power of the Spirit and to disciple those who respond to Christ in God's transforming Word.[37]

# A GENERAL BIBLICAL APPROACH TO THE ARTS

Many worldviews devalue the physical side of God's creation. This devaluation has taken the vague and curious form, so characteristic of American culture, of making "spiritual values" more desirable than "material values."

Every such form of devaluation flies in the face of God's affirmation of his creation. The sheer physicality or materiality of something is never a legitimate ground for assigning it a lower value in our lives. The important concern is the manner in which the physical or material is used.

Artists who see life and reality as Christians will not despise the creation in which they find themselves. They will not see creation as something from which to be liberated. And though an artist may on occasion produce highly intellectual, even perhaps conceptual, art, that artist will not do so

36. Ibid., 272-73.
37. Ibid., 273-74.

because he wants to free himself from the constrictions of his materials. Instead, he will see the world as a storehouse of materials from which he can select to do his work. He will think of those materials as having potentials to be realized rather than as something constricting the scope of his own self-expression.

Earthly existence is one of God's favors to us. The physical creation is good for human beings, since it serves human fulfillment. Earth is humankind's present home, the world our present dwelling place. This view is good soil for art. However, even though the Bible affirms the goodness of the physical, it never implies that the physical is all there is to life, which is an assumption of much contemporary art.[38]

Part of what it means to be human is to interact thoroughly with nonhuman reality. We should not see art as concerned chiefly with moving us beyond the material world to some "higher" realm of beauty, or see the heart of an artist's work as giving outward expression to inner, nonmaterial realities, as if the "real" work was carried out in the sanctuary of the self, and the piece of art merely served to externalize and convey this interior experience.

This is not to say that art can be explained entirely in physical terms, or that mental activity has no place in artistic creation, or that artists are never blessed with compelling visions. But, in the words of Jeremy Begbie, of Ridley Hall at Cambridge, there should be more room for a deeper sense of our embeddedness in creation and the rootedness of art in substance, in the human body, in pigment, in the twanging of gut, and the blowing of air on reeds. Accordingly, art will be seen as an engagement with the physical world involving our senses as much as our mental and emotional faculties.[39]

This approach is different from the New Age tendency to move away from the material to the nonmaterial, from physical reality to abstract aesthetic experience. The New Age emphasis undoubtedly has its roots in ancient Greek and Eastern thought. In more recent times, the emphasis is toward the feeling responses of the human subject.

According to philosopher Immanuel Kant (1724-1804) — in so many ways the father of modern aesthetics — aesthetic pleasure comes about when two mental faculties, the imagination and the understanding, engage in "free play." It is this free play which we enjoy. This distinctive experience arises when we contemplate beautiful objects characterized by what Kant calls "purposiveness without purpose." Yet Kant holds that aesthetic judgments are based not on features of the world to which we respond but rather on features

---

38. Nicholas Wolterstorff, *Art in Action: Toward a Christian Aesthetic* (Grand Rapids: Eerdmans, 1980), 69-72.

39. Jeremy Begbie, "The Gospel, the Arts and Our Culture," in *The Gospel and Contemporary Culture*, ed. Hugh Montefiore (London: Mowbray, 1992), 70.

of our response — specifically the interplay of the imagination and the understanding. Aesthetic experience and knowledge are quite distinct, Kant believes. When someone makes an aesthetic judgment, he says, "nothing in the object is signified, but [only] a feeling in the subject as it is affected by the representation."[40]

## Biblical Emphasis on the Incarnation

Although a Christian aesthetics, or theory of beauty, is concerned with the arts portraying God's good creation, humanity made in the image of God, the Fall, and redemption, it finds its center of gravity in the doctrine of the Incarnation. The material earth not only comes from the hand of God, but is radiant with God's presence. This means that philosophical idealism, which plays down the material earth, is not possible for the artist, a fact which even Plato recognized.

The Christian artist goes further in seeing that the physical and the material were judged worthy to contain Jesus Christ. The material world is thus radiant with both the glory of the creation and the new creation that proceeds from the Incarnation.[41]

## Redemption and Renewal

The Christian worldview, however, speaks of more than creation. It also speaks of redemption. Admittedly, there are those who perceive the message of the Christian gospel as the message of escape from our creaturely earthly existence. But the Christian drama tells of the renewal of human existence. This means that humanity may attain fulfillment both in the present and in the future. Artists are called to be God's agents in this cause of renewal. This means that art thus gains new significance. Art can serve as an instrument in our struggle to overcome the fallenness of our existence, while also affording us delight, which anticipates the kingdom beyond.[42]

The biblical teaching emphasizes that God himself has penetrated the very heart of the darkness of evil — represented by Gethsemane and Calvary. But redemption emphasizes not only the exposure of evil and the presence of God in the darkness, but also a transformation, a renewal of that which is

40. Ibid., 59-60.
41. John W. Dixon, *Nature and Grace in Art* (Chapel Hill, N.C.: University of North Carolina, 1964), 79.
42. John P. Newport, *Life's Ultimate Questions* (Dallas: Word, 1989), 561.

distorted, in such a way that we are given a promise of the ultimate transformation and consummation of all things. This is the gospel of Calvary and Easter.

Artistic creativity demands respect and courtesy for what is given to hand and mind, but the artist cannot leave the matter there. According to Begbie, new connections and novel meanings need to be established through enlarging and elaborating on whatever reality is encountered. Composers, for example, do more than discover and honor their material; they combine sounds in novel ways, explore fresh, melodic lines, juxtapose rhythms and harmonies to create new musical meanings.

The Christian artist cannot ignore the brutalities of war, the fear of death, and the suffering of the innocent. Sadly, some so-called "Christian" art has turned a blind eye to such realities and degenerated into a superficial kitsch, something encouraged all too often by art theories which insist that any hint of disorder in art is a mark of discredit. There should be no attempt to diminish the horror of the tragic by ignoring the tragic and portraying life only as a monistic and beautiful whole.

Beyond the tragic, Christian art emphasizes the raising of the crucified Son of God from the dead. Such art will inevitably resound with an inner joy, even though it may be a joy won only through despair. Such art will be "realistic" in the profoundest sense of that word, for, as D. Hardy and D. P. Ford remind us, "The resurrection of the crucified Jesus Christ is [the] logic at the heart of Christianity. . . . If this is basic reality then all existence can be thought through in the light of it. True realism will take account of this first, and live from it." Furthermore, insofar as art does take its final cue from the resurrection, there will be in it an anticipation of the ultimate goal of creation, a provisional manifestation of a future glory beyond compare.

Begbie sees something of this quality in Rembrandt's "Christ Healing the Sick" or El Greco's glowing representation of Christ in Gethsemane, "The Agony of the Garden." Examples of this art in our own day include Duke Ellington's "Come Sunday," the early works of Graham Sutherland, and the luminous portraits of Georges Rouault.[43]

## Biblical Emphasis on the Trinity

In *Foolishness to the Greeks*, English theologian and missionary Lesslie Newbigin writes that "the twin dogmas of Incarnation and Trinity . . . form the starting point for a way of understanding reality as a whole." Much has been written in recent years which questions the usefulness and the intelligibility

43. Begbie, "The Gospel, the Arts and Our Culture," 74-75.

of both these doctrines. And yet, in the area of the arts, there are good grounds for believing that together they provide us with a valuable resource.

In fact, according to Jeremy Begbie, the doctrine of the Trinity, far from being an ecclesiastical antique to be periodically pulled out, scrutinized, and then returned to storage, becomes quite pivotal. It tells us that reality as such, not the least human reality, is relational. According to the Christian faith, no one can be made whole except by being restored to the wholeness of that being-in-relationship for which God made us and the world, and which is the image of that being-in-relationship of God himself. The Christian gospel is about discovering our identity in relationships that respect our distinctiveness and uniqueness. It is about being related through the Spirit of Jesus and his Father to other persons and to the material world created and redeemed in Christ.

The biblical approach to art should reflect this relational character of human existence. The richest sources of artistic creativity are to be found not so much in the recesses of the artist's own soul, but in a dynamic interaction with the created world, society, fellow artists both past and present, and (for the Christian) fellow believers and the Father who fashioned all things out of nothing. Moreover, to see the created world as the product of a trinitarian God who is love in his innermost being will remind us that nonhuman creation is there not as an inflexible machine, but as an environment given to us out of love. This environment is appropriate for the development of free humans and therefore one which the artist should enjoy, respect, and develop to the fullest.[44]

## Biblical Respect for Order and Meaning

The biblical faith presents us with a vision of created existence possessing its own latent orderliness and meaning. Thus, a crucial part of human creativity is to be attentive to that inherent order, to discover it, and to bring it to light. This means that we will question views of art which lay the main weight on bringing value and meaning to a reality which is regarded as essentially lacking in value and ultimately unknowable. The imagination creates, to be sure, but only on the basis of an already established divine ordering. It is not that the artist contributes meaning to something which is meaningless and formless; it is rather that the artist enables creation to take on another, perhaps richer, more meaningful form.

The Christian sees creation's order as a gift from God whose nature it is to love. If we take this approach, the properties of an artist's medium can

44. Ibid., 69, 79-80.

be regarded as an opportunity for, and stimulant to, artistry, rather than a straitjacket to which the artist must grudgingly yield. Novelist Dorothy Sayers insisted that the business of the artist "is not to escape from his material medium or bully it, but to serve it; but to serve it he must love it. If he does so, he will realize that its service is perfect freedom."[45]

In the biblical tradition, genuine freedom is not constituted by independent self-determination, or by the absence of limits, or by multiplying the number of possibilities open to us; it is realized only in relation to real possibilities, by acting in accordance with the way things are. This refers to the way artists treat their material — notes, words, stone, or whatever. Artistic freedom in this respect entails an encounter and interaction with the chosen medium in such a way that its integrity is not violated.

This approach is quite different from the concept of the artist as chiefly an imposer, rather than a discoverer, of value and meaning. Clearly, there can be no such thing as pure discovery; all our interchange with reality involves a contribution on our part which affects the content and character of our experience. It is the Kantian stress on the mind's imposition of a fixed conceptual order on essentially unknown reality — the heart of the Enlightenment doctrine of knowledge — which needs challenging.

For Kant, art triumphs by working the wonders of the human mind upon the formlessness of the world, not by interacting with an order already given to the hand.[46]

## ART AND ACTION

The biblical teaching emphasizes that God has acted to restore our whole being — supremely in the person of Christ — in such a way that we are able to relate actively as whole persons not only to God himself, but to the world of space and time in which we are set. Instead of disengaging us from the contingencies of history, God has called us to participate in his purposes for creation as embodied agents in history. This is a call to a life of shared relationships in a world of living creatures and created things, to a life in which all our capacities and capabilities are to be united in obedience to him.

In his book *Art in Action*, Yale philosopher Nicholas Wolterstorff has argued that works of art are first and foremost instruments and objects of action. They are inextricably part of the fabric of human purposes, passions, and interests. They are vehicles through which we carry out our intentions with respect to the world, our fellows, and ourselves. Our society's institution of "high" or "fine" art encourages us to regard an artwork for its own sake

45. Ibid., 71.
46. Ibid., 60-61.

alone. Although "perceptual contemplation" is one of the uses to which some art can legitimately be put, to insist on it as the key idea of art is unduly restrictive.

It should be noted that the attempt to integrate art and action can easily be overplayed, leading to a "functionalist" view of art, where we value a work of art solely according to its usefulness. Questions of aesthetic worth and excellence cannot be reduced to pragmatic questions of utility, commercial or otherwise. However, we cannot abstract works of art from their context in human action if they are to be interpreted right and enjoyed to the fullest.[47]

## ART AND RELATIONSHIP

At the heart of the biblical faith lies the truth that we find our true being only in relationship, supremely in relations of self-giving love. Paradoxically, it is only as we exist for and with others that our particularity and distinctiveness are preserved. And this is so because God himself is not a single, monadic being, but is triune, existing as a free communion of distinct persons in relationship, eternally giving and receiving in love. The uniqueness of the Christian gospel is that we who pursue the quest for fulfillment through autonomous self-direction can in reality discover our authentic humanity as persons-in-relationship. We find this fulfillment by sharing in the eternal and perfect relationships of love revealed to us as we relate to the triune God of the biblical worldview.

The implications of this biblical emphasis on relationships has important implications for art. Art should be seen as a vehicle of communication between people. Of course, artists may say that they make things "only for themselves" or "only because they have to." But, instead of seeing an artwork as an "irrefutable object" or a "gift from the self to the self," we should regard it as a medium of personal exchange.

There is also an artist's obligation to society, which simply cannot be sidestepped. The artist will have to display sensitivity to the shared values and assumptions of his or her social setting.

Begbie affirms that artists should be suspicious of speaking of originality as the supreme artistic virtue. They also should seek to rehabilitate a sense of the importance of tradition. An infatuation with originality not only makes us immune to anything in the past which might criticize and challenge us, but it is ultimately self-defeating. For originality without tradition stagnates just as quickly as tradition without originality.

For Begbie, it is clear that the arts will flower best in the context of a community of open discourse in which conversation, undistorted communica-

47. Ibid., 73-74.

tion, and communal judgment inform our lives. Here Christian artists can and should remember that they are, first and foremost, members of a community which has access to resources which impart to it a genuine fellowship and openness. The church is summoned to be a provisional embodiment within this finite world of a type of human existence which mirrors, and shares in, the life of the triune God. It may well be that if the church is to play a significant part in the renewal of art in the days ahead, this will come about not through highly trained "performers" — which can so easily plow into a new individualism — but through the emergence of new forms of communal art. In such a setting, relationships generated and sustained by the Holy Spirit are allowed to affect the very character of artistic creativity itself.[48]

## FULFILLMENT

The Christian view accepts the fact that, by common grace, all people have spiritual longings and create religious myths. There is some truth in the Jungian view which identifies these "archetypes" as fundamental and universal symbolic patterns latent in all people. Religious phenomenologists such as Mircea Eliade have discovered these motifs in both primitive and sophisticated societies. Such images as creation, a fall, a hero figure, a dying and rising god, the demonic, and yearning for paradise, rebirth, and resurrection are in all people's mythic consciousness.

It is the Christian contention that these mythical longings and images are crystalized, historicized, and fulfilled in the biblical view. Around Christ, these images are reconstituted in a powerful way as the Incarnation, the Messiah, the New Covenant, the Word, the Cross, and the Kingdom. These master images, as transformed by Christ and the Bible, afford artists dynamic and balanced themes of universal interest and power.[49]

# BEING BIBLICALLY INFORMED

Thus we see that the Christian has always been involved in a war of myths or worldviews for human souls. There is a biblical background for this constant conflict of worldviews. In its originating years the biblical faith was in a continual war against pagan myths and worldviews. With the emergence of

48. Ibid., 77-79.
49. Amos Niven Wilder, "Art and Theological Meaning," in *The New Orpheus: Essays toward a Christian Poetic*, ed. Nathan A. Scott, Jr. (New York: Sheed and Ward, 1964), 414.

the gospel came a renewed activity in the areas of mythical and symbolic creation and evaluation and discourse. The new Christian imagery arose out of the drama of the cross and resurrection. The biblical faith was a worldview that contradicted the imaginations of Greece and Rome even as it borrowed from them and transfigured them.[50]

It is important that Christians in any epoch should have ability and knowledge in the area of biblically informed art criticism. Without violating the integrity of art forms, they should be able to grasp clearly the presuppositions of the various worldviews presented by artists. They should be able to analyze these worldviews and note their implications. They should then have the ability to evaluate these worldviews in light of biblical standards. In a more positive way, the informed Christian should be part of a Christian artistic vanguard which would provide compelling images and potent art forms rooted in a biblical perspective.

50. Ibid., 414.

# CHAPTER THIRTEEN

# The Meaning of History

The collision of the New Age and biblical worldviews — the theme of this book — is rooted in the disagreement between the New Age and biblical views about basic beliefs. This dramatic conflict can be traced to a different understanding of the meaning of history.

Simply speaking, the study of history can be approached from two different directions. First, there is the approach of the technical, or empirical, historian. According to this concept, the writing of history is to be governed by tough, critical, empirical rules. All the sciences are to be utilized by the historian for whatever information they may supply.

But even a scientific approach to history can never be as absolute and precise as natural sciences such as physics and chemistry. Even when historical evidence is obtained scientifically, the historian has to interpret that evidence. Thus, even the technical historian has to deal with some hidden philosophical implications.

The other approach to history goes beyond the technical, or scientific, approach, for there will always be a cry for interpretation of the human drama that does more than just uncover and analyze facts. The philosopher or theologian seeks this broader interpretation of history, asking questions such as: What is the ultimate significance of history? Is history merely the result of chance or inexorable fate? Or is it a divine drama with a plot, a plan, a goal? Is there a hidden master dramatist?

These questions are significant since they are related to human life and destiny, to our highest hopes and deepest fears. They zero in on the meaning of life, the purpose. For if there is no purpose, how can we do anything but despair? It can be said, then, that every person has a philosophy of history — a viewpoint from which to interpret life.

In the seventeenth century, there developed an Enlightenment view of history that had an emphasis on inevitable progress. Robert Heilbroner, in his disturbing book *An Inquiry into the Human Prospect,* says we have to come to the end of the Enlightenment. The Enlightenment dream of progress, which was to be inevitably attainable through the autonomous exercise of human reason translated into technological power and economic abundance, has been proven not only to be an illusion, but dangerous. It not only lied to us about the world and ourselves, but it has also cursed us and cursed future generations.[1]

As we will see, both the biblical and New Age views of history differ from the Enlightenment view of inevitable progress through unaided autonomous human reason. But they are in conflict at crucial levels.

## THE NEW AGE VIEW OF HISTORY

To understand the New Age, we need to understand the New Age perspective on history, a perspective that is becoming almost mythical. New Agers tend to be progressively shaped, energized, and directed by a common symbolic mythos. Their view is a vision of history through which they make sense of life. It is a vision *for* the world as well as *of* life. It is what Nicholas Wolterstorff of Yale calls a "control belief."

The basic idea of the New Age view of history is rooted in a spiritual doctrine of evolution. This evolution is based on the concept that we can achieve essential union with God through mystical spiritual evolution.

While retaining elements of humanism, naturalism, and existentialism, the New Age view has spiritualized the universe by making mystical consciousness, rather than matter, its essence. Reality is engaged in a process of evolution — an evolutionary spiral.

In some respects, New Age religion can rightly be classified as a Western expression of classic monistic Hinduism, which is called Vedanta. However, in other respects, it is very different from traditional Hinduism. It is life- and history-affirming. The key to this difference is that the New Age approach maintains aspects of the Western Enlightenment heritage. It affirms the value of temporal realities: people, nature, culture, education, politics, even science and technology. In fact, contemporary New Age thought represents

---

1. Brian J. Walsh, "Worldviews, Modernity and the Task of Christian College Education," *Faculty Dialogue* 18 (Toronto: Institute for Christian Studies, 1992): 22.

an effort to graft the fruits of higher learning onto the various branches of the mystical tradition.[2]

As we noted in the chapter on science, Fritz Capra and other New Age scientists have combined the mystical and spiritual with quantum physics. They call this a paradigm shift and a mystical holistic approach.

## New Age Idea of Evil and Ethics

For classic New Age advocates, good and evil do not exist. This statement by actress Shirley MacLaine is representative:

> All of life, technological or emotional, is a question of working with positive and negative energies and that *negative* doesn't mean wrong. It simply means the opposite polarity — the other end of the balance — of *positive*. Negative energy is as necessary as positive. . . . Understanding the basic tenets of this principle is helpful then in extending our understanding that "evil" exists only in relation to the point of view: If a child steals to live, if a man kills to protect his family, if a woman aborts a fetus rather than give birth to an unwanted child, if a terrorist murders because he has been raised all his life to believe that killing is his right and proper duty — *who* is evil? And if a person kills "simply" out of hatred or greed, *he* perceives his motives as *his need* — others make the judgment that his act is "evil."

According to Wouter J. Hanegraaff, of the University of Utrecht in the Netherlands, New Age sources *do* identify some kinds of action as undesirable. The most common distinction between what is and what is not desirable is based on whether such human action assists the process of *evolution*.

New Ager Erich Jantsch states, "We can define ethical behavior as behavior which enhances evolution. . . . As an integral aspect of evolution, ethics is not subject to revelation, as is the ethics of religions with a personal god."

Hanegraaff summarizes New Age ethics by stating that human actions are regarded as undesirable to the extent that they run counter to the cosmic evolutionary process, or to one's own personal evolution which is part of that larger process. The extent to which they produce suffering, or are motivated by evil intentions, is *not* a primary criterion. The will of the limited ego personality cannot possibly be condemned to bear the burden of full moral responsibility for its actions. It is for this reason that we mostly find a striking

2. Elliot Miller, *A Crash Course on the New Age Movement* (Grand Rapids: Baker, 1989), 22.

absence in New Age sources of moral indignation even in the face of overtly evil behavior. Instead, we find, essentially, a teaching reaction: evil behavior is regarded as the regrettable outcome of spiritual *ignorance* on the part of limited egos.

It is only to be expected that people who are ignorant of their inner divinity — out of touch with their own Higher Self — would engage in negative behavior. The New Age says they should not be condemned for the products of their ignorance. They literally "do not know what they are doing." It is in this context that we should interpret, for example, Kevin Ryerson's assertion, in his discussions with Shirley MacLaine, that "there is no such thing as evil": "It doesn't exist. That's the point. Everything in life is the result of either illumination or ignorance. Those are the two polarities. Not good and evil."

According to this framework, the supreme moral task is not to do what is good and avoid evil. Rather, it is to develop one's inner divine potential. The assumption is that ethical behavior, as normally understood, will naturally result from such inner development.

The exalted Hindu channeler Ramtha chooses to speak through his channel J. Z. Knight so he can teach humanity that its present patterns of behavior are destructive, and that "there is a better way." But he immediately goes on to emphasize that this better way is ultimately dependent upon the realization that evil does not exist.

> I have returned here simply to tell you that there is a better way. And also to tell you that you are already God. And that you've never failed. And you've never done anything wrong. And you're not miserable, wretched creatures. And you're not sinners. And there is no wonderful folly called a devil. When you realize these things, you can get down to the business of being *happy* — which is what God is.

If all of ethics is to enhance evolution, why should a person have compassion on a beggar? According to Shirley MacLaine, it is only the helper, not the beggar, who "profits. . . . If I fed a starving child, and was honest about my motivation, I would have to say I did it for myself, because it made me feel better. . . . I was beginning to see that we each did whatever we did purely for self."

Hanegraaff points out that this whole line of reasoning is an exact reversal of basic Christian ethics. The New Age does not see human beings as fundamentally flawed by "sin and guilt," which makes salvation possible only by outside grace. In contrast, the belief in the existence of such flaws *is* the flaw, according to New Age thinking. Similarly, fear is not justified by reference to a God who punishes transgressions; rather, it is this very belief in a holy Creator God that *produces* the problem in the first place.

It is not surprising, therefore, that the person many regard as the most influential Christian theologian in the New Age movement, Matthew Fox, identifies the root of our present problems as the persistent influence of "fall/redemption" thinking based on the doctrine of original sin. In short, the New Age teaches that sin and guilt do not exist, but it is the belief in their existence which produces negativity. A New Ager must profoundly realize that *nobody* is sinful or guilty, including oneself. Self-forgiveness means to get rid of negative, limiting self-images. "Forgiving" is ultimately done for one's own sake.[3]

Darwin's theory of evolution deprived humans of a spiritual base. If all of life arose strictly through chance mutation and natural selection, instead of from God's creative power, human beings were deprived of a spiritual base upon which to establish their ethics, hopes, and very identity. Without challenging evolution itself, several thinkers began looking for ways to overcome the futility that Darwinian evolution seemed to impose on humanity. It forecloses ultimate meaning.

## Hegel

A number of philosophical thinkers early in the nineteenth century provided a context for the spiritualizing efforts of New Age thinkers. The view of history of German philosopher G. W. F. Hegel was one such philosophy. His view of history as God in process envisioned the world and humankind moving ever forward — by thesis, antithesis, and synthesis — to new degrees of freedom. It was not difficult to find a place for biological evolution in such a scenario. It was only necessary to add to evolution a creative principle beyond mutation and selection to guide things upward and (in some fashion) to legitimize spirituality.[4]

For Hegel, the real world is secondary to the mind, and ultimately the mind is the only reality. Hegel's stress on the concept of mind came from his belief that the particular human mind is the manifestation of the eternal mind, which in Hegel's thought is the equivalent of God. In knowing the world, the human mind creates the world, because the human mind is part of the great creative mind, or God. Hegel is therefore classified as an absolute idealist; he believes the ideas of the mind are wholly responsible for the external world.[5]

3. W. J. Hanegraaff, *New Age Religion and Western Culture* (Leiden: Brill, 1996), 278-82, 289, 295, 301.
4. Miller, *Crash Course*, 64-65.
5. D. W. Bebbington, *Patterns in History* (Downers Grove, Ill.: InterVarsity, 1979), 119.

*Process Thinkers*

Through the writings of such thinkers as Herbert Spencer, Henri Bergson, Lloyd Morgan, Samuel Alexander, Alfred North Whitehead, and, most importantly for the New Age movement, Pierre Teilhard de Chardin, a process philosophy emerged which embraced evolution as the basis for, rather than the destroyer of, humanity's spiritual aspirations.[6]

According to the early twentieth-century French writer Henri Bergson, the basic fact of all experience is change. Reality, therefore, is to be understood on the model of process and change, which is basically evolutionary. "Becoming" — not being — is the essential mark of ultimate reality. For Bergson, God is exclusively the immanent life-force. In religion, Bergson said, human beings intuitively unite themselves with the life-force.[7]

As we will see, this process view of God and history has been adopted (because they identify the world with God) by New Age thinkers. However, they have expanded the evolutionary drama of process thought into a full-blown mythology.[8]

# New Age Use of Psychology

## HUMANISTIC PSYCHOLOGY

From a psychological perspective, the concept of evolutionary transformation can be traced back to the thought of Abraham Maslow, who was instrumental during the 1960s in developing what has come to be called "humanistic psychology."[9] In Maslow's *Toward a Psychology of Being*, the thesis is that human beings have a built-in urge toward inner growth and self-transcendence.[10]

Maslow found a positive, "self-actualizing" force within each person that is struggling to assert itself. Freudian psychoanalysis seemed to make humanity a victim of instinct and social conditioning; Skinnerian behavioralism made it a pawn in an environment of biological stimulus/response. Maslow and the other pioneers of humanistic psychology wanted to restore human dignity. What they offered was a psychology that glorified the self. It pronounced people's impulses essentially good, affirmed the unfathomable depths

---

6. Miller, *Crash Course*, 65.

7. Henri L. Bergson, *Creative Evolution* (New York: Modern Library, 1944), 166-67, 182, 194.

8. Miller, *Crash Course*, 65.

9. Duncan S. Ferguson, ed., *New Age Spirituality: An Assessment* (Louisville, Ky.: Westminster/John Knox, 1993), 116.

10. Brooks Alexander, "Last Exit Before Judgement," *SCP Journal* 19.2/3 (1995): 37.

of human potential, and held out personal growth as an individual's highest goal. The affinities between the new psychology and mysticism did not go unnoticed, even by its founding fathers. Moving from past to infinite potential and from personal growth to spiritual transformation required a virtually imperceptible shift.

Maslow, for one, placed the transcendent at the top of his list of hierarchical needs. He affirmed that humanity had a transcendent dimension that needed to be satisfied before self-actualization was complete. But the human longing for the transcendent was not, for Maslow, to be met by the wholly other God of biblical revelation. In fact, the transcendent dimension of which he spoke was not in the strictest sense an "other" at all: It was that dimension of an individual which intersected with the larger and more "all-is-one" spiritual realities of the cosmos. Maslow's self-actualized person was truly a self-satisfied person, a person fulfilled, one who was full of himself.[11]

Maslow emphasized so-called "peak experiences" — mystical states of religious understanding or illumination. His concept of the peak experience prefigures the New Age notion of the "transformative" experience.[12]

Maslow uses the word "metahuman" or "B-human" (meaning Being Human) in order to stress that his becoming very high or divine or godlike is part of human nature even though it is not often seen in fact. This is a potentiality of human nature and not a gift from God. Though an atheist, Maslow invested humanity with the attributes of deity. Such a realization, he thought, would be revolutionary.[13]

## HUMAN POTENTIAL PSYCHOLOGY

From the germinal thoughts of humanistic psychology grew more developed perspectives, forming what is now called the Human Potential movement, a prime component of the New Age. Ranging from the low-key pop-psychology of transactional analysis ("I'm O.K., You're O.K.") to the myriad of encounter groups begun by Carl Rogers, the movement stressed human goodness and potential. The Esalen Institute in Big Sur, California, has been a human potential "hothouse" for over three decades. Prominent at Esalen have been Michael Murphy and George Leonard, both pioneers of the New Age movement in America.[14]

11. Karen Hoyt, *The New Age Rage* (Old Tappan, N.J.: Revell, 1988), 29-30.

12. Ferguson, *New Age Spirituality*, 116.

13. Douglas R. Groothuis, *Unmasking the New Age* (Downers Grove, Ill.: Inter-Varsity, 1986), 77; see also Abraham H. Maslow, *Religions, Values, and Peak Experiences* (New York: Viking, 1970); idem, *The Farther Reaches of Human Nature* (New York: Penguin, 1979).

14. Groothuis, *Unmasking the New Age*, 78-79.

## TRANSPERSONAL PSYCHOLOGY

A logical extension of the humanistic school is "transpersonal psychology." This approach is called "fourth force psychology" and is interested in "ultimate human capacities" not incorporated into behaviorism (first force), classical psychoanalysis (second force), or humanistic psychology (third force). Among those capacities listed are unitive consciousness, peak experience, mystical experience, self-actualization, oneness, and cosmic awareness.

According to transpersonalism, the self, when divorced from a higher, transcendent power to whom it is accountable, quickly masquerades as the Self, a treasury of all meaning, power, and wisdom. The old-fashioned secular humanist (including the orthodox Freudian or Skinnerian) said, "There is no Deity. Long live humanity." The new transpersonal or cosmic humanist says, "There is no Deity but humanity." God is pulled into the human breast. Scientific prowess and rationality as the crowning human achievements are outstripped by psychic abilities and unlimited potential.[15]

As we will note in more detail, these developments in psychology prepare for and undergird the New Age view of history.

## Union of Physics and Mysticism

Fritjof Capra, a physicist at the University of California at Berkeley, has helped to promote the New Age view of history by synthesizing Eastern mysticism and modern physics. This synthesis is emphasized in his early popular work *The Tao of Physics* (1975). In a later book entitled *The Turning Point: Science, Society, and the Rising Center,* Capra united the strange discoveries of quantum physics with the intuitions of the mystics to reveal a different world: a universe intimately interconnected, interpenetrating, interdependent, and unified — more an organism than a mechanism.[16]

### GENERAL SYSTEMS THEORY AND MONISM

Douglas Groothuis points out that Capra argues for a scientifically supported version of monism — all is one. To this end Capra also enlists the speculations of more modern physicists like David Bohm. He summarizes by saying,

> In modern physics, the image of the universe as a machine has been transcended by a view of it as one indivisible whole whose parts are

15. Ibid., 80-81.
16. Ibid., 97-99.

essentially interrelated and can be understood only as patterns of a cosmic process.[17]

Capra further elaborates on and attempts to establish his view through a discussion of general systems theory. This view was first formulated in the 1930s by Austrian-born biologist Ludwig von Bertalanffy. By the 1950s his General Systems Theory had generated an interdisciplinary movement. Moving from the microscopic world of energy particles to the macroscopic landscape, systems theory views nature as an interlocking system of various subsystems made up of cyclical feedback loops. It sees the linear and mechanistic picture of sequential cause and effect as too narrow. The full holistic mosaic must be held in view. From this perspective the earth itself becomes a living being: "Mother Earth." The various subsystems are "self-organizing" and imbued with an immanent consciousness of their own. He argues for a panoramic, panpsychic worldview in which all is one (monism) and all is alive (panpsychism).

The systems view is a sophisticated cosmology that finds the whole greater than the parts without ignoring the parts; rather, they are placed into a more comprehensive picture. Consciousness itself is not strictly localized or individuated in living beings; it extends, in varying degrees of intensity, across the universe.[18]

## PHYSICS AND PSYCHOLOGY UNITE IN MONISM

Based on this holistic metaphysic, Capra endorses a "transpersonal" psychology in which normal and paranormal consciousness both fit into the total spectrum of human experience. Capra follows the human potential movement (Maslow, Rogers, etc.) in asserting "the farther limits of human nature" as ever evolving toward higher consciousness. Here, in one grand synthesis, systems theory, mystical experience, modern physics, and adventuresome psychology all synergistically fuse into a "rising culture" whose time has finally come. A transformation is imperative. The evidence is in; civilization must turn from its error and the New Age view of history must be adopted.

## REDEMPTION OF HISTORY IN CONSCIOUSNESS

The view of Capra and other New Age scientists has given the New Age movement what proponents call "scientific" support for their belief that con-

17. Fritjof Capra, *The Turning Point: Science, Society and the Rising Culture* (New York: Simon and Schuster, 1982), 92.
18. Douglas Groothuis, "Revolutionizing Our Worldview," *The Reformed Journal*, 21.

sciousness is the essence of all reality. To change consciousness will thus change history.

In summary, according to the New Age view, the meaning and redemption of history are to be found in consciousness. An enlightened understanding of the unity and harmony of all things and of our participation in the cosmic drama will quicken our minds and engage our wills. Consciousness itself can be our savior if resurrected from the mechanistic tomb. Then we may fully experience not only our oneness with nature, but our participation with deity itself.

Groothuis affirms that this New Age mysticism permits, even encourages, a variety of occult and paranormal experiences. The sophisticated panpsychism of systems theory is a close cousin to a belief in animism. The shaman returns in scientific guise.[19]

## THE CHALLENGE TO THE BIBLICAL VIEW OF HISTORY

Groothuis points out that nothing less than a carefully formulated biblical philosophy of history and civilization will effectively counter Capra's more than four hundred pages of encyclopedic effort. Biblical thinkers need to develop an informed theology and cosmology that is conversant with modern physics and systems theory but which compromises neither the biblical teaching of immanence nor the transcendence of God. Furthermore, biblical thinkers must explore the area of consciousness research in order to develop a biblical perspective in this area and restudy the meaning of biblical mysticism in relation to its counterfeits.[20] A description of an authentic biblical mysticism is found in Chapter 4, which deals with transformation.

## PIERRE TEILHARD DE CHARDIN AND THE OMEGA POINT

Pierre Teilhard de Chardin (1881-1955), philosopher, paleontologist, theologian, and poet, never saw his ideas gain currency during his life. In recent years, his work has enjoyed a renaissance as a philosophic system in support of various New Age conceptions, especially the New Age view of history. Several central aspects of his thoughts, such as evolution toward Omega Point, the idea of the noosphere, and the inwardness of matter, have their direct counterparts in New Age teaching.

Teilhard de Chardin was born in France and trained by the Jesuits, for whom he taught physics and chemistry for several years in Egypt. In 1912 he returned to France, where he decided to undertake a career in paleontology. At this time he became a confirmed evolutionist.

19. Ibid., 21, 23.
20. Ibid., 23.

After serving as a corporal in the medical corps during World War I, Teilhard de Chardin became professor of geology at the Institut Catholique. That position was short-lived as he soon clashed with his Roman Catholic superiors. He lived and worked in China for twenty years with only occasional visits to Europe.

Things did not improve significantly upon his return to France twenty years later. During this time he lectured widely, but ecclesiastical authorities were able to keep his ideas from being published. Eventually, in 1951, he was asked to leave the country. Teilhard de Chardin went to New York, where he lived until his death in 1995.[21]

Teilhard's philosophy, according to Brooks Alexander, co-editor of the *SCP Journal*, is a form of evolutionary pantheism (all is one and all is God), dressed up in theological language. Teilhard described a process of mystical "evolution" that went beyond mere biology. The process of Evolution, he said, guided by the Higher Mind, has finally produced human beings. But now we are about to begin the next evolutionary surge. According to Teilhard, our individual units of human consciousness will begin to merge together into a higher unit of consciousness, consisting of the earth as a whole and everything in it and on it: "We are approaching a time when the whole world will link up in one interfeeling organism. Teilhard called this advent 'Omega,' the 'Christification of the Earth'. . . ."[22]

Direct quotes from Teilhard's *Christianity and Evolution* augment Alexander's view: "What I am proposing to do is to narrow that gap between pantheism and Christianity by bringing out what one might call the Christian soul of pantheism or the pantheist aspect of Christianity"; "I can be saved only by becoming one with the universe"; "I believe that the Messiah whom we await, whom we all without any doubt await, is the universal Christ; that is to say, the Christ of evolution."[23]

Robert Muller, a prominent New Age leader, affirms the view of Teilhard. In *The Birth of a Global Civilization*, Muller said that this "archaeologist and theologian" (Teilhard), after a lifetime of study of the past of our planet and of the human species, concluded that humanity would enter a New Age of evolution and metamorphose itself into a higher, more peaceful, more responsible superconscious and a spiritual global species.

In *New Genesis: Shaping a Global Spirituality*, Muller said he often heard himself being described as "Teilhardian." He admitted that ". . . now after a third of a century of service with the United Nations I can say unequivocally

21. D. Gareth Jones, *Teilhard de Chardin* (Grand Rapids: Eerdmans, 1969), 16-18.

22. Alexander, "Last Exit Before Judgement," 37.

23. Pierre Teilhard de Chardin, *Christianity and Evolution* (New York: Harcourt Brace Jovanovich, 1971), 56, 95, 128.

509

that much of what I have observed in the world bears out the all-encompassing, global, forward-looking philosophy of Teilhard de Chardin."[24]

## ALICE BAILEY AND THE ARCANE SCHOOL

The Arcane School, an offshoot of Theosophy, was founded by Alice and Foster Bailey in 1923. Many of the Arcane school's doctrines are similar to those of Theosophy, including their teaching about Ascended Masters. Alice Bailey believed she was the "mouthpiece" of a Master known as the Tibetan. She produced nineteen books as the mouthpiece of this Master. Two of her more significant books — both of which are popular among New Agers — are *The Externalization of the Hierarchy* and *The Reappearance of the Christ.*[25]

Teilhard and current New Age leaders have been greatly influenced by Alice Bailey, who wrote and taught long before the New Age movement came on the scene with its updated Cosmic Christ. Alice Bailey has been called the "mother" of the New Age movement or at least a proto–New Age movement. For example, she adapted Madame Blavatsky's theosophical teachings and shaped them into the ideological/mythological system we now call "New Age."

In the Alice Bailey writings, a "Plan" for preparing the world for the New Age and a New Age Christ is described in much detail. Bailey claimed her works were telepathically received from "the Tibetan" Djwhal Khul. Khul predicted a new world government and world religion to be galvanized by "the reappearance of the Christ." This Christ is not Jesus Christ of the Bible but an advanced member of a spiritual hierarchy whose reappearance must be summoned by "The Great Invocation," a prayer widely distributed by Bailey's followers. Bailey expected the New Age to dawn after a global crisis occurred which could be rectified only by "the Christ." But, she believed, we can offset our present futility and frustration and find incentive toward building a new world through the belief in the essential divinity of humanity. A "new world religion" will result, eclipsing traditional Christianity. And it should be noted that over the last seventy years there have been self-conscious disciples of "Master D.K.," working to further the Plan.[26]

To this day, the followers of Alice Bailey speak about the inevitable advent of a great New Age teacher. In Bailey's writings he was called "Maitreya" and "the Christ." The juxtaposition of the two titles is slightly ironic, because the name "Maitreya" comes out of the Buddhist tradition and refers to a Buddha from the future. Bailey's disciples are fond of reciting the

24. Warren Smith, "Sign of the Times," *SCP Journal* 19.2/3 (1995): 57-58.
25. Ron Rhodes, *The New Age Movement*, Zondervan Guide for Cults and Religious Movements (Grand Rapids: Zondervan, 1995), 26.
26. Groothuis, *Unmasking the New Age*, 119.

Great Invocation, which in some circles functions as the New Age counterpart of the Lord's Prayer in Christianity. The Invocation calls for, among other things, the descent of the "Light" within "the Mind of God" to earth and its dwelling in the hearts of human beings, whereby the mysterious "Plan" of the ascended hierarchy will be put into operation on earth. According to some renderings of Bailey's teaching, Maitreya as the New Age "world teacher" is what the Hindus used to call the "avatar," or incarnate divinity, for our age.[27]

One of my students at Rice University was the area director of the Bailey followers. On many occasions I heard the Great Invocation.

## BENJAMIN CREME AND THE COMING MAITREYA

In 1972, a student of Bailey's writings named Benjamin Creme started to "channel" communiqués from ascended masters. Creme believed in a singular "Second Coming" involving the individual known as Maitreya, who would take the primary leadership role in the New Age. From 1977 to the present, Creme has traveled around the world proclaiming that the coming of Maitreya (Christ) is imminent. Maitreya, says Creme, is the leader of the "Planetary Hierarchy" — a group of exalted Ascended Masters who guide humankind's spiritual evolution. Maitreya has been living incognito among human beings since 1977, when his consciousness entered a specially created humanlike body called the "Mayavirupa."

In April 1982, a full-page ad appeared in fourteen major newspapers around the world — from Rome to Jerusalem, from Kuwait to Karachi, from New York to Los Angeles — announcing that "The Christ Is Now Here." The ad, sponsored by Creme's Tara Center in Los Angeles, predicted that "within the next two months [Christ] will speak to humanity through a worldwide television and radio broadcast. His message will be heard inwardly, telepathically, by all people in their own language."

Maitreya was to deliver his message on the "Day of Declaration," after which time a new era of peace and happiness would begin. This Christ would come not as a religious, political, economic, or social leader, but as an "educationalist" who would solve all the world's problems in these areas and usher in a New Age of love, peace, and shared wealth.

Obviously 1982 has come and gone and Christ has yet to appear. The reason given for why Christ did not appear was that the media prevented it by refusing to report the event. Since the media represent humanity, the media's apathy shows the broader apathy of humanity. Creme says that since Christ's manifestation cannot occur against the wishes of humans, his coming has been delayed.

27. Ferguson, *New Age Spirituality*, 116-17.

From 1982 to 1990, Creme continued to maintain that Christ would soon reveal himself to humanity. In April 1990, the Tara Center distributed a press release saying that Maitreya presented his credentials as the Messiah before two hundred media representatives and world leaders at an April 21-22 conference in London. Creme said that conference was a prelude to the Christ's Day of Declaration, though the date for that has not been revealed.[28]

Creme still expects Maitreya to appear shortly, possibly in a worldwide television broadcast during which he will make his presence known to all peoples. Meanwhile, Creme has emphasized the development of transmission groups (for whom he authored a manual, *Transmission: A Meditation for the New Age*) and the work of sharing, the inner decision necessary for the ultimate goal of world peace.

Creme's statements served as a catalyst in raising the consciousness of the larger evangelical Christian community to the emerging New Age movement. Lawyer Constance Cumbey's *The Hidden Dangers of the Rainbow* (1983), which became an evangelical best-seller, drew a picture of the New Age movement as a giant satanic conspiracy built around Creme and the coming Maitreya. The public response to Cumbey's book forced other evangelical leaders to confront the New Age movement even as most leaders distanced themselves from Cumbey's conspiracy theory.[29]

Creme has repeatedly stated that he has met the world teacher, who he says is living incognito in the slums of London. Traditional East Asian Buddhism has taught that the "coming" of Maitreya is not a historical event, but a breakthrough illumination and wisdom on the part of the seeker. That interpretation may be more in keeping with the spirit of the New Age than Creme's somewhat literalist eschatology would imagine.[30]

## JOSÉ ARGUELLES AND THE HARMONIC CONVERGENCE

In the summer of 1987, University of Colorado art historian and New Age theoretician José Arguelles announced a major cosmic event that came to be known as the Harmonic Convergence. The episode turned out to be a major historical rallying point for the New Age movement itself. Arguelles talked to the media about ancient Mayan calendars, great beams of light from stellar sources, the unlocking of the meaning of the myth of the Mexican savior-god Quetzalcoatl, and humming and chanting by clusters of like-minded seekers around the globe in an effort to boost the "vibratory rate" of the planet.[31]

28. Rhodes, *New Age Movement,* 70-71; see also Elliot Miller, "Benjamin Creme and the Reappearance of the Christ," *Forward* 6:1, 3.
29. J. Gordon Melton, *New Age Almanac* (Detroit: Visible Ink, 1991), 316-17.
30. Ferguson, *New Age Spirituality,* 116-17.
31. Ibid., 112.

Arguelles drew on Native American prophecies in the construction of his grand occult vision. According to Arguelles's timetable, an oceanlike wave peaked on August 16-17, 1987, causing a new energy and momentum to enter into the planet's life and acting as a prelude to the true intergalactic Harmonic Convergence in 2012.

Drawing on information in a Hopi prophecy as well as in Revelation 14:3, Arguelles concluded that 144,000 persons ("enlightened teachers") should gather together at power spots around the earth to meditate, chant, and visualize. This would ensure the earth's safe passage into the year 2012, the final stage of transformation.

As *The Mayan Factor* circulated through the New Age community and interviews with Arguelles were printed in the New Age press, excitement built. He was eventually noticed by the mainstream news media.[32]

One of the indirect results of the Harmonic Convergence was a sudden rise in interest within the New Age community in visits to the planet's "sacred sites" — places of "high energy" from the geomagnetic standpoint that had been the destination for religious pilgrimages and vision quests for untold centuries among the earth's indigenous peoples, including Native Americans. A sizable number of New Age votaries spent the days of the Convergence at Chaco Canyon in New Mexico and buried crystals in the ground in order to help "attune" the planet's vibratory patterns.

The underlying belief among those celebrating the Convergence was that concerted conscious action on a planetary scale would not only lead to peace and a reduction in political tension, but it would also empower hundreds of thousands of individuals in their quests for personal wholeness and self-understanding. Some celebrators of the Convergence also made love with each other in order to assist in the new vibratory alignment of Mother Earth.[33] Some New Agers even traveled to Egypt and to Machu Picchu, Peru, to participate amid metaphysically charged ancient pyramids. Thousands of people, including such celebrities as actress Shirley MacLaine, singer John Denver, and LSD guru Timothy Leary, participated. Arguelles later estimated that more than 144,000 persons had taken part in Harmonic Convergence activity.

Because the Harmonic Convergence was seen as the beginning of a period of radical transformation which called for action, several groups have attempted to continue the Harmonic Convergence emphasis.[34]

32. Melton, *New Age Almanac*, 369.
33. Ferguson, *New Age Spirituality*, 112-13.
34. Melton, *New Age Almanac*, 369-70.

## The New Age Use of Politically Oriented Leaders

Robert Muller is a veteran of leadership positions within the United Nations and is still an important presence at the U.N. and often represents the U.N. at significant gatherings. At the World Parliament of Religions held in Chicago in 1993, Muller gave a plenary address entitled "Interfaith Understanding." In his address, Muller emphasized his New Age philosophy. "There is one sign after the other, wherever you look, that we are on the eve of a New Age which will be a spiritual age. . . . We are on the eve of a new spiritual renaissance." Muller substantiated his claim of a coming renaissance by referring to an article in the Dalai Lama bulletin citing the predictions of astrologers that 1993 would be a turning point in human history.[35]

In his speeches, Muller announces an impending "cosmic age" wherein we will become "the planet of God." He sees humankind on a universal scale "seeking no less than its reunion with the 'divine,' its transcendence into ever higher forms of life." He then commends the Hindus, who "rightly see no difference between our earth and the divine." The United Nations, he believes, has been and will be a decisive catalyst for global transformation.[36]

Muller, more recently the chancellor emeritus of the University for Peace in Costa Rica, continues to be active in U.N. affairs. He also oversees several Robert Muller Schools. These schools are based on a World Core Curriculum that Muller authored in its skeletal form. The World Core Curriculum is now being uniformly introduced into public schools throughout the world. In the preface to *The Robert Muller School World Core Curriculum Manual* the reader is told, "the underlying philosophy upon which the Robert Muller School is based will be found in the teachings set forth in the books of Alice A. Bailey by the Tibetan teacher, Djwhal Khul. Bailey's *Education in the New Age* is also quoted in the preface.

The purpose of the curriculum is to provide students with a "global education" so they can assume their "correct place in the universe" as "true planetary citizens."[37]

## BARBARA MARX HUBBARD

Barbara Hubbard, futurist and New Age visionary, was born in 1929 in Washington, D.C., the daughter of Rene Saltzman and Louis Marx, the toy manufacturer. She described her family as a Jewish agnostic one from which she received no spiritual training as a child.

35. Smith, "Sign of the Times," 57.
36. Groothuis, *Unmasking the New Age*, 120.
37. Smith, "Sign of the Times," 56.

Hubbard's awakening to a new life was occasioned by three discoveries. First, Abraham Maslow's *Toward a Psychology of Being* taught her of real needs beyond mere subsistence, and she came to understand her problem as one of unused growth potential. Second, from Teilhard de Chardin's *Phenomenon of Man*, she learned that the world also has unused growth potential and that personal growth and planetary growth are parallel phenomena. Third, the new insights from Maslow and de Chardin were brought together for her by John Glenn's space flight, which led to a vision of the human race as a universal species possessed of a technology of transcendence. She became convinced that her generation stood on the threshold of a New Age. Some of her early insights were put into her first book, *The Search Is On* (1969), which was written with her husband, Earl Hubbard.

Barbara Hubbard became convinced not only that a New Age was imminent, but that humankind had to take control of the future and plan and direct it. To give visible expression to her insights, she formed the Committee for the Future in 1970. The committee began to hold conferences and create networks of future-oriented leaders.

During the last two decades, Hubbard has become one of the major spokespersons of the New Age movement and of the goals of the urgency of planetary consciousness.[38]

She waged a campaign for the 1984 Democratic vice-presidential nomination, but a New Age newsletter, "Renewal," lamented that "the transformational synthesis has yet to guide the voting behavior of a U.S. Senator or Representative."

Barbara Hubbard is an influential exponent of the New Age view of history. According to Brooks Alexander, she is influential because she has a great deal of money to put behind her deep New Age views (she is heiress to the fabulous Marx toy fortune and receives funding from one of Laurence Rockefeller's Foundations). She is controversial because she has clearly stated that classical Christianity and its believers are unfit to enter the New Age, and that both will therefore have to be extinguished before the New Age can properly begin. In support of her convictions, she teaches a dynamic mixture of evolutionary mysticism and her own "inner voice" of revelation that claims to come from "Christ" himself.[39]

Hubbard has expressed some of her views in her treatment of the book of Revelation. It has been published in a full-color, oversize paperback edition that is widely available in bookstores across the country. It is simply *The Revelation: Our Crisis Is a Birth*. Hubbard and her "Christ voice" claim that the book of Revelation's picture of judgment and suffering is only one

38. Melton, *New Age Almanac*, 410.
39. Alexander, "Last Exit Before Judgement," 32.

possible outcome of our "evolutionary moment of opportunity." We won't actually have to undergo those trials and tribulations unless we resist the urge to evolve. According to the "voice," the book of Revelation presents only one option among many; it is nothing more than a worst-case scenario, described in all its awfulness, as an incentive for us to wise up and choose the better path.

Barbara and her "Christ voice" not only claim that there are several versions of the future before us, but they plainly say that the version of the future we actually get depends on which one we hope for and concentrate on.

According to Hubbard, anyone who forms an expectation of the future based on the "negative" scenario of the book of Revelation and concentrates on that outcome contributes to the likelihood that it will come about. And that makes that person an obstacle to the coming of the New Age. Thus, believing Christians who take the Bible at face value become, by definition, enemies of evolution, hinderers of the New Age, and barriers to the fulfillment of human happiness.

## NEGATIVISM OF CHRISTIANS

In her discussion of the book of Acts, Hubbard states: "There is an anti-evolutionary cadre of orthodox Christian believers who focus on the limits of this life and the unworthiness of human nature. Now they would destroy our capacity to transcend. . . . These people unwittingly kill ideas. Unaware of our evolutionary potential, they prevent the action and response needed to transcend the terrestrial phase of our existence. They would annihilate the possibility of Universal Humanity by claiming we have no right to achieve it."

What is to be done with such "negative" people? According to Hubbard, the advent of the New Age depends on total consensus. The world will be perfect when everyone agrees that it should be and is. Humankind will be perfect when everyone agrees together to ascend to the next level of existence and *be* perfect. Those who refuse to merge with the collective mind thereby dilute our unity. People like that are just so much sand in the gears of evolution. By one means or another, she explains, they will have to disappear before we can fully enter into our divine potential. Evolution allows no dissidents. The penalty for resisting new consciousness evolution is extinction.

As one can see, Hubbard's view of history weaves together many different threads of gnostic, occult, anti-Christian thought.[40]

40. Ibid., 46-49.

## MARILYN FERGUSON

Marilyn Grasso Ferguson is one of the major theoreticians of the New Age movement. She was born in 1938 in Grand Junction, Colorado. She believes that at the deepest levels of society there is an underlying shift occurring in the values which dominate people's actions. This is accompanied by a shift in the manner in which people view reality. She derives her basic picture of the perceived shift from applying Thomas Kuhn's understanding of paradigm shifts in science to the broader social setting.

Five years of observation on the changes in society led to the 1980 publication of Ferguson's *The Aquarian Conspiracy*. The book, which quickly became a best-seller, has been accepted more than any other single book as a consensus statement of the New Age perspective. In the book's often quoted opening paragraphs, Ferguson describes what most people take to be the New Age movement in its broadest terms — a decentralized network of people who have idealistic, even mystical, ideals and have forsaken the past for a new world. Their numbers are large, far larger than may be supposed because of their invisibility, but they share a bonding because somehow each of them has experienced an inner transformation. The personal transformations led these people to believe that they could change society, and so they began to work in often quiet but effective ways in society's large institutions. Ferguson describes the emerging new movement in terms of "universal connectedness," with reference to the concept of "Segmented Polycentric Integrated Networks," or SPINs.[41]

*The Aquarian Conspiracy* offers its own expansive Wal-Mart of options for "personal change." It lists self-hypnosis, transcendental meditation, Sufi dancing, dream journals, the science of mind religion, mountain climbing and wilderness retreats, all the martial arts, humanistic psychotherapies, New Age music, pottery, biofeedback, LSD, the Congressional Clearinghouse for the Future, quantum physics, the U.S. Army, self-help networks, hospices for the dying, herbalism, Elderhostels, free universities, Tibetan Buddhism, Werner Erhard's hunger project, and the Unity Church as significant instances or players in the "Aquarian Conspiracy."

Even though all these seemingly disparate institutions or activities may not at one level seem connected, in Ferguson's survey they become "invisible beginnings" of a "revolution in consciousness" that leads to a "transformation of society."[42]

---

41. Melton, *New Age Almanac*, 400.
42. Ferguson, *New Age Spirituality*, 118.

## SIGNIFICANCE OF FERGUSON'S WRITINGS

Miller contends that Ferguson's writing has probably done more to promote New Age ideology on a popular level than any other single book. It provides an overview of a vast array of contemporary ideas and activities, and suggests that they may all be converging to produce a far-reaching social transformation — the "New Age."[43]

The New Age for Ferguson signals a transformation so radical that it may amount to an entirely new phase in evolution. By providing the movement with an optimistic view of itself, the book by Ferguson has probably done more to substantiate a sense of identity and vision for the New Age movement than has any other single event.

By the mid-1980s, *The Aquarian Conspiracy* had been translated into eleven foreign languages. The book became the focus of attacks by evangelical Christians, who used the idea of the "conspiracy" to create an image of the New Age as a satanic conspiracy.[44] Hubbard says there is a conspiracy, but it is a "conspiracy without political doctrine. Without a manifesto." The collusion she claims is one of shared assumptions rather than centralized planning.

Russell Chandler, of the *Los Angeles Times,* points out that it seems inconsistent to assume that such an unstructured, effervescent collection of movements and ideas embraced by the term "New Age" could be part of some gigantic, centralized conspiracy against the church headed by Satan.

A more moderate view is expressed by Douglas Groothuis in *Unmasking the New Age:* "The New Age movement is better viewed as a worldview shift than a unified global conspiracy. This is not to minimize its influence but to recognize it as an intellectual, spiritual, and cultural force to be reckoned with.

David Burnett, of WEC International, who agrees with both Chandler and Groothuis, considers the New Age movement as a paradigm shift resulting from a synthesis of themes. What we see with the New Age movement is the evolution of a new worldview based upon a joining together of Eastern and primal worldviews with the secular.[45]

But it should be noted that the New Age movement is part of a gathering social and cultural transformation that is increasingly coherent and increasingly hostile to Christianity.

43. Miller, *Crash Course,* 56.
44. Melton, *New Age Almanac,* 401.
45. David Burnett, *Clash of Worlds* (Eastbourne: MARC, 1990), 183-84.

## Optimistic Evolution

As we have seen, mystical spiritual evolution is central in the New Age view of history. For the New Age view, evolution is God in process; hence, mystical evolution is sometimes assigned a place in their world similar to that which the biblical God occupies for the Christian. According to Miller, without such faith in mystical evolution, the New Age view would be incapable of maintaining its distinctive optimism.

New Age leaders have a historic sense in some respects comparable to that found in some Christian circles: this generation may stand at the threshold of history's consummation. British science writer and New Age advocate Peter Russell affirms that "the majority of human beings now alive may experience an evolutionary shift from ego-centered awareness to a unified field of shared awareness."[46]

### "PUNCTUATED EQUILIBRIUM"

Even the gruesome developments of recent history have not deterred New Age optimism. Marilyn Ferguson describes the new model which the New Age view of history has adapted. Punctuationalism, or "punctuated equilibrium," suggests that the equilibrium of life is interrupted from time to time by severe stress. A crisis in a species's environment can disturb its "stasis," or equilibrium, and trigger rapid and radical evolutionary change.

The theory of punctuated equilibrium has thus been used to provide the New Age view of history with a positive context within which to interpret the negative realities of the world scene — a new world may be in the throes of birth.

Elliot Miller questions whether punctuated equilibrium can convert humanity's current megacrisis into an evolutionary leap forward. It should be noted first that even a serious punctuationalist would derive little hope from the fantastic New Age application of this hypothesis. Second and more importantly, punctuated equilibrium is not at all established as a scientific theory. Even many evolutionary scientists reject the model. *Newsweek* observed in 1980 that punctuated equilibrium is a point of bitter contention among geneticists and biologists.[47]

## New Age Vision of a Global Civilization

New Age leaders maintain that the New Age view will help humankind to reach the first global civilization. Robert Muller describes this development

46. Miller, *Crash Course*, 65-66.
47. Ibid., 68, 85.

519

by using the metaphor of the human brain. Each person, young or old, able-bodied or handicapped, is an important neuron in the emerging planetary brain that is constituted by the myriad "networkings" among people. The result is the nation of all humanity evolving into a single consciousness or civilization or oneness.[48]

## PLANETARY CONSCIOUSNESS

Planetary Consciousness is a perspective on life that became a benchmark of the New Age movement in the 1980s. It is a worldview that emphasizes loyalty to the community of humanity rather than local loyalties to nation, tribe, or other social groups.

The seminal idea for the concept grew out of the world federation and one-world government movements of the early twentieth century. Planetary consciousness, however, has moved away from the federationist focus upon political structures and concentrated instead on transcultural bonding in human relationships. The well-known pictures of the earth taken by the astronauts from space, which reveal the artificiality of human social boundaries, have become symbolic of the planetary vision. Merged with New Age visions and holistic health concerns, the concepts of planetary transformation and healing have emerged as guiding ideals for future action.

An important spokesperson of planetary consciousness has been William Irwin Thompson, who taught at Massachusetts Institute of Technology and York University in Canada, then left academic life. He traveled throughout the world, visiting such sites as the Findhorn Community, Auroville, and the ancient monastery at Lindisfarne. In 1972 he authored what has become a classic statement of planetary consciousness, *Passages about Earth*.[49]

Another prominent leader of the Planetary Consciousness movement is Donald Keys, a longtime consultant to the United Nations. This movement has also attracted such New Age luminaries as David Spangler and Peter Caddy (both formerly of the Findhorn community), futurist Willis Harman, former astronaut Edgar Mitchell, and Michael Murphy of Esalen Institute.

Humanity, says Keys, is evolving toward Omega, or the unification of consciousness and culture. Keys says that New Consciousness communities like Findhorn and growth centers like Esalen will lead the passage to planetization and will provide the "myths which will form and inform the emergent world order." According to Keys, the flagship of planetization is the United States.

Keys asserts that we are "already in the midst of the final planetary revolution" where "human consciousness is moving on to become a continuous,

48. Ibid., 70.
49. Melton, *New Age Almanac*, 425-26.

non-segmented medium" that will "become the normal moral medium for the new politics of the planet."[50]

### Worldwide Networking

Within the New Age movement, a constant attempt has been made to distinguish the new alternative society from that which New Agers hope is being left behind. In seeking to live as if the New Age is coming, advocates have consciously created new organizational patterns. They see the old aeon as one which was dominated by hierarchical top-heavy organizations, while the New Age will be one typified by egalitarian organizational forms such as co-ops and communes. According to Gordon Melton, the single most important New Age organizational form is the network.

A network is a very loose structure of people and organizations related to each other by a shared interest, connected primarily by a mailing list or directory with names, addresses, and phone numbers.

In this age of computers and information, networks have gained new prominence. The necessity and ease of linking resources to people, and of bringing individuals into contact with people of similar backgrounds, interests, and concerns, has reached a new height.[51] John Perry Barlow, a technovisionary, sees the eventual coming of a cosmic mind presaged even in something as pedestrian as e-mail:

> Watching e-mail messages come and go can give you a holy sense of mission. It's synaptic firing, across the web of a slowly evolving nervous system. In a couple of hundred years, every synapse on this planet will be continuously and seamlessly connected to every other synapse on the planet. One great wad of mind.

More recently Jean Houston, a New Age consciousness researcher, states that she frequently uses the Internet to converse with New Agers around the world. "It's an extraordinary confluence of consciousness. Teilhard's noosphere is alive and well."

According to Groothuis, a large number of technopagans are tapping into cyberspace as a realm for mystical discovery, magical powers, and evolutionary advancement. The use of cyberspace for these ends is often called technoshamanism. Although it is not an organized movement, technoshamanism represents a growing cultural trend to deify cyberspace.[52]

New Ager Marilyn Ferguson says networking takes place through

50. Hoyt, *New Age Rage,* 94.
51. Melton, *New Age Almanac,* 416.
52. Douglas Groothuis, *The Soul in Cyberspace* (Grand Rapids: Baker, 1997), 109-10.

"conferences, phone calls, air travel, books, phantom organizations, papers, pamphleteering, photocopying, lectures, workshops, parties, grapevines, mutual friends, summit meetings, coalitions, tapes, and newsletters."[53]

New Agers also exercise their political muscle through networking by joining together and pooling their efforts to influence the political process at a grassroots level.

The very existence of these networks creates an image within the New Age community of a growing movement that is permeating mainstream society, and of a public, far beyond the boundaries of the movement itself, which is participating in the creation of the New Age without knowing it.

### The Asian Influence

The development of networks of people interested in spiritual and social transformation in the late 1960s was an important, if not the most important, element in giving the scattered leaders of the New Age some awareness that they did not stand alone. Networks provided the geographically scattered New Age groups some sense of community. That sense of community was especially enlarged by the influx of Asian teachers into Europe after World War II and into the United States after the 1965 passage of a new immigration law. These Asian teachers began to establish centers of primarily young adult converts to Hinduism and Buddhism.

As the early New Age leaders began to travel throughout Great Britain, continental Europe, and North America, they encountered these new Asian centers. People attracted to an Asian teacher moved freely among all of the emerging groups, sampling each new guru and discovering the older occult and metaphysical organizations. Among these young converts to the new Asian faiths and members of the older metaphysical faiths, the New Age leaders found the greatest response to the idea of participation in the building of the New Age, and the earliest networks created by the New Age consisted of lists of these Asian and occult/metaphysical centers.

## DIRECTORIES AND PERIODICALS

In 1972 the first recognizable, professionally prepared New Age directories of the kind, which were to set the boundaries of the emerging New Age movement, were published. These were book-length volumes, each generated with the backing of one of the new Asian religions.

About the same time the first networking periodicals emerged. The

---

53. Marilyn Ferguson, *The Aquarian Conspiracy* (Los Angeles: Tarcher, 1980), 62-63.

initial copies were little more than primitive newsletters which carried announcements of New Age events and advertisements for groups with ongoing programs. By the mid-1970s they were superseded by a set of tabloid-size newspapers, most produced quarterly and directed, as were the originals, to a single metropolitan area. By the mid-1980s, almost every metropolitan area in North America had its own free New Age periodical/guide.

The New Age community depends upon networks as the major tool in keeping the movement connected. Given the mobility of the community, the number of directories will also increase, since they must be constantly revised.[54]

## The Importance of Discernment

Miller suggests that because agendas can at times overlap, it is conceivable that New Age and biblical advocates might cooperate on some issues. But when they do, discernment is crucial. For example, the evolutionary and "paradigm shift" models for interpreting the development of history make it appear self-evident that humanity will eventually embrace the New Age belief system. Therefore, a "pluralistic society" would no longer seem necessary.

Furthermore, the New Age understanding of "conscious evolution" makes it the moral duty of government and citizens alike to contribute to the New Age and the growth of Gaia, the living planet. Such concepts, according to Barbara Hubbard, leave no room for the separation of church and state, and would make resisting the New Age a serious offense. The biblical view could be considered anti-evolutionary: a threat to the global unity necessary for racial survival.[55]

New Age hopes are grounded entirely in human potential, the divine within, and the One for all. Once this psychic beast is unleashed, New Agers say, the world will change. The new mind will make a new world — as soon as the old mind is overthrown.

In contrast, the biblical worldview affirms that political realism must begin with the realization that human beings are sinners. New Agers place their hope in human potential, which is viewed as good and trustworthy. The New Age equates sin with ignorance, believing we can rid ourselves of such ignorance when we accept the enlightenment of pantheism, the idea that all is one.

The biblical view sees such New Age enlightenment as a deceptive counterfeit. The only way to permanent change is to recognize the reality of

54. Melton, *New Age Almanac*, 416-18, 420.
55. Miller, *Crash Course*, 121-22.

sin and the need of redemption through Jesus Christ. All detours around the centrality of Christ crash on the brutal rocks of reality.[56]

## The Biblical Meaning of History

As we will see, the biblical view offers an alternative to the New Age approach. The main question, however, is whether some Christian advocates are still too entrenched in Enlightenment culture to provide an authentic statement of the biblical view of history.

In place of this Christian entrenchment, we need to understand and commit ourselves to a radically comprehensive biblical view of history.

### PRINCIPLES OF THE BIBLICAL VIEW OF HISTORY

Following Brian Walsh of Toronto, N. T. Wright and Alister McGrath of England, and other advocates of the evangelical view, we will list some basic features or principles of the biblical approach to history:

#### Creation, the Fall, and Redemption

The biblical approach to history understands creation, the Fall, and redemption in comprehensive terms. All of reality is creaturely and all of creation is distorted by human disobedience and revolt against God. This situation calls for Jesus Christ to come to restore all things. Consequently, the biblical worldview is truly a *worldview* — all of reality falls within its compass. Since Christ is so crucial to humankind's future, an important and dominant part of the function of God's people and the churches is direct missionary and evangelistic sharing of the resources for restoration in Christ.[57]

#### Rejection of Dualism

The biblical view of history rejects dualism, which is rooted in Neoplatonism and Far Eastern philosophies. This dualistic view undercuts or short-circuits the dynamics of the biblical view by privatizing the biblical faith, thereby failing to grasp or be grasped by the world-transforming power of a biblical worldview.

56. Hoyt, *New Age Rage,* 101.
57. Walsh, "Worldviews, Modernity," 26; cf also Brian J. Walsh and J. Richard Middleton, *The Transforming Vision: Shaping a Christian World View* (Downers Grove, Ill.: InterVarsity, 1984), 41-90.

### Goodness of God's Creation

The biblical view is rooted in the goodness of God's creation. People who follow the Bible are to love, protect, and heal the creation because it is God's, not ours — the work of his wise and loving hand and the object of his redeeming work. Wanton destruction of ecosystems is not only unwise, but also a sin against the Creator and an undercutting of the biblical teaching of the significance and implications of the redemption achieved at the cross.[58]

### Satan, Sin, and Idolatry

The biblical view of history is rooted in the biblical understanding of sin and idolatry. Those who do not return to the Creator are in Adam. Such rebellion and self-idolatry result in death — personally, spiritually, and culturally.

The biblical view of history has an apocalyptic concept which recognizes the reality and continuing power of evil and Satan in history and anticipates their defeat. However, the New Testament teaches that Satanic forces continue to have a measure of substantial control in the world.

Though Christ's triumph through the Cross and the Resurrection and the coming of the Holy Spirit is a decisive triumph, a once-for-all victory, it does not immediately issue in the abolition of rebellion at the human or cosmic level. As the apostle John saw, the powers of this world are passing away, but they still constitute a power with which one must deal.

### The End Times

Elliot Miller, editor of the *Christian Research Journal,* points out that some sectors of conservative Christianity appear obsessed with the study of biblical prophecy relating to the end times. Scenarios are continually constructed and revised to show how current world events will shortly lead to the last great battle of Armageddon and the end of history.

It is not surprising that when those looking for signs of the end of the world discovered the New Age movement, they viewed it as ominous. Also, because some Christians see the New Age movement in terms of a sign of the end, several important moral and social issues that the New Age raises which should be considered by the church are ignored.[59]

In 1983 Constance E. Cumbey, a semi-retired lawyer from Detroit, in her book *Hidden Dangers of the Rainbow* contended that the New Age move-

58. Ibid.
59. Miller, *Crash Course,* 129.

ment is a sinister conspiracy led by Satan to take over the world. In so doing, both Christians and Jews would be eliminated and the universal worship of the Antichrist established. This so-called conspiracy theory was further developed by Texe Marrs, a retired U.S. Air Force officer, in his books *Dark Secrets of the New Age* and *Mysterious Mark of the New Age*.

Cumbey, Marrs, and other writers have tried to link biblical prophecy, particularly Daniel and Revelation, to New Age objectives. Their books have alerted many Christians to the reality of the New Age movement. However, their explanations have given an extreme and almost fanatical exposure of any seeming New Age influences.[60]

According to *SCP Journal* (Spiritual Counterfeits) staff writers, this conspiracy assumption tends to rationalize biblical prophecy. It uses Scripture as a picture of predictive detail rather than as a standard for discernment. At its base is a misunderstanding of apocalyptic prophecy and a misapplication of apocalyptic imagery.

### Teachings of the Book of Revelation

John's Apocalypse has much to say about specific events, and it predicts them in some detail. Nevertheless, its descriptions must be interpreted and applied in the light of the book's basic message. The book of Revelation is less revealing about the details of history than it is about the nature of history. It tells us that:

1. History is governed by God. His purposes are secure despite the turmoil of conflict. God triumphs not only over history but in history.

2. History has a climax. It has an end. It is not eternal or cosmically repetitive.

3. As history moves toward its end, there will be a final intensification of the fundamental conflict that pervades all of history. Conflict will be with us until the end of history because, in a fallen world, history is full of conflict.

This is a prophecy of the future, and it is clear that at some point this evil will manifest itself concretely in history, in a form as pure as that which the apostle John foresaw. The book of Revelation is also a commentary on the present: The spirit of Antichrist is always with us; its diluted influence can be discerned in many evil developments.

At times the spirit of Antichrist is stronger than at others. John's day was such a time; our own day is another. In times like these, the structure and dynamics of human society will more and more resemble the pure form of evil depicted in the Apocalypse. In John's time, this trend was eventually reversed. In our time, the issue is yet to be resolved.

60. Burnett, *Clash of Worlds*, 183.

In any case, the prophetic books of the Bible give us a scale of comparison by which we can evaluate any historical period, including our own. It will give us discernment of current events, but it will not give us the details of their development. The Bible is not so much a device for divination as a tool for discernment.[61]

The Spiritual Counterfeits staff writers admit that the conspiracy tradition is intriguing and suggestive. Sometimes it contains an element of truth. But the literature of "Conspiracy Apocalyptic" illegitimately mixes theological concepts with rationalistic speculations about human affairs.

## Postmillennialism and Reconstructionism

Miller points out that some Christians who do not share this obsession with the end of the world are ready to dispense with an "end-time" analysis of current events. A growing number have been attracted to the postmillennial teachings of the "Christian Reconstruction" movement. Its teachers (such as R. J. Rushdoony, Gary North, and David Chilton) affirm that the church is destined to conquer the world for Christ — both spiritually and politically — before he returns. Thus social and political involvement is understood to be part of the Great Commission to "make disciples of all the nations." The biblical basis utilized for social and political development is called postmillennialism and theonomy (the doctrine that the law of Moses is binding on all governments).[62]

### PREMILLENNIAL RESPONSE

It is undoubtedly true that both at the Tower of Babel and today we find an effort to realize humanity's collective potential for greatness apart from the redemption and rule of the sovereign God. By its all-out effort to overcome the global crisis by affirming human autonomy and self-sufficiency (the desire of which caused humanity to fall in the first place: Gen. 3:4-6) rather than by repenting before God, the New Age movement fits into the biblical eschatological scenario of self-centered, nonrepentant humanity. Although some conservative Christians have exaggerated this point, there are striking correspondences between it and a legitimate premillennial, futurist interpretation of biblical prophecy which sees the spiritual rebellion of humanity as an end-time sign.[63]

---

61. Hoyt, *New Age Rage,* 198-99.
62. Miller, *Crash Course,* 129-30.
63. Ibid., 132-34.

According to the historical-premillennial approach, the biblical view would state that each succeeding year brings us closer to the climax of history about which Revelation speaks. It is easy to see why many people today believe that the evils described in Revelation are increasing in our time. Humans possess an increasing ability to destroy themselves and their world by the powers of nature which they have harnessed. Legislation and diplomacy and conferences have not been able to get into the hearts of people permanently. In other words, the world process has accelerated greatly in the last fifty years. The Bible describes a climax when humankind asserts its independence of God under the leadership of one genius, the beast, and when God decides to reveal his ultimate authority through Christ, the Redeemer and Conqueror.

The historical premillennial interpretation of Revelation is taught by many outstanding evangelical scholars. If this view is correct, then the growth of good and evil will tend to keep pace with each other. As the gospel reaches to the uttermost parts of the earth, rebellion against it will become even more widespread. It is also true that much of the growth of the churches is based on a superficial type of Christianity which can be called a defection or renunciation of the faith.[64]

A biblical balance on how Christians relate to government can be found in passages like Romans 13:1-7 and Revelation 18:1-3 and 9-10. The apocalyptic viewpoint, which is developed especially in times of radical change and persecution, does not dominate the Old or New Testaments. More characteristic is the prophetic emphasis of the Old Testament and the view of Jesus and Paul. So, for the Christian, a pessimism regarding the world which releases the Christian community from responsibility for the world is not possible. God has not withdrawn himself, but he is able and will do signs and wonders for which we must diligently look and expectantly wait. Our responsibility is here and now, and there must be no evasion of it.

Evil and good continue to exist side by side. Conflict between the two continues. However, since Christ has won the victory, the ultimate outcome of the conflict is never in doubt. The enemy is fighting a losing battle.

## BIBLICAL EMPHASIS ON ALTERNATIVE LIVING

We need to recognize that in some respects the rise of the New Age movement is a criticism of Christian churches for their undiscerning identification with society's status quo and Christians' failure to take a prophetic view of social matters. New Agers are filling a "service void" — meeting needs in areas the church has neglected.[65]

---

64. John P. Newport, *The Lion and the Lamb* (Nashville: Broadman, 1986), 212.
65. Miller, *Crash Course*, 137-38.

The biblical view of history calls for positive and alternative ways of living that follow the revealed wisdom of God. The revealed biblical norms lead to the fulfillment and healing of life. Consequently, in place of economic self-interest, Christians will strive for an economics of sharing and care. Competitive individualism is replaced by community cooperation. An economics of exploitation gives way to an economics of stewardship. Unceasing economic growth is replaced by a contented lifestyle of "enough." And in the face of an oppressive politics of power and control, Christians will seek justice through service and cross-bearing.[66]

## BIBLICAL WORSHIP AND COMMUNITY

One way to discover and follow these revealed biblical norms is through the creation of authentic Christian community and worship. It is important to maintain the epic biblical drama in worship because it enables modern-day Christians to avoid both pragmatism, the bending of religion to fit personal goals, and psychological manipulation. Following the epic drama of the Bible in worship should help to establish a foundation which is objective and God-oriented, rather than just subjective and human-oriented.

## BALANCE BETWEEN MISSION AND MANDATE

The church following biblical guidelines has both a spiritual mission and a cultural mandate. Its primary goal is to bring the glad tidings of reconciliation and redemption to all races and nations, but it is also responsible for teaching people to be disciples of Christ in the very midst of the world's plight and dereliction.

It therefore follows that while Christian ethics has a personal and interior dimension, it must also have a public and exterior proclamation arising from Jesus' authority and based upon his conquest. This proclamation is the gospel of Christ, whose rule is not postponed to the chronological end of the age, but has even now begun. The chief purpose of New Testament teaching on the last things of history is not to encourage speculative fascination with world politics but, rather, to compel a deep and unremitting commitment to both evangelistic and ethical action in the world.

People who follow the Bible must steer clear of both a theocracy, where the church actively wields political power, and a rationalistic, egalitarian democracy, where the voice of the people is equated with the voice of God. Democracy in the Christian context is based on the axiom that all people are equal before God — all are created in his image and all have sinned and fallen

66. Walsh, "Worldviews, Modernity," 28.

short of his glory. We need today a democracy anchored in theonomy, in which ultimate authority is assigned to the living God rather than to the nation or religious institutions.

## GOD'S SOVEREIGNTY

Undergirding the biblical view of history is the concept of divine sovereignty. The idea of sovereignty emphasizes that Almighty God continues his activity in history despite the power and work of the Evil One. God plows up the soil of humanity, making it ready for the seed of authentic Christianity and an appreciation of God's revealed creational, ethical way of life. We should not be surprised that a Christless or even anti-Christian autonomy and ideology threaten to disintegrate life. However, these forces are repeatedly limited, held back, or turned back by the positive signs of Christ's reign in the world. This fact should constantly fill us with gratitude and amazement, giving us power to enter the future without fear and with the expectation of seeing new signs.

The Bible states that God used Assyria, Babylon, and Persia to discipline the Hebrew people and bring them back to his redemptive purposes. Later he used Rome and Greece to prepare for the ministry of Jesus and for the mission of Paul at the "kairotic," or key, time in history.

In our era, which is surely one of the most dramatic periods in human history, God is plowing up the soil of humankind in Asia, Africa, the former Soviet Union, Eastern Europe, South America, and even the United States, making it ready for the seed of the gospel.

## "ALREADY–NOT YET"

Christians understand the activity of God to be both *linear,* or sequential, and *particular.* The *linear* dimension is an ongoing process of divine action in history which reached a climax in the Christ event and will culminate in an act of final divine self-revelation and triumph. The *particular* dimension is the providential action of God between the first and second comings of Christ. Meaning does not wait for the final curtain — it exists in each line of the script.[67]

The impact of the nature of God is both through time and at each point in time. God's nature leads to activity that is positively directed to the benefit of the world and in particular to the rescue of men and women from their disastrous tendency to self-destruction. The name given to this divine

---

67. Hugh Montefiore, ed., *The Gospel and Contemporary Culture* (London: Mowbray, 1992), 31-32.

commitment is "grace." Again it is sequential — evidenced in the centuries of preparation for the coming of Jesus Christ, the Son of God, his life, death, and resurrection, and his ongoing life in the Church. Again, too, grace is immediate. It is experienced in particular instances and is in principle available in every circumstance.

The Christian church stands between the dawning of the Kingdom with power in the cross and resurrection and the coming of the Holy Spirit and its full consummation in the *parousia*, or second coming of Christ. Further, the church's preaching is not just a demonstration that the Kingdom has come with power. This preaching and witness is a precondition for the final glorious unveiling of the Kingdom. The full consummation cannot be made manifest until all nations have heard the good news. The Kingdom is already being realized in history. However, the full realization awaits the accomplishment of God's plan for the world mission.

Of course, the biblical view of history has a constant backward look. It has its basis and justification in God's central and decisive act in Jesus of Nazareth — in his life, death, and resurrection.

But the biblical perspective faces not so much backward as forward. With the risen Lord, the Christian faces forward and moves forward to the full realization at the end of the age. This means that Christians live with tension. The time of the church is the time in which God has begun his decisive redemption but has not yet fully completed it. This redemptive time must move forward under the lordship of Christ until the day when Christ comes to complete his work. Thus, the New Testament never floats off into the stratosphere of timelessness to seek there a perfect bliss.

In fact, the Christian understanding of the movement of history toward its climax helps to explain the dynamic of the early church. We should have a sense of spiritual responsibility. We should have moral courage that does not worry about immediate practical results. We should have incentive.

The "not yet" emphasis in the New Testament puts us in touch by way of the Spirit with the future. Our anchor is lodged in the "not yet," and our life is given direction and firmness. In the New Testament, the final hope remains as an undergirding emphasis. The church is, however, a colony of heaven, and the heavenly life may be enjoyed here and now. The New Testament is concerned with the present life in Christ, in the church and in the world.

An authentic Christian attitude is characterized by differences *with*, not withdrawal *from*, the world. It is also marked by radiation. Christians are not only to be a light in the world (Phil. 2:1; Eph. 5:8) but also the light of the world (Matt. 5:14).

But, once again, we must remember that the future expectation of the first Christians bestowed on them a unique vantage point from which to view every dimension of reality. It also impelled them to act in light of this hope. Their view of the last things was not merely a set of beliefs concerning future events but also the attitude or atmosphere aroused by their hope and conviction about the future.

The early Christians learned to live with the biblical paradox — the Kingdom is already here but it has not yet come in its fullness.[68]

## Relevance

Properly presented, the biblical view of history fills a prophetic void. Not only have Christians failed to take a clear stand against certain cultural sins and vices which New Age advocates decry (for example, materialism, racism, neglect of the poor and oppressed, and environmental abuse), but too often Christians have been caught up in these nonbiblical practices. Christians have often allowed their Christianity to be defined by the culture rather than challenging culture by biblical standards. Each generation needs to hear the prophetic voice against pagan culture.

The biblical view of history calls for innovation and attempts to find biblically acceptable solutions to the most strongly felt moral and spiritual needs created by our rapidly changing society. The biblical perspective needs to be integrated or reintegrated into such fields as education, science, politics, the media, and the arts.[69]

The New Age view of history is permeating our culture at many levels. Christians need to critique and resist New Age cultural penetration at both the personal and the societal levels. This calls for prophetic and creative responses to the New Age challenge. The biblical view of history calls for its advocates to incarnate and proclaim the biblical model in its delicate and profound biblical balance.

68. John P. Newport, "Facing toward the Millennial Year 2000 under Biblical Guidance with a Focus on the Resurrection," in *Ex Auditu* (Allison Park, Pa.: Pickwick, 1993), 117-21.

69. Miller, *Crash Course*, 137-40.

# CHAPTER FOURTEEN

# Modern Satanism and Black Magic

The New Age movement is founded on the premise that "all is one," which means that everything is God, including humans. There is no personal creator God or rebellious Satan in the New Age worldview. A person's primary concern is to change consciousness and realize godhood. Spirit beings who once lived but are now in a non-earthbound spiritual realm are ready to help through channeling. Various monistic religions — mostly from the East — are also available. Since a person is primarily a spirit, a person will never perish but will be reincarnated for further development. The New Age also emphasizes that prior to the coming of Christ, there were neo-pagans and white witches and goddess groups usually dominated by women. Modern-day representatives stand ready to help a person gain goddesshood. White magic can also help.

In contrast, the revealed drama of the biblical worldview portrays a personal creator God who is both transcendent and immanent. God created the earth, angels, and humans. Angels and humans were given freedom. Some of the angels and all of the humans rebelled against God. Respecting human freedom, God inaugurated a redemptive program culminating in Jesus Christ and the church to restore humans to their status at creation.

The rebellious Satan and his demonic cohorts continue to rebel against God and his redemptive plan despite their defeat by Christ. Humans likewise follow Satan and even worship him.

Throughout post-Christian history the Satanist movement has been the subject of sociological, psychological, and theological discussion and controversy. In this chapter we will give a historical and contemporary perspective on and use an evangelical approach to the crucial problem of radical evil and destructive Satanism in our time.

# MODERN SATANISM —
# DEFINITION AND INFLUENCE

Satanism is the worship of Satan — the tempter to sin, the accuser of God's people, and the proud rival of God's government in the world. At its base, Satanism involves a vow of reverence and obedience to the Prince of Darkness. Contracts with Satan surface even today from the occult underground.[1]

Some sociologists consider the concern over Satanism by law enforcement officers, school leaders, parents, therapists, and Christian evangelicals as excessive and exaggerated. The Satanic scare, they explain, is related to explainable and correctable sociological and psychological factors.[2]

But Carl Raschke, a University of Denver professor, disagrees. In *Painted Black,* he gives a forceful and factual survey of a Satanist subculture that is bringing random violence to the United States and to the world. Raschke marshals shocking evidence from police records and newspapers, as well as occult sources, that a Satanist movement not only exists but is working to destroy the very foundations of America's social values.

For Raschke, Satanism is not a formal organization but rather a growing network of "aesthetic terrorists" who seek to demolish all positive values through the use of games, music art, literature, cinema, and religion pervaded by the symbolism of evil.[3]

John Cooper uses the term "destructive occultism" to cover all cases of groups that seek to work evil and impair and harm.

Characterized as it is by rebellion against moral absolutes, Satanism leads in some cases to a disregard for human life, a destructive lifestyle, and various types of criminal behavior.

Satanism claims to be "unfreezing" the moral sensibilities of the biblical worldview. Now a widespread phenomenon, Satanism is assuming several forms across the American landscape. The plain facts show us that American popular culture spreads Satanism through music, books, films, computers, substance abuse, and the redefined sexual mores of the past quarter century that have legitimized and popularized deviant and immoral behavior. What was "hard rock" in the seventies has now become "heavy metal," which at times involves the devil's name along with drug abuse and respect for the Satanic values of cruelty, ugliness, insensitivity, violence, and self-indulgence.[4]

---

1. John Charles Cooper, *The Black Mask: Satanism in America Today* (Old Tappan, N.J: Revell, 1990), 33.

2. Roger E. Olson, "The Demons Next Door," *Christianity Today,* October 18, 1991, 56.

3. Ibid., 56.

4. Cooper, *The Black Mask,* 11, 19, 77.

Ted Peters, a professor at Pacific Lutheran Seminary, calls modern Satanism and black magic "radical evil," a form of evil that dishonors or reviles the name, being, or work of God through slander, cursing, or showing contempt. It employs the symbol of Satan for the purpose of disavowing all loyalty to the God of love and salvation. Worse, the symbol of Satan prevents others from gaining access to the God of love and salvation.[5]

## History of Satanism and Black Witchcraft

Black witchcraft, which is just another name for Satanism, is historically understood as arising from a pact with the devil agreed to by men and women at odds with the church and in rebellion against the established political order. According to *The Encyclopedia of Witchcraft and Demonology*, all the witch-hunters of the Inquisition, and later in Protestant England, saw witchcraft as revolving around a pact with the devil. This recanting of one's Christian baptism and making a vow to Satan were, in fact, the essence of the "crime" of witchcraft and were seen as the basis for any extraordinary powers a witch might possess. Thus in the earlier centuries, Satanic witchcraft was occultism with a definite evil, criminal, and antireligious cast.

### FOLK WITCHES

The hostile "black" witch can be distinguished from the folk or healing witches of Western history, who were actually healers and midwives. In fact, there were far fewer of the hostile "black" witches than people generally suppose. For these witches, the church seemed to stand for privilege and cruelty to the poor and weak, and Satan seemed a logical alternative as an object of worship. In various periods of history, under various rulers, these black witches became "political witches." They attempted to predict or cause the death of a ruler as a way of overthrowing the established order. Poison was their preferred weapon.[6]

### THE CATHARS

In the Middle Ages, from the 1140s, the Cathars, known in France as the Albigensians, used radical dualism to turn the tables on Christianity. Just as Christianity had demonized the pagan deities, so the Cathars demonized the Christian God:

5. Ted Peters, *Sin* (Grand Rapids: Eerdmans, 1994), 218.
6. Cooper, *Black Mask,* 33-37.

God created the material world for the purpose of entrapping spirit in matter. He imprisoned the human soul in a cage of flesh. The creator of the world, the God of the Old Testament, is the lord of matter, the prince of this world, and the Devil.[7]

The Cathars were not witches per se, but they were catalysts for the formation of witchcraft through their dualistic beliefs and their rejection of the church. Catharism generated an atmosphere in which Satan and his demons were seen as both powerful and available.

## The Gnostic Sects

Back of the fact that people turned to Satan as an object of worship was the influence of the gnostic sects. The gnostic sects of the first two centuries A.D. pulled strongly in the direction of dualism. For them, Satan was an anti-God of enormous power. This power was to be fought, exorcised, and struggled against. But because it was so vast, Satan's power could also be manipulated, harnessed to one's own will, and even, in extreme cases, worshiped. There was no organized Satanism in those early centuries, but some gnostic sects seem to have verged on it by practicing orgiastic sexual rites.

Many of the gnostics combined Iranian dualism with Greek dualism, which identified spirit with good and matter with evil. By naming the devil as creator and lord of matter, gnostics opened the door for extremists to worship this material lord to obtain material goods. Thus gnosticism bred both the self-denial of asceticism and, occasionally, gross orgies.[8]

## The Great Witch Hunt of the Middle Ages

Pope Innocent VIII issued a papal bull against witchcraft in 1484, authorizing Heinrich Institoris and Jacob Sprenger to investigate and prosecute charges of witchcraft throughout the lands under the pope's ecclesiastical control. In 1486, Sprenger and Institoris published *Malleus Maleficarum,* a textbook on witchcraft. This book became the "Bible" of the Great Witch Hunt of the late Middle Ages. It was the single most influential factor in promulgating false information about Satanism, witchcraft, folklore, and folk

7. Brooks Alexander, "Witchcraft and Neo-Paganism: From the Dark Ages to the New Age," *SCP Journal* 16.3 (Berkeley: Spiritual Counterfeits Project, Incorporated, 1991): 13.

8. James T. Richardson, *The Satanism Scare* (New York: de Gruyter, 1991), 43.

medicine and in providing a pseudo-documentary basis for civil and ecclesiastical courts.

Geoffrey Parrinder declares, "Sprenger, who was the principal author, was a dangerous and evil-minded fanatic. He claimed to have gathered disinterested information from eye-witnesses, confessions of witches maintained even to the stake. He revels in the preposterous and even more in the sensual. Altogether the *Malleus* is one of the wickedest and most obscene books ever written."[9]

Apparently the numerical high point of the witchcraft explosion occurred just before and during the Protestant Reformation in the early sixteenth century. By 1700, somewhere between thirty thousand and a million witches had been tried and executed.[10] It is generally accepted by historians that witchcraft was not a fantasy of the Inquisition, nor was it the product of popular hysteria, though both played their part in fueling the craze that eventually surrounded witchcraft. There is little doubt that many crimes attributed to witchcraft were an ugly fact of medieval society.

Unfortunately, it is also certain that the medieval church caused many people, perhaps hundreds of thousands of them, to be falsely accused. In many cases, these innocents were executed after first being subjected to torture that was demonically inventive in its cruelty.

The Inquisition pitted one form of sin against another. The sin inside the church clashed with the sin outside it. Drowned out in all the clamor was the biblical command to judge sin in sorrow and compassion. Only by stepping outside the hysteria could the church regain its perspective and begin to realize what was happening. Near the end of the seventeenth century, that began to happen.[11]

## Satanic Worship and the Black Mass

Another phase of Satanism, which is an overt dedication to the perverse, began in the eighteenth century in the ferment that led up to the French Revolution. It arose among the privileged, wealthy classes, beginning as a search for sexual perversion, sensual enjoyment, and power over others. This form of Satanism mimics and repudiates everything Christian: the devil replaces Jesus Christ as Lord, and the Black Mass replaces the Eucharist.[12]

9. Bob and Gretchen Pasantino, *Satanism,* Zondervan Guide to Cults and Religious Movements (Grand Rapids: Zondervan, 1995), 36-37.

10. John Warwick Montgomery, ed., *Demon Possession* (Minneapolis: Bethany, 1976), 91-104.

11. Alexander, "Witchcraft and Neo-Paganism," 23.

12. Peters, *Sin,* 221.

In the Black Mass, renegade Catholic priests would slash newborn babies to death over the naked bodies of young women, who served as the altars for these sacrileges. The attenders of these masses were members of the nobility, including several hundred of the highest courtiers of Louis XIV. Something like a contemporary drug ring existed. Ladies-in-waiting to the king's mistresses were recruited to "push" poisons on the jealous and quarrelsome women who vied daily for the king's favor — and the power that favor gave them.

These Black Masses, or invocations of Satan or his demons, were not done by pagans but by so-called Christians who were filled with lust for power, with greed for the wealth royal favor could give a family, and with sexual obsessions. Frustrated by the Christian condemnation of the sins of the flesh, these perverted "believers" followed a seventeenth-century "gospel of wealth" in an inverted worship of Satan. In these actions they were aided by members of the clergy who chafed under celibacy.[13]

The Black Mass is clearly a case of ritual rebellion against the established church. The services were oftentimes enlarged to include rebaptism in the devil's name and a reading of the Lord's Prayer backward. Similar services are widespread today in meetings of the Church of Satan and similar witchcraft and Satanist groups.

The upper classes devised even more horrible Black Masses and services in the fifteenth, sixteenth, and seventeenth centuries, and even into the eighteenth century. These services constituted a prototype for the writings of Marquis de Sade, whose fictional works such as *Justine* have gained wide attention in our time. In the novel *Justine,* de Sade includes a lengthy passage describing a Gallic Black Mass.

In the eighteenth century, in Great Britain, Black Masses were conducted by the well-known Hellfire Clubs. The masses were conducted over an altar consisting of a naked girl. The monks of these groups, known as the "Unholy Twelve," were influential political and literary figures.[14]

## The Influence of Manicheanism

Influential at this same time was the heresy of Manicheanism. In many ways Manicheanism was similar to the Cathars. It stressed the tension between the two cosmic powers, which could be overcome only through an influx of "higher

13. Cooper, *Black Mask,* 38-40.

14. John P. Newport, *Demons, Demons, Demons: A Christian Guide through the Murky Maze of the Occult* (Nashville: Broadman, 1972), 42-44; see also Arthur Lyons, *The Second Coming: Satanism in America* (New York: Dodd, Mead, 1970), 1.

knowledge" into the consciousness of the initiate. Manicheanism was transmitted to Western Christianity by way of the Middle East. It seems to have taken root along the trade routes of the Mediterranean in the wake of the Crusades.

The link between Manicheanism and Satanism, and ultimately with the modern occult underworld, can be found in the dualistic doctrine that "good" and "evil," or light and darkness, are equivalent. Since good has no priority over its opposite, the immersion of the devotee in the black abyss of things and what society might consider depraved conduct represents a valid part of the quest for "salvation." These people thought Satan would aid them if they venerated him. The nobility looked for help from renegade priests who befriended the devil.[15]

# TYPES OF MODERN SATANISM

## Classic Satan Worship

According to Peters, Satan worship today exists in small, highly secretive groups who engage in ritual torture and murder. In almost all contemporary cases, Satan worship is associated with illegal drugs. The purpose of ritual murder and the subsequent eating of human flesh is twofold: to gain power from the victim and to desensitize cult members, making them ready for criminal assignments.[16]

## Aleister Crowley as the Great Beast

No true-life personality has cast more of a shadow over contemporary Satanism than Aleister Crowley. He was born in 1875, the son of parents belonging to the fundamentalist Christian group known as the Plymouth Brethren. Much of Crowley's Satanism was a calculated and self-willed reaction against what he considered the extremes and stupidity of his fundamentalist upbringing, which at times included physical abuse. Crowley's mother, a dim-witted but pious woman, one time in anger branded him as "the Beast" of the Apocalypse. He cherished the insult and let the epithet stick to him for the remainder of his seventy-two years. In fact, Crowley publicly anointed himself the "Beast 666" of the book of Revelation. He also believed he was

15. Carl Raschke, *Painted Black* (San Francisco: Harper & Row, 1990), 88.
16. Peters, *Sin*, 221.

the embodiment of the mysterious figure of Baphomet. He presided over his own Satanic, pseudo-Masonic fraternity based on the legendary ideal of the "secret," non-Christian society founded in Jerusalem by the Templars — the Ordo Templi Orientalis, the "Order of the Oriental Temple" or O.T.O.[17]

His father, a brewer, left Crowley a fortune, which he spent with astonishing rapidity. He was educated at Malvern, Tonbridge, and Trinity College, Cambridge, where he became involved in a homosexual love affair and acquired the beginnings of a highly sinister reputation.[18]

## Order of the Golden Dawn

In 1898, Crowley joined the Hermetic Order of the Golden Dawn. This was a magical and pseudo-Masonic community founded by the occult scholar Samuel MacGregor Mathers. The Golden Dawn included such prominent literary figures as Irish poet William Butler Yeats. In the Golden Dawn, Crowley learned to elicit — today we would say "channel" — disembodied "angels" or spirits, the majority of which turned out, to Crowley's perverted delight, to be demonic.

### CHANNELED PAGAN MESSAGES

Later Crowley claimed that he "channeled" communiqués from the ancient Egyptian gods, including Thoth and Horus. But it was the revelations from a mysterious entity calling himself "Aiwass" that affected Crowley the most. Crowley said he had been commanded by the spirits to write down what came to be titled *The Book of the Law*, a kind of esoteric scripture that resembled the poetry of Robert Browning. In the book, Aiwass spoke of a "new religion" and a "new eon" that would be distinguished by complete self-fulfillment and the unleashing of private volition and desire. The great "commandment" of Crowley's new age, as dictated by Aiwass, has been recited over and over: "Do what thou wilt shall be the whole of the law." Crowley regarded magic, especially the black variety, as the best vehicle to attain mastery over all things. The key to magical sovereignty lay in the "will."[19]

Historians point out that Crowley's teachings were little more than inferior literary imitations of the German philosopher Friedrich Nietzsche, who was a generation younger than Crowley. These revelations, which Crowley termed "magick" with a *k*, promised unlimited satisfaction of instinctual wishes

17. Raschke, *Painted Black*, 92.
18. Richard Cavendish, *The Black Arts* (New York: Capricorn, 1967), 39.
19. Raschke, *Painted Black*, 92-94.

along with total liberation from both human and divine laws. Crowley spent the First World War in the United States, writing anti-British propaganda for the Germans. In 1916, living in Bristol, New Hampshire, he ascended to the high magical grade of Magus, going through a ceremony of his own invention in which he baptized a toad as Jesus Christ and crucified it.[20]

Crowley believed that the discovery of true willpower was the "Great Work" that made one a master, magician, or magi. This willpower could come only through the psychological downplaying of what is ordinarily considered the self and doing away with the mind's discrimination between good and evil.[21]

## CROWLEY'S LAST DAYS

In 1920 Crowley went to Cefalu in Sicily and set up his Sacred Abbey of Thelema ("the will" in Greek), with his then current mistresses, the Scarlet Woman and Sister Cypris (a name of Aphrodite, the Greek goddess of love and beauty). Very few disciples and very little money arrived. Crowley was in urgent need of both for most of his life. Rumors of abominable rites and orgies, some of them well founded, floated out from the abbey, and Mussolini's government expelled Crowley in 1923. He was later expelled from France as well and wandered forlornly from England to Germany and Portugal and back again, much in the eye of the popular press, which called him "the wickedest man in the world." He himself preferred the title "The Great Beast."[22]

Crowley popularized the use of cocaine and other psychoactive drugs among the avant-garde. While on cocaine, Crowley evidently had his first great insight that, as the "sublimist mystic in all history," he was the Beast of Revelation, the "self-crowned God whom men shall worship and blaspheme for centuries."[23]

Crowley died at Hastings, England, in 1947. His orgiastic "Hymn to Pan," the Greek god of shepherds characterized as having the ears, legs, and horns of a goat, was recited during his extremely odd funeral service in the chapel of the crematorium at Brighton, to the scandal and annoyance of local authorities. The last few lines show Crowley as he liked to think of himself:

> . . . I am thy mate, I am thy man,
> Goat of thy flock, I am gold, I am god . . .

20. Cavendish, *Black Arts*, 41.
21. Cooper, *Black Mask*, 49-50.
22. Cavendish, *Black Arts*, 41.
23. Raschke, *Painted Black*, 95.

With hoofs of steel I race on the rocks
Through solstice stubborn to equinox.
And I rave; and I rape and I rip and I rend
Everlasting, world without end, . . .
Io Pan! Io Pan Pan! Pan! Io Pan![24]

## CROWLEY AND DRUGS

One especially harmful influence of Crowley on the twentieth century was his advocacy of the use of cocaine and other psychoactive drugs among the avant-garde. In his *Diary of a Drug Fiend,* a fictionalized look at his own probing and playing with what occultists and addicts would call the "white lady" (cocaine), Crowley sees the drug, though dangerous, as an expedient for "increasing your natural powers." Drugs, particularly heroin and cocaine, were a sacrament for Crowley. At the time of his death Crowley had physically wasted away from overindulgence in drugs.

During the First World War, Crowley paid a visit to the Parke-Davis pharmaceutical plant in Detroit, Michigan, and discussed with them preparations of mescaline. He had probably learned about mescaline, or peyote, as the hallucinogenic substance in cactus during his ramblings through Mexico in 1900. Evidence also exists that Crowley first introduced Aldous Huxley, who stood as the gray eminence of the psychedelic drug culture in the 1960s, to mescaline. Their collaboration is not inconsequential, for in his autobiography, Timothy Leary, the sixties guru of social transformation through hallucinogenic mind-blowing, tells how Aldous Huxley had urged him in October 1960 to "become a cheerleader for evolution" by pouring "brain-drugs, mass-produced in the laboratories," into the streets of the Western democracies.

Crowley's new aeon, which he alternately described as the age of the hawk-god Horus whose talons would rip to shreds the body of Christ, was transmitted in the 1960s into the Age of Satan. In his writings, Crowley told of the inauguration of the "New Age" by the "bloody sacrifice."[25]

## INFLUENCE ON THE NAZIS

It is not clear whether Crowley had in mind an actual high ritual to be performed by his "gnostic" inner circle or whether he envisioned the kind of general, apocalyptic bloodshed that accompanies such calamitous historical events as revolutions and wars. In any event, Crowley, like the Satanists who

24. Cavendish, *Black Arts,* 41-42.
25. Raschke, *Painted Black,* 95-96.

would succeed him, repeatedly talked of the coming era of chaos and, to use the phraseology of Nazi occultism itself, the "triumph of the will." Anton LaVey in his *Satanic Rituals*, published in 1972, proclaimed the arrival of "the new Age of Fire" as the ascendancy of the order of Satan. There seems to be evidence, according to Raschke, that the influence and work of Crowley became one of the larger ideological streams feeding the subculture of Satanism and the drug culture, and even undergirded Nazism.

Crowley described his *The Book of the Law* as a "revolutionary" handbook with an implicit "magical model of society." To him it was "practical politics." By 1927 Hitler was introduced to the writings of Crowley. In the thick of World War II, Crowley annotated a copy of the book *Hitler Speaks*, in which he proudly pointed out how what Hitler had written corresponded with his *The Book of the Law*. He speculated that Hitler may have been swayed by reading his own "sacred text."

It is impossible to prove that Crowleyite Satanism was a straightforward "cause" of the Nazi holocaust or that Crowley's disciples ever really succeeded in seriously fashioning and coloring the program and philosophy of the Third Reich. However, there is a similarity in perspective.[26]

## Anton LaVey and the Church of Satan

Anton LaVey, a continuer of the Crowley tradition, is seen as the twentieth-century culmination of a strand winding through the Satanic world. Part of this Satanic strand is the passionate judgment that Christian civilization, which has persisted almost two thousand years, is corrupt and hypocritical. A new "natural" regime of instinctual spontaneity and untrammeled free will must burst the fetters of imposed Christianity. Such an attitude, which may be described as *neobarbarism*, runs all the way down the line from the French radicals of the 1700s, many of whom practiced a discrete and finely cultivated form of Satanism, to LaVey himself.[27]

LaVey is the best-known religious Satanist. With his shaved head, goatee, and black coat and hat, he was the subject of the cover story for the *Washington Post Magazine* in February 1986. Almost single-handedly, LaVey created contemporary Satanism.[28]

Howard Anton "Tony" LaVey was born April 11, 1930, in Chicago. He came from Russian, Romanian, and Alsatian stock. His grandmother, a gypsy from Transylvania, filled his ears with tales of vampires and the

26. Ibid., 95-97.
27. Ibid., 82.
28. Cooper, *Black Mask*, 51.

supernatural. With such a heritage he was reading *Dracula* at five. His family moved to San Francisco in the early thirties, and stayed until 1947. By his early teens, LaVey had developed a strong interest in the occult and was fascinated by such roguish magicians as Rasputin, Cagliostro, and Crowley. He dropped out of high school in his junior year and joined the Clyde Beatty circus.[29]

In the winter of 1947, LaVey was working for the Pike Amusement Park in Long Beach, California, where he became steeped in stage magic. He became aware of hypocrisy, he states, when he saw men lusting after half-naked sideshow girls on Saturday nights. On Sunday, when he played the organ for the tent show evangelists, he would see the same men sitting with their wives and children and praying that God would take away their carnal urges. But the next Saturday they would be at the carnival, lusting again. "I knew then that the Christian church thrives on hypocrisy and that man's carnal nature is stronger than his religion."[30]

The following year, 1948, chiefly to avoid the military draft, he enrolled in San Francisco's City College, where he studied criminology. In 1952 he acquired a job as a police photographer which, according to his own account, drilled him in the seamy affairs of life and made him completely cynical about the human condition. He quit his job as police photographer and took up playing the organ at the Lost Weekend nightclub. He formed weekly classes in ritual magic. From this well-attended endeavor evolved a magic circle that met to perform the black rituals that LaVey was uncovering in his study of historic black-magic groups.

## LAVEY AND HIS "MISSION"

In the late 1960s, LaVey proclaimed that he had a "mission" and a "legacy" to fulfill. He envisioned a time — the fruition of the Age of Satan — when Satanic emblems, rather than crosses, would rise from church roofs. LaVey said he was going to make hatred and defiance of authority not only respectable but a socially powerful force.

It was on the evening of April 30, 1966 — *Walpurgisnacht* in the occult calendar — that he declared the arrival of the Age of Satan. Headquarters was in his house at 6114 California Street in San Francisco. The house has a chilling black interior, art deco geegaws, and lifelike, automated mannequins of tarts and bar floozies. LaVey performed both "Satanic weddings" and "Satanic funerals" to gain the interest of the press. He also kept a full-grown circus lion that scared the neighbors with its roar. With deliberate parody,

29. Martin Ebon, ed., *Witchcraft Today* (New York: Signet, 1971), 86-87.
30. Ibid., 92.

LaVey called himself "the black pope."[31] Soon he was gaining considerable publicity by performing Satanic weddings of famous people, Satanic baptisms of children, and Satanic last rites for a sailor member who died — all deliberately staged as media events. LaVey sought celebrities as members, and for a time claimed such stars as Sammy Davis, Jr., and Jayne Mansfield as active participants, gaining national attention as a result. He also served as a consultant to the film *Rosemary's Baby,* even playing a part in the film.

## TEACHINGS

Like other Satanists, LaVey pirated both ritual and psychic ingredients from recognized religions or occult practices all over the world. In *The Satanic Rituals* LaVey writes that his religion is "a blend of Gnostic, Cabalistic, Hermetic, and Masonic elements, incorporating nomenclature and vibratory words of power from virtually every mythos."[32]

From a philosophical perspective, LaVey's Church of Satan actively rejects spirituality and mysticism of any sort. Instead, it espouses an elitist, materialist, and basically atheistic philosophy. Satan constitutes a worship of one's ego. In its major features, the Church of Satan takes a position of extreme Machiavellianism and cynical-realism toward human nature. Its major feature is its emphasis upon the importance of myth and magic and upon their impact in a world of people who can still be manipulated through such beliefs and emotions. The Satanist, then, is the ultimate pragmatist.

We can summarize his teachings by pointing out that Anton LaVey and the Church of Satan contend that if a person is to worship anything, it ought to be his own natural desires. Indulgence instead of abstinence is LaVey's theme. Satan is a symbol of the material world and the carnal nature. Rituals of the group include a rite of communal cursing in which members ventilate resentment and anger. Members are taught to follow physical lusts, the desire for revenge, and the drive for material possessions.

At its roots, LaVey's brand of Satanism represents an organized rejection of all conventional morality and religion. He has "transvalued all values" and proclaims evil as the ultimate "good" in the world. Worship of "Satan," who personifies all counterforces to good as normally understood, is a symbol of this rejection of morality. In LaVey's reasoning, Satan is really not the "enemy" but a person's life force, the libido, and so cannot be other than a good to be affirmed. Satan is the symbol of unrestrained egoism. If Satan is worshiped as God (God and Satan are considered one), people should live according to their inborn tendencies. For example, LaVey encourages his

31. Raschke, *Painted Black,* 118-19.
32. Ibid., 215.

followers to indulge in the Seven Deadly Sins. They were invented by the Catholic Church to instill guilt in the faithful. But in the Church of Satan, the Seven Deadly Sins are virtues. "If we didn't have pride, we wouldn't have any self-respect. Anger? If people exploded, there might not be ulcers. Lust? If it weren't for that we wouldn't be here. Envy? How could one get ahead if he didn't envy. It's the same for gluttony, greed, slothfulness," LaVey explains.[33]

In keeping with this philosophy of self-indulgence, the Church of Satan openly advocates the practice of any type of sexual activity which satisfies a person's needs, be it promiscuous heterosexuality, strict faithfulness to a wife, homosexuality, or even fetishism. LaVey rejects the supernatural, an afterlife, heaven, and hell. There is no sin. Humans are superior animals and should worship their own egos.[34]

## SATAN AS A SYMBOL

LaVey's theology can be summarized in a few of his statements. "We hold Satan as a symbolic personal savior, who takes care of mundane, fleshly, carnal things. God exists as a universal force, a balancing factor in nature, too impersonal to care one whit whether we live or die. The sons, such as Jesus, take care of the spiritual aspect, but the devil takes care of the carnal side of man. We literally want to give the devil his due. There has never been a religion before that has given him credit. We recognize that man is sometimes lower than the animals, that he is basically greedy and selfish, so why feel guilty about it? We accept ourselves as we are and live with it. The one great sin is self-deceit."[35]

In the Satanic Bible, LaVey declares, in relation to the founding of the Church of Satan: "A glow of new light is borne out of the night (of the Twilight of God; the Death of God) and Lucifer is risen, once more to proclaim: 'This is the age of Satan! Satan rules the Earth!' The gods of the unjust are dead. This is the morning of magic, and undefiled wisdom. The FLESH prevaileth and a great Church shall be builded, consecrated in its name. No longer shall man's salvation be dependent on his self-denial." His introduction concludes with: "Regie Satanas! [Satan Rules!] Ave Satanas! Hail Satan!" Those who saw the film *Rosemary's Baby* will recall that these are the words proclaimed by the Satanic coven at the birth of Rosemary's dreadful child, the son of Satan. LaVey was the consultant on the occult for that movie.[36]

---

33. Ebon, *Witchcraft Today*, 91.
34. Arthur Lyons, *The Second Coming: Satanism in America* (New York: Dodd, Mead, 1970), 190.
35. Ebon, *Witchcraft Today*, 88.
36. Cooper, *Black Mask*, 51-52.

John Fritscher, author of *Popular Witchcraft,* has conducted a series of interviews with Anton LaVey in which he summarized his teachings and viewpoints.

## SATAN AND PERSONAL DESTINY

"I have felt Satan's presence but only as an exteriorized extension of my own potential, as an alter-ego or evolved concept that I have been able to exteriorize. With a full awareness, I can communicate with this semblance, this creature, this demon, this personification that I see in the eyes of the symbol of Satan — the goat of Mendes — as I commune with it before the altar.

"I am not deluding myself that I am calling something that is disassociated or exteriorized from myself the godhead. This Force is not a controlling factor that I have no control over. The Satanic principle is that man willfully controls his destiny; if he doesn't, some other man — a lot smarter than he is — will. Satan is, therefore, an extension of one's psyche or volitional essence, so that extension can sometimes converse and give directives through the self in a way that mere thinking of the self as a single unit cannot. In this way it *does* help to depict in an externalized way the Devil per se."[37]

### Christian Hypocrisy

LaVey continues, "I think that the worst thing about Christianity is its gross hypocrisy which is the most repugnant thing in the world to me. Most Christians practice a basic Satanic way of life every hour of their waking day and yet they sneer at somebody who has built a religion that is no different from what they are practicing, but is simply calling it by its right name. I call it by the name that is antithetical to that which they hypocritically pay lip service to when they're in church."

### Morality

On morality and the "law of the jungle," LaVey says, "Satanically speaking, anarchy and chaos must ensue for a while before a new Satanic morality can prevail. The new Satanic morality won't be very different from the old law of the jungle wherein right and wrong were judged in the truest natural sense of biting and being bitten back. Satanic morality will cause a return to intrigue, to glamour, to seductiveness, to a modicum of sexual lasciviousness; taboos will be invoked, but mostly it will be realized these things are fun."

37. John Fritscher, *Popular Witchcraft* (Secaucus, N.J.: Citadel, 1973), 167.

### Satanism and Women

LaVey describes his book *The Complete Witch; or What to Do When Virtue Fails* as "a guide for witches. It smashes all the misconceptions that women have had, not only about witchery but about their own sexuality. Even if a woman is a man-hater, she can use her femininity to ruin that man. This book tells her how to do it. If she wants to enjoy men, this book will open her eyes to a few things."

### Vengeance, Violence, and Control

Regarding the movie *Rosemary's Baby,* LaVey says the role he played — the devil in the shaggy suit — "was not from my point of view anything other than it should have been: man, animal, bestial, carnal nature coming forth in a ritualized way. The impregnation of Rosemary in that dream sequence was to me the very essence of the immodest, the bestial in man, impregnating the virginal world-mind with the reawakening of the animalism within oneself. This impregnation was very meaningful because it spawned literally the Church of Satan. The end of the film shows Rosemary throw away her Catholic heritage and cherish the devil-child. The natural instinct of Satanism wins out over man-made programming."[38]

In the foreword to *The Satanic Rituals,* LaVey states that "All is chaos, and anything goes, however irrational, that is against established policy. Causes are a dime a dozen. Rebellion for rebellion's sake often takes precedent over genuine need for change. The opposite has become desirable, hence this becomes the Age of Satan." Satanism is utter selfishness, pure egotism in action, and a quest for personal power and unlimited sensual pleasure.[39]

In the realm of politics, LaVey would like to see benevolent dictatorships or even monarchies rule the world. For LaVey, too much freedom is not a good thing — except for the freedom of the flesh, which he likes to encourage. LaVey hates democracy and equality. In a 1986 interview with the *Washington Post Magazine,* LaVey told writer Walt Harrington that most people are useless and insignificant. They might just as well "never have lived at all."[40]

## RITUALS — THE VEHICLES OF POWER

The rituals held at the Church of Satan, in keeping with its philosophical tenets, are for the purpose of releasing and directing "magical power" rather

38. Ibid., 170, 177, 181-83.
39. Cooper, *The Black Mask,* 52-54.
40. Raschke, *Painted Black,* 137.

than as vehicles of religious worship. There are some inversions of Christian services. The altar room in which the ceremonies are held is completely black, an inverted pentagram (a magical symbol, as opposed to an inverted cross, a religious symbol) and is inscribed on the wall above the fireplace. All the services begin and end with a series of Satanic hymns played on an organ. The formalities are opened with a ritual invocation of Satan. A naked woman, a symbol of lust and self-indulgence, is used as an altar. The heart of the service is based on the efficacy of magic. The participants are taught to direct magical and psychic forces through the use of symbols.

LaVey makes the distinction between "greater" and "lesser" magic. Greater magic is that type of magic which involves the outpouring of will and directing the flow of vital emotional and psychic energies inherent in the controlling individual. It is the type of magic employed at Friday night services. The Friday night rituals are begun in pitch blackness to a medley of hymns played on the organ. Candles are then lit. The male participants all wear black robes and hoods, except for LaVey, who wears a black cape and a skullcap with horns. Female acolytes wear black robes without hoods. A bell is rung nine times to signal the beginning of the service. A leopard-skin cover is removed from the mantle, revealing the altar for the evening, the nude body of a volunteer female. Purification is performed by one of the assistant priests, who sprinkles the congregation with a mixture of semen and water, symbolic of creative force.

## SELF-GRATIFICATION

After the preliminaries comes the text of the ritual. Usually, the magical workings take the form of wish fulfillment. Members of the congregation are led forward into the center of a circle formed by the hooded priests and are asked what they desire. Accompanied by eerie organ music, the high priest touches the member's head lightly with a sword and asks the devil to grant the person's request. The request might be for material gain, to acquire a mate, or to receive a physical or emotional quality. After each member of the congregation goes through this process and all have returned to their seats, the proceedings are brought to a close, the bell being rung nine times clockwise, while the organ plays Satanic hymns.[41]

## AN EMPHASIS ON HATE

At another ceremony called the Shibboleth Ritual, Satanists are encouraged to take the role of somebody they hate or wish to scorn. At the end of the

41. Lyons, *Second Coming*, 193-200.

Shibboleth, curses are worked on the objects of scorn. It is from this kind of activity that the Church of Satan has derived much of its publicity.

## THE CASE OF MANSFIELD AND BRODY

One of LaVey's early disciples was the glamour queen and actress Jayne Mansfield. Tired of raw hedonism, Mansfield had begun to flirt with Catholicism. She was especially attracted to the incense, the golden altars, the solemnity of the Mass, and the august tonality of the cathedral settings. But it was difficult for her emotionally to remain the great American sex symbol and practice Catholicism. In the end, she chose something that used the candles, the altar, and ritual, but was very different. She chose Satanism.

As the high priest of the Church of Satan, LaVey escorted Mansfield through his home, which he told her was "the First Satanic Church of the Devil." He showed her some candles on the altar, which he said contained the power of death and would bring down a curse on anyone who touched them.

Mansfield's boyfriend, Sam Brody, who tried to keep a close rein on Mansfield, was not at all happy with her fondness for the Prince of Darkness. When LaVey returned to the altar room, Brody became angry. In order to spite LaVey, Brody lit the forbidden candles on the altar, which only the devil himself supposedly had the authority to light. LaVey became furious and proclaimed that Satan himself had cursed Brody and that he would be killed within a year.

LaVey called Jayne Mansfield into a back room and told her solemnly that "no one laughs at the Devil!" He then darkly prophesied that Brody would meet death in a car crash — not one, but a succession of them — and that anyone with him would also die. LaVey demanded that Jayne rid herself of Brody forthwith. The series of predicted car crashes began. Frightened, Mansfield went to a Catholic priest and asked if LaVey did indeed possess evil powers. According to Mansfield, the priest confirmed her fears and warned her about staying too close to LaVey or the world of black magic.

Whether produced by magic or not, the disasters in her life continued. The end came swiftly, within the year that LaVey had predicted. Early on the morning of June 28, 1967, Mansfield was killed in a car crash outside New Orleans. Her head was severed from her body during the accident. Brody and the chauffeur also were killed.[42]

---

42. Raschke, *Painted Black*, 121-23.

## SEXUAL MAGIC

In contrast to the higher magic practiced in the formal ritual, there is also a lower order of magic which enables an individual to control and manipulate his environment at a more basic level.

On Saturdays, LaVey holds courses for his female witches. Since the Satanic movement is aimed basically at a Machiavellian-type control, and since the most obvious means of control from a female standpoint is through the use of sex, the Church of Satan employs sex as a basic tool in the practice of lesser magic.[43]

LaVey's church is composed of people who experience powerful inner rebellion. They usually have strong drives for power or, alternately, desires to be slaves. They are mostly intellectual types, analytic and superficially "straight." However, they are frankly hedonistic people who feel a need for a religious rationale for their way of life, which has overtones of sensational rebellion.

One observer noted that in attendance at both the magic seminars and the rituals of the Church of Satan were physicians, lawyers, engineers, teachers, former members of the FBI, and IBM executives. At one gathering, half were either Ph.D.s or Ph.D. candidates.[44]

Grant Hardner states that the membership is widespread geographically and includes numerous persons in law enforcement, the media, the military, movies, government service, and teaching. At least in its early stages, membership was kept highly selective because LaVey said he was trying to assemble an elite group, one oriented toward stability and power. "The Satanic Church is the first organization of its kind," he proudly asserted, "whose membership consists largely of responsible, respectable people. Only by limiting our membership to individuals of this variety, rather than appealing to the lunatic fringe, can we be certain of becoming the strongest power structure in the world."

Michael Aquino, an army officer turned occult leader, contends that in more recent years LaVey started selling religious offices in the Church of Satan to anybody who would sign a check. LaVey's decision to set up a service business for mail-order magi was very much in keeping with his design both to compromise all and to lay bare the hypocrisy of all. This is how the Church of Satan became thousands, if not hundreds of thousands, strong. Raschke says that when LaVey decided in the mid-seventies to sell his own brand of indulgences to the masses, he made Satanism into a crude belief system. He stripped Satanism of intellectual pretense and made it

43. Lyons, *Second Coming,* 195.
44. Raschke, *Painted Black,* 118.

exactly what it has become — an ideology of hate and an incitement to "revolutionary" violence.[45]

In summary, the black occult represented by LaVey is much more interested in the performance of "magic" (seeking power) or in glorifying the devil than it is in mocking Christ. There are both "theistic" and "atheistic" Satanists. This means that some black occultists really do believe in the "existence" of Satan, while many others do not believe in the literal reality of either Satan or God. Many Satanists, like LaVey, believe only in themselves; they think of themselves as "the devil"; they are their own "god."[46]

## INFLUENCE ON YOUTH GROUPS

LaVey has had a strong influence on teenage Satanists. The liturgies used by these youth groups are generally eclectically devised rites, based on LaVey's *The Satanic Bible* and *The Satanic Rituals*.

LaVey states that he does not accept any responsibility for the evil done by Satanists. But Raschke points out that LaVey has been selling books by the millions counseling people not to take morality seriously. He has defended Satanism time and time again as nothing more than "psychodrama." Yet, according to Raschke, when LaVey's Satanism has been peddled worldwide for more than two decades to millions of people with virtually no discretion, it is difficult to take seriously the protestation that the Church of Satan should not be held accountable somehow for the many acts of perversity related to Satanism.[47]

## CONFLICTING INTERPRETATIONS
## OF THE CHURCH OF SATAN

In the last decade, LaVey has rarely spoken to the press. Once a flamboyant public figure — hanging out with Jayne Mansfield, making international press with his Satanic masses and weddings — his reclusiveness in recent years has fostered wide rumors of his demise. But Blanche Barton, who describes herself as LaVey's personal secretary and a church administrator, says he's alive and well, active in his sixties, and simply shunning publicity.[48]

Barton, an official spokesperson for the Church of Satan, agrees that "the influence satanism has had since 1966 is overwhelming." That's the year LaVey founded the church.

---

45. Ibid., 125, 137.
46. Cooper, *Black Mask*, 106-7.
47. Raschke, *Painted Black*, 135.
48. John Strasbaugh, "Making Book," *New York Press* 3.38 (September 19-25, 1990): 6.

Barton criticizes Raschke, author of *Painted Black* for misrepresenting and overstating her organization's activities. Yet, ironically, she maintains that it is conservative Christians and "people like Raschke who keep adding fuel to the flames" — so to speak — "by generating hysteria. Ultimately this publicity just sells more Satanic Bibles. It makes people curious to find out for themselves what satanism is about."[49]

Barton notes that *The Satanic Bible* has remained in print and in wide circulation since 1969. She does not know the number of copies sold. The figure often tossed around is "over a million copies."

According to Barton, the Church of Satan is "not an evangelical movement" or a religious movement but an "anti-religious" one — not a church, but a for-profit business incorporated in California. "We use the term church 'blasphemously,'" she explains. "We also do not believe in beings called God or Satan, but use them as symbols appropriated from Christianity." Rather than actively seeking souls — which they also do not believe in — she describes the church as "an elitist organization." Membership costs $100, and the application includes a daunting 40-item questionnaire. "We do not expect everyone to agree with us. We believe you are either born a satanist or you are not. In terms of recruitment, 'We're in the Yellow Pages. And the books are out there.'"

Barton does not deny that an increasing number of wacko killers and other perpetrators of violent crimes have espoused Satanic beliefs or claimed *The Satanic Bible* as a guide. But she ascribes it to a general increase in interest and rejects any direct responsibility. "It's like Mr. LaVey says: There are satanists and there are nuts. We don't tell people to kill their cats or whatever. There have always been people like that. They used to say 'Jesus made me do it.' Now it's more popular to say 'Satan made me do it.'"

Barton says the Church of Satan has always had "a very comfortable and mutually beneficial relationship with law enforcement agencies." LaVey has often played the role of consulting expert on cases with Satanic overtones.

## A DANGEROUS INFLUENCE

Carl Raschke disagrees with LaVey's and Barton's interpretation of the influence of the Church of Satan. For Raschke, LaVey is "sort of the Karl Marx of the contemporary satanist movement." Raschke calls *The Satanic Bible* "a mediology of pop satanism" which others have "picked up and cited and used." LaVey "started this thing and decided to sell it," he says, "and now he's trying to beg off since it's gotten out of control." He agrees that LaVey's books don't specifically advocate murder, but points to suggestive and equivocal references to human sacrifice and destroying your enemies. LaVey may well have meant

49. Ibid., 1, 6-7.

such talk metaphorically or flippantly, Raschke says, but there are evidently readers out there who take him at his word. According to Raschke, the bottom line is that LaVey teaches a belief system that actually condones and encourages violence and perverse sex.[50]

Raschke points out that "they talk in the *Satanic Bible* about human sacrifice and then they use this sort of weasel word at the end, a disclaimer that it's not meant to be taken literally. Well, I don't think Pete Roland [a teenager who confessed to a Satanic killing] was capable of that intellectual finesse. A lot of kids get this glazed look in their eye when they walk into an occult bookstore, and if they're being told by a friend, 'Well, let's kill a cat and drink the blood and read the *Satanic Bible*,' and when they read about the choice of a human sacrifice, do you think they're really going to figure out what Anton LaVey had in mind?"

In Raschke's opinion, Satanists are using volatile forms of psychological conditioning that can destroy lives, threaten our social fabric, and turn impressionable kids into drooling zombies with an insatiable appetite for bodily secretions. "I think people should have a right to destroy their minds, to indulge in weird fantasies. But that doesn't mean I don't have a right to speak out against something that I think is obnoxious in its influence, and try to warn people."[51]

In fact, it may be immaterial whether "traditional" Satanists, who assert their right to protection under the First Amendment, ever truly carry out the evil that they vaunt and relish in their writings. Like the cloning of IBM personal computers, Satanists' prized beliefs are often "cloned" and retailed by a host of entrepreneurs and even criminal cartels.[52]

A well-known historian of beliefs about Satan, Jeffrey Russell, of the University of California at Santa Barbara, sees LaVey's "The Satanic Bible" as a mix of hedonistic maxims and incoherent occultism. In it LaVey describes the devil as a good, creative power associated with sex, success, and freedom from restraints. Russell says the proposition that the devil is good rather than evil is literal nonsense, a proposition without meaning, for it contradicts the basic definition of the word.

Russell agrees that LaVey and his writings encourage interest in the devil. However, he sees the main cause of this renewed attention to the devil as the need to fill the void created by the disappearance of traditional religions. This need for some type of religion, he maintains, can assert itself in bizarre forms, one of which is the Church of Satan.[53]

50. Michael Roberts, "Beat the Devil," *Westword — Denver's News and Arts Weekly* 14.9 (Oct. 31–Nov. 6, 1990): 3.

51. Ibid., 5.

52. Raschke, *Painted Black*, 77.

53. Jeffrey Russell, *The Prince of Darkness* (Ithaca, N.Y.: Cornell University, 1988), 261-62.

# HARD-CORE AND CRIME-PRONE SATANISM

Until the 1960s, Satanism was seen by many people as a rejection of middle-class values and an expression of chronic adolescent "alienation." With its eroticism, its mysticism, its sheer and mischievous nonsense, it was not taken seriously by a large sector of Americans.

But with the Manson murders in 1969 and the Matamoros murders discovered in Mexico in 1989, that notion has ended. Satanism is now seen by a substantial majority as involving the dangers of nihilism and terrorism. There is evidence of a broad and powerful ideology which is in collision with the biblical world and its belief system and moral sensibilities.

## Charles Manson and the Manson family

Charles Manson is representative of those individuals with deep-seated criminal tendencies for whom Satanism provides a vocabulary to symbolize and act out deviant, patterned behavior. Very often these persons can be serial killers, sexual deviants, or child molesters. They may be skilled in mind-control techniques, stage magic, and mood setting.

### EARLY LIFE

Manson, who called himself the "Devil" and would frequently use demonic symbols, is a premier example of the self-styled Satanist. Manson was abused severely as a child and eventually abandoned. He became a hardened criminal who spent more of his years behind bars than in a normal social environment. The details of his life are spelled out by Los Angeles deputy district attorney Vincent Bugliosi in *Helter Skelter*.

He was born "no-name Maddox" on November 12, 1934, in Cincinnati, Ohio, the illegitimate son of a sixteen-year-old girl named Kathleen Maddox. His mother lived with a succession of men. One, a much older man named William Manson, whom she married, was around just long enough to provide a surname for her son.[54]

### SCIENTOLOGY AND THE PROCESS CHURCH

Though uneducated, Manson was extremely street smart. The result was that he plunged into the kind of career that befitted his warped genius — he

54. Vincent Bugliosi and Curt Gentry, *Helter Skelter* (New York: Bantam, 1974), 184-85.

became a con artist. During one of his brief stints between jail sentences, Manson studied pop psychology, hypnosis, magic, and the occult — in particular, Scientology. Scientology, an outgrowth of science-fiction writer L. Ron Hubbard's Dianetics, was just coming into vogue at that time. Manson continued his studies of Scientology in prison. His teacher, or "auditor," was another convict, Lanier Rayner. Manson would later claim that while in prison, he achieved Scientology's highest level, "theta clear."[55]

Manson's familiarity with Scientology made him particularly susceptible years later to receiving Robert de Grimston's Process teachings. (De Grimston split from Scientology and organized the Church of the Process of the Final Judgment in England in 1964.) Manson's criminal connections were extensive because of his life as a jailbird. This gave Manson the "business" clout and savvy to translate de Grimston's revolutionary teachings about the urgency of end time revolution into occult action.[56]

Paul Watkins, Manson's second-in-command, said of his Master Satan: "Manson was big on Scientology and black magic. He picked it all up in San Francisco. It was pretty powerful stuff. He was continually hypnotizing us . . . like mental thought transference."[57]

## RITUAL SLAYINGS AS AN APOCALYPTIC TRIGGER

Manson was a tactician with tremendous personal skills and a baroque imagination. Even the murder of Hollywood actress Sharon Tate in 1969 was more an artistic "happening" than most people realize. Watkins told of Charles Manson's desire for human sacrifice and the delight of the Slaves in the torture-slaying of musician Gary Hinman, one of twenty-five supposed victims of the Manson family.

According to Raschke, the killings were not political assassinations so much as they were ritual, or sacrificial, slayings. In keeping with the symbolism of Crowley and the fantasies of aesthetic terrorists, the slayings were intended as supernatural "triggers" for the apocalyptic upheavals that magicians since early in the century had been expecting.

Manson's idea of helter-skelter had some obvious relation to Process Church theology. It connoted, in effect, the unleashing of the cataclysmic evils of the end times in order to align the powers of Satan with the majesty of Christ.[58]

<hr>

55. Ibid., 195-96.
56. Raschke, *Painted Black,* 113.
57. Fritscher, *Popular Witchcraft,* 133.
58. Raschke, *Painted Black,* 113-14.

## THE BEATLES AND THE BOOK OF REVELATION

Manson had taken the name "helter-skelter" from the Beatles' song and the concept from what he regarded as the "secret" meanings behind the "Revolution 9" on the *White Album*. "Revolution 9" was the apocalyptic substantiation of the Bible's Revelation 9. This is the chapter that tells of the blowing of the "fifth trumpet" and the opening the "bottomless pit" from which fly scorpionlike creatures "with hair like women's hair," which are commissioned to torture a third of humankind.

Bugliosi makes much of the influence of Revelation 9 and the Beatles on Manson's thoughts and actions. On different occasions, Manson interpreted Revelation 8 and 9. The "four angels" were the Beatles, whom Manson considered "leaders, spokesmen, prophets." The line "And he opened the bottomless pit. . . . And there came out of the smoke locusts upon the earth; and unto them was given power" (Rev. 9:2-3) was still another reference to the English group of musicians. Locusts — Beatles — one and the same. "Their faces were as the faces of men," yet "they had hair as the hair of women" (Rev. 9:7-8). This was an obvious reference to the long-haired musicians. Out of the mouths of the four angels "issued fire and brimstone" (Rev. 8:5). According to Gregg Jackson, a student of Manson's philosophy, this referred to the spoken words, the lyrics of the Beatles' songs, the power that came out of their mouths.

The reference in Revelation 9 to their "breastplates of fire," according to Poston, a follower of Manson, was to the Beatles' electric guitars. Their shapes, "like unto horses prepared unto battle," were the Manson family's dune buggies (Rev. 9:7). The "horsemen who numbered two hundred thousand" and who would roam the earth spreading destruction, were predicting motorcyclists (Rev. 9:16-17).

Another verse, Revelation 9:4, states: "And it was commanded them that they should not hurt the grass of the earth, neither any green thing, neither any tree; but only those men which have not the seal of God in their foreheads." The mark or seal would designate for Manson whether they were with him or against him. With Manson, it was either one or the other; there was no middle road.

Again, Manson quoted Revelation 9:15, 11: "And the four angels were loosed, which were prepared for an hour, and a day, and a month, and a year, for to slay the third part of men. . . . And they had a king over them, which is the angel of the bottomless pit, whose name in the Hebrew tongue is Abaddon, but in the Greek tongue hath his name Apollyon." The Manson family noted that the king also had a Latin name, which, though it appears in the Catholic Douay Version, was inadvertently omitted by the translators of the King James Version. This name was Exterminans. Exterminans, they believed, refers to Charles Manson. "The important thing to remember about Revelation 9," a Manson colleague said, "is that Charlie believed this was happening *now*, not in the future. It's going to begin now and it's time to choose sides."

## A PROPHECY OF REVOLUTION

Manson believed that "the Beatles were spokesmen." He considered their songs prophecy, especially the songs in the so-called *White Album*. The *White Album*, Manson said, "set up things for the revolution." An album entitled *His*, which was to follow, would, in Charlie's words, "blow the cork off the bottle. That would start it." Almost every song in this album had a hidden meaning which Manson interpreted for his followers. The *White Album* contains two songs with the word "revolution" in the title. Manson took this to mean that the Beatles, once undecided, now favored the revolution.[59]

Manson believed his "family," with their long hippie tresses, were in fact the appointed agents of wrath and mutilation. He even holed up his "family" at a remote location in Death Valley, a site he thought was the entrance to the bottomless pit. When "helter-skelter" was finished, he would return with his legions of doom to their foul abode inside the bowels of the earth.

Raschke sees evidence of the influence that the Process Church of de Grimston had on Manson. Until 1969, Manson had proselytized for the Haight-Ashbury belief of "love is all, love is groovy." In 1969 he was pronouncing the "opposite," which he said was not really a contradiction. The distinction between hate and love, he explained, is an illusion clutched by the unenlightened soul. Manson's crowd began to dress up like Process Church members in black capes and other forms of black attire in order to practice "getting the Fear."

The pages of the *Fear* issue of the Process Church publication are filled with images of holocaust. On the back is a flaming pink skull. Out of the skull's mouth marches a phalanx of Nazi storm troopers parading over masses of people burning up in a fire. At the lower right can be seen the evil visage of Hitler and a Buddhist monk in flames. The head of page one reads, "Next issue: DEATH."[60]

Death did come on August 8, 1969, at the lavish and highly protected home of actress Sharon Tate and her movie producer husband, Roman Polanski, in the Hollywood hills.

59. Bugliosi and Gentry, *Helter Skelter*, 322-28.
60. Raschke, *Painted Black*, 114.

## MANSON'S MOTIVE

The motive? There is some evidence that there was a "ritual" structure to the acts of the Manson family. Was it related to a vast drug and pornography procurement racket in which Manson was enmeshed and which implicated many of the Hollywood stars, including Roman Polanski? One hypothesis is that Sharon Tate was killed in vengeance for a drug deal that had gone sour. But Sharon, who was pregnant, seems to have not been involved with drugs during the pregnancy.

In any case, the Manson episode is part of a common ideology and a common set of passions. Susan Atkins, one of Manson's followers, at one time worked as a dancer for Anton LaVey in his collusion with a nightclub impresario. It is known that Manson had a close association not only with members of the Church of the Process, but with the remnants of Crowley's organizational structure — the O.T.O. in Southern California. But the personal and institutional ties are much less important than the collusive strength of the total occult experience.[61]

In January 1996, the A&E television network presented a biography of Charles Manson. The program reviewed his life and included interviews with the three women sentenced to life imprisonment in 1971 along with Manson. On the program the three women claimed Manson broke their will. They expressed regret for their participation in the 1969 killings. Manson did not. He calmly denied any responsibility. He has been denied parole nine times.

## The Rancho Santa Elena cult and drugs

John Charles Cooper, a specialist in the occult, contends that the Matamoros drug-smuggling cult of Adolfo de Jesus Constanzo amply illustrates the connection between drug use and destructive occultism. Constanzo's group has received little continuing follow-up except the efforts of the "trash" media.[62] This is a shame, for the uncovering of the Matamoros tragedy is evidence of the real demonic underground of destructive occultism that does exist.

Before discovery of the gruesome remains of the fifteen victims of cult kidnappings and "sacrifice" on that remote ranch west of the Mexican border city of Matamoros in April 1989, there had been reports of "occult-related" crimes throughout the country, from southern California to New England. These reports, handled by local police, had frequently been met with suspicion and even ridicule by some authorities.

---

61. Ibid., 114-16.
62. Cooper, *The Black Mask,* 126.

After Matamoros, the climate changed.

The horror of Satanic crime — often entailing deliberate and brutal torture, mutilation, or dismemberment of victims — could no longer be dismissed as merely Christian fundamentalist ravings or social hysteria. The bodies of the victims were visible to an international television audience and the cultists' confessions were given in detail to journalists on both sides of the border.

The Matamoros case conformed to what many criminologists and a few anthropologists had been saying for decades about the darker facets of the occult. The occult was a "bonding" mechanism that ensured both loyalty and control within tight-knit, conspiratorial groups. It was a setting for criminal enterprise of the most elaborate and dangerous type. The Matamoros cultists were related to the vast underground empire of Latin American drug runners stretching from Peru and Colombia through the central Mexico mountains to the streets of America's cities. Their "religion" had been improvised from a variety of sources encompassing Mexican peasant folk magic, the Hollywood horror movie *The Believers,* and the warped fantasies of Adolfo de Jesus Constanzo. This blend of the ancient and the contemporary make up what is most appropriately called Satanism.[63]

## THE MATAMOROS MURDERS

During the early morning of March 14, 1989, a 21-year-old University of Texas student, Mark Kilroy, was abducted from the streets of Matamoros, Mexico. On April 11, Kilroy's body was recovered from a shallow grave on a ranch outside Matamoros owned by the Hernandez family. The body had been mutilated, as had most of the other fourteen corpses recovered on the same site. Investigation determined that Kilroy and others had been sacrificed in rituals designed to obtain supernatural protection for the drug-smuggling activities of the Hernandez family.

## ADOLFO CONSTANZO

The sacrificial rituals had been directed by Adolfo Constanzo, a 26-year-old Cuban-American hired by the Hernandez family to provide them with magical protection and to revive the flagging fortunes of their drug-smuggling empire.

What we know now is that Adolfo de Jesus Constanzo was born in 1962 and raised in Miami by his mother, who introduced him to the mysterious practices of Santeria, a cult religion from her native Cuba that combines

63. Raschke, *Painted Black,* 3-4.

elements of primal religion and Roman Catholicism. After moving to Mexico, Constanzo became a sort of ecumenist of the black arts. He appears to have apprenticed himself to sorcerers in various Afro-Cuban and Haitian voodoo cults, including Palo Mayombe and Abakua.

Constanzo admitted to practicing a combination of Santeria and Palo Mayombe, but since it is the custom among Mexican members of these sorts of religions to associate themselves in public conversations only with religions that are closer to legitimacy (a practitioner of Santeria will publicly admit only to practicing "Christian Santeria" or "white Santeria"), we can assume, based on the evidence and the confessions, that he was most probably a practitioner of Abakua. The Abakua engage in torture, human sacrifice, and mystical cannibalism.

In Mexico, the ripping out of a beating human heart calls to mind ancient Aztec rites of sacrifice. This practice was revived by the Constanzo cult. Constanzo's ritual chants were in the African Bantu language, so his practice was also known as Regla de Congo or simply Congo.

Before joining the Hernandez family, Constanzo had established a reputation, extending to the upper echelons of Mexican entertainment and government, for personal charisma and for the supernatural powers of his *limpias* (ritual cleansings). He lived a flamboyant lifestyle in Zona Rosa, Mexico City's gay district.

After the discoveries at Santa Elena Ranch, Constanzo and his inner circle of followers (Alvaro de Leon Valdez; his lovers Omar Francisco Orea Ochoa and Martin Quintana Rodriguez; and his "high priestess" Sara Aldrete) were linked to a series of particularly sadistic ritual murders in Zona Rosa.

Constanzo had earned money by performing religious rites of cleansing — limpias. His clients consisted of narcotics traffickers, government officials, and the elite of Mexico's entertainment business. Each limpia included a ritual of human sacrifice. A homosexual or prostitute from the Zona Rosa district would be invited to attend or perhaps kidnapped. The victim would be stripped naked and placed willingly or unwillingly on the ritual altar. At Constanzo's priestly instruction, assistants would slit open the individual's chest and remove the heart, and then all present would drink blood directly from the heart. The victim's brain and other body parts would then be removed and placed in a cauldron along with other symbolic items connoting death, and the resulting mixture would be consumed by all present. Inflicting terror and pain just prior to death was deemed important, because it was assumed that fear placed the victim's soul totally in the killer's hand. The priest typically tortured the victim prior to execution as a means of capturing the dead soul's power so that it could be redirected for the use of the living. Constanzo explained that this procedure guaranteed his paying customers mystical power for professional success. He performed two to three limpias per week. His wealthy customers paid $30,000 to $40,000 for the sorcerer's service.[64]

## CONSTANZO'S "HIGH PRIESTESS"

Although the practices that led to this series of murders borrowed features of Afro-Caribbean religions such as Santeria, to which Constanzo had been introduced by his mother, other influences proved far more important to the final form the rituals took. Among these was Sara Aldrete, who became Constanzo's "high priestess."

Prior to her involvement with Constanzo, Aldrete had been a student at Texas Southmost University in Brownsville, Texas, and had studied the anthropology of religion. More importantly, she had become obsessed with the 1987 film *The Believers,* which focuses on a cult that practices human sacrifice to acquire supernatural power and protection. Her obsession led to Constanzo's cult using the film as an indoctrination tool.[65]

The breakthrough for the Matamoros case occurred on April 9, 1989. Serafin Hernandez Garcia, a nephew of reputed crime boss Elio Hernandez Rivera, ran a roadblock. In fleeing he led officers to Rancho Santa Elena, owned by his family and used for smuggling activities. Here authorities found the bodies and occult apparatus — a bloody altar, "voodoo" paraphernalia, La Palma cigars, cheap rum, human body parts, animal bones, chicken and goat heads, thousands of pennies, gold beads, and an iron kettle filled with the most foul mixture of blood and flesh — a veritable witch's cauldron. The fluid in the cauldron, which contained brains, hearts, lungs, and testicles, had been drunk in regular rituals by the cult members to "sanctify" themselves "so the police would not arrest them, so bullets would not kill them, and so they could make more money."[66]

## THE CONFESSIONS

The Hernandez family confessed to the murder of Kilroy, describing in lurid detail the sacrificial ritual. They revealed some of the workings of the cult and its leaders. They fingered Adolfo de Jesus Constanzo as well as Sara Villarreal Aldrete, who acted as the "high priestess" of the group. At Aldrete's home in Matamoros, police found an assortment of "voodoo" paraphernalia and a blood-spattered altar of sacrifice. She characterized the ritual paraphernalia as "santeria cristiano."

64. Peters, *Sin,* 234-36.
65. Richardson, *The Satanism Scare,* 237-38.
66. Raschke, *Painted Black,* 9-11.

The cult members had been convinced that the kidnapping and sacrifice of an American would secure them supernatural protection on the north side of the river. That they lacked such "protection" was obvious from a recent series of drug busts and the breakdown of their supply lines. Kilroy's body parts were boiled in an iron kettle with animal blood. The cult members then passed around and drank the "witch's" brew as a kind of sickening "communion" among themselves. They believed that the blood and the energies of violence it contained would make them unconquerable soldiers in the war of evil.[67]

The final episode in the Constanzo story came when the police surrounded Constanzo's gang in their Mexico City hideaway. Constanzo ordered Alvaro de Leon Valdez to execute him with machine gun fire, which he did.

The arrested gang, still confident in their magical powers, snickered and laughed as wobbly kneed police, overcome by the stench and horror of what they were seeing, rushed off one by one to vomit. Finally, police called in a curandero, a witch doctor, to exorcise the premises and burn everything to the ground.

But the bodies, the photographs, and the confessions remain, a reminder of the Satanic horror of Constanzo.[68]

## THE BLACK MAGIC OF MATAMOROS

Before Constanzo, Matamoros was a drug boomtown. Among the drug traffickers, there were vicious, frequent, and barbaric incidents of killing. There was also mounting pressure from the American anti-narcotics crusade.

When North American journalists began probing the cultural context of the Matamoros murders, they learned that the practice — and the fear — of black magic was pervasive in the Rio Grande Valley. They discovered a vast black magic belief system and witchcraft that could be traced all the way back to the Spanish conquest.

Scholars continue to argue and speculate whether Constanzo really practiced "classical" Palo Mayombe or whether he was a Satanist. Raschke points out that all forms of occultism by their very nature are entrepreneurial and experimental. The occult, strictly by definition, is opaque, private, and elusive. (The word itself derives from the Latin meaning "obscure" or "concealed.") For that reason occultism can be easily changed to suit the needs of the entrepreneur, even though most occultists insist that they are embroiled in a form of religion that is unchanging.

67. Ibid., 7-8, 21.
68. Peters, *Sin*, 237.

The history of the occult is the chronicle of thousands of strange, constantly shifting, and half-intelligible "systems" of very personal belief. Constanzo appears to have been trained in Palo Mayombe and the black facets of Santeria. Then, under the pressure to succeed in the drug business, he imported the practice of human sacrifice, which he adopted from well-established top-secret strands of Mexican occultism. Following are some of the beliefs behind the Matamoros incident.[69]

## HUMAN SACRIFICE AND THE AZTECS

Constanzo's followers reported that he had educated them in the correct magical procedures of the Aztec priests. These priests would rip the heart from the victim's body cavity and gulp down the blood before it drained away. The belief on which the ritual system of the greater Aztec empire had been built was that the throbbing heart contained the energy of the sun, which had to be "fed" with constant sacrifices. The ancient ritual sites at Mexico City were stained red with the blood of hundreds of thousands of victims killed in this manner. After a sacrifice, the body parts — particularly the brain and vital organs which contained the "soul-life" of the sun — were boiled with blood in an iron kettle for ritual consumption. Spanish soldier Bernal Diaz, who accompanied Cortez on his conquest of Mexico from 1519 until 1521, reported seeing many pots — the kind used by Constanzo — near the Great Temple of Tlatelolco.[70]

## GUARDIAN SPIRIT, OR NAGUAL

Constanzo also adopted the very old Mexican folk magic of the *nagual*. The *nagual* is a guardian spirit — frequently a bird or some other animal of "power" — with whom the magician identifies in order to both master and participate in the universe of black magic. The popular American author Carlos Castaneda has written extensively about a version of nagualism in his stories of the Yaqui Indian sorcerer Don Juan.

Nagualism is basically an underground warrior religion. The nagualists thought that through their magical techniques they could render themselves totally invisible to their enemies and impervious to their enemies' weapons. In effect, Constanzo trained the Hernandezes, "warriors" in their own right, in nagualism.[71]

69. Raschke, *Painted Black*, 22.
70. Ibid., 23.
71. Ibid.

## PALO MAYOMBE

Palo Mayombe is primarily an African sorcery cult. It is, perhaps, a loose term applicable to the Matamoros group. Some of the documented elements of "conventional" Palo Mayombe were discernible among the artifacts found at the shed on the ranch. The use of the big iron cauldron with blood and human and animal parts mixed together is one recognizable feature. The cutting of the arm, the burning of candles, and the smoking of cigars to "attract" the energy of the spirits — these items could be documented. Even obtaining the brain of a *mundele,* or "white person," as a special prize can be seen in the selection of Kilroy. However, the slaying and torturing of enemies in preparation for sacrifice have never been typical of even the most bizarre cultic form of Palo Mayombe in the past. Constanzo was obsessed with death. It was his hatred of his victims, especially Anglos, that distinguished his black magic.[72]

## AFRICAN BLACK MAGIC

The Brownsville-Matamoros cult is a New World variant of a West African sorcery cult. John Charles Cooper, a professor at Eastern Kentucky University, contends that the drug cult of Brownsville, Texas, and Matamoros, Mexico, is most closely related to an African black magic sorcery cult but shares similarities with Santeria (from Cuba) and Brujeria (from Mexico).

Brujeria is a sorcery cult of northern Mexico and the American Southwest. It mixes Santeria-like elements with old European magic and the sorcery or witch cults of Native American tribes. It has some similarities to the black witch cults of the Pueblo and Navaho Indians. The Navahos, for example, still have a great fear of these witch cults. Indeed, the large Indian reservations of the Southwest are now experiencing Satanic activity and have recently held seminars in an attempt to combat it.

Brujeria is a malevolent black-magic cult that appeals to evil spirits for protection. Because of this, it is proper to refer to it as Satanic.

A classic example of such a cult existed among black rebel soldiers in the Congo rebellion of the 1960s. The sorcerer's magic then was designed to protect the rebels against bullets and make them "invisible" to their enemies. The influence of this African cult undoubtedly reached the Western hemisphere because of Cuba's involvement in Angola and in other parts of Africa. More than thirty thousand Cuban soldiers a year served in Africa for over a decade — perhaps for twenty years.[73]

72. Ibid., 23-24.
73. Cooper, *The Black Mask,* 71-73.

The Brownsville-Matamoros cult is thus a New World variant of a West African sorcery cult. Sorcerers gain power over spirits by elaborate rituals and sacrifices (witches come by their supposed powers naturally). Therefore the cult leader (or "patron" or "father") who uses these sacrificial rituals is a sorcerer, not a witch.

It should not be overlooked that a Matamoros cult member who confessed spoke of sacrificing to "the devil." Nor should the goat's head (associated with the devil) or the inverted crosses tattooed on at least one cult member be forgotten. This hybrid cult was fundamentally designed to be Satanic — evil.[74]

## SANTERIA

This religion from the Yoruba tribe of southwestern Nigeria is mingled with the practices of old Spanish Roman Catholicism in Cuba. In the United States there are about eighty thousand Santeria followers.[75] A woman who knew Constanzo's family in Miami, where he had grown up, told newspapers that his mother, Delia Gonzales Del Valle, "was in *santeria*." His grandmother, Delia's mother, had apparently been a practitioner in Cuba. Norma Brito, who bought the family's home in Miami, said she found altar remains of *santeria* ceremonies.

The *New York Times* reports that Santeria is going public. For decades it has operated in a muted underground in New York City, but recently it jumped out of the shadows. It has burst onto the Internet. It has smitten musicians and in 1997 hit Broadway in a musical. And it has slowly seeped into city life through its African and Cuban cultures.

## A MOVIE AND AN OBSESSION

Constanzo claimed to base his rituals on the movie *The Believers*. His high priestess, Sara Aldrete, was also obsessed with this movie. *The Believers* tells the story of a bizarre and unnamed African religion that has been adapted by Hispanic followers and white cultists in New York City. It centers on child sacrifice as a means of achieving divine powers and averting personal harm.

It is not at all surprising that Constanzo and Aldrete were infatuated with the movie. The practitioners of the religion in the film are portrayed as insuperable and almost all-knowing. In one telling scene, a victim of the fictional cult screams in a jail-cell interview that the "believers" can even "walk through walls." *The Believers* theatrically strives to hammer home the sense

74. Ibid., 76.
75. Ibid., 71

that the cult, though protected by its own facade of upstanding citizenry, is "everywhere," and therefore its influence cannot be resisted. In a less stagey manner, the real-life saga of Constanzo and his troop of "believers" revealed similar themes.[76]

## VIOLENCE TO THE EXTREME

An anthropologist called in on the Matamoros murders stated that Constanzo was a "psychopathic killer who took the practice of Palo Mayombe into his own hands." The anthropologist said Constanzo's concern was attainment of power for oneself and the warding off, if not the destruction, of adversaries.

The issue of where the Santeria of his mother shades off into Palo Mayombe and where Palo Mayombe lapses into Satanism touches directly on the degree of potential criminal application of all occult practices.

Satanism is the carrying of magic and intrigue to the utmost extremes. Constanzo *was* a Satanist because he went beyond the basic moral and cere- monial boundaries established by the magical traditions, which he had learned at his mother's knee. Constanzo's mastery of occult mind control was a talent he took with him from Miami to Mexico City, and it accounted for his rapid rise to power in both high society and in the tightly controlled Colombian- based drug cartels.

Constanzo was, in fact, a Hispanic "New Ager," the Latin American equivalent of a California psychic who nonetheless converted his understand- ing of metaphysical mumbo-jumbo into a particularly successful criminal conspiracy. He combined his knowledge of Afro-Cuban magic with mysteri- ous and secretive Mexican traditions of human sacrifice dating back to the Mayans and Aztecs.

It was not the Afro-Cuban or "Santerian" elements that gave Con- stanzo's cult its ghastly nature. It was the "Mexican mystique" of blood and the inflicting of torture on human captives, witnessed by the Spaniards during the conquest. According to their worldview, Constanzo and his followers were not irrational. They were merely reverting to a worldview of black magic and logic that had been starkly imprinted in the pre-Christian strata of their society.[77]

## THE IMPACT OF THE MATAMOROS INCIDENT

Within a month after the first reports in the press, investigators began making connections that placed the Matamoros situation in a much more sweeping

76. Raschke, *Painted Black,* 20.
77. Ibid., 12-14.

context. Customs agents realized that the slayings at the ranch bore a striking resemblance to mass murders committed about the same time at the Mexican border town of Agua Prieta, about 120 miles southeast of Tucson, Arizona.

In June 1989 federal drug agents raided a house in San Mateo County south of San Francisco and came across a sacrificial altar, animal organs, human skulls, and a human spinal column used in rituals. The remains and paraphernalia were almost identical to what had been discovered at Matamoros just two months earlier.

Now information gathered before Matamoros began to fall into place. One year earlier, during a drug raid in Houston, law officers had found an altar and paraphernalia that resembled those discovered later at Matamoros. Convicted mass killer Henry Lee Lucas had told authorities that he had been connected with a Satanic cult operating along the border of Texas and Mexico, but authorities had done nothing about that statement. After Matamoros, with Lucas still waiting on death row, the Texas attorney general's office took a second look at those statements.[78]

In December 1989 when the U.S. Army invaded Panama to arrest General Manuel Noriega, who had been indicted in Miami on drug trafficking charges, soldiers entering Noriega's apartment found many of the same paraphernalia Constanzo had owned. A picture of President Ronald Reagan was covered in red candle wax. Buckets of blood, Buddha statues (which Constanzo also kept), and representations of frogs were found. Like Constanzo, Noriega had mixed a wide assortment of native Hispanic black magic with European Satanism.[79]

On the American side of the border was the Satanic ritualistic murder in 1987 in Joplin, Missouri, which brought a confession from Pete Roland, a teenager.

Tragically, some teenage dabblers order Satanic paraphernalia and read LaVey's *Satanic Bible*. They're experimenting. Some have committed suicide. Others, like Roland, have become killers.[80]

## Satanism and Human Sacrifice

A danger lurking behind the beliefs of black occultists and Satanists is the trivialization of human life, the fact that a human can so easily be killed as a sacrifice, that the killing is not even done humanely but with torture to enhance the benefit of the sacrifice.

78. Ibid., 16-17.
79. Ibid., 25-26.
80. Ibid., 28-29.

According to Raschke, Satanism, formally begun in the United States by LaVey, has gone from mere "wicked and ungodly" deportment, as the mark of innate human depravity, to a rude metaphysics of vengeance and violence.

For Satanists there is a transvaluation, or complete reversal, of all values. In the case of murder, the self-styled Satanists explain their actions by saying they killed to see what the experience was like. The sense of power, of utter control over someone's life and death, has greater value to such killers than the victim's life.

The selfish search for pleasure encouraged in Satanism builds a gateway to immoral behavior. And as the pursuit of physical pleasure continues, the person involved demands more intense stimulation. At that point, the sadistic abuse of others, or the masochistic abuse of one's own body, may begin.

## CHILD ABUSE

A controversial and widespread discussion relates to the many reports of child abuse connected to Satanism. Some public officials have discounted the Satanic element in these cases. Others, such as occult investigator and former FBI special agent Ted Gundersen, allege that the Satanic involvement reported in a number of these cases is real.

What has been proved is child abuse in several new religions, or "cults." In such groups, *discipline* is often a code word for "sadistic mistreatment of little children." Therefore, on the basis of the actual abuse we know took place and still takes place in certain of the new religions (which Cooper has called "destructive cults"), it is not difficult to believe that such child abuse takes place in underground, or criminal, Satanic cults.[81]

## EXTENT AND INFLUENCE OF THE SATANIST MOVEMENT

In 1991, I attended the fifth annual International Conference on New Religions, at Santa Barbara, California. At that conference, sociologist David G. Bromley called for a reappraisal of the claims and reports of the anti-Satanist movement. As a result of that conference, theologian Ted Peters has identified three basic facets of the Satanic phenomenon: the Satanism movement, the anti-Satanism movement, and the anti-anti-Satanism movement.

The anti-Satanists, according to Peters, are convinced of the existence of a massive underground network of organized Satanic groups who practice ritual worship of the devil, sponsor molestations of children in preschools, kidnap or breed their own children for ritual purposes and the production of child pornography, torture animals and sacrifice human beings in versions of

81. Cooper, *Black Mask,* 115-21.

the Black Mass, practice cannibalism, and continue to recruit our nation's young people through heavy metal music and games such as "Dungeons and Dragons." Supporting the anti-Satanists are television personalities Geraldo Rivera and Oprah Winfrey and scholars such as Carl Raschke.

Against the anti-Satanists are the anti-anti-Satanists, who include social scientists, law enforcement personnel who are disenchanted with their anti-Satanist colleagues, and Satanists themselves. Many anti-anti-Satanists doubt that Satanism exists in any widespread organized conspiracy. And some oppose anti-Satanism simply because it has been linked with evangelical and fundamentalist Christian forces.

The anti-Satanists claim in a flyer put out by the Schiller Institute that 1.8 million children have disappeared in the United States, abducted by Satanists for ritualistic sacrifices. The anti-anti-Satanists disagree, saying no proof exists.

Anti-Satanists describe complex Satanic rituals sponsored by a huge and complex underground network of Satanists. The anti-anti folks say there is no evidence of any common belief system, set of rituals, or Satanic organizational apparatus.

The stories of Satanic cult abuse reported to therapists by people suffering from Multiple Personality Disorder also fall into the two camps. While anti-anti-Satanists do not casually dismiss these reports, they consider them unconvincing as evidence of widespread Satanism. Skeptic Jeffrey Victor contends that those with multiple personalities have a chameleonlike, manipulative personality and feed therapists the kinds of stories they feel the therapists want to hear. Therapists who want to hear stories of cult abuse get them.

Also at issue is the credibility of law enforcement people who specialize in cult crime. Anti-anti-Satanists such as Robert Hicks, who is a law enforcement officer, are critical of so-called specialists in cult crime, claiming they lack professionalism. Hicks argues that cult cops gain their knowledge from seminars and workshops rather than from actual encounters with Satanic groups. He calls for restraint and careful investigation: "Some cult survivors may be telling accurate accounts of human sacrifice; satanic cults may be running day-care centers; and playing Dungeons and Dragons may lead some children to acquire the Black Arts. If such phenomena exist, then they must be proved."[82]

Some are against the anti-Satanists merely to combat the influence of conservative Christianity. They try repeatedly, through guilt by association and innuendo, to reduce the anti-Satanist movement to nothing more than an expression of Christian fundamentalism rather than a force to combat the Satanic threat. They attribute to anti-Satanists the following hidden agenda:

82. Peters, *Sin*, 224-29, 231-33.

if an anti-Satanist effort gets people to believe in Satan, it can also get them to believe in God. As proof of this reasoning Jeffrey Victor reported finding a therapist at a conference on cults who said that the existence of Satanism had confirmed her belief in God.[83]

But Peters disagrees that Christian fundamentalists are the single push behind the anti-Satanism effort. He notes that the amalgam of groups supporting the anti-Satanism position does not represent a single unified theology, let alone any fundamentalist Christian theology. Many of the psychotherapists associated with the anti-Satanism sentiment are Jewish or secular or otherwise unlikely to subordinate their psychological theories to a fundamentalist ideology. Groups rallying to expose or prevent preschool child abuse contain random mixes of individuals, including parents from a variety of religious and political backgrounds. The police departments of our states and municipalities are arms of government, not from churches.

What appears to be happening between the anti-Satanists and the anti-anti-Satanists is that each side is characterizing people they disagree with as a group that is conspiring to undermine our society.[84]

David Bromley, a secular sociologist, attributes both the religious cult scare of the 1970s and the Satanism scare of the 1980s and '90s to heightened social tensions caused by the turning over of previously family-held responsibilities to businesses or contractual agencies. To put it simply, Bromley says the growth in the child-care industry marks one more way that parents have been losing control over their children's socialization process. Parents who drop their children off at day care can be vulnerable to projection, self-justification, and the scapegoating of day-care workers. Chaos threatens the family order.

Although this argument covers only one area, it does afford some insights. There is trouble, but the troublemaker is not just an external force — a Satanic underground. Rather, the trouble is also rooted in the vulnerability families feel to any and all external forces.[85]

Peters notes that even though one cannot rightly characterize anti-Satanism as solely a movement of Christian fundamentalists, it is true that conservative Christians of both fundamentalist and evangelical persuasions are deeply involved in it. Peters is disturbed by much evangelical literature because it falls into the trap of crying wolf. He claims that if we are told to walk in the fear that Satan is hiding behind every bush, we will eventually either condemn as the devil's work everything that is the least bit unconventional or begin to dismiss the whole idea of Satan as nothing more than a sham.

83. Ibid., 233.
84. Ibid., 241.
85. Ibid., 243-45.

The problem is that Satan, the wolf of radical evil, does exist, and we need to consider the threat from him with utter seriousness. If we trivialize radical evil by identifying it with every point of view with which we disagree, we may fail to recognize the real Satan when he does appear.[86]

For an evangelical Christian, the current threat from Satanism calls for presentation of a balanced view of the biblical approach to both radical evil and Satanism.

## Radical Evil

We have noted individuals and groups such as Crowley, LaVey, Manson, and Constanzo who have given themselves up wholly to radical evil and who take pride and delight in doing so. Globally radical evil expresses itself in genocide, terrorism, and preparations for nuclear war. Individually it appears in actions of callousness and cruelty. On August 24, 1987, *Time* magazine described the state of mind of Michael Hagan, a 23-year-old who methodically shot a young girl six times in the back, killing her "just for kicks." Hagan had never met Kellie Mosier or her family. He did not care about Kellie or her dreams of being a model or the fact that she never belonged to any gang. "I done did something, and I'm known," he boasted, smiling broadly as he lounged behind the bars of the Los Angeles County jail.

Jeffrey Russell, a noted scholar of the history and concept of Satan, contends that there is a will to destruction, a focus of annihilating malice, existing like a sucking void within humanity, unlimited except by the practical boundaries of our physical power to destroy. Two psychiatrists long associated with the New York State penal system observed that some people have no desire at all for good. Their lives have been turned over to the void. Radical evil has always existed; it now threatens to overwhelm us entirely.[87]

## The Early Biblical Worldview and Radical Evil

The biblical worldview includes belief in the real existence of Satan and principalities and powers. It recognizes these powers as angelic beings belonging to Satan's kingdom. Their aim is to lead humanity away from God through direct influence on individuals as well as through wielding control over the world religions and various other structures of our existence. Belief in the real existence of these powers continued through almost the entire history of the

86. Ibid., 246-48.
87. Russell, *The Prince of Darkness*, 273.

church, including the Reformation. Martin Luther, like all of his contemporaries, had no doubt about the terrible power of the devil and his hosts of darkness, as is evident from his classic hymn "A Mighty Fortress Is Our God" and his many writings.[88]

## The Enlightenment Critique

Clinton Arnold points out that the Copernican overthrow of the dominant Ptolemaic view of an earth-centered universe was the catalyst for a new scientific spirit that swept through Europe in the seventeenth and eighteenth centuries — an age known as the Enlightenment. The advances made in the sciences were astounding. They were made possible through the development of a scientific method based on reason, observation, and experiment.

The thinkers of this so-called "Age of Enlightenment" began to apply this scientific method not only to science and technology but also to the humanities. The enthusiasm for the method produced a distrust of authority and tradition in all matters of intellectual inquiry. This distrust included the traditions of the church and the authority of Scripture. Consequently, many of the Enlightenment scholars rejected religion, with the majority becoming deists, believing in the laws of nature and the universe rather than God, and some even turning away from God entirely and espousing atheism.

The new supremacy of a materialistic and rationalistic worldview called into question the reality of the miraculous and supernatural, even that which was recorded in Scripture. The references to demons and angels now became regarded as "myth," perhaps important for conveying theological truth but devoid of any historical substance.[89]

## PARTIAL AND INADEQUATE EXPLANATIONS OF RADICAL EVIL

The "Structures of Power" model contends that personal pathology, distress, and alienation are not due to a flawed personal psyche or demons but are instead caused by capitulation by the person to oppressive structures of power. Such a perspective is held by some liberation theologians, Marxists, and a wide spectrum of social theorists. According to those who see the cause in structures and society, people are held in submission to alienating structures and ideologies. They cannot be liberated by personal insight unless that insight

---

88. Clinton E. Arnold, *Powers of Darkness: Principalities and Powers in Paul's Letters* (Downers Grove, Ill.: InterVarsity, 1992), 169-70.
89. Ibid., 170.

includes the ways in which their inner demons are the internalized product of brute institutional power. Help is to be found primarily in social struggle, reform, or revolution.

The "Psychological Model," which is held by a large number of people in the Western world, holds that while structures and systems may contribute to personal breakdown, psychopathology is primarily the consequence of developmental malfunctions. Help is given through personal analysis, behavioral modification, or lifestyle change.

Sigmund Freud (1856-1939) took religion as a mere psychological phenomenon whose origins and nature can be not only explained but explained away. Freud developed a theory about the devil, the central point of which was that "the Devil is clearly nothing other than the personification of repressed unconscious drives." The devil always represented whatever element of the unconscious was most in opposition to the conscious will. The devil is the projection onto a metaphysical being of the whole hostility of Christian society.[90]

## The Question of Evil Spirits

Science is not qualified to decide the question of evil spirits. Just as it is beyond the scope of science to adjudicate on matters of morality, so it is beyond the parameters of science to make a decision on the question of the existence of the devil and evil spirits, or angels and God. Jeffrey Russell states, "The fact that most people today dismiss the idea [of evil spirits] as old-fashioned, even 'disproved,' is the result of a muddle in which science is called on to pass judgment in matters unrelated to science."

The question of the existence of evil spirits depends not on scientific observation, but upon revelation, worldview, and human experience. As we will see, the Old and New Testaments affirm that these writers believed in the existence of the powers. The tradition of the church corroborates it. The worldviews of many societies give credence to the idea of evil spirits.[91]

Purely naturalistic explanations are not adequate to describe many forms of evil in the world today. To give one example, I participated in a conference composed of psychiatrists, anthropologists, psychologists, and theologians to discuss this problem. Basil Jackson, professor of psychiatry at the University of Wisconsin, opened the conference with this statement: "A sense of desperation has come upon some of us. We cannot cope with certain problems that we have been faced with clinically. These people make little

90. Russell, *The Prince of Darkness*, 242-45.
91. Arnold, *Powers of Darkness*, 178.

response to our professional ingenuity. Perhaps we have missed something quite important both psychologically and spiritually because we have ignored the material in the Bible about Satan and the demonic."

Researchers are coming to a common conclusion, that some evil force is at work in the world. In his book *Christ Triumphant*, Graham Twelftree demonstrates that psychologists and counselors today are faced with an "unexplained residue," situations in the problems of clients that they can't explain. Anthropologists face the same unexplainable phenomena in the interpretation of their fieldwork. Jeffrey Russell has spent much of his academic life in a quest to find an explanation for the horrific evil in the world. He has become increasingly convinced of the existence of the traditional devil — "a mighty person with intelligence and will whose energies are bent on the destruction of the cosmos and on the misery of its creatures." For Russell, the potential global annihilation insured by nuclear war, the untold suffering and killings of an Auschwitz, and the fact that a mother could put her four-year-old child in an oven and burn her to death (Auburn, Maine, 1984) cannot be explained by mere human destructiveness. There must be a powerful force leading humanity to destruction.[92]

## Neglect of Biblical Traditions

Russell also points out that the Jewish, Christian, and Muslim traditions have for 2,500 years thought seriously about the problem of evil. No other religions or ideologies have confronted the problem so directly and courageously as these three, which formulate it in such a poignant way: How can radical evil exist in a world created by a good God? How can it, yet it does?

This creative tension within the theology of the great Western religions for two and a half millennia has produced thousands, even millions, of serious, truth-seeking people, many of them brilliant intellectuals, many others deeply spiritual, still others astute psychologists, who have wrestled with the problem. This creates a reservoir of wisdom that is ridiculous to dismiss, yet leading voices of our dominant worldview have done just that. The concept of the devil and of radical evil is one of the fruits of these two and a half millennia of wise reflection, and we have much to learn from it.[93]

92. Ibid., 179.
93. Paul Woodruff and Harry A. Wilmer, eds., *Facing Evil: Light at the Core of Darkness* (LaSalle, Ill.: Open Court, 1988), 59.

## Denying the Reality of Demons

Arnold points out that the West needs to realize that it is the only contemporary society that denies the reality of evil spirits. The field of anthropology reveals that throughout Asia, Africa, the Pacific islands, among folk Muslims — virtually anywhere that the Western worldview has not permeated — the idea of evil spirits is an integral part of the worldview of many groups.[94]

On the basis of extensive missionary experience, Donald R. Jacobs notes that in Africa, Latin America, and Polynesia the worldview of the people resembles that of the New Testament world, a world populated with spirits. Modern missions have dealt almost exclusively with the sin-forgiving aspect of the Christian faith. But the demons remained and they were exorcised, as they had been for centuries, by traditional shamanistic practices. Christian faith, therefore, had its limits. What Christ was not expected to do, the local practitioners claimed they could! According to Jacobs, by failing to introduce Jesus to all levels of spiritual beliefs in a culture, an undergirding is given to a sort of spiritual dualism in which Jesus answers some questions and other questions are answered by other spiritual powers.[95]

For many Westerners, such worldviews that continue to give the demonic a place are discounted as prescientific. Often there is an assumption that once these people are educated, they will eventually see that their ways of perceiving reality were wrong. It is supposed that they will eventually begin to think of evil in "correct" abstract terms.

After working in India, anthropologist Paul Hiebert came to the conclusion that Western culture has a significant blind spot when it comes to the question of spirits and evil powers — a blind spot he has termed "the flaw of the excluded middle." He describes Western evangelicalism as answering questions of life experience either in empirical (scientific) or theistic (divine) terms, but neglecting the middle zone of spirit forces that are believed by non-Western cultures to influence life. He paints the results of this dichotomy in rather startling terms, making clear the implications for missions: "When tribal people spoke of fear of evil spirits, Western missionaries denied the existence of the spirits rather than claim the power of Christ over them." The result, as missionary Leslie Newbigin has pointed out, is that Western Christian missions have been one of the greatest secularizing forces in history. Gordon Fee, professor at Regent College in Vancouver, affirms that the cloistered existence of the Western university tends to isolate Western aca

94. Arnold, *Powers of Darkness*, 179.
95. John Warwick Montgomery, ed., *Demon Possession* (Minneapolis: Bethany Fellowship, 1976), 183-87.

demics from the realities that many Third World people experience on a regular basis.[96]

## THE RESURGENCE OF BELIEF IN TRANSHUMAN EVIL POWERS

The Naturalistic or Materialistic view of the West has never convinced the entire population of the nonexistence of Satan and evil spirits. In fact, belief in the spirit world and spirit possession has found many devotees during the last two hundred years. There also was an upsurge in spiritualism in the Victorian era, especially after the publication of Darwin's *Origin of the Species* in 1859.

### Charismatic and Pentecostal Groups

Many Christian groups have continued to affirm the real existence of evil spirits. Protestant Pentecostal and charismatic groups unanimously believe in the reality and power of evil spirits and minister to people on the basis of that assumption. Numerous other Protestant denominations, subgroups, independent churches, and individuals within some of the mainline churches affirm the existence of this realm. Even the Roman Catholic Church continues to maintain an office of exorcist.[97]

### Evangelicalism

In recent years, evangelicalism has grown increasingly open to the idea that evil spirits do exist and need to be reckoned with on a spiritual basis. This concern is evidenced in part by the vast number of books and pamphlets published over the past decade on the topic of "spiritual warfare." Much of this literature is coming from the writings of evangelicals who are neither Charismatic nor Pentecostal. The formation of the "International Center for Biblical Counseling" in Sioux City, Iowa, is representative of this growing concern to factor principles of "spiritual warfare" into the counseling ministry of the church. A recent symposium at Fuller Theological Seminary brought together forty participants from a wide variety of traditional evangelical institutions (only seven participants represented classic Pentecostal/charismatic institutions) to discuss the issue of evil spirits in relation to local church

96. Arnold, *Powers of Darkness,* 180.
97. Ibid., 181.

ministries and world evangelization. All of the participants assumed the reality of the demonic.[98]

## Literature and the Media

Russell points out that many modern writers and filmmakers have continued to accept and portray belief in the devil. By the middle of the twentieth century, cynicism and skepticism had made it difficult to portray the traditional devil effectively without disguising him either mythologically or in a horror tale.

J. R. R. Tolkien (1892-1973) cast the struggle between transcendent good and evil in the fantasy world of Middle Earth, with Sauron, the dark lord of Mordor, representing Satan.

Twentieth-century mythology and science fiction tended to transfer demonic or angelic qualities from "supernatural" entities to supposedly "scientific" extraterrestrials. The films *2001* and *2010* (1968 and 1985) present angels in the form of disembodied space aliens, and the 1978 remake of *The Invasion of the Body Snatchers* featured extraterrestrials whose hissing, darting tongues, cruelty, and ability to replicate human appearance reproduced traditional demonic characteristics.[99]

The statements truest to the biblical tradition appeared in the work of C. S. Lewis (1898-1963). Lewis suggested that demons are motivated by both fear and hunger. Cut off from God, the source of real nourishment, they roam the world seeking human souls to consume. If thwarted, they turn and devour one another. No amount of feeding can mitigate their infinite emptiness, for they refuse the bread of life, which alone can satisfy. Lewis set forth this idea in *The Screwtape Letters* (1942), which he feigned were written by a senior demon, Screwtape, to his nephew Wormwood offering practical advice on the corruption of humanity.

In *Perelandra* (1943) and its companion "deep space" novels, Lewis imagined that each planet is ruled by an "oyarsa," an angel. Earth has fallen under the power of a "bent oyarsa," an evil archon.

Georges Bernanos (1888-1948) was the leading novelist of the French Catholic revival. Without belief in Satan, he argued, one cannot fully believe in God. The scale of evil in the world far transcends what humans could cause by themselves or collectively, and all efforts to improve the world without understanding this are doomed to failure.

To penetrate comfortable illusions was the purpose of Flannery O'Connor (1925-64), who described her subject as "the action of grace in territory

98. Ibid., 182.
99. Russell, *Prince of Darkness*, 262.

held largely by the Devil." The Evil One has helped us to construct around our souls a thick rind that can be pierced only by the action of grace. The modern materialist "puts little stock either in grace or the Devil" and "fails to recognize the Devil when he sees him," so O'Connor took pains to make it clear that she believed in the devil as an external personal entity. "Our salvation is played out with the Devil," she said in a lecture, "a Devil who is not simply generalized evil, but an evil intelligence determined on its own supremacy. I want to be certain that the Devil gets identified as the Devil and not simply taken for this or that psychological tendency." Flannery O'Connor urged the devil's existence in the midst of a society increasingly dominated by materialism and relativism.

Despite Satan's ability to produce real suffering, affirms O'Connor, he is also comically absurd, for God turns his every effort into an occasion of good so that he is "always accomplishing ends other than his own." Whenever the Evil One assaults a character for his own ends, God uses the break opened in the character's defenses to pour in his own grace and love. "The Devil teaches most of the lessons that lead to self-knowledge," she said in another letter. Demonic assault is always an occasion for grace.[100]

## Proving the Existence of Satan

Jeffrey Russell contends that natural reason offers certain indications that there exists a devil who is a person or personality with consciousness, will, and intelligence, whose intent is entirely focused upon causing suffering and misery for his own sake.

The first reason is that we do not experience a morally neutral world. Psychology confirms that we begin to experience things as good or evil at a very early age, though with maturity we learn the refinements of ambivalence. We also extrapolate evil to whatever other intelligent beings may exist in the cosmos, whether angels or extraterrestrials. Whenever we imagine extraterrestrials as real persons having intellect and will, we imagine them as capable of good and evil, of suffering and of inflicting suffering. There is no reason to assume that the active evil in the universe is limited to humanity.

There is also no reason to assume that the cause of human evil lies in human nature alone. We possess weapons for a nuclear war that at the least would bring desperate suffering to thousands of millions of people. Many assume that this unlimited destructiveness is an extension of individual human destructiveness. It is true that there is evil in each of us, but adding

100. Ibid., 262-63, 265, 267-68.

together even large numbers of individual evils does not enable anyone to explain an Auschwitz, let alone the destruction of the planet. Evil on this scale seems to be qualitatively as well as quantitatively different. It is no longer a personal evil, but a transpersonal evil. Natural reason indicates that there is a truly transcendent evil, an entity beyond as well as within the human mind.[101]

## A Changing Worldview in the West

As we have noted, the West is experiencing an "occult explosion," which the rapid growth of the New Age movement is now fueling. The end result is that more and more people are opening themselves up to believe in the supernatural, the paranormal, and the realm of spirits. Western culture (quite apart from the influence of Christianity) may very well be far down the road of change.[102] In fact, the revival of the occult after 1965, part of the counterculture movement of those years, included a component of diabology, a belief and worship of the devil. The popularity of such films as *Rosemary's Baby* (1968) and *The Exorcist* (1973) encouraged interest in the devil.[103]

As New Age leaders claim — and seek to substantiate — the West is involved in a change in paradigms or worldviews, which is breaking the dominance of the so-called "Enlightenment Age." This opens the door for a fresh study and even reappropriation of the biblical view of the Satanic and demonic.

This restudy of the Western worldview does not mean that we ignore the contributions of empirical science in the physical realm. We do not call for belief in a flat earth or a geocentric universe. We laud the utility of the scientific method for helping us to discover innumerable secrets about our world. However, we should correct the West's bias against the supernatural and its role in human evil and redemption. Russell states that philosophically we must break out of the narrow limitations of materialistic reductionism and investigate radical evil as a real phenomenon. Satan and the powers of darkness are real. We need to be conscious of their influence, and we need to respond to them appropriately.[104]

101. Ibid., 274-75.
102. Arnold, *Powers of Darkness*, 182.
103. Russell, *Prince of Darkness*, 261.
104. Arnold, *Powers of Darkness*, 182.

# A Biblical Response to Evil

## OLD TESTAMENT

The Old Testament points out that the Hebrew people were living in the midst of four cultures which were overwhelmed by the occult and the demonic — the Egyptian, the Assyrian, the Babylonian, and the Canaanite. The people of the Old Testament recognized Satan and the spirit world. But the Old Testament shows that Satan and the spirit world were powerless when confronted by the power of Yahweh, or God. Satan was created. He was not, as the Persians later were to at least suggest, co-equal with God. He could tempt but not force. God alone, said the Hebrews, was to be feared. In fact, many people think that one reason why there is a limited discussion about Satan in the Old Testament is that God wanted to get before the Hebrews that they must concentrate on the one God — Yahweh.

## NEW TESTAMENT

In the New Testament, especially in the first three Gospels, Satan and the demonic appear openly and in a more extensive way. It is the contention of C. K. Barrett, James Kallas, George Ladd, and others that the demonology-eschatology motif is dominant, constituting some three-fourths of the material in the first three Gospels and the books written by Paul. The New Testament teaches that Satanic forces have a measure of real control in the world.

Nearly everyone living in the Mediterranean world during the Old and New Testament eras — Jews, Greeks, Romans, Asians, and Egyptians — believed in the existence of evil spirits. Rather than questioning the existence of demons, people sought ways to control these spirits and to protect themselves. Most people, regardless of religious background (even some Jews), believed magic was helpful.

It was in this environment that Jesus ministered and the early church came into existence. Jesus and the early Christian writers shared their peers' belief in evil spirits, but with some important modifications. They believed there was only one true God, the God of Israel. They believed that the "gods" of pagan religions were really the manifestation and working of demons, opponents of the one true God working a deceptive influence. They believed that these evil spirits were organized under the leadership of the one prime adversary — Satan. Further, the early Christians believed that the practice of magic, witchcraft, and sorcery — popular among the common people — represented the work of Satan and his forces.

In addition, Scripture assumes some kind of hierarchy within the realm of the hostile supernatural powers, but it never gives any delineation of the

581

chain of command. Satan is "the ruler of the kingdom of the air" (Eph. 2:2, NIV), and he has within his sphere of authority a vast group of powers, dominions, thrones, angels, demons, unclean spirits, elemental spirits, and rulers.[105]

An important focus for determining how the powers operate is found in Ephesians 2:1-2, where Satan is described as the ruler of a host of forces who hold humanity in a slavery apart from God. He creates this bondage by supernaturally influencing individuals to disobey God — that is, by inciting them to sin.

## How Satan Works

Arnold maintains that this passage in Ephesians and other parts of the New Testament suggest three ways in which Satan accomplishes this aim: through direct and immediate influence, by exploiting the inner impulse to do evil, and by influencing the environment and social structures.[106]

The Bible never portrays evil spirits as possessing their own bodies; rather, they work their influence in the lives and bodies of people. For instance, John tells us that Satan "entered into" Judas in order to betray Jesus (John 13:27). The account of the Gerasene demoniac (Mark 5:1-20) demonstrates that a person can be afflicted by more than one evil spirit at a time, perhaps even hundreds. All of the exorcism stories also portray evil spirits as intelligent and capable of exercising will. They frequently talk to Jesus, usually expressing their fear, by speaking through their victims' vocal apparatus. Satan is depicted as a clever strategist constantly plotting against the purposes of God.[107]

Like God, Satan can manifest himself in and through material beings, but he himself is not material. Scott Peck tells of one case of therapy involving exorcism in which Satan manifested himself through the patient's writhing serpentine body, biting teeth, scratching nails, and hooded reptilian eyes. But there were no fangs, no scales. Satan was, through the use of the patient's body, extraordinarily and dramatically and even supernaturally snakelike. But he is not himself a snake. He is a spirit. His power is exercised through the patient's body.[108]

105. Clinton E. Arnold, "Giving the Devil His Due," *Christianity Today*, August 20, 1990, 17.

106. Arnold, *Powers of Darkness*, 183.

107. Arnold, "Giving the Devil His Due," 17.

108. John P. Newport, *Life's Ultimate Questions* (Waco: Word, 1989), 203; see also M. Scott Peck, *People of the Lie: The Hope for Healing Human Evil* (New York: Simon & Schuster, 1983), 182.

Although the Satanic and demonic emphasis is central in the New Testament, after Christ won the victory over Satan through the cross and resurrection, there is less in the New Testament about exorcism (driving demons out) and more about the Great Commission with its emphasis on preaching, teaching, and baptizing. George Ladd feels that a more satisfactory translation of Colossians 2:15 is that of the Revised Standard Version, which understands the verse to mean that Christ has disarmed the spiritual powers, stripping them of their insignia of rank and of their arms. Thus the verse states that by his death and resurrection Christ triumphed over his spiritual enemies, winning a divine victory over the cosmic powers. The fallen angels are ultimately helpless before the power of God and his angels. Furthermore, in the New Testament, all such spiritual powers are *creatures* of God and therefore ultimately subject to his power.

Nevertheless, despite Christ's saving work, the forces of evil continue their hostile activity. The cross represents the major victory of the war, but the battle continues. There is a vital difference, however, between before the cross and after.[109]

In the progressive work of Satan, there is first the level of temptation, contagion, influence, and impression. The second level is one of oppression or obsession. At this stage we still have some freedom in our personalities. But we are becoming slaves of sin (Rom. 6). At this level we are oftentimes depressed, discouraged, and disillusioned. At this stage there is often a non-receptivity to divine things, deep doubt, disillusionment, continued compulsions, and chronic fears.

The third and final stage is possession. It is quite rare. The authentic marks of demon possession are very extreme and seldom seen. Demon subjection is perhaps more common. Peck agrees with Malachi Martin, a Catholic leader, that most of the cases we call possession should more properly be termed "partial," "incomplete," or "imperfect."[110]

## Exorcism

Missiologist Timothy Warner, of Trinity Evangelical Divinity School, points to the early church practice of exorcism of demons and a clear renunciation of Satan as integral parts of their ritual of conversion and baptism. "It's tragic that on the mission field, particularly, we have not had this dramatization of turning from Satan and giving ourselves to the Lord. We have them squeak by on some minimal act of affirmation of Jesus, and it's no wonder they go

109. Arnold, "Giving the Devil His Due," 17.
110. Newport, *Demons, Demons, Demons*, 75-77.

on having problems." Warner thinks the problem is that "our worldview says that spirits are not real."

Missiologist C. Peter Wagner agrees: "Many missionaries are seeing tremendous acts of God out on the mission field, but say they cannot talk about it here [in North America]."

In England, the Anglican Bishop of Exeter has pointed out that in Western countries today, the widespread apostasy from the Christian faith, accompanied by an increasing recourse to black magic and occult practices, is revealing the presence and the power of evil forces and the contaminating influence of an evil atmosphere in particular places and environments. He asserts that the need for the restoration of the practice of exorcism is becoming steadily more urgent and more evident.

*Demonic possession*    There are some generally accepted criteria and symptoms of demonic possession.

- The exorcist discerns an evil presence or personality that is alien to the individual being exorcised.
- The person possessed speaks in voices distinctly other than his or her own, or in foreign languages unknown to the victim. The demons are able to speak, presumably using the vocal equipment of the person possessed (see Matt. 8:29, 31; Mark 1:24, 26, 34; 5:7, 9, 10; Luke 4:41; 8:28, 30).
- The person possessed utters blasphemies against God and everything sacred. Often this appears in total contrast to the person's usual demeanor.
- The person possessed displays "impossible" physical contortions and undergoes convulsions. Although contortions and convulsions may attend demonic possession, they are not alone adequate criteria for identifying a phenomenon as demonic.[111]

Nigel Wright, a professor at Spurgeon's College in London, gives some warnings in the area of exorcism. He states that it is wise to be highly reluctant to conclude that a person is demonized. Every other avenue needs to be explored first. Wherever possible it is wise to have medical and psychiatric support in ministering to an individual. Where it is possible to consult a more experienced minister, this should be done. Some church structures appoint consultants for this task. Deliverance should never be attempted alone. There should be at least two mature and experienced Christians present, and it is preferable that one should come from another

111. Newport, *Life's Ultimate Questions*, 210-16.

church to provide objectivity. Obvious care needs to be taken when ministering to members of the opposite sex. Intense situations of mutual dependence should be avoided and a sense of critical distance maintained about the deliverance process.

Persons believed to be possessed by demons should be treated with gentleness and respect at all times. Avoid aggressive words, gestures, or expressions. Rely upon the authority of Christ. Demons should not be talked to, argued with, or given any attention other than that of rejecting, refusing, and scorning them. The use of holy water, crosses, sacred objects, communion wine, anointing oil, or the Lord's Prayer in this context should be discouraged. It is the name of Christ alone which has power. The use of physical means in a quasi-magical way heads in the wrong direction. It is not the minister who drives out demons. It is Christ. The name of Christ brings about the confrontation which sets people free.

Deliverance should not be used for its sensational value in Christian testimony but should be discussed only when it is necessary and then in a discreet, sober, and undramatic way. It should be subject to the same ethics of confidentiality as any other form of counseling. It should take place within a structure of accountability.

Exorcism is an area in which excesses are commonplace, according to Sidney Page, an evangelical scholar. He came to that conclusion after critical reflection on the reports given by those engaged in exorcism. In his book *Powers of Evil,* he notes that superstition and speculation are widespread. He says there are a number of dangers in proposing a diagnosis of demon possession. First, since some people are susceptible to the power of suggestion, one may unconsciously induce simulated possession. Second, a person may encourage exaggerated views of the power of the demonic and an unhealthy paranoia. Third, one may furnish those who are inclined to deny personal responsibility for their actions with a convenient scapegoat. All who attempt to engage in exorcism must be careful to base their beliefs and practices upon Scripture and must use discernment in deciding how best to help those under their care.[112]

# A Tendency toward Evil

Satan and the demonic forces exploit our inclination or proclivities to evil. British theologian J. Stafford Wright points out they will find a passion alive

---

112. Nigel Wright, *The Satan Syndrome* (Grand Rapids: Zondervan, 1990), 126-27; see also Sydney H. T. Page, *Powers of Evil* (Grand Rapids: Baker, 1995), 181.

in us and intensify, heighten, glamorize, and glorify it. They capitalize on tendencies such as lust and hatred.[113]

According to Clinton Arnold, a professor at the Talbot School of Theology, Satan works in concert with an individual's inclination toward evil ("flesh"). If a person is naturally inclined toward anger and bitterness, in some way an evil spirit may directly encourage that attitude. If the malice continues and intensifies, demonic involvement in the person's life may become more direct. This situation is what Paul referred to as giving "place" to the devil. In principle, it appears that those who persistently and willfully continue in certain patterns of sinfulness may experience increasing amounts of direct demonic influence.[114]

In *The Screwtape Letters*, C. S. Lewis envisioned each of the powers of darkness as having an assigned "patient." Throughout the book Lewis depicted the younger demon (Wormwood) as keeping careful track of everything in his patient's train of thinking and then working to influence the subject's thoughts in the areas in which the demon considered him to be the most vulnerable. Lewis provokes his readers into thinking about Satan's potential involvement in the hour-to-hour mundane affairs and decisions of everyday life. While Lewis's account moves far beyond the few insights given to us in Scripture, I do not think he contradicts what we know about the work of the evil powers from Paul's writings.

Jeffrey Russell suggests that Satan works with our own proclivities: to ambition, or avarice, or sexual irresponsibility, or backbiting, or power, or lying, or anger, or physical violence, or whatever. What Russell suggests that is different from that which most psychologists believe is that underneath these individual destructive proclivities is a focus of malice and destructiveness that unites and energizes the variety of destructive, hateful forces within us. This focus of destruction creates its own hidden agenda, its own policy, which is destruction for its own sake.

Take avarice as an example. At some point, the focus of evil within us seizes that greed, energizes it, and utilizes it for its own purpose of destruction far beyond the scope of the original avarice. This focus of evil, which has an agenda, a purpose, and a will of its own, is what we know as the personal devil.

The focus of evil may completely dominate some people. What is one to say of Adolf Hitler? With most of us it does not dominate, but it is always there, threatening to dominate. We need to keep in mind that the devil disguises his intentions well. Repression of malice and failure to face it in ourselves produce the self-righteousness that provides us with ready justifica-

---

113. J. Stafford Wright, *Mind, Man and the Spirits* (Grand Rapids: Zondervan, 1971), 132.

114. Arnold, *Powers of Darkness*, 188-89.

tion for our cruelty and insensitivity. It enables us to claim vices as virtues, justifying our violence, our prejudice, and our intolerance on the grounds that evil is not found within ourselves but in others.[115]

Becoming a Christian neither removes the impulse to do evil nor deters the powers from trying to exploit it. Indeed, Paul envisioned the believer as coming under rather intense pressure from the hostile spirits to displease God, especially during vulnerable times (as in periods of depression or crisis). For Christians the main difference is that they can draw on the enabling power that God offers as a means to resist these influences.[116]

Paul saw the work of evil spirits as extending beyond their hostile influence on individuals and the church. However, Paul says the powers unleash their greatest hostility when they hinder the proclamation of the gospel. They use the flesh and, indeed, the structures of the world to blind people from discovering the truth about God's redemptive work in the Lord Jesus Christ. Those who affirm faith in Christ are rescued from the deadly clutches of Satan's kingdom and delivered from the community of Adam, which is moving toward its death.

## Evil People and Networking

Paul described unredeemed humanity as trapped in a pattern of transgression and sin against God because "the present age" so heavily influences them (Eph. 2:2). Becoming a Christian involves being crucified to the world (Gal. 6:14) and being rescued from the present evil age (Gal. 1:4). When Paul spoke of "the world" in a moral sense, he was thinking of the totality of people, social systems, values, and traditions in terms of its opposition to God and his redemptive purposes.

Nevertheless, people control governments, corporations, the media, and various other structures of our existence. If the powers of darkness can gain significant influence over the lives of key people, through them they can create oppressive dictatorships, evil drug rings, exploitative multinational corporations, and all kinds of horrific, destructive mechanisms bent on destruction and terror. In the twentieth century we have witnessed the extensive repression and exploitation that corrupt rulers can wield over millions of people. Mention the names of Adolf Hitler, Nicolae Caeusescu, Idi Amin, Manuel Noriega, and Saddam Hussein, and one easily sees images of untold atrocities. Certainly, Satan and his forces make people of such power the objects of particular attack because of their political authority.

115. Woodruff and Wilmer, *Facing Evil,* 53-54.
116. Arnold, *Powers of Darkness,* 185.

The powers exert their influence to corrupt the various social orders of the world as a further means of drawing humanity away from God. Working through people, the powers can pollute a society's traditions and values. They can influence authors, television producers, political thinkers and analysts, pastors, university professors, composers, artists, screenplay writers, economic policy makers, architects of defense strategies, and journalists. Through a unified networking influence, it is not difficult to imagine how the powers can influence the direction of an entire culture. In one decade something may be considered morally outrageous and in the next morally acceptable through a change in public opinion. The powers themselves, however, are not the structures. Although the powers do their best to influence the structures, evil can reside in the structures only to the degree that the people involved are evil.

Arnold notes that Satan, by coordinating the activity of his innumerable powers of darkness, attempts to permeate every aspect of life in his attempts to oppose God and his kingdom. The work of the Evil One moves far beyond the simple notion of tempting an individual to sin. Satan appears to have a well-organized strategy. He aims strongly at the people with power and influence. The moral lapse of one pastor can send one church reeling. Inciting the moral lapse of numerous prominent ministers devastates Christians all over the country and makes society perceive the fragrant aroma of the gospel as a stench to be avoided.[117]

## Christians as Rescuers

Christians are to be rescuing agents. Christians are not to seek to escape completely from the present world and withdraw from involvement in the social order and the structures of our existence. Jesus called Christians to be salt and light. God demands that Christians engage in social action based on their love for humanity and their responsibility to be careful stewards of creation.

From the perspective of the new order of God brought by Jesus, both the personal and the structural views are correct, but only in tension with each other. The notion that people are solely the victims of outer oppressive structures is materialistic and denies human capacities for self-transcendence. The view that humanity's problems are rooted exclusively in the person is individualistic, and isolates people from the social context, without which human existence is impossible.

A truer understanding sees persons as the network of relations in which

117. Ibid., 201, 203-4.

they are embedded. This means that the individual can never be considered in isolation from the political, economic, and social conditions in which the person was born and by which the person has been, to a significant degree, formed. Increasing numbers of therapists and theologians are recognizing that personal healing is impossible to attain if it ignores the political, economic, and social conditions that helped produce the problems in the first place. On the other hand, some liberation theologians are recognizing that long-term struggles for justice require more than tools of political analysis and a praxis, or strategy, for social transformation. Also needed are therapies capable of removing "all the flaming darts of the evil one" (Eph. 6:16) that have carried the poisons of self-doubt, fatalism, and personal sin directly into the bloodstream of the oppressed.

## Satan and Mass Violence

The personal darkness or evil in the depths of the human soul is not confined to the individual. It is attracted to its collective expressions in society. It can even erupt into a frenzy of violence in the permissive context of a riot, revolution, or war. Feelings of inferiority can be played on by dictators to produce monsters compensating for their low self-esteem and seeking revenge on those whom they blame for having caused it. An evil person like Hitler would get nowhere if he were not riding the cresting wave of resentment from millions of would-be evil people longing to be released from the restraints of truth and civility. Together the institution and the individual form a united front of hostility to the redeeming purposes of God.

Danish philosopher Søren Kierkegaard, writing in the nineteenth century, noted that diabolical possession in modern times happens en masse. People gather into groups, in order that natural, animal hysteria may take hold of them, in order to feel themselves stimulated, inflamed, and beside themselves.[118]

My first serious interest in the demonic came at Basel University in Switzerland where I was rooming with Martin Nieden, who had been caught up in Hitler's youth corps as a young man. He convinced me that there was a Satanic manifestation in the Nazi movement which arose in one of the most culturally advanced countries of Western Europe. In more recent times, we have seen Satan working in the drug culture and in social patterns of adult behavior such as excessive drinking, racial hatred, materialism, and greed.

118. Newport, *Life's Ultimate Questions*, 205-6.

589

## Evil Explained

In his best-seller *This Present Darkness,* Frank Peretti unveils the strategy and networking of those hostile opponents who come from the realm of spirits, demons, and powers. He depicts these forces of darkness mobilizing to gain control of a typical small town in America. They try to accomplish this takeover through a variety of means, but primarily through a plot to draw people away from Christ via an organized expression of the New Age movement. His conceptual framework is much the same as that of Lewis's *Screwtape Letters.*

While C. S. Lewis gave the Christian community a thought-provoking assessment of how an evil spirit may exert influence over a person in day-to-day life, Peretti builds upon this insight to help us imagine how the powers might work in concert to attain a much larger diabolical goal. He describes the individual workings of demonic powers, but he also shows their collective purpose. Assuming a well-defined hierarchy with a chain of command, Peretti depicts various ranks of powers carrying out their orders as part of a large-scale plan to usher in an occultic philosophy first to one strategic city, and then, from that base of operations, to the entire country.

Some of Peretti's work is extreme and does not match biblical emphases. For instance, why is so much said about the countermanding work of God's angels and so little about the work of the Holy Spirit?[119]

James Lewis, editor of *Magical Religion and Modern Witchcraft,* notes that Peretti's art has created an exciting imaginative world that enables Christians to understand and respond to the demonic threat. But the cost of this literary tour de force, he points out, has been to bring conservative Christianity closer in spirit to the very phenomenon in which the forces of darkness are most clearly evident: the New Age movement. Peretti's narratives have imaginatively transformed the realm of the ordinary and the everyday into a kind of real-life game of Dungeons and Dragons. While Christians have traditionally believed in the guidance of the Holy Spirit, the vivid picture Peretti draws of highly personal angels conveying guidance to the minds of God's saints makes "Christian" inspiration appear a close relative of New Age psychism and channeling. Peretti also pictures angels as capable of materializing to help God's chosen, as when the angel Betsy materializes to give one of the heroines, Bernice Krueger, a short motorcycle ride. Once Bernice has reached her destination, Betsy evaporates like some eerie figure out of an occult novel.[120]

119. Arnold, *Powers of Darkness,* 205.

120. James R. Lewis, ed., *Magical Religion and Modern Witchcraft* (Albany, N.Y.: State University of New York, 1996), 346-47.

In a recent visit to North Texas to promote his book *The Oath,* Peretti stated that his books are meant to inspire. They should not be classified as theological treatises. The popularity of groups such as the Promise Keepers is evidently creating a need for entertainment and aesthetic experiences that are within the broad parameters of the Promise Keepers' worldview or lifestyle.

In his intriguing and broad-sweeping book *Fire from Heaven,* Harvey Cox of Harvard examines what a recent group of evangelical Christians and Pentecostals call the "Third Wave." These people view classical Pentecostalism as the first modern outpouring of the Spirit, the charismatic movement in "mainline" churches as the second, and themselves as the "third wave." Peretti sees himself as part of the "Third Wave." Peter Wagner of Fuller Seminary is also included. Wagner asserts that "Satan delegates high-ranking members of the hierarchy of evil spirits to control nations, regions, cities, tribes, peoples, groups, neighborhoods, and other significant networks of human beings throughout the world." Demons of the higher rank have the responsibility of directing the work of the lower-ranking ones.

Although Cox feels that many "Third Wave" advocates have an excessive fixation on demons, he is convinced that a significant number of modern liberal theologians have too easily discarded the idea of transpersonal forces of evil. Instead of trying to understand what references to evil spirits in the Bible point us to in our own age — which Cox believes is quite real — they have discarded the whole notion of the demonic as implausible. Cox states that perhaps what Frank Peretti and the Pentecostals who teach Satanic conspiracy theories are doing is similar to what missionaries have observed among Pentecostals in Asia, Africa, and Latin America. They adapt facets of popular piety into their theology. Such a Pentecostal absorption calls for careful biblical evaluation to find weakness as well as strength.

Cox's statements remind us of the spiritually insightful ideas of C. S. Lewis. For Cox there is a quotation from *The Screwtape Letters* that seems to give a balanced perspective. "There are two equal and opposite errors," Lewis writes, "into which our race can fall about the devils. One is to disbelieve in their existence. The other is to believe and to feel an excessive and unhealthy interest in them. They themselves are equally pleased by both errors, and hail a materialist and a magician with the same delight."[121]

Evangelical scholar Clinton Arnold suggests that those who appreciate Peretti's novels need to remember that Satan may very well find his best line of attack against a church through something other than through what Peretti calls an organized conspiracy. In fact, is it not more often the case that sexual impropriety, ethical misconduct, deeply entrenched feuds

121. Harvey Cox, *Fire from Heaven* (Reading, Mass.: Addison-Wesley, 1995), 281-87.

between church members, and similar matters do more to dim the light of the church's testimony in its community than the inroads of occultism or Satanism? This is certainly not to minimize the danger of aberrant (or Satanic) teaching, but it does emphasize Satan's use of a wide variety of schemes (Eph. 6:11).[122]

## Satan at Ephesus

Arnold gives an example of how Satan worked in Ephesus during New Testament times using an occult, counterfeit religion (the cult of Artemis, a Greek moon goddess) and political, economic, and civic structures. The Artemis cult controlled major economic and civic structures of western Asia Minor. It was the major savings and loan institution for the entire region. Athletic contests were held in her honor, and even one of the months of the year was named after her. Christians would have been forced to decide on such questions as whether they should refuse to borrow money from the cult and whether they should decline participation in the "Artemisian games." The eyes of Christians would certainly have seen the pervasiveness of her influence on their society.

The demonic is able to influence any existing human structure. The cult of Artemis is merely one example of a first-century structure that Satan used to delude people and lead them away from devotion to the one true God.[123]

## Satan and the Holocaust

Jeffrey Russell detects Satan's work in the Nazi Holocaust. Satan was active with his own agenda and purpose, a composite of evil raised to a new dimension of intensity and malignity. Russell explains that, having will and purpose, Satan works as a malign force with its own will and agenda, operating within humanity as a whole.

When we experience the devil within ourselves personally, or when we observe his appalling social manifestations, we immediately realize that it is essentially a force bent on destruction. The biblical idea of the devil is precisely that of a force intent upon destroying and annihilating the cosmos to the greatest degree possible.[124]

122. Arnold, *Powers of Darkness*, 206.
123. Ibid., 207-9.
124. Woodruff and Wilmer, *Facing Evil*, 56-57.

## Conclusion

In light of what we have seen of radical evil in history and in our time in society and in our own lives, each of us should surely appreciate in a renewed way the biblical approach to radical evil and the demonic.

As Christians we should relive our status as rescued members of Christ's kingdom. The New Testament is clear that becoming a Christian does not bring about automatic immunity to the influence of evil spirits. Becoming a Christian does link one to a new resource for dealing with these hostile forces. Jesus teaches his disciples the possibility and necessity of "abiding" in him, like a branch in a vine, in order to be infused with his divine enabling power (John 15:1-8). In a similar fashion, Paul constantly affirms our identity as being "in Christ." Just as Christ holds a position of superiority to the powers, so believers have a position of superiority and authority over the forces of the devil. Paul tells the Colossians, "You have been given fullness in Christ, who is the head over every [demonic] power and authority" (Col. 2:10, NIV).

## Importance of Prayer

Clinton Arnold reminds us that wearing a magical charm or even a crucifix does not impart God's power to Christians. Nor should we expect God's power through some magical use of Jesus' name. God cannot be manipulated. His power is bestowed on his people through devoted trust in him. Prayer is one of the most natural expressions of trust in God. The apostle Paul modeled this activity throughout his letters. This kind of communication with God acknowledges his sovereignty and our dependence on him for all of life.[125]

One distinct advantage of having a biblical worldview that teaches the real existence of evil spirits is the impact it can have on our prayer life. Knowing that Satan and his demons do exist and that they are constantly scheming and attacking us, seeking our destruction, gives us great reason to pray. God is there — Father, Son, and Holy Spirit. He hears, he understands, and he wants to help us survive in the context of rampant supernatural hostility.

Arnold notes that despite his excesses, Frank Peretti has rendered a service to the church in his fictional accounts *This Present Darkness* and *Piercing the Darkness*. These novels seek to lift the veil hiding the unseen world. Peretti startles us with his vivid and grotesque depictions of the powers of darkness and forces us to consider afresh the real and pervasive hostility of this evil spiritual domain. One comes away from reading Peretti's novels with a re-

125. Arnold, *Powers of Darkness*, 213.

newed incentive to pray because, if he is anywhere close to the truth in his fictional depictions, what else can one do but turn to God? God will fight for his people.[126]

## Spiritual Warfare

In Ephesians 6:10-20, Paul portrays spiritual warfare as primarily concerned with Christian conduct — not with exorcism or eradicating structural (institutional or societal) evil. Spiritual warfare is therefore *resistance*. It is a defensive posture. It involves appropriating the power of God to make progress in eradicating moral vices that already have a place in one's life. The Bible portrays every Christian as engaged in spiritual warfare and the struggles as primarily religious and moral. It would be wrong to focus on the sensational and unusual to the neglect of the more common. Demon possession appears to be a rather rare phenomenon, but all believers experience Satanic trials and temptations.

The Christian life is carried out in a community, in dependence on other people. The apostle Paul especially stressed this point through his analogy of the church as the body of Christ. God has chosen to strengthen and build up individual Christians through their relationships with other Christians, particularly when the church assembles for worship, edification, and fellowship.[127]

Spiritual warfare also takes the offensive. Paul calls the soldiers of Christ to advance on enemy territory by proclaiming the gospel. According to Paul, the primary aggressive action the Christian is called to take is to spread the gospel — the good news of salvation through Christ. In other words, Christ has given the church the task of "proclaiming release to the captives" of Satan's kingdom. In the context of Paul's teaching on spiritual warfare, this represents the offensive part of that warfare.

According to the biblical drama, God delays the Second Coming of Christ to give time to the church to engage in this mission. Paul urged his readers to "redeem the time" which God gives for this task. It is furthermore the task of the entire church, each individual member, not just those perceived to be uniquely gifted, to carry it out.[128]

126. Ibid., 214.
127. Ibid., 214.
128. Ibid., 216.

## The Devil's Way Will Never Work

In dramatic, nonecclesiastical language, Jeffrey Russell states that it is easier to go the devil's way, with hatred and violence. But the devil's way is not only morally wrong, it is stupid. It will never work. It has never worked. Violence always provokes violence; hatred everywhere provokes hatred. Daily we are reminded of this, and reminded too that we have not yet learned. The devil stands like a blind man in the sun, seeing only darkness when he stands among the green and brilliant fields of God's creation.[129]

We have thought the devil's way long enough. It is time for a new way of thinking. This new way of thinking is to pursue the life of redemptive love, not by denying and repressing the work of the devil within ourselves, but by recognizing it, facing it, and transforming it into positive energy. We have no other choice: we will learn to understand and live out the Christian way and proclaim Christ as the Savior.

In more distinctly Christian terms we affirm that the resources to confront and combat both personal and collective evil are described in the biblical revelation. There we find the cause of evil and the presentation of deliverance from evil in Jesus Christ.

The recent fascination with Satan and demons is partially a reaction to an earlier disbelief. Satan and the demonic are active and powerful.

But the main emphasis of Christianity is on the availability of God's power and love in Jesus Christ and the Spirit. By virtue of Christ's victory on the cross and our identification with him, believers share in his present power and authority over Satan and the evil powers.

129. Russell, *Prince of Darkness*, 277.

# CHAPTER FIFTEEN

# New Age:
# Critique and Transformation

Everyone has a worldview, or vision of life, that determines his or her values and principles of action. And each worldview is built around faith in something. That something can be a myth, a story, a vision, or a narrative.

According to James Olthuis, a professor at the Institute for Christian Studies in Toronto, our worldview is a framework of fundamental beliefs through which we view the world and our calling and our future in it. Our worldview gives direction and meaning to life. Our worldview is what we believe is the truth about history, life, and existence.

Although each worldview is built around a central faith, there are other factors motivating a worldview. Also playing a role in the formation of our worldview, as revealed by Marx, Freud, and Nietzsche, are our socioeconomic interests, rationalizations, personality type, and the unconscious.[1]

For Christians, faith is a commitment of self to the biblical God, in whom we trust and from whom we receive certainty, connection, and ground for our existence. Our faith is a trust in which we meet God in ourselves and in creation, even as God meets us in salvation in Christ. We are graciously renewed. We experience connection with self, with others, with creation, and with God. God is the healing power and sustaining ground of our lives. God constitutes the final ground and ultimate power of and for all other grounds and power.[2]

1. James Olthuis, "On Worldviews," *Christian Scholars Review* 14.2 (1985): 3-4.
2. Ibid., 5.

## THE PARADOX OF FAITH AND REASON

As a vision rooted in faith a worldview is in its basic tenets not argued *with*, but argued *from*. However, a worldview is also confronted by the demands and experiences of life. This means that the worldview must do more than exhibit internal conceptual coherence and consistency; it also must illuminate experience and guide human action. As the historical process continues, re-articulations will become necessary as aspects of reality remain unillumined, and refurbishing will necessarily take place as insight increases and faith deepens. Thus, worldviews can and ought to be argued with, even though, since a worldview is based in faith, it is in the end argued from rather than argued with. This seeming paradox needs to be accepted. Olthuis suggests that honoring this paradox opens a path which allows us to slip through the either-or, "fideist" (faith only) versus "evidentialist" (rational argument) dilemma.[3] Both the faith only and rational approaches have validity when used in the proper balance.

## MODERNIST, POST-MODERN, AND NEW AGE DEVELOPMENTS

The biblical worldview, or at least a sometimes distorted version of that view, was very powerful in Western culture until the seventeenth century, when the modernist, or Enlightenment, worldview began to undercut its dominance. In recent years, the modernist view in turn has been attacked, with postmodern critics saying it is not only relative but tends to be totalizing, repressive, and violent.

Stepping up to take over now is the New Age worldview, predicting that it will replace modernism, or secular humanism, and what New Agers call the outdated, propositional, non-fulfilling, compromising biblical world-view. This New Age view surfaced in American life with Transcendentalism, Theosophy, and Mind Sciences in the middle to the latter part of the nineteenth century.

The New Age has now become a major cultural and religious option. Some people who were devoted to the modernist view have turned to the New Age. Some professing Christians have privately or openly affirmed New Age views.[4]

This study focuses on the fact that the worldview one holds is the key

3. Ibid., 7.
4. Ibid., 10.

to understanding what is happening in our world today. It is important to point out that no matter how sound a worldview may be, if adherents do not understand their worldview and are not emotionally and willfully committed to it and to others who share the same worldview, they cannot properly live out that vision as a way of life.

That is why it is important for Christians, in the current collision between the New Age and biblical worldviews, to know their own biblical worldview, to understand it, and to be committed to it and to other Christians who share the same view. Only then, with a thorough understanding of their own worldview, can they detect the problems in the New Age worldview. Christians must become people of discernment, worldview watchers and evaluators.

# DIALOGUE

The enlightened Christian does not call for a return to the rigid dogmatism and closed system of earlier years. Evangelical Christians see the importance of both formal and informal dialogue with New Agers. Both Jesus and Paul were concerned with understanding the context of their target audiences and sensing their needs and establishing common ground and using questions to prompt interest and understanding before they proclaimed in a clear and sensitive manner their perspective, or worldview.[5]

## Person-Centered and Content-Oriented Dialogue

As adherents of the biblical worldview, Christians have genuine respect for the integrity and dignity of others as human beings made in God's image. This respect calls for a willingness to listen and to take seriously the other person's most basic worldview commitment. You start with what the other person believes.

In order to effectively communicate the biblical view to a New Ager, you must understand the basic assumptions and values of the New Age worldview. Listen carefully to what its adherents have to say, ask pointed questions for clarification, and contrast the answers with basic biblical beliefs.[6] This is one reason why, through the years, I have attended New Age seminars, lectures, and conferences. The objective is a more accurate understanding of the basic beliefs

5. Harold A. Netland, *Dissonant Voices* (Grand Rapids: Eerdmans, 1991), 297.
6. Ibid., 298-301.

of the other party and clarification of any similarities or differences between these beliefs and the central claims of the biblical worldview.

This is not unlike a commitment to witness. With this approach you seek to persuade someone of Christian truths. You help real people become convinced of the truth of the biblical worldview.

But first, you must begin with a clear grasp of presuppositions. Key issues should be presented with openness, honesty, cross-questioning, and listening. This process does not require compromise. It does require a willingness to listen, understand, and seek mutual enrichment. There should be a reverence for reverence. Christians have been accused of being both ignorant of other people's views and arrogant. Such a track record calls for Christians to seek knowledge, display sympathy, and practice humility.[7]

## Understand Felt Needs

One aspect of this approach is to seek to understand the needs of people. For example, the secular worldview seems to provide for the physical needs of humans, but it has failed to answer some basic questions concerning the meaning and power for living.

The Hindu law of karma says a person reaps what he sows. It meets a certain human need for justice. It also has a biblical link in Galatians 6:7, "A man reaps what he sows." The Hindu view seeks to help people to become liberated from the law of karma and become identified with God in a mystical union. The concept of karma may be a useful starting point for Christians to go beyond karma and present the gospel of forgiveness, which is related to the cross of Christ and the atonement.[8]

## Correcting Misunderstandings

Another aspect of dialogue is to attempt to correct misunderstandings of biblical teachings. For example, properly understood, the authentic biblical view is not self-centered, an ego trip, or withdrawal into the self. The biblical faith sees the self as essentially related to other selves, to God, and to a world of suffering and need. Christianity does not encourage ruthless conquest and exploitation of nature.

For clarity and a full understanding it is important to define terms such as God, Christ, spirituality, and "born again" from a Christian perspective.

7. David K. Clark, *Dialogical Apologetics* (Grand Rapids: Baker, 1993), 103.
8. David Burnett, *Clash of Worlds* (Eastbourne: MARC, 1990), 244.

Otherwise, the same word or term can give different meanings. For example, in the New Age understanding, Jesus was just a man who obtained an awareness of the Christ consciousness, which is an impersonal, divine essence. For the New Age, Jesus is Christ only because he realized his divine potential. New Agers believe that we can realize our divine potential just as Jesus did. A core Christian doctrine of the atonement is seen by the New Age believer as "at-onement," an awareness that all is one. No blood atonement by Christ is necessary, as in Christian belief, because there is no real separation to be overcome. In the New Age view, there is no sin, only ignorance of the great cosmic oneness.[9]

Christians need to explain to others that the basic tension in the biblical worldview is not between God's love and justice, but between God's will and our will. Because we have chosen to assert our will against his, we have alienated ourselves from God and our own welfare and salvation. Although God seeks us with his love, our prideful nature keeps us from admitting our weakness and depending on him and his way of salvation. We consistently reject him. God allows our desire for autonomy to result in eternal separation from him. But God does not want to be eternally separated from us. The choice is ours.[10]

As Christians we do not fear dialogue because we do not fear the truth. Rather, "it is the truth that sets us free" (John 8:32).


# EVALUATION

## The Approach of "Critical Realism"

As we have seen, the postmodern view is skeptical and relativizing. This view has been influenced by what is known as deconstructionism. Christians believe that there can be bridge building between different worldviews based on creational truth and the basic capacity of humans for knowledge. Even though this creational capacity has been damaged by sin, Christians advocate some form of "critical realism" and believe there is helpful truth in the coherence theory of knowledge. All humans have at least a residue of the human capacity for reason so that we can compare beliefs.[11]

---

9. Douglas Groothuis, *Confronting the New Age* (Downers Grove, Ill.: InterVarsity, 1988), 70-71.

10. Karen Hoyt, *The New Age Rage* (Old Tappan, N.J: Revell, 1989), 219-20.

11. Ted Cabal, "Worldview and Postmodern Skepticism," Ph.D. Colloquium, Southwestern Baptist Theological Seminary, 1996, 13, 16-17.

The approach of "critical realism" moved to modify the extreme pre-suppositional view of Cornelius Van Til of Westmister Seminary, which affirms that Christian believers and unbelievers have no common intellectual ground, no common knowledge commitments or understandings. Because of the destructive effects of sin on knowledge, according to Van Til, non-Christians cannot understand the world as it truly is. Although God shed his light throughout nature, human minds darkened in sin cannot see it.

A milder presuppositional view would state that a non-Christian has enough insight both to recognize that worldviews should make sense and to understand what "make sense" means. It assumes that unbelievers understand and accept some primary concepts. They would admit that worldviews that make sense of human life and experience are better than those that do not. This is common ground between Christians and non-Christians.[12]

This view, called evidential apologetics, views human reasoning in a somewhat more positive light. Human beings can grasp some knowledge bout God despite being hampered by finiteness and sin.[13]

There is limited truth in the work of Thomas Reid, of Scotland, in what is called "commonsense realism." Reid said that all humans share the ability to evaluate. There is an objective, external world. God has given all humanity a limited amount of common sense and some self-evident principles, which include matters such as belief in an external world, in other minds, and in others' testimony, empirical evidence, and memory beliefs. This most basic level of reason is necessary for human existence. So there is at least a limited validity, despite sin and finiteness, in the classical conceptions of correspondence and coherence. Various worldviews can be tested.[14]

## The Approach of "Critical Certainty"

Most postmodernists who claim that there is no objective reality independent of personal interest disagree with the view of "critical certainty." In contrast, Christians reason to affirm an underlying objective order beyond subjective distortions.

However, the evangelical Christian would not accept the view of "uncritical certainty" held by some unthinking Christians. This view maintains that a person can obtain an unbiased understanding of reality. Christians would

12. Clark, *Dialogical Apologetics*, 105-6.
13. Ibid., 107.
14. Cabal, "Worldview and Postmodern Skepticism," 17-18; see also Nicholas Wolterstorff, "Can Belief in God Be Rational If It Has No Foundations?" in *Faith and Rationality: Reason and Belief in God* (Notre Dame: University of Notre Dame, 1983), 150.

also not advocate relativism. This view holds that little or no knowledge can be gained by historically and culturally limited thinkers. Rather, evangelicals would have more sympathy with the perspective of "critical certainty," admitting the genuine limitations which historical conditioning and sin place on a thinker. At the same time, there are valid tests for truth.[15]

Evangelicals will admit that factors other than rational are important in leading people to build their lives around a certain worldview. But these factors do not displace a necessity for sound reasoning. Even though worldview commitment is often passionate, it should not dispense with careful reasoning.

Following the view of "critical certainty," evangelicals would say that the verification method is important because it involves both logical consistency and factual adequacy. An adequate view must satisfy the whole person, not just certain aspects of existence. It must also meet people's deepest psychological needs and resolve their moral predicament.

Generally accepted questions of "critical certainty" that should be asked when a person is considering accepting a particular worldview as a way of life are:

- Does this worldview include all kinds of human experience?
- Does this worldview hang together, make sense?
- Does it encourage renewal and a forward look?
- Is this worldview satisfying? Does it bring joy, happiness, and fulfillment?
- Which worldview has fewer difficulties?
- Which worldview answers more questions, corresponds with more facts, and gives a better explanation of experience as a whole?[16]

## The Experiential Emphasis

Although the use of rational arguments both to uphold the truth of Christianity and to refute New Age beliefs are crucial, it is also important for Christians to rely on their experiences as Christians when talking with New Agers. Christian experience is both unique and convicting.[17]

Although rationality should be affirmed, "rationalism" should be avoided. Existentialism posts a warning sign against dry rationalism. As we have contended, Christianity is a worldview capable of rational defense, but

---

15. Cabal, "Worldview and Postmodern Skepticism," 19-20.
16. William Dyrness, *Christian Apologetics in a World Community* (Downers Grove, Ill.: InterVarsity, 1983), 53-69.
17. Clark, *Dialogical Apologetics*, 103-4.

it is also an experiential way of salvation. The Christian does not rule out powerful, spiritual experiences as long as they meet certain criteria. The biblical wouldview maintains that the divine communication or inspiration found in the Bible is personal and moral but also cognitive so that it can be discussed logically.[18]

For more than thirty years, I have spoken at international student conferences. Students generally agree that the primary problem in their personal lives and in their culture is egocentricity, pride, greed, and hate. Individual students would then share how their particular religions or worldviews seek to solve this problem. Then I would tell them about my conviction that the biblical worldview is the most adequate to answer life's questions. I would tell them how the biblical view undergirds the worth and dignity of persons, how it provides motivation for education and scientific research, how it justifies and sustains a visionary and noble humanitarian program, and how it provides an answer to the deepest longings about ultimate meaning and salvation, moral power for the individual, and the cosmic process.

# SEPARATION, TRANSFORMATION, AND CRITICAL ENGAGEMENT

## Separation

Throughout the Bible, the idea of separation was central when God's people faced alien views. Separation is also crucial in confronting aspects of the New Age worldview that are basically opposed to the biblical worldview. Certain contrasts between the two views suggested by Douglas Groothuis can be noted. God is either personal or impersonal. He cannot be both. God is either moral or amoral, not both. People are either nondivine or divine, not both. There is either resurrection or reincarnation, not both.[19]

## Transformation

The biblical worldview proclaims a world to come; it does not consider this world the final, or ultimate, frame of reference. However, the biblical worldview is passionately concerned with this world as the theater for redemption and as the scene of the beginning of restoration. This kind of approach does

18. Groothuis, *Confronting the New Age*, 74-75.
19. Ibid., 49-50.

not repudiate the culture so much as it strives to harness it in the service of God. It sees the kingdom of God extending into secular culture and seeking to bring the principalities and powers under the dominion of Jesus Christ. The kingdom of God is not an island separate from the culture but a leaven that is at work in the culture, seeking to transform its values and attitudes.

Although Satan has reached into this world as an evil force, he does not own or control the world. Rather, the world is the theater of the glory of God, the field in which the kingdom of God advances. The world and all its achievements rightfully belong to Jesus Christ. However, the world in its sin refuses to acknowledge this fact and must therefore be brought into submission by the forces of righteousness.[20] Cultural concepts united with the biblical message can become means the Spirit uses to exalt Jesus Christ in the world.[21]

## EXAMPLES OF TRANSFORMATION

Christians do not merely separate from a worldview such as that of the New Age movement, but they also seek to transform wrong perspectives or frameworks. History has been witness to the fact that Christians have transformed the pagan world in terms of the sanctity of life, charity, proper education, and other problems. This transformational dynamic is both unmistakable and imperative. It is demanded by Scripture.[22]

Some New Age practices are condemned by the biblical worldview and should be avoided. These include spiritism and various forms of divination. Other New Age practices may seem neutral and, because of beneficial effects, even desirable. However, the interpretative framework in which these practices are embedded makes them problematic. Examples would be certain types of body manipulation and meditational approaches if they are used to inculcate the New Age worldview.[23]

Selected New Age ideas can be brought into the biblical worldview. We have noted some of these possibilities in the areas of transformation, health, ecology, the arts, education, and business.

God has left signs of himself even in the New Age movement. The theme of spiritual transformation is a high New Age priority. Many of their writings refer to the need for spiritual awakening and change. New Agers admit that something is wrong with humanity and contend that the individual

---

20. Donald G. Bloesch, *A Theology of Word and Spirit* (Downers Grove, Ill.: InterVarsity, 1992), 263.

21. Donald G. Bloesch, *God the Almighty* (Downers Grove, Ill.: InterVarsity, 1995), 30.

22. Groothuis, *Confronting the New Age*, 52-54.

23. Hoyt, *New Age Rage*, 49.

must be transformed before we can have individual fulfillment and global harmony. The Christian would respond by noting that the problem is deeper than can be solved by a mere humanly induced change in consciousness or by the adoption of a new monistic worldview. Christian transformation extends to more profound levels of human nature. We have within us the seeds of death, but God wants to give us renewed life and redemption through Jesus Christ and the practice of biblical principles.[24]

There is considerable debate today about how some church leaders have unwittingly used New Age thinking. New Age critics like Roy Livesey believe that some Christian leaders have distorted biblical truth. One such distortion is the emphasis of positive thinking that centers on prosperity and health. Robert Schuller of Crystal Cathedral in California has been criticized for facets of his teaching concerning possibility thinking and self-esteem. Some forms of holistic medicine also need to be investigated and critiqued.[25]

The Greek Logos concept originally referred to the all-pervading, organizing principle within all things. The apostle John emptied the Logos term of its impersonal nature and gave it flesh and form in the person of Jesus Christ. In a similar way, Christians try to lead persons holding certain concepts of the New Age movement into a new understanding of these meanings when couched in the biblical worldview. The New Age concept of total self-acceptance strikes a positive chord within us. We want to feel good about ourselves. We want to know we are valuable as individuals. We therefore would agree that we need personal transformation and personal affirmation.

# EMPTY WORDS WITHOUT GOD

But there is a problem. Although New Agers assert the value of the individual on the psychological level, their belief system denies this value on the ultimate spiritual level. And if ultimate reality is impersonal, the individual is worthless. New Agers may be asserting a kind of affirmation of the person, but their words are empty without God as the foundation for reality.

Christians should be careful not automatically to call terms such as holistic, human potential, networking, paradigm, rainbow, self-realization, and spaceship earth New Age and thus to regard them as negative concepts. They should avoid the danger of seeing a New Age distortion wherever they look.[26]

24. Ibid., 208-11.
25. Burnett, *Clash of Worlds*, 185.
26. Ibid., 185-86.

Instead, Christians need to address the same sorts of issues addressed by the New Age movement. Christians can best defend the biblical worldview by recognizing truth wherever it is found and by integrating it into a biblical framework. James Orr, a theologian at Glasgow University, holds that Christians need to show that the portions of truth found in other systems can be included in the biblical worldview. The Christian view completes the body of truth, including revealed discoveries peculiar to itself.

Douglas Groothuis illustrates this process. He contends that Christians should preserve a spiritual view of human psychology, but must separate themselves from any pantheistic view that asserts that humanity is divine. Christians should also not be involved in occult practices such as supposed past-life hypnotic regression, which the Bible forbids. Groothuis maintains that Christians can take the truths they find in certain psychologies and reposition them within a system more consistent with the biblical view. In that way they can transform psychology in a way that advances the Kingdom of God.[27]

# A CRITICAL ENGAGEMENT

According to Groothuis, the biblical view held by many evangelicals is one of "critical engagement." All thought must be brought under the scrutiny of the biblical worldview. In some areas we need to separate ourselves from the alien New Age view, both in thought and action. Yet we are called to be engaged. This means that we must seek to transform culture for the glory of God and to conserve those aspects of culture that please him. According to John Stott, a British theologian, Christians cannot be totally world-affirming or world-denying, but must be some of both.[28]

Some evangelical Christians see today's New Age groups as similar to religions that existed at the time of Christ. In the first century, the mystery religions, the worship of Greek and Roman gods, and Greek philosophies aroused the people to reflect on ultimate questions. In a similar way, New Age groups today are revealing the limitations of scientism, modernism, and forcing people to think of life's central spiritual concerns. It was in the fullness of time that Christ came in the first century. In much the same fashion, the New Age groups are helping to constitute a new fullness of time for a fresh witness to the Christian way.

27. Groothuis, *Confronting the New Age*, 55-57.
28. Ibid., 57.

# A TIME TO WITNESS

Evangelical Christianity cannot embrace the New Age worldview. But it can and must establish contact with those who have turned to the New Age movement in their search for spiritual meaning. Their religious needs can be satisfied only by biblical religion.

Christianity offers the world a dynamic and superior alternative to the New Age — the historical and cosmic Christ who is the foundation for all creation. Christianity not only appropriates spiritual resources for life on earth, but it affirms the hope of a personal and fulfilling life beyond death.

Christ has already won the victory over the powers of evil. He has paid the price and offers salvation to all who will accept.

It is the responsibility and privilege of every Christian to share the "good news" of that victory.

# Index

Acupuncture, 349-51

Alchemy, 21

Aliens: in movies, 485-86. *See also* UFOs

Alpert, Richard. *See* Ram Dass, Baba

Alternative medicine, 328-29. *See also* Ayurvedic medicine; Healing and health; Holistic medicine

Aquarian Age, 2-3, 13

*Aquarian Conspiracy, The,* 517-18

Arcane School, 160, 510-11

Arguelles, Jose, 512-13

Art, visual, and artists: evaluation of New Age approach, 474-75; Kandinsky, 472; Frantisek Kupka, 473; Kasimir Malevich, 473; Mondrian, 472; New Age and, 470-75; Jackson Pollock, 473

Arts, biblical approach to, 490-98; New Age and the, 470-90

Association for Research and Enlightenment (A.R.E.), 161

Avatar, 14

Ayurvedic medicine, 335-36, 344-49

Bailey, Alice, 290, 510-11. *See also* Arcane School

Biblical worldview, 17-18, 38-39, 48-49, 202-204, 444-45, 459-60; and art, 482-84, 490-98; and business, 415-17; ecology, 312-14, 316-19, 320-21, 323; and education, 439-30, 440-42; and evil, 572-77, 581-83; and evil spirits, 574-75; and health, 373-77; and magic and witchcraft, 260-61, 264-65, 273; and the New Age, 598-600; and possessions, 403, 405-8; and science, 458-59, 464, 465-69

Blavatsky, Madame, 27-28, 158-60, 471, 472

Buckland, Raymond, 234

Buddhism, 83-87; and ecology, 284; Four Noble Truths, 84-85; Mahayana, 85-86; Mind-only, 85-86; and physics, 454; Tantric, 87; Zen, 86

Cabot, Laurie, 218

Capra, Fritjof, 14, 40-41, 54, 237, 290-91, 453-55, 457-58; critique of, 506-8

Castaneda, Carlos, 64-65, 100-102, 230-32, 564

Cayce, Edgar, 161-62

Channeling, 11, 145-211, 394; analysis of, 188-89; 193-95, 197-98; and biblical teachings, 210-11; content of, 198-201; Aleister Crowley, 540-41;

and demon possession, 197, 209-10; with dolphins, 181-82; evaluation of, 148-49; explanations of, 193-98; history, 146-62; and Jesus Christ, 201; and *Jonathan Livingston Seagull*, 181; J. Z. Knight, 166-71; Ramtha, 166-79; Jane Roberts, 163-64; Kevin Ryerson, 171-72; Seth, 163-66; types of, 191-93; and UFOs, 182-86

Charismatics. *See* Pentecostalism

Chiropractic, 351-52

Chopra, Deepak, 344-49

Christ, Jesus: and the arts, 492-93, 495; and channelers, 201; Christian understanding of, 203-4, 206, 211; and the demonic powers, 583; in New Age thought, 58, 60, 179, 510-11

Christ principle, 58

Christ the Savior Brotherhood (I AM Movement), 28, 29, 160-61

Christian Science, 30-31

Christianity, 202-10; and business, 406-47; and channeling, 148-49, 197-98; and *A Course in Miracles*, 176-78; and drug use, 102-3; and ecology, 276-79; and feminism, 238-59; and Greek thought, 280-81; and Hindu groups, 83; and magic/witchcraft, 259-73; and Satan, 582-83, 588-89, 590-92, 593-95

Church of the Process of the Final Judgement, 556-58

Church of Satan: interpretations of, 552-54; rituals of, 548-51. *See also* LaVey, Anton

Church Universal and Triumphant, 179-80

Communes, 36

Computers: and the New Age, 487-88, 521

Consciousness, altered states of, 57-58; as creator of reality, 53

Corduan, Wilfred, 122, 125

Correspondences, Theory of, 4, 10, 23, 25

Cosmic energy, 4-5

*Course in Miracles, A*, 35, 172-78; Christian critiques, 176-78; New Age critiques, 176; reasons for appeal of, 175; teachings of, 173-74; teachings on health, 342

Cox, Harvey: on Pentecostalism, 129-31, 137-39, 401-2; on the Third Wave Movement, 591

Creation: and art, 492; biblical view of, 316-19, 465-66, 524

Creation spirituality, 126-27

Creme, Benjamin, 180-81, 511-12

Crowley, Aleister, 539-43; and drugs, 541, 542; and the Nazis, 542-43

Crystals, and healing, 352-53

Davis, Andrew Jackson, 154-55

de Chardin, Teilhard, 45, 126, 508-10

Deconstruction. *See* Postmodernism

Demon possession, Demons, 197-98, 209-10, 224; biblical approach to, 207, 372, 574-75; Christian response to, 593-95; and exorcism, 583-85; in literature, 578-79; modern belief in, 577-89; Western rationalism and, 576-77

Dewey, John, 421

Dialogue, Christian/New Age, 51-52, 598-600

Dianetics. *See* Scientology

Dominion theology, 400-402

Don Juan. *See* Castaneda, Carlos

Drugs, Drug use, 97-103, 559, 563; and Christianity, 102-3; and Aleister Crowley, 541, 542

Earth Mother Goddess, 63, 218-19

Eastern spirituality, 64-82, 422, 454, 455; growth in the west, 11, 32-33, 66-68, 87, 522; and healing, 335-36, 344-51; and modern art, 471, 472; and New Age music, 476, 477, 478

Eckhart, Meister, 123-125

Ecology: Rachel Carson on, 285-86; and Christianity, 276-81, 308-10, 311-23; Christian response to, 308-10, 311-23; deep ecology, 292-94; ecofeminism, 294-300; and Greek and

Roman thought, 279-80; and "Harmony with Nature," 285-86; in Japan, 284-85; and the New Age, 274-310
Eddy, Mary Baker, 29-31
Education: biblical view of, 440-45; Christian response to New Age view of, 433-39; Beverly Galyean, 424; evaluation of New Age view of, 428-30; New Age view as religious, 427-28; New Age view of, 423-28; problems of New Age view, 432-33
Emerson, Ralph Waldo, 25, 28, 382
Enlightenment, 41-43, 44, 500, 573, 597; and civil religion, 419-20
Erhard, Werner (John Paul Rosenberg), 93-96, 384-86
Eschatology, End times: biblical view of, 525-28; and ecology, 278-79
est, 93-96; Christian evaluation of, 96, 385-86; the Forum, 386; teachings, 94-95; and Zen Buddhism, 94, 95
Ethics: Christian, 408-17; New Age, 501-4
Evil: biblical view of, 581-82; Christian response to, 588-89
Evil Spirits. See Demons, Demon possession
Evolution, Evolutionism, 12, 503; mystical, 519

Faith healing, 361-66
Feminism, Feminist religion, 238-59; Elizabeth Achtemeier, 238-39, 245; and the Bible, 240-44; Christian response to, 244-59, 265-66; Mary Daly, 238; Marilyn Ferguson, 54, 517-18, 519; Elisabeth Schüssler Fiorenza, 242-43; and the Gaia Hypothesis, 290-91, 294-300; Daphne Hamson, 239-40; and Native American religion, 222-23; Rosemary Radford Reuther, 241-42; Sophia, 243-44; Aida Besancon Spencer, 246-47, 248, 251
Filmore, Charles, 383. See also Unity School of Christianity
Findhorn Community, 303, 342
Fox, Matthew, 126-29

Fox sisters, 155-56
Freemasonry, 22
Freud, Sigmund, 104, 106-8, 574
Future: biblical view of, 466-67; New Age view of, 13. See also End times, Eschatology, History

Gaia hypothesis, 229-30, 281-91, 293-98, 301-2; and Christianity, 302; critiques of, 288-89, 305-8; and eco-feminism, 294-300; and the Findhorn Community, 303; Richard Lovelock and, 286-89, 290-91, 301-2; modern development of, 296-98; and the New Age, 301-2, 307-8; primitive versions of, 287; scientific support for, 289; and Taoism, 283, 284; and Zen Buddhism, 284
Galyean, Beverly, 424
Gardner, Gerald B., 234, 235
Gimburtas, Marija, 234, 236-37
Globalism, 427, 519-20
Gnosticism, 20, 456, 536
God: Christian view of, 530; as the individual, 9-10; within the individual, 5-6; as life force or energy, 343; pantheism, 5; present in the world, 25; reached through the unconscious, 10; as Ultimate Unifying Principle, 58; as working only in the mind, 47
Goddess religion, 235-37, 238, 298-300; and Christianity, 238-39, 246-47, 269. See also Earth Mother Goddess
Groothuis, Douglas, 4, 518, 606; on business, 416; on Fritjof Capra's monism, 506-8; on cyberspace and the New Age, 186-87; on the paranormal, 461-62; on science, 462; on visualization, 392-94
Guided Imagery. See Visualization
Gurdjeff, George, 89-90
Guru, 9, 68

Hagin, Kenneth, 397-98
Hare Krishna, 69-70
Harman, Willis, 53
Harmonic convergence, 512-13

Harner, Michael, 232-33

Healing and health, 37, 324-28; acupuncture, 349-51; biblical view of health, 373-81; evaluation of, 368-73; lessons from, 367-68; mind/body collaboration for, 356-58; mind therapy, 356; New Age healing, 349-61; role of energy in, 343-44; spiritualist healing, 157, 304; therapeutic touch, 353-56; visualization and, 358-61; Word of Faith Movement/faith healing, 361-66. *See also* Alternative medicine, Holistic health

Heaven's Gate, 185-86

Hegel, G. W. F., 503

Hermeticism, 21

Hill, Napoleon, 383

Hinduism, 14, 24-25, 65-71; and America, 66-68; basic concepts of, 68-69; and Christianity, 83; and New Age transformation, 55; "Protestant," 26-27; science and, 453, 454, 463; yoga, 72-82; yogakananda, 67-68

History: biblical view of, 524-32; New Age view of, 500-501

*History and Power of Mind. See* Ingalese, Richard

Holistic health: and Christianity, 329-34; contemporary origins of, 337-38; dominant themes in, 338-44; historical origins of, 334-37

Home, Daniel Douglas, 156-57

Hubbard, Barbara Marx, 514-16; critique of Christianity, 516

Hubbard, L. Ron, 91-93, 388-89

Humanism, 420-22; and New Age, 422

Human Potential Movement, 119-22, 168, 505

Human Potential Seminars, 386-87

Human sacrifice, 559-69

Huxley, Aldous, 99-100

Hypnosis, 391

I AM Movement, 28, 29, 160-61

Ingalese, Richard, 382-83

Insight seminars, 187-88

ISKCON. *See* Krishna Consciousness, International Society for

Islam (Sufi), 88-90

John-Roger. *See* Insight seminars

Jung, Carl, and Jungianism, 10, 21, 91, 103-17; archetypes, 108-10; and channeling, 194-95; Christian evaluation of, 111-17; and Christianity, 104-6, 110-17; and Abraham Maslow, 118, 119-20; on UFOs, 182

Kant, Immanuel, 491, 495

Krishna Consciousness, International Society for (ISKCON), 69-70

Kuhn, Thomas, 451, 158

LaVey, Anton, 224, 543-54; influence on youth, 552; life of, 543-45; teachings, 545-48

Leary, Timothy, 97, 98, 102

Lewis, C. S: and evil spirits, 578, 586, 590, 591

Lovelock, James, 286-89, 290-91, 301-2

MacLaine, Shirley, 78-79, 169, 170, 171-72, 188-89

Magic, 212-35, African, 220, 565-66; biblical response to, 259-64; black, 224-25; Brazilian, 221; mana, 217-18; Mayan, 220-21; Native American, 222; principles of, 225-27; white, 224. *See also* Shamanism

Maharishi Mahesh Yogi. *See* Transcendental Meditation (TM)

Maitreya, 180-81, 510-12

Manicheanism: and Satanism, 538-39

Manson, Charles, 555-59

Maritain, Jacques, 420-21

Maslow, Abraham H., 118, 120, 452, 504-5

Master Mind group. *See* Hill, Napoleon

"Matamoros Incident," 559-69

Mayan religion, 512-13

Mesmerism, 23-24

Monism, 4-5, 533; in *The Dark Crystal,* 486; and Islam, 89

Mormonism, *Book of Mormon*, 151-53
Movement for Spiritual Inner Awareness (MSIA), 387-88
Movies: *The Believers*, 566-67; *ET* and *Close Encounters*, 485-86; *Ghostbusters*, 486-87; *The Last Temptation of Christ*, 486; and the New Age, 484-87; *Rosemary's Baby*, 546, 548; and Satanism, 566-67, 578; *Star Wars*, 484-85
Muller, Robert, 514, 519-20
Murray, Margaret, 233
Music: Christian evaluation of New Age, 479-81; Christian view of, 481-84; New Age, 475-79
Mysticism, 102-3, 122-29

Naess, Arne, 292-94
Naropa Institute (Buddhist), 87
Native American religion, 34, 63-64, 222-23, 513
Neopaganism, 212-73; beliefs of, 214-19; and the Gaia hypothesis, 290-91; key leaders of, 233-35; and the New Age, 215; overview of, 229-30; and polytheism, 216; worship, 227-29
Neoplatonism, 20-21
New Age: as a business, 16; and the business world, 382-405; Christian response to, 596-607; and Christianity, 1, 2, 10, 12, 16-17, 18, 51-52, 202- 11; "Churches," 15; definition of, 1, 3-4; ethics in, 501-4; and the future, 2-3, 13; growth of, 46; impact on Christianity, 47-52; institutes, 15-16; and the media, 488-90; optimism, 13, 14; origins of, 19-39; as a theosophical term, 28; view of history, 500-501
New Age worldview, 3-15, 18, 53-54, 56-58, 60-61, 62, 210, 281-82, 299, 324-25, 371-72, 423
New Thought, 29-30, 31, 32, 120, 361-62. *See also* Unity School of Christianity
Noll, Richard, 107, 110, 115

Nostradamus, 149

Occult, 2, 38-39; and art, 473-74; and computers, 456. *See also* Magic, Satan, Satanism, Satanists
O'Connor, Flannery: and Satan, 578-79
Order of the Golden Dawn, 540
Otto, Rudolph, 124
"Out-of-body" experiences, 219

Paganism, 260-61; Celtic, 21. *See also* Neopaganism
Palo Mayombe, 565, 567
Pantheism, 5; in *The Last Temptation of Christ*, 486; in *Star Wars*, 485
Parapsychology, 196-97; and physics, 455
Parliament of Religions (1893), 32-33, 66
Pentecostalism, 129-42; critique of, 141-42; growth of, 132-34; and jazz, 137-39; and the New Age, 129-32, 139; and spiritual transformation, 134-36; and tongues, 139-41
Peretti, Frank, 590-91
Peters, Ted: on creation spirituality, 127-29
Philosophy/Philosophers: Enlightenment, 41-43, 44, 500, 573, 597; Gnosticism, 20; Greek, 465; G. W. F. Hegel, 503; Hermeticism, 21; Aldous Huxley, 99-100; monism, 4-5, 465, 533; Neoplatonism, 20-21; postmodern, 43-44, 600-601; Process, 504; Transcendentalism, 25-26, 285, 382, 398
Pike, Bishop James, 157-58
Planetary consciousness, 520-23
Polytheism, 216-17
Positive thinking, 31-32; Christian, 395-96
Postmodernism, 43-44, 600-601
Primordial realm, 216-17
Process thought, 504
Promise Keepers, 270-73
Prophecy/Predictions, 13-14, 135; biblical, 205, 207-8
Prophet, Elizabeth Clare, 179-80

Prosperity consciousness, New Age prosperity, 382, 383, 384, 396; problems with, 391

Prosperity gospel, 396, 397-98, 401; problems of, 402-5

Psychic mysticism/Psychic phenomena, 460-62; and ecology, 304

Psychology: Sigmund Freud, 104, 106-8, 574; Human Potential Movement, 119-22; humanistic, 118-19; Carl Jung, 103-11; New Age use of, 504-6; Carl Rogers, 119; Transpersonal Psychology, 120-21; Wilhelm Reich, 120

Rajneesh, Bhagwan Shree, 77-78, 97-98

Ramtha, 11, 146, 166-70, 502

Ram Dass, Baba (Richard Alpert), 34-35, 98-99, 194

Rancho Santa Elena, 559-69

Raschke, Carl, 3, 553-54

Reality, biblical view of, 533; New Age view of, 17, 423, 457

Reincarnation, 6-7

Renaissance, 22

Right-brain learning, 425

Roberts, Jane, 163-64. See also Seth

Ryerson Kevin, 171-72

Sagan, Carl, 446

St. John of the Cross, 125-26

Santeria, 566

Satan: biblical view of, 582-88, 592; and the holocaust, 592; and mass violence, 589. See also Satanism, Satanists; Witchcraft

Satanism, Satanists, 213, 533-80; biblical view of, 572-73; and black mass, 537-38; in the entertainment world, 486-87; and human sacrifice, 553-54, 556; influence of, 569-72; modern, 539-69. See also Witchcraft; Satan

Schucman, Helen, 172-73

Science: Bacon, 449; biblical view of, 462-63, 464, 469; early Greek approach, 446-47, 463-64; Einstein, 450-51; Galileo, 448; holistic, 451; modern science, 447-51; New Age

and, 452-62; Newtonian, 448; problems with New Age approach, 457-61; Ptolemaic, 447; quantum theory, 450-51, 452-53; "Scientism," 449-50

Scientology, 90-93; and Charles Manson, 555-56

Secret Doctrine. See Madame Blavatsky

Self worship in the Church of Satan, 545-46, 547-49

Seth, 163-66

Sex: biblical approach to, 82; and holistic health, 339; and Tantric Yoga, 76-82

Shamanism, 33-34, 64, 222, 232-33

Silva mind control, 394

Smith, Joseph. See Mormons, Book of Mormon

Spiritualism (Spiritism), 24, 154-58, 394; and UFOs, 182-83. See also Channeling

Spirituality, biblical, 45; New Age, 142-44

Starhawk, Miriam, 212-13, 218, 219, 227, 228, 236, 299

Swedenborgianism, Emmanuel Swedenborg, 22-23, 150-51

Taoism, 283-84

Tao of Physics. See Capra, Fritjof

Television and the New Age, 487, 488

Terrikyo, 153

Theosophy, 27-29, 32, 158-61; and modern art, 471, 172

Therapeutic touch, 353-56

Transactional Analysis, 505

Transcendental Meditation (TM), 70-71, 344, 388, 390; and Christianity, 72, 83

Transcendentalism, 25-26, 285, 382, 398

Transformation, 6-7, 8, 37-38, 55-59, 60-64; and Buddhism, 83-87; central to New Age belief, 56; Christian views of, 59-60, 122-44, 603-5; of consciousness, 8, 389-90; critique of New Age, 142-49; and Hinduism, 55; "Transformational Technologies," 385, 386; Western views, 90-144

Transpersonalism, 506, 507
Trine, Ralph Waldo, 399-400

UFOs, 182-88
Unitarian Universalism, 237
Unity School of Christianity, 31, 383,
   398, 399
Universalism/Syncretism, 12, 32-33,
   38-39, 47

Values clarification, 426
Visualization, 304, 358-61, 392, 425;
   Christian reaction to, 392-94

Witchcraft, 212-73; biblical response to,

259-65; Raymond Buckland, 234-35;
and the Cathars, 535-36; folk witches,
535; Gerald B. Gardner, 234; Marija
Gimbutas, 234; and magic, 223-24;
medieval, 536; Margaret Murray, 233;
in Salem, MA, 213
Word of Faith Movement.
   *See* Prosperity gospel
Worldview, 596-604; apologetic use of,
   598-604; modernist, 41-44; nature
   and definition, 40-41. *See also* Biblical
   worldview; New Age, worldview of

Yoga, 72-82